THE RIFLE BRIGADE
IN THE SECOND WORLD WAR
1939 - 1945

[*Photo: A. E. Rice, Winchester*]

H.R.H. THE COLONEL-IN-CHIEF AT THE WAR MEMORIAL SERVICE, WINCHESTER, 19th OCTOBER, 1949

Behind His Royal Highness are Field-Marshal Lord Wilson and Captain Sir Charles McGrigor, Bart. The Guard of Honour was composed of Riflemen from the 1st Battalion, London Rifle Brigade and Rangers

Frontispiece]

THE RIFLE BRIGADE
IN THE SECOND WORLD WAR
1939-1945

By
MAJOR R. H. W. S. HASTINGS, D.S.O., O.B.E., M.C.

Foreword by
H.R.H. THE DUKE OF GLOUCESTER
K.G., K.T., K.P., G.M.B., G.C.M.G., G.C.V.O.

The Naval & Military Press Ltd

Published by

The Naval & Military Press Ltd
Unit 5 Riverside, Brambleside
Bellbrook Industrial Estate
Uckfield, East Sussex
TN22 1QQ England

Tel: +44 (0)1825 749494

www.naval-military-press.com
www.nmarchive.com

In reprinting in facsimile from the original, any imperfections are inevitably reproduced and the quality may fall short of modern type and cartographic standards.

CONTENTS

		PAGE
FOREWORD BY H.R.H. THE DUKE OF GLOUCESTER		xi
ACKNOWLEDGMENTS		xiii
INTRODUCTION		xvii
CHAPTER I	MECHANIZATION	1
CHAPTER II	CALAIS	7
CHAPTER III	THE PRACTICE OVER	31
CHAPTER IV	THE ARRIVAL OF THE AFRIKA KORPS	61
CHAPTER V	THE INEFFECTIVE SUMMER	67
CHAPTER VI	SIDI REZEGH—THE FORGOTTEN BATTLE	80
CHAPTER VII	THE SECOND ADVANCE TO AGHEILA	94
CHAPTER VIII	THE MSUS STAKES AND THE GAZALA LINE	102
CHAPTER IX	GAZALA TO ALAMEIN—THE RETREAT OF 1942	114
CHAPTER X	THE WORST SUMMER—EL ALAMEIN, 1942	134
CHAPTER XI	THE BATTLE OF ALAMEIN	148
CHAPTER XII	SNIPE	162
CHAPTER XIII	THE THIRD PURSUIT	181
CHAPTER XIV	MARETH, AKARIT AND THE FOREST OF OLIVES	195
CHAPTER XV	NORTH AFRICA: ALGERIA AND TUNISIA	207
CHAPTER XVI	THE FALL OF TUNIS	223
CHAPTER XVII	AFTER THE DESERT	238
CHAPTER XVIII	NO GENTLEMAN'S WAR—ITALY AND THE FORMATION OF THE 61ST INFANTRY BRIGADE	251
CHAPTER XIX	ADVANCE ON ROME	262
CHAPTER XX	PERUGIA	272
CHAPTER XXI	THE ARNO VALLEY AND THE GOTHIC LINE	282
CHAPTER XXII	WINTER IN THE APENNINES	299
CHAPTER XXIII	TOSSIGNANO: ATTACK AND DEFENCE	311
CHAPTER XXIV	THE LAST CAMPAIGN IN ITALY	328

		PAGE
Chapter XXV	The Second Front	344
Chapter XXVI	The Dog-fight	355
Chapter XXVII	The Break-out and the "Swan"	366
Chapter XXVIII	The Low Countries	381
Chapter XXIX	Into the Reich	401

Epilogue .. 413

Appendices:

"A": Copy of Leaflet dropped by German Aircraft upon the Defenders of Calais .. 415

"B": Message from the Colonel-in-Chief .. 415

"C": The Snipe Action .. 416

"D": Message from H.R.H. The Duke of Gloucester to all Battalions of the Regiment at the end of the War .. 417

"E": The 9th Battalion .. 418

"F": Roll of Honour .. 419

"G": Honours and Awards .. 445

Index .. 461

ILLUSTRATIONS

H.R.H. The Colonel-in-Chief at the War Memorial Service at Winchester, 19th October, 1949 .. ..*Frontispiece*

	FACING PAGE
Calais, March, 1944	13
Sollum Bay	44
Last Stand of the Italians—Sollum, 15th December, 1940	44
Air Dispersion in Typical Desert Country	58
Sidi Saleh	58
Life in the Desert	61
The Coast Road; General Sir Claude Auchinleck and Brigadier Hugo Garmoyle; The Italians observe us	84
The Enemy on Every Front	140
General Sir Henry Maitland Wilson inspects the 2nd Battalion ..	140
Lieutenant-Colonel V. B. Turner, V.C.	172
The Snipe Position: Sergeant C. V. Calistan, D.C.M., M.M.; Major T. A. Bird, D.S.O., M.C.; Rifleman D. A. Chard, D.C.M.	173
North Africa—Djebel Kournine	228
Lieutenant-Colonel Adrian Gore, Brian Shepherd and Dick Fyffe	228
North Africa—the 10th Battalion	228
Mr. Anthony Eden visits the 7th Battalion in Egypt, Autumn, 1943	245
Italy—the 1st Battalion	245
The 7th Battalion in Italy	260
Italy—7th Battalion Mules	300
Snow in Italy	300
A 10th Battalion Patrol	316
Tossignano	316
Battalion Headquarters, 1st Battalion, before crossing the Somme	372

	FACING PAGE
Colonels Vic Turner and Victor Paley	372
Three Sergeants and a Cat	372
The Maas at Maastricht	381
A Half-track in the Snow	381
Attack at St. Joost	396
A Carrier (not on Patrol!)	396

MAPS

	PAGE
CALAIS	27
SIDI SALEH	56
SIDI REZEGH	84
OPERATIONS AROUND SIDI REZEGH	91
EGYPT AND LIBYA	139
BATTLE OF ALAMEIN	153
POSITIONS AT SNIPE	173
WESTERN DESERT, 1940-1943	facing 180
THE THIRD PURSUIT—ALAMEIN TO TRIPOLI	facing 236
TRIPOLI AND NORTH AFRICA TO TUNIS	facing 236
OPERATIONS WEST OF PERUGIA	273
ITALY	facing 310
TOSSIGNANO	319
ADVANCE INTO AUSTRIA	343
VILLERS BOCAGE	351
THE PLAINS OF CAEN	361
LE BAS PERRIER	369
FRANCE, 1944	facing 380
THE LOW COUNTRIES	facing 400
CROSSING OF THE RIVER WESER	407
INTO THE REICH	facing 412

YORK HOUSE,
ST JAMES'S PALACE.

  This History of The Rifle Brigade for 1939-45 covers not only the war services of the two Regular Battalions but also those of the 7th, 8th, 9th and 10th Battalions which were formed originally from the London Rifle Brigade and the Tower Hamlets Rifles.

  The pages that follow add yet another eventful chapter to the annals of the Regiment which has played a conspicuous and memorable part in so many theatres of war since its embodiment 150 years ago.

  This stirring record of courage and endurance, which shows how faithfully the Regiment, of which I have the honour to be Colonel-in-Chief, has guarded the traditions of its past, will, I know, be read with special interest and pride by all Riflemen, past, present and future.

Henry.
Colonel-in-Chief.

ACKNOWLEDGMENTS

THE principal source from which the material for this book has been drawn is *The Rifle Brigade Chronicle*. Throughout the war years, despite paper shortage and censorship regulations and the difficulty of extracting suitable articles from battalions and individuals who were busily engaged in the fighting, Major H. G. Parkyn, O.B.E. ("Parkyno"), managed to keep the *Chronicle* going. Without his efforts it would have been almost impossible in the time available to trace the story of the Regiment in the war. Even after the war he set about filling in the gaps and getting somewhat reluctant officers to search their memories of those periods in the campaigns of the battalions which had not been dealt with already. "Parkyno" always had an eye to the future historian and all Riflemen should be grateful to him for that—I, myself, most of all.

Apart from the *Chronicle*, a number of personal accounts, diaries, letters and reminiscences were sent in by Riflemen of all ranks and by relations of those who were killed. Such papers have proved most valuable. Even though some of them may not have been quoted directly, they have all helped to make up the background against which the story of the events has been written. Too many documents were sent in for it to be possible to acknowledge each one here by name.

It would be unfair, too, not to mention with gratitude the authors of those much-maligned documents the war diaries. Knowing the conditions in which they were sometimes written and the horror with which adjutants and intelligence officers often regarded them, it is surprising and satisfactory to find how useful they could sometimes be.

All these papers I have used quite shamelessly, borrowing whole sentences and even paragraphs, editing extracts to suit myself and being guilty, consciously and often unconsciously, of plagiarism of the most irritating kind. I hope their authors will not mind. I have regarded these sources as the property of the

Regiment and used them without acknowledgment, except in a few cases where long extracts have been taken.

The three most flagrant cases of lifting other people's stories bodily into my own are:

Calais.—The account by Major A. W. Allan, D.S.O., is used almost entirely, almost word for word.

"Snipe."—The account by Lieutenant-Colonel V. B. Turner, V.C., has been used with his permission but edited once or twice behind his back.

The Italian Campaign.—The main chapters concerning the 61st Infantry Brigade are almost identical with those in *The History of the 61st Infantry Brigade*. Brigadier A. C. Gore, D.S.O., has been kind enough to allow this book to be used. I hope the anonymous author will not take too unkindly to the editing and alterations which have seemed to me to be necessary.

I would like also to acknowledge a debt to Messrs. Cassell and to Messrs. Houghton Mifflin for giving permission to make certain extracts concerning the defence of Calais from Mr. Winston Churchill's *Their Finest Hour*; to Messrs. Macmillan for allowing me to quote the last sentence of the Introduction from Thomas Hardy's *Tess of the D'Urbervilles*; and to Messrs. Chatto & Windus for permission to quote a phrase ("chance's strange arithmetic") from a poem of Wilfred Owen's.

I am most grateful to all those who sent in photographs, many of which have been reproduced without specific acknowledgment.

My thanks are due to the various people, commanding officers and others, who have been kind enough to read parts of this book in draft and have corrected some of the inaccuracies and definite errors which have crept in.

I would like also to thank Major T. C. Sinclair, M.C., for his assistance in compiling and checking the Roll of Honour.

Finally, I would like to acknowledge my gratitude to the History Committee, at first under the chairmanship of Lieutenant-General F. W. Festing, C.B., C.B.E., D.S.O., and later of Brigadier A. G. V. Paley, D.S.O., O.B.E., and to those who have read the proofs at various stages, particularly Brigadier Paley (and Mrs. Paley, who not only read pages of proofs but was of the greatest assistance in checking the list of decorations) and Major Parkyn, to Lieutenant-Colonel C. N. C. Boyle, M.C., and to Major H. Hubble, M.C., who as Secretary of the Rifle Brigade Club was always being bothered for help and information of one sort or another.

I make no claim for consistency in the spelling of Arabic place-names or even always of Belgian place-names, since there seem to be at least two versions of the spelling of each village in some parts of those countries.

INTRODUCTION

THIS is the story of the battalions of The Rifle Brigade at war from 1939 to 1945. It is a story which takes long enough to tell; for battalions were continuously in contact with the enemy for remarkably long periods of the war. It is because there is so much to tell of fighting that no mention is made of the training and administration at home on which the success of the Regiment was founded. There is no room for an account of the Motor Training Battalion (or Charles McGrigor, its Colonel for so long) in its various forms and different locations—its final home was as the 9th Battalion at Ranby—which turned out a succession of trained Riflemen of all ranks capable of taking an immediate part in the battle as soon as they joined a battalion. There is no room for mention of the Greenjacket Officers' Cadet Training Unit and the organization of the Colonels Commandant's Office, although it is to them that we owe the high standard of young officers who were sent out to the battalions, officers worthy of this description of one of them in a letter from another: "The bravest of all is one whose life is charmed beyond all doubt. He is the quietest of men, very shy and dreamy and embarrassingly modest, but yet if there is a battle in the neighbourhood you would always find him in the forefront, usually quite unprotected, standing on the top of something, looking through his field-glasses."

For the same reason hardly any mention can be made of the years of training which all the battalions except the 2nd spent in England before they were committed in battle, years which probably bulk as large in the memories of those concerned as do the periods of active service which followed them. There is no room to mention the activities of the 70th (Young Soldiers) Battalion. There is room only to mention in passing the debt we owe to the Ceylon Planters Rifle Corps, who provided reinforcements of a high quality, particularly to the 2nd Battalion, at a time when they were urgently needed, almost all of whom were soon commissioned as officers. Ceylon is now an independent member of the Commonwealth: the Ceylon Planters Rifle Corps has ceased to exist and its affiliation to the Regiment has unfortunately come to an end.

No account is included of the 3rd Battalion Tower Hamlets Rifles, since they did not fight as part of the Regiment, but as the 5th Reconnaissance Regiment.

The contribution of a regiment in war is not measured only in the part played by its battalions. Besides forming fighting units we had to provide commanders and staff officers, to send officers, non-commissioned officers and riflemen to various establishments and units. No record of the Regiment in war is complete without passing reference to those officers and many other Riflemen who had served in the Regiment and who distinguished themselves as commanders and staff officers and to whom battalions owe a great deal in their pre-war training, such officers as Field-Marshal Lord Wilson, General Sir Montagu Stopford, Lieutenant-General Sir Ralph Eastwood, Lieutenant-General Frankie Festing, Lieutenant-General Sir Ronald Weeks, Major-General Jack Reeve, Major-General Lord Bridgeman and Brigadier Tim Massy-Beresford. There were, too, Riflemen serving in the Long-Range Desert Group, where Pat Hore-Ruthven was killed and Vivian Street was saved in mid-Mediterranean by a miracle. Riflemen dropped by parachute in Yugoslavia with Brigadier Fitzroy Maclean, among them Vivian Street, John Henniker-Major and John Earle. John Harington was a successful saboteur in Greece. Most of those mentioned are officers because we were lucky enough to keep the majority of non-commissioned officers and riflemen in the battalions, though you hear of Company Sergeant-Major Endean distinguishing himself, when serving under command of a Rifleman, in the Libyan Arab Forces or of Sergeant Stockdale and Corporal Blundell at Dieppe.

In war the Regiment expected to produce more than its quota of staff officers. But in the summer of 1943 a further inroad was made into the officer resources of the battalions. Various officers were taken away to command battalions of other regiments. We provided two commanding officers for the 60th Rifles, one for the Green Howards, one for the Royal West Kents, one for the Wiltshire Regiment, one for the Royal Northumberland Fusiliers, one for the Yorkshire Dragoons, one for the 5th and one for the 44th Divisional Reconnaissance Regiments—the list is far from exhaustive and does not, for instance, include those Riflemen who commanded Italians (Free Italians) or Libyans or Burmese.

All these burdens fell on a regiment which had already lost one Regular battalion, complete, in the defence of Calais.

Early in 1942 the Regiment suffered a grave loss of a different sort. On the 16th of January His Royal Highness The Duke of Connaught, Colonel-in-Chief since 1880, for sixty years, died at his home at Bagshot Park. He had served in the Regiment, commanding the 1st Battalion from 1876 to 1880, and for more than half a century had been our friend and our protector against the assaults of the outside world. No colonel-in-chief could have taken a more active, or a more useful, interest in the affairs of the Regiment. For years he saw all officers who were to be commissioned in the Regiment, and those who had to visit him soon found that it was no mere formal interview. In those sixty-two years his influence on the fortunes of the Regiment was incalculable and to him belongs much of the credit for the selection of officers, not only those who fought in two wars and particularly in the war with which this book is concerned, but those, too, who trained and moulded the battalions through the difficult days of peace.

In August, 1939, he had arranged to inspect the 1st Battalion near Bagshot. But preparations for war made this impossible. However, in November of that same year, during a sudden move of part of his old battalion from the South of England to the East Coast, he was able to watch it, now completely conveyed in motor vehicles, pass the gates of Bagshot Park. The following June, when almost all that battalion had been engulfed at Calais, his was the best-remembered of all the messages received at that time.

He was succeeded as Colonel-in-Chief by His Royal Highness The Duke of Gloucester.

It is customary to apologize in advance for the errors and inaccuracies which inevitably arise in accounts of operations of this kind. It would be too much to hope that there are none; certainly none are intentional. But those who may feel that their actions have been belittled or over-praised, or left out altogether, who have had their names spelt wrongly or their initials confused, should apply for redress not to the Colonels Commandant or to the Secretary of the Rifle Brigade Club, but to me. For, although this is the History of the Regiment in war, it is also to an extent my book, save in one respect—that the use of "we" in the text refers to the Regiment and does not necessarily imply that I was there.

For this book is intended to cover all the campaigns of all the battalions. It is not the story of certain companies, or the reminiscences of individual officers, or a record of only the bravest riflemen. It is the collective story of all Riflemen who fought at the front in the war, of those who are still living, and of those who are not—"every one of whom walked in his own individual way the road to dusty death."

CHAPTER I

MECHANIZATION

By 1937 the news from Europe was already ominous. The Rhineland had been reoccupied; the German Army was rapidly increasing in strength and armament; the Luftwaffe had achieved something more than air parity with the Royal Air Force. Italy, prodded by sanctions which irritated her people without seriously affecting her war effort in Abyssinia, had already taken sides with Germany. In England a government, by nature and conscience absolutely opposed to rearmament, attentive, perhaps, to the gruesome warnings of Mr. Churchill, was at last taking steps to increase the strength of our defences.

It was with this background of events that the plans for forming an armoured division were implemented. An early decision was taken that tanks would require specially trained infantry to work with them in close support. These infantry would have to be fully mobile so that they could keep up with the armoured advance. Their main role would be to restore the momentum of the attack when the armour was temporarily held up by the enemy in built-up areas or in rough or mountainous country where the tanks could not operate by themselves. Many subsidiary tasks were to emerge later.

The motor battalions, as they were called, were to be formed from the 60th Rifles and The Rifle Brigade. So the Regiment, which had fought throughout the First World War as infantry, was destined for a new role in the war against Hitler. All the battalions who made contact with the enemy fought as motor battalions until, in May, 1944, the 2nd and 7th Battalions were reorganized as lorried infantry to form part of the 61st Infantry Brigade in Italy—a decision forced on the Higher Command by the mountainous nature of the country. The new mobile role was not inappropriate to a regiment which had fought with such distinction in the Light Division. For the qualities of quickness and independence of thought, of mobility and of individual initiative were just those which were required by Sir John Moore and exhibited by the 95th throughout the Peninsular campaigns. At any rate, this change of role was to have a profound effect on the fortunes of the Regiment in this new war.

In 1937 the 1st Battalion was in England at Gosport, where it was reorganized under Lieutenant-Colonel (now Major-General) Jack Reeve as a motor battalion. It was no small task to change from an infantry battalion, who marched, to a motor battalion, able to drive everywhere in their own vehicles. First there was the necessity of teaching drivers to drive, and above all to maintain trucks and carriers and motor-bicycles. There was the really important task of training wireless operators. There were the administrative changes, not least of which was to accustom Riflemen, used to the inverted vocabulary of the quartermaster, to the even more complicated system for recognizing and accounting for the vast assortment of tools and spare parts, almost all with strange names, many of which to a layman looked exactly the same as each other.

There was then the more interesting problem of tactics. For a new type of battalion a new tactical outlook was required. It was difficult enough to drive as a battalion along the road; to take part in the battle required a new technique. The fact that they were pioneers in this role gave an added interest to training, which took place, for the most part, on Salisbury Plain at first from camp and then from barracks at Tidworth. The 1st Battalion soon found that the essential requirements for a motor battalion were quickness of thought and action, initiative among junior leaders, ability to work wireless communications perfectly and a high standard of maintenance of vehicles. The principles worked out by the Battalion, mainly by men who on account of the defence of Calais had no opportunity to act on them, held good for the other battalions throughout the war. It is extraordinary how right they were. They did, perhaps, over-estimate the importance of the motor-bicycle, that democratic vehicle which would refuse to start for an officer but would respond to the first kick of a rifleman, and many of which were to stick in Tunisian mud or be lost in the open spaces of the desert.

There was one advantage of being motorized that affected the existence of all Riflemen vitally. You did carry your bedding with you and, what was almost more important, your food and your cooker as well. Instead of having your meals cooked centrally by professionals and brought up to you, each vehicle cooked its own meals at whatever moment in the battle appeared most suitable. The "brew-up" became an institution of the greatest importance; it was often the high-light of the day. And Riflemen preferred cooking for themselves. However uneconomical in rations it may have been, there were advantages in being able to cook your food just as you liked it, whether it were bully done in one of twenty ways or biscuit "burgoo" or the kidneys, perhaps, of a gazelle or eggs scrounged from an Italian farm or a chicken "run over" in France. In vehicle-cooking speed was more important than cleanliness; a good team could brew tea at vast expense of petrol during a twenty-minute halt, probably saving the tea-leaves in an old sock for use later in the day. There were many who held that a good dose of sand improved the brew. Whatever the theatre, however fierce the fighting, vehicle-cooking played its all-important part. It is not surprising that the chief regret of the 2nd and 7th Battalions at being reorganized on an establishment more nearly resembling that of normal infantry was that they would lose their "brews": nor is it out of place to find in a rifleman's diary, describing a withdrawal in the desert, telling of Stukas and enemy tanks, of shelling and being shelled, of all the horrors of war, the entry for the 2nd of January, 1942: "Cold morning. Made a duff. One of the boys dropped a cigarette in it"! For shells and aeroplanes were incidental to a life in which "brews" were essential.

Tactically the introduction of wireless was a vitally important development. Orders could be given out at great speed without collecting company commanders together: reconnaissance elements could send in information from longer distances and more quickly than ever before. The whole process of fighting a battle was speeded up immeasurably. The advent of wireless introduced, incidentally, a whole new vocabulary, code signs, code names, the phonetic alphabet: "Ack," "Beer," "Charlie," "Don" in the early years, "Able," "Baker," "Charlie," "Dog" later on. There were codes to be fumbled with and compromised so that resort had to be made to veiled language. For the enemy, also, could listen to our wireless and spend, like us, harassed hours thumbing the captured "Codex" or the map-reference code or translating thinly veiled references to the "big chaps" or "our friends with the Hats" or "the green men" or "the tin-bellies"—for those who had lost the code name of the Household

Cavalry. The more senior the officer on the wireless the more likely he was to break the code. There were hours, too, particularly after dark in the desert, when no voice came through clearly, if at all, when the wireless roared and oscillated and signallers yelled at each other "Your speech is distorted" and "Hear you strength one." It was its proficiency in the use of wireless that made a motor battalion capable of working with the armour and using its mobility to the full. Wireless was a great benefit. If there were occasions when the companies or the carriers asked for advice instead of getting on with their task, the use of wireless enabled the great commanders, the Jock Campbells and the Herbert Lumsdens, the Hugo Garmoyles, to keep a personal hold on the fortunes of the battle. But those who had to sit with the earphones glued to their ears and their wits at their sharpest for hours and days on end, sometimes wished it had never been invented.

Association with armour brought with it one remarkable piece of good fortune. Throughout the war we worked with and were supported by the regiments of the Royal Horse Artillery. In the early days the 3rd R.H.A., at first with anti-tank guns and afterwards with 25-pounders, and the 4th R.H.A. with 25-pounders were in the Support Group. At Sidi Saleh Geoffrey Goschen's guns halted the German advance; at Sidi Rezegh it was three riflemen who recommended two officers of the 3rd R.H.A. for Victoria Crosses. The battalions worked with the 1st R.H.A. and 2nd R.H.A. when they, too, arrived in the desert and, when columns were the fashion, we often depended for our survival on the speed of their guns into action and the accuracy of their fire. The 1st Battalion and, later, the whole 7th Motor Brigade came to know the 11th R.H.A., and when, before Alamein, the 5th R.H.A. joined the 7th Armoured Division, an alliance with the 1st Battalion was struck up which was to end only on the Baltic. The 10th Battalion and the 12th R.H.A. fought together in North Africa; the 8th Battalion and a battery of the 13th R.H.A. became, with the 23rd Hussars, as formidable an armoured regimental group as could be met with in 21st Army Group. Though the Horse Gunners are mentioned frequently in this book, it is the story of the Regiment which is being told, and the part played by supporting arms may often seem to be taken for granted. But none of those who were there could underrate our assistance from the Royal Horse Artillery.

MECHANIZATION

When the decision was taken to turn The Rifle Brigade into motor battalions, the 2nd Battalion was coming to the end of a four-year stay in Malta and was about to move to Meerut, India. It was still organized and trained as an infantry battalion. During the winter of 1938-39 it was one of the reserve battalions for the North-West Frontier and many officers and non-commissioned officers learnt about mountain warfare. In June, 1939, in the middle of the hot weather, the Battalion moved to Palestine, where there were still considerable disturbances in progress, our opponents at that time being almost always Arabs. The Battalion came under the command of a general officer of the name of Montgomery, who left on sick leave as soon as we arrived. We were again to serve in his command. Although the troubles were dying down, there was a great deal of internal-security work to be done. At the same time, the Battalion had to be mechanized, so that driving instruction and lessons in wireless procedure had to be sandwiched in between expeditions to surround villages perched on the top of considerable hills. The experience of officers and non-commissioned officers of the 1st Battalion was invaluable in learning the new role. At the outbreak of war Arab disturbances ceased and there was some opportunity for training. The Battalion moved to a camp near Nathaniya, where they were attacked by rabid jackals and all the vehicles were stuck in the sand. After occupying various stations in Palestine, a move was made in January, 1940, to Egypt to join the Mobile Division, shortly to become the 7th Armoured Division. The Italians had not yet entered the war and here at last there was an opportunity to train as a motor battalion and prepare for a desert war. Colonel Teddy Williams and, later, Colonel Callum Renton seized this opportunity with avidity.

As a result of their reorganization the battalions of the Regiment were associated with armour throughout the war. In the desert conditions were such that motor battalions more often than not acted independently so that the Regiment had a good Press. Later on in Italy and North-West Europe the armoured regiments with whom we worked made a more direct appeal to military correspondents. That does not mean that battalions of the Regiment were less heavily engaged during the last two years than they were in the early stages of the war. It has sometimes been suggested that motor battalions take part in patrolling and skirmishing with the armour and leave the heaviest fighting to the infantry. Certainly motor battalions were in contact with the enemy for long periods when little serious activity occurred and in pursuits when there was little opposition; but they were also to be found at the critical stages of most of the important and decisive battles, at Sidi Saleh and Sidi Rezegh, on the Snipe position at Alamein, at El Hamma, in the advance to Tunis, at Perugia, on the Orne, crossing the Weser, in the Gothic Line, and fighting to the last round in the defence of Calais.

CHAPTER II

CALAIS

THE English are inured to military disaster at the outset of wars. There has always been time to recover from the initial setbacks. While the Allies on the Continent have taken the first shock and held on or gone under with as good grace as they can muster, the English war machine has gradually geared itself up until it is able to produce an effort sufficient to turn the scale. Great Britain owed its immunity from the blitzkrieg to an unassailable financial position and the existence of the English Channel. Since the defeat of Napoleon it had been generally agreed that the presence of an enemy in the Channel ports was the worst military disaster which could befall us on the Continent of Europe. Much English blood had been shed to save the Channel ports in the First World War. The attempt to hold the most important of them even temporarily was to prove fatal to the 1st Battalion in this one. In the history of the Regiment the story of the defence of Calais forms something of a link between the two wars; for, in reading the accounts of these days, one is often struck by incidents which recall the spirit of 1914-18, tales of officers who would not withdraw until their orders had been confirmed, of wounded men who refused to be evacuated, of the naval officer who directed the traffic with his left arm when his right had been blown off, all indications that this operation was carried to its conclusion on a note of high endeavour, less obviously present in the more matter-of-fact atmosphere of future battles.

In May, 1940, the 1st Battalion and the 2nd Battalion 60th Rifles formed part of the 30th Infantry Brigade. They were both organized as motor battalions. The third battalion in the Brigade, the 1st Battalion Queen Victoria's Rifles, was a motor-bicycle battalion and, at that time, was employed in an independent role in Kent. The 1st Battalion had been part of the Support Group of the 1st Armoured Division and as such had travelled up and down England and across to Northern Ireland The 30th Infantry Brigade was formed in great haste for the purpose of landing in Norway as part of an armoured force designed to capture Trondheim. The invasion of the Low Countries put an end to this enterprise before the force could sail but not before the Battalion had had the full benefit of orders and counter-orders and all the confusion resulting from sudden changes of military plans at the latest of last minutes.

On Tuesday, the 21st of May, the Battalion, dispersed in Suffolk villages, had done a hard day's work constructing road-blocks in anticipation of the German invasion of England, then regarded as imminent. Orders received at 7 p.m. for an immediate move to Southampton resulted in the whole Battalion being under way in fully packed vehicles at a quarter past eleven. An exhausting drive in pouring rain ended at Southampton at midday on the 22nd. Vehicles were taken straight to the docks and loaded as they were, with all ammunition and weapons (except for forty rounds per man and eight Bren guns) on to the vehicle ship. Some two hours later the Battalion marched in hot, sunny weather to embark on a personnel ship, s.s. *Archangel*. The German armoured thrust was then at, or approaching, Abbeville.

The men spent the night packed like sardines, only those not on duty being able to get a few hours' fitful sleep, as the convoy of two personnel and two vehicle ships, with the 2nd Battalion 60th Rifles and the 1st Battalion, steamed up-Channel to Dover. Here Brigadier Nicholson received his orders to move, on disembarkation at Calais, to operate somewhere beyond St. Omer on the right flank of the British Expeditionary Force. It was known that the 3rd Royal Tank Regiment had gone to Calais the previous night with similar orders. The third unit of the 30th Infantry Brigade had crossed from Dover on the 21st and were awaiting the arrival of the rest of the Brigade at Calais.

The convoy sailed from Dover under escort of one destroyer, and during the crossing the Brigadier issued orders for the battalions to move to dispersal areas clear of the harbour on disembarkation, and to await the unloading of vehicles. As these arrived, units were to concentrate right and left of the Calais—Boulogne road, the first unit to disembark to take the right. This order had, in the event, the effect of determining the tasks of the 60th and Rifle Brigade, for, as the personnel ships steamed into Calais Harbour at one o'clock on Thursday, the 23rd of May (after an ineffectual attempt by German aircraft to bomb them and amid depth charges dropped by the escort), the 60th's ship berthed first.

From the moment of arrival it was plain that the battle for Calais was on. A movement control staff officer and a few khaki-clad figures only were there to handle the warps and one or two short gang-planks. Broken glass from the station and hotel buildings littered the quays and platforms, in which many bomb craters were visible, besides overturned and bombed trucks on the lines. As he stepped ashore the Brigadier was informed by the movement control staff officer that all telephone communications at the quay with England and France were cut by fifth columnists and Germans; that the town was full of snipers; that the location of B.E.F. Headquarters, last heard of near Hazebrouck, had not been known for some time and could not now be conjectured; and that German armoured columns were already operating between Boulogne and Calais. The 3rd Royal Tanks were still unloading the last of their "B" Echelon, but the regiment had already moved south of Calais and were rumoured to have met opposition. The battalions filed off the ships to their dispersal area, the men gazing curiously at the piles of abandoned kit lying on the quays, jettisoned by crowds of soldiers and airmen who were being shepherded on to the ship recently vacated by the 3rd Royal Tanks, homeward-bound. These troops were in the main non-combatant personnel, Royal Air Force ground staff and clerks, who had suffered a severe battering by the Luftwaffe on their travels to the coast. They bore every sign of this, and made a far from cheerful welcome to the theatre of war.

The dispersal area for the 1st Battalion was in the sand-dunes to the east of the harbour mouth. The Colonel was quickly called away and John Taylor, who had temporarily taken over Second-in-Command in the absence of Alex Allan, on special duty, set companies, after a hasty meal, to digging trenches. It was well that he did so, for such protection as was then prepared was used throughout the battle and it was in this area that the last rounds were fired. The afternoon wore on, with the vehicle ships still churning up the mud in the falling harbour tide in the absence of tugs to haul them in to the quays, and it was not until five o'clock that the 60th's vehicle ship berthed and unloading began. She got the benefit of three cranes, while the Rifle Brigade ship, last in, had only one. Soon after unloading began the first enemy shells fell on the far side of the harbour. This shelling, combined with an excited mob of civilians yelling "Les Allemands," was in full view of the Battalion, which could also see that some form of engagement was taking place down the coast towards Boulogne. Now came the news that the 3rd Royal Tanks had fought an action only a few kilometres south of their position, and were withdrawing into Calais itself, having lost about a squadron of tanks, and officers began to feel more than impatient for the arrival of their weapons and equipment.

Unloading proceeded very slowly. The British stevedores had worked for thirty-six hours at unloading a supply ship of rations for the B.E.F. on to lorries, and were almost too tired to stand. There was no French dock labour, with the exception of the operators of the cranes. Parties from each company standing by to take away vehicles did what they could to help, but it was found that unskilled labour was more inclined to delay unloading than otherwise. So darkness fell, with little that was required ashore, and already there were new orders for the Battalion requiring the use of all transport urgently.

There were really four phases of the action at Calais, corresponding with fresh orders received by Brigadier Nicholson. These orders varied in accordance with information as it was collated by higher authority. The first, as has been said, was the preparation for concentration south-west of the town, with a view to advancing inland and operating against enemy light troops on the flank of the main battle. At this time it was believed that enemy armoured cars only were operating in the areas Abbeville—Calais. Next, the urgency of the supply situation for the B.E.F., now withdrawing on Dunkirk, pressed for the delivery of the 350,000 rations unloaded on the 22nd of May at Calais, and the Battalion was ordered to escort them halfway to Dunkirk, while the 60th and the Queen Victoria's Rifles held the enemy from Calais. It was now realized that the enemy were stronger than formerly supposed (for Boulogne was to be evacuated), though they were still thought to have only light armoured forces. Thirdly, early on the 24th of May orders were received for the defence of Calais; but the Brigadier was informed that evacuation of defending troops would probably be undertaken that night. Later this evacuation was postponed until the 25th. Lastly, at some time on the 25th Brigadier Nicholson received the order, directly inspired by the Prime Minister, to hold out to the last, and that every moment the enemy could be held off was of the utmost importance to the safety of the B.E.F. This last order reached the 1st Battalion some time shortly before midnight on the 25th and was repeated continually throughout the 26th by various means.

As the evening of the 23rd drew on, Colonel Chan Hoskyns gave out the orders to "A" and "I" Companies for concentration areas north of the Calais—Dunkirk road preparatory to picketing the route for some twelve miles, after which protection would be taken over by troops from Dunkirk. "B" Company was detailed as escort to the supply column, with a detachment of the 3rd Royal Tanks under command. The column was to start at midnight. These orders were not destined to be carried out, for various reasons, the first being the desperately slow rate of unloading of vehicles. "A" Company's scout platoon, under Tony Rolt, was made up to strength and drove to its rendezvous some seven miles to the east. On arrival there, local information indicated that enemy tanks were already in the area and surrounding the platoon. A despatch rider arrived from Peter Peel, who had taken over "A" Company, with withdrawal orders; but, as the despatch rider gave these orders only verbally, Tony Rolt asked for confirmation and leaguered for the night with all-round defence. During the night a number of fires were lit in his neighbourhood on all sides. These proved to be the enemy forward tanks lighting signals to show their aircraft the limit of their advance. It was only by the exercise of considerable skill that this platoon extricated itself without loss the following morning after receiving confirmatory orders to withdraw.

Meanwhile, as vehicles slowly became available, Arthur Hamilton-Russell, commanding "B" Company, with Mickey Smiley as his second-in-command, received four composite platoons made up from all companies, and was ready at the appointed hour for his escort duties. It was not until nearly five o'clock on the 24th that the column got under way.

The companies still awaited their vehicles, but "I" Company's scout platoon (David Sladen), mounted in trucks, and Charlie Weld-Forester's platoon (dismounted) were placed to the east of Calais, the 60th Rifles having by now taken up positions to the west and south-west on the outer defences of Calais, with their left about the St. Omer road. The Queen Victoria's Rifles still held the thin line of advanced positions west and south of Calais to which they had been directed on arrival. During the night a complete hiatus had taken place on the quay: all the staff having gone away to sleep in utter exhaustion, and the men who worked the cranes had disappeared after several shell splinters had landed in the holds of the ships. It was mainly by the superhuman efforts of Robin Gordon-Duff that the cranes were got working again, and slow unloading resumed.

Several ships of the Royal Navy came in during the night, one destroyer bringing Major-General McNaughton, commanding the 1st Canadian Division, to reconnoitre. Despite desultory shelling and bombing during the night, the Battalion suffered no loss so far as is known, and the first casualties occurred in Arthur Hamilton-Russell's column. This met opposition within some two miles of Calais amongst the suburban "ribbon development" and allotments. A strong enemy road-block defeated the advanced-guard tanks, which found flanking movement impossible. A gallant effort by John Surtees, with carriers, was also unsuccessful, but, while he pinned the enemy so far located, Edward Bird's platoon of "B" Company was sent round the right flank, while Platoon Sergeant-Major Stevens covered the left flank with "I" Company troops. Touch was lost with Edward Bird (who, in fact, had become involved with enemy infantry posts south of the road) and several casualties were incurred from well-directed enemy mortar fire on the reserve platoons, a motley-mounting truck receiving a direct hit. Arthur Hamilton-Russell's orders were interrupted by accurate fire wherever his command post was moved.

The Commanding Officer and Brigadier were present during a considerable part of the five-hour effort to break the passage, and, after reports from David Sladen and other posts which strongly confirmed that Arthur Hamilton-Russell's command was rapidly being surrounded by superior forces, he received orders to withdraw. Edward Bird's platoon rejoined just as the withdrawal began, well pleased with having inflicted ten or more casualties on the enemy. They had, however, lost Corporal Cross (killed) and three or four riflemen were carried back wounded. The column was back in Calais by eleven o'clock on the 24th, and "B" Company (less 6 Platoon) now took up positions in

CALAIS, MARCH, 1944

The dock area is now quite unrecognizable, only the sand-dunes and Le Bassin remain unchanged from 1940

[*Official Photo: Crown Copyright Reserved*]

Face page 13]

reserve near the cellulose factory, while the remainder joined their companies.

Much had occurred during their absence. The 60th's vehicle ship, which carried Brigade Headquarters vehicles, completed unloading at about half past four and was then filled with wounded from the first of two hospital trains which had been standing in the station before its arrival. Unloading of the Battalion's ship continued, but at about half past seven orders were given by the quay staff, who stated that they had Brigadier Nicholson's permission to close down the holds and load with the wounded of the second hospital train. Both train-loads of patients were transferred by the Battalion, but more than twenty men who had died in the train were left on the quay, which had now for some hours been under shell fire. The stevedores and their officers and some of the quay staff embarked, and the ship sailed at eight-thirty, followed some time later by the 60th's vehicle ship, which carried the remainder of the quay staff (except one) as well as the brigadier lately commanding the Boulogne base, and other persons who had escaped from that place. The ships were shelled from a south-easterly direction as they left the harbour, but not hit.

The 1st Battalion's deficiency in equipment was now severe. All scout cars and the six Bren guns they carried had been handed to the 1st Armoured Division just before embarkation, and the premature departure of the vehicle ship left them some fifty per cent. short of weapons and equipment; the Signal Officer (Jerry Duncanson) had only one truck, only "B" Company had its wireless truck; carriers were barely enough to make up two scout platoons; the doctor had no medical stores or transport, and "B" Echelon no tools. Fortunately the reserve ammunition had come ashore. Much was done to remedy this state of affairs. By the efforts of Dick Tryon and others, vehicles were, in many cases, replaced from the mass of abandoned material in Calais, several Bren guns even being "scrounged" and at least one scout car. Wally Straight was most successful in finding rations in various places under sniping and other fire, and in distributing them. The men, in fact, were never short of food but rather of time in which to eat any. A limited amount of 3-inch mortar ammunition (not issued to the Battalion up to the time of embarkation) was brought in by the Royal Navy, as well as quantities of petrol and gelignite for demolition purposes.

The Royal Navy demolition party reported, however, that the primers brought were the wrong size, and at about one o'clock they, and the Admiralty wireless ship, left Calais, the quay now being entirely deserted of officials.

For some time the increasing enemy fire had added considerably to the difficulties in movement and "sorting out." Fires were blazing everywhere; oil tanks were smoking; Robin Gordon-Duff, who had been put in charge of the protection of the quays with two scratch platoons of spare drivers, was hard put to it to keep them clear of refugee civilians. He and his men also succeeded in saving some light tanks out of several set on fire, but the 3rd Royal Tanks were already sadly reduced in tank strength by the afternoon of the 24th.

During the morning the 60th had been fighting in the outer defences of Calais in extended positions interspersed with two companies of the Queen Victoria's Rifles. The remaining half of that regiment was put under Colonel Chan Hoskyns's command, and was reinforced by platoons of the 1st Battalion. Francis Reed, with 10 Platoon of "C" Company, had put himself under command of Captain Bower, of the 60th, at the point of junction with that regiment. Here at five o'clock two German prisoners were taken, and at six o'clock two light tanks were driven off.

Little is known of the adventures of Willy Welch's platoon ("B" Company), posted on the Dunkirk exit, from the time the column returned until four o'clock. David Sladen (13 Platoon) reported at about eleven large enemy forces moving from south to north across his front, and the Colonel ordered this and 14 Platoon posts to be withdrawn to the line of battlements. This was effected successfully. The enemy took no action. At a quarter to twelve, after the Queen Victoria's Rifles had reported the outer perimeter no longer tenable, the Colonel ordered "I" and "A" Companies to occupy the inner perimeter: "I" Company on the right from the end of the bridge under the Mairie clock tower (in touch here with the 60th Rifles), then southwards four hundred yards to the canal junction, thence eight hundred yards eastwards to the junction of the battlements with the canal (here "I" Company was in touch with "A" Company). "A" Company held from this corner (inclusive of the bridge) facing east along the battlements to the Bassin des Chasses, with their scout platoon from there to the sea, but this platoon was kept as a reserve under the Colonel's hand. Both companies had an uncomfortably long frontage, and Fitz Fletcher's platoon of "B" Company (about half-strength only) and later Willy Welch's platoon also were sent to Peter Peel. Headquarters and the remaining two platoons of "B" Company were held in reserve near a large, heavily bombed building south of the quays, known as the cellulose factory. "C" Company, under Vernon Knollys, were still digging in on the dunes, held in reserve, while Harry Coghill, with H.Q. Company, was never required to leave his original position to the east of the harbour entrance throughout the battle.

Before midday on the 24th the 30th Brigade was clearly involved in a desperate attempt to defend the town and harbour of Calais. To do this, Brigadier Nicholson had few troops and all too little material. There was no artillery. Some execution had been done the previous evening and earlier this day by French shore artillery turned inland, but the men manning these weapons had put them out of action and departed to sea in a fleet of tugs before midday. A detachment of an anti-tank unit under a Gunner officer had arrived with eight 2-pounder anti-tank guns. These were all out of action by the afternoon of the 25th. The 1st Battalion had two or three 3-inch mortars, and the 60th one per company. A few anti-tank mines were landed by the Royal Navy and distributed by Anthony Bampfylde equally between the two regiments' fronts on a lorry drive which he must have found somewhat hectic. For the rest, apart from the machine guns in the few tanks left, and two Vickers brought by the Royal Marines, reliance had to be placed on Bren guns, Boys anti-tank rifles and the rifle.

Large numbers of troops continued to make their way into Calais on the 24th from the lines of communication, bombed-out anti-aircraft and searchlight positions, and Royal Army Service Corps units, but the large majority of these were unarmed except for revolvers. Useful work was, however, done by many in the heavy fighting to come, in particular by one anti-aircraft unit from Belgium. It was clear that demolition material was of the first importance, for Calais was intersected by canals which in those days made excellent anti-tank obstacles if the bridges could be destroyed or well blocked. It had been arranged that demolition would be the responsibility of the French, with the exception of the docks area, for which the Royal Navy were to make arrangements. The French had no material and no demolitions were in the event carried out. Most of the many bridges were, of course, of heavy masonry and considerable size, and the plan advanced by the French commander at the Citadel for attempting their destruction by placing under them some prodigious shells which he said existed in his store, and having them fired in some mysterious way by officers prepared to sacrifice themselves "pour la patrie," was adjudged to be at that state of the battle impracticable. H.M.S. *Wolfhound* tied up to the outer jetty during the early afternoon with a view to spotting for some destroyers which were engaging German batteries on the coast between Boulogne and Calais. At least one such battery was put out of action. The Colonel went aboard with the Adjutant (Tom Acton) to ask for demolition material, and was offered the ship's complement of gun-cotton, with any other assistance the Captain could give. Unfortunately, the matter was not pursued. H.M.S. *Wolfhound* remained until the evening, several times coming into action against attacking enemy aircraft. At about six o'clock a motor torpedo boat brought a commodore, who once more took over naval control of the docks, and, having brought the necessary primers, wirelessed for the naval demolition party to return. A swing bridge over the docks was prepared for demolition, and the party returned home, the commodore himself remaining until the 26th.

During the afternoon the enemy attacks on the 60th's front had intensified to such a degree that the Colonel found it necessary on several occasions to send assistance from his reserves. Robin Gordon-Duff took a platoon of spare drivers, with whom he held a section of the 60th's front, being about the last to be withdrawn from the outer perimeter at dark. At 4 p.m. Arthur Hamilton-Russell, with 8 Platoon (Platoon Sergeant-Major Easen) and half his scout platoon, was sent in trucks through "I" Company's position into the town to support the 60th and the Queen Victoria's Rifles. There was sniping by fifth columnists in "I" Company's area at this time, and a part of Brigade Headquarters withdrew past the Mairie to its new location at the Gare Maritime. At about four o'clock also Tony Rolt received an order through the Intelligence Officer to take his mortar section and 11 Platoon of "C" Company (Platoon Sergeant-Major Criss), to the 60th's area. There he was to get into touch with the Colonel of the 60th (whose headquarters were not known to the 1st Battalion) and put down mortar fire on an area of the Rue Gambetta which Michael Price showed him on the map. On passing through 15 Platoon he was told that enemy tanks were already in the 60th's area, and that he was likely to meet them at any moment. All parties of the 60th and Queen Victoria's Rifles confirmed that the enemy had got a footing in the town. After reconnaissance the area indicated was plastered with thirty bombs at long range from the gardens near the Mairie square. This random shoot actually helped a party of Queen Victoria's Rifles according to information given later to Tony Rolt by an officer who was present. However, he rightly decided to use no more ammunition and withdrew to report to the Colonel. Arthur Hamilton-Russell returned through "I" Company at about half-past five to the road-block near the cellulose factory. His company ("B") still had two platoons (6 and 7) detached and was destined to remain so for the remainder of the battle. At 7 p.m. these platoons were both in position with "A" Company, and at about the same time 12 Platoon, "C" Company (David Fellowes), and 11 Platoon, "C" Company (Platoon Sergeant-Major Criss), were sent to reinforce "I" Company. Both these platoons were placed by Peter Brush in reserve about two hundred yards in rear of 16 Platoon on the transverse road (and yet they were in a front-line position, as the Battalion was forward of the 60th's line here from now onwards). The 60th were fighting in the Rue Gambetta, about three hundred yards south-west of "I" Company, while withdrawals from the battlements south-west and south of the town were taking place. The Queen Victoria's Rifles, less two companies, were withdrawing to the neighbourhood of Headquarters of the 1st Battalion, and the 60th (the majority of whose retirements did not take place until dusk) were brought back to the shorter line in the old town ordered by the Brigadier. By nine o'clock the new positions were taken up, leaving, as arranged, "I" Company in a forward salient with the nearest 60th post in view of 15 Platoon's bridge overlooking the Hotel de Ville. At midnight enemy activity in the town ceased, apart from isolated bombing and shelling, Battalion Headquarters having some close "overs" of heavy stuff which fell in the Bassin near by at about one o'clock in the morning of the 25th.

Friday, the 24th, had been a day of great tension. At about 7 p.m. the Colonel sent a message to companies that positions then occupied were to be held to the last man and the last round. Apart from enemy action, the general confusion as to the situation, the fantastic stories put about by enemy agents (in a letter to the Colonel-in-Chief from hospital in England, Colonel Chan Hoskyns drew particular attention to the effect of the so-called fifth-column activities on this and the next day), and the fact that no commander ever had a moment from the time of landing to look around him and think and plan for more than the immediate future, all tended to intensify fatigue. Nobody had slept except for a few hours on the ships, or ceased to work hard since the morning of Tuesday, the 21st.

The 1st Battalion "stood to" at 3 a.m. on the 25th of May. After the successful repulse of the enemy on Friday, and the lull during the hours of darkness, Brigadier Nicholson asked the 60th and ourselves whether there were signs of enemy withdrawal. Peter Brush reported that he had himself patrolled the Rue Gambetta from five-thirty in a car and discovered no sign of the enemy.

Peter Peel reported little activity on the eastern face, and the 60th reported similarly. Forward moves were ordered by the Brigadier; but these soon met German anti-tank guns and infantry. Advance Brigade Headquarters had left the Gare Maritime for the Citadel with a view to close liaison with the French commander there at 6 a.m. At 7 a.m. Germans were reported by "I" Company in the Rue Gambetta. Sniping began from the western side of the canal, and a bombardment of "A" Company's position also took place at about this time, as well as a certain amount of small-arms fire from the woods to its front, coupled with fifth-column sniping from the houses behind them. Tony Rolt's 3-inch mortar (Corporal Blackman) engaged Germans in the Rue Gambetta at a quarter to eight from 11 Platoon's position. At eight o'clock Peter Brush was shot through the throat by a sniper, but refused to leave his headquarters. At half past eight a German tactical reconnaissance plane flew along "I" Company's positions and indicated them to its artillery by a line of smoke. At nine-thirty the enemy *strafe* came down with accuracy. At ten o'clock John Taylor arrived with orders to send Peter Brush to the regimental aid post and to take over his command. All positions were now under intense fire, except the north-eastern portion of the defences, from which the company of Queen Victoria's Rifles extending "A" Company's left, nevertheless reported observations of considerable enemy movement.

Throughout the remainder of the morning enemy pressure was very strong at the southern face. Apparently a German wireless message was intercepted by the French indicating that if the attacks now being launched failed they proposed to attack heavily on the left, i.e., the 60th's right. The Brigadier decided to attempt a diversion in rear of the enemy from the 1st Battalion's left, and at one o'clock Colonel Holland (formerly Base Commandant), accompanied by Charles Clay, returned with duplicate orders to the Colonel to take a mobile column of all tanks and carriers and at least two motor platoons through the perimeter east of the Bassin des Chasses, and to sweep round to attack the enemy's right rear in order to relieve pressure on the 60th. All reserves had become involved from the previous day with the exception of Headquarters and two platoons of "C" Company. "I" Company relied particularly on their three carriers and Corporal Blackman's mortar section of Tony Rolt's carrier platoon to cover bridges on their extended front, and both these and "A" Company's bridges were now in imminent danger of being forced. The Colonel made a formal and energetic protest, which was rejected by Colonel Holland, and preparation for collecting the necessary troops was put in hand. The Colonel stated that he would try to start at half past two. Tom Acton made a personal reconnaissance of the route along the southern edge of the Bassin des Chasses, and, finding it impracticable, returned to report and to get the vehicles, now collected, turned round and in order (for the only other way out was by the sand-dunes and beach), a very difficult task on the narrow road past the railway yards which was all the time under heavy fire.

At this time Tony Rolt, while engaged in collecting Sandy Sanderson and his carriers from "I" Company's line, became involved in the streets behind the main positions with enemy infantry who had infiltrated. Meeting three light tanks of the 3rd Royal Tanks, he led them with his carriers in a successful counter-drive to clear the streets, inflicting several casualties and finding particularly good targets down the streets across the canal to the west of David Fellowes's house and south of the 60th's left. Jerry Duncanson shot down a German reconnaissance plane with a Bren gun in "A" Company's area.

Meanwhile, the Colonel had already sent Vernon Knollys

with "C" Company (less two platoons) on foot along the dunes to the eastern end of the Bassin, but now, realizing the practical impossibility of taking wheeled vehicles through the heavy sand, he at last succeeded in getting through to Brigade by wireless and receiving Brigadier Nicholson's permission to cancel the column. The leading tanks and carriers had already started, and were in trouble in the sand. Where possible, the return of troops to their previous locations began, but the damage was already done when the defence was weakened by the collection of the column. Before the Colonel left finally to start the movement (taking practically all Battalion Headquarters with him), he had already received reports that breaches had been made in the front line and left Alex Allan to organize another position through "B" Company's main road-block. This was accomplished, the troops used being headquarters of "B" Company with one Bren-gun section, Headquarters and one company of the Queen Victoria's Rifles, the remains of an anti-aircraft battery half-armed with rifles, about thirty men of a searchlight battery, and Rear Brigade Headquarters.

The enemy had by three o'clock succeeded in breaking through the forward positions in two places and, working through the streets, in getting round the back of company headquarters and platoons holding the front line. Desperate close fighting took place, during which John Taylor was severely wounded and David Sladen killed while attacking the enemy in one of the many small counter-actions which took place. The second-in-command of "I" Company, Adrian Van der Weyer, was eventually killed defending the point of junction with the 60th, where Platoon Sergeant-Major Williams had already lost his life and shortly afterwards George Thomas too was killed. Small detachments continued to defend houses in this area after being surrounded, and Platoon Sergeant-Major Stevens (16 Platoon), with some sixteen men of "I" and "C" Companies, having fought until all their ammunition was exhausted, hid in the houses round their positions for fourteen days before starvation forced them to surrender. Few of "I" Company and the two platoons of "C" Company attached were extricated from this imbroglio in spite of a determined effort on the part of Peter Brush, who had left the regimental aid post and had received the Colonel's permission to attempt to retrieve the situation on his company's front with the assistance of Edward Bird's platoon of "B" Company (now returned from the cancelled column) and the remaining tanks. None of the latter were, however, made available, and the small party were brought to a stop a short distance beyond "B" Company's block by intensive light-automatic fire. While trying to deal with this, a French camion appeared full of wounded men belonging to "I" Company in charge of Corporal Lane, and driven by a fifth columnist at the point of the revolver. In spite of being waved on, the driver stopped under fire, and while the wounded who could were getting out to try to crawl across the road, Edward Bird ran forward, climbed into the driver's seat, and endeavoured to restart the lorry. In this gallant effort he was shot in the head, dying soon afterwards. After this, Peter Brush, having only a handful of 5 Platoon unwounded men left, was forced to abandon the attempt to reach the original company area. "A" Company, although suffering many casualties, was still fairly intact and was fighting the enemy on three sides of it, Platoon Sergeant-Major Johnstone being killed at the road-block formed to protect the rear of Peter Peel's headquarters. But the two attached platoons of "B" Company were overwhelmed by enemy tanks on this evening while attempting a flanking movement to retake the bridge which had been lost at the junction of "I" and "A" Companies' fronts. Willy Welch was killed during the counterattack.

At about half past three a shell had landed in one of H.Q. Company's trenches where the Colonel was with Harry Coghill and John Taylor, who had been brought there. John Taylor was again wounded, as was Company Quartermaster-Sergeant Clifton by the same shell, and Chan Hoskyns received such severe wounds that he subsequently died in England. Alex Allan duly reported to Brigade that he had taken over, and in time he, Arthur Hamilton-Russell and Peter Brush became aware of each other's presence, each having received false reports that the others were casualties and believing himself to be the senior officer left. This was a critical moment in the battle. Between half past three and half past four Tony Rolt's carrier platoon (dismounted after the cancellation of the column) was now remounted and sent by the acting Colonel on a foray into the old town across the Place de l'Europe as a result of reports that enemy tanks had broken in and the danger of a break-through between the two regiments. At about half past four the bombardment intensified upon the whole Brigade's position, and soon the Citadel was a vast sheet of flame. From this time Advanced Brigade Headquarters were out of touch on the wireless. While Tony Rolt was away, Arthur Hamilton-Russell reported with a well-worked-out scheme for ordering and covering the withdrawal of "A" Company, the company of the Queen Victoria's Rifles extending "A" Company's left, and as many elements of "I" and "C" Companies' platoons as possible to a shorter line behind the cellulose factory.

He already had arrangements in hand at his headquarters, and Alex Allan now approved the plan and ordered Arthur Hamilton-Russell to take charge of this operation, while he himself dealt with the point of pressure at the junction with the 60th and "B" Company's right flank. Subsequently, withdrawal proceeded with little interference from the enemy, Mickey Smiley directing platoons to their new positions as they came back. The Queen Victoria's Rifles reported that they would not be able to get all their men in before dark, and in fact some elements did cross the canal in the wrong direction, and, becoming involved with the Germans on the dunes to the east, were not recovered. Terence Prittie came back via the beach with a few men of "A" Company and, reporting to Jerry Duncanson with H.Q. Company, was ordered to join John Surtees in "C" Company's old trenches. John Surtees, after his carriers had become stuck in the sand, had been informed of the cancellation of the column during the evening by Tom Acton, who was not, however, able to retrieve the rest of Vernon Knollys's command from the dunes east of the Bassin, where the Colonel had sent them early in the afternoon. Vernon Knollys, joined by some Queen Victoria's Rifles from the eastern perimeter, had moved to positions farther east for the night. On the following morning he engaged the enemy, who had tanks in this area, for some hours before being surrounded and overwhelmed. During this action George Kane carried out a most successful fighting patrol amongst the sandhills, in which he, with Rifleman Eagle as his second-in-command, destroyed three enemy machine-gun sections, until, when disarming a fourth with an empty revolver, he was severely wounded by a German non-commissioned officer who appeared from behind a knoll at the wrong moment.

At about five o'clock Alex Allan, who had failed to get

through to the Brigadier, did succeed in speaking to Colonel Euan Miller (commanding the 60th) and ascertained that he was being very hard pressed everywhere, and was still very nervous about his right flank. Not long after this, enemy aircraft dropped showers of leaflets on and around the Gare Maritime giving an hour's grace for surrender, from six until seven. In the hot weather of these days and the dust and grime of battle drinking water was of importance, and trouble was caused from Saturday onwards by damage to the mains in the town and Gare Maritime area, but this difficulty was overcome by recourse to wells which were found and by constantly repairing main supplies. Water had to be carried for some distance to the sand-dune positions.

As on previous nights, enemy activity died down at dusk and the Battalion, now settled in its new positions for the night, breathed again. Enemy attacks had all but succeeded this evening, and great credit is due to the 60th for their magnificent defence of the old town. Chan Hoskyns and John Taylor were found in the regimental aid post at the station, both in a bad way, but the former expressed his delight at the way in which the enemy had been held off. It is difficult to write more of this fine officer, who had now seen the last of the battalion he had loved and commanded so well. John Taylor, who had been a tower of strength throughout, was a grave loss to the Battalion at this time. Though damaged beyond complete repair, he fortunately recovered enough to do much more for the Regiment during the war.

At about half past eleven the Brigadier arrived at the station yard, just as wireless touch with the 60th had been regained, and expressed himself in most complimentary terms on the Battalion's efforts. He then received the Colonel's rather meagre reports (for patrols sent out to locate troops beyond the Bassin and on the beach were not yet back) and approved his proposed dispositions for the following day. The Brigadier now gave the latest order from home that Calais was to be held to the last, and this was duly repeated during the night to responsible commanders. He then asked if it would be possible, in the event of the 1st Battalion and other troops in the vicinity being heavily attacked, to withdraw them all into the town and, with the 60th, make an all-round defensive ring to include the Citadel. Alex Allan replied that he did not think so, and the Brigadier agreed that it would be most difficult, especially in view of the failure so far to locate the remnants of the 3rd Royal Tanks, "C" Company (less two platoons) and some of the Queen Victoria's Rifles. Permission was given to wireless for a hospital ship, and this was done by the Commodore later in the night. The Brigadier wished the Battalion luck and said good night, returning to the Citadel. No further order was received from Brigade, except for a repetition of the Government and War Office message to hold to the last, brought by Colonel Holland the next morning.

At dawn a small yacht took off Colonel Chan Hoskyns and John Taylor and other wounded from the quay, where Surgeon Lieutenant Waind, R.N., had done wonderful work, and was to do more on the 26th, when he was the only medical officer present. The aid post in the tunnel was shared by Captain Cameron, R.A.M.C., the Battalion's Medical Officer, and Lieutenant Gartside, Medical Officer of the Queen Victoria's Rifles, helped by the two Padres, Wingfield-Digby and Heard. Here they had been intensely busy for two days. All their efforts deserve the highest praise. Unfortunately, during the afternoon this regimental aid post was moved on some stranger's orders farther along the beach, and so it fell, with all its patients, into enemy hands at the end.

During Saturday the 1st Battalion had used all its ammunition, including reserves, and had issued twenty thousand rounds more brought by the Royal Navy, most of which had been used up. There was, besides, a grave shortage of weapons available for the next day's battle, a shortage more serious than man power, which in itself, so far as the Battalion was concerned, was now serious. Expectations of an enemy dawn attack on the 26th were fortunately not realized. Apparently the two defeats suffered by the enemy on the Friday and Saturday imposed on the enemy corps commander such caution that he decided to relieve his forward troops (probably for the second time) and stage a new full-dress attack with more extensive artillery preparation, continuous dive-bombing attacks and heavy mortar and machine-gun support—certainly a compliment to the tired defenders. Subsequent accounts of German origin made much of the resources called upon. Artillery of a complete corps was stated to have been in action since early on the 24th, and much was made of the fine supply effort which replaced their ammunition expenditure. In consequence of this extended preparation some measure of reorganization was possible on the Battalion's front. New forward positions on either side of the Bassin des Chasses were manned by the least tired of the troops available, with as much advantage taken of cross-fire positions as possible. Bren guns were very short, and, though thoroughly cleaned during the hours of darkness, became, like the rifles, badly clogged with sand in the positions held on this side of Calais, and many excellent targets must have been inadequately dealt with on this account during Sunday's fighting while weapons were cleaned again and again. Ammunition, however, was now so short that few rounds can have been wasted; and the capable efforts of Regimental Sergeant-Major Goodey and Sergeants Phillips and Welch, of the new skeleton Headquarters formed, eked out what was left for replenishment to the best effect. The last 3-inch mortar rounds were fired during the morning with accurate results by Sandy Sanderson, who had, with Corporal Morton, already done good execution with a salvaged machine gun. There were no other weapons to use. The heavy German strafing preparation had little effect on the riflemen, who fired from their exposed positions at the attacking Stukas as coolly as participants in a pheasant shoot. That some positions became, as the day drew on, untenable goes without saying, but on no occasion was a withdrawal made of more than a few yards, and more than once the original position was retaken. The spaces between the portions of the defence on the Battalion's front entailed great difficulty of control and communication, and distances between sub-units were greatly increased by battle obstacles. In this kind of fighting a man often knows nothing of what is occurring within ten yards of him. Smoke, fires, dust and falling masonry, line after line of railway track holding scores of goods wagons and other rolling stock, thin but high cement walls, heavy sand on the dunes and bunds combined to make movement as fatiguing as observation was difficult. In spite of all this, the defence, by no means badly damaged or deterred by the preparatory bombardments, continued throughout the morning to hold the enemy's attack, which was now being pressed very strongly at all points; but from about one o'clock onwards the situation deteriorated. Accurate German heavy mortar fire was mainly responsible for helping on their infantry.

It had been hoped that these and other enemy support weapons might be dealt with by naval bombardment and this had been asked for at a quarter to eleven on the 26th in the last message ever sent over the air from the Gare Maritime. Targets considered easily recognizable were indicated as well as a clear line beyond which it was safe to shoot. In the evening an effective bombardment was in fact carried out by the Royal Navy on this line, but it was by then too late. Lieutenant Millet, of the Royal Corps of Signals, who, with his section of Brigade Headquarters Signals, had been of inestimable value throughout, was ordered to be prepared to destroy all wireless installations and files early in the afternoon. Later this was done for him, before the final order was given, by enemy mortar fire, all vehicles of value in the station yards being burned out. By half past four or thereabouts the last rounds were fired, and all organized resistance ceased. The enemy infantry had indeed treated the exhausted defenders with respect and taken their time in coming to grips. This they eventually did at all points simultaneously, from the 60th's right, into the Citadel itself, and all along the circle of attack to the beaches in the rear of the Battalion's positions. Men of the Battalion were shot from across the harbour mouth at the end.

Much more could be written of the fighting on this last day: of the tough resistance put up on the right by Tony Rolt's scout platoon, Platoon Sergeant-Major Easen's platoon of "B" Company (he later died of wounds) and others; of Arthur Hamilton-Russell, mortally wounded in an attempt to gain observation from the most exposed point near him, after as hard a four days' fighting and work as ever a soldier did; of Tony Rolt's final gallant effort, almost alone, to seize a possible point of vantage; of the accurate fire still being directed from the French shore-battery emplacement by men of "A" Company, Royal Marines and others, including Major Coxwell Rogers, the Staff Captain, who was killed here while firing a Bren gun at Germans on the beach behind this position; of the hours of steady and accurate shooting put in by Peter Brush's command based on John Surtees's trenches on the sand-dunes, where Rifleman Gurr (one of the Battalion's best Bisley shots) got badly wounded in the leg he was to lose; Sergeant Welsh, shot through the jaw, Rifleman Murphy, who had found and got into working order a Lewis gun; David Fellowes, of "C" Company, with a large hole

CALAIS

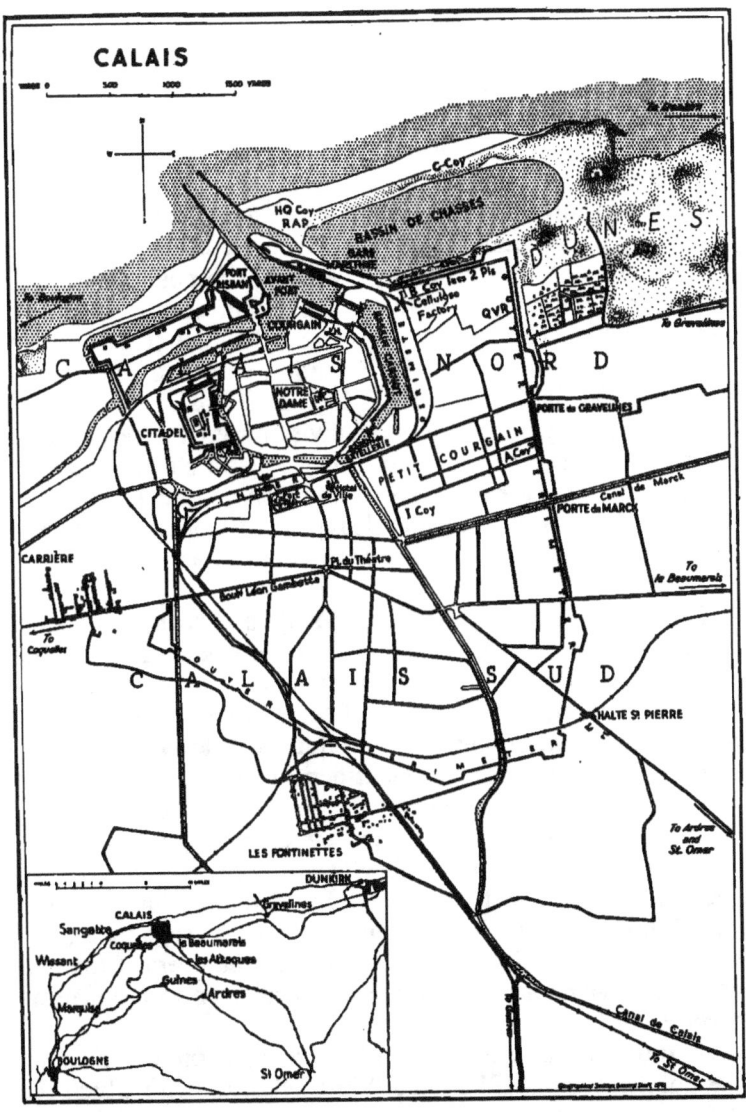

in his head from the fighting in "I" Company's area the day before; Peter Peel and John Surtees, both wounded, and Peter Brush wounded again, with Charlie Forester, Michael Price and a few other riflemen sniped and hit (for that was all that was now possible) to the end—until Jerry Duncanson, who had never for a moment ceased to chivvy the enemy at every possible opportunity, and who had enjoyed every moment of it, stood up to kill the last German to be shot in this area, and inevitably received his mortal wound. It is invidious to dwell upon individual efforts when all did their utmost. Of those who died, although the deeds of some are not known in full, it would be impossible to write too much. Of those who survived a great number were wounded, most of whom had to recover as best they could in German hands. If all ranks of the 1st Battalion who had reached by keenness and hard work such a high standard of training for mobile warfare with an armoured division were disappointed of their fun in a war of movement, they at least still enjoyed the excitements of the early days of this action, and in the grim realities of the last days took pride in their discipline and fighting qualities as Riflemen under any conditions of war.

For the Regiment the losses at Calais had been calamitous. At one blow we had been deprived of the whole of one of the two Regular battalions. It is on the framework of trained officers, non-commissioned officers and riflemen whose experience enables them to teach others and to command at levels above their peace-time ranks that a regiment depends for its expansion in war—the more so as pioneers in the new role of motor infantry. In the 1st Battalion was collected almost one-half of the total resources of the Regiment. They were, too, our friends. There were months of anxiety before the full details of the casualties were known. In the relief brought by the knowledge that many were prisoners we did not forget that large numbers of the best officers, non-commissioned officers and riflemen would take no further part in the war.

Against this disaster, as some faint consolation, we could set the public acclaim, led by the Prime Minister, with which the defence of Calais was greeted. There is something about a gallant failure against heavy odds which appeals—or used to—to the British public. After the war those concerned were to receive some recognition for what they had done. But for the

Regiment it was not simply a question of praise and medals. If the loss of one battalion would shortly be forgotten by the public in the rush of events which were soon to deal in corps and armies and army groups, it was still to us an appalling calamity. What we required was an assurance that our personal loss had been to some purpose.

The idea of sending a brigade to Calais had originated at the highest level. When it was clear that so far from attacking the flank of the enemy the troops would have difficulty in holding the port, it was in a message drafted by the Prime Minister that the news was sent to the Brigadier.

> "Defence of Calais to the utmost is of the highest importance to our country and to our Army now. First, it occupies a large part of the enemy armoured forces, and keeps them from attacking our line of communications. Secondly, it preserves a sally-port from which portions of the British Army may make their way home. Lord Gort has already sent troops to your aid, and the Navy will do all possible to keep you supplied. The eyes of the Empire are upon the defence of Calais, and His Majesty's Government are confident that you and your gallant regiment will perform an exploit worthy of the British name."

And when the pressure of events elsewhere was such that it became necessary to hold the town to the last round and without help, it was again the Prime Minister, with his unfailing flair for "command," whose message was sent to the defenders.

> "Every hour you continue to exist is of the greatest help to the B.E.F. Government has therefore decided you must continue to fight. Have greatest possible admiration for your splendid stand. Evacuation will not (*repeat* not) take place, and craft required for above purpose are to return to Dover. . . ."

Mr. Winston Churchill had been a soldier. He was quite clear about the implications of telling Riflemen that there would be no withdrawal: he understood the difficulties attendant upon the earlier talk of relief for the garrison. At the time the utmost importance seemed to attach to the possession for a few hours longer of the port of Calais. And nine years afterwards, giving his considered judgment, the Prime Minister was once again quite clear that great results had in fact been achieved, that the defence of Calais was worth it.

"Calais was the crux. Many other causes might have prevented the deliverance of Dunkirk, but it is certain that the three days gained by the defence of Calais enabled the Gravelines waterline to be held, and that without this, even in spite of Hitler's vacillations and Rundstedt's orders, all would have been cut off and lost."

CHAPTER III

THE PRACTICE OVER

IF the 1st Battalion's introduction to war was calamitous, a forlorn hope in an unaccustomed role, the 2nd were let down more easily. At the end of the first spell in the desert an officer could write home: "It is a great bit of luck to have been able to have a practice over or two, so to speak, with the Italians—what more delightful people to fight could there be?" That was written at the end of a successful campaign. It is not so certain that many members of the Battalion as they sat in Egypt waiting for the Italians to attack would have dismissed the dangers of the future so lightly. The fighting qualities—or lack of them—of the Italians had for years featured as a standing joke in English music-halls. But there were a great many Italians in Libya. We believed them to be well equipped: they had had recent experience of fighting in Spain and Abyssinia; they had a large air force. In fact, their air superiority had a decisive effect on the dispositions of the Battalion throughout the campaign. It is always easy after the race to predict the winner. In April, 1940, few prophets would have predicted the eclipse of the Italian Army within ten months.

The Italians were bad fighters. But they were not a negligible quantity. There were some few divisions, generally recruited from the North, which fought really well, such as the Folgore, the "Lightning" Division, which was well up to the standard of the Germans. Some Italian pilots pressed their attacks home with great determination and their gunner officers reached a reasonably high standard. But on the whole they were more concerned with putting up a show of resistance sufficient to satisfy their honour than with fighting for the glory of the Fascist State. When our attacks began—and often when nothing was happening at all—a tremendous barrage of defensive fire would issue from the Italian positions and, since there is nothing like bright colours to cheer those of uncertain morale, a high proportion of "tracer" in the most varied colours was included in their armament. One of our earlier—and unsuccessful—attacks was described by a rifleman as more like the Crystal Palace than anything else, though the same occasion reminded Brigadier Strafer Gott of the Ypres Salient. When the war opened in the desert, no one could know that once these initial fireworks had been braved there were thousands of prisoners ready for collection. Fighting the Italians had this disadvantage, that few of their sentries dared sleep upon their watch, though those who did slept sound.

In April, 1940, the 2nd Battalion was at the Citadel in Cairo. It formed part of the Support Group, 7th Armoured Division. This formation consisted of ourselves and the 1st Battalion 60th Rifles, who were a motor battalion organized as we were, and the two Royal Horse Artillery regiments in the Division, the 4th equipped with 25-pounders and the 3rd armed, if that is the right word, with Bofors anti-tank guns. The Regiment began thus early an association in the war with the Royal Horse Artillery which was to last until Austria and the Baltic had been reached. The motor battalions were at this time organized with four motor companies each of three motor platoons and a carrier platoon. Such was the shortage of equipment that we began this war with only five carriers per platoon. Brigadier Teddy Williams, until he was called home to command an infantry brigade, was the first Brigadier of the Support Group. It was held in readiness in the Delta to be rushed to the Western Desert as soon as the Italians showed signs of entering the war. Meanwhile the Battalion concentrated on training and on making the most of the fleshpots of Cairo before they were left behind. General Jumbo Wilson was at that time in command of the British Troops in Egypt. Colonel Callum Renton asked him to come to lunch in the officers' mess on the 1st of May to celebrate the birthday of the Duke of Connaught and the sixtieth anniversary of His Royal Highness's appointment as Colonel-in-Chief of the Regiment. The toils of practice mobilization were set aside: preparations were made to entertain the General and for him to be photographed with the officers of the Battalion after lunch. During the morning the Adjutant's telephone began to ring at unusually frequent intervals. Sometimes it was an inquiry about the cocktail party to be held in the mess the next evening; but more often messages arrived indicating that something was about to happen. The General drove up an hour late. When he arrived he said that the photograph had better be taken at once, since the Battalion would be moving at extremely short notice with the rest of the Division to the Western Desert. It was a difficult and complicated mobilization and movement problem to take place with the utmost secrecy.

On the 2nd of May the Battalion moved out for the first time along the Mena road to take the field in the Western Desert.*

Since the Regiment was to fight for some three years in this desert and eventually four battalions were to be concerned, it may be worth describing in some detail the country, the climate and the conditions of life.

Most Englishmen picture the desert as a series of rolling sand-dunes stretching endlessly across Africa, traversed only by caravans of camels and the Legion described so graphically by Mr. P. C. Wren. In the Western Desert there were, fortunately, comparatively few dunes. The surface was generally stony, although in many places there was deep sand. It was not uniformly flat, since in most areas definite features existed. Along the Mediterranean there was a narrow belt of sand-dunes, consisting for the most part of sand of an almost dazzling whiteness. The coast from Alexandria to Mersa Matruh, with its glaring white beaches and its intensely blue sea, has an exotic beauty all its own. Inland there is a wider belt of country chiefly remarkable for short scrub and a kind of molehill, known as a camel hump or to some as "porridge country." These are so placed that one of the wheels of a vehicle is always in contact with a camel hump, so that its movement across them becomes a trial to the nerves and temper of its occupants. It did have the advantage of forming a more suitable background than the bare desert to stationary vehicles and was thus the nearest thing to cover from air to be found in Libya. Farther inland there is generally an escarpment or rocky cliff dividing the coastal strip from the desert proper. The most famous escarpment runs from west of Tobruk, parallel with the coast as far as Sollum, where it juts out as a cliff over the sea and then describes a half-circle to the south, gradually decreasing in height until it peters out in the desert. Above, that is south, of the escarpment the desert is,

---

*By this time the company commanders were: "A," Squeak Purdon; "B," Hugo Garmoyle; "C," Dick Poole; "S," Dick Basset; H.Q., Douglas Darling. Tony Fulford was Second-in-Command.

generally speaking, more level and more sandy, although there are many hollows and hills and large areas or belts of stony ground. On the whole, the farther south one goes, once one is clear of the stony belt parallel with the escarpment, the more sandy is the surface.

The nature of the desert has been well described in a letter written by an officer in 1940. "The ground for the most part is fairly hard sand, covered sometimes with scrub, sometimes with stones, which vary in size from small pebbles to quite large boulders. Some areas are covered with furrows from Bedouin cultivation, but of course there are no crops now and these areas are given over to scrub. The whole area is divided up into huge terraces by escarpments which run east and west. As they approach the west these escarpments converge on one another, until at Sollum they coalesce to form a formidable obstacle. . . . These escarpments, together with other physical features such as depressions, tablelands, hills and spurs, give a fair amount of variety to the scenery, so that you cannot say that one bit of desert is just like another, although it is very nearly true. Other landmarks—very important for navigation—are Arab graves, which are simply large cairns of stones, and wells and cisterns. These are fairly plentiful, although few of them have water, and they can always be recognized a long way off by the conical mound of excavated sand. These cisterns are most remarkable. They were made by the Romans; some are huge subterranean chambers cut out of the limestone underneath the sandy surface."

For most of the year the desert is a dull, dry brown. In the autumn and winter there are occasional rains, particularly near the coast. After them you can almost see a faint green sheen appear, like a bad shave on a man's chin, over the surface of the desert. In the spring a remarkable number of wild flowers make an unexpected appearance. One April, as the 2nd Battalion was on the way up for a spell of fighting which was to end with his death at Alamein, Mike Mosley counted over thirty different varieties of wild flowers at one place where his company had halted for the night. Nor was the desert devoid of wild life. There were numerous birds, wagtails and an occasional English robin, larks, and a few bustards, which found their way, rarely, into the cooking-pot of a company officers' mess. There were scorpions and lizards. Chameleons were often caught and kept as pets by riflemen, with pieces of string tied round their tails to prevent them escaping. Jerboas, or desert rats, were shy and not often seen. They were not unlike miniature kangaroos, with long tails having a feathery tuft at the end. Gazelle, of course, were the swiftest, the most beautiful and, for them unfortunately, the only edible animals in the desert. They showed a great turn of speed and it needed a very level piece of desert to give a truck a chance of keeping up with them.

The climate was almost perfect with the one terrible exception of the khamseen. There was more often than not a breeze, and even in the summer there were few days which were unbearably hot. The nights were cool in summer and definitely cold in winter. There were many days in winter, and a few even as late as May, when the weather was cold enough to call for pullovers, leather waistcoats and greatcoats. When the desert was cut up by vehicle tracks a strong wind was always apt to blow the dust about unpleasantly. But in the spring a boiling-hot wind would blow at times from the south, from the centre of the African continent, whipping the dust to fury, dragging down tents, filling every corner with particles of hot sand. These khamseen (sandstorms carried by a roaring and scorching gale) had the most irritating effect on the skin. There was no refuge from them; it was impossible to see for more than a few yards; cooking was out of the question; washing was unthinkable; the body became unutterably weary; the mind refused to think. A bad khamseen is one of the worst experiences that the weather can require a man to endure.

At the times when there did not happen to be a battle in progress, life in the desert was healthy but dull. The ground was hard for sleeping on; the nights were often cold; at midday the wind sometimes dropped and it was hot. The food for the first two years consisted almost entirely of bully and biscuits, helped out by an occasional tin of "meat and vegetables." Fresh meat, bread and butter seldom arrived. The shortage of water made washing difficult and cut down the amount of tea that could be drunk, particularly since water was needed for radiators as well as for drinking and washing. Its issue was generally one gallon per man per day for all purposes, sometimes half a gallon, more often one and a half, and even at half a gallon there was seldom any real excuse not to shave—if anyone wanted one. But it was a revelation to those who complained in peace time, if they had to miss one bath a week, that life was still endurable on no baths for three months at a stretch—and sleeping at night time fully clothed. Those lucky enough to be near the sea could avail themselves of Mediterranean bathing and sea-water soap.

It was on the whole a healthy life. There were cases of sandfly fever; there were several severe outbreaks of jaundice, to which, for some reason, officers were more prone than riflemen. But the real scourge was a form of blood-poisoning called "desert sores." Those—and there were many—addicted to this infuriating disease, found that the smallest cut or prick went "bad" and could spread into a large sore. Even sunburn could lead to the appearance of these sores. Whether they derived from vitamin deficiency or the sand of the desert, they were a curse and an affliction to many people. For some reason the stretch of desert south of the escarpment was more healthy than the coastal belt. On one who was not suffering from sores and did not find himself gradually growing yellow the desert air had something of the effect of a tonic.

As the sharpest possible contrast to the dull level of existence in the field, to the inevitable bully, the monotonous routine, the exclusively masculine company, stood Cairo, the home of every luxury, every amusement, every vice. After living in the open for three or four months the Rifleman on leave suddenly found himself in the most comfortable of hotels, surrounded by cold drinks, by baths, by food that, at any rate, did not appear to be bully, by barbers, by salesmen of every conceivable ware, by women of all sorts and descriptions. It was a city as unreal as a cinema picture. Yet it was only a day or two's journey from the front. It had most excellent welfare services "laid on" by the authorities on the one hand; on the other there were to be had the most extraordinary, the most sordid experiences for the asking in the murky depths of the Berka. For the picture of luxury and comfort was only the enamel which covered as dirty and fly-ridden a city as there is in the world. It was the fashion in the desert to imagine to yourself or aloud what you would do when you first set foot in Cairo or it might be Alexandria, whether the bath would precede the whisky-and-soda, what you would eat and where you would go. "Leave" meant to those in the desert an immediate transition from the most primitive conditions and the simplest life to all the material advantages of civilization imposed on a city that was essentially Oriental at heart.

The military significance of the desert which most affected a motor battalion was that you could drive a vehicle anywhere. Distances were immense; maintenance of any force in the field was difficult. There was always a cry for petrol and for water, and the armour was obliged to wear out its tracks in lengthy journeys before the enemy were met at all. Since there was little cover and few obstacles to movement, the power of the tank was greater than in other theatres of war. The Regiment worked with armoured formations until their "track mileage" had been consumed, often covered the whole front in advance, withdrawal or in static periods and in addition took part in the infantry battle when it materialized. That is why there was hardly a moment in the desert campaigns when one or more battalions of the Regiment were not in the forefront of the battle.

There were many Italians in Cairo. From the days of the Abyssinian War some of these Italians had taken a keen interest in any military plans the British Troops in Egypt might make for defending the Delta against invasion from Libya. The Italians had had several years to consider these plans. They knew that a fortress had been constructed at Mersa Matruh, some three hundred miles west of Alexandria and a hundred and fifty miles east of the frontier town of Sollum. Here there were water and a small harbour. Sitting over coffee and cakes in the Delta, these interested strategists had spared a contemptuous thought for the British soldier digging sweatily in the desert. They knew also that an armoured force was training in the desert near Cairo. It soon became generally accepted in Cairo, as in Rome and London, that on the outbreak of war the frontier would be watched by a screen of light forces and the main armoured force would concentrate on the southern flank of the fortress of Mersa Matruh. The experts in the cafés in Cairo, knowing the British inferiority in numbers, never doubted that these were the plans being prepared. The Italian General Staff banked on a defensive policy on our part.

The British Higher Command, and General Jumbo Wilson in particular, had, however, quite other ideas. With great secrecy plans for a "forward policy" were hatched. Despite our inferior forces it was decided to attack the frontier posts the moment war was declared. This would at least have the effect of hindering the

Italian preparations for the march to Cairo. The secret was well kept. Few outside the planning staffs in Cairo knew of it, so that agents and gossips continued to congratulate themselves on the discovery of the British plan. It was to implement this forward policy that the 2nd Battalion moved to the desert, not that they knew it at the time.

The Battalion first took up a defensive position to the west of Mersa Matruh along the Wadi Halazin. They soon realized how cold the desert could be, even in May. They were under the command of the Support Group Commander, then Brigadier Strafer Gott; they were supported by some anti-tank guns of the 3rd Regiment, Royal Horse Artillery, shortly to be commanded by Lieutenant-Colonel Jock Campbell from "C" Battery, 4th Royal Horse Artillery. No account of the Regiment's operations in the desert would be complete without mention of these two officers. Strafer Gott had been commanding the 1st Battalion 60th Rifles. He had also been G.S.O.1 of the 7th Armoured Division. He was a Rifleman: he understood the desert; he had formed and trained a motor battalion. You could not talk to him for long without realizing that he had a deep understanding of the military situation. He was a leader who was to have under his command battalions of the Regiment as Brigadier, Divisional Commander and Corps Commander, and it was a sad misfortune that he was killed at the moment when his abilities were at last to have their reward. He was a great friend to the Regiment, as well as a great leader. In these days, when we remember more clearly the comparative plenty of 1944, it is difficult to do justice to Strafer, who used his meagre resources to such effect and achieved great results at small expense. Anyone who served with the Regiment in the desert in the years before Alamein will remember the feeling of security and confidence which resulted from a visit from Strafer. For one thing, in moments of the most serious crisis, his sense of humour never allowed him to miss the opportunity of making us laugh.

The fortunes of the Battalion were intimately connected with those of Jock Campbell. A Horse Gunner who had trained for war on the polo ground and out hunting with the Pytchley, he possessed tremendous drive and energy, the quickest possible eye for country, an offensive spirit and a tactical sense unmatched in the desert, and the intelligence, not universal among commanders, to use his motor infantry in the right way. If the enormous figure of Jock Campbell, striding into Battalion Headquarters, groping with a huge hand for his notebook, was greeted sometimes with apprehension, his vast enthusiasm, his determination and obvious insight into enemy intentions carried all before him. He was a friend to all the Regiment, but particularly to the 2nd Battalion. It was not altogether a coincidence that during the battle of Sidi Rezegh, where Brigadier Campbell was awarded the V.C., he was accompanied in his car throughout the action by two officers of the Regiment, Ian Whigham and Philip Flower.

After a fortnight of holding this position, all the indications were that the Italian entry into the war had been delayed. The Battalion soon moved back to the outskirts of Mersa Matruh. Here training was continued, companies were sent off on such tasks as the building of dumps; and every day the news from Europe became worse. It was on the 4th of June at a party for Etonians given by the 60th that we heard of the fate of the 1st Battalion at Calais.

By the 7th of June it was clear that the Italians were about to enter the war. On the 10th of June orders were received to move at once to the frontier area, though it was not known definitely that war had been declared. At Sidi Barrani, as the first brew of the morning was being made, a British bomber appeared from the west, passed over the landing ground, turned back as if in trouble, and suddenly dived straight for the ground—a crash, an explosion, a sheet of flame, and then a great cloud of black smoke, broad at first, gradually tapering away. It was a sight that Riflemen were to know too well.

The success of the "forward policy" was complete. The frontier posts were taken, Capuzzo and Fort Maddalena with a satisfactory number of prisoners. The 60th had the larger share in these attacks; but at least the silk pyjamas of the commandant at Capuzzo fell into the hands of Oscar Chichester. As soon as the initial capture of these posts had been completed the 7th Armoured Division reverted to the defensive, the armoured brigades remained forward on the line of the frontier wire, covered by the 11th Hussars, and the 2nd Battalion took up a defensive position at Sollum. It was here that the first night patrols were undertaken.

In the life of a member of a motor platoon night patrolling bulked large. For the subaltern in command such patrols were a heavy responsibility. Their object might be to capture a prisoner or lay mines or recover a tank knocked out in enemy territory, or, more often, to find out information about enemy dispositions or habits. It is always distinctly unpleasant to wander about in the dark when you know the enemy may be somewhere about. But in the desert there was a further problem. Owing to the open nature of the country the enemy were seldom, as it were, within walking distance. It was a case of bumping over the desert in a truck for some five to fifteen miles, then patrolling for the remaining three or four miles on foot, finding out the information, returning to the truck and driving home. One of the biggest problems was, of course, to find your way. More than one officer has been lost for a whole night between the mess and his bed, although the total distance involved was only two or three hundred yards. A night patrol was a much greater problem. If you drive the truck too close the enemy hear the engine and are ready for you. If you do not go far enough there will not be time to complete the task in the dark. All these hazards crop up before the enemy are encountered at all. A man standing still at night in country that he has seen in daylight has a great advantage over a stranger stumbling about in the dark. Sentries are not often surprised. The Italian sentry was just occasionally fast asleep, in which case you did not find him at all, or, much more often, so trigger-happy that the slightest sound would elicit a considerable flow of highly coloured tracer ammunition. Apart from navigation and the alertness of the enemy, the patrol commander was continually harassed by the apparently inevitable irritations that attend any movement by night: the rifleman who cannot see in the dark, the man who trips over every stone, the non-commissioned officer who mistakes you for the enemy, the coughers, the whisperers, the sleepers-at-every-stop, the pointers-out-of-bushes, and the men whose Bren guns jam. Patrols were a great strain on everyone; few activities call for a higher standard of leadership. The Battalion at this time did much patrolling. If there were rumours that Bardia was being evacuated, carrier patrols went in daylight to investigate. When Capuzzo was reoccupied by the Italians, night patrols reconnoitred the new positions. Those early lessons were useful for the future, and luckily were attended by few disasters.

The greater part of the Battalion was at the bottom of the escarpment, with Sollum Bay on its flank. Here there was some of the best bathing on the coast. But proximity to the sea involved the Battalion in an incident almost without parallel in naval history. One morning the Commander of the Western Desert Force, General O'Connor, was visiting the positions by the shore. Colonel Callum Renton was going round with him. While he was talking to riflemen, four destroyers were seen approaching from out to sea. This was indeed co-operation from the Navy. They had not, however, given the General much information about what they intended to do. He was, in fact, surprised that they were there. Everyone got out of their trenches and stood up to welcome the Navy. They came in closer and closer, very close indeed. Riflemen waved; people hoped to recognize their friends from Alexandria. Suddenly someone realized that they were Italian. The excitement was intense: everyone returned to their trenches; two Brens were switched to oppose the Italian Navy. They came so close that it seemed that they intended a landing—a landing which would have been extremely difficult to oppose. When they had come near enough for every detail of the ships to be visible, they opened fire over the heads of the Battalion, their shells falling with little damage at the foot of the escarpment. Then they turned about and disappeared as quickly as they had come. There cannot be many occasions in the history of war when British troops have been bombarded from the sea, certainly not by the Italian Navy. If there had not been such illustrious witnesses of this incident, the Royal Navy might well have claimed that there are none.

By early August it was clear that the tanks of the armoured brigades were wearing themselves out to no purpose. They were therefore withdrawn to the Mersa Matruh area for refitting and the 11th Hussars, less one squadron, went back to Bug Bug. The front was taken over by the Support Group. The 2nd Battalion was relieved in the Sollum area by the 3rd Coldstream Guards and moved south of the escarpment, where its front stretched for something approaching sixty miles. This was a return to the original plan so well known to the Italians, by which light forces held the frontier area ready to fall back, imposing delay on the enemy, while the armour was concentrated south of Mersa Matruh. It was the old plan. But the "forward policy" had already delayed the Italian advance for two months. It was a suitable role for a motor battalion, supported by 4th R.H.A. and covered on the south flank, inevitably, by a squadron of the 11th Hussars. It was none the less a strenuous one, since great distances had to be covered and, owing to the general shortage of armoured vehicles, much patrolling had to be done in unarmoured 15-cwt. trucks which should really have been done by armoured cars. The Italian command of the air made this role particularly trying. Although the appearance of one Hurricane had effectively scattered a formation of Italian biplane fighters, the Italians were numerically superior in aircraft, at any rate temporarily. There were no anti-aircraft guns in the Support Group or indeed at this stage in the Division.

It was early in September before the Italians began their much-vaunted advance. There were signs that their forces were concentrating behind Bardia. A rifleman on an observation post reported seeing "a wog beating a donkey," which information was construed by a smart intelligence officer to be evidence that mule-borne mountain artillery were to be employed in this desert advance. Early in the morning of the 13th of September there was a sound of engines being run. Hundreds of those great, black Diesel lorries so soon to be familiar were "revving up" for the advance to Cairo, and soon after first light a large-scale artillery barrage began to fall on an area forward of the Coldstream Guards unoccupied by our troops. To the accompaniment of this encouraging noise the Italian advance began.

The 2nd Battalion's front was not immediately affected by these events. It was clear that they would soon have to conform to the Coldstream Guards when they began to withdraw, according to plan, along the coastal road. Before this happened the Battalion captured its first prisoner, an event worthy of its description in a letter home. "It was a fine bit of action! A shape was seen wandering about in the desert mirage, and for about ten minutes we shot at this shape until finally it stopped and we went out to see what it was. It was a dear old Italian, quite bald, who had got lost on his motor-bicycle. Eventually we had hit one of the wheels and he had fallen off. I did feel sorry for him. But I think he was far too old for fighting and much better off in a nice prisoner-of-war camp; and I think he thought so too." Tom Bird, who wrote that letter, was to fight for years in the desert, to be wounded four times, to command the anti-tank company on the Snipe position at Alamein, and to see the capture of thousands of German and Italian prisoners by various battalions of the Regiment. This bald one was the first.

The Italians plodded along on the coastal belt. The gunners did a great deal of damage to them and they were seriously delayed in the passes down the escarpment at Sollum and Halfaya. Their advance crossed the Battalion's front between the frontier and Halfaya, so that after that they did not follow us up directly, though it was necessary for the Battalion to withdraw to conform to the Coldstream Guards on the coast. Although we were not seriously engaged, this was a trying operation, because, apart from the hot wind that blew unceasingly, the Battalion attracted much attention from the Italian air force. Medium level bombing by Savoias in formation was not generally particularly effective. But this time they scored some lucky hits. Being without armoured vehicles except a few ancient carriers, the Battalion was obliged to send patrols in ordinary 15-cwt. trucks miles out into the desert. Tony Palmer and Tony Franklyn took two of these round the flank of the enemy and remained for almost two days right behind the enemy's main force. Their information kept the rest of the Battalion in touch with the movements of the Italian forces, ponderously moving forward into Egypt. What with the threat from the air and the vulnerability of their soft-skinned vehicles and the dry, khamseen-like weather, it was two tired and dusty patrols which rejoined the Battalion as they moved back farther east.

On the 17th of September, rather to the surprise of most people concerned, the Italian advance halted. They had advanced beyond Sidi Barrani and spread out from there in a half-circle to the south. There they proceeded to build themselves "fortified" camps surrounded by stone walls, while the Axis radio regaled us with one of the best jokes of the whole war, boasting of the restoration of tram services to the town of Sidi Barrani, in reality a small collection of squat, stone dwellings centring round the white building of the Frontier Force barracks. Even these were soon to be obliterated by bombardment from the sea.

It was necessary to contain these Italian camps, to reconnoitre them, to prevent the enemy reconnoitring our position, and to make life as unpleasant as possible for the enemy while using up as few of our own troops as possible. For this task the first columns were formed. There will be more to say about columns later, for the battalions of the Regiment were to spend many months fighting in this formation. It is difficult to find anyone who is not prejudiced on the subject of columns. At one time to claim to be a member of one of Jock Campbell's columns would earn respect in every bar in Cairo; later such an admission would have been treated with contempt. For military fashion had changed: columns and the "new look" were incompatible. In fact, the issue is a good deal simpler than that. It is an old-established principle of war to decentralize for movement and to centralize for the decisive battles. Columns grew up to fulfil a particular purpose. The armoured cars in observation were apt to be driven in by comparatively weak enemy forces and therefore required artillery support. The guns, in turn, needed infantry protection at night. Close reconnaissance was only possible by night patrolling with infantry. Columns were formed round a battery of guns as a nucleus, with one or two companies of motor infantry as protection and for night patrolling, a troop, perhaps, of anti-tank guns, a small party of sappers. It was at about this time that a very few Italian anti-aircraft guns, captured, it was said, at sea, became at last available. A column such as this required a commander and a staff officer. It was extremely mobile; orders were given almost entirely by wireless. Its task was to support the armoured cars, to harass the enemy by artillery fire and night patrolling, and to prevent an enemy reconnaissance being successful unless in considerable force. The most valid criticism of column tactics is that they were often employed in such a way that they detracted from the main effort. In June, 1940, they covered very suitably an area to the south of the main pivot, Mersa Matruh. In the autumn of 1942 they merely constituted a dispersion of effort.

As soon as the Italian advance had halted, two columns were formed, the infantry element being found alternately by the Regiment and by the 60th. They set about locating and reconnoitring the "camps" put up by the Italians. When the armoured cars retired to leaguer at night, the Battalion's night patrols took over. It was on the information gathered by these columns that the plans for the December offensive were based. The Battalion concentrated in particular on two camps, Tumar in the north and Nibeiwa farther south. A series of night patrols resulted in the production of a fairly accurate picture of the minefields in the area. To patrol the Tumar camps required a turn-round of twenty miles. Nibeiwa, though nearer, was not without its difficulties.

SOLLUM BAY
Well known to four battalions of the Regiment

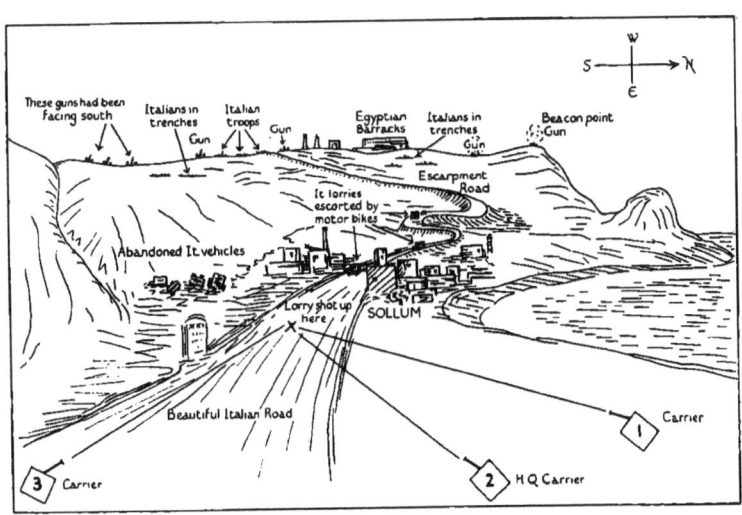

LAST STAND OF THE ITALIANS—SOLLUM, 15th DECEMBER, 1940
Sketch by Merlin Montagu-Douglas-Scott

Two patrols by Charles Liddell on the nights of the 2nd/3rd and 7th/8th of December were particularly valuable. The important thing was to find out where the minefields were so that the attack by "I" tanks planned for the 9th of December would be directed at the right place. On the first occasion he, with Corporal Brown and Acting Corporal Field, worked round behind the camp, crawled through the outer perimeter between enemy sentry groups only fifty yards apart, and found a gap in the defences. They also located the minefield. Returning five nights later with the same non-commissioned officers, he found enemy tanks with sentries patrolling between them stationed apparently in the minefield. These tanks were only twenty yards apart; but he managed to crawl between them unseen and located the gap in the minefield, a discovery which was later to be of inestimable value. This patrol, though it had more spectacular and far-reaching results than most, was typical of many carried out in the desert.

On the 22nd of October the Battalion was employed as bear-leaders for the Camerons, who were to attack by night the most forward of the Italian camps at Maktila. These duties included securing a start line and leading the attacking infantry up to it. It also entailed receiving a share of the enemy's defensive fire. The attack was only partially successful, though the bear-leaders carried out their role efficiently. It was the first time that a full-scale display of pyrotechnics had been drawn from the Italians and it demonstrated that their lethal effect was not commensurate with the lights and the colours and the noise. Everyone within the perimeter fired something; but few of them took aim.

The Italians showed no signs of advancing. They were greatly superior in numbers: their equipment was at least the equal of ours. It seemed that they stood every chance of marching straight on to Cairo. Why they halted for so long is not clear, unless it was that the difficulties of maintenance were greater than they expected. They were certainly building a road along the coast. Perhaps they had been prepared only for a token war, grabbing what they could of the spoils secured by the Germans. Although they did not advance, it hardly seemed that the British had sufficient forces to attack them or, if that attack was successful, to follow it up. Middle East Headquarters had also to consider the enemy forces in Abyssinia.

The arrival of two tank regiments to make the 7th Armoured

Division up to strength, the presence for the first time of "I" tanks in this theatre, and the ill-conceived defensive tactics of the enemy gave an opportunity for what was originally planned as a raid. In November rehearsals were carried out near Mersa Matruh. The secret was well kept. The concentration was covered by a dust-storm. On the 9th of December the blow was struck. The Italians were astonished at being attacked at all. They were unable to cope with the "I" tanks, who entered Nibeiwa through the gap in the minefield discovered by Charles Liddell. Resistance at first was fierce: General Maletti was killed manning an anti-tank gun himself. Once the crust was broken the Italians surrendered in thousands, one division caught on the march towards Sidi Barrani giving up almost without firing a shot. The raid was indeed successful. Before the last prisoners had been rounded up, the 4th Indian Division were on the road back to the Delta on their way to Abyssinia. But besides prisoners, quantities of supplies and transport vehicles had been captured, and these vehicles turned the administrative scale. Exploitation became a possibility.

The 2nd Battalion took no part in the early fighting, but "C" Company had soon to be detached to help in the collection of prisoners. Tony Palmer, the company commander, found himself with fifteen thousand prisoners to look after—a division practically complete. Michael Cubitt spoke Italian and he soon succeeded in translating the divisional commander's cook to "C" Company officers' mess. There "Rifleman" Antonio remained for some four weeks unknown to the authorities, although sharing for ten minutes the shelter of a cave with the Colonel during an Italian air raid. "C" Company received many congratulations on the standard of their mess and might long have continued to enjoy his services if he had not overdone the garlic so that the officers of the company had practically to live by themselves.

The rest of the Battalion took up the pursuit first along the north of the escarpment, as far as Sofafi, again attracting the attention of the Italian Air Force, and then to Bug Bug and along the coast road. The carrier platoons were invaluable at this stage for gathering information and cutting off occasional parties of stragglers. The enemy were strong in artillery and did not allow patrols to follow up too closely.

This phase is best described by Merlin Montagu-Douglas-

Scott, who led the advance in "A" Company's scout platoon:

"On the 12th I was told to take a carrier patrol (a wireless carrier and three others) forward and see if the Italians were still holding a large rambling camp known as Halfway House situated on top of the escarpment and some fourteen miles ahead of our position. We set off at 6.45 in perfect weather, but by the time we had done seven miles a furious khamseen or dust-storm was blowing and visibility was reduced to two hundred yards at best and at times was nil. However, we eventually arrived at the camp. It was surrounded by a low, rambling, stone wall, about three feet high, quite reminiscent of the low walls one occasionally sees in Dorset. Every fifty yards there was a sangar or small circle of wall inside the main one where normally a sentry would be standing. There was no sign of any anti-tank defences. As I expected, the whole place appeared deserted, so we cautiously nosed our way through a gap in the wall until all four carriers were well inside. There was certainly no sign of enemy activity, but there were plenty of signs to show that the occupants had left in a hurry.

"Inside the place was a mass of small, circular trenches, dug out to some two feet in depth and then surrounded with a stone wall, a waterproof canvas being stretched over the wall and held down by stones—the whole, in fact, providing rather a snug little dug-out—especially as most of them had wire bedsteads and some even had little canvas windows and small, stone shelves.

"The contents of these dug-outs were not very exciting; most of them were full of broken lemonade and a few wine bottles, some rolls of blankets, equipment, letters, tattered photographs and coloured pictures of girls.

"The whole camp was very 'deathody' and seemed especially so in a sandstorm—full of odd noises, chiefly the flapping of torn canvas and the creaking of two very rickety-looking structures about thirty feet high which were obviously look-outs for sentries.

"We stayed in this desolate camp for about half an hour, when I received fresh wireless orders to make contact and report the position of the enemy, who were now said to be retreating along the Sollum track about nine miles in front of us.

"Once again we set off down the track and had gone two and a half miles when we came up with the first fugitive, who was very glad to be taken prisoner. He had with him a useful light-automatic gun and plenty of ammunition, so we bundled him into a carrier and went on. After that we encountered odd stragglers every half-mile or so, sometimes singletons but generally in groups of four or five; sometimes they were dragging themselves wearily along, sometimes lying exhausted on the ground, only getting up when they heard our carriers coming towards them. We simply disarmed them and went on; we only kept our first prisoner as a token. (One prisoner we found had a dog on a lead.) After we had gone about six miles, abandoned lorries started to appear and then about seven or eight small tractors; most of them had run completely out of petrol and one or two of the lorries had nothing more wrong with them than a puncture.

"At ten miles there was still no sign of anything but stragglers, when quite suddenly I saw a dark thing looming up in front of me. When fifty yards from it I made it out to be two huge Italian lorries, one towing a light field gun, the other containing a Breda gun—in addition, a good thirty Italians standing round. However, I rushed in with the three other carriers, shrieking and yelling, and we took the whole outfit prisoner.

"Just as we were about to start searching and disarming them the khamseen suddenly lifted and two hundred and fifty yards ahead of us we saw four more lorries towing guns and surrounded by a good number of Italians; beyond this again we saw the Italians marching steadily away from us in close column. It was a perfect picture of a rearguard (or rather army in retreat)! Our carriers dashed forward until we were within one hundred and fifty yards of the vehicles and guns. Then followed a pause during which both sides just stared at one another. Then I grabbed hold of a Bren gun and tried to fire it from the hip. One shot came out and hit the ground about thirty yards in front of me. I feverishly recocked and fired again; this time a burst of about five rounds came out and went rather high over the lorries.

"Meanwhile the Italians were galvanized into activity. In a matter of moments they had their light guns off the back of the lorries and into action at pretty well point-blank range. We all turned round and fled back as hard as we could go. As we passed the lorry with the men who had previously surrendered someone fired a shot at me which was certainly very close, the bullet fizzing past my ear.

"Shells were soon falling uncomfortably close, columns of

sand going up all round us, and so it continued until we were four miles back. Their shelling was surprisingly accurate, considering that we were on the move and could not have been seen.

"When we stopped I found that one carrier would go no farther and would therefore reduce our active force to two. We had a breather until 3.30, when I went forward to recontact; we never came up with the main force again and I did not dare go more than two miles forward of where we had contacted in the morning owing to the petrol difficulty (a carrier does only three to five miles per gallon). At five o'clock we stopped by a certain cairn where we were going to be relieved. It was just beginning to get dark. From all round stragglers rose up from the desert and came slowly and wearily towards us. We gave a few of them a little water and biscuits and they were very grateful. Some of them made signs indicating that they did not think much of Mussolini! They were nearly all very young and obviously fed up with the whole business. I'm afraid a good many must have died of exposure up there on top of the escarpment, as we simply had not enough vehicles or time to go round and pick them all up.

. . . .

"We arrived at our new position (Ilwet el Naas) at noon and I immediately got out my valise and lay down for a feverish sleep—not that I got much, as the Italians started sending over Savoias and soon general dog-fights with Hurricanes were in progress, much to my inconvenience. Quite a number of Italian stragglers—I think there were nine altogether—came in and gave themselves up during the course of the day. One of them obligingly showed us how to strip and use their light machine gun!

"Night brought with it a solitary Savoia, which circled round and round, occasionally dropping a bomb just close enough to make sleep impossible. When its load was exhausted it was replaced by another Savoia, and so on throughout the night. I think it is a very effective way of demoralizing people, as it keeps one so long in a state of suspense.

"At 10.30 a.m. on the 14th of December we were once more on the move and we went forward some ten miles on to the coast track which runs along about four hundred yards off the sea, which itself is hidden from view by a long line of very high sand-dunes.

"We had to go four miles along this track of flattened sand; on the left of it there was a high ridge of rocky ground; on the right a flat salt-marsh which eventually gave place to the sand-dunes.

"A most extraordinary sight confronted us—an Italian column had been retreating in haste along the track and I think they must have been machine-gunned from the air. The inevitable paper lay strewn about the track—letters, envelopes and perfectly good writing blocks and files. Every few yards were huge lorries which had gone off the track, heeled over and become stuck in the marsh, their contents scattered all round. There were also very ancient-looking field guns abandoned on the road and quantities of shells which we took care to avoid when we found them on the road.

"In one place I saw an Italian who had evidently been killed just as he had got out of his car—the door of his small Fiat saloon wide open—he himself lying on the ground by the door, his face pale, yellowish-green, his hands crossed on his already swollen stomach.

"And so we moved, or rather felt, our way slowly forward, past the deserted lorries, guns and paper which blew about the road or caught on pieces of scrub or rock at the sides. Eventually after some four miles we could see dark blobs quivering in the mirage and so we stopped and the company took up a position on the strip of high, rocky ground on the left of the road (Bir Thidyan el Khadim).

"I was immediately sent forward with a carrier patrol to reconnoitre. We moved very slowly forward (three carriers) so as not to raise too much dust, one carrier on either side of the ridge and the headquarters carrier moving from side to side to keep contact with the other two.

"We proceeded in this manner for some three miles, when, on getting out of my carrier, I saw eight Italian lorries about two miles off on the flat ground to my half-left. Straight ahead I could see the guns mounted on the top of Halfaya Pass and away to the right Sollum shimmering white and a large number of Italian lorries fiddling about in front of the town.

"I thought that we might get a shoot at the eight lorries on the left, so on we went even slower than before so as not to raise a speck of dust. Unfortunately when we had got to within a mile of them I saw a man get up and dash towards them and knew that we had been spotted. A few moments later the inevitable barrage came down, luckily all falling about a hundred yards to our left on the flat ground. I could see the guns firing from the top of Halfaya Pass, their flashes resembling the glint of glass a long way off when suddenly caught by the sun.

"I now decided to go back four hundred yards out of range and establish an observation post (just short of Alam el Kidad). This we did and spent a fairly peaceful day sunning ourselves and staring at Italian transport returning home via the road at dusk.

.   .   .   .   .   .

"*December 15th.* We got away in good time and fairly tore down the road to the observation post (Kidad). I went up to the heap of stones and had to spend a very cold half-hour before any observations could be made at all. I then saw that the guns were no longer on the top of Halfaya Pass, though the eight vehicles I had noted yesterday had not moved and there still seemed to be a good many vehicles on the ground in front of Sollum. I sent back a message to this effect and was told to move forward and investigate. As I had expected, we found the eight vehicles deserted and as we approached Sollum it became apparent that all the vehicles on the outskirts of the village were deserted too. My wireless operator intercepted a message from 'S' Company carriers to say they were sending a patrol into Sollum itself. I resolved to beat them to it and had got to within a quarter of a mile of the outskirts of the town when I suddenly realized that the escarpment above the town was bristling with guns and troops—in fact, as I watched, two of the guns on the extreme left flank suddenly opened fire on something facing due south. I now called a halt to send off wireless messages and as these were being sent three vehicles, escorted by four motor-bicycles (two with the leading one and two in rear), started coming down the escarpment road into Sollum. I was amazed, but on they came, and when they had passed through the town and were within one hundred and fifty and two hundred yards of us we opened fire with Bren and rifle. This accounted for the leading lorry and motor-bicycles, but the others made their escape back into the town. Both motor-bicyclists got behind a blockhouse to shelter from our fire. The occupants of the lorry —seven in all—were less fortunate, having one man killed, five wounded and one unhurt. After this brief and very slight action we went on towards the town with the whole carrier platoon (eight carriers) which had come up to join the original patrol of three. By now the Italians on the escarpment had realized what was happening—the guns which had been firing to the south, together with the other escarpment guns, were turned round on to us and these, together with the Italian infantry in positions a little way down the hill, opened up on us. The position was most unpleasant, as the Italians, being above us, could fire straight into our carriers. After a few ineffectual shots at them with a rifle we turned, the shells following our path of flight with an almost devastating accuracy. Luckily, however, we got into the shelter of a small wadi and the firing died down, the only signs of action on the carriers being a few bullet marks.

"After about an hour's breather I had to take a patrol forward to establish an observation post overlooking the escarpment and Sollum on a small, flat-topped hill some four hundred yards from our wadi. I *knew* we would be spotted going forward in our carriers, and so we were! Shells fairly rained down upon us, but we got under the shelter of the hill without incident, and I then chose a small sangar or circle of stones as our observation post. The firing had again died down, but unfortunately we were seen (two of us) getting into the sangar and then almost every gun on top of the escarpment opened up on us. We could practically see the Italians loading their guns; at any rate, we quite clearly observed them bustling around their gun positions. The shells simply tore across towards us, some falling within ten yards, some dislodging several stones from the sangar. There was none of the whining which shells make when coming from some distance—these just screamed over—then followed a shattering explosion, a cloud of dust and above this would hang, as though suspended, a cloud of evil-looking black smoke. When this had drifted away one could see a small cavity, a mere pock mark, in the sand. In fact, the shells did no material damage at all except that at the end of the day the sand around our area was heavily pitted with these marks.

"At about three in the afternoon we had a great piece of luck; a sudden dust-storm sprang up which lasted for about only twenty minutes and under cover of this I managed to effect a relief of the observation post. When I got down to the wireless carrier I was greeted with the news that I had got to take a patrol out into Sollum under cover of darkness to 'draw fire' and report whether it was clear of enemy!

"Accordingly, at 6 p.m. the observation post was closed down and we rattled off towards Sollum, roaring down the beautiful road which the Italians have built. We 'drew fire' when we got up to the spot where we had destroyed the Italian lorry in the morning, so we simply turned round and drove back again, this time going straight for our company position."

Halfaya was captured; the frontier wire was crossed. It seemed for a moment that the enemy might not hold Bardia. When it was clear that they would, the Battalion was ordered to move round to the west of the town with the role of cutting communications with the garrison and preventing reinforcements arriving or enemy leaving the town. Meanwhile the Australian Division were to prepare to assault the defences from the south-east. Apart from patrols towards the defences and diversions during the attack, there was little incident in this role. The cold and an epidemic of jaundice made more impression on morale than the attacks of the enemy air force. Rations were augmented by small captures of Italian food, of which none was better received than tinned tunny-fish.

Battalion Headquarters took up residence in that rare phenomenon in the desert, a house. It was a white house by the road, comfortable to sleep in and an excellent situation in which to enjoy Christmas. The rest of the Battalion was envious and viewed, perhaps with quiet satisfaction, the sharp Italian air raid which ensued early one morning and the rapidity with which the occupants abandoned the house, never to return. For the capture of Bardia they lived, like everyone else, in the open and watched from a safe distance Kit Barclay's carriers demonstrate against the defences and draw much shell fire while the Australians attacked from the south.

As soon as Bardia was captured the Support Group was off again to get round behind Tobruk and cut the road to the west. Starting on the 22nd of January, 1941, the Battalion moved along the desert south of the town and established itself between the main road to Derna and the track from Acroma to Tobruk. The 60th were on the left, responsible for the main road; the 7th Hussars were covering the approaches from the west. Again the Battalion was ordered to make a diversion while the Australians put in their attack.

The Battalion's area looked over the town to the sea beyond. The shell-bursts gave some indication of the progress of the battle on the right. Our diversions drew heavy retaliation from the guns in that sector of the perimeter. Progress in the main attack was slower than had been hoped; and early on the second day the Battalion was ordered to press its attacks home. This was a very different business from dodging about and drawing shell fire, to which our activities had so far been confined. However, before our attacks began, the Italians set fire to the oil by the harbour. An enormous black cloud rose up from the town, as depressing to the defenders as it was encouraging to us. With evidence of Italian defeatism hanging over them, the attacks on the perimeter began. Against Medawwar Fort little progress could be made; but Tom Bird, commanding "S" Company carriers, managed to penetrate the defences, got round behind the fort and soon reported the capture of nine big guns, about forty smaller guns, some two thousand prisoners and the contents of a particularly well-stocked officers' mess. He was ordered to hand the guns and prisoners over to the Australians, but to bring the rest back with him.

Before the capture of Tobruk was complete the Battalion moved off west of Segnali, a place whose exact location has never been agreed by any two navigators. "B" Company, commanded by Hugo Garmoyle, went ahead with the armour to Mechili, where they narrowly missed cutting off the Italian flank guard. Owing to difficulty in deciphering a fairly inadequate map, the 4th Armoured Brigade had left some tracks uncovered and when the Support Group finally closed the trap the enemy had already pulled out. The rest of the Battalion followed up and concentrated at Mechili on the 3rd of February. It seemed that administration had at last been outrun: it was said that there would be no move before the 15th. The Battalion settled down to rest.

The Battalion had some two hours' rest. Every truck had its bonnet open; for they had most of them already exceeded the useful mileage of their make. Washing operations were everywhere in progress as far as one gallon of water a man a day allowed. Hair was being cut; vehicles were being unloaded. Hugo Garmoyle went on leave and Brigadier Gott was due to leave the next day, Colonel Callum Renton having actually taken over command. The Adjutant had already been overtaken by piles of paper. Then General Wilson drove up. The enemy were showing signs of quitting Benghazi, of giving up Cyrenaica altogether. The plan was to send an armoured force straight across the desert for a good one hundred and fifty miles to cut the road from Benghazi to Tripoli where it ran along the edge of the Gulf of Sirte. The Battalion would take part in this gallop. There was no time to lose.

That evening orders arrived. The next day, the 4th of February, the 4th Armoured Brigade Group set off across the desert. The armoured cars, the 11th Hussars, were sent right ahead. The tanks led the main column, the 4th R.H.A. and the 2nd Battalion bringing up the rear. The going was stony so that progress was so slow that half-way through the morning Brigadier Caunter was ordered to send a wheeled force on ahead. It was to consist of the 2nd Battalion supported by "C" Battery, 4th R.H.A., and one battery, 106th R.H.A., Territorials from Liverpool armed with anti-tank guns. This party was to move under command of Colonel Jock Campbell and to join the 11th Hussars, who, with one squadron of the King's Dragoon Guards under command, were already about a hundred miles ahead near Msus. Colonel John Combe, commanding the 11th Hussars, was to assume command of the whole force, Dick Poole being attached as liaison officer to his headquarters.

The bad going made it particularly difficult for the carriers to keep up. They also had a petrol problem and it was by no means certain that their supplies would allow them to reach the road. They were brigaded under Tom Bird and ordered to follow on as best they could with the 4th Armoured Brigade. The rest of the force made fair progress until towards dark, when they encountered what were known as "thermos bombs" dropped from Italian aircraft. These bombs resembled a thermos flask in appearance, did not go off when they hit the ground but were exploded by touch after that. It was decided not to try to drive through this patch in the dark but to leaguer for the night. Colonel Campbell characteristically disregarded the possible presence of the enemy, turned on the head-lamps of his car and drove on to join up with the headquarters of the 11th Hussars. The next day the force moved on, harried occasionally by Italian aircraft. A hot east wind followed behind and made most of the vehicles boil, and Colonel Callum Renton in his car was the

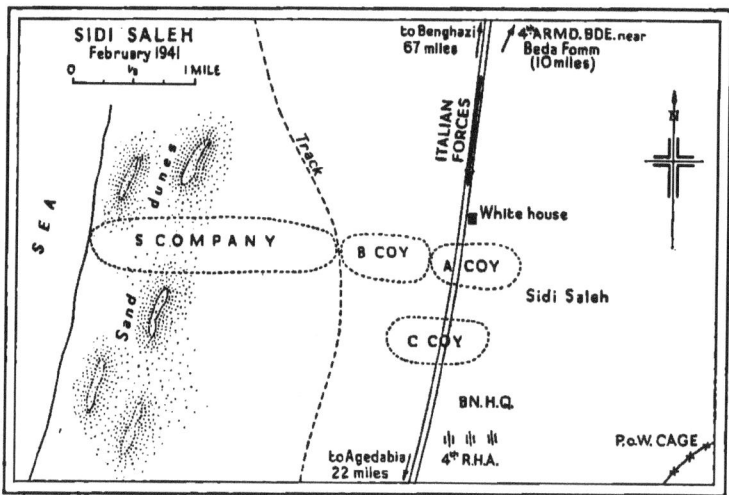

object of a particularly savage but inaccurate attack by Italian fighters. But on the afternoon of the 5th of February they reached the road. The 11th Hussars reported that traffic was still travelling in both directions. They had arrived in time.

The Battalion's role was primarily to protect the guns. Provided that these were secure, they were to cut the road and to prevent the enemy moving down it. The leading company, which was "A" Company, under the command of Tom Pearson, was sent forward to cut the road, which it reached at a place called Sidi Saleh. The remaining three companies were left with the guns about five miles away. Almost as soon as "A" Company had got across the road, about a thousand Italian infantry appeared from the north, the leading elements of the army which was making its way to Tripolitania, all unconscious that its way was blocked. These infantry never really knew what hit them. It was a feature of this battle that the Italians never caught up with what was happening. They had imagined that the British were some one hundred and fifty miles away. Now that their way of escape was closed they simply piled up in a road block stretching for miles to the north and delivered a number of unco-ordinated attacks straight down the road. Each attack was in itself of strength enough to envelop the Battalion; a flanking movement would have made its position impossible. But the Italians were caught on the wrong leg: the Riflemen had their tails up. The leading Italian formation set the example when their attack was repelled by "A" Company and they sat down to think their way out of the trap that had closed so unexpectedly. The vision of Tripoli faded.

The Colonel came up to "A" Company and decided to bring up "B" Company, now commanded by Chris Sinclair, to the left of the road. Tom Pearson took command of all troops on the road who now included anti-tank guns, and arranged for a minefield to be laid across the road, to be increased in size as opportunity offered. During the night he hit on an expedient which would further confuse the enemy as to our strength. Mike Mosley took a patrol, which included two anti-tank guns, northward parallel to the road and to its west, to fire at intervals into the enemy columns who were now piling up along its length. This patrol was skilfully carried out, set fire to more than one vehicle and succeeded in utterly confusing the enemy as to our strength and positions. One effect of this action may have been to prevent the Italians moving round our right flank during that night, an apparently obvious manœuvre. At any rate, they did not do so.

The next morning news came that the Armoured Brigade were approaching the road about ten miles north of the Battalion near Beda Fomm. This lessened the danger to the guns, and the whole Battalion, less half a company detailed to guard the prisoners, were moved up to the road. "A" and "B" Companies were astride the road; "S" Company, under Douglas Darling, stretched from the road to the sea, and "C" Company, under Tony Palmer, were in reserve about five hundred yards behind. During the morning three more anti-tank guns joined the Battalion. Battalion Headquarters were established just to the east of the road a few hundred yards behind the reserve company. It was here that John Harington, the commander of H.Q. Company, arriving in a lull, misappreciated the fury of the battle and erected a large canvas structure to act as a mess. It remained there throughout the battle with a slightly surprised expression on its countenance and acting as a splendid aiming mark for the Italians.

The enemy began attacking on the morning of the 6th of February and continued throughout the day and night and the next morning. These attacks varied in strength and cohesion. Most of them were supported by artillery and tanks. The fire of

"C" Battery continually broke up their attacking formation; they suffered heavy casualties from small-arms fire. A continual stream of prisoners came in, to be hastily disarmed and sent off unescorted in the direction of the improvised "cage" guarded by a platoon of "C" Company. Arrived here, one Italian who had surrendered easily enough when armed with his weapon, suddenly decided to make a break for freedom and attacked the platoon commander, Michael Cubitt, with an axe, scoring a near-miss. The majority were docile enough.

The enemy attacks were carried out with little originality; but, owing to the open country and the numbers of Italians involved, there was always a grave danger of their breaking through. However, throughout the day they were held. The Battalion was covering a wide front and a well-directed night attack would have been almost impossible to deal with. But the enemy's attacks were unco-ordinated and were practically confined to small parties hoping to slip through. There was enough moonlight for almost all these attempts to be prevented—not that the night was devoid of incident. On the sand-dunes near the sea Platoon Sergeant-Major Jarvis was commanding an isolated platoon of "S" Company. He saw in the moonlight two enemy medium tanks approaching along the beach. Accompanied by Rifleman O'Brien, he ran up to the tanks and both fired through the slits with their rifles, wounding the crews. One of the officers fired at the Platoon Sergeant-Major from the door of the tank. Jarvis hit him over the head with the butt of his rifle; and so completed the capture of two medium tanks.

By the next morning the attack of the 4th Armoured Brigade on the northern part of the enemy column had made the Italians realize that a break-through was essential if the whole force was not to be destroyed. One can guess that here General Bergonzoli, the Italian Commander-in-Chief, known in the English Press as "Electric Whiskers," took personal command. Most of his tank resources were engaged in fighting the 4th Armoured Brigade, but he had twenty or thirty medium tanks under his hand. With these and the support of all his guns he launched a determined attack on a narrow front straight along the road early on the morning of the 7th of February. It came near to succeeding. The anti-tank guns had a very bad time; one by one the crews were knocked out. The enemy tanks got right up among the forward companies. Several passed through these and

AIR DISPERSION IN TYPICAL DESERT COUNTRY

SIDI SALEH

Lieutenant-Colonel (later Major-General) Callum Renton inspects the Italian tank which penetrated farthest. In the background Battalion H.Q. Mess

made for Battalion Headquarters. The command party hastily evacuated and withdrew over a slight rise. Geoffrey Goschen, commanding "C" Battery, asked for and received permission to fire on the positions of the forward and reserve companies. Major Burton, who commanded the battery of the 106th R.H.A., collected a scratch crew, consisting of his batman, a cook and himself, and manned a gun which had lost its crew. He drove it to a flank where there was some slight cover from a mound. From there he managed to knock out the leading tanks, one of them about ten yards from the command vehicle. It is said that one of his guns accounted for five tanks with its last five rounds. The destruction of the leading tanks took the heart out of the enemy attack. The forward companies had held their ground although overrun, so that the enemy infantry had not been allowed to advance. Soon the white flags began to appear. The attack had failed. It was not long before General Bergonzoli himself surrendered to Tom Pearson and with his surrender the Italian army in Cyrenaica ceased entirely to exist.

Six Italian generals were collected in the mess. There were twenty-seven medium tanks abandoned outside it, one within twenty yards. About fifteen thousand prisoners had somehow to be fed and disposed of. Well over a hundred guns had been captured. Along the road for mile after mile stretched the wreckage of the defeated army, vehicles of every make and shape, full not only of military stores but of whatever comforts and valuables the Italians had hoped to save from the abandonment of their colony.

The Battalion's losses had been infinitesimal—three killed and four wounded—though the anti-tank gunners had suffered more severely. There were few vehicle casualties. In fact, the Battalion had moved at speed in worn-out vehicles across one hundred and fifty miles of desert, much of it rough, stony going, with the loss of one truck out of a hundred and forty. The carriers had eventually run out of petrol almost within sight of the battle and had been unable to obtain any more from the 4th Armoured Brigade.

This operation was described by General Jumbo Wilson, in a letter to His Royal Highness The Duke of Connaught, as "an epic in the history of the Regiment." Seldom can the efforts of one battalion have brought so great and so tangible a reward. If the companies astride the road had given way, a large part of the Italian army would have escaped and, however sceptical one may be about the fighting value of these soldiers of the Fascist Empire, the fact that the whole army had been captured made a great impression on friend and enemy throughout the world. Though our casualties were light and the final result was absolutely decisive, it is worth remembering that there was a moment on the last morning when enemy tanks were at Battalion Headquarters and the Italians had almost broken through. It was in this crisis that the Battalion realized how lucky they were in their field and anti-tank gunners and in the quiet, sure efficiency of Colonel Combe's command.

Had administration allowed it, an immediate advance might have been made to Tripoli. Preparations were made to dispatch a wheeled column along the main road. Administrative difficulties—the shortage of transport would have appalled anyone used to the Rolls-Royce scale of 1944—and impending events in Greece caused this project to be abandoned. Instead, the Division moved in easy stages to the area between Agheila and Mersa Brega, the obvious bottle-neck to any advance from the west. The 2nd Battalion took up a defensive position astride the road, waiting with undisguised impatience for the appearance of the 2nd Armoured Division and with them the 9th Battalion of the Regiment. But before the relief had taken place there had appeared the first German aeroplane in the skies over the Western Desert and with its arrival a change came over the whole character of the war.

On the 27th of February the 2nd Battalion handed over an awkward position at the end of a long line of communication to the 9th Battalion and departed on the long journey to the Delta. They had been broken gently to war. They had known a withdrawal and taken part in the tremendous excitement of the first great offensive into enemy territory—an experience not to be equalled for most of them through any of the phases of the war. They had ended up with an operation the success of which was not likely to be repeated by any single battalion. And during this "practice over" there had hardly been any casualties at all.

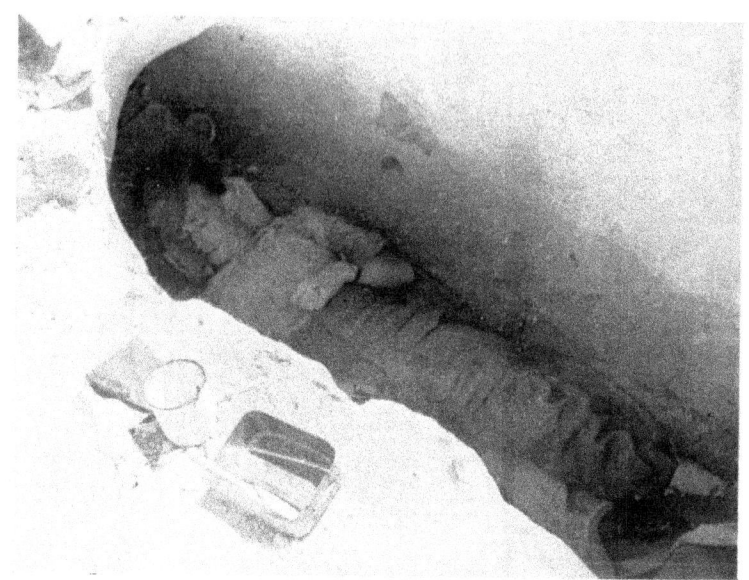

LIFE IN THE DESERT
Bed-Sitting Room

LIFE IN THE DESERT
—Kitchen

CHAPTER IV

THE ARRIVAL OF THE AFRIKA KORPS

THE campaign in Cyrenaica had been unbelievably successful. It was this very success that drew the Germans into North Africa. Mussolini, disappointed to find that gains were not to be had without fighting, lost no time in demanding assistance in Libya. That the Germans responded is in some ways surprising. Perhaps they imagined that they could march at little cost to the Delta—and how nearly they did—securing the Libyan coast for their airfields. Perhaps their enterprise had a grander conception: for, as the two armoured divisions were crossing the Mediterranean, larger forces were concentrating to overrun the Balkans. The armchair strategist is tempted to imagine a plan for the two pincers to meet in Palestine or a year or two later in the Caucasus. In any case, there was a chance of achieving valuable results at the expense of comparatively small effort, to seize the Nile Valley, while drawing from the main fronts but three divisions. Whatever their intended strategy, far-reaching or opportunist, the presence of German troops in Africa entirely altered the situation of our army in Libya. It coincided, as luck would have it, with the decision to send a British force to Greece. With half the troops they had expected, the Western Desert Force had to face something like twice the odds. Transport resources were inadequate; maintenance was a problem in itself. The situation in the air was just as bad as it was on land.

The 9th Battalion (1st Battalion Tower Hamlets Rifles), under command of Lieutenant-Colonel Eric Shipton, with Joe McGaw as second-in-command, landed at Port Said on the last day of 1940, at the time when the 2nd Battalion was cutting the escape route from Bardia. The new battalion formed part of the 2nd Armoured Division, a formation destined to be cut in half almost at once. They spent five weeks at Ismailia being reorganized after the voyage out. They were issued with desert equipment. They learnt something of how to navigate by compass across the open, although they had no chance to send an advance party to the front. But, while they prepared for a desert war, the news of successes in the field must have made them wonder if they would ever be called upon to fight in such country. In fact, their first role was one of policing an area around Cyrene in the Djebel of Cyrenaica. The "hump" of Africa, which sticks out northward into the sea, stretching roughly from Derna to Benghazi, is a hilly, almost a mountainous, district, fertile compared to the desert. Here there was a reasonable annual rainfall and the Italians had established many settlements. Squat dwellings, splashed with Fascist slogans, dotted the hillsides: tractors had ploughed the soil. The Arabs had watched this activity with intense jealousy. Now their opportunity for retaliation seemed to have arrived. It was the task of the 9th Battalion to keep the peace between the two, protecting our enemies from our friends. After a fortnight the Battalion was moved to Benghazi to carry out a similar role in that area. The town, with its white houses, oleanders and intensely blue sea, was not without its attraction. Damage to houses was not yet excessive and you could sit down in the Italian hotel to ministrone and spaghetti and cheese at the next table to the Italian chief of police. When next the British Army came to Benghazi the Italian civilians did not wait to receive them.

On the 22nd of March the Battalion moved south some one hundred and fifty miles from Benghazi to Mersa Brega, where they took over the front. The first patrol, led by Jack Cope, identified Germans opposite the Battalion and soon afterwards the information was elicited that one German armoured division and part of another had moved up from Tripoli to join the forces already collected by the Italians near Agheila. German reconnaissance aircraft were already busy. Ground patrols became more and more aggressive. The Mersa Brega position was not a strong one to be held with the troops available, the more so since a dry winter had made many salt-pans dry enough to drive over. It was, in addition, at the end of a long line of communication. The Air Force, with no suitable aerodromes forward enough for effective support of the ground forces, had to keep looking over their shoulder in the direction of Greece, and could spare only one squadron of Gladiators for the forward areas. In these circumstances the 2nd Armoured Division, at half strength, was ordered to be prepared to withdraw in front of the enemy, delaying him as long as possible. In any country such an operation is difficult in face of superior and highly mobile forces. In this particular stretch of desert there were many pitfalls in the shape of treacherous salt-pans which would not take the weight of a vehicle, and belts of deep, soft sand almost impossible to negotiate.

The Support Group of which the Battalion formed a part had lost half its troops to Greece. There remained, in addition to themselves, the Essex Yeomanry (104th R.H.A., armed with 25-pounders), one battery of anti-tank guns of the 3rd R.H.A., a machine-gun company (Fifth Fusiliers), two anti-aircraft guns and a field ambulance. There was also one company of Free French. The right flank rested on the sea; on the left there was a five-mile gap between them and the two armoured regiments who made up the 2nd Armoured Brigade. One armoured regiment, believe it or not, was equipped with captured Italian tanks. These regiments had yet to discover the inferiority of even their British equipment compared to that of the Germans, a factor we were to learn to appreciate only too well. The nearest formation to the rear was the Australian division at Benghazi, not nearer than one hundred and fifty miles.

It was on the 31st of March that the attack began. The carriers, operating about a mile and a half forward of "C" Company, commanded by Jack Andrews, were attacked at about eight o'clock in the morning. It is recorded that the enemy forces consisted of armoured cars, tanks and motor-cycle combinations. But no one at that moment had the time to derive a little quiet satisfaction from the idea of sweating Germans, new to the desert, struggling with desperate determination and no sense of humour to get their vehicles through the softest sand. The carriers withdrew, on orders, to "A" Company on what was known as Cemetery Hill, giving much useful information before they left. This locality was held until about 10.15, when all but one platoon and the carriers were withdrawn. These held on for a further half-hour, although subjected to a heavy dive-bombing attack, sufficient reminder, if any was needed, that the Germans were taking a hand in this hitherto Italian war. This brought the enemy, led by some fifteen tanks, face to face with the main position, held by "A" and "B" Companies, "D" Company being back at Agedabia digging a reserve position. These tanks were effectively engaged over open sights by the Essex Yeomanry—

how often in the desert had field guns to be used for this! (Some intrepid riflemen actually brought their anti-tank rifles into action.) One or two were knocked out and the remainder withdrew. Their place was taken at about midday by a party of infantry and guns, who occupied Cemetery Hill and overlooked the main Battalion position unpleasantly.

The attack followed closely the pattern so dear to the Germans. For several hours, while the sun was hot and the mirage at its worst, the enemy made no move. They had done their reconnaissance: their tanks were now "topping up" with petrol; their infantry were deploying; the commanders were making their plans; some of the soldiers no doubt were sleeping. In that midday lull one can imagine the flower of the Afrika Korps preparing for this their first attack in the desert with the complete confidence they were always to display from Agheila to Sidi Rezegh, to Alamein and back across all the desert to Cap Bon. On the other side there were the Riflemen, in their first battle, knowing that the German tanks had gone behind the hill and waiting for them to reappear, as it was certain they would, at a time and place to suit themselves. Such was the psychological value of the midday lull.

At half past two "A" Company were heavily dive-bombed by sixteen aeroplanes and lost five vehicles. At half past four the enemy attacked the right flank resting on the sand-hills of the coast with four tanks and a company of infantry. Their attacks were held off by a small party consisting of one platoon of "C" Company, two sections of "A" Company and a machine-gun section of the Fifth Fusiliers. They held them off until dusk—one wonders how. But the pattern of the German advance was worked out inexorably to its end. There were more dive-bombers: a larger force supported by twelve tanks again attacked the right flank. For over an hour these attacks were held. But just before dark the enemy tanks and infantry were infiltrating—ominous word—into our main position. "B" Company had already begun its withdrawal; "C" Company slipped away successfully. But "A" Company were extricated only with difficulty and the loss of one platoon and four vehicles. The Battalion withdrew in the darkness to an intermediate, unprepared reserve position twenty-five miles in the rear.

The Afrika Korps had begun their operations with an attack that was a model of German technique. Few could have guessed

The Arrival of the Afrika Korps

how unchanging and how successful that technique was to be. The Battalion had done well to hold them for a day, nor had the Germans succeeded in enveloping the inferior forces in front of them.

Twenty-five miles is a short distance in the desert. But on the next day, the 1st of April, the enemy ground forces did not attack the Battalion, although the Luftwaffe did. Besides the air attacks they probably made an air reconnaissance, because their plan for the 2nd of April was more ambitious than before. At dawn the carriers observed enemy armoured forces about three miles in front of the main position. These scout platoons did excellent work and before they were driven in reported enemy infantry debussing astride the main road running through the Battalion's position. At half past ten these infantry attacked, supported by tanks, and at the same time other parties of tanks moved round both flanks. The Support Group ordered the Battalion to withdraw. But "B" Company, finding their previously reconnoitred withdrawal route cut off by tanks, drove in their vehicles into a treacherous salt-pan and despite the efforts of their company commander, Clifford Bass, only some half-dozen men escaped capture. The withdrawal, more or less complete, was made possible only by the action of "C" Company's carrier platoon, who were themselves too heavily engaged to get clear.

The Battalion withdrew to a position just north of Agedabia. They were quickly followed up and by four in the afternoon enemy tanks and infantry were attacking. This attack soon penetrated our defences almost to the gun positions, where a counter-attack by our tanks drove the enemy back and enabled the Battalion to be extricated with few casualties. They withdrew to Antelat.

The rest of this story of withdrawal followed a curious pattern. In February it was the Italians who were surprised by our rapid movement across the desert. Now our route was by Sceledima, then Msus to Maraua and along the main coast road to Derna. It was a path littered by our tanks burnt out for lack of fuel or because of mechanical breakdown. There was no alternative but to burn them, and one rifleman, snatching a tin of sizzling bully as he passed, offered it round, saying: "The most expensive meal you have ever had; cost £20,000 to cook." The Battalion passed through Derna at about eight o'clock on the 6th of April, but the enemy had taken a straighter course. As the vehicles of "C" and H.Q. Companies were winding their way up the steep, twisty hill from the town to the aerodrome, they were attacked by tanks and anti-tank guns which had driven up from the south-west. After a sharp engagement, in which some guns of the Essex Yeomanry, two Bofors anti-aircraft guns and four cruiser tanks managed to destroy some sixteen enemy armoured vehicles, the road was cleared but not before Battalion Headquarters and the remnants of "C" Company had suffered severely. Four officers were killed in this engagement.

The remainder of the Battalion reached Tobruk by ten o'clock on the 7th of April. On the next day a mobile column under Brigadier Jock Campbell was formed from that part of the Battalion for whom transport could be found. The remainder were left in Tobruk as a dismounted party to help in the defences of the town. About a month later they were evacuated to the Delta; so the Regiment played no part in the defence of a town which it had originally assisted to capture, and in whose attempted relief it was to be heavily involved.

The mobile column withdrew gradually by Gambut to the frontier wire and thence to Bug Bug. On the 22nd of April it moved to the top of the escarpment at 'Sofafi, where it was engaged in patrolling for a week. After an uneventful fortnight at Samalus it was withdrawn at the beginning of May to the Delta to reorganize and refit. But by this time the 2nd Battalion was already back in contact with the enemy, for there was hardly a day of the three years' fighting in the desert when some battalion of the Regiment was not taking part in the battle.

The 9th Battalion had reached the front when our forces were at their weakest and our lines of communication most stretched. The Afrika Korps made at the same time its first appearance, superior in numbers, mechanically sounder and more powerfully armed. Besides these obvious advantages they learned at once to use the wide stretches of the desert to exploit the mobility of their forces. They used in reverse the route which had been travelled so successfully by the 2nd Battalion in February and in so doing almost succeeded in cutting off the 9th. In the eight days' withdrawal the Battalion lost sixteen officers and some three hundred and fifty men. No battalion could have timed its arrival at the front more unluckily, nor could any have acquitted themselves better in circumstances where everything conspired against them at their first introduction to war.

CHAPTER V

THE INEFFECTIVE SUMMER

THE 2nd Battalion had moved back to the Delta in March. The intention was to refit and to train; for in contact with the enemy the finer arts of individual training are neglected and as casualties occur new and half-trained replacements take on the responsibilities of a rank above their own. There was something more serious to do besides tasting the enjoyment of baths and cold drinks. But at first there was a task to be done on the Suez Canal. The Germans were trying to close the Canal by dropping mines into it from the air. Our job was to line the banks, to observe where the mines fell and so to assist the operation of clearing them up. As many anti-aircraft guns as were available were deployed along the banks and a scheme was launched by which most of the Canal was to be covered during the night by a net. Holes in the net would show just where the mines had fallen. At the first demonstration of this new technique there is a story that two aeroplanes, instead of one as expected, flew up the Canal and dropped their burdens into the water. Investigation showed that one of these was German.

The Battalion was centred on Ismailia, but at night an unpleasantly large proportion was spread out along the Canal. This was a hindrance to training and prevented the full enjoyment by the officers of the amenities of the French Club. It did, however, bring at least one company in close contact with the questionable delights of Port Said. However, everyone appreciated a move to Mena, where the remainder of the time in the Delta was spent. It was while the Battalion was at Ismailia that Colonel Callum Renton was posted away, to command the Middle East Officers' Cadet Training Unit. It is not for the author of this History to pass judgment on commanding officers of the Regiment, but his departure must call for some recognition of the outstanding part he had played in training the Battalion and launching it into the desert war. He was succeeded by Colonel Archie Douglas, and Hugo Garmoyle became Second-in-Command.

While the Battalion watched the Canal the 7th Armoured Division was refitted with tanks in the Delta. The general opinion, if not the official policy, was to forget the peculiarities of the desert war and to concentrate on more normal activity. There was an odd disposition to regard the clearance of Cyrenaica as final. But even while speculation on the new theatre was ranging from the Balkans to the Caucasus, the Germans' appearance at Agheila made our return to the desert inevitable. When the Divisional Commander began to lecture in Turkey on the story of our remarkable victory the enemy were on the Gulf of Sirte and the Turks were all attention. In a few days the Germans were at Derna and the General departed from the now-empty lecture halls to return to his division in Egypt.

New officers, among them Quintin Hogg, and a draft of riflemen arrived. Vehicles were drawn from Ordnance. There were in this base area all the signs of an impending upheaval. Brigadier Gott was sent for, as usual, to reorganize the scattered forces outside Tobruk. It was on the 30th of April that the 2nd Battalion once more took its way along the road to the Pyramids while the bougainvillea was in flower and the orange blossom smelt its strongest, turned to the right before it reached Mena and left civilization firmly behind it for the second time.

The move was to Bug Bug, midway between Sidi Barrani and Sollum. Here the Battalion came at first under the 201st Guards Brigade, consisting of the 2nd Battalion Scots Guards and the 3rd Battalion Coldstream Guards and commanded by Brigadier Ian Erskine. This formation, with the 1st Battalion 60th Rifles, the 11th Hussars (armoured cars) and the remains of the 9th Battalion, were practically the only troops between Tobruk and the Delta, where the armour of the 7th Armoured Division were still refitting. The Germans had pushed on to the frontier with light forces while concentrating for the attack on Tobruk. They had contained Tobruk and faced our columns on the line of the frontier wire. The immediate problem for the Army was to raise the siege. The naval forces were suffering severely in keeping the garrison supplied: the attacks on the town might at any moment succeed. The rest of the spring and summer was spent in attempts to break through to the besieged, culminating in the offensive which took place in November. The task of the 2nd

Battalion was to hold the ring while the attacks were being prepared and when they were launched to play a part of their own. In September the 9th Battalion returned from the Delta and took part in similar operations.

There was nothing, no landmark on the ground, to indicate where Bug Bug was. The coast road ran parallel to the sea and a track from Sofafi wound vaguely along to join it. There were blinding sand-dunes near the beach white as bleached bones: the sea was a brilliant blue. There were patches of dark-green scrub, and in some springs the asphodel grew in profusion, though it is hard to imagine why the coarse stems and pale-blue blossom of the heavenly flower should have picked on Bug Bug. Since the first campaign the Italians had built a stone roadway, soon to be covered with clay stamped down to a smooth surface, which was to prove fatal to General Jock Campbell within a year. Much of this spring was spent by the Battalion at Bug Bug, supported often by one squadron of the 3rd Hussars until they were spirited away to Java and the Japanese bag, and afterwards by the 7th Hussars.

There were two attempts to relieve Tobruk by attacks for which the preparations were comparatively hurried. There was then a longer period while an offensive on a much larger scale was mounted.

The first attempt was on a minor scale. The Battalion were concerned in this attack and in the reconnaissance that preceded it. During this reconnaissance on the 8th of May a khamseen made visibility bad and Merlin Montagu-Douglas-Scott drove much closer to the German position at Halfaya than he had meant to. His carrier was hit and so, despite the efforts of Sergeant Wightman to recover him, he became the first officer to be killed since the Battalion went into action in June, 1940. He was much missed personally and as a fine carrier-platoon commander. At about the same time German armoured cars, making the most of the dust-storm, captured Geoffrey Goschen, a famous Royal Horse Artillery battery commander who had supported us at Sidi Saleh.

The attack took place on the 15th of May. The operation was designed to capture the whole of the quadrilateral formed by Halfaya—Capuzzo—Sidi Aziz—Sidi Omar, and, had that succeeded, to have been exploited towards Tobruk. The 7th Armoured Brigade, who had "A" Company under Chris Sinclair with them, moved off unopposed to Sidi Aziz. Meanwhile the Guards Brigade, with some Matilda "I" tanks of the 4th Armoured Brigade, captured the enemy positions at the top of Halfaya Pass. "S" Company, under Dick Basset, were at the bottom of the escarpment and were told to exploit the success of the Guards and get forward if they could. The carriers, ably handled by Tim Marten, made ground under the escarpment and the company got near enough to prepare for an infantry attack. As always in a motor battalion, there was a shortage of swords to go in with the assault. The Australian anti-tank gunners who were with "S" Company insisted on downing tools and joining in the infantry assault, and the position was captured with about a hundred and thirty Italian prisoners. It is recorded that "Quintin Hogg, dressed in ill-fitting shirt and shorts and a topi, brandishing his pistol in a very dangerous way, took charge of them." (Not every constituency was represented by its member at the front.) "S" Company went up the Sollum Pass on to the aerodrome, and, as a battalion of the Durham Light Infantry, who formed part of the Guards Brigade, had taken Capuzzo, the operation seemed to be going well. In the late afternoon the Germans launched a counter-attack with tanks and infantry, the first of those devastating counter-attacks in a long chain of desert battles that were so often to alter the fortunes of the day. The Durham Light Infantry lost the greater part of two companies and on the morning of the 16th were forced to withdraw. "S" Company, who had leaguered behind them on the aerodrome and been soundly bombed in the moonlight, were obliged to make a quick get-away down the pass before dawn. The 7th Armoured Brigade were withdrawn and the only advantage to us from the operation was that we had a precarious hold on the Halfaya positions now occupied by the 3rd Coldstream Guards. The Battalion were concentrated at Bug Bug and warned by Brigadier Strafer Gott, now in command, to stand by to help when the inevitable counter-attack descended on the Coldstream Guards. He had wanted to withdraw them earlier, but had been ordered to hang on. All we could do when the Coldstream were heavily attacked was to send vehicles to help in their withdrawal.

The "June Battle," the code name for which was "Battleaxe," is described as follows by Tim Marten, at the time commanding the scout platoon of "S" Company:

"The next three weeks were devoted to the preparations and concentration for the operation which was to take place on the 15th of June (later notorious as the 'June Battle'). The object of this operation was to relieve Tobruk. Old 4th Indian Division returned for the operation. They had taken part in the attack on the Nibeiwa and Tummar camps in the first few days of Wavell's campaign; they had then moved down to Eritrea, where they played the chief part in the capture of Keren, and now they were back in the desert again. Supported by the Matildas of the 4th Armoured Brigade and the Guards Brigade, they were to capture Halfaya and Capuzzo. Meanwhile, the 7th Armoured Division, with the 7th Armoured Brigade and the Support Group, was to break through the German defences between Musaid and Sheferzen, defeat the armoured division which Rommel had at that time on the frontier and then advance on Tobruk. There, presumably, the plan was to join up with the Tobruk garrison and defeat the remainder of the Afrika Korps, consisting of the other armoured division and elements of the newly arrived 90th Light Division.

"The Support Group was again organized in columns, commanded by Jock Campbell. The four columns which under his command took part in the battle were commanded by Dick Basset, Harry Withers (4th R.H.A.), Jack Christopher (4th R.H.A.) and Christopher Consett (1st Battalion 60th Rifles). Dick Basset's column had 'S' Company and 'C' Battery, Harry Withers had 'B' Company and 'F' Battery. 'C' Company, under Tony Palmer, was in reserve, and 'A' Company, under Chris Sinclair, was again operating with an armoured brigade. The columns concentrated in the Rabia area in the week before the battle began. Never before had we had such a concentration of tanks in the desert, about two hundred and seventy all told, including a number of the then brand-spanking-new A15 cruiser tanks (Crusaders mounting a 2-pounder). When we saw them rolling by disguised as three-tonners we were filled with confidence. It only needed the issue of 1/100,000 maps of the area between Sollum and Tobruk to make this confidence complete. Little did we know how ill-founded this confidence was, how lamentably under-armoured and under-gunned these tanks were in comparison with the German tanks, and how ill-prepared we were to deal with German anti-tank guns. It took us a long time to learn the lesson.

"The columns moved forward to battle positions pivoting on Bir Dignaish on the night of the 14th of June. On the 15th of June the battle started. The 4th Indian Division, with the Guards Brigade, captured Musaid and Capuzzo, but failed to take Halfaya, where units of the 90th Light Division put up a magnificent defence. The 4th Armoured Brigade lost most of its tanks during this fighting. Two years later we heard from a German officer prisoner who was an inmate of our prison cage at Hammam Lif after the German surrender in Tunisia that about twenty of our Matildas broke clean through during the fighting, and advanced on a defenceless Bardia, which contained only German administrative units. There were German 88-mm. flak guns in Bardia for anti-aircraft defence of the harbour. The officer commanding them stopped a German supply column which was passing through Bardia at the time, waylaid a truck which contained 88-mm. anti-tank ammunition, lined his guns up south of the perimeter defences and gave battle to our tanks. After a short slogging match eleven tanks were left and one 88-mm. gun. This gun destroyed all the remaining tanks, a feat which matches Colonel Turner's and Sergeant Calistan's at Snipe. The officer was awarded the Ritterkreuz of the Iron Cross. He deserved it.

"The German armour on the frontier was fully engaged, and Rommel himself, with the nearest reinforcements, was on the Tobruk perimeter some eighty miles to the west. During the night of the 15th he moved the other panzer division to the relief of his hard-pressed forces on the frontier. Meanwhile the Support Group columns had seen comparatively little of the enemy, apart from severe Stuka attacks. But during the night the remaining forces of the Support Group and the 7th Armoured Brigade were concentrated on a line from Bir Sheferzen to Sidi Omar Nuovo, where on the 16th the cruiser tanks of the 7th Armoured Brigade attempted a break-through. At first light the carrier platoon of 'S' Company, commanded by Tim Marten, occupied Libyan Sidi Omar, and remained there during the rest of an exciting day. At about 1000 hours our tanks attacked, apparently with success, and various observation posts saw them inflict severe tank casualties on the enemy. They then charged the Hafid Ridge, where the enemy had a well-dug-in and well-concealed anti-tank-gun screen. This destroyed almost all our attacking tanks. The situation was temporarily saved by a fine action by

Kay Wood (4th R.H.A.), an observation post of Dick Basset's column, and by our possession of Libyan Sidi Omar, which disconcerted the enemy. Kay Wood fired one thousand four hundred rounds from 'C' Battery in an hour, and at one moment could have had three hundred prisoners for the picking up, but alone in his eight-cwt. pick-up he could not do anything about it.

"During the afternoon the small party in Libyan Sidi Omar watched the enemy massing. At 1400 hours Tim Marten reported thirty enemy vehicles about a mile to his west; at 1900 hours he reported about two hundred and thirty, including 'some very big guns.' This was our first view of 88-mm.'s. In the mirage they looked like Big Berthas, than which they were anyhow much more effective. At 1930 hours the enemy attacked with the sun behind them. A very frightened [sic] Tim Marten was ordered to hold Libyan Sidi Omar at all costs. He had four 2-pounder guns commanded by Ronnie Colt-Williams (3rd R.H.A.) and eight carriers. It seemed to him improbable that he could do much to halt a panzer division. At 2030 hours, to his great relief and in the nick of time, he was ordered to withdraw. The counter-attack advanced towards a gap between the 4th Armoured Brigade and the 7th Armoured Brigade, which the enemy had located through his wireless intercept, and tank fighting went on into the darkness. There we first saw that most depressing sight—the tracer of the solid shot from our 2-pounder guns describing graceful parabolas in the air and bouncing anything up to five or six hundred yards short of the enemy tanks, while the tracer from enemy weapons flew on much flatter curves and 'brewed' our tanks up one after the other. When the 7th Armoured Brigade concentrated at Bir Khireigat the next morning they had nine 'runners' left."

Battalion Headquarters, sitting without any particular job, since the companies were out with their columns, saw a small aeroplane fly over and land near Divisional Headquarters. It contained General Wavell and as a result of his visit the attack was called off. This defeat was a bitter disappointment to the defenders of Tobruk. It was to cost the Navy dear; for their losses were heavy in keeping the garrison supplied.

The visitors withdrew. The desert was left once more to the columns of the Support Group. It was lucky for them that the enemy did not follow up his success. Perhaps he had lost more tanks than he was able to replace. The situation remained very much the same as it had been before the "June Battle" began, with an Indian brigade on the low ground between the escarpment and the sea and the "Forward Group" above the escarpment. This force was formed around the 2nd Battalion and the 4th R.H.A. and remained organized in the four columns which had fought the battle. It was commanded by Jock Campbell, promoted local brigadier for the purpose, and the Battalion and the 4th R.H.A. made up a composite Brigade Headquarters. Brigadier (local Major-General) Strafer Gott commanded all the forces in the forward area. There were no tanks to support the columns, but a party of dummies near Sofafi attracted frequent attention from the enemy air force. They were not the only derelict vehicles in the desert. The area of the battle was strewn with damaged vehicles and equipment, and even with some which had been stuck in soft sand. The more daring spirits on either side would make expeditions to try to salvage likely looking derelicts in this no-man's-land. In the mirage of the summer it was difficult to distinguish between those which were "alive" and those which were "dead," and it was not unusual for Oscar Chichester and the recovery vehicle to set out for some abandoned pick-up, only to find it bristling with Germans bent on a similar errand to his. By this time the Battalion felt that they were already old soldiers and regarded a selection of derelict equipment left by those formations who came up to the forward areas only for the more important and fashionable battles as a natural perquisite, theirs by right.

The summer was spent without great incident, with at least two columns harassing the enemy on a line which ran roughly from Libyan Sidi Omar to Bir Suweiyat, while two more columns prepared two defensive positions in the Sofafi—Habata area, called North Point and Playground. During this time Hugo Garmoyle began to establish a reputation as the commander of Hugo Column, of which "C" Company, under Tony Palmer, formed the nucleus. Although there was little sensational action during that summer, column work was active enough for those who were in them.

During the war Tim Marten described them in a letter for the use of the future historian:

"The column as a tactical unit has gone out of fashion in European warfare, though one can detect its re-emergence in an analogous form in Wingate's 'Chindits' in Burma. The similarity is perhaps only a superficial one, for the Chindits are now a large-scale organization, amounting almost to an airborne division. But one feels that the same spirit must animate them as animated us, and column warfare largely depended on the spirit of the officers and men. Columns, as Jock Campbell said, could do any job except two. They could not capture ground from the enemy or deny ground to the enemy. As war consists mostly of doing one or other of these things, their value might seem small. But handled by a master like Jock they proved capable, by dogged and aggressive action, of turning at least one defeat into victory.

"It was a strenuous life. We broke leaguer about an hour before first light (0430 or 0500 hours in the summer). The component parts of the column then went to their allotted stations, spread over an area of four or five square miles and centred on an R.H.A. battery, which provided the main hitting power. Round the battery were normally grouped the platoons of the motor company as local protection. The other main task of the motor infantry was doing night patrols. Also near the battery were the 2-pounder guns which always fired portee from their vehicles at this time. Radiating out at a range of five or six miles were the observation posts and carrier patrols; these were sometimes combined, and they interlocked with the armoured-car troops in a cohesive patrol line. During the early morning and late evening there was occasional cutting and lunging at the four-wheeled and eight-wheeled armoured cars of the 3rd and 33rd Reconnaissance Regiments (the armoured-car regiments of the 21st Panzer and 15th Panzer Divisions respectively). As the enemy armoured cars were frequently supported by small detachments of tanks, this was an exciting game. In the middle of the day the mirage made movement risky, and there was usually a lull. After last light the horns were drawn in, the column concentrated, and moved off three or four miles into leaguer. There everybody listened to 'Lilli Marlene' (broadcast from Belgrade at 2200 hours) while awaiting the arrival of 'B' Echelon.

"The arrival of 'B' Echelon was the great moment of the day. Would there be bread or tinned pineapple on rations? Would there be a N.A.A.F.I. up? Would there be a mail? A mail meant not merely letters from home, which were our chief consolation in the desert, but books, papers, cigarettes and perhaps a crate of delicacies from Fortnum & Mason's. The Colour-Sergeants (Atkin, Antoine, Tucker and Hart) were unbelievably swift and expert at the distribution of rations—and they needed to be, for by this time officers, non-commissioned officers and riflemen were all dropping with sleep. Only the column staff officer still remained awake, sending in final 'sitreps,' ammunition states, etc., to Brigade Headquarters, dealing with official correspondence, codes for the next day, orders and ration returns. If he was lucky he got to bed by midnight, with the earphones lying beside him on his pillow in case there was an urgent message during his four or five hours of well-earned rest. This solitary, self-contained life induced a great sense of independence among those who experienced it, and with it a remarkable self-reliance. The units of the old 7th Support Group —11th Hussars, 3rd R.H.A., 4th R.H.A., 1st King's Royal Rifle Corps and 2nd Rifle Brigade—had their own ideas and went their own way. In the Sidi Rezegh campaign and in the summer withdrawal in 1942 they learnt to operate up to a hundred miles or more from the nearest supply dumps, to penetrate areas dominated by the enemy, to remain unconcerned for days and sometimes weeks while the enemy were surrounding them in superior strength and to make deadly and damaging thrusts, which he found it hard to parry, against the enemy supply lines. Admittedly columns, as a method of fighting the Germans in Africa, had their limitations and had considerable moral and military drawbacks. But in the days of our weakness they provided an economical means of tying down superior enemy forces and of inflicting daily casualties on the Germans which in the aggregate constituted a 'running sore' that they could ill endure.

"Columns were composite groups, and the friendships and loyalties which they evoked cut right across orthodox regimental ties. I think the 2nd Rifle Brigade had a genius for making friendships, and certainly the Battalion had unique opportunities for using this aptitude. Witness our deep personal pleasure and pride when the 11th Hussars were first into Benghazi, Tripoli and Tunis during the 1942-43 advance, coupled with Lieutenant-Colonel Trevor Smail's letter of congratulation to the 2nd Rifle Brigade after Snipe. The 11th Hussars were the oldest and most famous of the desert armoured-car regiments, but we also had many links with The Royals and the 4th South African Armoured Cars. For skill and virtuosity the performance of the South Africans during the 1942 retreat was perhaps unrivalled. It never received adequate recognition. From time to time we also operated with the King's Dragoon Guards, the 12th Royal Lancers and the 13th (Indian) Lancers. Among tank regiments we had many friends. In the early desert days, the 3rd, 7th and 8th Hussars and the 2nd and 6th Royal Tanks were our most frequent collaborators. Later we worked with the Gloucestershire Hussars and the Greys. When the 7th Motor Brigade joined the 1st Armoured Division before Alamein we often co-operated with the regiments of the 2nd Armoured Brigade, and we never saw finer tank gunnery or more skilful tank fighting than that carried out by the Bays, the 9th Lancers and the 10th Hussars at Alamein, at El Hamma and at Lake Kourzia. Among gunners our greatest friends were the 4th R.H.A. For months at a time in the desert the 2nd Rifle Brigade administered and commanded batteries of the 4th R.H.A., and the 4th R.H.A. companies of the 2nd Rifle Brigade. Occasionally we fired their guns and they directed our carrier patrols. There was never a happier or more fruitful partnership, and the commanders like Jock Campbell and Hugo Garmoyle who fostered this friendship employed motor companies and 25-pounders with equal facility and success. The 'stars' of this desert fighting, Jock and Hugo, Chris Consett, the Hobbs brothers, Dick Basset, Harry Withers, Mike Mosley, Hugh Barrow, Len Livingstone-Learmouth, Tom Bird, Jack Lomas, Robin Hastings, Peter Greenfield, Peter Innes, Dick Flower, John Sharpe, Oliver Newton, Sandy Goschen, and all the others, belong not so much to their own regiments as to the columns, of which all were equal and indispensable members. Among the gunners with whom we had successful associations were the 1st, 2nd, 3rd and 11th R.H.A., the 60th Field Regiment and the 64th Anti-Tank Regiment, R.A., which was latterly commanded by that great desert figure Whirley Birch. This list could be prolonged almost indefinitely. I think special mention must be made of the 15th Light Field Ambulance and 550 Company, R.A.S.C., who unfailingly supplied our medical and material wants, and of the 4th Field Squadron, R.E. This co-operation with other arms and units undoubtedly broadened our tactical minds and was of inestimable value to us."

After that fly-ridden summer the 2nd Battalion moved back to Gerawla on the sea, a few miles east of Mersa Matruh. Here there were bathing, recreation, re-equipping and such forgotten luxuries as drill and weapon training. There were various changes in the composition of the Battalion at this time, necessitated partly by a request to send officers and non-commissioned officers to the 9th Battalion, who were re-forming in the Delta, now under command of Colonel Squeak Purdon. Among those who went to this battalion were Paddy Boden, Charles Liddell and Eddy Gibbons. At the same time David Wilson went to the staff of XIII Corps and Ian Whigham as Intelligence Officer to the Support Group. Tony Franklyn was given command of "B" Company. After a fortnight's bathing, a week's leave in Cairo and a few drill parades taken by Regimental Sergeant-Major Pinnock, the Battalion was much changed in appearance and health from that which had returned, covered in dust and dirt, from the arduous months in the column.

On the 14th of September the Germans launched what was probably a reconnaissance in force. It caused sufficient disturbance to put an end to the Battalion's rest by the sea and it penetrated as far as some of the dummy tanks. When the Germans had retired and the excitement subsided, the Battalion returned to its old hunting grounds at the top of the escarpment to relieve the 60th in the columns. After only a fortnight the 201st Guards Brigade, of which the 9th Battalion now formed a part, came up and took over. The Support Group moved south to a remote but clean and, so to speak, virgin piece of desert, where they were not in contact with the enemy. Throughout October and until the offensive of the 18th of November neither battalion was seriously engaged, although the 9th did much patrolling and took part in the usual activities of column work. They were lucky to be with the Guards Brigade and this comparatively gentle rebreaking-in of what was a much-changed battalion before the new battles began was a great help to all concerned. While the 9th Battalion was thus engaged the 2nd Battalion had a peaceful time in the south. Had they known it, it was the end of a period of the war, when their battles would be attended by few casualties. They now sat in what passed in the desert for luxury, the Battalion Headquarters mess, an enormous erection attached to a lorry and organized by the Medical Officer, Captain Picton, now a member of The Rifle Brigade Club.

"He was an encyclopædia of knowledge. Among other

abstruse but vital pieces of information he possessed were how to cure desert sores, how to fire a battery of 25-pounders, the price of an oke of potatoes in the Cairo black market, where to get M.&B.693 when even the A.D.M.S. and D.D.M.S. could supply no more, how to write an operation order, how to run a dressing station and emergency surgery in no-man's-land, how to bring the Battalion's establishment of vehicles up to strength, how to cook desert snails *à la française,* how to dispose of all unwelcome visitors—British, Allied and enemy—and a hundred and three ways of disguising bully beef."

Meanwhile anyone from the Battalion who visited on military errand the "rear areas" could not fail to see the signs of another, greater, offensive on the way.

CHAPTER VI

SIDI REZEGH—THE FORGOTTEN BATTLE

THE bold decision to hold Tobruk in the spring of 1941 had been rewarded. The Germans had halted their advance into Egypt: they had turned aside to assault the town. But the successful defence had raised difficulties politically in Australia and had cost the Navy dearly. The Australian Division were relieved; the garrison were kept supplied. The Luftwaffe had a unique opportunity to strike at British shipping. Although the enemy's attacks on the perimeter had failed, they had retained enough forces in the frontier area to hold off our attempts to raise the siege. The two ill-fated operations in May and June had been broken by the 88-mm. gun. It was obvious that only a large-scale offensive could now relieve the town. An army was built up in Egypt during the summer of greater size and more powerful than any yet seen in the desert. The New Zealand Division and two South African divisions arrived; the 4th Indian Division returned from Keren; and, since the German invasion forces had turned east against Russia, the 1st Armoured Division set out from England to sail by the Cape route to the Middle East. With this division came the resuscitated 1st Battalion. It was considered that the need to start this offensive was so urgent that the arrival of this division could not be awaited, although one armoured brigade, the 22nd, was sent on ahead and arrived in the desert in time to take part in the battle under the 7th Armoured Division.

There were great changes in command. An Army Headquarters was set up, to be called the Eighth—"Where," said the riflemen, "were the other seven?"—and to be commanded by General Cunningham, fresh from a victorious campaign in Eritrea. The XXX Corps was formed under General Norrie; Strafer Gott assumed command of the 7th Armoured Division; Jock Campbell took over the Support Group. The face of the desert was covered by innumerable trucks and vehicles. The railway was being extended westwards from Mersa Matruh. To one who had known already more than a year of desert war, the preparations seemed greater and more far-reaching than anything visualized before. It even seemed possible that air superiority might be obtained.

The plan for this offensive consisted briefly of an armoured left hook aimed at establishing our forces in such a position that the enemy armour would be obliged to attack us on ground of our own choosing, coupled with a frontal attack on the defences in the frontier area. It was expected that the enemy would fight the main armoured battle somewhere just south of or on the Trigh Capuzzo and that a suitable opportunity would occur for the defenders of Tobruk to break out to meet us. The administrative preparations included the establishment of a dump west of the frontier wire and south of the area in which the main battle would be fought. The selection of the site for this dump was luckily in the hands of General Gott.

The 2nd Battalion was to take part in the left hook to be made by the 7th Armoured Division, now consisting of three armoured brigades, the 11th Hussars and the Support Group. The 9th Battalion, still in the 201st Guards Brigade, was to be held in reserve with a role in the tradition of the Wavell campaign, a dash across the desert to cut off the enemy on the Gulf of Sirte, somewhere even farther south than Sidi Saleh. Details of this plan are not worth discussing, since circumstances arose which prevented its ever being put into effect. The 9th Battalion was in the meantime to be involved in protection of dumps, a task which was soon to entail sufficient excitements on its own. So, while the 1st Battalion was still travelling and the 9th Battalion was in reserve, the 2nd was clearly destined to play a prominent part in the early stages of the battle.

If one is to understand the story of this offensive it is necessary to realize one important factor. The Germans were possessed of tanks and guns capable of knocking out any armoured vehicle of ours at two thousand yards. The maximum effective range of any of our 2-pounder guns in tanks or out of them was six to eight hundred yards. There were no 6-pounders in the desert; we had no 75-mm. tank guns. The only method of knocking out enemy tanks which proved effective was by the use of 25-pounder field guns firing over open sights. No one could call this method satisfactory, since the crews were devoid of cover and, anyway, were intended to fire indirectly at targets more like ten thousand yards away. Two of our armoured brigades were armed with new cruiser tanks, pitifully under-gunned and suffering from mechanical defects, such as an imperfect cooling system, from which they were never to recover. The 4th Armoured Brigade had Honeys, American light tanks, whose guns had no pretensions to compete with the German in a tank battle. We set out on this great offensive to relieve the garrison of Tobruk without question, and drive the enemy from Cyrenaica at this moment in the war, when the Germans had received their first check outside Moscow, with a tank armament incomparably weaker than the enemy's, to fight in a country where movement was unrestricted and few anti-tank obstacles existed, where tanks and mobility had an influence never exerted elsewhere. And we succeeded.

For the advance into Libya the 2nd Battalion was much split up. "A" Company, commanded by Christopher Sinclair, were under command of the 7th Armoured Brigade. "B" Company (Tony Franklyn) were part of a column under Hugo Garmoyle which included one squadron of the 11th Hussars. Their task was to move to the west of the main advance and to make contact with the enemy position at Bir Gubi. They were to become closely associated with the 22nd Armoured Brigade. "C" Company (Tony Palmer) were to protect the Brigade "B" Echelon, while Battalion Headquarters and the remaining company—"S" Company (Dick Basset)—moved with the Support Group organized as a column with a battery of the 60th Field Regiment, a troop of 2-pounder anti-tank guns of the 3rd R.H.A. under command of Ward Gunn, and a troop of Bofors anti-aircraft guns under Pat McSwiney.

At dawn on the 18th of November, 1941, patrols of the 2nd Battalion cut gaps in the frontier wire. In the early light, the autumn sun bright but not hot, the tanks moved forward into Libya. As the great columns of vehicles spread out into the desert our aircraft appeared punctually overhead. There was no mirage and as far as the eye could see were tanks and vehicles streaming forward towards Tobruk, a sight to be remembered three years later when the convoys sailed from the Isle of Wight, and, across the water, saw the fleet from Weymouth making out to sea.

The first part of the Battalion to gain contact with the enemy was "B" Company with Hugo Garmoyle's column. The patrols of the 11th Hussars with this column reported that the enemy held Bir Gubi and that there were tanks with them, identified later as those of the Italian Ariete Division. "B" Company watched the attack made by the 22nd Armoured Brigade on this position, the nearest thing to a cavalry charge with tanks seen during this war. It scored an initial success. The Ariete never recovered from their tank losses. The infantry and anti-tank-gun positions were overrun. The lack of infantry to exploit this success enabled the enemy to recover their nerve, to furl up their white flags and to destroy some of our tanks returning to rally. "B" Company spent much time collecting prisoners.

"A" Company were with the 7th Armoured Brigade, who led the advance to the Trigh Capuzzo. Towards evening they heard the sound of a tank battle to their east, which proved to be the 4th Armoured Brigade—in Honeys—engaging German tanks. The next day the 7th Armoured Brigade pressed on to Sidi Rezegh aerodrome, where they destroyed a number of enemy aircraft on the ground, driving their tanks through the fuselages. It was decided to form a pivot consisting of the Support Group in the area of Sidi Rezegh from which the armour could operate and on the evening of the 19th of November the Brigade moved up to take up an all-round defensive position. The pivot was in place. But the armoured brigades were widely scattered, this dispersion being dictated partly by political as well as by military necessity; for it was not possible to leave the Dominion forces entirely unsupported by armour, however ineffective our tanks were likely to prove against the heavier armament of the Germans. The 4th Armoured Brigade were still heavily engaged to the east; the 7th Armoured Brigade were on the aerodrome; the 22nd Armoured Brigade were reorganizing near Bir Gubi after their first battle. The attack by XIII Corps on the frontier was making slow progress and the time for a sortie from Tobruk had not yet been reached. The German armoured forces, though not concentrated, had interior lines and a shorter way to go.

When Battalion Headquarters and "S" Company arrived at their destination they found it a bare, rocky ridge, with a gently sloping valley to the north between them and the rising ground on which the tomb of Sidi Rezegh and the aerodrome were situated. To the south and east the ground was flat. Contact with the enemy infantry to the east and north-east was established

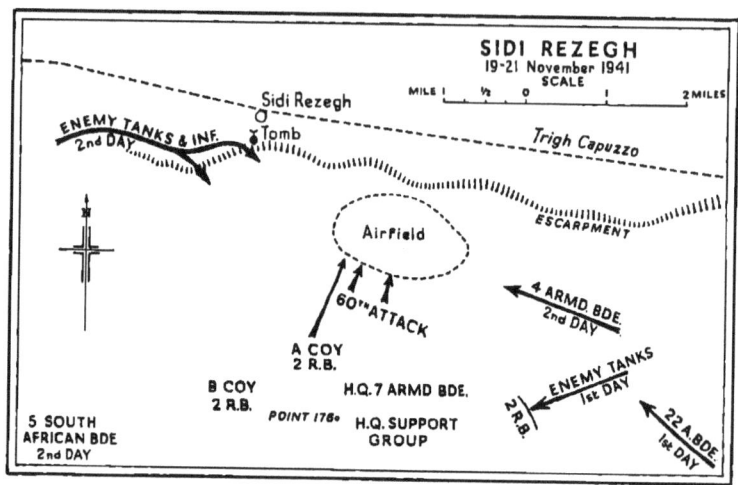

by a patrol of "S" Company's carriers under Jack Ling. There was some intermittent shelling and everyone lay down to sleep apprehensive of what the next day would bring.

At about eight o'clock the next morning an attack was carried out by the 1st Battalion 60th Rifles, with "A" Company under command. The objective was the ridge beyond the aerodrome overlooking the "Axis Road," built by the Germans to bypass Tobruk at a place called El Duda. A firm hold of this ridge would have dislocated traffic between the enemy on the frontier and those round Tobruk. This threat was certain to cause the enemy to react. The attack was supported by such guns as were available and tanks of the 7th Armoured Brigade. Despite fierce opposition and some casualties, the ridge was taken, Rifleman Beeley of the 60th gaining a posthumous V.C. "A" Company on the left of the attack had considerable trouble from machine guns from their left and the tanks whose task it was to protect them from this direction were prevented by anti-tank-gun fire from doing this effectively. They gained their objective, but not without casualties, among whom was one officer, John Copeland, wounded. They consolidated at the far end of the aerodrome, from where they could look over the escarpment in front of them towards the defended perimeter of Tobruk. This attack, carried out in face of heavy opposition across open ground with little opportunity for reconnaissance, was one of the outstanding exploits of the desert war.

The Coast Road near Derna
Captured German photograph

Official Photo:
Crown Copyright Reserved!
General Sir Claude Auchinleck and Brigadier Hugo Garmoyle

The Italians observe us
A captured photograph showing flat, scrub-covered desert and a portly Italian officer with field glasses

The South African Division were ordered to come up to a position to the west of the Support Group to strengthen and enlarge the pivot. They were new to war in these conditions and, since the 2nd Battalion were split up and only one company was left to Battalion Headquarters, Colonel Archie Douglas was sent off to the South Africans to help them. Dick Basset took over command in his absence. The morning was spent in digging as far as was possible in the stony soil. At about ten-thirty some eighty or ninety tanks of the 21st Panzer Division appeared from the east and launched a counter-attack, while a Fieseler Storch aircraft did a reconnaissance for them over our area. The 7th Hussars were quickly engulfed, though they went down fighting with their inadequate armament, and their Colonel, Freddy Byass, was among those killed. The enemy advanced towards "S" Company. Sixteen tanks appeared over a ridge moving slowly westwards about eight hundred yards away into the valley to the north-east. The two 2-pounders on the ridge to the north under command of Ward Gunn opened fire on them. The 25-pounders of the 60th Field Regiment engaged them over open sights. Four of them went up in flames. The remainder halted, dodged about and, finding that they could make no headway against our fire, but having had a good look at our positions, withdrew just out of sight. They had returned our fire and the two anti-tank guns had been knocked out. It was quite clear that the enemy's retirement was only temporary. They had made their reconnaissance, not without loss. The gunner observation posts could see them topping-up with petrol and shelled them soundly. Everyone in the Battalion knew that the Germans were choosing their own time and their own place of attack and that not sixteen but sixty tanks might appear at any moment over the ridge. Ward Gunn collected his remaining anti-tank guns. The 60th Field Regiment prepared for action over open sights. Messages and officers were sent to warn Brigade Headquarters of our situation and to ask for tank assistance. These enemy tanks had approached from an unexpected direction. The Brigade Major was incredulous; the 7th Armoured Brigade accused us of firing on the 7th Hussars. To Battalion Headquarters and "S" Company theirs was the only battle. But "A" Company on the ridge beyond the aerodrome could already see signs of a counter-attack in preparation. "B" Company with Hugo Garmoyle's column were moving fast towards the battle from the south, and "C" Company, protecting the "B" Echelon, found themselves threatened from the most unexpected directions.

When the Germans were ready their attack began. There were several attacks by dive-bombing Stukas, though these were well clear of the Battalion. Enemy field guns shelled the position. In the rocky ground the motor platoons had been able only to scrape inadequate trenches. They were pinned to their weapon pits as soon as the enemy tanks came in sight. Battalion Headquarters were in full view, three eight-cwt. pick-ups with wireless masts, isolated on this bare ground. Realizing that these would be an obvious target for the enemy tanks, the members of Battalion Headquarters crouched behind their vehicles, reporting while they could on the wireless what dismal information they had and requesting armoured help in a tone that made it quite clear that friends were not being mistaken for foes. Five Crusader tanks were sent over. These were set on fire before they could get near enough to engage the enemy with their 2-pounders. Two of the vehicles of Battalion Headquarters—and the Adjutant's best hat—were soon in flames. Corporal Warner, of the Signal Section, jumped into the third, started it up, and drove it to safety without being put out of action—one of the unaccountable miracles of this desperate battle. The enemy tanks were now being engaged by the 25-pounders of the battery of the 60th Field Regiment and some guns of the 4th R.H.A. which had come into action behind them. Apart from these, unsuitable but brilliantly fought, there were three weapons capable of taking on the enemy tanks—two 2-pounders on their unarmoured portees under Ward Gunn (3rd R.H.A.) and one Bofors anti-aircraft gun commanded by Pat McSwiney. These three engaged the enemy as best they could, outranged and unarmoured as they were. The Bofors fired self-destroying 40-mm. anti-aircraft ammunition and, though it had the range, its effect on the Mark III and IV tanks was not decisive.

The small party round the blazing pick-ups watched these three guns firing away at the enemy, watched the crews, completely composed, completely undaunted, picked off one by one. The enemy gave everything they had: machine-gun fire from the tanks and the supporting infantry, mortars, shells from the Mark IV's and the field guns. One 2-pounder was destroyed; the Bofors gun was set on fire. All the crew of the

SIDI REZEGH—THE FORGOTTEN BATTLE

remaining gun were either killed or wounded, and the driver not unnaturally began to drive it out of the battle. Ward Gunn, at Battalion Headquarters, was joined at that moment by Bernard Pinney, the commander of "M" Battery, 3rd R.H.A. He said to Ward: "Go and stop that blighter!" and even then it seemed hard to be so described for driving a useless gun and dead crew out of action. Ward immediately ran out and stopped him and, together, they dragged the bodies off the portee and got the gun into action, Bernard Pinney joining in. No one could gauge the effect of this fire, because to look over the edge of a slit trench was suicidal. Dick Basset had already been wounded in the head and Tom Bird in the heel. A little dog was running round from trench to trench, trying hard to find its master and being distressingly friendly to each person in turn—distressingly because its movements attracted a hail of machine-gun fire. The Germans concentrated their fire on the burning vehicles of Battalion Headquarters and the one remaining gun. But at least the two nearest enemy tanks were blazing.

In a matter of seconds the portee was on fire, the off-side front wheel had been hit, and the tyre was blazing; two boxes of ammunition held in brackets behind the passenger seat were also in flames. Pinney took the Pyrene fire extinguisher and got the fire in the tyre under control; but the ammunition boxes continued to burn. Ward Gunn, who had kept on firing throughout, was hit in the forehead and killed instantly. Pinney pushed his body out of the way and went on firing until further hits made the gun unusable. He drove away unscathed. The next day in a comparatively quiet area a stray shell landed close enough to kill him. The driver, in normal times the sergeant, No. 1 on the gun, crawled away to join Battalion Headquarters and got out with them later in the day. Both Ward Gunn and Bernard Pinney were recommended for Victoria Crosses and the award was given to Ward Gunn posthumously. One of the three Riflemen who witnessed the citation was Tom Bird, the future commander of "S" Company, the anti-tank company, whose exploits on the Snipe position were to rival those of Gunn and Pinney.

"S" Company and Battalion Headquarters were now hopelessly pinned. The slightest movement above the top of a slit trench drew a hail of fire. The enemy tanks, held off from further advance by the fire of the field guns, swept every inch of our position. An attempt by Jack Ling in his carriers to collect any survivors was the signal for an even more furious burst of firing. The guns of the 60th Field Regiment were gradually being silenced, all the ammunition having been used or destroyed by fire, the crews casualties or the guns themselves hit. Small groups of enemy infantry were filtering slowly forward. It seemed as if the whole position would be overrun. Two things prevented this. The 22nd Armoured Brigade, having moved fast from Bir Gubi, attacked the enemy on his left flank. His attention wavered. Some of his tanks turned to meet this new threat. At the same time Oscar Chichester, unconscious of this new tactical feature of the battle, had made his way to within four hundred yards of the burning headquarters, and from ground which was not in view of the enemy shouted to those who were pinned to try to make their escape. Under cover of a few wisps of smoke from the burning vehicles and the occasional distraction of friendly aircraft flying overhead, most of Battalion Headquarters and subsequently most of "S" Company crawled away, all being shot at as they did so. One platoon was lost almost complete. The survivors spent the night near Support Group Headquarters and the next morning took up a position on the escarpment to their west, there being no battery left for their support.

Hugo Column and "B" Company, who had spent most of the 20th on the move and had listened on their wireless to the expiring cries of Battalion Headquarters, came up and by the morning of the 21st were established with their battery in the valley just south of Sidi Rezegh aerodrome.

By nightfall on the 20th the 7th Armoured Division was almost completely concentrated in the Sidi Rezegh area. The 4th Armoured Brigade were still some thirty miles to the east; but the 22nd Armoured Brigade's arrival had halted the attack of the 21st Panzer Division. The Support Group still held the aerodrome and the ridge beyond, but had already taken a hard knock and suffered serious losses in casualties and guns. The 5th South African Brigade were not far away to the south. But disaster had already overtaken the 7th Armoured Brigade and their tank strength was greatly reduced. The battle was far from won.

The night in the desert always belonged to us. The enemy made no move. The next morning, too, was comparatively quiet except for occasional shelling. But the 60th and "A" Company could see much movement from east to west across their front and rightly interpreted this as a concentration of the enemy against them. The 7th Armoured Brigade had few tanks left; ammunition was short. The lull was uneasy.

The 5th South African Brigade were due to attack the enemy on the escarpment to the west of the Support Group. But at about half past two, half an hour before the zero hour for the South Africans, the Germans began to attack the 60th from the west with about a hundred and twenty tanks and infantry, mainly of the 15th Panzer Division. The few remaining tanks of the 7th Armoured Brigade were powerless: some of the 22nd Armoured Brigade in their new but ineffective cruisers engaged the enemy across the aerodrome. It was obvious that the position could not stand. There remained one hope. The 4th Armoured Brigade were approaching from the east. If they could arrive in time the enemy might be halted. From the tomb of Sidi Rezegh one could see to the north-west the smoke and dust of explosions gradually drawing nearer, and, to the east, in the far distance, the dust of the Honeys hurrying up to join battle—for they were Honeys, light tanks excellent for their purpose of reconnaissance but not for taking on German medium tanks, and for those who looked so hopefully over their shoulders there was in reality no chance of rescue. Jock Campbell was one of those who saw the 4th Armoured Brigade approaching. He had driven about the battlefield in an open car all day, regardless of shells and bullets, always accompanied by Ian Whigham or Philip Flower, both of the Regiment. Now he drove out towards the Honeys and, unarmoured, led them into the battle. But no amount of personal bravery could redress the balance of unequal armament. The Honeys and the Crusaders were no match for the enemy. Gradually, but not without considerable loss, they withdrew to the south of the valley. With their departure the 60th and "A" Company were lost.

This left "B" Company in the centre of the battle. To their left they saw the 5th South African Brigade unsuccessful in their attack, so that the enemy to their west could concentrate their attention on Hugo Column. To their right front they could see the shell-bursts of the battle for the aerodrome. The 4th Armoured Brigade withdrew piecemeal through the column's position. The carriers on the aerodrome were slowly forced back. Suddenly enemy tanks appeared on the ridge to the south of the aerodrome, not eight hundred yards from our guns. It is an uneven battle between 25-pounder field guns in the open and tanks eight hundred yards away. The battery commander, too, had just been killed while driving in a pick-up with Hugo Garmoyle. But the crews stuck to their guns. Hugo walked slowly from one to another encouraging and giving orders. Every time an enemy tank appeared over the ridge it was engaged over open sights. There is a story that as Hugo was going from gun to gun, deliberately and full of purpose, one rifleman said to another: "Look, there's a shell fallen right on top of the Major."

"What did he do?" said the other.

"Took a longer stride," was the reply.

The action of these guns and the personal efforts of Hugo Garmoyle, who understood his battery almost as well as his company, had a great deal to do with preventing the enemy following up their success on the aerodrome. At any rate, they did not come on. Towards dusk the remainder of the Support Group were withdrawn to the south of the valley. As the order for this was given, the Headquarters of Hugo Column was hit by a shell and Jimmy McGrigor and Martin Crowder, two of our best and most popular young officers, were added to a list of casualties already long. The wireless being out of action as a result of this direct hit, there was much difficulty in getting the orders to withdraw to the carrier platoon, which was still on the near edge of the aerodrome almost among the enemy tanks. Having seen the rest of the column on their way, Hugo Garmoyle characteristically turned round to fetch his carrier platoon himself.

That night, the 21st/22nd of November, the scattered parts of the Battalion were miraculously collected together—except for "A" Company. They leaguered uncomfortably just south of the valley of Sidi Rezegh. In the early hours of the morning Christopher Sinclair walked in. He had been captured with most of the company when they and the 60th had been overrun. As he was being marched away the party he was with were accurately shelled by our guns and in the confusion he managed to make his escape. John Davies-Scourfield, who was captured with him, finally made his escape from Benghazi after several unsuccessful attempts.

This unexpected arrival was the last good news that day.

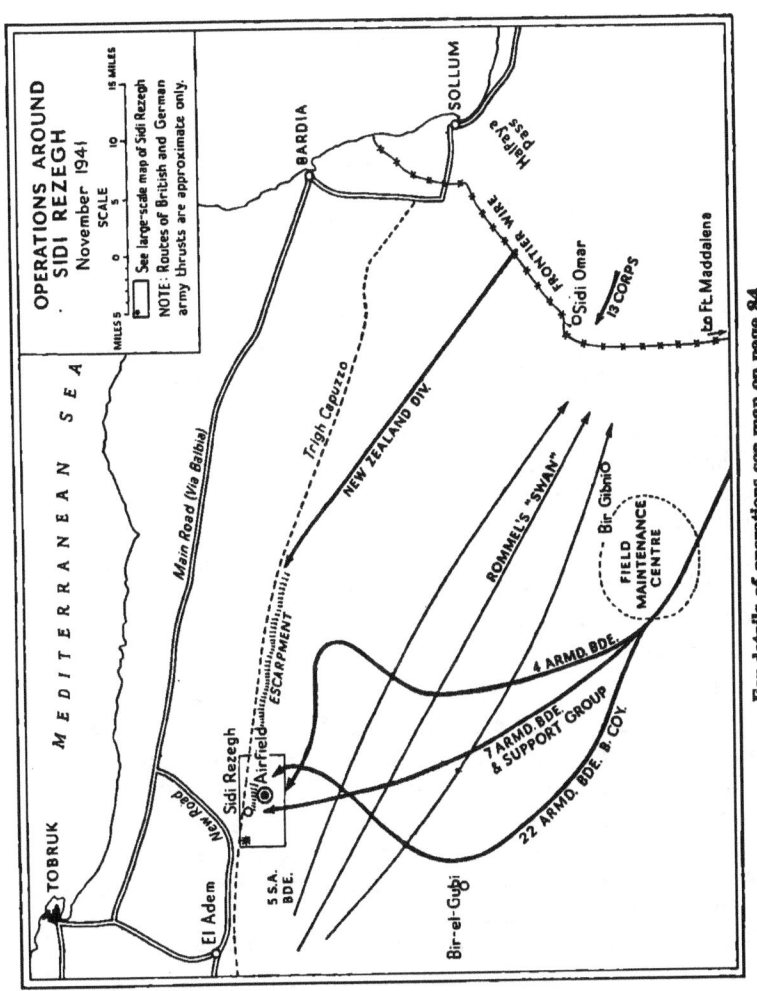

As the Battalion were cooking their breakfasts the Support Group were attacked from east and west by enemy tanks which had broken through the 8th Hussars on one side and the South African Brigade on the other. Jock Campbell organized personally such resistance as was possible, ordering his liaison officer, Ian Whigham, and Tony Palmer, who happened to be passing, to man an anti-aircraft gun. But the Support Group had to withdraw—and that quickly—away from the defenders of Tobruk with whom they had so nearly linked up.

In the initial confusion the Battalion Headquarters wireless vehicle was hit and lost. But, on the whole, most of the Battalion were got on the move. They streamed eastwards among a heterogeneous collection of vehicles, remnants of the 7th Armoured Brigade, supply echelons and the huge covered lorries which had carried the South African Brigade to their fatal battle. They had not gone far before it was seen that a German column was moving parallel and to the south towards the frontier wire. Throughout the day these forces moved at speed across the desert, occasionally shelling each other but generally hurrying eastwards. Just before dark the Support Group received orders to move to the south and to protect the vast supply dump south of Bir Taieb el Essem, which had been planted before the offensive began. This meant a night move across the line of advance of the enemy.

To those who took part in it that move was a nightmare. It was pitch dark. The column which formed up, close together and four abreast, contained various extraneous elements. Jock Campbell sat astride the bonnet of his armoured command vehicle, hoarse with energy expended, so that his voice reverberated like a ghost's whenever the engines were turned off. At intervals Very lights would go up, showing that there were parties of Germans in every direction. The column moved by fits and starts. At halts other vehicles would be heard approaching, sometimes the ghastly clanking of tanks, quite unidentifiable until they were right on top of the column. Once a German motor-cyclist shot through the column and away before anyone could engage him. One party of Germans met our column about half-way up and in the confusion and shooting and excitement many vehicles went astray. But as dawn broke the Support Group found themselves on the edge of the vast dump on which the continuance of the offensive depended. The Germans in their rush towards the wire had left it a few miles to their south.

That morning the dust blew miserably. The 2nd Battalion had had little to eat for four days: there had not been much time for sleep. For those who thought, morale could hardly be high. Our forces in the desert had been beaten before, just as they had had their victories. But the preparations for this enterprise had been on a greater scale than anything known before in this theatre involving more and newer tanks, fresh divisions, a new Army Headquarters. It was the disaster to the armour which had the most depressing effect. To see our tanks knocked out before they came within range for their own guns, to watch our tracer falling short or bouncing off while the enemy were "brewing up" our tanks, apparently at will, made the tired Support Group feel that we were powerless to advance to the relief of the garrison of Tobruk. We were in perfect tank country without a suitable weapon for dealing with tanks. Some indication of the fierceness of the fighting is given by the award of three Victoria Crosses to the Brigade, the citations for two of them witnessed by members of the Battalion—the only unit which did not receive this award, a deficiency to be remedied at Snipe. It was, perhaps, more disheartening to have failed when we knew we had fought well.

Even as these melancholy thoughts were exercising some of the Battalion among the whirling dust devils of the dump, General Strafer Gott was laying the plans which were to change this temporary setback to a definite victory. The Air Force had already begun to turn the scale in our favour; the base installations were replacing tanks at a rate hitherto unheard of: the genius of the Divisional Commander was to turn these reinforcements to good account. In the defeat of Rommel's counterstroke and the resumption of the offensive, the columns were to play a worthy and valuable part.

H

CHAPTER VII

THE SECOND ADVANCE TO AGHEILA

It was the practice of the great desert commanders—and more fashionable generals afterwards—to spend some time trying to account for the manœuvres of the German generals and even to anticipate their moves. Jock Campbell or Hugo Garmoyle would puzzle over the reported presence of two enemy armoured cars at an unusual location: General Strafer Gott tempered his plans as a result of his appreciation of the enemy's reactions. But it is doubtful if any of these could have made more than a guess at the intentions of Rommel in his dash to the frontier wire. He may have aimed at destroying railhead or even at Mersa Matruh; he may have made a bad shot at hitting off the dumps on which our offensive was to draw; he may have merely intended to link up once more with the defended positions on the frontier. The German campaigns in the desert depended for their success on the exploitation by an opportunist of openings secured by forces which were not really adequate for a major operation. It may be that he seized this particular tactical opening without waiting to decide upon his ultimate objective. In any case "Rommel's swan" failed to take into account either—and understandably—the strength of the Desert Air Force or the resilience of the 7th Armoured Division.

When, on the 22nd November, Rommel's forces set out for the wire, the 9th Battalion was still officially part of the reserve brigade which was to exploit a victory yet to be won. After cutting the wire for the initial advance of the 7th Armoured Division, the Guards Brigade had been employed in looking after the newly established field maintenance centre south-west of Bir Gibni. In the early stages of the battle, when things seemed to be going well, the 9th Battalion was ordered to leave one company at the field maintenance centre and, with a field battery, to move north-west to engage the enemy on the left of the main battle. The Battalion was in action against scattered forces north of Bir el Gubi, when news was received in the afternoon of Rommel's break-through. The force was ordered to return with all possible speed to their original area for protection of the dump, a course which entailed travelling parallel and to the south of the Germans. When it was clear by the next morning that the enemy had missed the field maintenance centre the Battalion was ordered back eastwards to the frontier wire. Here it met one of the German columns which had taken part in the rapid advance from El Adem and must have thought it was all set for a free run to Cairo. It was attacked by "C" Company and driven northwards, where it was severely dealt with by the Air Force. This little action, coming at a time when the Germans seemed to have broken clean through and had only the echelons to deal with, had considerable effect on the local situation.

As soon as the immediate crisis was over, the 201st Guards Brigade were re-formed and the 9th Battalion rejoined them. Their first task was to go to the assistance of the 11th Indian Infantry Brigade, who were making slow progress in an attack on the position at Bir el Gubi, held by the Italian Ariete Division. As the battalion commanders joined the Brigadier for an order group, a strong mixed column of Germans appeared from the north-north-west and was engaged by the battalions from the positions they happened to be in at the time. The 9th Battalion came in for much shelling from enemy guns and tanks and were subjected to several Stuka raids. But, although there was no adequate anti-tank weapon in either brigade, the enemy held off and contented themselves with shelling vehicles and any movement which attracted their attention. The 4th Armoured Brigade appeared from the east and with their help the Indian battalions were withdrawn through the Battalion. Just before last light the German column, rather surprisingly, withdrew and it was found that the Ariete Division, whose withdrawal the Germans had presumably come to cover, had cleared off also—a piece of Italian-German co-operation of a kind rare at the time and to become yet rarer.

On the evening of the day—the 22nd of November—that they retired to the dump the 2nd Battalion was re-formed into columns. Colonel Archie Douglas returned from the South Africans. At first the whole of the Battalion formed one column with one battery of the Field Regiment. Later a composite company of "A" and "B" Companies, commanded at first by Chris Sinclair and later by Wriggy Wrigglesworth, joined the 4th R.H.A. column under command of Lieutenant-Colonel Currie, who gave his name to the column. The 2nd Scots Guards joined the Support Group in place of the 60th, who went back to Cairo to re-form. The Support Group were now to the south of the enemy and behind them. When the columns set off from the dump they soon began to meet small, isolated parties of Germans, sometimes four or five men with a broken-down vehicle, sometimes a single motor-bicyclist lost, sometimes more formidable bodies on the move. Many of these Germans were taken prisoner and the spectacle of those who were captured, dirty, lost and unhappy in the desert, was a tonic to the riflemen. So were the bombing and strafing attacks of the Royal Air Force, which surpassed anything we had seen before.

For over a week the Support Group operated on the flank of the enemy. Every day the harassing grew bolder. The columns worked their way farther north until there was no enemy movement south of the Trigh Capuzzo. The New Zealand Division, advancing along the line of the main Bardia—Tobruk road, made steady progress. The 4th Armoured Brigade joined forces with them near Sidi Rezegh and the Tobruk garrison made an attempt to break out. But the New Zealanders were counter-attacked and driven back: XIII Corps Headquarters could only escape into Tobruk. Most of the enemy positions on the frontier still held out.

All this time, while the fortunes of the battle were still in favour of the Germans, the columns continued to exact a heavy toll in prisoners taken and vehicles knocked out. It was a strenuous life, breaking leaguer as it got light, moving out to a gun position, changing position several times during the day, engaging the enemy, shelling and getting shelled, often attacked by aircraft, moving at dusk and not settling down in leaguer until eleven or later at night. The nights were short. There was little sleep, hard rations and few comforts. With all the various moves the riflemen had little idea of what was going on. The enemy might be anywhere. There was no front and no safe rear. Occasionally there were good days when results spoke for themselves, such as one when a liaison officer from Rommel's own staff was captured carrying a marked map. On the whole, all

The Second Advance to Agheila

this activity did not seem to be achieving very much. But there gradually grew up a feeling that the enemy were being worn down, that their losses were mounting, that they were more and more on the defensive, until the columns were directed on Acroma, and in the first days of December the whole situation changed and it was suddenly clear that the enemy were on the run. The relief of Tobruk was complete.

The Support Group led the advance across the desert well south of the main coast road. It was hardly yet a pursuit. The 4th Armoured Brigade, who had the 9th Battalion temporarily under command, made a wide turning movement and failed on a dark night to cut off any significant enemy force: the 4th Indian Division had to drive off a serious counter-attack by tanks. The composite company with Currie Column took part in a rapid advance to the north to shell the road near Derna. Early in December Colonel Archie Douglas left, having commanded for nine months, and Hugo Garmoyle took over. The 2nd Battalion's column was active but took some punishment from the air. Godfrey Carter was badly wounded by Messerschmitts which attacked his carrier platoon, and in sight of the fort of Mechili we lost Tony Franklyn in an air attack, a regular officer who had come with the Battalion from India, had survived with distinction every desert battle since June, 1940, and now or at any time could ill be spared.

Many people expected another dash across the desert to Sidi Saleh, as had been done the year before, but for some reason it was only the Germans who remembered the story of Wavell's campaign. They had taken the reverse route once already and next spring would take it again. The Support Group were at first directed a good deal farther north towards a point just south of Benghazi. This route took them along the foothills of the Djebel. The going was bad and stony, so that progress was slow. It was obvious that we should be too late to cut off the enemy's retreat and prevent him destroying the harbour installations in Benghazi. The Royals, in armoured cars, were sent ahead with "C" Company under Tony Palmer. When they reached the escarpment south of Benghazi the only way down was barred by an anti-tank gun. "C" Company engaged this effectively and opened up the road for The Royals. But their arrival in Benghazi was too late to prevent the Germans from blowing up the port facilities and doing much damage in the town.

Too late it was decided to cut the road farther south with mobile forces. The Support Group and the Guards Brigade, which still included the 9th Battalion, were directed on points on the coastal road north of Agedabia. From the top of the escarpment at Sceledima it was plain that the enemy were moving with flank guards well out to the east. But the advance was continued in the hope of cutting off any stragglers from the main body.

The Support Group were to the north of the Guards Brigade. The 2nd Battalion had been merged into Currie Column, and now consisted only of headquarters and two companies. On Christmas Eve the column moved down the escarpment and across the plain towards the road. It was planned to lie up for the night a few miles from the road and to cut it at first light the next day. Jock Campbell arrived just before last light, so that he would be on the spot for the excitement of the morning. He managed, as usual, to infuse his own enthusiasm into many of those under his command and people went about talking in whispers as though the road was a hundred yards and not ten miles away from us. To those used to leaguering in the empty spaces the Bedouin encampments in this coastal plain, with their lighted lamps and the sound of their beasts, added to the feeling that we were in a strange and enemy land. There was, indeed, reason to lie low if we were to fall on the unwary stragglers the next day.

It was late before Battalion Headquarters got to sleep. They felt that their heads had hardly touched the pillow before they were awakened by the sound of small-arms fire within the leaguer, punctuated by Very lights and louder bangs. Everyone leapt to their arms. Then, above the sounds of battle, Jock Campbell's voice could be heard shouting: "If you don't put that fire out in five minutes the whole leaguer will move five miles!" An ammunition truck of the King's Dragoon Guards had caught fire, and it was that which was causing this furore. The blaze continued and, Christmas morning or not, the whole party picked up their beds, got into their vehicles and drove off five miles into the night. But the uproar had made no difference, for, when the road was reached the next morning there was no movement in either direction and it was clear that the Germans had declined, as they would once again, to fall into the trap which had closed so successfully on the Italians.

The Germans had made a planned withdrawal. It was not a rout comparable to the Italian debacle. The enemy had suffered heavily in tank losses, in prisoners and in prestige. But they had pulled out in time and the speed of their retirement was definitely dictated by themselves. They retained a tank force strong enough to discourage any too rash a pursuit, and at least one counter-attack in fair strength had been delivered at the expense of the 4th Indian Division. The 9th Battalion, being to the south of the Support Group, presented the more serious threat to the retreating German forces. Early one morning, before they had broken leaguer, the enemy attacked one of their columns with tanks, and Charles Liddell's company had to make a very hasty withdrawal, only just in time.

The Germans pulled back in their own time through Agedabia and halted on a series of sandy ridges a few miles south of the town. It was clear that they would have to be attacked or manœuvred out of this position. The area between Agedabia and Agheila was always unhealthy. By the time we got there we were at the end of a long line of communication; vehicles were in need of repair and maintenance; there were some particularly tricky stretches of soft sand; and, worst of all, we were temporarily out of range of the support of our own Air Force. The Luftwaffe always took advantage of this absence of air cover to attack the spearhead of our forces, using the comparatively adjacent clusters of airfields round Agheila for the purpose.

The 9th Battalion, who ever since the extinction of the 2nd Armoured Division had been a stray motor battalion without a permanent master, was a victim of a series of changes of command confusing and bewildering to a degree. Having started this battle under the Guards Brigade, they had already left them for the 4th Armoured Brigade, only to change command to the 22nd Armoured Brigade, north of Agedabia. Apart from these variations in command for the Battalion as a whole, companies were continually being sent off on one errand or another, so that Ted Jones (Quartermaster) never knew from day to day how many he had to supply or what brigade staff he had to deal with. Three days after Christmas the 9th Battalion found itself under command of the 22nd Armoured Brigade in the area of

Hasseiat, with Charles Liddell's company detached in the area of Benghazi.

South of Agedabia was a comparatively flat expanse of desert covered with small patches of scrub and camel humps. South of that again were some sand-hills running north-east to south-west which marked the beginning of the unpleasant, difficult country, full of soft sand patches and treacherous mud-flats, ridges and deep hollows, which stretched down to El Agheila between the sea and the Wadi Faregh. It had been expected that the enemy would put up no serious resistance between Agedabia and El Agheila. In fact, they made a stand on the line of these sandy ridges. The 22nd Armoured Brigade was ordered to dislodge the enemy and advance south. For the battle Paddy Boden's company ("C") was under command of the 4th County of London Yeomanry, Bing Baylay's ("B") under the 3rd County of London Yeomanry, and Battalion Headquarters and "A" Company (Mark Clayton) were directly under Brigade. The remaining armoured regiment, the Gloucestershire Hussars, was reduced to one squadron in strength. On the evening of the 28th the enemy light forces were driven in and the next morning the Brigade advanced into the rough country to the west. Four miles south of Hasseiat they bumped a strong enemy force and an armoured battle ensued, in which all the tanks and the motor companies with them were soon involved. While the attention of the Brigade staff was focused on this fighting another enemy column appeared swiftly from the north directed at Battalion Headquarters and "A" Company, who engaged it. It was some time, despite the eloquence of the Adjutant over the wireless, before Brigade could be persuaded that these new arrivals were not friendly. Since the "soft" vehicles of the armoured regiments were up with the Brigade, the appearance of this column caused some confusion and necessitated a withdrawal. In the middle of this upheaval "D" Company drove up happily to report their return from Benghazi. By last light the Brigade was back at Hasseiat, having lost a number of vehicles by enemy action and in the rough going. "A" Company had suffered heavily, losing as prisoners Mark Clayton and almost all the company headquarters. The Germans might be retiring; but before they went they left their mark.

As a result of this attack the enemy moved back to the Agheila area. The 9th Battalion returned to their old area,

The Second Advance to Agheila

forming part of three columns which operated between Mersa Brega and the Wadi Faregh. They remained there until the 19th of January, enduring air attacks and patrolling the enemy positions. They were then moved about a hundred miles to the rear to the area of Saunnu for what was intended as a rest. The 2nd Battalion, now reduced to two companies, were in position to the east, inland of the Guards. Here there was much soft sand and some determined air attacks by the enemy. The Colonel, Hugo Garmoyle, flew back to Cairo. On the way his Royal Air Force aircraft flew over the Halfaya Pass position which was still held by the Germans, with the inevitable result that it was forced down. It came to rest without injury to the Colonel in no-man's-land between the Germans and the South Africans, and there were some anxious moments before the passengers and crew were picked up by South African armoured cars and brought safely to our lines.

News gradually reached the front that the 1st Armoured Division, one of whose motor battalions was the 1st Battalion, was on its way to relieve the 7th Armoured Division. The 2nd Battalion waited anxiously for its arrival. It was an unpleasant area, what with soft sand and hostile aircraft. The two remaining companies were tired, their vehicles worn out. They were under no illusion as to the probability of an armoured attack by the Germans as soon as they were ready. For the second year running they prepared to hand over what was an unsavoury position to another battalion of the Regiment, whose first taste of the battle would be in circumstances unfavourable to anyone but particularly so to those who were new to the desert and to the peculiarly local hazards of the Wadi Faregh. In the second week of January the 1st Battalion arrived and took over from the 9th, and the 2nd started on the long trek to Cairo, the ancient vehicles and weary drivers spurred on by the thought of cold drinks and baths and haircuts, of Shepheard's and Gezira and the more democratic amusements of the Berka, of food not from a tin.

CHAPTER VIII

THE MSUS STAKES AND THE GAZALA LINE

AFTER the fall of Calais the 1st Battalion had to be reconstituted entirely. It was re-formed in England under the command of Colonel Jimmy Bosvile. Colonel Tim Massy-Beresford succeeded for a short interval but was soon recalled to the staff. The Battalion became part of the 1st Armoured Division and trained to work with the armoured regiments, the 9th Lancers, the Bays and the 10th Hussars with whom a close liaison and a firm friendship soon grew up. Training continued in England until, on the 28th of September, 1941, the Battalion embarked for an unknown destination. Looked at afterwards it was quite obvious where they were going, but at the time there were several alternative destinations in the air. Suspense was kept up, even after leaving the wonderful hospitality of Capetown, and it was not until the convoy left Aden and began to steam up the Red Sea that everyone knew that they were destined for the desert.

The Battalion landed at Suez, curiously enough in the rain, at the end of November, a few days after the offensive to relieve Tobruk had begun. After a short time among the dust-storms at Amariya, where the fundamentals of desert navigation were learnt under the guidance of Dick Poole and several other officers lent by the 2nd Battalion, the Division moved up on the 13th of December to Matruh, then across the desert through the frontier wire and on south of Tobruk, much training being done on the march. From there the Division moved up to the front to take over from the 7th Armoured Division, who by now had reached the area of the Wadi Faregh and Agheila. Before they moved up to take over, there was a halt near Antelat, where the Battalion provided two columns to take over from those already at the front. "A" Company, under Hugo Anson, was left some miles behind, and Colonel Jimmy Bosvile assumed command of one column and kept "C" Company with him. "I" Company went off to reconnoitre the going towards Maraua. Mike Edwardes and Mark Kerr went ahead to have a look at the columns in action before they were withdrawn.

The circumstances of the arrival at the front of the 1st Battalion were very similar to those of the 9th a year before and in the same area. The Sidi Rezegh campaign had been a tactical, but not a decisive, success. It is clear now that the Germans behind the marshes were preparing to go forward once more, although at the time there were intelligence reports that their tank strength had been disastrously depleted. Owing to the shortage of petrol, the main tank force of the 1st Armoured Division had to be placed to the north-east of Agedabia, and it was planned that the columns would fall back on them. The difficulty was that the going south of Agedabia was bad, but that once north of the track running east from that town there was ample room for manœuvre. It had been planned to establish a division in a defensive position at Agedabia, but there was insufficient transport to bring it up or to maintain it. So the 1st Battalion were bombed and occasionally shelled, took part in numerous patrols—their first in battle—and waited for the Germans to advance, despite the confident assertions by those who should have known better that they were in no position to do so. The 9th Battalion, after holding the position near Mersa Brega, were withdrawn a hundred miles to the rear to rest and refit.

On the 20th of January, in perfect summer weather, the Germans began their advance. George Millar's scout platoon gave the first news of their approach. The Afrika Korps were now experienced desert fighters. They moved faster and more purposefully than they had the year before, and the story of our retreat must be told more briefly. The enemy almost encircled the Guards Brigade on the main road, so that they had to move back rapidly. The 1st Battalion's companies out with their columns, who had heard for some time "a tremendous throb of engines," had a bad time, as they withdrew, from Stukas, from shelling and from soft sand. "I" Company farther north had the first news of the advance from the B.B.C. news. When night fell the Germans did not halt. Soon friends and enemies became inextricably mixed. As the columns leaguered for the night they saw German Very lights going up in every direction. Recognition was particularly tricky, because some of the Germans were in captured British vehicles, and on the second day, as the "Well-with-a-Wind-Pump" was approached, confusion was extreme. Here the armoured regiments of the 1st Armoured Division took a hand. But their counter-attacks, handicapped as they were by lack of petrol, against an enemy with superior armament were unable to halt the Germans for long. The Afrika Korps, reared on the doctrine of the blitzkrieg, knew that once the wide spaces of manœuvrable desert were reached they must drive as hard as they could to exploit their mobility and to reach those echelons of "soft" vehicles which were so vulnerable a target for their tanks. Some of these echelons and some of the dumps might furnish the petrol for further advance.

From "Well with a Wind Pump"—quaint name in a dry desert, but there it was, marked on the map and visible on the ground—the 1st Battalion's columns withdrew to Msus. From there the rate of progress became fast enough to be known as the Msus Stakes. Lack of petrol became a nightmare. The route was north to Charruba, just south of the Djebel, thence east to Mechili. Here it was clear that the Germans had been outstripped and a forward move was made to Charruba once more. But the German advance continued, until the Battalion had withdrawn behind what became known as the Gazala Line. The withdrawal had taken four days and nights to Charruba. This bare account gives little idea of the various battles fought by the columns, in which not a little damage was done to the enemy. The withdrawal was not all "run." It succeeded in preventing the enemy from cutting off any significant force. The Battalion lost four officers, Regimental Sergeant-Major Munday, about a hundred other riflemen and many vehicles; but on the whole it came well out of an unpleasant ordeal.

There were many stories of individual adventures. People tacked on to enemy columns in the dark and drove off unscathed when the mistake was discovered. Nearly a hundred enemy drove into our leaguers and were captured. The night, full of German Very lights, gave an illuminated picture of the confusion. No one had a more exciting experience than Vic Turner, whose vehicle had been knocked out in the early stages of the operations. He, together with Geoffrey Fletcher and several riflemen, set out to walk back across that endless desert. To anyone who knows the desert the idea of walking across it is quite fantastic. But they set out, lying up by day and walking at night. After six nights, during each of which they walked for ten hours, torrential rain added to their discomfort and they decided that they must somehow secure a vehicle. They laid an ambush, featuring the apparently bloodstained body of a rifleman, and waited. For two days nothing came. On the third day a German staff car appeared and stopped to investigate. They set on the crew, seized the car and drove off across the desert, leaving the astonished Germans still standing with their hands above their heads. Their troubles were not over, although the car was full of petrol and carried a reserve. When they were almost within our lines, the car broke down and the little party had to start off again on foot. They rejoined the Battalion after a memorable trek, avoiding capture chiefly by refusing to accept the apparently inevitable. They must have covered a hundred sandy miles on foot!

The 9th Battalion made a habit of avoiding, as a result of last-minute orders from above, some of the more disastrous operations by a few days or even hours. Twice they were spared from Tobruk; once the insistence of a French general saved them from Bir Hacheim. This habit made for a dull life, though by no means a safe one, but it saved them, temporarily, from complete extinction at the hands of the enemy, though not in course of time from the "A" Branch. On this occasion the Battalion moved back on the 19th of January and the very next day it was certain that the Germans' advance would begin. The Battalion had gone to Saunnu, a stretch of desert like any other, with some patches of Arab cultivation producing thin crops of corn. Here with the Northumberland Hussars (anti-tank gunners) and the 2nd R.H.A., it was hoped that some degree of rest might be had. In case of emergency this force was put under command of the 2nd Armoured Brigade. On the 20th of January vehicles were unloaded to ease the springs for the first time for months and the usual curious collection of possessions was uncovered: objects appeared which had not been seen since the Battalion left the Delta; the existence of some had been forgotten; others had already been replaced. During this day of complete confusion before refitting could begin, while much washing was done and the bonnet of every vehicle was opened, news was received that no move was envisaged for some days and that petrol issues were to be restricted.

There were some cynics who interpreted this order as a certain prelude to a quick move.

On the morning of the 21st a liaison officer was sent as a routine measure to report to the 2nd Armoured Brigade Headquarters. He found them gone. Another was sent to look for them, but before he returned news was received that the enemy advance was in full swing. In fact, by that time the 1st Battalion was already struggling back through the soft sand. The 9th did not take part in the counter-attacks of the Armoured Brigade; instead it was placed under command of the 1st Support Group, but, since this formation was unable to take over effective control, was soon placed under Vaughan-Hughes Force, a composite force of three columns, formed from the three regiments resting in the Saunnu area. This force came under command of XIII Corps direct.

By the morning of the 22nd of January all three columns, each with its motor company, were in contact with the enemy and much damage was inflicted on the rather scattered parties which they met. But the situation was distinctly confused. Not only were vehicles of both sides appearing at speed from the south and south-west but many British vehicles were being driven by Germans. It was impossible to know when to shoot. Eventually orders were received to "withdraw to the east," and partly owing to the confused situation and partly to the scattered salt-pans to the south of Msus, the columns became separated and acted independently. Squeakcol, commanded, as its name implies, by Colonel Squeak Purdon, having shot its way through a German column in a lively little action with the guns of the 2nd R.H.A. battery firing over open sights, found itself out of wireless range of any headquarters. Petrol was short and there was no means of telling the whereabouts of any other troops. The decision was taken to turn north and, putting some forty prisoners in three captured vehicles which had not been burnt, and some of the "extra" spare petrol always carried by provident motor battalions into the 2nd R.H.A. gun-towers, it went north for half the night and leaguered. Moving on at first light, it eventually bumped a patrol of the 11th Hussars, who directed it to the Charruba area, which it reached in the afternoon, to find a varied assortment of troops under XIII Corps, among them the column which included "B" Company. The next day a further withdrawal was ordered through Mechili to the Meikhtila area. In the course of this move "C" Company rejoined the Battalion after an adventurous period, during which the column commander had been captured and Paddy Boden had taken command, shot the 2nd R.H.A. guns himself and extricated the party from an awkward situation south of Charruba. That was the end of the second withdrawal which the 9th Battalion had made across the wide spaces of open desert between Agedabia, Msus and Mechili.

The Battalion had escaped lightly. The subsequent wearisome period of odd-job work on the Gazala Line to which it was subjected gave an opportunity to re-form "A" Company, extinct since the battle at Hasseiat on the 29th of December. The Battalion guarded dumps and gaps in minefields and workshops, and sent occasional patrols to the west which attracted much attention from the Luftwaffe, so that two officers were wounded at this time. In April the 9th Battalion went back for a three-week rest and refit at Bug Bug by the sea, to resume the unloading and washing and unpacking which had once been interrupted at Saunnu.

The 1st Battalion had not escaped intact during the withdrawal. The 2nd Armoured Brigade were kept as the immediate counter-attack force behind the Gazala Line, on which the front had been stabilized. While the infantry—the 50th Division, South Africans and Free French—held static positions covered by minefields, the Brigade and the 1st Battalion were in reserve behind them at short notice to move. It was necessary to send "B" and "I" Companies to the Tobruk area to re-form and refit. Later it was sometimes possible to send one company at a time to the sea to a delightful site at Mersa Aula. The role of the Battalion allowed scope for training and various wireless exercises and manœuvres were held. There were occasional excitements. On the 14th of February a column of fifty enemy tanks, probably of the 21st Panzer Division, were reported at Bir Temrad. Everyone expected an attack; but after some bombing by the Air Force the enemy column withdrew. Again, on the 15th of March, three columns, one an Italian force including the Ariete Division, were reported on the move. That threat also came to nothing. The South Africans repelled one serious Italian attack successfully, taking many prisoners. But on the whole the period from February to the end of May was spent by both sides in preparing for another offensive.

We hoped to build up forces strong enough to retake Benghazi and to recover the aerodromes so essential for command of the Eastern Mediterranean. While the base, which could only be Tobruk, but a short drive by desert standards from the front, was being built up, while the tanks in the Delta were being repaired, and while all the various preparations were mounting daily in intensity, there was little activity at the front. The launching of this new offensive was urged continually by those in England. It was strategically necessary. On the ground there were some who would have preferred to remain on the defensive, based more securely farther east; for it was clear that the Germans, too, were getting ready for a march to Cairo. As always in the history of the desert war, each successive offensive had to be planned on a bigger scale than the one before.

The role of the 1st Battalion was not entirely passive. Columns were found from the 1st Armoured Division to operate forward of the Gazala Line to harass the enemy and observe what they were doing. The role of the Riflemen was much as usual, chiefly patrolling and protecting the guns. On one of these patrols Paddy Biddell had crept up to an Italian encampment round a tumulus. He was within twenty yards when the sentry suspected movement and threw a stone at him. He did not, however, pursue his inquiries and it looked as if the patrol might get near enough to capture a prisoner, when the sentry saw Acting Corporal Hancock, who was just behind the patrol commander. Paddy Biddell, seeing that surprise had been lost, shot the sentry with his revolver and in so doing called down on the patrol a considerable barrage of the Italian type—much noise and many colours but less lethal than it appeared. The patrol managed to withdraw during this display, more or less without hurt. There were surprisingly few nights during the three years of the desert war when there was not a patrol out from some battalion of the Regiment, creeping wretchedly across a bare desert, waiting for some Italian to shoot off or groping by compass with no landmark and perhaps no stars to help, or bumping over stony wastes on the return journey, the riflemen asleep in the back of the truck, the driver fighting to keep his eyes open, the subaltern's eyes glued to his compass, expecting a volley of rounds to whistle at any moment past his ear, proclaiming either that the guard on his company leaguer were taking no chances or that he had navigated into the

German lines. In the winter those nights could be cold. March, 1942, was notable for nearly two days' continuous rain.

On the 2nd of May the 1st Battalion was visited in the field by His Royal Highness The Duke of Gloucester, who had recently been appointed Colonel-in-Chief of the Regiment. It was his first visit to a battalion since he had taken over and his presence was much appreciated by all ranks. He also visited the 9th Battalion, who were resting by the sea at Bug Bug. Soon afterwards, on the 7th of May, the King of the Hellenes also came to see the 1st Battalion, and he too went on to the 9th. These visits were luckily not attended by the Luftwaffe, who were active all this time and had already succeeded in wounding Gilbert Talbot. In February all vehicles were painted with large, white St. Andrew's Crosses so that our own aircraft should recognize their own side. This experiment was not universally successful. For one thing it made the vehicles stand out prominently against the background of the surface of the desert. The 25th of February must have been a bad day—or a good one for the Luftwaffe. The war diary of one battalion records a "Tewt" for all senior officers of the Brigade and then follows the entry, almost with relish: "The Divisional Commander's kit lorry; vividly painted with St. Andrew's Crosses, was selected and completely destroyed by three Messerschmitt 109's this morning." There follows a short sentence, which someone on maturer reflection decided to cross out—to the extreme disappointment of the reader. These remarks intend no disrespect for the Divisional Commander personally nor do they really reflect indiscipline. The English soldier in the last two wars was always prepared to regard with amusement and even with satisfaction disasters to the personal arrangements of the formation above his own: the brigade headquarters mess lorry overturned, the salvo of shells which lands uncomfortably near to "Division." It is as if Falstaff should sit on a chair that gives way or a builder's bucket upset suddenly upon the head of the Prime Minister. It is an attitude derived to a degree from the English sense of humour; but it also goes some way towards explaining the electoral defeat of Mr. Churchill in 1945. This was a war in the main of good generals; and there was little, if any, feeling against the staff. But many a rifleman cooking his bully in the rain has laughed and felt much better for it when a passing staff car breaks a spring.

I

It was during this period of preparation that two changes in organization were made which were profoundly to affect the motor battalions. Early in February it was decided to equip one company of each battalion with anti-tank guns. This policy was a reflection of the nature of war in the desert, where the tank had an unrestricted run. It was a direct result of the experiences of the Sidi Rezegh campaign, when there were all too few methods of dealing with enemy tanks. It reduced the strength of the Battalion in the assault, a deficiency which was to be felt more strongly in close or European country than in the desert. It was said with some truth that the anti-tank gunner was either bored to tears or qualified for a posthumous V.C. The anti-tank guns of the Regiment were to fight glorious actions in the next few months, below Alam Halfa, at the Snipe position and on many other less-famous occasions. Later some guns were to be towed from Alamein to the Baltic without firing a shot. The possession of anti-tank guns is an insurance policy, the necessity for which decreases with the decline in the enemy tank strength. If you are English, the time when you need them is in the early stages of a war; and the lessons drawn from the victorious ending of the previous war will have taught that they are not much use! In any case, the guns issued to the 1st, 2nd and 9th Battalions in February and March, 1942, were 2-pounders, carried portee on vehicles, and their range was clearly inadequate.

The other change in organization was the reintroduction of the Vickers machine gun. At this time it was decided to give each company one platoon of four medium machine guns. No modern gun can give quite the same rate of continuous fire; certainly no gun makes a noise more calculated to assure the morale of those it is supporting. The Vickers were welcomed in a country where one seldom got to within small-arms range of the enemy in daylight at all.

The Regiment was armed with both these weapons until the end of the war, the 2-pounders soon being replaced by 6-pounders. There were many arguments about how they should be organized, let alone employed. Eventually they were generally centralized in the Support Company. In Italy there were variations according to the nature of the country, and no two commanding officers ever had identical ideas about what should be done with either weapon. The first introduction of these

The Msus Stakes and the Gazala Line

weapons deserves mention and consideration in the story of the Regiment, for their arrival changed the lives and occupation of many Riflemen in all the battalions.

For the second year running the 2nd Battalion had been withdrawn to refit just before the German advance had begun. While the 1st and 9th Battalions were retreating towards the Gazala Line, the 2nd were enjoying the comparative advantages of Beni Yusef Camp outside Cairo. It was while they were there, training and bathing and draining cold drinks, that they heard the news that General Jock Campbell, recently appointed commander of the 7th Armoured Division, had been killed. He had been unable to keep away from the battle and had gone up to the desert to see what was going on. On the way back his car skidded on the road between Sollum and Bug Bug, and Jock, whom the Germans and Italians had failed, despite every opportunity that he had given them to destroy him, was killed. The death of this inspired commander, who had known the 2nd Battalion through every battle since the beginning of the Italian War, was a grave blow and an irreparable loss. He had been with the Battalion at Sidi Saleh; he had commanded their Brigade at Sidi Rezegh. There was no battle or skirmish or incident where he had not been present and his hand had been evident in all the successes of these years. As well as being a great fighter he had been a kind and considerate friend—and even, I suspect, an admirer—of the Riflemen who had fought with him in the desert.

The 7th Armoured Division had been reorganized, having one instead of two armoured brigades. This armoured brigade included a motor battalion. The 7th Motor Brigade had been formed, consisting of the 2nd and 9th Battalions 60th Rifles, the 4th R.H.A. and the 2nd Battalion. It was commanded by Brigadier Callum Renton, who had left us after the first spell in the desert. This motor brigade was intended to form, to use a now-unfashionable expression, a "box," an all-round defensive position capable of holding attacks by enemy armoured forces while our own tanks manœuvred to engage them. The Brigade had also certain mobile qualities which were to prove invaluable. Those who knew the Brigade Commander had no doubts about the seriousness with which training would be undertaken. In February the last baths were taken, the last nights were passed under a roof, and the Battalion moved out along the

Mena road for a spell of training in the desert. It was expected that this would last six weeks. But from the efforts the enemy were making to sink the island of Malta in the Mediterranean it was clear that an offensive was impending. In March the Division moved up to the forward areas.

The Division were in a counter-attack role to the south of the 1st Armoured Division. The 7th Motor Brigade were to operate with columns some thirty or forty miles in advance of the Gazala Line in the area of Segnali, and on the 10th of May to dig in with two battalions at Retma. These columns were to support the armoured cars, the 12th Lancers, the King's Dragoon Guards and the 4th South African Armoured Cars in their role of observing and harassing the enemy. The 2nd Battalion at first provided the motor infantry component of the columns. The Colonel, Hugo Garmoyle, who had with him "A" and "C" Companies, under John Davies-Scourfield and Desmond Prittie, commanded one column. "B" and "S" Companies, with Robin Hastings and Tom Bird, went to a column under command of Major Harry Withers (4th R.H.A.), a well-known desert figure, experienced and wily as a column commander. The weeks spent in this role were strenuous without being spectacular and were remarkable for one particularly undignified and rapid withdrawal at breakfast time and a magnificent fighting patrol by Tom Bird, who found a German leaguer with no sentries and blew up several trucks. When their place was taken by the 60th Rifles, the 2nd Battalion returned to the construction of a "box." For almost the first time in the war digging was taken really seriously. The position was to be held as long as possible, but no reserves of ammunition or stores were to be dumped, for the 7th Motor Brigade was a mobile formation.

The rain in March had made this spring one of the best for flowers that we were to know. Even the barren dust of Bug Bug grew many varieties of small wild flowers, and in the evening and early morning one could smell them as one broke leaguer or closed in for the night.

As May went on, the tempo of the preparations of both sides became more feverish. The Gazala Line was held by the South Africans, by the 50th Division and, in the south, by the Free French at Bir Hacheim. In front of this line the armoured cars, supported by columns of the 7th Motor Brigade, kept a watch on the enemy forces. Between Tobruk and the defensive line were the two armoured divisions, ready to counter-attack or to advance, strengthened by a few 6-pounders and some American Grant tanks. It was clear, as the desert dried up and the flowers withered and the faint green in the hollows gave way to dust, that the battle was imminent. The Regiment would be thoroughly committed. In the north the 1st Battalion was ready for immediate counter-attack; in the south the 2nd Battalion was digging its defences; in the centre the 9th Battalion, cast apparently for the least spectacular, though not the least hazardous, role, was guarding a field maintenance area midway between Acroma and Bir Hacheim. By whatever route the enemy struck it was certain that a battalion of the Regiment would be involved.

CHAPTER IX

GAZALA TO ALAMEIN—THE RETREAT OF 1942

As the war went on we became more and more sophisticated about "intelligence." In the early days all we knew was that we were fighting the Italians—and I suspect one or two Riflemen of being a bit vague about that. With the arrival of the Germans it became gradually more usual to know one's opponents better, until one would hear the names of the 21st and 15th Panzer Divisions, the 90th Light Division and, later, the Hermann Goering Division bandied about with a familiarity that would have surprised General Rommel. The "I" service began not only to identify the enemy formations but to forecast their moves. There was an understandable tendency to decry these prophecies. Often one had "stood to" in the miserable cold because of some intelligence rumour that the enemy were about to attack and the whole front had remained quiet. There was, too, an unfortunate period when the enemy were always said to be "just going" or, worse still, "just gone," when they were all too clearly visible to the forward troops and had no intention of departing. The worst habit of all, personally decried by General Strafer Gott, was that of the intelligence officer from somewhere far behind who would tot up the reports of enemy tanks which were claimed to have been destroyed and announce with complete confidence that the enemy now had no tanks left at all. In May, 1942, the sceptics and the believers were about evenly divided. While some formations were sleeping in their boots, others had sent parties off to the sea to bathe. This time the great brains of Intelligence were not crying "Wolf! Wolf!" For one thing, the organization of Intelligence had been improved beyond belief from the early struggling days when its resources were so thin. They said now that the Germans would begin their offensive on the 25th of May and punctually on the afternoon of that very day the patrols out to the west of the

Gazala Line reported that large columns were advancing towards them.

The experts had had three months to think about what form this attack would take. The Germans could either pierce the defences in the north by the main road or in the centre, or they could drive round to the south of the end of the line, leaving Bir Hacheim on their left, or they could combine the two courses, a straight punch and a right hook. It is not, I suppose, really surprising that the Germans should have understood the use to which the wide spaces of the desert could be put. The Italians were never happy away from the main road; the German High Command used the desert as a friend, though German soldiers never grew used to it and would rather huddle in crowds of vehicles than launch out in small parties across the open. On the 25th of May they set out to outflank the Gazala Line to the south and, in conjunction with this wide sweeping movement aimed at Tobruk, to attack the defences from the front. We were caught off our balance by the swiftness of their advance so that subsequently we were always being forced to react to any threat to our main base at Tobruk, which was too near the forward areas for security. To make things more difficult, the lines of communication, both road and rail, did not conform to the celebrated maxim of Clausewitz that they should be at right angles to the front.

The story of the three battalions in the confused operations of the next month is not easy to follow. There were many days of continuous fighting; the moves were constant and many of them apparently pointless. The best that can be done is to trace the main outline of the battle and enlarge upon a few of the more spectacular incidents.

The 2nd Battalion were the first to be engaged. They were dug in to the south in what was known as the Retma Box. There were with them the 9th Battalion 60th Rifles, just returned from column work near Segnali, the 4th R.H.A., some of whose gunners were absent at the sea, and the Rhodesian Anti-Tank Battery, commanded by Major Whirley Birch. The Battalion occupied the eastern of the two battalion positions in the "box." A minefield to surround the area was still incomplete. Like the other motor battalions, they were in the process of changing their 2-pounder guns for 6-pounders, though none of the latter had yet arrived. On the evening of the 25th the news of the enemy advance had been heard. They were still some distance away; they had yet to pass Bir Hacheim: there was another Indian "box" in process of construction to the west. The Retma Box was so placed that any column making a wide sweep round Bir Hacheim and heading for Tobruk would pass within range of its guns. The Battalion lay down to sleep realizing that the battle had begun but not expecting to be involved in it themselves for at least another day.

The German columns moved by night. The 4th South African Armoured Cars shadowed their movements and gave accurate reports of their progress. The Indian "box"—the 3rd Indian Motor Brigade—was swept aside, despite the gallant gesture of its Liaison Officer, Admiral Sir Walter Cowan, a sailor famous at Jutland, who fired all the rounds in his revolver before surrendering to a German tank. The next opposition that the enemy met was from the Retma Box. The Battalion had just finished brewing their breakfasts and were beginning to lay the mines which had that very night arrived, when large numbers of German vehicles appeared, all moving rapidly north-east and stopping apparently for no one. At first the anti-tank guns had a good shoot at the passing columns, setting several vehicles on fire, the Rhodesian battery, already armed with 6-pounders, being particularly successful. Then the Germans turned their attention to the 60th's position to our west. They mounted a heavy attack with tanks and infantry, crossed the minefield and overran the forward companies of the 60th. The 2nd Battalion were involved only in stopping the "overs" from the main battle. But with the 60th overrun our position was untenable. We had dug these positions where we were to fight our battle; before our breakfasts were well digested, Brigadier Callum Renton and the Colonel, Hugo Garmoyle, were driving round the companies in a staff car, making nice practice for a German anti-tank gun and telling us to get ready to go. The 7th Motor Brigade and the Battalion moved out to the east with, all things considered, little further loss. The Germans who were heading for Tobruk did not follow up and the move continued to the area of Bir el Gubi, where a halt was made amid a large crowd of startled "B" Echelon vehicles which had suddenly found themselves in the centre of a battle. The Brigade quickly reorganized into columns. During the evening these columns moved out to the north-west and were soon engaging the enemy forces still streaming across their front.

The 9th Battalion was guarding a corps field maintenance centre east-north-east of Bir el Gubi. The first wave of the German advance bypassed them completely. They remained until the 30th of May out of range of the main battle, although they did manage to capture a few stray Germans with the help of their newly acquired 2-pounders, which they fired for the first—and last—time in anger at the enemy.

On the 24th of May the 1st Battalion sent most of their 2-pounder anti-tank guns in "B" Company away to be replaced by 6-pounders. Two days later the Battalion "stood to" on hearing the news of the German advance round Bir Hacheim. The plan was for the 4th Armoured Brigade, who had a proportion of Grant tanks with them, to attack the enemy. The 2nd Armoured Brigade and the 1st Battalion were to be prepared to move south-east to assist them. But by 10.30 in the morning it was clear that the enemy had bypassed the 4th Armoured Brigade, except for one regiment, which had been caught unawares and had been severely dealt with, and were advancing north. The 2nd Armoured Brigade moved about five miles and faced west to meet the enemy head-on. They drove them back: the Bays overran some enemy anti-tank guns; "A" Company's scout platoon took about a hundred prisoners. The enemy made off to the north. It seemed that the first enemy attack had been repulsed.

From now on the Battalion was split up, one motor company with each armoured regiment. The role of the scout platoons in carriers was to do reconnaissance for the armour and to clear up the battlefield in the wake of the armoured advance. The motor platoons had in the day time the task of protecting the field battery of the 11th R.H.A. in each group and at night they had to be ready to patrol. The story of the Battalion's part is therefore that of the Brigade. Placed as they were to the south and rear of the South African positions and to the east of the 50th Division, the task of the 2nd Armoured Brigade was to prevent the enemy attacking the main infantry positions from behind. An escarpment ran east and west parallel with the main road and the coast which was impassable in most places to tanks and vehicles. As a result of a "war game" held by XXX Corps, a "box" had been constructed at a position which commanded the easiest ways down the escarpment and the tracks along the top of it towards Tobruk. It was dug and occupied by the Guards Brigade, less the 9th Battalion, and had been given the name "Knightsbridge"—incongruous among the "birs" and "wadis," the "abus" and the "gots." The Knightsbridge Box was the pivot round which the armoured brigades operated. It was attacked again and again. The armour fought off the German tanks continually and the 1st Battalion, involved in all these battles, watched our tank strength gradually whittled down, as inferior armament and thinner armour told despite the skill and gallantry with which these cavalry regiments fought.

When the Germans were first encountered Vic Turner was in command in the absence of the Colonel and Adjutant on leave. His command vehicle was penetrated by an armour-piercing shell, wounding Charlie Simeon fatally and the driver seriously but leaving Vic and the vehicle unhurt.

On the morning of the 27th the 10th Hussars fought a successful battle, assisted by "I" Company, destroying several anti-tank guns and taking some forty prisoners. That afternoon the 2nd Armoured Brigade fought the main enemy and again drove them back, overrunning more guns. In the night "A" Company's scout platoon and the Sappers blew up five enemy tanks and some seventeen anti-tank guns left abandoned on the battlefield. Every day until the end of the month the story is the same. The 2nd Armoured Brigade was engaged with at least one panzer division, with the 22nd and 4th Armoured Brigades joining in on either side. On the 29th, in a severe sandstorm, the Germans tried to break through to the west to join up with the Italian Ariete Division. This attempt was foiled. On the 30th twenty-five enemy tanks were chased south towards Bir Hacheim. But the main battle raged round Knightsbridge and Bir Aslag. The enemy brought up more guns; their aircraft strafed and bombed, once almost hitting the Battalion Headquarters White scout car. There were always night patrols by Sorbo Soboleff, Bill Apsey, John Lentaigne and all the subalterns of the motor platoons. Locally these battles were successful. But successes cost dear. By the 31st of May the total tank strength of the 2nd Armoured Brigade had sunk to forty. All these remaining tanks were handed over to the Bays and 9th Lancers, and the 10th Hussars went back to collect more tanks, so that the Brigade had to be reorganized as one armoured regimental group with "A" Company and two "support groups," each formed round the nucleus of one battery and one motor company. These two support groups were commanded by Colonel Jimmy Bosvile.

While the 1st Battalion was so heavily engaged in the armoured battle of the north, the 2nd was fully occupied farther south and the 9th was moved from its role of protecting the field maintenance centre to take part in the fighting. We had left the 2nd Battalion after being chased from the Retma Box, re-forming in columns on the afternoon of the 26th of May to attack the flank of the enemy columns moving north-eastwards towards Tobruk. This enemy thrust struck at the administrative base from which the forward elements of the Eighth Army were supplied. We were forced to react to this threat. The Headquarters of the 7th Armoured Division had been overrun on the first day; XXX Corps Headquarters were being chased round the desert in a manner reminiscent of the bad days after Sidi Rezegh. But orders came from somewhere on the 27th of May for the 2nd Battalion to move northwards and protect the administrative base at Belhamed, just south of Tobruk. The leading elements arrived just too late to prevent one dump being set on fire and a few wisps of blue smoke were all that was left of the N.A.A.F.I.'s supply of whisky. Recovering from this severe blow to morale, the 2nd Battalion moved the next day to Acroma, which was threatened by elements of the enemy. From there they moved south and spent the next few days until the end of the month attacking the enemy lines of communication between their forces at Bir Hacheim and those which were involved in the armoured battle in the north. This was a profitable role. Many prisoners were taken and stray vehicles captured. The enemy supply situation was chaotic. In one place some fifteen enemy tanks were found abandoned for lack of petrol. Colonel Hugo Garmoyle was eminently suited to make the most of the opportunities he was offered.

It might be as well at this stage to take stock of the larger picture of the Eighth Army's battle. It had begun disastrously with the break-through round Bir Hacheim by the enemy's armour. Part of the 7th Armoured Divisional Headquarters had been captured and much of the 4th Armoured Brigade had been seriously damaged; enemy armoured cars were loose among the echelons and supply dumps, the 3rd Indian Motor Brigade had been overrun, and the Retma Box had been abandoned. In the next phase, largely through the efforts of the 2nd Armoured Brigade, the tide had turned in our favour. The enemy armour had been driven back. They had only a narrow gap through the minefield, vulnerable to fire from both sides. The main defensive positions still held, since the Free French had driven off the attacks on Bir Hacheim, and the supply difficulties of the forward enemy columns were immense. We had more than recovered our balance. We were on the threshold of a considerable victory. Someone issued a jubilant order that enemy tanks found abandoned were not to be destroyed, since they could be recovered and put to our own use later on. Perhaps that order tempted Providence too much. We have seen that the 2nd Armoured Brigade had already lost more than half their effective tank strength. From the end of May onwards the fortunes of the battle steadily favoured the Germans. The infantry battle in the north to drive the enemy out of the position they had captured in the minefield—the battle, as it was called, of the Cauldron— ended disastrously for us, perhaps because the attack was delivered at half-cock, neither as an immediate counter-attack, which might well have succeeded, nor as a fully prepared set-piece operation. The divisions concerned in the attack suffered heavily; the 150th Brigade of the 50th Division were overrun. The Regiment were not directly concerned in the Cauldron itself, but Colonel Ted des Graz, commanding a battalion of the Fifth Fusiliers, was killed fighting a gallant action which came near to earning him a Victoria Cross. After the batttle of the Cauldron the fighting round Knightsbridge wore down our strength until finally the evacuation of Bir Hacheim made necessary the withdrawal which was to end at the Alamein Line.

The stories of the three battalions of the Regiment must be fitted into this larger picture before they are described individually in detail. The 1st Battalion continued to operate in the Knightsbridge area. The 9th Battalion was drawn into this northern battle on the 3rd of June. The 2nd Battalion, after two raids to the west of the Gazala minefield, remained in the south, continually tapping-in on the enemy's communications and keeping contact with them when the withdrawal began.

For the first four days of June the 1st Battalion took part in the confusing series of battles centring round the Knightsbridge Box. Their main object was to prevent the enemy moving north and so cutting off the South Africans and the 50th Division.

Their success was largely due to General Herbert Lumsden's inspiring leadership. Bir Aslag and Maabus el Rigel are the names which most frequently occur. On the 4th the Brigade had to turn about and face enemy advancing from Harmat. During the night of the 4th/5th the Brigade made a night march through the minefields, but failed to prevent the enemy gaining a temporary hold on Belefaa Ridge. The two support groups drove them off the ridge. But almost at once they were ordered round the "box" again to the north, where a determined attack by the enemy overran some of the anti-tank guns and infantry with the 22nd Armoured Brigade. This was a bad day. From the 5th to the 9th the enemy slogged away at the Knightsbridge Box. The 1st Battalion, guarding the guns round Rigel, came in for their share of shelling, bombing and strafing. Every night there were night patrols; every day the carriers—Ed Garnier, Tommy Redfern, Mark Culme-Seymour and Francis Dorrien-Smith—did the reconnaissance for the Brigade. Sometimes, but not often, there were definite results to report. On the 6th of June Bill Apsey's patrol killed two enemy; on the next night Paddy Biddell managed to blow up an enemy ammunition lorry; on the 7th John Lentaigne recovered a tank of ours within a few hundred yards of the Germans. But more often than not there was little enough that was concrete to show for the desperate efforts which had to be made on each successive night, at a time when days were long and darkness lasted for only a few hours. The 10th of June was a quiet day. But by the 11th the Brigade was reduced to one armoured regimental group, the Bays, and one "support group," which was commanded by Tommy Whittaker. The next day was chiefly notable for a particularly heavy bombing attack on the Battalion.

In the accounts of the tank battles at this time various attempts have been made to pick on one day when the issue was decided and the strength of the armoured regiments dropped dramatically to a figure which made it impossible to go on. In war, events are seldom so clear-cut as the reports and communiqués would have us believe. It is a gradual wearing process, a process of attrition which often drains away the resources of one side or the other before the generals are aware of what has happened. I do not believe that there is one day in this June which should be made a scapegoat. There may be no fatal 11th or decisive 13th. But it is clear that on the 13th of

June the enemy attacks developed which resulted in our having to withdraw from the Knightsbridge Box. In the morning the enemy tanks could be seen forming up. In the afternoon heavy shelling began. For the rest of the day the 1st Battalion was involved in the attempts to maintain contact with the Scots Guards in their defensive positions, attempts that were not without their local successes and resulted in the destruction of, anyway, six enemy tanks. But by evening orders were given to withdraw to Bir el Tmer and positions south of Acroma. The withdrawal was not merely local; for, two days before that, the Free French had intimated that they would have to pull out from Bir Hacheim, an event which concerned the 2nd Battalion closely and must be dealt with in the story of their operations. At any rate, on the evening of the 13th it was clear that the Eighth Army was in retreat.

The next day, with the pivot of the defences uprooted, the South Africans streaming eastwards down the main road towards Tobruk, and the 50th Division breaking out by a great detour to the south, was almost the hardest day for the Battalion since the operations began. The Germans put all their efforts into the struggle to cut through by Acroma to Tobruk. The 1st Battalion was in the centre of the battle. When the infantry "box" in front of the Battalion was overrun by enemy tanks it was Sorbo Soboleff's motor platoon in unarmoured vehicles who rescued many of the retreating infantry. The Battalion, trying to cover the withdrawal, were heavily involved once more. In the evening enemy tanks got right up to the battery position, where Dick Jepson-Turner had two 6-pounder guns in action. A bare desert gives a great advantage to the tanks. The two guns took the enemy on and scored hits on no fewer than six tanks before the whole crew of one gun became casualties. Jepson-Turner then took over and loaded and fired the gun single-handed until his right arm was shot off.

The 1st Battalion was now ordered to move down the escarpment towards the coast road and then east to Tobruk. Since all known passable tracks downwards were mined or already occupied by the Germans, this was not so easy as it seemed. But at about eleven in the evening of the 14th of June a start was made along some sort of pathway down the escarpment and it was owing to Hugo Baring, the Adjutant, that a way was found at all. It was not a very good way. For seven hours the vehicles bumped, crashed, stopped, restarted, stuck on boulders, got ditched, drove in the dark and without lights into the truck in front and found their way at a snail's pace to the bottom. Those who had no brakes ran into the vehicle in front. Drivers slept and sometimes failed to wake when the others in front of them went on. It was like a nightmare dream, for everyone knew that behind them the German tanks were approaching, that we must be clear of the escarpment before it was light and yet the appalling going made progress desperately slow. As the last platoon was just reaching level ground and it was getting light enough to see to shoot, someone reported that there were twenty enemy tanks on the top of the ridge. But by the time they could see to engage us almost all the Battalion was out of range and only one carrier received a direct hit. In seven hours the Battalion had moved three miles.

The 1st Battalion passed through Tobruk to Gambut and then for ten days was out of the battle. Some of this time was spent in bathing and refitting at Bug Bug and "I" Company went right back to the Delta to refit. The period of rest was uneasy, for the withdrawal of the Eighth Army which had begun with the fall of Bir Hacheim was gathering impetus with every day.

We left the 2nd Battalion operating in the south against the right of the German lines of communication between Bir Hacheim and the Cauldron battle. At the end of May, when the cry was that the enemy had been defeated, the 7th Motor Brigade were sent round the minefield south of Bir Hacheim to attack the enemy supply line well west of the Cauldron battle. This entailed a long march right behind the enemy lines. It took them entirely by surprise and for two days the Brigade, and particularly the 2nd Battalion, had a successful time, destroying tanks on transporters, over a hundred enemy trucks, and a number of guns, capturing some three hundred enemy prisoners and releasing even larger numbers of our own who were being escorted back. It was one of the few occasions when we laid mines on their main supply route by night and actually saw the result the next morning in the daylight. If such were the results achieved by columns, one wonders if the appearance of an armoured brigade might not have proved decisive. But the main battle was going badly. We could see that the enemy were reinforcing the Cauldron and that the reports that they were pulling out were the product of wishful thinking. The Brigade was withdrawn to an area south of Bir Hacheim. The task here was to assist General Koenig and the Free French, who were still being attacked continuously by the enemy. Here the columns were less effective, though they did make contact with the French. Tony Palmer and Tom Bird were among those who made their way through the enemy and the minefields to escort supplies to the defenders. Of these expeditions Tom Bird wrote: "My own most exciting time was round Bir Hachiem fort. Two days before it was evacuated, I took some food and ammunition in to them, and in order to do so had to go through the middle of the enemy—all this during the night with enormous, unwieldy lorries. Then I saw General Koenig inside the fort, collected information, and had to get out, which fortunately went O.K., though I won't say without mishap." At first the French seemed in great heart and pointed triumphantly to the derelict tanks around their positions. But they were bombed continually by large concentrations of fifty or a hundred Stukas. When the garrison refused to take some supplies which could with reasonable safety have been got to them, it was clear that Bir Hacheim would not be held much longer.

Meanwhile permission had been sought to return to the area of Mteiffel behind the Cauldron where the columns had already had such outstanding success. One column—the 2nd Battalion's—under Colonel Hugo Garmoyle was allowed to go. The expedition was a great success. The column moved out to a position from which it could shell the main track running east and west on which the enemy depended for their supplies. There it was over fifty miles from the rest of the Brigade to its south and separated from the remainder of the Eighth Army by several minefields and the bulk of the German army. There were many "soft" vehicles to attack. On the 9th of June traffic on the track was brought more or less to a standstill. Some fifty more of our prisoners were released and a number of enemy were captured. The Germans were more prepared than they had been when the 7th Motor Brigade had first appeared from this unexpected direction, so that they lost no time in sending out parties of eight-wheeled armoured cars and then tanks to hold us off their supply route. The column was alone and unsupported. It was the sort of situation in which Hugo Garmoyle excelled. He seemed to have an eye in every direction. We were always on the move, dodging an enemy thrust or creeping up to attack the track at another point. In the three days while the column was behind the enemy lines it destroyed over forty lorries, four tanks, six guns and one self-propelled gun. The day before we moved back a formation of over fifty Stukas appeared from the south at hedge-hopping height—if such a term can apply in the desert. After a moment of consternation the column suddenly realized that they would certainly be mistaken for Germans in this unlikely position, far behind the orthodox front line. Everyone who possessed a weapon fired it and it is said that two of these sitting birds were seen to fall, while another was brought down by a patrol of armoured cars a little to the north. While the 2nd Battalion was making its presence felt to the north-east events elsewhere were progressing much less well. On the 12th of June the Free French were forced to evacuate the "box" at Bir Hacheim.

The 2nd Battalion were now by many miles the most westerly troops in the Eighth Army. They withdrew gradually south while the rest of the Brigade superintended the evacuation of Bir Hacheim. The column then moved due east, keeping contact with and harassing the enemy. There was one hazardous day when the dust blew and visibility was restricted to a few hundred yards and the "B" Echelon vehicles of the 4th South African Armoured Car Regiment found themselves suddenly surrounded by the enemy. But on the whole the column was in good control of the local situation. After gradually stepping back for several days, orders were received to move north and to assist the defenders of Tobruk. This was the first indication that the South African garrison was seriously threatened. Tobruk had once been held; and, as our fortunes in the battle gradually receded, we had pinned our quite unjustified hopes on its ability again to resist a siege. As the 2nd Battalion pushed northwards the seriousness of the Eighth Army's situation began to sink in. Most of the enemy we met were hurrying to the east. We did some damage to these. But in the anxiety to assist the garrison, risks had to be taken; parties of enemy were bypassed, and vague figures in the mirage had to be taken on trust. The columns were approaching the escarpment at Sidi Rezegh when, in the distance to the north, straight in the direction of the fortress, a great black cloud began to rise. Many of us had seen that cloud before, the token over a year before of the impending surrender of the Italians. Now we knew that the dumps, the great oil tanks, the supplies accumulated for our offensive to Benghazi had been set on fire by the defenders. In 1941 endless columns of Italian prisoners had filed past under the black curtain of the burning oil drawn across the winter sun. Now, as the smoke-cloud grew larger and larger until it covered the whole horizon to the north, we saw a small column of vehicles approaching from the direction of El Adem. After some preliminary circling its identity was established as British and, when contact was made, we discovered that it was a party from the Guards Brigade, bringing the melancholy news that the garrison of the fortress had been ordered to surrender, an order which this party had refused to obey. It was the 20th of June, just eight days after the fall of Bir Hacheim and almost a month since the beginning of the German offensive.

Operating, as they were, many miles behind the leading elements of the enemy, the columns could expect to be attacked from any direction. There was no knowing where the Germans might be: nor could the enemy expect to find us so far from the rest of the Eighth Army. Those experienced in this form of fighting cultivated a habit of having reconnaissance in every direction, for, if the opposition was too strong, there was safety in sensible movement. Although the German Higher Command was alive to the potentialities of wide, sweeping movements in the desert, small parties of the Afrika Korps were always apt to get lost and demoralized by the open spaces. Just at the time that Tobruk fell Peter Innes's carrier platoon of "B" Company was out on patrol watching to the north of the rest of the column. The platoon commander saw the figures of two large vehicles approaching through the mirage. On closer inspection these were identified as a large, half-tracked troop carrier and a Mark III tank—German vehicles. Peter Innes gave orders for the carriers to remain still where they were. As the enemy approached they could see that the tank was being towed and that the crew were sitting outside on the turret, paying little attention to where they were going. They were, after all, some fifty miles behind the main battle. When they were within a few hundred yards, the Germans suddenly saw the carriers. They halted and had a look at them through their glasses. They were clearly puzzled. The platoon commander gave the order for the whole platoon to advance as hard as they could go from all directions towards the tank. The enemy were still not seriously disturbed. But as the carriers got closer the tank commander fired a Very light as a recognition signal. When this was not answered the Germans realized that these small vehicles approaching them at full speed were not friendly. They opened the turret and manned the guns. By this time Peter Innes's carrier had got so close to the Mark III tank that its guns could hardly be depressed low enough to take aim at him. The gun crew tried frantically to aim at him: the driver tried to start up so as to back to a better range. Sergeant Pevalin, seeing that at any moment his officer's carrier would be blown up at pointblank range, drove right up to the back of the tank and with Rifleman Rowett clambered up on to the platform behind the turret. From here they managed to fire inside the tank and forced the crew to surrender. The carrier platoon commander was able to come up on the wireless with a message which his company commander, who had seen him ten minutes before in an apparently empty desert, will never forget: "I am coming in now with a Mark III tank, a large troop carrier and twelve prisoners, two of them wounded." Such were the advantages of operating behind the lines.

Not all actions met with as few casualties, however excellently they were carried out. One day at this time a party of German vehicles, apparently unescorted, was seen by the Gunner observation post and an operation by John Henniker-Major's carriers supported by Jack Toms's 6-pounders was planned. Before they had gone far towards the enemy it was clear that, so far from being unescorted, the "soft" vehicles were accompanied by some anti-tank guns. The carriers, however, went straight in and John Henniker-Major ordered his driver to drive within grenade range of the guns! The carrier just overshot the mark, was blown up at point-blank range, and the officer and crew were wounded. However, the wounded were extricated, assisted by the fire of the 6-pounders, and the platoon retired, leaving a number of German lorries in flames and the whole column in confusion. Such local successes made it harder to understand why the Army's withdrawal persisted.

When it was clear that the columns could no longer influence the battle for Tobruk, the 7th Motor Brigade moved on to the east, not before John Reeve had been killed in a night patrol. They acted as the rearguard of the Eighth Army. The plan at first was that they should cover the occupation of a position at Sollum. The momentum of the withdrawal continued, and in a few days we were told that it was Mersa Matruh which was to be held. The whole force moved back east of the frontier wire. "B" Company and the light squadron of the 5th Royal Tanks were probably the last formed body of the Army to cross the frontier into Egypt. It was a fine clear evening and the 4th Armoured Brigade, formed up in battle formation to the east of the wire, were an impressive sight. But the withdrawal continued across the old battlegrounds of Jock Campbell and the earliest columns to the outskirts of the fortress of Matruh.

It was at this time that Brigadier Callum Renton assumed command of the 7th Armoured Division and Colonel Hugo Garmoyle went off to command the 7th Motor Brigade. Mike Edwardes took over temporary command of the 2nd Battalion. To say that the Battalion owed its survival to Hugo Garmoyle would be less than the truth; for it was the faith and confidence of every Rifleman in the judgment and leadership of the Colonel that had made it possible to operate continuously, offensively and successfully for so long and often at such great distances from the rest of the Army.

Someone said in a letter home: "After Hacheim was evacuated we started withdrawing and for some reason never clear to me seemed unable to stop." We could not at any rate stop to hold Matruh, and the fortress, specially constructed in peace time at the cost of so much sweat and labour, was abandoned just before it was invested. The effectiveness of this fortress depended on the existence of an armoured force to its south and such a force was no longer in being. There is a story that the enemy crossed the minefield to the south of the town by driving a herd of camels before them. Whether that is true or not, they did not hesitate for long. They were soon driving hard for Cairo and in front of them, or at any rate driving in the same direction, were three battalions of the Regiment. It was a time, not unnaturally, of the utmost confusion. There were bewildering changes of command; orders and counter-orders were frequent and complicated. Every day fires appeared on the horizon as dumps of supplies and N.A.A.F.I. goods were burnt. Beer and chocolate were unrationed, if you happened to arrive at the right time. The biggest fire in the open desert was at Bir Thalata, where the smoke darkened the afternoon. One particularly disturbing feature of the withdrawal was that by this time most of the vehicles were badly in need of repair: 15-cwts. would tow each other; carriers would limp and grind along. When the 1st Battalion reached the frontier wire, such was the appearance of their transport that the Military Police nicknamed them, a little unkindly, "Dodgy Column." When the 9th Battalion was sharply attacked by tanks during the last days of the withdrawal a herd of camels looked after by Bedouin Arabs became involved in the battle and had the same ideas about withdrawing as the carrier platoon, which was nearest to the enemy. The carriers, having by then completed some two thousand miles, had the worst of the race. As Mac McColl said: "I didn't mind much when the camels going fast shot past me; it didn't really worry me when a wog galloped past us on a donkey—but I did begin to get a little anxious and think the carriers weren't much good when a wog passed me on his own two feet." There are few more unpleasant situations than to be withdrawing with an enemy close behind you across an endless desert in an ancient and rickety truck.

All three battalions were involved in rearguard actions during the last stages of this retreat. The 1st Battalion found itself at one point well behind the leading elements of the enemy. There are stories of companies driving through vast columns of Italians all going the same way. One sergeant, unconscious of the identity of his fellow-travellers, is said to have stopped and calmly changed a wheel in the middle of the "B" Echelon of the Italian Ariete Division; an officer asked a man in the dark where company headquarters was and found that he was an Italian. There was one advantage of approaching the enemy from the rear and that was that you could pick up the stragglers from the main columns and quietly take them prisoner. You can imagine the astonishment on the faces of those Germans who had halted their truck for a smoke or to top-up with petrol, their minds already intent on the pleasures of Cairo, when a truck of The Rifle Brigade drives up from the east and requests them immediately to surrender. But the 1st Battalion was far from having it all its own way. For some distance it travelled as the centre of three columns, two of them German, and when identities were eventually established a difficult battle ensued. Near Bir Khanayis the Battalion leaguered between two parties of Germans and came in for a rough night at the hands of Wellingtons of the Royal Air Force, who were not helped by the fact that the Brigade had not received the recognition signal for the day. Apart from this understandable error, the Air Force support was magnificent and it was galling for the Army to be withdrawing when the Royal Air Force had complete control of the air. The final nightmare came when it was clear that the supply echelons could not arrive to replenish them with petrol owing to the presence of the enemy all round them, and it was far from certain that they would have enough petrol to reach the Alamein Line. Some companies had to stop and share out their petrol among all the vehicles equally. There was a further hazard when an escarpment was met which was all but impassable—an unexpected hazard, since there were few maps in possession of the fighting troops showing an area as far to the east as this.

The experiences of the 2nd Battalion were similar. They, too, made their way through the confusion to the Alamein Line. It was, of course, in these circumstances that the administrative training and experience of the three battalions paid. No one ever went hungry and few, if any, vehicles dropped out.

Throughout these operations the story of the 9th Battalion has been hard to trace, mainly for reasons which are explained in the next chapter. At the end of May they were guarding supply dumps in an area near the Gazala Line which was not in the area of the battle. This role was interrupted by a proposal that the Battalion, with a 60th battalion, should take over the defence of Bir Hacheim. The move to Bir Hacheim and the preliminary reconnaissance were completed without incident, although "a concentrated attack by Junkers 88 bombers on the position was regarded by some as an ominous pointer to the enemy's intentions in the neighbourhood."* The French were reported as confident, "though at the same time delighted at the prospect of relief from this dismal spot. . . . The following morning further measures for the relief were abruptly interrupted by the arrival in a sandstorm of a strong, mixed German force of tanks, infantry and guns. As we had neither tanks nor field guns we were in no position to argue with the enemy, and accordingly cleared out, doing what damage we could. Unfortunately the enemy was assisted by a strong khamseen which cut down visibility almost to zero and caused most of the Battalion's rather antiquated trucks and carriers to boil like so many kettles." The machine-

---

*The quotations here are from an account by Major P. A. D. Boden.

gun platoons and anti-tank guns, firing "portee," got off a few rounds into the sandstorm with unknown effect. The Battalion was then ordered to move off to Bir el Gubi. From there the 9th Battalion was drawn into the main battle round Knightsbridge and occupied a "box" at Elvet el Tamar on the 8th of June. They were much involved in the confused fighting in this area, which has been referred to, if not described, in the story of the 1st Battalion. When Bir Hacheim was evacuated "C" Company, under command of Paddy Boden, was detached to form part of a column which was to attempt to hold off the enemy advancing from the south. From the 11th to the 13th of June "C" Company were in contact with the enemy and had to watch superiority in tank armament once again tell decisively in the Germans' favour. They were then withdrawn to Acroma, where they took part in the battles to prevent the enemy cutting the main road from Gazala to Tobruk before the South Africans had been withdrawn. After a march through Matruh and a short time under the 1st Battalion 60th Rifles, the company rejoined the 9th Battalion near Matruh on the 26th of June.

In the meantime the Battalion had taken a fair measure of punishment at Elvet el Tamar. But they were not without luck. They were withdrawn from this "box" only to see it overrun the next day by German tanks. They moved to Tobruk and settled into a position as mobile reserve in the centre of the defences. Battalion Headquarters found a comfortable dug-out and remembered, perhaps, how nearly they had remained in the town the year before and how a change of plan had prevented them taking part in the siege. Once again a change of plan was to affect their fortunes; for, after only one day in their comfortable headquarters, they were ordered to move out to the east, much, it is said, to the annoyance of those concerned. After this reprieve the Battalion operated in columns in the area of Sidi Rezegh for several days, was ordered back to an area south of Matruh, and in the last days of June was making for the Alamein Line in close company with the Afrika Korps.

In the later stages of the withdrawal the 9th Battalion had two successful actions. On the first occasion "A" Company captured intact an Italian light tank and knocked out several vehicles of an advanced guard of the enemy. The second operation is described by Paddy Boden:

" 'C' Company was ordered to try to defend the main road a

few miles west of Dabaa in order to cover the evacuation of that place. It was believed that in fact Dabaa had already fallen, but the Company set out just before midnight to occupy a position chosen from the map. On nearing the road the sound of heavy vehicle movement was heard and investigation soon confirmed that German trucks were moving east along the road, thus confirming the suspicion that Dabaa had in fact already been captured.

"The company commander decided that the only course was to attempt to cut the road temporarily and with this end in view disposed the company behind a small hump some eight hundred yards south of the road. The anti-tank guns and machine guns were sighted portee to cover the road and the motor platoons to protect the flanks. The plan was to shoot up the road as soon as it got light, the carriers being used to help towards this end.

"As dawn broke, the carrier platoon was pushed forward to a small hill overlooking a further stretch of the road and on a given signal everyone opened up at the numerous targets that presented themselves. The enemy were completely surprised by this manœuvre and it was nearly two and a half hours before they were able to produce the necessary force to dislodge 'C' Company. During this period sixteen odd vehicles were knocked out, many more were put to flight, twenty-five prisoners were taken and all traffic on the road was stopped, which meant in effect that the German advance forces were temporarily cut off from their troops behind, as no alternative route exists between the road and the sea at this point. This little affray was hugely enjoyed by the company, coming, as it did, after a rather depressing month."

By the 2nd of July the withdrawal had come to an end, though the troops on the ground were not to know it. It was to take some three weeks before the position was definitely stabilized. During those three weeks of hard fighting one might have expected the morale of the battalions to fall low. But the Riflemen were now experienced in war. They had all known retreats and they had had their share of successes. After the Wavell campaign it had seemed that the desert was cleared for ever of the enemy. After Sidi Rezegh, when the armour for which we had cried had been smashed by the 88-mm., spirits had indeed been low. Now, in July, 1942, though the disaster was greater than any we had known, we saw the situation in better perspective. While the Afrika Korps, drawn from an army which had never known defeat, must have been quite confident that the Nile Valley was at their mercy, those Riflemen who had survived two years of desert war were unlikely entirely to despair. What was sad was the knowledge that the battle had so nearly been successful. No one could have forecast on the 1st of June that the Eighth Army would be at Alamein in a month's time. The Regiment, who had been among the first to meet the enemy on the 26th of May, had some of the credit for the successes of the first few days, had been the last to withdraw, the last through the wire, and, in a collection of vehicles which would have disgraced a circus, were among the last to reach Alamein.

CHAPTER X

THE WORST SUMMER—EL ALAMEIN, 1942

IT is nonsense to talk of the Alamein "Line." Such an expression conjures up a picture of deep-set fortifications, underground headquarters, great guns and tons of ammunition. The battalions came to a temporary rest at about the time when the defensive merits of this position were being canvassed in the Press. When the Riflemen heard the suave voice of the B.B.C. announcer reporting that the Eighth Army had reached the Alamein "Line" they looked round at the empty desert on either side, indistinguishable from the miles of sand to east and west, and commented as only Riflemen can. For at Alamein there was in no sense a series of fortifications. It happened that at this one place the area of navigable desert was sufficiently narrow to give the defenders a chance of holding it without being outflanked. To the south lay the Qattara Depression, a sand sea in the tradition of P. C. Wren, an area below sea-level composed of soft sand, which was considered impassable to any significant number of vehicles. It was the gap between the north of this depression and the sea which formed a bottleneck, in some ways similar to that at Agheila. Here in the days of comparative success the Higher Command had ordered a defensive position to be dug. The preparations were far from complete. Astride the coast road a strong position was almost ready for occupation. In other areas defences had been begun, rations had been dumped and some minefields had been laid. Unhappily more than one of the positions considered vital to the defence were lost before the Germans were checked at all. In fact, the battalions of the Regiment arrived in a bare desert, like any other, dominated in the south by a gaunt, conical hill called Himeimat and level enough in the centre for such inconsiderable features as the Ruweisat Ridge to be important. It was clear to them that the Alamein Line, on which the uninitiated, the listeners and the general public had perforce to place reliance,

THE WORST SUMMER—EL ALAMEIN, 1942

since Tobruk, Sollum and Mersa Matruh, the better-known fortresses, had failed, was a flimsy foundation on which to base their hopes for the defence of the Nile Valley. At Alamein there was no Maginot Line; but it is to the credit of the authorities, who had twice seen the Army at Agheila, that they should have built anything at all within a few miles of the Delta.

By July Rommel's army was at the height of its success. It must have seemed that nothing could prevent it from reaching the Delta. The Eighth Army had been continuously in retreat since the 12th of June. It has never been clear how in those first weeks of July the Germans were prevented from continuing their advance. The South African Division held firm in the north; the New Zealanders performed tremendous feats in the centre; the 5th Indian Division recovered from their early setbacks. The three battalions of the Regiment were all heavily involved in the fighting. The 9th Battalion had, as usual, the least spectacular but not the easiest role. They were used to plug every gap in the line from Alamein to Himeimat, never remaining long in one place or under one command. They had a stay in all the more unpleasant places and yet were never lucky enough to be able to show any substantially concrete results for their efforts. The 1st Battalion with the 2nd Armoured Brigade bore the brunt of the fighting south of the Alamein Box, where the main enemy armoured thrusts were directed. The 2nd Battalion was farther south, where the enemy's efforts were less persistent. Centred round the low ground of Deir el Ragil, the Battalion was none the less continuously in contact with the enemy and was more or less heavily involved in all the attacks to its north. Finally, on the 22nd of July, the 7th Battalion made its first appearance in the field, a decisive date, although an unfortunate battle.

For the 1st Battalion July must have been one of the worst months of the war. They were continually engaged. On the 2nd of July, in a battle personally inspired by General Herbert Lumsden, the enemy withdrew before our tanks for the first time since Knightsbridge. On the 3rd of July the 6-pounders under Bill Jepson-Turner and "A" Company's machine guns under Ed Garnier took a prominent part. Twenty enemy tanks lined up in the valley south of the Ruweisat Ridge and advanced east. They were driven back and the results for that day were said to include thirty tanks destroyed, four hundred prisoners taken, and forty-four guns and some hundred vehicles captured on the whole front. On the 4th of July the enemy again attacked and was driven back. But the "B" Echelon on its way up to the Battalion was bombed and Regimental Sergeant-Major Willis was killed while trying to pull a rifleman out of a burning vehicle. Operations were a little less strenuous for a few days, but the Battalion was concerned, though not directly, in the attacks by the New Zealand Division on the 14th and 15th of July. It was still hoped that by striking at once the enemy might be caught off their balance at the end of a tenuous and unorganized line of communications and driven back farther west. We ourselves had twice rebounded from Agheila. Although the New Zealanders fought a gallant and successful action and captured over two thousand prisoners, they suffered themselves in a counter-attack by tanks and the success was not more than local. On the 15th of July "B" Company captured some two hundred prisoners, and there was a story that nine German officers had surrendered to the New Zealanders, saying that they were "fed up."

To some of the Afrika Korps the vision of Cairo was fading. But the Eighth Army was far from secure. On the 17th of July the Battalion saw a New Zealand unit overrun and were remotely concerned in the subsequent fighting, which cost the Germans some seven hundred and fifty prisoners, including twenty-nine officers. The 21st of July was the first "quiet day" since the end of the withdrawal. That was only one day before the largest attack launched in these operations by the Eighth Army, an attack which concerned the 7th Battalion more than the 1st. For the rest of the month the Battalion was engaged every day. On the 22nd of July Hugh Meldrum's anti-tank guns claimed two tanks; but, on the 25th of July, John Lentaigne went out to locate and deal with a German sniper, was stalked himself and shot dead, one more irreplaceable young officer to add to the continual drain of casualties at this time. His death was immediately avenged, for Sergeant Bradbury, a name well known at Bisley, went out and shot this sniper, subsequently killing four and wounding two more. The Battalion continued in the insalubrious area of Ruweisat Ridge, which flies and dust and heat and dead, unburied bodies made among the foulest ever met in the desert, and were daily involved in fighting until, at the end of the month, they were withdrawn a short way into reserve.

Space compels the writer to dismiss three vital weeks in a paragraph. The fighting round Ruweisat Ridge decided the immediate fate of Egypt. It was the 1st Battalion, inspired as they were by General Herbert Lumsden's unfaltering determination, who played as large a part as any one unit in halting the Afrika Korps. It was the ability of the Eighth Army, and particularly the New Zealand Division, to fight back after the weeks of retreat that turned the scale. The number of German officer prisoners taken in these operations is an indication of the fierceness of the fighting. When reading contemporary accounts of this period, written by those who had every reason to be disheartened, one is struck by the frequent references to figures of prisoners taken and tanks destroyed, set down in black and white in the face of misfortune, as if this concrete evidence were required to reassure the writer of the reality of this eventual success.

For the first week of July the 2nd Battalion operated on the southern flank of the enemy's advance. But as their thrusts farther north failed, the Germans tried to advance by a move to the south. Their efforts in this direction were short-lived and the role of the Battalion became one of holding a line while a system of minefields was laid by both sides. The area was dominated by a bare, conical hill called Himeimat which stood above the Qattara Depression and was the most easterly of a line of low, rocky hills running east and west along the edge of the depression. At this stage Himeimat was in our hands. Although not in the centre of large-scale operations, the 2nd Battalion was constantly in contact with the enemy throughout July and August. The high-lights of this period were probably the repulse of a heavy German attack on the 7th of July and a model fighting patrol on the night of the 25th/26th of July. On the first occasion the enemy made a determined attempt to penetrate our positions in the area of Deir el Ragil. When the battle was at its height Colonel Vic Turner arrived to take over command. Somewhat characteristically he first appeared at a point, subsequently known as Lob Bowler's Alley, where "B" Company's 3-inch mortar was just coming into action for the first time in its life. At first spotting for it and then loading bombs at a hitherto unprecedented rate, he certainly ran through all available ammunition and probably did some useful damage to the enemy. At any rate, the enemy withdrew and the new Colonel's reputation in "B" Company was already made.

The patrol, which met with a success deserved by many others, was led by Tom Bird. It took place near Gebel Khalakh towards the south of the Battalion area and its object was to identify the enemy, since changes in their dispositions were suspected. The plan was to attack a post certainly defended by wire and probably by mines. The approach was across two thousand seven hundred yards of open ground and was in clear moonlight. Owing to the moon they were seen earlier than they had hoped and were subjected to heavy machine-gun fire. The only thing to do was to press on as fast as was reasonable. A hundred yards from the post they encountered a wire fence and had to negotiate it under intense fire. They then attacked the post with such determination that they captured two officers and fifteen men, including the entire crew of an anti-tank gun, and inflicted further casualties. The patrol commander then extricated his men except for Corporal Whatson, who was killed, and returned with his prisoners. Few patrols have ever been carried out more successfully.

It was in the first week of July that Brigadier Hugo Garmoyle was killed. He was returning from a visit to a neighbouring armoured brigade when he was hit by a shell and died from his wounds. We have never produced a better soldier nor one who inspired more confidence in those he commanded in battle. A month later General Strafer Gott was killed at the moment when he had been given command of the Eighth Army. The Regiment lost a good friend and a brilliant commander under whom we had been lucky enough to serve so often and with such success. These two great desert fighters and Jock Campbell died within six months of each other on the threshold of the abiding successes of the Army. In the more fortunate battles which were to follow, many of us were to remember those three, who had achieved substantial results with inadequate forces and without whose exertions for two difficult years the triumphant advances of the Eighth Army would not have been possible.

It was in August that the sad decision was made at G.H.Q. that the 9th Battalions of The Rifle Brigade and the 60th Rifles should be disbanded. It was calculated that there would be insufficient reinforcements in the Middle East to maintain four

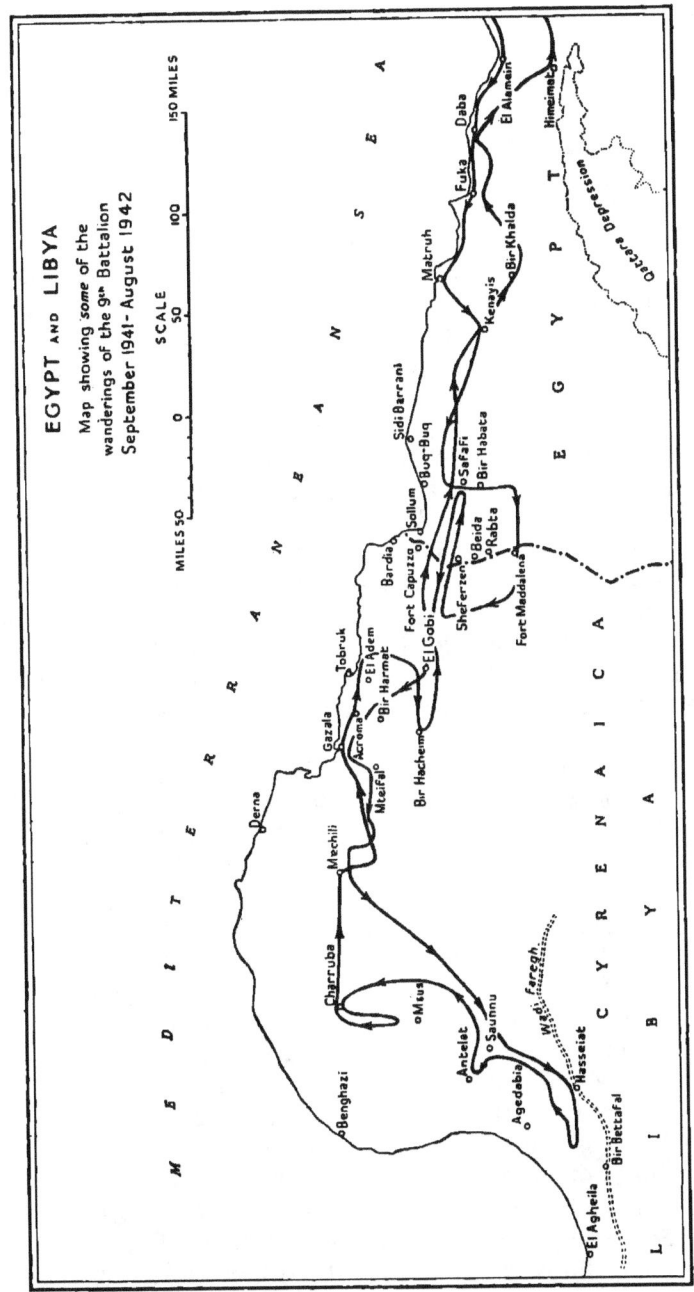

battalions of the regiment in being. The 9th Battalion had the highest number and was in the process of refitting in the Delta. If any battalion was to be disbanded it must be the 9th. Accordingly the 9th Battalion ceased to exist, except for its name and a cadre which eventually made its way to England and took up permanent residence at Retford.

The 9th Battalion were seldom lucky in the desert. They arrived as part of a division which was split in half shortly after their arrival. Subsequently the Battalion never remained under the same command for long at a stretch: at twenty-four hours' notice or less they would be switched to another brigade or division. Their longest connection—and a happy one—was with the Guards Brigade, and when they finally left their command the Brigadier (now Major-General) Marriott, wrote Colonel Squeak Purdon a charming letter in appreciation of their services in the brigade. Because of these constant changes of role and command the story of the Battalion is almost impossible to tell. For one thing, the most spectacular battles were generally fought by complete divisions, while the 9th Battalion stood by for emergencies or took over a task which released others for the main battle. The following list of changes of command and the map on page 139 showing their various locations may give some idea of the bewildering nature of their operations:

15th Sept. to 13th Dec.	22nd Guards Brigade.
14th to 21st Dec.	4th Armoured Brigade.
22nd to 31st Dec.	22nd Armoured Brigade.
1st to 19th Jan.	7th Support Group.
20th to 21st Jan.	2nd Armoured Brigade.
21st to 27th Jan.	Vaughan-Hughes Force.
28th Jan. to 12th Feb.	1st Support Group.
13th Feb. to 21st May	200th Guards Brigade.
22nd to 29th May	XXX Corps.
29th May (a.m.)	7th Motor Brigade.
29th May (p.m.)	29th Indian Brigade.
30th May to 1st June	XXX Corps.
1st to 3rd June	Gray Force.
3rd to 4th June	201st Guards Brigade.
4th to 5th June	2nd Armoured Brigade.
5th to 6th June	4th Armoured Brigade.
6th to 8th June	1st Armoured Division.

THE ENEMY ON EVERY FRONT
A captured photograph of an 88-mm. gun with crew and towing lorry

[*Official Photo: Crown Copyright Reserved*
GENERAL SIR HENRY MAITLAND WILSON INSPECTS THE 2nd BATTALION
Behind, Brigadier Jimmy Bosvile and Colonel Tom Pearson

Face page 140]

THE WORST SUMMER—EL ALAMEIN, 1942

8th to 12th June ..	.. 22nd Armoured Brigade.
13th to 15th June	.. 2nd South African Division.
16th to 17th June	.. XXX Corps.
17th to 22nd June	.. 7th Motor Brigade.
22nd to 26th June	.. 3rd Indian Motor Brigade.
26th June (a.m.) ..	.. 7th Armoured Division.
26th June to 4th July	.. 1st Armoured Division.
5th to 18th July ..	.. Wall Group.
19th July to 3rd Aug.	.. 4th Light Armoured Brigade.
4th to 8th Aug. ..	.. Eighth Army.

The Battalion was for long periods in contact with the enemy. It visited every well-known place in the desert from Alamein to Agheila. The fact that it was continually changing command did not make it any easier for the Riflemen, who were engaged like anyone else in night patrolling, in escorting guns, in being bombed and shelled, in evading enemy tanks, in contracting desert sores and going short of water, in brewing tea in twenty minutes and cooking bully in twenty ways, and in navigating across miles of desert. The story of the life of its individuals would be much the same as in other battalions of the Regiment, except that they were hardly concerned in the famous battles, the Beda Fomms and the Snipe positions. In one thing the 9th Battalion was lucky. It was twice reprieved from taking part in the defence of Tobruk and once from trying to hold Bir Hacheim.

On the Regimental Birthday Colonel Squeak Purdon, who had commanded so ably for a year, and the remaining officers gave a farewell party in Cairo attended by General Jumbo Wilson, and then to all intents and purposes the Battalion ceased to exist. It is sometimes difficult to understand the complex working of the Higher Command. Presumably they were happy at this critical moment in the fortunes of the Eighth Army to dispense with the services of an experienced battalion, proved and tried in eighteen months of desert fighting.

The arrival of the 7th Battalion has already been mentioned briefly. The 1st Battalion The London Rifle Brigade, embodied in the Regiment as the 7th Battalion, was a motor battalion like the rest of The Rifle Brigade. It was commanded by Colonel Geoffrey Hunt, and Kenneth Hicks was Second-in-Command. It formed part of the 8th Armoured Division. During the operations of May and June this formation was on the sea. As the convoy approached Aden it must have seemed as if the Eighth Army would meet it on the Canal. They made a record run for ancient troopships up the Red Sea and the 7th Battalion disembarked at Suez on the 5th of July. There was then a race to get equipped in time to take part in the battle. Wilfrid Suter went up to the 1st Battalion to get a picture of what was happening in the war, and Alastair Dudgeon took "C" Company off to Cairo to re-form as an anti-tank company. Between the 14th and 23rd of July it was re-equipped, resorted and retrained and joined the Battalion on the 26th of July, four days after their first introduction to battle.

By the third week in July the situation in the Alamein area was still critical. No one quite knew how the Germans had originally been checked. Perhaps it was due to the fact that they had outrun their supplies. Perhaps the magnificent efforts of the Royal Air Force turned the scale. Certainly the fighting on the Ruweisat Ridge in which the 1st Battalion were concerned played a vital part in halting the Afrika Korps. As soon as the battle showed signs of stabilizing we turned over to the offensive and tremendous efforts, mainly by the New Zealanders, were made to catch the enemy unbalanced. These attacks achieved local success and resulted in the capture of many prisoners; but they did not entirely remove the threat to the Delta. It was with this background, a critical situation still unresolved, that the 23rd Armoured Brigade of the 8th Armoured Division was pushed and hurried up to the front. The 7th Battalion, less "C" Company, went with them. The tank regiments were equipped with inferior tanks mounting 2-pounder guns. The preparations for the whole Brigade were hasty in the extreme. They began to land on the 5th of July and on the 18th of July the Battalion moved out to Burg el Arab. Three days later they were in the forward area and in two more they were in the middle of a major battle. Apart from deficiencies in equipment and such incidental irritations as batteries corroded by sea water on the voyage, there had been no time to learn about the desert, to practise navigation, to identify American tanks or decipher the figures of Germans far away in the midday mirage. To move armoured brigades after a long sea voyage straight from the boat into battle is to invite disaster. But in those critical days such risks had to be accepted.

From the point of view of the Brigade the battle was a tragedy. It took place on the 22nd of July. There was a large-scale set-piece battle in the area of El Ruweisat in which an advance by the new armoured brigade was to play a part. "D" Company, under Stephen Trappes-Lomax, was detached to work with an armoured regiment with the Australians to the north of the main battle. "A" and "B" Companies, under Wilfrid Suter and John Francis, remained under the Colonel's command. They watched the tanks with whom they had trained and worked launched into an area that was full of mines. Some tanks got right through the minefield and penetrated well into the enemy position, it was said to the German corps headquarters. Few of them returned. At the end of the day there was little left of the armour, and the 7th Battalion had lost a fair proportion of vehicles. Their casualties had not been heavy, although Peter Coryton had been killed by a mine. This battle had little to show for the expenditure of so many casualties and so much equipment. But the fact remains that from that date the enemy pressure relaxed and the immediate threat to the Delta receded. For the next month the Germans settled down to prepare for the set-piece attack which would presumably carry them to Cairo. They flew in a new division from Crete and increased their armoured strength as far as their administration would allow. The 7th Battalion dug in on a rocky strip just south of Alamein and for a few days there were four battalions of the Regiment in contact with the enemy.

When Hugo Garmoyle had been killed on the 4th of July command of the 7th Motor Brigade had been given to Colonel Jimmy Bosvile, a reward for steering the 1st Battalion so successfully through six months of heavy fighting. He was succeeded in command by Colonel Freddie Stephens, who had been on the staff of the 1st Armoured Division. On the 11th of August the 7th Battalion joined the 7th Motor Brigade, which at that time consisted of the 2nd Battalion and the 2nd Battalion 60th Rifles. The 1st Battalion remained as the motor battalion of the 22nd Armoured Brigade, commanded by Brigadier (later Major-General) Pip Roberts, who was to have a battalion of the Regiment under his command from now until the end of the war—and there was no armoured commander under whom it was better to serve.

Apart from the visit of the Prime Minister and the impact of

General Montgomery on the Eighth Army, August was a comparatively quiet month. But it was clear that the Germans would resume the offensive as soon as they felt strong enough to do so. The three battalions of the Regiment were at this time all in the south. The 2nd and 7th Battalions in the 7th Motor Brigade were watching the minefields, which now stretched the entire length of the Alamein Line. The role of these battalions was to prevent any minor advance by the enemy and, in case of a major offensive, to withdraw through the Deir el Ragil, covering the desert route to the Delta. Before he was killed General Gott had done a careful reconnaissance of the area and had come to the conclusion that if the enemy attacked in the south they would be likely to turn north after leaving Ragil and make for the comparatively high ground of Alam Halfa. It was here that the tanks of the 22nd Armoured Brigade were dug in and camouflaged. The motor companies of the 1st Battalion were with their armoured regiments, but the anti-tank guns were dug in on slightly lower ground forward of the armour. It was in these positions that the German advance was awaited.

The Germans had reinforced their African forces by one moderate division from Crete whose previous station lent it a rude but not inappropriate name. They hoped by this small addition to make certain of securing the Nile Valley, to capture the main base of our Army, to seize the Suez Canal, and to have the Middle East at their feet. It is idle to speculate what would have happened if they had taken one more first-class formation of the calibre of, say, the Hermann Goering, from Russia, where it would not have been missed for a moment. But the Germans regarded the Western Desert as a minor theatre, where an adventurer with a small but brilliant corps could be allowed to make the most of his self-made opportunities, provided that he did not bother them with too many requests. In any case, their administrative difficulties were such that the maintenance of another division would have been difficult. So they hung on in insufficient numbers with tenuous communications, while dreams of the Nile Valley grew dimmer and the British Army gradually collected its strength and regained its balance until it could throw the Germans out of Egypt and eventually into the sea.

Rommel's attempts in July had been chiefly concerned with the area north of the Ruweisat Ridge. His final effort to reach Cairo was made in the south. The chief disadvantage of this approach was that it was overlooked by Gebel Himeimat. However, he did his best to minimize this risk by starting off in the dark early on the 31st of August. Large columns of enemy vehicles met the minefield more or less opposite the 2nd Battalion. The enemy drove straight into it. At first they presented excellent targets for the field guns and the Battalion's 6-pounders sited along the eastern edge. George Emerson-Baker's carrier platoon had a particularly good time. But when it got light it became evident that our forces were stretched too thinly on the ground to deal with an offensive on this scale, and a gradual withdrawal began in accordance with a prearranged plan. The German Air Force visited most of the headquarters in the area soon after first light. The Gunner observation posts and the 60th's post on Gebel Himeimat had a grandstand view of the German and Italian columns passing below them. The withdrawal of the 2nd Battalion through their own minefields and under fire from the ground forces and strafing from the air was a complicated business. The 7th Battalion, who had begun the battle in reserve, were soon involved and withdrew gradually due east. The Motor Brigade therefore passed below and across the front of the 22nd Armoured Brigade on Alam Halfa. The enemy hardly showed the dash usually associated with the Afrika Korps, but by the afternoon they had emerged from Deir el Ragil and were directed, exactly as General Strafer Gott had forecast, straight at Alam Halfa. Their guns outranged the Grants of the 22nd Armoured Brigade and one of our squadrons on a forward slope was destroyed almost completely. At the same time news was received of an attack being launched by the enemy on the Ruweisat Ridge. Rommel presumably hoped that these two forces would unite.

Before they could close with the rest of the 22nd Armoured Brigade, the German tanks in three waves, totalling nearly ninety, had to advance farther. This brought them right on top of the 6-pounder guns of "B" Company of the 1st Battalion and the machine guns of "I" Company. Paddy Biddell's and Tommy Ross's platoons took the full brunt of the enemy's attack. They reacted magnificently: they held their fire to within three hundred yards, and Sergeant Griffiths's* gun knocked out five tanks. It is said that nineteen enemy tanks were destroyed by

---

*Later granted an emergency commission in the Regiment.

these guns alone. Although one platoon was overrun, this action had a decisive effect on the battle. The enemy withdrew temporarily. They were engaged by two divisional artilleries and by the 22nd Armoured Brigade, while the Greys in their first battle executed what was almost a cavalry charge from the east. From that moment the enemy's attack had failed. They remained in the hollow below Alam Halfa that night and there the Royal Air Force found them. The next day the whole desert was covered with enemy vehicles and these were attacked continuously from the air, while they were engaged by all available guns from the north and harassed from the east and south by the Motor Brigade. For two days they remained in this area, never making any serious attempt to break out, although the Luftwaffe tried to retaliate and killed Henry Browne, among others, in doing so.

The attacks opposite Ruweisat were driven back. Then the great concourse of vehicles between Himeimat and Alam Halfa began slowly and deliberately to withdraw. They were attacked from the north by the New Zealand Division and the 132nd Brigade; the 4th Armoured Brigade harassed them from the south; the 7th Motor Brigade, led by the 2nd Battalion, followed up; and all the time the Royal Air Force kept on bombing and strafing, so that the desert was littered with abandoned vehicles and unburied dead as the Afrika Korps fell back. By the 5th of September the enemy had withdrawn almost to where they had started, with two important exceptions that were to cost the 1st Battalion dear. The Germans retained in their possession the peak of Himeimat and the main minefields that we had laid. For the time being the threat to Cairo was removed; and once again the Regiment had played a great part in removing it. Indeed, the action of the anti-tank guns of the 1st Battalion had had a decisive effect in stopping the enemy at the nearest point to the Nile Valley that the 15th Panzer or the 90th Light Division were ever in their lives to reach.

When it became clear that the German offensive had been defeated the Eighth Army settled down to make their own preparations to break out of the Alamein Line. These preparations involved many changes of command. Up to now incidental changes of command affecting the Regiment have seldom been mentioned. The 1st Battalion was generally in the 1st Armoured Division; the 2nd Battalion was almost always

THE WORST SUMMER—EL ALAMEIN, 1942 147

in the 7th Armoured Division. The 9th Battalion had no such continuity and suffered in consequence. In September, 1942, a rearrangement was made which affected the Regiment intimately. While two corps held the line, a "corps de chasse" for the break-out battle was to be formed and trained, ready for the advance to Benghazi and Tripoli. The 1st Armoured Division was to form part of this corps (X Corps) and the whole of the 7th Motor Brigade was to come under its command as a permanent formation of the Division. At the same time the 22nd Armoured Brigade, including the 1st Battalion, was to become a permanent part of the 7th Armoured Division.

As the war went on various loyalties outside the Regiment arose. There was a genuine "divisional spirit." The 50th Division were quite sure that they were better than the 51st, and no one in the Highland Division imagined that any other formation could approach the smartness or performance of his own. So it is not really surprising that whatever energies were left over from the recent strenuous fighting were sometimes devoted to inter-divisional squabbles. Now the 1st Battalion, after years of wearing a rhinoceros on their tunics and their vehicles, had to put on a desert rat. The 7th Battalion took on the rhinoceros, and the 2nd Battalion, after fighting for two years with the 7th Armoured Division, had also to put on this sign. When it came to painting signs on vehicles some Riflemen were unable to repress their feelings and senior officers were shocked for a day or two to see pictures of enormous rhinoceroses tossing jerboas to the winds, or gigantic jerboas belabouring rhinoceroses to their deaths. Time and discipline soon restored equilibrium; for these affiliations were more or less permanent. Indeed, this change of command was to lead the 1st Battalion from Tunis to Italy, to England, through France, Belgium and Holland to the Elbe, and to last until armoured divisions had ceased for the time being to exist.

CHAPTER XI

THE BATTLE OF ALAMEIN

IT was often said in the summer and autumn of 1942 that the Eighth Army had locked the door on Egypt and thrown away the key; for, while for geographical reasons the Alamein position was a strong one to defend, it was also a difficult one from which to break out. If Rommel decided to stay, a major battle would be needed to dislodge his army, for its flanks rested securely on the Mediterranean and the Qattara Depression. But if he had pulled back the main part of his forces and held these forward positions with a few of his mobile troops he would have kept an army in being at less administrative cost to himself. Because he stood and fought we were given a chance of destroying his army in the battle.

In outline the plan for the break-out at Alamein was for the infantry to make a gap in the enemy defences and minefields through which X Corps—the "corps de chasse"—was to force its way. At the same time, in the south the XIII Corps was to make a feint attack so as to contain one enemy armoured division, and, should opposition be less determined than expected, to exploit any success it could obtain. In the event the infantry dog-fight and the armoured break-out became inextricably mixed, until after some ten days of heavy fighting the enemy was obliged to pull out. The 7th Motor Brigade, with the 2nd and 7th Battalions, first made gaps in the minefields for the armour, then met the counter-attacks of the enemy armour, and finally forced a way out for the armoured brigade to make their break into the open. The 1st Battalion had a prominent part in the feint attack beneath Himeimat which was pressed home at considerable cost to the enemy and to ourselves. It was then moved to the north and with the Armoured Brigade fought a way out on the left of the 7th Motor Brigade.

By October, 1942, the mine had come into its own. During the four months on the Alamein Line both sides had laid a series of minefields of a depth and complexity not previously encountered. These minefields consisted mainly of anti-tank mines which were designed to blow up any type of vehicle. But anti-personnel mines were frequently planted on the edges of these fields so as to make it more difficult to pick up the mines by hand. Various forms of anti-lifting devices and booby-traps were employed. One of the features of mine warfare was the ease with which it was possible to blow up one's own side, so that, in the hope of preventing this, the inner edges of minefields were often marked by low fences, generally of a single strand of wire. Such markings were not universal and it would be a bold man who could say with certainty that where there was no fence there was no minefield. On the other hand, much simple fun could be had by the Royal Engineers in making dummy minefields, the edges of a perfectly barren piece of desert being marked by a fearsome-looking fence.

One of the main problems of the break-out battle at Alamein was that of passing the armour through the minefields and out into the open. This was technically the task of the Royal Engineers, who had to pick up the mines and mark the clear tracks with tape. They were assisted by the flail tank, an invention at that time in its infancy, consisting of a contraption composed of heavy chains which was constructed so as to fit on to the front of a tank and beat the ground before it, thereby setting off the mines harmlessly as it advanced. Since they worked with armour, the motor battalions were closely connected with mine clearance. The 1st Battalion in the south had to pass through the gaps as soon as they were made and form a bridgehead on the far side of the minefield while the armour passed through. The 2nd Battalion had to take on not only the local protection of the gaps made by the Sappers but the control and command of all troops in the immediate area and, in the initial stages, of traffic control. They were fitted for this by reason of the large number of wireless sets in the Battalion. In the fighting at Alamein two things became apparent to those who had to hang about gaps in minefields. One was that vehicle congestion became worse than in the narrowest street at Epsom on Derby Day, and the other was that the enemy were apt to concentrate all available fire of machine guns and anti-tank guns and field guns on anywhere where they suspected that a gap was being made.

During October, 1942, the 1st Battalion, as part of the 22nd

Armoured Brigade, was occupied in holding the line of two minefields, known for some reason as Nuts and May. About ten thousand yards west of these were January and February, similar minefields laid by ourselves in July and August and captured by the enemy in their advance of the 1st of September. January and February were about three thousand yards apart. They extended almost to the foot of Gebel Himeimat, and this hill, held by the enemy, overlooked the whole of the area where the battle was to take place. For a month before D Day the Battalion had been patrolling on this front, collecting information on which the plan for crossing the minefields was based, an activity which involved many unpleasant nights and cost several casualties, among whom was Joe Persse, killed in leading his patrol to attack an enemy post. One thing that these patrols disclosed was the identity of the enemy opposite—the Folgore (Italian) Division. This was an Italian parachute division, recruited from the North of Italy and about the best Italian formation in existence. The men were of stronger physique than the average Italian, were possessed of high morale and compared favourably with the general run of German divisions. Unlike the usual Italian prisoners, the men of the Folgore Division would give little information when interrogated.

The plan, which was rehearsed three times, was for four gaps to be made in our own minefields by the Sappers twenty-four hours before the battle started. The next night the Brigade was to go through these gaps. The advance guard consisted of the 44th Divisional Reconnaissance Regiment, Battalion Headquarters, "A" and "B" Companies of the 1st Battalion, and the Greys—in that order. The remainder of the Brigade followed, "I" Company being under command of the 1st Royal Tanks and "C" Company under the 5th Royal Tanks. The 44th Divisional Reconnaissance Regiment, commanded by a 60th Rifleman, Lyon Corbett-Winder, was to make four gaps in January corresponding to those in Nuts and May. As soon as these gaps were complete "A" and "B" Companies were to push through and take up flanking positions—"A" to the north and "B" to the south—facing outwards and thus forming a corridor through which the 44th Divisional Reconnaissance Regiment could pass to repeat the gapping operation on February. The Greys were to support the advance guard throughout and when the gaps were finally completed to take up positions on the other side of the last minefield, where the rest of the Brigade would join them. The 131st Infantry Brigade would then take over the Battalion's job between the minefields so that it could join the rest of the Armoured Brigade in their battle position to the west. The gaps around which all this activity centred were in two pairs—a pair in the north and a pair in the south, with about two thousand yards between pairs and some two hundred yards between gaps. The whole operation was to be supported by a barrage which was to creep forward two hundred yards ahead of the leading troops, a heavy barrage but not comparable to the tremendous uproar at the northern end of the line.

That was the plan. By half past six on the evening of the 23rd of October the Brigade was drawn up in four lines ready to move forward to begin the Battle of Alamein. It was a clear desert evening, the white dust blowing about like flour but keeping low, so that the Royal Air Force, much in evidence above us, must have been able to see the Army quite clearly set out like crocodiles at a girls' school, heads towards the west. Perhaps the worst of the suspense was over: we were now committed: no luck, no accident had transported us to the base. It was no good wishing we had spent more time maintaining the carrier or learning to read a map or had written more punctually home or behaved a little better in Cairo. In a quarter of an hour we would start to advance through the minefields which we had sat opposite for the best part of two months. It was better to concentrate on what was important at the moment—was there time to have a "brew"?

At a quarter to seven the Brigade moved forward and by nine o'clock the head was through the minefields and in no-man's-land. There was then a delay of half an hour, during which someone's carrier (not one of the Battalion's) went on fire for reasons entirely unconnected with the battle. The enemy immediately began to drop a few haphazard shells about the area.

At ten o'clock our guns all along the line opened up the great barrage which General Montgomery had devised. It was the most impressive supporting fire that anyone had yet seen. The noise and the flashes were not to be forgotten. Encouraged by this, the Brigade started forward and after some groping to find the eastern edge of January located it at eleven o'clock. The enemy brought heavy fire from artillery, mortars and machine guns to bear on those waiting for the gapping to be completed. "A" Company suffered casualties almost at once. Already the area was as crowded as the car park at Cheltenham Races, and there was no room anywhere to manœuvre. At the end of half an hour "B" Company reported that No. 3 gap was impassable because of soft sand. In another twenty minutes No. 2 was nearly through, but was directly in the line of fire of an anti-tank gun whose flashes were identified by Colonel Freddie Stephens in the moonlight about two thousand yards away. He ordered up "A" Company's machine-gun platoon, who engaged the anti-tank gun with all four Vickers guns from their vehicles. The Italian gunners stopped firing at once. "A" Company went straight through the gap at the best speed they could make. They were then ordered to turn south and clear the western ends of gaps Nos. 3 and 4. "A" Company overran two enemy machine-gun posts almost at the end of their gap. But the situation remained critical. Progress in the southern gaps was slow and it was not until after half past one that "B" Company appeared at the end of gap No. 4.

It became clear that the Brigade would not get through the second minefield that night and the Battalion faced the prospect of being discovered at the western openings of January as soon as it was light. That would have meant almost certain destruction. The Colonel ordered "A" and "B" Companies to make more ground at all costs before it was light. He hoped to get the support of the Greys, although while it was dark they could do little. As it was getting light the two companies went forward supported only by their own machine guns, overran three strong Italian posts and by a quarter past seven were some three thousand yards short of the northern slopes of Himeimat. "A" Company had been reduced to about forty men and was amalgamated with "B" Company, both being put under command of Tony Palmer, the Second-in-Command. Casualties had been heavy, but they had taken over three hundred prisoners. The anti-tank gun which had caused so much trouble in the night was found abandoned with its crew dead. It was turned round and its entire stock of ammunition was fired at an enemy strong-point with considerable effect. Throughout the 24th the Battalion sat in this exposed position, wedged between two minefields and overlooked at short range by the enemy on Gebel Himeimat. One of the earliest casualties from shelling in

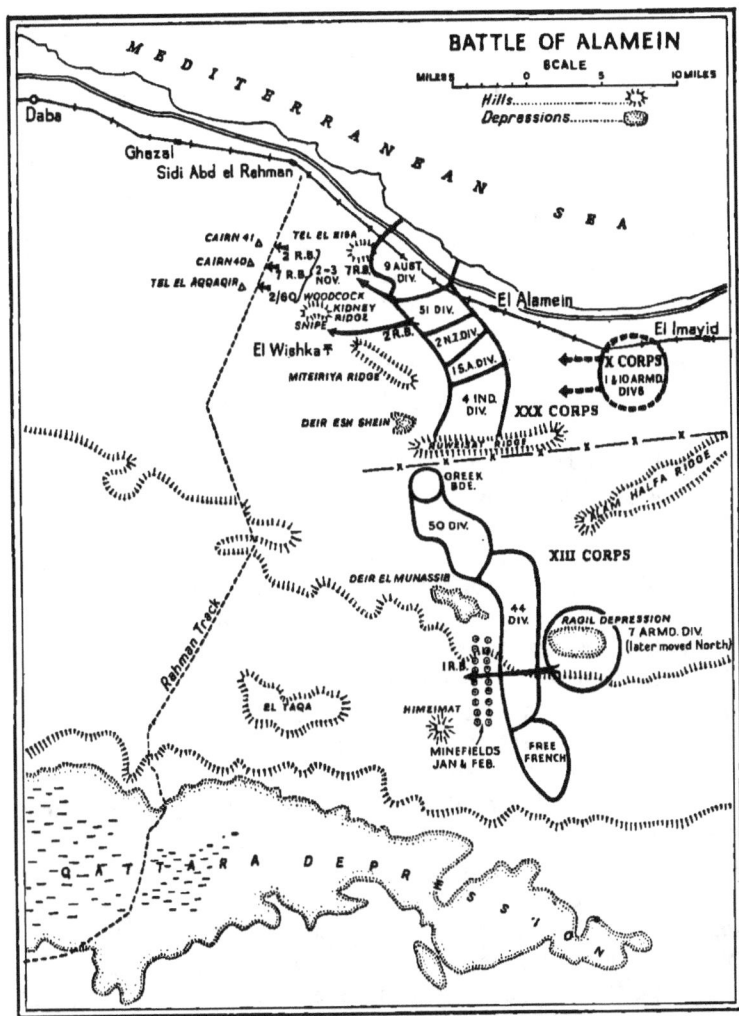

this position was Tony Palmer, who was hit in the arm, and it was during this phase that the Padre was killed while conducting a burial service.

After this unpleasant day the Division made one more attempt during the next night to breach the February minefield. Only "I" Company of the Battalion took part in this operation. The 4th County of London Yeomanry got one squadron through to the west, but lost some fourteen tanks. The result was that the

Battalion had to spend one more day under the baleful shadow of Himeimat in dead, flat, open, stony desert with minefields on every side; and when the armour was withdrawn on the night of the 25th/26th of October the Battalion was still left holding the line until the early morning, when the 132nd Brigade took over. It was then withdrawn to reorganize before moving up to the northern sector on the 31st.

The 7th Armoured Division had had a thankless battle. In the preparations for the attack they had been regarded very much as a second eleven, particularly in the share-out of new equipment. They had succeeded in their main purpose of keeping one enemy armoured division engaged in the south, but they had failed to penetrate the minefields opposite them and their casualties had not been light. In this minor role in a great battle the 1st Battalion had nineteen officer casualties and had lost many of the best non-commissioned officers and bravest riflemen.

It was in the north that the main battle took place. The 7th Motor Brigade was engaged in this area, the plan being that the 1st Armoured Division would force its way out of the minefields through the gap in the enemy defences torn by the infantry. The 2nd Battalion were trained for the particular task of forming the "minefield task force." It was their job to organize the gapping and protect the Engineers who were to pick up the mines. They practised the methods of achieving this, working directly under Divisional Headquarters with the Sappers and the three troops of tanks which were to support them. The 7th Battalion had to learn no peculiar tricks. Its role was expected to be to pass through the minefields with the armour, smoothing the rough edges and removing pockets of enemy bypassed by the infantry and then to use its mobility in the pursuit.

The pattern of the battle was rather different from what had been expected. The "corps de chasse" expended most of its energies and much of its reserve of petrol in the dog-fight, a role which planning had allotted to the infantry divisions. As far as the Regiment was concerned, there were four phases in which the battalions took part. On the night of the 23rd/24th of October and for the next two nights the 2nd Battalion was engaged as the minefield task force. On the 25th the 7th Battalion moved through the first minefield to a position where they were heavily counter-attacked by enemy tanks, fourteen of which they destroyed. After this the Battalion was withdrawn for a few days to refit. On the night of the 26th/27th the 2nd Battalion became involved in the now-famous action on the Snipe position. After a very short rest the 2nd Battalion was again part of the minefield task force on the 29th of October. In this role one more gapping operation was done with the New Zealand Division, happily without encountering much opposition. On the night of the 2nd/3rd of November the 2nd and 7th Battalions were engaged in an attack designed to clear the enemy from a ridge from which they could block the further advance of the tanks. It was not until these actions had been fought that the mobile forces intended for the pursuit were able, still licking their wounds, to start off across the open desert. The rest of this chapter deals with the 7th Battalion's story and the attacks by the two battalions on the 2nd/3rd of November. The Snipe action has earned a separate chapter to itself.

The 7th Battalion spent most of the 24th of October in an assembly position behind the area of the main battle. Everyone sat round their vehicles and brewed their tea and discussed the inevitable rumours which fluttered round the Battalion. Some said the New Zealanders were in Dabaa and others that the Germans were in Cairo. "Monty," it was said, was dead or in the leading tank or had been seen in the Battalion area. Nobody is better at producing rumours than the average rifleman and there is no more fertile ground than an assembly area in which to sow them. This particular spot was near the beginning of what was known as Sun Track. The congestion of vehicles was beyond belief. There was a constant stream of trucks bumping forward; ambulances, boxes on wheels, lumbered back. Elements of every formation and unit in the Army seemed to be represented among the hundreds of stationary trucks. Dreary columns of prisoners were walking aimlessly back. An occasional shell-burst would sound unpleasantly close. Our own barrage and the enemy's reply seemed to go on without pause. The dust, ground into the finest white powder, enveloped everything but did not altogether hide the succession of Boston bombers in close formation on their way to attack the enemy. Every now and then the anti-aircraft guns would start off and a Messerschmitt would appear low out of the dust cloud, dropping a bomb or firing its machine guns at random among the crowded vehicles.

At five o'clock in the evening the Battalion was ordered forward. In the dust and noise the intention behind the move was not clear to everyone. After hours of despairingly slow progress through traffic blocks and shelling, past Riflemen and Military Police controlling the flow, the Battalion passed through the gaps in the foremost minefields at about four o'clock on the morning of the 25th. It was still dark and some Australians were apparently engaged in dealing with a counter-attack. Only Colonel Geoffrey Hunt could say with certainty where we were. He interpreted the role of the Battalion and its location correctly and allotted to the companies defensive areas in what turned out to be a gap between the left of the 9th Australian Division and the right of the 51st (Highland) Division. Here in haste before it got light everyone set about digging in. It often seemed in the desert that when you wanted to drive a truck there was nothing but soft, deep sand on all sides, but when you wanted to dig, the surface was composed entirely of rock. This time it was rock. So, while the carriers went forward to cover the occupation of the position, picks were broken and arms bruised and by the time it was light most people were reasonably well dug in.

This was as well; for at dawn the carriers were heavily shelled and withdrew, bringing with them a good few prisoners and some wounded. The enemy soon turned their attention to the rest of the Battalion, whose vehicles in this bare area were an obvious and vulnerable target. Shelling was heavy and accurate. The machine guns and 3-inch mortars did have some chance to reply. Philip Flower's (until he was killed and Sergeant Jones took over), Mike Bird's and Peter Lockwood-Wingate's platoons kept firing throughout the morning and did some damage to the enemy infantry. There was a continual drain of casualties from the enemy's fire and these included the Adjutant, Kyrle Simond.

It was in the afternoon that the enemy tank attack came in. They appeared suddenly from behind a ridge with the dust blowing in front of them, a mixture of Italian M13's and German Mark III's. The majority of them came up against Jack Salt's guns, but a gun under Sergeant Allen in Jim West's platoon had a good shoot. The Riflemen in the motor companies kept up a continuous and accurate stream of small-arms fire, which had the effect of making the tanks close their lids and also caught the crews as they baled out of tanks which had been hit. The enemy could make no headway and soon withdrew into the dust. They had lost a number of tanks and the Battalion could claim to have knocked out fourteen of these and to have damaged others. The significance of this short, sharp attack was that the Germans had appreciated that here was the main thrust and had called on their armoured divisions to drive the infantry back into the minefields before they could gain a firm foothold. It was in this process of attacking anti-tank guns, dug-in in infantry positions, that the enemy tank strength was whittled away. But the result of these encounters was never a foregone conclusion. The 7th Battalion's was the first major success, the first good score of tanks destroyed to be credited to the Eighth Army in this battle. At a time when the number of tanks knocked out was more important than the amount of ground gained, this short, dusty, little action had an importance of its own.

The Battalion remained in this unpleasant area until the 29th, enduring much shelling and gradually being crowded out by new arrivals, making the congestion ever more acute as they prepared for the next attack. As the 7th Battalion moved back twelve miles to reorganize, the 2nd Battalion, who had been given only a few days to recover from the action at Snipe, moved up to take their place.

The first role of the 2nd Battalion, now commanded by Tom Pearson owing to Colonel Vic Turner's wounds, was to act as minefield task force during a successful attack by the New Zealand Division. The next morning, the 30th of October, the Battalion rejoined the 7th Motor Brigade. It was clear that the enemy were gradually giving way. The whole army in the northern sector was making progress. There was always a chance that this next minefield would be the last, that if the enemy could be dislodged from this one ridge he would pull out altogether or his main position would be penetrated with the most decisive results. That phase is always a dangerous one for the motor battalions. Commanders are anxious to loose the armour: each delay seems unnecessary: the motor infantry must tear a way through. On the 2nd of November the armour was held up by a screen of 88-mm. guns on a ridge. Throughout the day the battalions sat opposite this ridge, which ran along the line of the track south from Sidi Rahman and took their share of punishment from the guns on the reverse slope, so much so that the casualties included Peter Shepherd-Cross and Barry Holt-

Wilson, making a total of two company commanders and two seconds-in-command of companies since the Battle of Alamein began. Three of our anti-tank guns were also destroyed by shell fire. It was here that the 7th Battalion, who had moved up the Diamond track to Tel el Eisa station, rejoined the Brigade and immediately came in for a heavy dose of shelling, George Russell being killed and Freddie Hicks wounded.

This enemy anti-tank screen, supported as it clearly was by medium guns, appeared likely to be effective in holding up the armour while the bulk of Rommel's army pulled out. To the Higher Command such delay was intolerable. There were, as usual, those who took the view that the enemy would withdraw or, at any rate, thin out after last light. It was for just such a situation as this that the motor brigade was intended, to push the anti-tank defences aside and restore the momentum to the armoured advance. So in textbook battles does an armoured division fight. But now there were two factors which made the situation different from what had been taught on Salisbury Plain. The motor infantry had already suffered severely in the dog-fight of the past ten days: the Germans, as so often before and afterwards, resolved to stay in their positions long after they could logically be expected to have left. The 7th Motor Brigade were ordered to attack that night. The objective of the 2nd Battalion 60th Rifles was Tel el Aqqaqir. Then came the 7th Battalion, who were to make good the line of the Sidi Rahman track. On the right the 2nd Battalion were to advance up to the track and for a thousand yards beyond it. These objectives presupposed that the enemy immediately to the front had pulled out. The 60th were to have all available artillery support: our two battalions were to carry out silent attacks. The information about the enemy was meagre and even had guns been available it would have been difficult to pin-point the enemy's positions so as to fire concentrations on them. The attack was to be simultaneous by all three battalions and was timed for two o'clock in the morning of the 3rd of November.

The 60th's attack was successful after severe fighting—a success which should rank in the 60th's history with the attack on Sidi Rezegh aerodrome. The 7th Battalion led off with "D" Company, followed by "B" Company. They went off on a compass bearing in extended line accompanied only by desultory shelling and no small-arms fire. Stephen Trappes-Lomax thought that "D" Company had just about reached their objective. It was desert navigation at night and the Colonel decided that it was best to go forward a little farther to make sure. As soon as they started off the enemy opened up with every weapon he had. The Germans had held their fire until the last moment and cover was very scarce. The leading platoons, commanded by Bill Brownlow and Frank White, went straight in, supported by Mike Bird's machine guns from the left. They disappeared into the darkness and for the moment contact with them was lost. Any movement drew heavy fire and no further progress could be made. In the middle of the confusion the anti-tank guns, thinking that the success signal had gone up, began to drive slowly up on to the position. They were disillusioned in time to beat a hasty retreat. It was soon clear that the position was untenable and before it was light Brigade gave the order to withdraw, leaving "D" Company, some of whom did not at first receive the order and, indeed, penetrated as far as the line of the telegraph poles on the track, where they linked up with the 2nd Battalion, to come in by a longer and different route. When later in the day the company commander, Stephen Trappes-Lomax, himself turned up, the count of casualties was rather less severe than had at first been feared, though in "D" Company it amounted to about fifty.

The 2nd Battalion went in on the right. Tom Pearson had rightly doubted the more optimistic reports of the enemy's withdrawal. He was particularly concerned about the positions on the Sidi Rahman track itself and was told that if these were indeed occupied he was to take them and then dig in on the spot. The Battalion attacked two companies up, with the carriers ahead in line abreast, the direction of advance being due west. The leading companies were to advance straight through to the Sidi Rahman track and deal only with enemy immediately opposing them, while the third company was to mop up. Such was the plan. The leading companies made their way as far as the track despite considerable machine-gun fire, but the enemy came to life behind them and were more than the mopping-up company could deal with. An area around Cairn 40 containing enemy anti-tank guns, machine guns and infantry was cleared at considerable cost in casualties and the two companies set about digging in on hard, rocky ground which offered little cover. The next step was to call up the anti-tank guns. As soon as the vehicles appeared they were met with heavy mortar and machine-gun fire and it was clearly impossible to get them up to the position. While they were coming forward the enemy counter-attacked with about ten tanks whose movement was much assisted by flares dropped by the Royal Air Force west of Tel el Aqqaqir. Without the anti-tank guns the situation of the motor companies was perilous. They did contact elements of "D" Company of the 7th Battalion, but these could give little information of the whereabouts of the rest of their unit. At about four o'clock, seeing that the Battalion had bitten off more than it could chew and that the motor companies would be easy meat for the German tanks at first light, stranded as they were without the 6-pounders, the Colonel obtained permission from Brigade to withdraw. There were not many more than sixty officers and men remaining on the objective. The wounded were piled on the five remaining carriers as well as as many others from the companies as there was room for. The withdrawal was not the least hazardous part of the operation; for to rejoin the rest of the Battalion the carriers had to drive through the enemy tanks, who had by now worked their way to the rear of the defensive position which it had been hoped to hold. They succeeded in passing through without further casualties. Near Cairn 40 at least one 88-mm. gun had been knocked out and some four of the enemy's medium machine guns destroyed with their crews. Our own casualties for those twenty-four hours—one day being shelled and one night attacking—were heavy and included another seven officers.

On the 26th of October the Battalion had fought the celebrated action of Snipe with the loss of ten officers and thirty-eight riflemen. On the 2nd and 3rd of November, one week later, in this trifling, inconsequent, nameless battle, of which no one has ever heard and which ended in undignified retreat, the casualties were nearly as many and individually quite as important. Such is the fortune of war; and, as if to underline the logic of "chance's strange arithmetic," it was in this second battle that Mike Mosley, who had survived each of the early battles, who had commanded the roving patrol during the night of Sidi Saleh and dug deeper than anyone at Retma, now commander of "B" Company, for whom in these years he had done so much, was killed by a machine-gun bullet as he was standing by the Colonel awaiting the order to withdraw.

The Battle of Alamein

Although this battle had been unpleasant and unsuccessful for those who took part, it cured the enemy of any idea of holding on longer. The Eighth Army drove out clear of the maze of minefields and set off at last across the open desert. The battalions had a wonderful feeling of release from congestion. It was as if out hunting one had galloped round the deep rides of endless woodlands, never able to see far ahead, never able to get clear of the crowd and then suddenly, and after so long, unexpectedly, hounds had broken cover and sped off across the best of the vale. From now on the battle became a pursuit. Everyone was conscious of a great victory achieved, the long trails of prisoners, the tanks and vehicles strewn derelict along the route, the dead bodies of Germans and Italians lying about unburied on the sand were visible evidence of the Axis defeat. By breaking through in the north after days of bitter fighting the Army had cut off the Italian divisions abandoned without transport in the south. At the cost of some thirteen thousand casualties to the Army on the whole front, the Italians had been utterly broken and much of the flower of the Afrika Korps had been killed. But the dog-fight had been so long and so bitter that X Corps, intended for the pursuit, had been fully employed in the fighting and the petrol reserves, some of the administrative precautions for the immediate follow-up, had been partially used up. The motor battalions, whose mobility would have been invaluable in cutting off the retreating enemy, had suffered heavily and the formations to which they belonged were not in a fit state for a prolonged and immediate advance.

Now that the door was open one reflected a little sadly on the energies used up in the dog-fight. But news that had struck us soon after the beginning of the battle began to sink in with its full import, news entirely unexpected to nearly everyone in the Army, so well had the secret been kept. We were no longer the only British army in Africa. The First Army and the Americans had landed in Algeria and it seemed that we should now motor steadily westwards to meet them while the Germans pulled out across the Mediterranean. The order of battle was unknown to the Eighth Army; but, in fact, a company of the 10th Battalion had landed early with the First Army and there were now four battalions of the Regiment in active contact with the enemy.

CHAPTER XII

SNIPE

It is a curious feature of English history that the great defeats are remembered with as much pride as the great victories. Rupert at Edgehill, Sir John Moore at Corunna, the charge of the Light Brigade, Gallipoli, and Dunkirk are as famous as Naseby and Waterloo and Alamein. More people could tell you that Nelson died at Trafalgar than could count the French losses in that battle. Such a view of the history of war has, perhaps, a sounder basis than many of the popular misconceptions of what has happened in the past. The most successful battle is not always the one that is fought in the best way by the generals and the most gallantly by the troops. As with the battles of armies so it is with the operations of regiments and battalions.

It would be wrong to single out the Snipe action as necessarily the greatest fought by the Regiment in the war without a thought for the many occasions when individuals or companies or battalions fought just as well, as gallantly, and as successfully. It was the circumstances in which it took place and the results, the concrete results, measured in tanks knocked out, that have made the battle on the Snipe position—and deservedly—the most famous of our war.

The 2nd Battalion began the Alamein battle by providing the minefield task force. It had been envisaged that the infantry divisions would make good the ground, the Sappers would lift the mines and then the armour would sail out into the open to meet the German tanks. The 2nd Battalion was to protect the Sappers, organize the passage through the gaps, clear up the pockets of enemy left by the attacking infantry and beat off any counter-attacks that might occur.

The Battalion went into action on the night of the 23rd of October divided into three route parties, each consisting of a motor company with Sappers and a tank troop under command. "A" Company (David Basset) took the right route behind the

Australians and had completed their task by dawn. The Australians were experienced fighters and mopped up thoroughly behind their leading troops. "B" Company (Mike Mosley) and "C" Company, commanded by Charles Liddell, who had returned from the now-defunct 9th Battalion, took the centre and left routes behind the 51st (Highland) Division, whose first major battle this was. Well as they fought, they had reached only the second enemy minefield by dawn. These two companies had some opposition to subdue on the first minefield before gapping could begin. Dawn on the 24th found us trying to gap the second minefield in the face of considerable fire from enemy machine guns, 88-mm.'s and medium artillery. The armoured regiments had been pushed up close behind and the congestion in the area was stifling. When the second minefield had been gapped by seven o'clock in the morning, it was found that a third and fourth existed with an all-in depth of two thousand yards; for the Germans had not been idle in these months on the Alamein Line. The whole area was overlooked by a ridge to the west, strongly held by enemy infantry and a party of some thirty Mark III and Mark IV Special tanks. The Highland Division attacked this ridge, but were unable to clean it up completely. Under cover of this attack the gaps were pushed forward at the cost of casualties from shell fire. "B" Company lost Company Sergeant-Major Nobel and three sergeants in the course of the morning. By last light we had the gaps through, mainly owing to the extreme gallantry of the Sappers and the fine work of the carrier platoons under Peter Innes and Dick Flower. Just as "B" Company's task was complete, Peter Innes was badly wounded, having both legs broken by shell fire as he stood beside his carrier. Dick Flower with his party got through in the face of direct fire from 88-mm. guns and small arms, and was able to report the way clear for the armour.

That night no one in the Battalion had any sleep—the second night running—as they were engaged in traffic control for the armour moving up through their gaps. That duty continued throughout the next day, the 25th, while the 2nd Armoured Brigade tried to break out against a formidable array of 88-mm. guns. It was proposed that the Battalion should attack these guns at night; but the project was cancelled and, to add to the relief of the Battalion, the Divisional Provost took over traffic control on the gaps. Cheered by the news of the 7th Battalion's success against enemy tanks, most of the Riflemen got a few hours' sleep that night.

By the 26th it was clear that no decisive success had yet been gained by the Eighth Army. In the south the XIII Corps' attacks had been called off; in the north, though substantial ground had been gained and many prisoners captured, no break-through had yet been achieved. There were many more minefields in existence of greater depth than had been expected, so that the armour, cramped in congested gaps and unable fully to deploy, was an easy target for the mobile anti-tank guns of the Germans. It seemed that the enemy had appreciated that the main thrust was being delivered in the north and had collected their tank forces in this area so as to drive our infantry back into the minefields before tank support could arrive. It was a stage in the dog-fight when a definite success was a psychological necessity and when the ability of the infantry to fight off a counter-attack by tanks on their own still required to be proved. The 7th Battalion had already shown the way. The 2nd Battalion's attack on the night of the 26th/27th of October was an attempt to gain more elbow-room for our own armour. In fact, it showed that there was no better way to ensure the eventual defeat of the enemy than to destroy his armour piecemeal with the anti-tank guns of the infantry.

The story of Snipe is told from two angles. There is the full account by the Commanding Officer, Colonel Vic Turner, covering the whole action, and there is an account from a captured enemy document of what one phase of the operation looked like from the other side. At the end of the book are two citations for awards as an example of the gallantry of individuals. With the passage of time one might have been tempted to remember the Snipe action as a model battle in which nothing went wrong. That would not be a true picture of war. There has never been a battle in which things have not gone absurdly wrong, usually through no one's fault, and it is the side which adjusts itself to the unexpected that generally wins in the end. I have not cut out of the Colonel's account the accidents, the mistakes, the omissions, the Gunner observation post who was lost, the circumstances in which the Doctor got left behind, the confusion about map reading, or the shelling by our own side. The account is the true account as the Colonel saw it, altered only in two respects, that some of the more technical military expressions have been demobilized and certain details, such as orders given in full, and all map references have been omitted. For one patch of sand is much like another to anyone who may visit the site of these happenings, stray Bedouin with camels or foolhardy tourists, unconscious of the acres of unexploded mines which must still lie under the surface of this now-empty desert.

"On the 25th of October, 1942, the Commanding Officer of the 2nd Battalion The Rifle Brigade received a warning order that his Battalion was to be prepared to carry out an attack on the night of the 26th/27th of October on an unspecified objective. This order was cancelled, as it later became known that the 51st Division was doing an attack in the same area at the same time, but the Colonel was warned that the attack by his Battalion would probably take place the following night on an enemy strong-point known as Snipe.

"The Colonel and all company commanders therefore carried out a reconnaissance during the morning of the 26th of October. The party reconnoitred Star track as far as a hillock thought at the time to be the Double Pimple marked on the map. Forward of this point such intense fire was encountered that it was not possible to observe the ground over which the attack was likely to be made. The Colonel contacted the Commanding Officer of the 5th Battalion The Black Watch, who stated that he was about to attack Stirling. This did not agree with the Battalion's reckoning, and the party returned from the reconnaissance in considerable doubt and confusion of mind.

"The Colonel went to Headquarters, 7th Motor Brigade, during the evening and received orders for the attack. He returned and at once dispatched Lieutenant R. A. Flower (O.C. 'C' Company carriers) to reconnoitre a start line, and if possible to determine its location. He then issued verbal orders to company commanders, O.C. 239th Battery and O.C. Detachment, 7th Field Squadron R.E.

"The following is an order of battle for the 2nd Battalion The Rifle Brigade for the Snipe operation:

"2nd Battalion The Rifle Brigade (with sixteen 6-pounder anti-tank guns and twenty-two carriers), 239th Battery, 76th Anti-Tank Regiment, R.A., with eleven 6-pounder anti-tank guns, and Detachment, 7th Field Squadron, R.E. (Lieutenant N. Graham and sixteen other ranks).

"The 6-pounder anti-tank guns had already been allotted as follows:

" 'A' Company and 13 and 15 Platoons, 'S' Company, 2nd Battalion The Rifle Brigade: eight guns.

" 'B' Company and 239th Battery (less one troop): seven guns.

" 'C' Company and 14 and 16 Platoons, 'S' Company, 2nd Battalion The Rifle Brigade: eight guns.

"Battalion Headquarters and one troop of 239th Battery: four guns (as central reserve)."

The Colonel now issued verbal orders. The enemy had an anti-tank screen along Kidney Ridge with strong-points at the northern edge and at Snipe at its southern end. The 2nd Battalion 60th Rifles were to capture Woodcock. The 7th Battalion was in reserve. The 2nd Battalion was to attack, capture and consolidate Snipe. There was to be a barrage fired by a large concentration of artillery for thirty minutes from five minutes before zero until twenty-five minutes past. At four in the morning the armour was to move up and the 2nd and 24th Armoured Brigades were to exploit as soon as it got light. Dick Flower had been sent off to reconnoitre a route and a start line, a difficult enough task in the prevailing uncertainty about our whereabouts. "A" Company on the right and "C" Company on the left were to lead the attack, the carriers forming a screen across the front and the motor platoons following on foot behind, with "B" Company in reserve. Tom Pearson on the start line was to be ready to follow up with the 6-pounder guns of "S" Company, the wireless control set and rear link and section trucks. In consolidation the company sectors were to be: "A," 315° to 90°; "B," 90° to 225°; "C," 225° to 315°. Such a method gives a fair indication of the featureless nature of the country. Zero hour was to be eleven o'clock.

"Shortly after this Lieutenant R. A. Flower returned and stated that he had reconnoitred a route as follows:

"Star track to Double Pimple—a thousand yards on 280°; south-east down a track for four hundred yards.

"There there was a space approximately three hundred yards broad between two Highland Division battalions which was the only possible start line by the 1st Armoured Division's reckoning. The Colonel therefore said that the line of attack would be one thousand seven hundred yards on 233° unless the barrage came down in a very different place, in which case the attack would be directed on the southern end of the barrage.

"The approach march did not go according to plan.

"Owing to short notice, 'A' Company was unable to arrive at the start line by 2100 hours, and 'C' Company led off. The going was very bad, the moon was not yet up, the dust was stifling, and it is a matter for congratulation that only two portees ran into each other during the march. These two portees took no further part.

"The start line was reached at 2235 hours. The Battalion formed up under intermittent fire from 88-mm. guns. At z minus 5 the barrage started, and at 2300 hours was in full blast. It was then perceived that the southern end of the barrage was on a bearing of 270°. The line of attack was therefore altered to two thousand yards on 270°. The change of front necessitated a delay of ten minutes. At 2310 hours the carriers, followed by the infantry and Engineers, advanced.

"Only spasmodic fire was encountered during the first thousand yards, and no enemy opposition on the ground. After a thousand yards wire was encountered, possibly marking the edges of an enemy minefield. The infantry continued, but the carriers were forced to halt for five minutes while the Engineers discovered that the minefield was dummy.

"Thereafter the fire became heavier. Confusion was caused, as the carriers, though halted, continued to fire, with the infantry directly in front of them. The going was bad (the Colonel's jeep went into a slit trench twenty yards from the start line and had to be pulled out by a carrier). About twenty prisoners were captured during the advance, but the enemy put up no resistance on the ground. Scattered groups were seen running westwards in front of the advance. After two miles 'A' and 'C' Companies halted. This was farther than originally intended, and took the Battalion one thousand five hundred yards beyond a pronounced ridge.

"The success signal was given by wireless and by firing a Very light at approximately 0015 hours.

"Meanwhile the trucks waited on the start line. There was considerable shelling by 88-mm.'s and at about 2330 hours a lone plan flew over and after releasing a parachute flare dropped a stick of bombs which hit and set alight two vehicles, causing three casualties. The Medical Officer was sent for and was still engaged in dressing their wounds when the success signal was given and the trucks advanced. For this reason the Doctor and ambulances failed to leave the start line and were afterwards never able to reach the position.

"Consolidation proceeded rapidly. The Colonel issued orders to company commanders and allotted sectors to companies on the principle laid down in his original orders. The carriers advanced on to a ridge which formed the south-western and western edges of the position, and 'C' Company carriers captured another twenty prisoners. Wire was encountered and it appeared as if there was another minefield in front of the carriers. 'C' Company carriers observed much enemy movement beyond this wire and advanced five hundred yards towards the enemy through a gap. About a hundred and fifty enemy stood in a huddle, and appeared ready to give themselves up. The motor platoons of 'B' Company were sent for to collect them. Before they could arrive enemy tanks counter-attacked 'C' Company carriers, some advancing from the south-west, some, as it were, springing to life all around them in the area in which the carriers already were. 'C' Company carriers set alight an enemy truck. By the light of the flames the enemy were easily able to see our carriers. They were forced to withdraw and one carrier was knocked out. The prisoners bolted. They were soundly shot-up by machine-gun fire from both sides. Finally about thirty-five prisoners remained, from the 220th and 33rd Pioneer Engineers (164th Division and 15th Panzer Division respectively).

"Meanwhile the trucks, on receipt of the success signal, left the start line at about 0020 hours. The going was extremely bad, with long ridges of soft sand. Only ten vehicles, with four 6-pounder anti-tank guns among them, arrived with the Second-in-Command and Adjutant at about 0145 hours. The remainder were stuck, but finally thirteen 6-pounder anti-tank guns from 'S' Company and six from 239th Battery arrived on the position. Sufficient section trucks arrived to provide ammunition for all machine guns, and rations, water, etc., for all in the position. Off-loading was complete by 0345 hours and the trucks assembled and left under command of the Second-in-Command at 0545 hours.

"The Battalion position was in the middle of a German sapper dump and Battalion Headquarters were established in an officers' dug-out bedroom. Although in the prevailing confusion the situation was obscure, it now appears that there was a leaguer of tanks and vehicles (mainly Italian) about eight hundred yards south-west of the position (into the middle of which 'C' Company carriers penetrated) and a German leaguer of tanks and vehicles about a thousand yards north of the position. Both were visible during the night. The Italian leaguer broke up on being penetrated by 'C' Company carriers and tanks started advancing straight towards the German leaguer, entering the Battalion position on their way. In the ensuing action, which was very confused, a Mark IV tank was hit and set alight at thirty yards' range and one self-propelled 7.62-mm. gun at two hundred yards' range. One of the crew of the Mark IV jumped into a slit trench, from which he sniped the Battalion position until dawn. A grenade was then thrown at him, and landed in the slit trench.

"It became light enough to see at 0600 hours. The scattered remains of the Italian leaguer moved away westwards and the German leaguer to the north also started moving westwards. Both offered excellent targets and both were engaged. The bag claimed after this drive was six tanks destroyed and two hit to the north, and eight tanks destroyed to the south-west and south; two 7.62-mm. self-propelled guns were also hit. The Battalion position was heavily shelled. One 6-pounder anti-tank gun of 'S' Company was hit and knocked out and two ceased firing and could not afterwards be repaired. On the whole, the gun positions were found to be satisfactory, but one gun (Sergeant Pearson), after firing a few rounds, became so deeply embedded in the soft sand in which the pit had been dug that it was unable to fire until moved by a carrier at about 0730 hours.

"The 2nd Royal Horse Artillery observation-post officer, Captain Noyes, had disappeared during the night. He was last seen in the Battalion Headquarters dug-out at about 0400 hours. He did not go back to his vehicle but apparently got lost, as at 0747 hours he was reported as having arrived at the 7th Battalion a 'vehicle casualty'! In fact, his vehicle was still in the Snipe position and still intact. He is believed to have tried to walk back to the Snipe position in daylight, which would have involved crossing the strong German position on Woodcock. No replacement observation-post officer was able to reach the

Battalion during the day. The lack of one was greatly felt, as numerous targets offered but were never engaged, and there was no means of countering the intense enemy fire during the morning and again between 1600 and 1800 hours.

"Shortly before 0730 hours Sherman tanks of the 24th Armoured Brigade appeared on the ridge about two thousand yards to the east of Snipe. They immediately started to shell us intensively with 75-mm. guns and other fire. In the face of this the Intelligence Officer (Lieutenant H. J. F. Wintour) made his way in a carrier across to them, and informed the leading tanks of our identity. This caused the leading squadron to desist from shelling us, but the remainder of the brigade continued unabated.

"At 0807 hours the leading tanks advanced westwards towards our position. The enemy tanks started forming up about one thousand five hundred yards to our south and south-west hull-down behind a ridge. There appeared to be about twenty-five of them, almost all German tanks with long-barrelled 'special' guns with muzzle-brakes. We engaged these tanks with success and a gun of 14 Platoon claims to have hit and set alight three at one thousand one hundred yards. The crews of two of these were killed by machine-gun fire from the Shermans as they baled out. When the leading Shermans had entered the Snipe position at 0830 hours the battle became intense. Smoke screens were laid by both sides which had the general effect of entirely obscuring any possible targets from our tanks. The enemy, however, made effective use of his tanks and 88-mm. guns. Within fifteen minutes seven Shermans had been set alight in our area, and the 24th Armoured Brigade very sensibly started to withdraw. It is doubtful whether our tanks ever saw anything to shoot at at this time, while they presented excellent targets to the enemy, who employed interesting tactics: they put down a round of smoke most accurately (within twenty yards) on to an individual Sherman and then shelled the smoke with 88-mm. guns.

"As they withdrew at 0900 hours the Shermans were engaged by tanks and guns from the north (Woodcock area) and it was at a Mark IV among these that the 239th Battery had its first shoot. The range was extreme (one thousand eight hundred yards) and Sergeant Binks was with difficulty persuaded by the O.C. 'B' Company to have a go. With his third shot he hit and halted a tank, which was immediately towed away by another German tank. The two right-hand guns of 239th Battery were by now out of action.

"With enemy tanks and guns making such excellent use of ground, the great need was for artillery fire to silence them. At 0905 hours a wireless transmission was sent to the 7th Motor Brigade saying: 'Our crying need is a Gunner O.P.' The reply was that one would be with us shortly. He never arrived. The need of an observation post was also felt because much of our own artillery fire was landing in the Snipe position, probably because it was covered with tanks and guns (derelict) which appeared to distant observation posts to be suitable targets. At 1036 hours we sent by wireless: 'What we most need is artillery support. We have a suspicion that own artillery is landing on us.' This latter was an understatement. The matter was eventually cleared up at about 1230 hours when the Second-in-Command contacted Regimental Headquarters, 4th R.H.A., back on the gun positions.

"At 0900 hours a carrier of 'B' Company commanded by the company second-in-command, Captain P. Shepherd-Cross, and two carriers of 'A' Company commanded by Sergeant Sampher made a dash from the position carrying severely wounded. All got through, though the 'B' Company carrier received a direct hit from a 75-mm. *en route*. Captain Shepherd-Cross intended to fetch the Medical Officer, ambulance and more ammunition up to the position. This never in fact proved possible. Major T. C. H. Pearson, D.S.O., the Second-in-Command, had a convoy standing by all day to make a dash for it, but when he himself tried to cross the ridge to our east it attracted such heavy fire that he decided that it was not physically possible to get vehicles across to Snipe.

"After the withdrawal of the 24th Armoured Brigade to hull-down positions on the ridge south-east of Snipe the enemy developed two attacks. The first was an attack by thirteen M13's against the Snipe position from the west. Two 6-pounder guns (Sergeants Brown, D.C.M., and Dolling) were moved up to the west flank to reinforce this sector; the difficulty of moving guns in the soft sand was very great. The tracks were hitched on to carriers with a tow rope; during the process the vehicles and men offered good targets to enemy fire, and one officer and three riflemen were killed while shifting these two guns. This attack was beaten off fairly easily and four M13's were hit. Meanwhile, twenty-five to thirty German tanks moved forward from their hull-down positions and moved slowly forward to attack the 24th Armoured Brigade passing across our southern front at about a thousand yards. We engaged the enemy, which caused him to detach half his strength to attack Snipe from the south and south-west. All these tanks were successfully engaged by the 24th Armoured Brigade; those attacking our tanks presented broadside targets to the 6-pounder anti-tank guns in Snipe, and those attacking Snipe presented targets to the 24th Armoured Brigade. At least eight were set alight. (Of these none now remain on the ground and there are no traces of this action left.)

"After this phase the anti-tank-gun position became serious. The following guns remained in action:

"*West and South-west.*—Five: Sergeants Brown, Calistan and Dolling; Corporal Savill's gun (manned by Lieutenant A. B. Holt-Wilson, Sergeant Ayris and Rifleman Chard), and Corporal Cope's gun at very short ranges only, as its field of fire was limited to the top of the ridge a hundred and fifty yards away.

"*North-west and North.*—Four: Sergeants Hine, Miles, Brett and Newman.

"*North-east.*—Four: Sergeants Hillyer, Cullen, Binks and Woods of 239th Battery.

"Those guns, firing to the west and south-west, were extremely short of ammunition. The company commander, Major T. A. Bird, M.C., and Corporal Francis carried up more ammunition under heavy fire in jeeps, but when the midday attack developed only Sergeant Calistan's gun was able to fire.

"Shelling continued to be intense and six of 'C' Company's carriers which were in hull-down positions on the ridge on the western flank were hit and set alight. At 1300 hours nine M13's attacked this flank. Only Sergeant Calistan's gun was able to fire. It was manned by Sergeant Calistan, who did No. 3, the Colonel, who loaded and observed, and Lieutenant J. E. B. Toms, M.C. (the troop commander), who did No. 1. One member of the crew was suffering from shell-shock and the other two had crawled two hundred and fifty yards to fetch ammunition and had not yet returned. The Colonel ordered Sergeant Calistan to hold his fire until the tanks were six hundred yards away. Six were then hit and set on fire. The gun ran very short of

[Photo: *Navana Vandyk, London*

LIEUTENANT-COLONEL V. B. TURNER, V.C.

Rifleman D. A. Chard, D.C.M.

Major T. A. Bird, D.S.O., M.C.

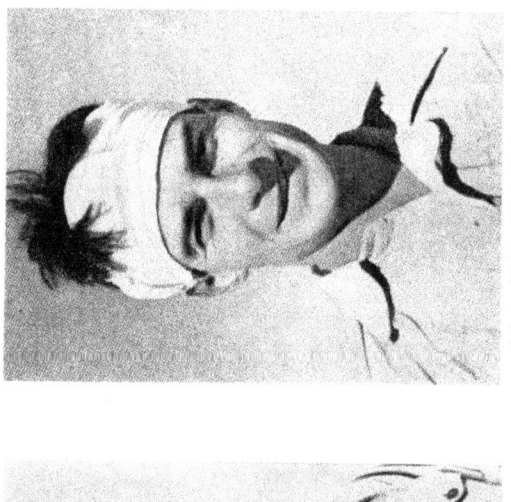

Sergeant (later Lieutenant) C. V. Calistan, D.C.M., M.M.

THE SNIPE POSITION

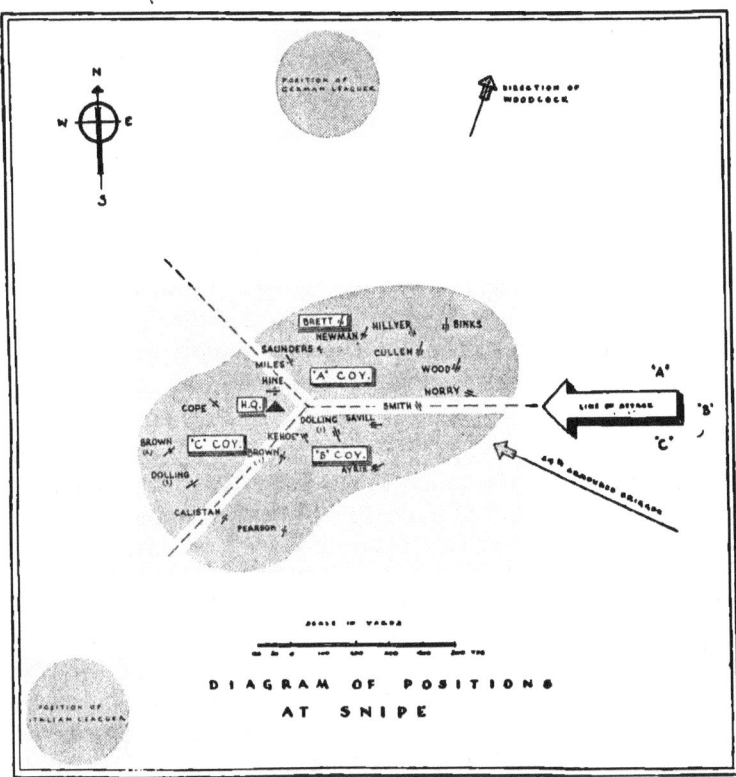

[*Drawn by Major T. A. Bird*]

The Company positions are roughly those occupied from p.m., 24th May, to p.m. 25th May. Names are those of N.C.Os. in charge of anti-tank guns.

ammunition (two or three rounds left). The remaining tanks continued to advance, machine-gunning hard. Lieutenant Toms ran to his jeep, which was a hundred yards away, on to which he loaded several boxes of ammunition from Sergeant Pearson's gun (out of action). He drove back under heavy fire, and the jeep was riddled and set on fire about ten yards short of Sergeant Calistan's gun. The Colonel and Lieutenant Toms took the ammunition off the burning jeep and reloaded the gun. The Colonel was wounded in the head at this moment, and was persuaded against his will to go and lie down behind some bushes about ten yards away. With the three remaining tanks at about two or three hundred yards' range, Sergeant Calistan took careful aim and scored a hat-trick, setting all three on fire.

"After this there was a comparative lull. Major Bird and Lieutenants Toms and R. A. Flower were wounded at about 1400 hours and no officer remained on the western ridge. Sergeant Brown, D.C.M., was put in command there until Lieutenant J. M. F. Lightly was sent to take over. This officer later went right forward to get better observation and was never seen or heard of again.*

"At about 1600 hours there was activity on the ridge to our east, and shell fire again became intense. Tanks of the 2nd Armoured Brigade appeared on the ridge and their guns shelled our position at Snipe intensely. During an unpleasant day this was the most unpleasant thing that happened.

"The German tanks now started forming up for an attack. They were in two main bodies. In the Woodcock area and spread out between Woodcock and Snipe were approximately thirty German tanks and ten M13's. About two thousand yards north-west of Snipe was a concentrated party of thirty German tanks. At 1700 hours the Woodcock party moved rapidly south-east in the direction of the 2nd Armoured Brigade. These were engaged by our 6-pounder anti-tank guns. It is believed that these tanks were newly arrived in the area (possibly the 21st Panzer Division from the south), as about seven tanks passed Snipe at two hundred yards' range, obviously quite oblivious of the fact that our anti-tank guns were there. It is inconceivable that the tanks which had been engaging us all day should have been so unwise. The 239th Battery were able to get their first real shoot of the day, and claim to have set on fire nine tanks during the action (Sergeants Hillyer, Binks and Woods) with several more hits. Two of their guns (Sergeants Cullen and Binks) were hit and put out of action. Meanwhile 15 Platoon, which had not been seriously engaged since the action against the German leaguer at first light, also had a good shoot, and Sergeant Newman's gun claimed four tanks "brewed up," including one 7.62 self-propelled gun and one Mark II, from which a man wearing a three-quarter-length white jacket baled out. He is thought to have been the commander. Undoubtedly 15 Platoon and 239th Battery were engaging the same targets. 'A' Company's machine-gun platoon had good targets. They trained their guns on the turrets of the nearest German tanks.

---

*He was, in fact, taken prisoner.

When these were knocked out and the crews baled out through the top of the turret they were picked off like sitting birds. The 2nd Armoured Brigade also had an effective shoot during this attack, which halted at 1725 hours. The remaining tanks of the Woodcock group took up hull-down positions.

"The second group now became active and detached about fifteen Mark III's to attack Snipe. These advanced hesitantly head on to the position. Only two guns were in a position to engage these tanks: Corporal Cope's gun, now being operated by Sergeant Hine and his crew (Sergeant Hine's own gun had been hit by shell fire at about midday), and Sergeant Miles's gun, which was exposed to intense machine-gun fire.

"Sergeants Brett's and Newman's guns had been hit and knocked out fifteen minutes before. Lieutenant Holt-Wilson was able to turn his gun right round, and he with Sergeant Ayris and Rifleman Chard also engaged these tanks. These three guns had an average of ten rounds per gun left.

"The enemy tanks were unfortunately able to secure hull-down positions behind the western ridge about five hundred yards from Battalion Headquarters. They overlooked the whole Snipe position, and continued to fire viciously with their 50-mm. and machine guns until 2030 hours. No anti-tank gun was in a position to engage them. When the three leading Mark III's were about a hundred yards' distance from Sergeant Miles's gun Sergeant Swann crawled across from Battalion Headquarters area to the gun—about fifty yards—loaded the gun, aimed and fired it. He scored two hits on the tank, one on the turret and one on the body, which halted it. The crew baled out. The crew of the gun, who had been lying in a shallow trench about eight yards in the rear of the gun under intense machine-gun fire, joined Sergeant Swann and continued to operate the gun. The other two Mark III's were set alight, one hit by all three guns and the other hit by Corporal Savill's gun. Sergeant Hine's gun put one shot right through the nearest Mark III (range about a hundred yards) and hit another tank about ten yards behind it. This second tank backed away to a hull-down position at about eight hundred yards' range and machine-gunned the Snipe position. About three rounds per gun remained to the guns firing on this front. Providentially no further attack developed, although one was expected at any moment. At 1844 hours a wireless transmission to the 7th Motor Brigade stated: 'Twenty tanks lying doggo in valley to the north of us at about one thousand yards. We are being swept by machine-gun fire from tanks. Expect attack any moment.'

"During this action a little comedy had been enacted. At about 1740 hours the 7th Motor Brigade started to transmit withdrawal orders in codex. Almost at the same time it became necessary to burn all codes, which the Adjutant (Captain F. W. Marten) did by popping his head out of the dug-out between bursts of machine-gun fire and pouring petrol over them and setting them alight. They burnt satisfactorily. The orders received had therefore to be transmitted in veiled language. The points made by the Brigadier (Brigadier T. J. B. Bosvile, D.S.O., M.C., commanding Motor Brigade) were:

" '1. Friends will come and take your place at dinner time.
" '2. You are to wait until they are happily settled in your place.
" '3. Your transport will then arrive and bring you home.'
"*Question:* Will it be an early dinner or a late dinner?
"*Answer:* The fashionable time.

"At last light (1930 hours) the enemy tanks pulled away to the north-west. They were nicely silhouetted against the pale patch in the sky until 2000 hours. At about 1950 hours we shot off our remaining ammunition at their retreating shapes, more as a gesture of relief than with any hope of hitting them. One hit was scored at one thousand two hundred yards. The enemy tanks leaguered about one thousand two hundred yards north-west of Snipe.

"At about 2015 hours company commanders and the Adjutant held a conference (the Colonel and Major Bird had by now been knocked out by the effects of their head wounds and the heat).

"At this conference it was decided that:

"1. That all wounded should be immediately evacuated.
"2. That the remainder should stay on the position and hand it over to friends at about 2100 hours. When the transport arrived loading would take place immediately and companies would withdraw independently for two miles due east to the start line of the previous night and rendezvous at the Double Pimple.
"3. In the event of an attack, action to be taken was left to the discretion of company commanders. It would

probably be necessary to destroy all equipment which could not be carried, and get away on foot by companies.

"Almost immediately after this 'C' Company's position was very heavily machine-gunned by the three tanks which remained in their hull-down position. The forward motor platoon and machine-gun platoon of 'C' Company started closing in on company headquarters, creeping towards it with the machine-gun tracer bullets passing over their heads. This looked exactly as if an enemy infantry attack was coming in, and a report of an infantry and tank attack reached Battalion Headquarters from 'C' Company. O.C. 'C' Company therefore decided to withdraw his company immediately. In fact, no attack developed and it is doubtful whether one was ever launched by the enemy.

"The remaining jeeps and one three-tonner were loaded with wounded. One jeep, with the Colonel and Major Bird on board, made its way to a 51st Division dressing station. The other two, carrying Lieutenants Crowder and Naumann and several wounded, ran over a minefield (Hawkins mines) which had been laid since our arrival on Snipe across our line of withdrawal. The damage was not serious and none of the wounded was further injured.

"Lieutenant Holt-Wilson went round every gun position and ensured that each gun had been rendered useless to the enemy.

"By 2130 hours there was no sign of any 'friends' or of our own transport. Os.C. 'A' and 'B' Companies therefore decided to withdraw their companies on foot at 2230 hours if no relief arrived. During this time the enemy were active recovering tanks and wounded and towed away the tank which Sergeant Swann had hit a hundred yards in front of the position. It was not, however, considered advisable to take offensive action, as our own wounded were still being evacuated and the enemy were in force to our north.

"At 2230 hours 'A' and 'B' Companies started withdrawing. Soon afterwards our own artillery started firing a barrage, which landed nicely in the enemy leaguer one thousand two hundred yards to our north-west. To avoid this fire the enemy started moving towards us. About twenty or thirty minutes later the barrage thickened and the enemy tanks and vehicles were again shifted, and made straight for the Snipe position. At about

2315 hours Battalion Headquarters and the remaining men withdrew and reached our own lines without incident."

The enemy engaged in these attacks were Germans and Italians mixed. The following is an account of one attack by the 12th Battalion 133rd Tank Regiment of the Littorio Division, mainly from the pen of the Italian commander, who was working under the orders of a German. This battalion formed, with the Stiffelmayer Group of German tanks, the force under command of the German Colonel Teege which attacked Snipe from 0330 to 1330 hours on the 27th of October. The battalion, commanded by Captain Preve, had nineteen M14 tanks, with nine Semoventi (self-propelled 105-mm. guns in M13-tank hulls) of Major Barone's battery in support, at last light on the 26th of October. Colonel Amoroso commanded the 133rd Tank Regiment. According to this account, the Italian attack ceased by 1130 hours; yet the action by Sergeant Calistan's gun in which nine Italian tanks were knocked out took place from 1300 to 1330 hours. There are two possible explanations of this.

Perhaps the Italians or ourselves made a mistake in the time. It is unlikely that we did, as the times are taken from the timings of the wireless reports noted in the Brigade log-book; Brigade Headquarters presumably had the correct time.

The other possibility is that this account refers to the attack by thirteen Italian tanks mentioned in Colonel Turner's account, and our claim of four M13's as a result of that action is an understatement. The second attack at 1330 hours might have been carried out by another battalion of the 133rd Tank Regiment and would not therefore be mentioned in the 12th Battalion's account.

"*27th October, 0400 hours.*—Colonel Teege's adjutant, accompanied by an interpreter, confers with Captain Preve. He carries the order that the whole group (Raggrupamento) is to move to Point 426 to attack enemy forces who are withdrawing north-east.

"*0425 hours.*—An order arrives from Colonel Amoroso to move between the 250 thrust line and Point 426 to attack the British forces in front in co-operation with the Barone battery and in close collaboration with the Stiffelmayer Group—direction north-east.

"*0530 hours.*—The battalion and the Barone battery are near 4 and 5 Companies, who are in the first wave: behind follow two Semoventi groups in line with 6 Company in the second wave.

"*0630 hours.*—The battalion is ready to attack. Strength: tanks, nineteen; Semoventi, nine. In front of us, covering the British withdrawal, are at least ten 56-mm. anti-tank guns, dug in flush with the ground (as events proved later). Distance of the anti-tank guns from our starting line, two thousand metres.

"*0645 hours.*—Two tanks of 5 Company hit and immobilized. The Semoventi troops open fire on the forward anti-tank gun.

"*0700 hours.*—The battalion attacks. In spite of the violent enemy fire and the resultant initial losses of tanks and men, the battalion advances firmly but keeping a certain distance from the anti-tank guns, which are extremely well dug in and camouflaged. Suddenly there is most violent fire from another eight or ten anti-tank guns hidden on our left and in depth. A number of victims in the battalion, which halts too suddenly. Enemy fire becomes more and more violent. The survivors then give incredible proof of valour. Second-Lieutenant Camplani from outside his turret urges his own tanks on to the attack at the head of them, drives his own tank at full speed on the most forward anti-tank gun. He is stopped by a belt of mines in front of the anti-tank positions and by a shell which breaks his tracks.

"Second-Lieutenant Stefanelli has his tank hit by an armour-piercing shell, which penetrates and explodes.

"Lieutenant Pomoni's tank at the head of his company is hit in the engine and the crew miraculously saved.

"Lieutenant Bucalossi's tank is hit and set on fire.

"Lieutenant Zilambo is wounded in the right leg and saved by Lieutenant Luciano (the Adjutant).

"Second-Lieutenant Delfino continues the attack and is only stopped by the minefields.

"At 1130 hours Colonel Teege gives the order to withdraw to the start line and disperse in the wadi behind. The tanks not burnt out were recovered.

"The following losses are reported:

"*Tanks.*—Burnt, nine; hit, immobilized, recovered, three.

"*Personnel.*—Dead, four; wounded, eleven.

"Colonel Teege's adjutant and his interpreter followed the action from their own tank and reported the actions of the battalion in battle to their commander. Colonel Teege expressed his admiration for the magnificent courage shown by the battalion and for the way in which Captain Preve commanded the movement of his own tanks and the Semoventi."

In this account the Italians admitted considerable losses. It is always difficult to be certain of the "bag" after a battle against tanks. Two guns often claim the same tank; some tanks which are hit are towed away by the enemy. There is seldom an opportunity immediately after the firing is over to go round and count the victims by type, to distinguish between German and Italian, between tanks and self-propelled, semi-armoured guns. In the excitement which succeeded Snipe it was at first claimed that over fifty tanks had been destroyed. The action gained such fame throughout the Army that, when the battle had passed on, a committee of investigation, on which were co-opted representatives of the 2nd Battalion, examined the ground over which the fighting took place. The final conclusion reached was that the minimum number of tanks destroyed was thirty-two, twenty-one German and eleven Italian, as well as three self-propelled guns. Others, of course, were hit and damaged; it is quite likely that more were destroyed. Thirty-two is as good a number as any other. It is certainly a very large total for any one battalion in an unprepared position to destroy. The defeat of the enemy armour at the hands of infantry anti-tank guns was a substantial blow to them at a moment when they still stood a good chance of driving us back into the minefields; as such it was one of the decisive factors in winning the dog-fight at Alamein. The Battalion had more to show for the battle than a long casualty list and an intense desire to sleep. There were the carcasses of the derelict enemy tanks; there was a personal message from General Montgomery; and there was the Victoria Cross won by the Colonel, not only for his own personal endeavours, great as they were, but awarded in recognition of the performance of the whole Battalion.

WESTERN DESERT 1940 – 1943

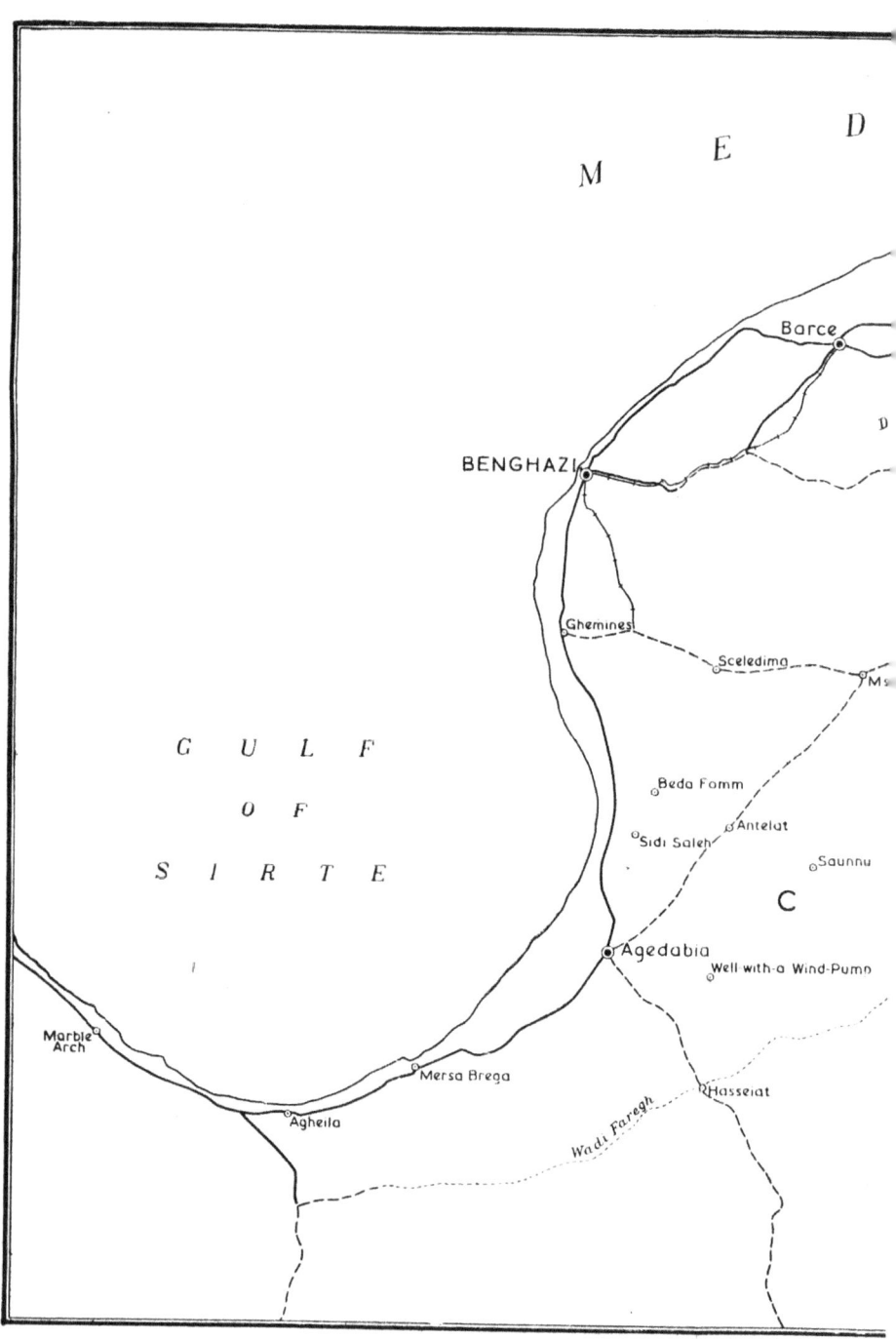

WESTERN DESERT 1940 – 1943

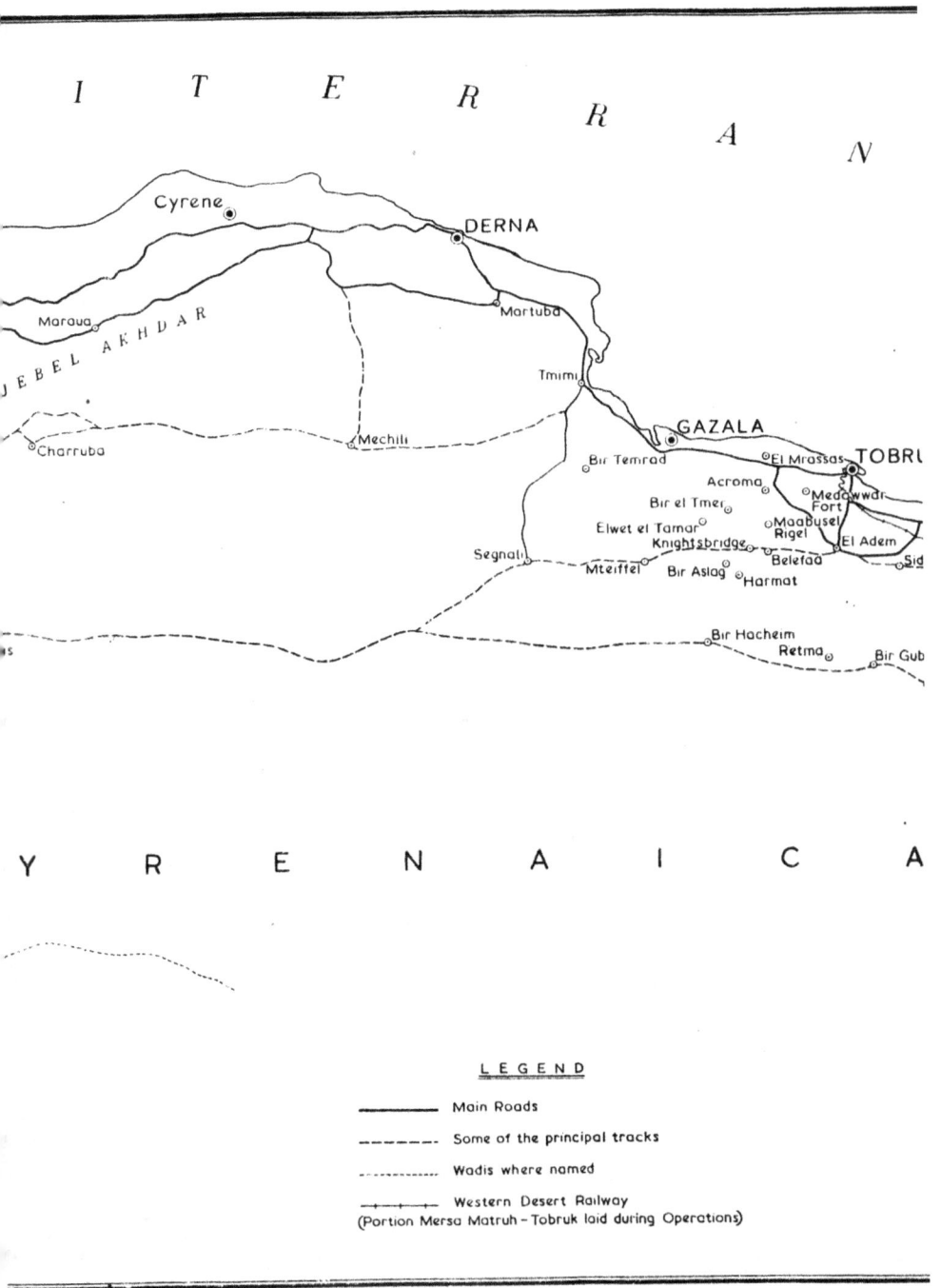

WESTERN DESERT 1940 – 1943

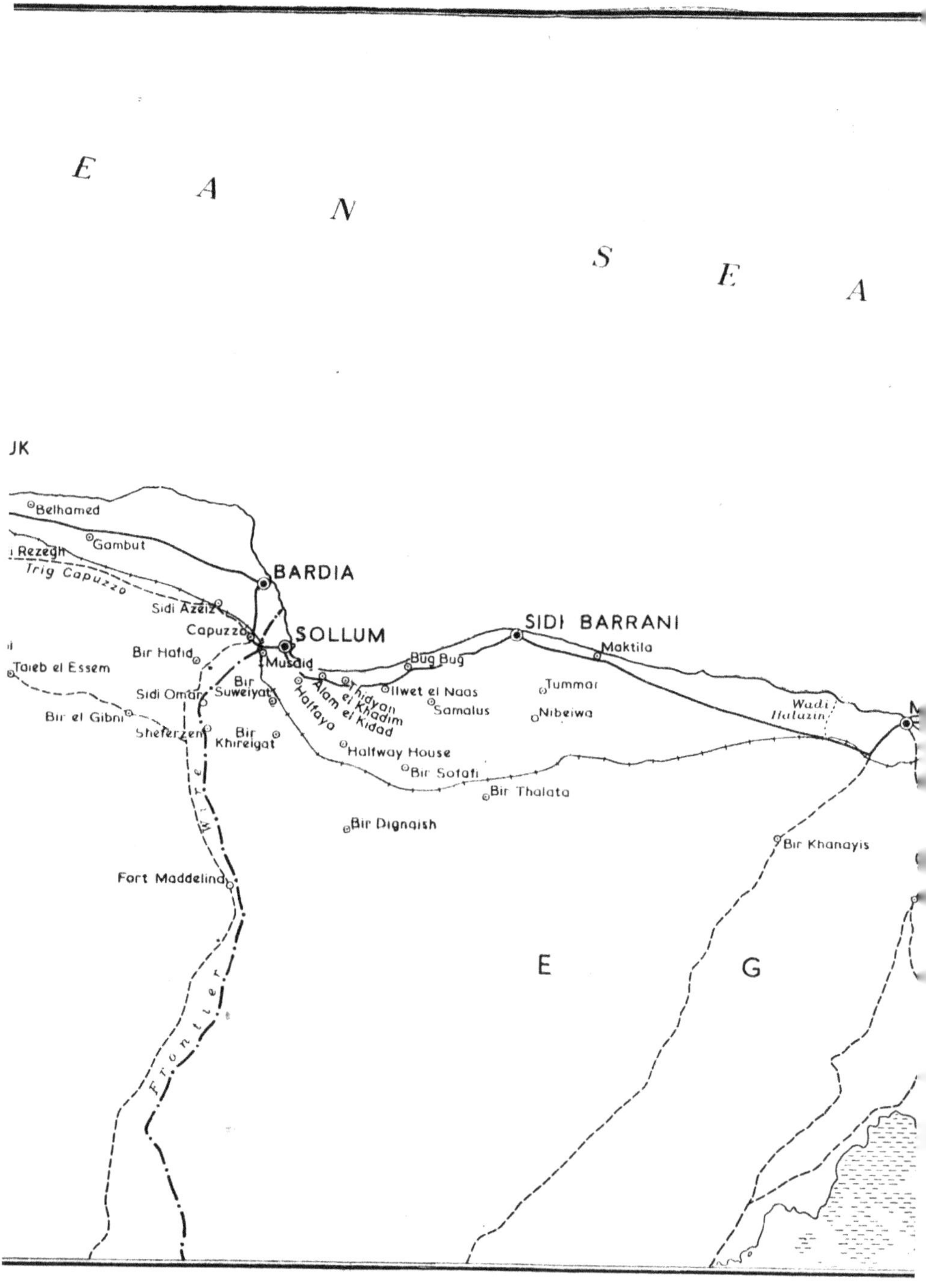

WESTERN DESERT 1940 – 1943

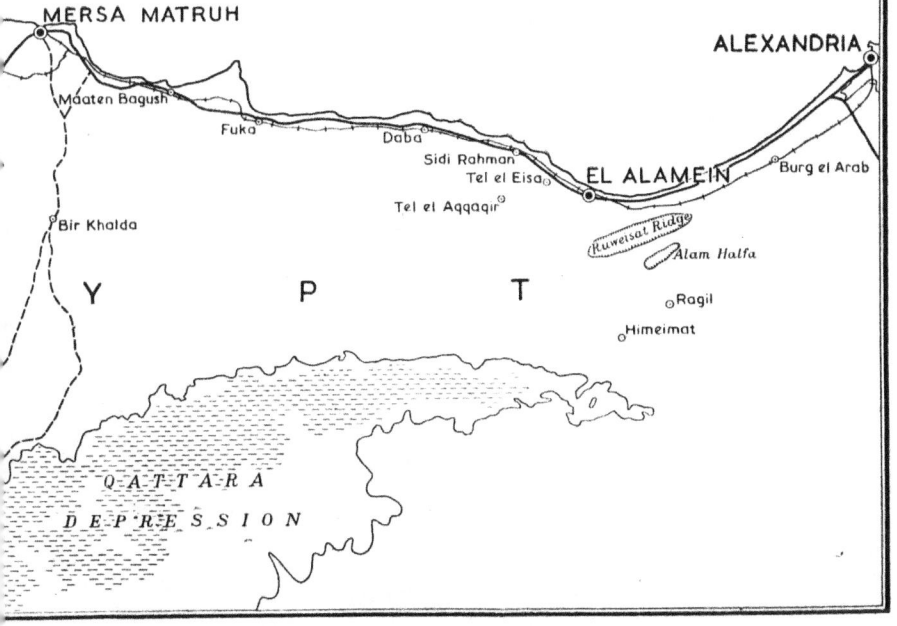

CHAPTER XIII

THE THIRD PURSUIT

In modern armies, despite the mammoth production of armaments which is undertaken in war, there is never quite enough equipment to go round. A branch of the General Staff allocates what there is to those most likely to put it to effect in the near future according to the plans for the battle, and tells the rest of the army to wait. So it was that before Alamein the bulk of the new equipment went to X Corps, who were to take the most prominent part in the break-out battle. The 7th Armoured Division, with whom the 1st Battalion was now serving, had been in the desert since the Italians first came into the war. They had had a hard battering in the summer of 1942. It was decided that they should hold the front while X Corps re-equipped and trained in the rear. After playing a minor role in the main battle itself there would be ample time to sit down and refit while the rest of the Army chased Rommel to Tripoli without them. Events worked out quite differently. The 1st Battalion, as part of the Division, played a secondary part, though an unpleasant and expensive one, in the opening phases of Alamein. Then, as the dog-fight absorbed more and more armour in the north, it was moved up in its rickety trucks and part-worn carriers close behind the leading troops so as to take part in the break-out when opportunity offered. The Division had a very determined commander, General Harding, and instead of a rest and a refit he led his Division out of Egypt, through Cyrenaica and all Libya and was not caught up by the rest of the armoured divisions until he was far into Tunisia. The 1st Battalion went with him; and so, while the limelight at Alamein was taken by the 2nd and, to some extent, the 7th Battalions, the Regiment's story in the advance from Alamein to Mareth is mainly concerned with the 1st Battalion.

After the expensive fighting for the Sidi Rahman track the 7th Battalion was sent to the rear to re-equip and rest, leaving one company under Alastair Dudgeon with the 2nd. Tom Pearson commanded this composite battalion and started off with the 7th Motor Brigade in the pursuit. They narrowly missed cutting off the tail of the enemy at Dabaa and set off on a long, turning movement which was aimed at the junction of the main coast road with the Khalda track from the south, some fifteen miles west of Mersa Matruh. This move showed promise of cutting off large numbers of enemy. But on the night of the 6th of November it rained, unexpectedly, and very hard. Rain in the desert did not often fall as early as November nor often for long enough to make the ground impassable. In the Sidi Rezegh campaign rain in the coastal area on the 19th and 20th of November slowed up the advance: this rain a year later has been blamed for the escape of the remains of the enemy forces. It certainly stopped the 2nd Battalion; for the echelons were stuck on Fuka escarpment and the 1st Armoured Division was stranded, bogged down and without petrol before it could reach the road. The enemy, on the good, hard surface, suffered from no such disadvantage and motored hard towards Sollum. But Rommel must have had some anxiety lest a force dispatched straight across the open desert, south of the area of the rain, might not catch up with him somewhere in the neighbourhood of Bardia.

That ended the part taken by the 2nd Battalion in the advance. It made its way by stages to Martuba and then to Tmimi. There the 7th Motor Brigade, rejoined now by the 7th Battalion as well, got down to rest and training with X Corps until it was eventually called forward for the Mareth battle.

The 1st Battalion was still under command of the 22nd Armoured Brigade. It had not been possible to re-form "A" Company yet and a composite "A" and "B" Company remained under Battalion Headquarters, "C" Company being with the 1st Royal Tanks and "I" Company with the 5th Royal Tanks. While the break-out battle was still in progress the Battalion was close up behind in a series of unpleasant areas full of dust and mines and other people's vehicles, generally close to one of the main tracks along which the debris of the battle limped to the rear: prisoners, damaged tanks, ambulances. On the 3rd of November some Hurricanes, returning from strafing the Germans and misled no doubt by the dust and sand blowing about, let off a few rounds without effect at the Battalion. That evening the Battalion moved down the Diamond track for some way and leaguered for the night while the 4th Indian Division carried out one last clearing attack. The next day, the 4th of November, they moved off at first light and after a sticky start with soft sand and no enemy they found themselves going due west across open desert, at last clear of the Alamein minefields and congestion. They continued moving until midday, when large parties of Italians were met, who were apparently prepared to fight. The tanks knocked out six M13 tanks and an 88-mm. gun, the motor companies collected some prisoners and the advance continued. The course steered by the Division was parallel to but well south of the rest of the Army, who were moving along or just south of the main coast road. It is always a temptation on such occasions to turn up too soon to the road, to bite off too small a chunk, to aim off too little and so arrive when the retreating enemy have passed. General Harding had long experience of these campaigns; he made his way due west with as little deviation as his orders allowed. From the moment he left the outskirts of Alamein it is probable that he aimed at Bardia. But his Division had not been intended for the pursuit and had no special supply echelons attached. The problem of petrol was soon to be a serious one.

On the 5th of November the Battalion made good progress, covering fifty-eight miles. During the day the motor companies had to escort some thousand prisoners to the rear. The next day the advance continued without serious opposition until a large column appeared moving across the Brigade's front towards the road. Some vehicles in this column were knocked out, including an armoured car containing Germans of the 33rd Reconnaissance Regiment, who were, no doubt, escaping from the south, where they had left the Italians to march hopelessly on foot. By the evening the Battalion was roughly south of Fuka and was delayed by a minefield put down quite ineffectively by our Sappers in June to hold up the German advance. On the 6th the advance continued until the Battalion was a few thousand yards east of the track which runs due south from Maaten Bagush on the coast. Here a curious battle developed, in some ways a model armoured battle under desert conditions. The remnants of the 15th and 21st Panzer Divisions, a collection of Mark IV tanks, Mark III Specials and 88-mm. guns was drawn up across the track, presumably with orders to halt the Division, whose left hook threatened to cut off the main body of the enemy moving along the road. As the firing began it started to rain steadily, a development which was to our advantage, since it denied the enemy the advantage, usual in Africa, of having the light behind them in the evening. The two leading armoured regiments, with their motor companies, engaged the enemy frontally. The third regiment was in reserve, to be used at a suitable moment. On the right flank the anti-tank guns and machine guns of the 1st Battalion prevented any enemy move round towards our rear and were able to have a good shoot on to the track running north from the enemy position. The field guns, Brigade Headquarters with Brigadier Roberts, and the Divisional Tactical Headquarters with General Harding were all close up behind the leading troops, laid out like figures on a cloth-model demonstration at the Staff College. At the psychological moment the reserve armoured regiment was ordered up into action and the enemy began to thin out, giving our machine guns an excellent shoot at effective range as they went. It looked as if most of the German force might be caught, but visibility grew worse and the enemy seized the opportunity to retire into the darkness. They left behind them thirteen Mark III Special tanks destroyed by our fire and two 88-mm. guns. "C" and "I" Companies collected about two hundred prisoners between them.

The rain, the scapegoat for the escape of the Afrika Korps, continued all night. Many vehicles in the morning were bogged down. Yet only two miles to the west the ground was hard and firm and, had the echelon not done some wandering about in rain and dark, the Brigade might have been able to replenish and push on one day earlier. For the next few days the move continued steadily west, meeting no enemy and making only fair progress, about thirty miles a day, which was all that petrol would allow. On the 10th motor platoons of "C" and "I" Companies went forward with the Sappers to the frontier wire to make gaps and reached it at kilo 68. The Battalion was bombed by six Messerschmitt fighters without damage, and at half past four in the afternoon passed through the wire out of Egypt and into Libya for the last time.

The 22nd Armoured Brigade was now the leading formation of the Eighth Army. The troops on the coast road were not far behind but were about to be faced by the enemy defences at

THE THIRD PURSUIT

Sollum and Halfaya Pass. The coast road at Sollum makes a turn north through Capuzzo to Bardia, names to bring memories of 1940, and then turns left and parallel again to the coast. The original intention was for the 22nd Armoured Brigade to cut the corner and go straight from the wire to hit off the road west of Bardia. Unhappily those orders were changed and the advance was directed farther north to meet the road east of Bardia, since it was hoped to turn in behind the garrison of the Halfaya Pass, capture them and assist the main forces on the coast road, threading their way through hundreds of vehicles bombed by the Royal Air Force and now derelict, to get up the passes and into Bardia. The petrol situation was such that the main part of the Brigade could do one thing or the other, but not both.

That evening, the 10th of November, as we sat in close leaguer inside Libya, waiting as often before to cut a road and attack an enemy who we hoped was still unconscious of our presence, the 11th Hussars brought in to Battalion Headquarters to be guarded a truckful of men of the German 90th Light Division whom they had chased and captured crossing the wire near Sheferzen. It was obvious from the bearing of these prisoners that the disaster of Alamein had not been enough to affect the morale of these Germans, confident and well disciplined in defeat.

The next morning the Battalion set off at five o'clock before it was well light. But when they reached a point north of Bir Hafid from which the road was in view, all that could be seen was the tail of a long line of lorries waiting to pass through Bardia and the flashes of a few field guns and 88-mm. guns of the rearguard firing to hold us off. A railway engine and one truck made off at speed down the single track, being fired at by every tank in the Brigade—and continuing unscathed. Towards Sollum there was no sign of movement. For lack of petrol only a few carriers with some light tanks could be dispatched to the west of the town to cut the road there. They did much damage and caused casualties to men and vehicles; but they could not stop the traffic altogether and the long columns trickled past them towards Tobruk. It was clear that the last chance of cutting off a slice of the Afrika Korps had gone as a result of a day's delay, a change in plans and a few gallons of petrol. But the only Germans left in Egypt were now prisoners and Rommel was never again to threaten the Nile Valley.

In the afternoon the Colonel, with the composite "A/B" Company and one company of the Queen's, was ordered to go and clear up Bardia town and particularly to secure the water point. There were no enemy about, although mines and booby-traps abounded. The first road-blocks were destroyed by 6-pounder fire. The main bridge across a deep wadi was blown and so the occupation had to be done on foot. This was achieved without incident; but the mines and dirt and flying dust made the town an unpleasant place, so that Battalion Headquarters and "A/B" Company were glad to rejoin the Brigade on the 12th.

By the time Tobruk was reached and found not to be held it was obvious that the Germans were well on the run. Air reconnaissance showed that they were likely to leave Benghazi without a fight. The Army, however, was faced with great administrative difficulties, having started this time from Alamein, and for several days there was no move forward from Tobruk. On the 14th of November the 11th Hussars set off across the desert to Msus by the route taken two years before by the 2nd Battalion. "A/B" Company, commanded by Ed Garnier, went with them. They had little to do in a ground role, but had a hard time from the Germans in the air, who were sensitive about any move which might threaten their flank. "Soft-skinned" vehicles were very vulnerable in the open desert. Having reached Msus on the 19th and captured some sixty Italians, they then turned north to Soluch, and one platoon set a night ambush on the main road near Ghemines. But the last enemy vehicles had already departed to the south. On the 22nd of November the company moved north and into Benghazi, being, with the 11th Hussars, probably the first British troops to enter the town on this its third capture since the war with Italy had begun. Apart from some aimless snipers and looting Arabs, there was no opposition to be found. Nearly a hundred and fifty Germans, mainly dock operators and sailors, gave themselves up. The company then set itself up as a report centre for escaped Allied prisoners, some eight hundred of whom were soon collected.

Meanwhile, on the 18th of November, the anniversary of the start of the campaign of Sidi Rezegh, "C" Company, under Noel Kelly, had been put under command of the 1st Royal Tanks, who were ordered to move across the desert to Antelat and hurry the enemy on his way. Battalion Headquarters and

"I" Company remained at El Mrassas, at a reasonably pleasant site near the sea some fifteen miles from Tobruk, to rest and refit and prepare for the advance to Tripoli. They stayed there for over a month.

"C" Company and their armoured regiment reached Antelat on the 23rd. The regimental group was ordered to clear Agedabia, but strong anti-tank-gun opposition was met and the day was spent in dealing with these guns by tank fire, field guns and the company's machine guns. The bag was satisfactory. At last light the Company were ordered to push on into the town. This they did cautiously, moving from ridge to ridge, for there were mines and booby-traps and enemy sprinkled about the place. They entered the town at three in the morning and captured the last six Germans who remained. During the next few days the company moved on slowly to Mersa Brega, picking up a fine selection of mines on the way. "A/B" Company rejoined the Brigade from Benghazi on the 29th. The two companies held a line between the sea and the marshes, patrolling into the enemy positions, identifying the Spezia Division and being soundly bombed, until on the 7th of December a brigade of the Highland Division took over. In each succeeding campaign the area between Agheila and Agedabia was noted for the fierce activity of the German Air Force, who made the most of the period before the Royal Air Force could establish bases near enough to give effective air cover to the troops. This year was no exception, so that the two companies were profoundly thankful to move north away from it and rejoin the Battalion at Mrassas.

By the time the 1st Battalion's rest was over the enemy had been forced back from Agheila. This was something new in desert warfare. The British Army had never before gone as far west. The Agheila position had always before been used by the enemy as a springboard from which to start off on an offensive towards Egypt. But now, in December, 1942, there was sufficient transport to ensure administrative backing: a fighter wing could be flown in self-contained to operate from Marble Arch. There was no question of a serious counter-attack by the Germans, who knew that the First Army had landed behind them and that Allied forces were building up for the capture of Tunis.

The Brigade moved forward on the 20th of December from

Tobruk, travelled across the desert by Bir Hacheim and Msus to Agedabia, thence south past the Agheila position to an area near Marble Arch which was reached on the 23rd. Mussolini had erected a great stone arch across the road at a point about a hundred miles east of Sirte to mark the border between Cyrenaica and Tripolitania. The landing ground in that area was called Marble Arch and it was in this rather flat stretch of desert that the Battalion were able to fit in a few days' training. Christmas Day was remarkable only for a Brigade conference, followed by a conference for company commanders. However, the Battalion, having taken the precaution of having one Christmas dinner before leaving Mrassas, found another waiting for them in the forward area. On the 30th the Army Commander visited the Battalion. It was not until the 9th of January that a forward move was made to close up with the troops who were in contact with the enemy. It was a sign of the times that all the carriers were moved by tank transporters to the new positions west of Sirte.

This Tripolitanian desert was different from the level stretches of stony sand in Cyrenaica, almost all of which was passable for a truck. Near the coast there were deeper sand and fewer stones: inland there were rocky hills. The line of advance was intersected every few miles by deep, often impassable, wadis running towards the sea. The waterless area where the Battalion assembled was something like twelve hundred miles from Cairo. As far as Misurata the land was barren and uncultivated. Here there was cultivation, and Italian settlers eked out an existence along the coast until from Homs onwards the area of cultivation extended inland for about twenty miles in a half-circle with Tripoli at the centre.

On the 10th of January Colonel Freddie Stephens attended a conference at XXX Corps Headquarters, where General Montgomery gave out his plan for the coming battle for Tripoli. This habit of the Army Commander's of explaining personally to battalion commanders and those of equivalent rank how the battle was to be fought was one which gave enormous confidence to the Army and had great influence in raising morale throughout the entire Army. Everyone down to the private rifleman could consider himself to be in the Army Commander's mind: lack of information and the feeling that the soldier is being run in blinkers were notably absent from these battles.

THE THIRD PURSUIT

The plan for Tripoli was briefly that the Highland Division was to advance up the axis of the coast road through Misurata and Homs to drive the enemy from positions astride the road, to clear the road of mines, repair the culverts and put it in order for use as the main artery of supply. The New Zealand Division, with the 4th Light Armoured Brigade, were to carry out a left hook by Beni Ulid and Tarhuna. The 7th Armoured Division, with the 8th Armoured Brigade, were on their right. The 1st Battalion was still in the 22nd Armoured Brigade, whose role was to go up the centre, between the coastal column and the inland column, to keep touch with both and to be slipped into the plain of Tripoli when opportunity offered. The Brigade was under the personal command of the Army Commander, who moved close behind in his tactical headquarters. There was much speculation and some rivalry between formations as to who would be first into Tripoli. General Montgomery took a keen interest and a personal part in such rivalries and trusted to the 1st Battalion to clear his pathway of mines and not to lead him into an impassable sea of sand. For administration and navigation across this difficult country, well mined and booby-trapped by enemy whose main forces had retired, were the chief problems before the Army.

For the battle the Battalion sent "A" Company to the 4th County of London Yeomanry and "I" Company to the 5th Royal Tanks. The remainder of the Battalion had the task of left-flank protection. On the 14th the advance began. We had a dull day, motoring sixty-four miles, crossing the Wadis Tamet and Chebir and meeting with scarcely any opposition. On the 15th of January we were lightly shelled, and bombed, without damage, by Messerschmitts, and were successful in making contact by patrols with both coastal and inland columns. On the 17th the advance continued to the Wadi Soffegin and on the 18th turned north towards Zliten, still scarcely opposed. The Highlanders had taken Misurata without much difficulty, but the enemy appeared to have extricated himself easily, leaving few prisoners to be picked up.

On the 19th the Battalion Group went forward independently, parallel with the coast road, to try to outflank the Homs position. They met with steep-sided wadis and bad patches of deep sand so that by four o'clock they were forced to give up this venture. Patrols went forward as far as Homs—tall palms, white sand-dunes, Leptis Magna, standing complete and dignified in this arid land—where they made touch with the 51st Division, who were held up by enemy opposition on a large, round hill west of the town called by the Highlanders Edinburgh Castle. On the 20th the Battalion Group moved forward to the left of the 51st to a place with the Italian name of Baldagano. Here 9 Platoon of "C" Company, moving round to the rear of the enemy on Edinburgh Castle at the same time as the Highlanders attacked up the road, found that the enemy had slipped away. The 21st was a day of rest, among trees near running water such as had not been seen for twelve hundred miles.

On the 22nd, in face of little opposition, we moved off astride the road to Tripoli. It was the last lap. The going across country was impassable and the Brigade, the motor companies being with their armoured regiments, was strung out like a string of sausages along miles of road, a strange experience for the Desert Army. At about four in the evening "I" Company, with the leading tank regiment, bumped the Tripoli defences astride the road. There was heavy mortar fire and the leading tanks came under anti-tank fire. The Battalion was too strung out to be collected in time for an attack before it was dark. However, Geoffrey May was dispatched with a strong fighting patrol to try to outflank the position. The patrol cut the road a thousand yards west of the enemy, exactly where it had been ordered to, a good performance in the dark over strange, rough, difficult country. They must have missed the last of the enemy by five minutes, as they heard them motoring away when they were within half a mile of the road. The next day, the 23rd of January, three months to a day after the Battle of Alamein began, the Colonel and the Second-in-Command, Tony Palmer, entered Tripoli behind the Army Commander.

An advance into enemy country carries with it an excitement peculiarly its own. Everyone is intensely curious to see what these new places of which they have heard and talked about so much can look like. This was particularly so to troops accustomed for years to nothing but bare, uninhabited desert or an annual visit to Derna or Benghazi. To drive now into the capital of Libya, the first civilized town since Alexandria, gave to the 1st Battalion a thrill of pride and a sense of achievement which are among the few compensations that war can offer. Tripoli at that time had an importance to the Army which Tunis and Rome, Paris, Brussels and Berlin were later on to acquire. After Sidi Saleh in 1941 the 2nd Battalion had dreamed of driving on behind the Italians to their capital. Since then its capture had seemed less and less probable. Before the advance across the Wadi Zem Zem great expectation had deliberately been aroused. Now the Riflemen saw a city of white houses in the blazing sun, always bright in Tripoli even in January, a blue Mediterranean harbour dotted with bombed ships, oleander trees along the pavements, Jews and Arabs and frightened Italians lining the streets.

On the 31st there was a Victory service and a march past, in which the Battalion was represented. On the 4th of February the whole Battalion lined the road for the Prime Minister to drive past. But by the 9th the celebrations were over, even training had been interrupted and the Battalion moved on to near Zuara for the purpose of continuing the war.

The advance at first was slow and hampered by the going. The Brigade had the unusual experience for them of being bogged down in the salt marshes near the frontier. The Battalion did various reconnaissances to find suitable routes. On the 14th of February the motor companies went out to their armoured regiments and the whole Brigade advanced across the border to Fort Sidi Toui, six miles inside Tunisia and which the Germans had evacuated the day before. On the 18th the companies returned from the armoured regiments and the Battalion as a whole took over defensive positions from the Buffs south of the road from Ben Gardane to Medenine. The Eighth Army was gradually squaring up to the Mareth Line. It was likely that the long spell of advancing without casualties would come to an end. The Germans held the town of Medenine as an outpost of the line. Of itself the town was of little importance, being a small collection of white houses and mud huts centred round a square. But just to its west was a landing ground and three miles to the west of that a high, rocky hill jutting out of the plain, surmounted by a white house. This hill was called Tajira Chir on the map, but with a startling lack of originality came to be known as Edinburgh Castle. It had a certain tactical importance. From it you could see across the narrow plain to the Matmata Hills, on which the defences of the Mareth Line had been built. Edinburgh Castle was well within range of the guns of that line. With the lower hills to its north it gave some cover in its lee from observation from the defences. The main road to Tunis passed along its northern slopes.

By the 20th there were cries of distress from the First Army. Some of these were heard quite literally by the Battalion, whose forward control wireless frequency coincided with that of an Allied unit which was clearly finding it necessary to issue orders for a hasty retreat. It was decided to undertake an operation which, while materially assisting the preparations for the assault on Mareth in the future, might relieve the immediate pressure on the Americans at Gafsa. The 131st Brigade were to clear Medenine, while the 22nd Armoured Brigade were to swing round the north flank and cut the main road. We started off at eight-thirty, "I" Company carriers leading. There was a mist hanging about the low ground, but despite this the Brigade moved fast and by ten o'clock had bypassed Medenine to the north. "C" Company and the 4th County of London Yeomanry cut the road beyond Tajira Chir, seven miles to the west of the town, taking some enemy transport and a few prisoners. As the mist cleared, the enemy both from the Mareth positions and Tajira Chir had perfect observation of the whole Battalion, whom they shelled heavily all day. It was a situation reminiscent of Alamein, where Himeimat had overlooked the Battalion, lodged uncomfortably between the minefields. This time casualties were few: but one of them was Company Sergeant-Major Ridley of "I" Company, killed by a shell. He was one of the few remaining Regular warrant officers; as such and in his own right he was a grievous loss. That night, when the enemy slipped back to Mareth, abandoning Tajira Chir, we were hopeful that "C" Company's road-block on the main road would get a good haul. But the enemy found an alternative route to the south. All the same, it was a satisfactory operation. "C" Company particularly had done well.

The rest of the month was spent in holding defensive positions, which were not attacked, patrolling up to the outskirts of the Mareth defences and being shelled intermittently. On the night of the 25th/26th Timmy Cohen took out a reconnaissance patrol in the area of Zehmoula which was typical of many. The patrol found that in the dark there were so many loose stones to kick about that silent progress was impossible. They lay up close to what they thought was an enemy post. The enemy heard them and sent out two men to investigate. These made a great noise and by their voices appeared to be Italians. They came to within fifty yards of the patrol without seeing them. At moonrise the patrol moved off and located another post, which gave the alarm and stood-to; two men appeared on the skyline and eight others were seen running about. None the less, the patrol commander crept forward and found a trip-wire apparently marking a minefield. No amount of prodding could discover a mine and after more investigations in the area, watched probably by the enemy, who made no sound and were therefore unlikely to be Italians, the patrol withdrew and took home such useful information as they had gained. It is from patrols like these, nerve-racking for the participants, dull for the reader, that information for subsequent attacks is built up.

By the end of February the Germans, fresh from a successful attack on the Americans to the west of Tunis, were expected to turn on the Eighth Army. Rapid movements of formations from Tripoli and Cyrenaica to the front restored the Army's balance just in time. As a result of the arrival of these new formations, the 22nd Armoured Brigade was pulled back into reserve. When the German armour swept down from the Matmata Hills towards Medenine it was halted by the forward troops and the concentrated fire of the Corps artillery, without the reserve being called upon to go into action, although "C" Company had to take over an unpleasant piece of ground, overlooked by the enemy, when a company of the Queen's was overrun. So the 1st Battalion can hardly be said to have played much part in this model defensive battle, in which the Germans lost over thirty tanks in half a morning, although "C" Company's carrier platoon had a sight of the German divisions moving down from the hills and deploying in full view in the plain. The rest of the Battalion had to be satisfied with strafing by Messerschmitts and occasional overs from the enemy guns. They were lucky to have no casualties.

Having repelled this attack, the Army began to prepare for the assault on the Mareth Line. While the 1st Battalion remained in reserve there were signs that the 2nd and 7th would soon be moved up from the Djebel in Cyrenaica. At one time the administrative situation of the forward troops was so uncertain that all the wheeled vehicles of the Motor Brigade—and of the whole of X Corps—were taken away and used to carry supplies up the endless road from Benghazi to Tripoli. The two battalions spent the time in the Djebel Akhdar training, washing and even indulging in athletic meetings and a vehicle gymkhana. Colonel Geoffrey Hunt and Kenneth Hicks left the 7th Battalion, and on the 6th of December Douglas Darling took over command. There had been much rain at Martuba when the Brigade first arrived and as a result the desert round Tmimi was comparatively green. Many migrant birds cross the coast in this area; varieties of wild duck would alight in the sea on their way north or south. There were many reminders of civilization and a more temperate climate. While the Brigade was being fattened up for the battles to come there was leave to Cairo, and those who were wise sat about quietly enjoying a rest while they could or taking the advice of Doctor Picton on any subject under the sun or walking off to a neighbouring pool, strange to find after years in the desert, on the off chance of surprising a mallard.

On the 1st of March General Jumbo Wilson flew up to inspect the battalions. He had come to see the 2nd Battalion the day before they started for Sidi Saleh. This visit also portended a move; for the next day they started off along the main road to drive through Derna, Benghazi, Agedabia and Agheila, names of the desert campaign, to the new, strange places in Tripoli, and on to Medenine in Tunisia, where the preparations for the Battle of Mareth were by now approaching completion.

CHAPTER XIV

MARETH, AKARIT AND THE FOREST OF OLIVES

It was always an impressive proceeding to drive up to the front along the lines of communication of the Eighth Army, particularly for those who had known the small beginnings of the Western Desert Force. There was so much going on. Signallers were stringing wires on telegraph poles; Sappers were improving diversions and erecting new bridges; landing grounds were springing up in hitherto virgin desert. In the ports there was tremendous activity, strange machines fishing the debris of the enemy's parting demolitions out of the harbour waters. Immense numbers of huge vehicles were driving in both directions, on the whole with a lack of traffic blocks which was a credit to the Military Police. One gained the impression of a powerful machine working inexorably to bring back life to the country and to build for the Army foundations from which to step off on the next offensive.

The 7th Motor Brigade passed through all the administrative areas of the Army; skirted the town of Tripoli, crossed the border into Tunisia, and on the 15th, thirteen days after they had left the Djebel Akhdar, they passed through Medenine and took over a part of the front. Their area was on the western slopes of the hill known as Edinburgh Castle. The 7th Battalion had a perfect reverse-slope position, from which the Guards Brigade had repulsed the German attacks a week before. From here the two battalions looked across the open to where the main road passed through the Matmata Hills on the way to Gabes. Ten days were spent in patrolling actively by day in carriers and at night on foot to contain as many troops as possible opposite them. At first the Guards Brigade, much weakened by their disastrous attack on Horseshoe Hill, were on the right. It was typical of the methods of command in the Army that on the 19th, four days after their arrival, General Montgomery came to visit the 2nd and 7th Battalions and spent some two hours going round and talking to officers and riflemen in each position. He now had three battalions of the Regiment under command, the 1st Battalion being with the 22nd Armoured Brigade as a central reserve.

The Mareth Line, unlike the Alamein Line, was a system of fortifications prepared at leisure in peace time by the French to face an Italian invasion from the east. The Eighth Army had pushed on from Tripoli with a faint hope of "bouncing" the enemy out of the defences, but with the intention of assisting the First Army in Tunisia as their principal aim. They had held off the enemy counter-attack on the 6th of March, repaired the harbour facilities in Tripoli and now were administratively sound enough to drive the enemy out of their fortifications. In its original form the plan for the battle promised a minor role to the three battalions. In the north near the sea the 50th Division, consisting of two brigades but having a call on one Indian brigade, was to break into the defences on a narrow front. The success of the operation seemed likely to depend to a considerable degree on the ability to get tanks and anti-tank guns across the Wadi Zigzaou which formed the basis of the defences in this sector. This attack was to have support from artillery and the Royal Air Force on the grand scale. The 22nd Armoured Brigade, with the 1st Battalion, was prepared to pass through any gap made by the infantry and advance towards Gabes. Among those who were to carry out a holding role in the centre were the 2nd and 7th Battalions. While the enemy's attention was to be concentrated on the infantry assault against the main position, the New Zealand Corps, reinforced by the 8th Armoured Brigade and an assortment of Free Frenchmen, a total of twenty-four thousand men, was to make a wide detour round the left flank, a distance of some one hundred and sixty miles, and descend on the enemy from the rear through the El Hamma Gap. The popular conception that this stretch of desert was entirely impassable to vehicles had been dispelled by reconnaissances of the Long Range Desert Group in operations planned months before, perhaps by someone who remembered that every Maginot is apt to have its adjacent Ardennes.

The 7th Motor Brigade were to hold a part of the line centring round the western slopes of Tajira Chir while these battles were taking place. For those who had spent years in the desert it was a pleasant area. The 1st Battalion had experienced a gradual transition from the desert at El Agheila, through Homs and its palms, stopping in the comparatively fertile country near Tripoli, where they had leaguered "in an orchard in full bloom," to the edge of the Tunisian Plain. The 2nd and 7th Battalions had driven straight in a few days from the barrenness of Tmimi to this half-cultivated land, where in the spring green barley grew with patches of almond trees near the houses and small olive groves, even occasionally running water in the valleys. The surroundings of Medenine could hardly compare with the Vale of Evesham; but in this spring with a wonderful profusion of wild flowers the country looked surprisingly refreshing to these new arrivals from the desert proper. It may be that in these semi-desert countries all the soil's energy is devoted to the spring flowers before everything is withered up in the sun. However that may be, the war from now on until Tunis was captured was fought on a carpet of wild flowers such as few had ever seen.

It was clear after two days of fighting that the pattern of the battle would have to be changed. The brigades of the 50th Division who had penetrated into the defences on the 20th of March, were being heavily counter-attacked and the Wadi Zigzaou behind them was found to be practically impassable to tanks and entirely so to anti-tank guns. At the same time the left hook of the New Zealand Corps, after a brilliant initial success, had bumped serious opposition on the hills south of El Hamma. Once again the Germans were refusing to react to a threat to their rear which made their present positions logically untenable. The 1st Battalion was almost drawn into the 50th Division's battle. Colonel Freddie Stephens was ordered up to the 50th Division's Tactical Headquarters in the middle of the night. This entailed a nightmare drive along the dimly lighted track, threading his way through dust and prisoners and wounded, until among small sandhills and a great deal of shelling the Tactical Headquarters could be found. The noise was terrific: our own guns were firing defensive tasks; the whole machine-gun regiment was in action within a few hundred yards; the enemy mortars were plastering the area. An infantry battalion was slogging doggedly forward. There were miserable groups of stragglers wandering back to the assembly area. The 1st Battalion was due to take over the defence of the crossings. While the Colonel was waiting for his orders the plan of the whole battle was changed. General Montgomery decided not to persist with the 50th Division's operation but to exploit the success of the New Zealanders and at the same time to drive the enemy from the Matmata Hills from the south-east. The new plan affected all the battalions. The 1st Battalion, reprieved from its singularly unpleasant task in the north, was to take over the line in the area held by the 7th Motor Brigade. The 2nd and 7th Battalions, as part of the 1st Armoured Division, were to motor round by the desert route to join the New Zealand Corps.

While the Motor Brigade set off on their long journey the 1st Battalion was left holding the line. The companies were not entirely inactive. On the 25th of March the Battalion sent patrols to an intermediate feature on their left front called Djebel Saikra—intermediate because it formed one of the foothills of the Matmata Hills, rising sharply out of the plain but overlooked by higher ground to its west. They found that it was strongly held by the enemy. But the news of the left hook was good and the 4th Indian Division had begun to drive the enemy from the south of the Matmata Hills. It was clear that efforts would be made all along the Mareth Line to distract the enemy's attention from the increased weight of armour to his rear. An attack on the Djebel Saikra was ordered. On the 26th the Battalion moved up into a concealed position from which it was possible to observe the feature. The ground in front of it was open and heavily mined, except for a wadi some four hundred yards from the ridge itself. On the evening of the 26th "C" Battery, 5th Royal Horse Artillery, and a squadron of Sherman tanks of the 4th County of London Yeomanry came under command of the Battalion with a view to an attack on the feature in the morning. But that evening Bill Edwards, one of the best subalterns and son of a Rifleman, was blown up and killed by a mine when on patrol with his carrier platoon, sufficient reminder of the difficulties of the operation proposed for the next day.

The attack was made at dawn on the morning of the 27th of March by "I" Company, under Geoffrey Fletcher, on the right and "C" Company, under Noel Kelly, on the left. The battery and the Sherman squadrons were to concentrate their fire on the feature for five minutes before the attack went in. At a quarter to five all the companies had arrived on the start line on foot, "A" Company to remain there as a reserve and a firm base in case anything went wrong. At five o'clock the barrage lifted. The companies went straight in, at speed and without hesitation up the steep, bare slopes of the hillside in the face of heavy machine-gun fire from the deep-dug positions at the top. They went through two unmarked minefields, over a double-apron wire fence and straight at the opposition. By seven o'clock the south buttress of the feature was in our hands: it consisted of a narrow ridge running north and south and on it were captured about two hundred Italians of the Pistoia Division and all their equipment. By nine o'clock the remains of the regiment—three battalions in the Italian Army—had decamped and we were in possession of the entire feature. It was a distinctly unpleasant place, precipitous and isolated from the rest of the Brigade to the east, a difficult problem for maintenance with food, water and ammunition through a single lane in a minefield. Looked at from the enemy's position it was remarkable that we had succeeded in taking it. Owing to the pace at which the Battalion attacked, our casualties were only five riflemen killed and nine wounded. But the loss of officers was grave. Noel Kelly, described by his Colonel as "the best commander of a motor company I have ever seen," was killed in the hour of success, just as his men reached the summit. Geoffrey Fletcher, who had seemed to have a brilliant career as a scholar and games player in front of him, was killed early on in the attack. The loss of two such leaders seemed intolerable. Further, Timmy Cohen, though not killed, was desperately wounded in the minefield, losing a leg and breaking both arms. Yet none could deny the success of the attack, without great fire support and against long-prepared, seemingly impregnable positions on a rocky and horrible hill.

Meanwhile the 2nd and 7th Battalions had started off on the night of the 23rd of March on their approach march of a hundred and sixty-odd miles. In the prevailing excitement no fewer than four different battalions came in turn to take over from the 7th Battalion, with the result that they moved late and were hardly out of sight of the German observation posts when it grew light. The beginning of this trek was inauspicious, since the 4th Indian Division had been ordered to move to the south end of the Matmata Hills on the same night. The Eighth Army were unused to road movement. On this occasion there was only one route through Medenine. Both divisions arrived at the town at the same time and applied themselves at great speed to getting through it. The situation was further complicated by the fact that some Indian drivers, bewildered not unnaturally by the traffic signs put up by the rival divisions, drove in a circuit round and round the square. When the two battalions had sorted themselves out from Medenine they moved down the track to Foum Tatahouine and into the desert beyond. The route across country was rough and rocky. It had been churned up by the large number of vehicles which had already used it, and was by now feet deep in fine dust and, to make matters worse, a warm, south-easterly wind sprang up behind us. Progress was so slow that it was not possible to stop for any rest on the night of the 24th nor was there any halt on the 25th until about midnight on the 25th/26th, when the 2nd Battalion stopped for a few hours' sleep, though the 7th Battalion had no chance to stop at all.

By this time the vehicles had been on the move for forty-eight hours, covering about a hundred and forty miles. It was about 2 p.m. on the 26th of March by the time that the 2nd and 7th Battalions had concentrated in the assembly areas south-east of El Hamma and they were told at once that an attack would be put in at four o'clock in which they would be involved. There was just time to "brew up," wash off some of the worst of the dust and make preparations for this new battle in strange and unreconnoitred surroundings. This approach must rank with the greatest of the desert marches, comparable to that of the 2nd Battalion to Sidi Saleh in 1940, though this time it was the New Zealanders who had paved the way; a hundred and sixty miles of strange desert had been covered and the weight of the Eighth Army's punch had shifted decisively to its left.

Such a march should have been rewarded by a more successful battle. But the part played by the motor battalions in the battle for El Hamma was small. Perhaps if they had been used as a lead to the armour there might have been more to show for their efforts. The situation was that the New Zealanders, after initial success, mainly against Italians, found themselves opposed by Germans who had been hurried to the hills south of El Hamma to hold off this threat to the rear of Rommel's army. The plan was for the New Zealand Division, supported by the 8th Armoured Brigade, to force the enemy off the hills on either side of the El Hamma track so that the 1st Armoured Division, after their hasty move from Mareth, could push up the track and through El Hamma to cut off the main line of the German retreat from Mareth. The Royal Air Force, as a prelude to the New Zealanders' attack, were used for the first time in close support of the ground forces and gave a magnificent display of strafing and fighter-bombing.

During the afternoon the hot, south-easterly wind was still blowing, bringing with it, on this day, a swarm of locusts—the only occasion on which they are recorded as having intruded on the campaign. Visibility improved in time for the Royal Air Force attacks to go in. The New Zealanders drove the 21st Panzer Division from their positions. By last light the 1st Armoured Division, led by the Armoured Brigade, was advancing northwards along the track and, as it grew dark, the flames of burning enemy tanks shone brightly on either side. The Motor Brigade followed on behind them. It was a miserable night's march, without contact with the enemy but consisting of innumerable starts and stops, bumps and jerks, as drivers of the Armoured Brigade's echelon vehicles in front fell asleep or drove into slit trenches or failed to follow the tail light of the truck in front. It was all to no purpose. The enemy improvised anti-tank defences for El Hamma. The advance bogged down. When at last the Motor Brigade were employed it was to cut the track to the east of El Hamma in the hope of preventing the escape of the 21st Panzer Division. This manœuvre failed; for the enemy slipped away by a subsidiary track not marked on any of our maps. So by the end of the month the two battalions were almost more tired than they had ever been in the war and had to show for their extraordinary efforts and succession of sleepless nights nothing more concrete than a great many miles chalked on the speedometers of their trucks.

Although the battle from the point of view of the 2nd and 7th Battalions had been less conclusive than had at one time seemed likely, it represented a considerable success for the Army. The Axis forces had been driven out of the most formidable defences yet encountered in Africa and that with considerable loss to themselves. The Army was now well within Tunisia and finally out of the desert. Gabes was a small but definitely civilized town with white houses and gardens, and French civilians living not as colonists but as citizens of Metropolitan France. It was something strange and new to the Eighth Army to find such a civilization and to be confronted with any civilian problem at all.

It had at first been thought that the forcing of the Mareth Line would open the way for a swift advance to Sfax and Sousse. But a few miles west of Gabes the Wadi Akarit and the line of hills to its south offered a natural defensive position, flanked on one side by the sea and on the other by some utterly impassable country composed of rocky hills and salt marshes. When the last of the enemy had slipped away from El Hamma the Motor Brigade had at last struck the front. On the evening of the 30th of March the 7th Battalion, who had trailed across from Medenine as the last battalion in the whole division, was now the leading battalion of the Brigade and was slipped through El Hamma so as to be able to continue the advance the next day. At dawn on the 31st of March the 7th Battalion was ordered to send forward carrier patrols to find suitable routes for wheeled vehicles and to regain contact with the enemy. No contact was made; but one suitable route over difficult country which wheeled vehicles could traverse was found by "D" Company, although in doing so Eddie Gibbons, the company commander, was killed by a mine. By midday on the 31st the whole Eighth Army was approaching the Wadi Akarit positions, with the 1st Armoured Division on the extreme left. West of Gabes there was a stretch of broken, rough country with large patches of tall palms, much rock and in places deep, soft sand. It was drier and more of a desert than the Medenine Plain, although there was much barley under cultivation. Out of this comparatively low ground the hills of Akarit rose, dry, rocky and sharp-toothed. Those who have passed through Aden and have seen in the hills a glimpse of the mountains of Hell can best imagine the appearance of this range. Only in the early morning when the sunrise caught and tinted them or in the evenings with a series of bright-coloured spring sunsets as a backcloth did the Akarit Hills seem part of the habitable world.

Horrible or not, there was just a chance that a passage might be forced through these hills and the main Akarit positions turned. At about 2 p.m. Brigadier Jimmy Bosvile, commanding the Motor Brigade, ordered his three motor battalions to try to work their way through by one of the four tracks which appeared from the map and from local information to be passable. The 60th Rifles and the 2nd Battalion early discovered that their routes were either impossibly rough or strongly held. Perhaps their information, entirely correct in their own areas, may have influenced the commanders too readily to give up all serious idea of penetrating this difficult country.

The 7th Battalion's task was to try to force the most westerly pass of all between Djebel el Beida and Djebel Hadoudi. It was, perhaps, because the approach was so intricate that the manœuvre so nearly succeeded. The Battalion marched for seven miles in the dark. "A" Company went astray, but the remainder found themselves at the mouth of the pass. They went straight in to the attack, "D" Company led by Billie Becher fixing swords and charging. The attack was successful and by five-thirty in the morning the pass was very definitely in our hands. As it got light it was clear that the enemy on the hills on either side of the track held commanding positions from which they overlooked the companies. From the beginning there was much machine-gun fire and shelling, and within an hour or two of first light the enemy, severely shaken by this unexpected penetration into the heart of their position, had rushed German reinforcements and anti-tank guns to the area. The Battalion looked anxiously over their shoulders for the appearance of the 2nd Armoured Brigade, whose way through the defile was still open. But no armour could be seen. To make matters worse, the field guns were out of range to support us and the medium regiment originally on call to the Royal Horse Artillery observation post had been moved away elsewhere. By the time the leading armoured regiment came in sight the enemy's forces were stronger, the Battalion already much weakened. It hung on in the teeth of mortar and artillery fire, more than usually effective on this rocky ground, until ten o'clock. Then the order was given to withdraw.

It was a sorely battered Battalion that reassembled. Three officers had been killed, nine wounded and two wounded and missing. Of the other Riflemen, four were known to be killed, seventy-five were wounded and sixty-two unaccounted for, of whom over twenty were later known to have been killed and most of the rest wounded. This was a heavy list of casualties, particularly when the assaulting strength of a motor battalion is remembered, at this time perhaps forty or fifty to a company. The attack had, in fact, achieved nothing. Yet had it been, as originally envisaged, followed up by the Armoured Brigade with the support of the Divisional artillery, there would have been every chance of a complete break-through, of turning the whole Akarit position, probably cutting off great numbers of the enemy and at any rate making unnecessary the Battle of Akarit and the casualties which that entailed. It was one of the few occasions when a single battalion could influence the immediate course of the campaign. The 7th Battalion came near to achieving a decisive and far-reaching success. It was not their fault that their dash, opportunism and gallantry were not exploited at all.

The Army now set about, in its by now usual and inexorable manner, the preparations for a set-piece attack on the Akarit position. During this process the luck of the 7th Battalion remained "out." Three riflemen were killed by bombs, and Regimental Sergeant-Major Worboys was wounded by a shell. The 1st Battalion moved up through the minefields and booby-traps of the Mareth defences and by the 6th of April was waiting at El Hamma for the main battle to begin. In complete contrast to earlier operations of this magnitude the assault was to be made not at the full moon in the first half of the night but now at once in the early morning after a dark night. The 4th Indian Division was to attack the hills silently in the dark—and how well they did it! For the Gurkhas in particular it was good casting. The 51st (Highland) Division were to attack across the Wadi Akarit at dawn, supported by a large number of guns even according to the standards of the time. The armoured divisions, with the battalions of the Regiment, were to exploit the breakthrough and surge up the main Tunisian Plain through the Forest of Olives to Tunis. The attack was timed for the 7th of April.

As a result of the success of the attack on the Akarit position the 1st Armoured Division moved through the gaps in the defences made by the 4th Indian Division and out into the plain. This part of Tunisia, particularly in the spring, is very definitely not desert. The olive groves stretch for miles: there are orchards of almonds and other fruit trees: much corn is cultivated: in April grass and wild flowers cover the land. Though the country was farmed it was still possible to move with considerable freedom off the roads, cactus hedges being the most serious obstacles to be met. Threatened by the Americans from Gafsa as well as by the Eighth Army, the Germans had decided not to try to hold the southern end of the plain, although they intended to deny us the use of the ports of Sfax and Sousse for as long as possible.

The Motor Brigade spent the first few days of the pursuit following the armour and taking over prisoners. It was not seriously engaged with the enemy and was halted for administrative reasons near the cluster of airfields at La Fauconnerie. The 7th Battalion made themselves at home in the village of Bouthardi, where they were welcomed warmly by the French inhabitants but with some reserve by the Arabs. Here they were introduced for the first time to the latest of the German inventions, the butterfly bomb, a cluster of which landed unannounced in Battalion Headquarters in the night.

The 1st Battalion, with the 22nd Armoured Brigade, followed up the 51st (Highland) Division at Akarit and passed through them at about 7 p.m. in pursuit of the enemy. Their advance was nearer the coast than the Motor Brigade's and they had, therefore, a more eventful time. On the first day "A" Company, with the 4th County of London Yeomanry, had a successful little action, capturing some five hundred prisoners. On the 8th of April a thousand prisoners had been taken by midday. That afternoon "C" Company, with the 1st Royal Tanks, came up with a column of German vehicles near El Aggareb. It was the first battle they had had since Noel Kelly had been killed. They went straight in, mounted in their vehicles with every weapon firing, and within ten minutes twenty-three German lorries were burning, while the tanks had destroyed three Mark III's and two half-tracked armoured cars. No pause was made to count the dead, but the number of German and Italian bodies made an impression even on the experienced fighters of the 22nd Armoured Brigade. The pursuit was continued through the vast Forest of Olives towards Sfax, parallel with the Highlanders on the main road. Occasional tanks and self-propelled guns lay up hidden to delay our advance; mines and booby-traps abounded. Olive trees hold their branches at an awkward height for those in armoured vehicles and both sides blundered on occasion into each other. Colonel Freddie Stephens at one time drove in the Battalion control car straight up to a German Mark II tank which was luckily looking in the other direction so that a hasty and unreconnoitred retreat could be made in time.

On the 9th the Battalion blocked the northern exits from Sfax. But most of the enemy had already gone. Some of the Battalion had a glimpse of the destruction wrought by the Royal Air Force in the town. The advance continued and the Brigade moved westwards through Kairouan, disappointing to the casual passer-by, although it holds wonderful carpets and tapestries for those who have time to look. By this time—the 13th of April—the Army was closing up to the Enfidaville Line, the last natural defensive position before Tunis. Once again hills rose out of the plain. The Battalion operated on the left of the Army from Sidi Abdul Kader, about twenty miles inland from Enfidaville, and from the 19th onwards pushed patrols north towards Pont du Fahs. The French, under the First Army, were operating in this area and touch was kept with them. Prisoners were taken in these patrols, but no opening was found to lead into the enemy's stronghold.

It was clear that an operation on a large scale must be made by the First and Eighth Armies together to break into this defended area. It had become a habit to expect the main offensive from the direction of the Eighth Army. After the extreme gallantry of the New Zealand attack on Takrouna a plan was hatched to drive round the coast, where the plain is three thousand yards wide and thoroughly overlooked by the defences on the mountains. On the 27th the 1st Battalion was prepared and waiting with some apprehension for this unpalatable operation to begin. The plan was changed: the emphasis was shifted to the west; the final assault on the last foothold of the Axis in North Africa was to be launched from the area of the First Army. The 2nd and 7th Battalions had already moved round to the command of this army. Now in the last days of April the 7th Armoured Division and with it the 1st Battalion set off to join them. The 10th Battalion was there already. Four battalions of the Regiment were to be engaged in the last battle in Africa.

CHAPTER XV

NORTH AFRICA: ALGERIA AND TUNISIA

WITH the exception of the isolated expedition to Calais, the fortunes of the Regiment had been bound up with the war in the desert, a type of country which had suited the characteristics of a motor battalion. Mobility was not complicated by the incidence of traffic blocks. But while the four battalions were operating in Africa two Territorial battalions embodied in the Corps of the Regiment at the outbreak of war were training in England for the invasion of the continent of Europe. The 2nd Battalion The London Rifle Brigade, now the 8th Battalion of the Regiment, was a motor battalion in the 11th Armoured Division. As such it came near to being employed in the North African fighting. But the Division was reprieved to continue its training for what was generally considered to be a more important task. The 2nd Battalion Tower Hamlets Rifles, embodied as the 10th Battalion, formed part of the 6th Armoured Division and in the autumn of 1942 was commanded by Colonel Adrian Gore. It had trained as a motor battalion for use in European country and had taken part in the various exercises in England designed to prepare for the capture of Paris and Berlin. It had already made the acquaintance of two of the enemies in any war outside the desert; mud and the traffic block were as familiar to its members as they were strange to the desert battalions.

It was the 10th Battalion which was involved in the surprise invasion of Algeria. Troops in England in 1942 had not, I think, expected to take part in a landing in North Africa; certainly most of the Eighth Army were taken by surprise by the wireless announcement of the Allied landings to their west. The First Army's training in England was not wasted, for the coastal areas of Algeria and Tunisia bear little resemblance to the wide spaces of the Libyan desert. This part of Africa enjoys a considerable annual rainfall, a fact which was to strike the 10th Battalion only too forcibly on arrival, so that the whole of the area in which fighting took place, the north-west of Tunisia, is under cultivation. Along much of the coast are cork forests such as are found in Spain. The motor battalion was not employed in this country—for forests and armour do not go well together—and thus missed any chance of making the acquaintance of what must be about the only pack of hounds in North Africa. South of the cork forests the hills rise sharply. There is a ridge on the borders of Algeria and Tunisia as green as anywhere in England and in the winter as muddy. In the spring the hawthorn and apple blossom are far from African in appearance; you can hear a cuckoo or see a pair of otters cross the road. The French have given one of the villages on the main road across these hills the name of La Verdure. East of these hills the country has been described as resembling Ayrshire, only that the valleys are wider, shallower and more sandy but including belts of sticky clay. Constantine, seen from a distance, is said to have reminded one officer of a Cotswold town, standing on two high hills with a deep cleft between. Towards Tunis itself the steeper hills give way to rolling uplands, cultivated with arable, not unlike the uplands of Syria or even the Berkshire Downs in a dry year of drought. There are other places where pine trees and a local species of ling are like nothing so much as Chobham Ridges or a part of Bagshot Heath.

The whole of this area is farmed. There are vineyards and acres of olive groves, rolling cornfields, almond trees and cactus hedges. Farm buildings, huddled together surrounded by trees, are dotted everywhere. The farmers are often Frenchmen; for the Arabs live mainly in the villages. The country carries a fair head of stock, strongly built cattle and oxen, and everywhere it is evident from the horses tethered about the pasture that this is the home of the Barb. The French are naturally proud of their success in developing and colonizing the coastal areas of these two countries, and their predominance is visible particularly in the architecture of the coastal towns.

The character of war in such a country was certain to differ from that in the desert. For one thing there were large areas in which it was impossible to move vehicles off the road. In the desert anyone finding a house and occupying it was asking to be bombed or shelled, since it would be the only conspicuous target to be seen for miles around. In Tunisia there were enough houses and farm buildings to make their occupation a justifiable risk. With houses there arose the problem of dealing with their inhabitants. The French, despite the Vichy Government, could be expected to be friendly; and the vast majority of them were. The Arabs had been promised independence by the Germans, and by their nature could hardly be as helpful or as useful as the French. In either case the existence of civilians at all was another element in the fighting which had been absent in the Western Desert. Refugees would be a problem; the movements of inhabitants would give some indication of the whereabouts of the enemy; their reports would serve to increase the fog of war; their property would provide a temptation to the soldier such as had not been offered by the sparse contents of a Bedouin tent.

The British forces involved in the operations in Algeria were not to be employed in the initial landings. It was thought that memories of Oran would still be fresh. But after the Americans had paved the way the British were to attempt to slip a small, mobile force—a strong column and a parachute brigade—through to Tunis before the Germans could garrison that town. The 6th Armoured Division was to provide the armoured component and "B" Company of the 10th Battalion was to go with this party as the motor company to work with the armour. The remainder of the Battalion was to land later with the rest of the Division as soon as the administrative build-up allowed and take part in any operations that might be necessary after that.

So it was that "B" Company embarked before the rest of the Battalion. David Elkington commanded and Teddy Goschen was his second-in-command. The convoy sailed from England without anyone knowing officially where they were going. The voyage was uneventful. In mid-Atlantic the news of the company's destination was given out. On the 8th of November, 1942, the Americans made their first landings and four days afterwards the convoy sailed into the Bay of Algiers and "B" Company landed in that strange mixture of Eastern squalor and French civilization, the white-walled city of flies and beggars and the best Parisian scent.

During the next two days "Bladeforce" assembled at Arba, just outside Algiers. It consisted of the 17th/21st Lancers, "C" Battery, 12th Royal Horse Artillery, "A" Battery of the 72nd Anti-Tank Regiment, Royal Artillery, "B" Company of the

10th Battalion, "B" Squadron of the 1st Derbyshire Yeomanry (Armoured Cars), a troop of Sappers, a troop of light anti-aircraft guns and a transport platoon of the Royal Army Service Corps. The whole force was commanded by Colonel Dick Hull with an improvised headquarters and a small staff. While they collected their vehicles and prepared to go forward, the intricate political wrangles of Admiral Darlan and the Vichy Government followed their unedifying course. On the 11th of November the Germans had marched into "unoccupied" France: most of the French in Africa were gradually declaring against the Axis. But when Bladeforce moved forward from its concentration area it was not certain that the Germans and Italians would seize Tunis or that the French would oppose them.

On the 15th of November the wheeled part of Bladeforce set off by road. The tracked vehicles moved by train to the assembly area. They were to concentrate at Souk Arras, just short of the Tunisian border and some sixty miles from Tunis itself, there to form the armoured component of the small British force which was to try to capture the city by a *coup de main*. It was a drive of four hundred miles, accomplished in pouring rain within forty-eight hours. On that memorable drive they passed through Constantine, across the mountains and over the frontier into the foothills which border the plain, of which Tunis on the sea is the centre. There were friendly, though hardly enthusiastic, French farmers, sullen Arabs and endless strings of horse transport plodding towards the east. The road itself—the route nationale—is a good one, according to the standards of Africa, though more than one motor-bicycle left it far enough to stick in the mud.

On the 18th the company was told to take up a defensive position east of Le Kef—an Arab town high in the bare hills on the railway from Tunis. When they reached the place they found French troops already in position and apparently determined to fight the Germans. They took up positions behind them. By this time the administrative situation and particularly petrol supply had become hazardous in the extreme. There followed a series of short moves north to Souk el Arba, to Terboursouk, then to Testour with a detachment at Sloughia. On the 21st German aeroplanes made the first of many appearances, Stukas bombing the buildings in Testour. That same day the rumours of German ground forces in the vicinity took definite shape and the French made contact with them at Sloughia. Out of the fog of war there emerged the answer to the two most pressing problems which had faced Bladeforce before they set out. The Germans had arrived in unknown strength in time to bar the road to Tunis: the French were on our side—and fighting. It was no longer a race to reach an undefended Tunis. In the race to build up forces to capture the city the German Air Force, with its adjacent airfields, was to play a decisive part.

On the 22nd the company was relieved by the 2nd Battalion The Northamptonshire Regiment and moved south again to Le Kef, where contact was made with an American tank battalion. By now it was a case of harbouring in the olive groves hoping that the enemy aircraft would not detect the vehicles. On the 24th Bladeforce, with slightly more adequate supplies of petrol, moved north to Beja with the object of finding a way into Tunis and Bizerta by the northern route south of Mateur through the Chouigi Pass. Despite the rumours of landings in force by the Germans at Sfax and Sousse it was hoped that this way would still be open.

The advance began at half past six and by half past nine the Derbyshire Yeomanry reported that enemy, who had apparently come from the north, were in occupation of some farm buildings on high ground at the junction of the main road and that leading south from Mateur. The carrier platoon, commanded by Ken Dale, did a reconnaissance on the right of the road and reported the ground suitable for our tanks: an enemy tank was identified on the position. Soon after eleven o'clock the 17th/21st Lancers put in an attack, the company following up to mop up. Jim Wilson's platoon on the right cleared its area; but on the left Tony Nauman's platoon met more formidable opposition. A carrier went up on a mine; the platoon commander was wounded so badly that he lost his sight. The reserve platoon with further tank support took a hand and by one o'clock the area was clear of enemy, and a hundred and ten prisoners, mainly Italian but including some Germans, and three Italian tanks had been captured. The company had lost Corporal Mister and Rifleman Hooper killed and one officer and five riflemen wounded in its first action. They were within ten miles of Tunis.

For the rest of that day the company took up a defensive position facing north on the ground they had won, as a flank guard to the main advance. Throughout the 26th, 27th and 28th they remained there, not in contact with the enemy but subjected to bombing and machine-gunning at frequent intervals by day and night. It was impossible to continue the advance on Tunis while enemy forces from Mateur threatened the left flank. To hold off these forces a parachute battalion also took up a position to the north of the company. The toll of casualties to men and vehicles increased as time went on. Meanwhile the tanks had been held up at Djedida and on the 29th we were relieved by the Lancashire Fusiliers and moved off to hold the pass at Chouigi. Here on the 1st of December German tanks and infantry appeared soon after dawn moving south towards them. The Luftwaffe began to strafe and bomb: the enemy moved round to the left of the position. The Royal Horse Artillery and then our own tanks engaged the enemy, but by nine o'clock a story already familiar to the desert battalions, though strange as yet to the 10th, could once again be told. Our tanks were outgunned and outnumbered. The order was given to withdraw to the north-east corner of Tebourba. By this time 8 Platoon was practically cut off and a heavy air attack on its vehicles and riflemen made matters worse. Only a small part of this platoon could be extricated. The carriers were, however, able to withdraw across country, although they lost three by enemy action on the way. When the force reorganized near Tebourba, harassed by the now usual air attacks, everyone knew that the *coup de main* had failed. The Germans, with the shorter lines of communication, though at great risk from naval and air attack as they crossed the Mediterranean, had succeeded in building up their forces more quickly than we could. Yet our thrust had nearly succeeded: it had got closer to Tunis than would any of our troops until the following May, though no one at the time could have thought it.

Until the 21st of December "B" Company took no part in operations, as they were awaiting an opportunity to re-equip. But when our positions at Medjez-el-Bab were threatened the company found itself again in the line for a few days, though not seriously engaged, in position on what became known as Banana Ridge, the scene later of some of the fiercest fighting of the winter and spring. However, by the 27th the situation was such that the company could rejoin the 10th Battalion at El Arrousa for the first time since leaving England. Their total casualties had amounted to two officers and forty-five riflemen, and they had taken part in a memorable march and a series of operations which, had they succeeded despite the power of the hostile air force, would have become historic and of far-reaching importance out of all proportion to their scale.

While "B" Company were concerned in the attempted *coup de main* to capture Tunis the rest of the Battalion loaded up and set sail for North Africa as part of the build-up of the British forces in that theatre. For the majority of the Battalion the only excitement of the voyage was a collision between two ships at Gibraltar which necessitated the transfer of "A" and "D" Companies to a smaller vessel. On the 7th of December, a month after the initial landings by the Americans, the Battalion disembarked at Bone. On this date two companies of the 1st Battalion returned from the front at Agheila to Tobruk and the 2nd and 7th Battalions were continuing their training at Tmimi. Bone is a small port, very French in appearance with cobbled streets and tall, grey-gabled houses, such as you might expect to find in Normandy. Besides its importance as a harbour there are various factories and wine warehouses in the town and its neighbourhood. The Battalion was at first billeted in a tobacco factory. But Bone at that time was attracting the attention of the Luftwaffe, and a move was made every evening to bivouac in the sand-dunes in comparative safety. By the 19th of December the vehicles had arrived, with the exception of "D" Company's carriers, which had been sunk complete. Sergeant O'Brien, who was with them, fortunately survived, drifting ashore on a raft. From Gibraltar he went to Bone on H.M.S. *Dido*, but by the time he arrived the Battalion had moved on and he was sent back to Gibraltar in a minesweeper, as he had no equipment and was therefore suspect to the military mind! Undeterred, however, he stowed away, and after hiding during the voyage he landed in Algiers, whence he hitch-hiked five hundred miles to rejoin the Battalion near Bou Arada.

With the arrival of their vehicles the Battalion was ready to take part in the war. The campaign as far as it was concerned can be divided into three phases. There was first the initial attempt to reach Tunis with which "B" Company was concerned. Soon after it was clear that this had failed it also became apparent that the Germans, with their interior lines, were likely to build up a local superiority in strength and equipment and particularly in aircraft, if not in numbers. Throughout the winter the 6th Armoured Division was employed to stop the various gaps that appeared from time to time in the heterogeneous line which stretched southward from the sea. In this second phase the Battalion had much fighting and many moves and was often obliged to detach companies or even platoons for long periods. As the weather improved and reinforcements arrived and the Eighth Army approached from the east, the time came for the final offensive to capture Tunis and clear North Africa of the Germans. In these operations the 10th Battalion had again a prominent part.

When the Battalion moved eastwards to Testour on the 19th of December the repulse of Bladeforce and the rumoured arrival of numbers of German tanks were the talk of the rear areas. It was a two-day drive to Testour. The country there was described as "not unlike Scotland" and they enjoyed "Scotch weather, although it can be really hot on a fine day and really wet on a wet one." Continuous and torrential rain, endured in the inadequate shelter of an olive grove, was a suitable introduction to the Tunisian winter. There were also rumours of an attack to be made on Christmas Day which failed to materialize owing to the weather. On the 24th of December the Battalion moved to Sidi Ayed, about twenty miles to the southward. It was from this area on Christmas Night that the Battalion's active participation in the campaign began. Two patrols were sent out, and one of these, commanded by Ronald Sturgess, had an encounter with the enemy, one rifleman being wounded. It was here, too, that the Battalion had their first experience of working with their French allies in the form of a battalion of Spahis, who were holding the Bou Arada area. In co-operation with them an ambush was laid at a farm which German armoured cars were said to visit daily. Despite the evacuation of the buildings by the French inhabitants to the accompaniment of much noise and many lights and an attempt by some Arabs to warn the enemy of our presence, two Germans were killed and much experience was gained of the best method of dealing with enemy, allies and inhabitants. On the 26th of December "B" Company rejoined the Battalion, which they had last seen in England. On the 30th of December two German eight-wheeler armoured cars swooped down on the drivers of the Colonel's Humber and a scout car while they were "brewing

North Africa: Algeria and Tunisia

up," killing one driver and capturing the other, and removed the scout car to their lines. On the next day the Adjutant, Tony Henley, and Mike Welman drove over a mine and the latter was badly wounded. Such incidents are typical of a period when our troops were in contact with the enemy on an indeterminate front, neither side indulging in anything more spectacular than patrolling and daylight reconnaissance.

On the 2nd of January the Battalion moved to the area of Bou Arada. This was a small town in the centre of what came to be known as the Bou Arada Vale, a comparatively low-lying stretch of country of rolling cornfields surrounded by hills. All four battalions were to know it before Tunis was captured. For the first week activity was confined to night patrolling and laying ambushes. But the Germans in the Bou Arada Vale were seldom quiet for long. There was in the Battalion area a feature known as Two Tree Hill, manned daily by the Derbyshire Yeomanry as an observation post and occupied by them each morning at first light. From this hill a good view of the German positions could be had. It was therefore not unnatural that the Germans should ambush the Yeomanry troop as they arrived. This occurred on the 10th of January and the enemy then began to install themselves on a neighbouring ridge which dominated Bou Arada and the roads leading into it. "A" Company and a squadron of the 17th/21st Lancers were ordered to turn them off this ridge. They were successful in this at the cost of two casualties, although they were opposed by two infantry companies, who after some early resistance withdrew at last light. "C" Company were sent to help consolidate on the high ground north of Bou Arada. The enemy, however, remained on Two Tree Hill and the next day "D" Company, supported by one squadron of the 17th/21st Lancers, attacked this position. Preliminary reconnaissance had disclosed little sign of the enemy and the company approached the hill riding on the tanks. But the Germans were occupying positions on the reverse slope of the hill from which they brought down heavy mortar and machine-gun fire on "D" Company, who were quite unable to get forward. They eventually retired with the loss of two officers wounded, three riflemen killed and ten wounded. Only smart work by the tanks enabled them to get off so lightly. Two Tree Hill was attacked by forces of varying sizes three times after this during the campaign, but was never taken, being evacuated by the Germans at the end of April when outflanked by the British offensive up the Goubellat Plain.

About three miles east of Bou Arada was another feature, called the Argoub el Hanech, similar to Two Tree Hill and also manned daily by observation posts. In order to forestall the enemy in any attempt to seize this high ground two platoons of "C" Company were sent on to it on the 17th of January. These platoons were reinforced on the 18th by the remainder of "C" Company and all "B" Company, who arrived on the Argoub just before first light. The rest of the Battalion remained at Bou Arada. Before they had well settled in they observed a German tank battalion, followed by infantry and self-propelled guns, coming down the road by which they had themselves just driven to their present position. The Germans passed within half a mile of them. Since, as a result of this manœuvre, they were some two miles behind the enemy and in an area which the Germans might well consider worth clearing, the two companies watched the battle for Bou Arada with some apprehension. They saw the enemy driven off with loss, but had one more taste of the inferiority of British armour when the Valentine tanks which followed up the German withdrawal were easily dealt with by the Mark III's. That Bou Arada was held was a distinct relief to "B" and "C" Companies, since its loss would inevitably have meant that they were cut off from the rest of the Division. They made no contribution to the battle themselves except for sending a patrol commanded by Tony Pawson to lay mines across the road down which the Germans were withdrawing. These succeeded in blowing up a German jeep in full view of the minelayers. On the 19th the whole Battalion moved up to the Argoub. This resulted in heavy enemy shelling, particularly on Battalion Headquarters and "D" Company, during which Dick Elkington was killed.

For the next three weeks there was a constant succession of moves centring round the Argoub. Sometimes one company would occupy this feature, sometimes the whole Battalion. At other times a parachute battalion would take over. Whether on the Argoub or elsewhere in the Bou Arada Vale during that winter, the Battalion had to contend with torrential rain and icy winds. It was particularly unsuitable weather for those motor-bicyclists whose machines had not already succumbed to the mud. Many night patrols had to be done during this time.

Most of them passed without incident and are forgotten by all except those who took part in them. But one patrol vanished completely to the accompaniment of much firing by the enemy, and during another Tony Pawson, having climbed a tree to observe the locality, found at first light that he was in the middle of a German platoon area—and marched out straight between two sections without being challenged!

It was the 14th of February before the game of general post and night patrols was over. By that time the success of the German offensive against the Americans in the south was sufficient to cause readjustments to be made on the whole front. On that date—it was the day on which the 1st Battalion crossed the Tunisian frontier from the east—"A" Company were ordered to move off south to Kessera with the rest of the 16th/5th Lancers Regimental Group. It was clear that the German advance had made rapid progress across the plain. They were now approaching the hills through which movement of vehicles was impossible except by the various passes where roads had been constructed. "A" Company were sent off to El Ala to hold the road there. But the German armour, after a preliminary reconnaissance and exchange of shots, made off in other directions.

By the 19th of February "C" Company, though not the anti-tank platoon, had rejoined the Battalion just north of the town of Thala. As soon as they had arrived Colonel Adrian Gore was ordered to take a small composite force south to the Kasserine Pass. This force was to consist of one squadron of tanks of the Lothians and Border Horse, a battery of 25-pounders and a troop of anti-tank guns, Battalion Headquarters and "C" Company. "B" and "D" Companies remained in position near Thala. The value of this force was largely discounted by the fact that the tanks were Valentines, no match, however gallantly they were fought, for any of the German tanks. The object of the dispatch of this party was to prevent the enemy infiltrating round the flanks of the Americans, who were holding the Kasserine Pass. The road here rises from the plains and ascends by a series of ridges with high, bare hills on either side. By the time the Colonel reached the pass it was four in the morning of the 20th of February and the situation was far from clear. The Colonel wisely but narrowly avoided motoring into the Germans himself and used "C" Company's carriers under Bob

Fairweather to make contact. This they did, losing two carriers in the process. Some confused fighting followed, both American armour and our Valentines being concerned. But before long it was clear that German tanks had broken through the defences on the pass. They were therefore well placed for an inroad into the rear areas of the whole First Army. The Colonel's force must delay their advance at all costs, since every hour that was gained offered more chance of concentrating the 26th Armoured Brigade in the rear. "C" Company was dug in with the anti-tank guns, while the rest of the force fought for as long as they could. The German self-propelled guns did great damage and as the day went on all the officers of the Royal Horse Artillery battery were killed. The Lothians fought their way gradually back until at dusk the last Valentine was set on fire. The force, having lost all the tanks and one anti-tank gun, moved back some four miles nearer Thala, where an anti-tank defence was organized and four American-manned Grant tanks were added to its strength. By two o'clock on the morning of the 21st the enemy tanks had come up and had begun to fire tracer in the direction of the Grants. As soon as these replied they were set on fire by the German tanks, who advanced to deal with the anti-tank guns by the same process, a task made easier for them by the light from the glare of the burning Grants. The force, which by this time consisted to all intents and purposes of "C" Company only, now retired and at dawn passed through the rest of the Brigade, having delayed the enemy as best they could. While the Brigade fought a desperate tank battle, outranged and under-gunned as they were, and a battalion of the Leicestershire Regiment dug in just south of Thala, the Colonel's force was withdrawn behind both of these and was joined by "B" Company. "A" Company were holding a position west of Thala, but the Germans bypassed it and the company sat unmolested throughout the battle, hearing the sounds of fighting to north and south.

As it grew dark on the evening of the 21st of February the Lothians and the 17th/21st Lancers, after a day of fierce, uneven fighting, came in to harbour near the Battalion. Suddenly some tanks following behind them opened fire on "B" and "C" Companies. They were enemy who had passed through the Leicestershire Regiment, led, according to one story, by a captured Valentine, and motored into the harbour close on the tails of the Brigade—a stratagem used at one time by German aircraft, who followed our bombers when they came in to their airfield, but hitherto unknown on land. One of these tanks, passing near a rifleman of 12 Platoon who was digging a slit trench, was invited by the digger to "keep away from my ——— trench, you're knocking it in," a remark which sent a revolver bullet whistling past his ear. Confusion in the harbour was extreme. The Germans shouted in good English "Hands up —come out; surrender to the panzers." It was almost impossible to distinguish which were our tanks in the dark until a gunner scored a direct hit on a German tank so that it went up in flames. By the light of this fire nine German tanks were soon ablaze and their daring attempt was thwarted. No German motor infantry were in evidence, although for the rest of the night alarms were many and firing profuse.

Throughout the 22nd, while the tanks tried unsuccessfully to dislodge the enemy from what was now known as Leicester Ridge, the Battalion was shelled, dive-bombed and strafed. There was every indication that an attack was imminent. But nothing materialized. On the 23rd reconnaissance showed that there were no enemy on Leicester Ridge, which was occupied by "C" Company, being reinforced at night by the Coldstream Guards. The German offensive had petered out just when it had seemed most dangerous. The Armoured Brigade must have been largely responsible for halting it and the 10th Battalion thus had a part in one of the decisive actions of the campaign.

It remained for "C" Company, as part of a regimental group, to follow up the enemy's retirement towards the Kasserine Pass, a process which gave them early experience of German thoroughness in mining and demolitions. On the 25th of February, when the 24th Guards Brigade had retaken the pass, the whole Battalion retired to Ebn Ksour to rest.

In three days' time there was a move at speed to Medjez-el-Bab in anticipation of a German attack. No such attack developed and after a spell on the Argoub once more the Battalion finally concentrated on the 17th of March west of Le Kef, a town in the hills inhabited mainly by Arabs, where the armoured regiments were being re-equipped with Sherman tanks, so that their inferiority in range and armament no longer existed and they could meet the Germans at least on equal terms. While the Brigade was training with its new equipment Brigadier Charles Dunphie left it and the Battalion came under the command of

Brigadier Pip Roberts, who had already known the 1st Battalion in the 22nd Armoured Brigade and was to have the 8th in his division.

The failure of the Axis offensive against the First Army and at Medenine put a term on their continued existence in Africa. The First Army was built up with new arms and more modern equipment; and the Eighth drove the enemy from Mareth and Akarit into the Tunisian Plain. With the spring came an improvement in the weather and the 10th Battalion, who had borne the various vicissitudes of the campaign, early success followed by disappointment, the defensive battles of the winter, the depth of the German thrusts, was now on the crest of the wave. But the battle for Tunis was to be no walk-over. It is not enough to put the Germans in a hopeless position: they must always be utterly defeated.

In conjunction with the Eighth Army's attacks at Akarit the First Army was to burst out into the Tunisian Plain, thus threatening the communications of the Afrika Korps with Tunis. The 6th Armoured Division's part in this operation was to force its way out into the plains of Kairouan through the Fondouk Pass, a narrow descent made by road and railway dominated on either side by steep hills. On the 4th of April the Brigade moved south to Maktar over roads where the mud had now become dust, to concentrate near Jebltrozza. The plan for the capture of the pass envisaged a joint operation by the Americans and ourselves.

The infantry attack was, as so often, only a partial success. The pass was still overlooked by the enemy, who brought down heavy fire upon the approaches to it. At that moment—it was the 8th of April—news was received that the 10th Panzer Division retiring in front of the Eighth Army was about to present a vulnerable flank to us if we could cross this last barrier between ourselves and the plains. The Armoured Brigade was ordered to "force the pass." The 17th/21st Lancers suffered heavy losses on a minefield and "C" Company with them came under intense fire. Towards evening the 16th/5th Lancers found a way round the left flank and turned the enemy's anti-tank screen. "A" Company, under Bobby Selway, were with them and it was largely due to the scout platoon that the action was successful. Four enemy anti-tank guns were sited on two steep hillocks which could be approached only over completely open country. Owing to difficulties of deployment in the narrow area of passable going these guns were holding up the tanks effectively. Two sections of the carrier platoon motored across this open ground under cover of the tanks' guns, dismounted and, led by Jack Toms, charged the guns on the nearest hillock, killing or capturing their crews. From this position they then brought fire from their Bren guns to bear on the other hill, killing or driving away the crews of the remaining guns. The 16th/5th Lancers were thus able to resume their advance.

Although the other two armoured regiments were passed through this gap, there was still much mine clearance to do and the Battalion had to sit for hours under heavy shell fire, suffering casualties at intervals throughout the day, and imagining that with every moment the 10th Panzer Division was escaping across their front to the north.

The next day the 10th Battalion had their first taste of pursuit. They were clear of the hills and into the plains, now covered with wild flowers such as few had ever seen. The dead-flat country—and desert formation—was a new experience. For three days Bobby Selway "sailed along in his carrier in a sea of tanks with all guns firing, and Germans giving themselves up for miles around." No Germans surrendered more readily than the members of a penal battalion whose officers had decamped with all their transport. Towards evening on the first day the 16th/5th Lancers and "A" Company caught up with the tail of the 10th Panzer Division, and destroyed some fourteen enemy tanks. But the next morning just as we were starting off on the pursuit "A" Company were heavily dive-bombed and Jack Toms, fresh from his notable action at Fondouk, was hit by a bomb and killed. On the foothills north of the Kairouan Plain the enemy had reorganized with anti-tank guns and Tiger tanks and were strong enough to call a halt to this short and sharp pursuit. The Battalion did advance the next day as far as Sbikha, where Sergeant Metcalfe took forty prisoners with his carrier section. But now it was clear that a further battle would be needed to drive the Germans from Africa. The 10th Battalion was withdrawn and on the 17th of April went into a concentration area north of Bou Arada in a valley screened from the enemy by a large, scrub-covered hill.

The 1st Armoured Division from the Eighth Army, with the 2nd and 7th Battalions, now appeared in the Bou Arada Vale and, I think, from the point of view of the 10th their own private war with the Germans was over. A joint effort by troops of both armies was required to complete the capture of Tunis. In this final round the 10th Battalion was to play as great a part as it had in all the fighting in Tunisia, in Bladeforce, on Two Tree Hill, in the vital operations at Thala, in forcing the Fondouk Pass and in the innumerable night patrols and minor unrecorded actions which make up the real history of campaigns for the individuals of a battalion and take a constant toll of killed and wounded and steadily wear out the nerves.

CHAPTER XVI

THE FALL OF TUNIS

THE decision to make the principal effort to capture Tunis from the west threw the two armies together. For the first attempt the 1st Armoured Division, including as it did the 2nd and 7th Battalions, drove round from the Tunisian Plain through the mountains to the Bou Arada Vale. The move was a deep secret and of the highest importance. The leading elements of the Division were therefore surprised to find the Arab townsmen of Le Kef turned out in force to meet them along the streets above which they had stretched banners bearing the sign "Welcome to the Eighth Army." Certainly the inhabitants of Northern Tunisia, fed presumably by B.B.C. propaganda, had an intense curiosity about the appearance of the Desert Rats. At least one rifleman is suspected of having sold to some gullible Arab the dirt from the bottom of his jeep, guaranteed as the genuine "sable d'Egypt."

Englishmen at war often seem to have enough energy to spare from fighting the enemy for use in disparagement of their friends. Since the Regiment was represented in both, the meeting of the First and Eighth Armies cannot pass without comment. From the point of view of the Eighth Army an impression of this meeting is given quite clearly by Paddy Boden:

"Here we saw for the first time the British troops of the First Army. It was interesting to compare the difference in outlook, technique and appearance between the members of the two armies. The first and most obvious differences were those of appearance and technique. First Army lorries were all painted dark green and brown, and when in harbour were parked in huddles, making the best use of any available cover. Eighth Army transport was painted the colour of sand and the drivers continued to rely on dispersal as the best protection against air attack. There is little doubt that the best solution would have been a compromise between the two methods, both of which were carried to absurd extremes. The officers and men of the First Army were readily distinguishable from those of the Desert Army by their dress. The former were more or less correctly dressed and, more often than not, wore steel helmets as a matter of routine. In the Eighth Army it was almost unheard of for an officer to wear battledress trousers, and steel helmets were worn only on very rare occasions. More important than these relatively superficial differences were the differences of outlook.

"For nearly three years the Battalion had been fighting in the Western Desert, more or less isolated from all contact with England, which could be reached only by air and round the Cape. Other units had, of course, arrived from England more recently, but the average regiment in the Eighth Army had been in the desert for two years. It is true that reinforcements were continually arriving from England, but these newcomers quickly identified themselves with and assumed the habits of the 'veterans,' doing this either as a matter of policy or purely from a natural desire not to be different. One example of an officer quickly adopting 'local' dress was General Montgomery, who was to be seen one day very soon after his arrival in the desert in August, 1942, at the Headquarters of XXX Corps wearing a *khaki drill jacket* and *Sam Browne belt*.

"Thus it was that the Eighth Army, a large body of men sharing a common experience over a period of months and even years, isolated from all contact with their home country, whether England, Australia or New Zealand, developed a set of habits, customs and even a jargon of their own. We felt different from, and, by reason of our longer experience and of the flattering accounts of our exploits which appeared in the Press, superior to, the men from England, sometimes mockingly referred to as 'those bloody Inglese.' There were, too, certain grudges which we bore against the Army in England. It was felt, sometimes with some justification, that when drafts were sent out to the Middle East the best men were kept by the units in England; it was said that there had been a tendency, before the Battle of Alamein, when things were going badly, for senior officers recently arrived from England to be rather free with their advice, quoting in support of their theories the lessons of Exercise 'Bumper' or Exercise 'Tiger' in which they had recently taken part. This was hardly tactful and we rather naturally preferred to trust to the lessons drawn from our own experience,

experience bought at rather greater cost than the discomfort of manœuvres in England. There was thus ground for friction between the two armies and we were disposed to be unreasonably critical of our colleagues of the First Army.

"These differences of outlook seem rather petty in retrospect, but they were real at the time. I like to think that our stupid conceit and our failure to appreciate the efforts of the First Army were short-lived and I hope that our friends in the First Army were not unduly offended by the 'blood and sand' we threw at them."

I have nowhere so full an account of the views of the First Army about the Eighth. There were, of course, rumours that the Desert Rats were often referred to as "having chased tankless Italians round the desert in Shermans." There were certainly two grievances which the First Army could legitimately voice. For the assault of the Eighth Army on the lavish N.A.A.F.I. supplies in the area of the First was remarkable in its vehemence and in the number of subterfuges employed, particularly to acquire whisky. The 10th Battalion harboured the second grudge. For the pig brought up for weeks by an anti-tank platoon which had survived the attacks of the Luftwaffe and the German Army and had lived unmolested alongside Americans and French, disappeared at Sbikha at the first contact with units of the Eighth Army.

The two armies were from now on intermingled. They were, after all, both fighting the same war. As if to leave no doubt of this in the minds of the Riflemen, as soon as the 7th Motor Brigade arrived at Le Kef the battalions were visited by General Sir Harold Alexander, Commander of the 18th Army Group.

On the 23rd of April the First Army began an offensive towards Tunis all along the line. It involved the three battalions in an armoured advance across the Goubellat Plain. The 10th Battalion, with their armoured brigade, followed up the infantry advance, met many minefields and were heavily shelled. When the high ground north of the Salt Lake was reached the 6th Armoured Division had shot its bolt. On the 25th of April the 1st Armoured Division tried to take up the running with the tanks leading. But they could make little progress and the battalions of the Motor Brigade were hardly involved. The advance was halted and the 1st Armoured Division was given the role of containing as much of the German forces as they could, while further attacks were made to their north. The 6th Armoured Division and the 10th Battalion were withdrawn into reserve. Although this Battalion had been subjected to heavy shell fire for long periods, the companies had not been seriously involved in the fighting, their most interesting incident being provided by Norman Hedges's 3-inch mortars, which engaged some tanks in dead ground until they had scored a direct hit on one of them and caused the remainder to move off.

During this unsuccessful attempt to drive an armoured thrust into the German defences the area of the fighting had been dominated by a mountain called Djebel Kournine. It was a gaunt, rocky, two-humped feature which may have reminded some of the 2nd Battalion of Gebel Himeimat at the south of the Alamein Line. On its top the enemy had apparently installed an observation post which had a good view of the rolling cornfields towards Bou Arada. On the 25th, while the battle in the minefields was still in progress, "B" Company of the 10th Battalion sent a patrol at night to the top of this mountain and reported it clear of the enemy. Much trouble would have been saved for the 2nd Battalion if the patrol had remained there. At the time it was never the intention that it should. In fact, the enemy were probably always in occupation, but had lain low on the reverse slope while the small party stumbled round in the dark on the rocky and precipitous slopes. The importance of this mountain was so obvious that three other units had tried to capture it at various times. The 2nd Battalion was ordered to make another attempt.

Kournine rose to something like fifteen hundred feet. It would have made an excellent medieval fortress in the days of boiling oil. Its sides towards the summit were composed of a series of cliffs and ledges, hard rock and loose boulders. On this foundation the Germans had constructed a most ingenious defensive system, where every booby-trap and device known to their sappers was employed. One of the more original of these took the form of mines which could be dangled on lines over the cliff's edge at suitable moments. There was no natural cover round the mountain and a daylight attack was out of the question. It was also impossible to deploy more than two companies to attack such a narrow objective; and the difficulties which confronted the Gunners in attempting a barrage on such knife-edges are obvious even to a layman.

The Battalion's attack was on the night of the 29th/30th of April. A fighting patrol was first to cut, without being detected, the enemy's telephone wires leading to the position. The main position was then to be attacked by two companies. The preliminary patrol was successful. But the main attack met with great difficulties, largely because the steep surface of the mountain, which was smooth and covered with shale, made movement on it noisy and difficult. Anti-personnel mines were encountered. The enemy kept putting up flares which, in the absence of all form of cover, enabled them to engage our troops with aimed small-arms fire. John Verner's platoon got almost to the top. There they found that the final ascent was unscalable. While they were searching for a way round, John Verner was hit and it was clear that he was badly wounded. Repeated attempts to reach him failed before heavy and accurate fire. Nor were other platoons more successful in scaling the mountain, although Mike Leyland got near enough to the enemy to be able to throw grenades into their position. Just before dawn the attack was called off.

Kournine was never captured, but when the advances on either side of it had caused the enemy to leave, a party of the 2nd Battalion went off to look at it. They found John Verner's body on a ledge near the top. Close inspection confirmed that the position was, from the enemy's point of view, virtually impregnable, the natural hazards had been improved by the sappers' ingenuity, and the defenders could have held out for as long as they still possessed food, water and the will to fight.

As soon as the 26th Armoured Brigade (and the 10th Battalion) were called back into reserve the 7th Battalion became involved in a series of operations in the Goubellat Plain to the north of the 2nd Battalion. On Easter Day the Padre, Hugh Gough, held a service in the high cornfields near Bou Arada. That same afternoon the 7th Battalion took over from the 10th. That night "D" Company, commanded by Billie Becher, made a successful night attack, covering over two thousand yards to a feature called Argoub el Megas—not the Argoub known to the 10th Battalion—lying between a salt lake or chott on its right and rough, broken, tank-proof country on its left. Its occupation gave the tanks more elbow-room to manœuvre. The feature itself was a ridge, with "D" Company holding our side and German infantry and tanks on the other reverse slope. The ridge itself was the happy hunting ground of artillery and mortar observation posts and snipers of both sides. On Easter Monday morning at dawn in a ground mist Colonel Douglas Darling, going up to "D" Company in his jeep, met a German Mark IV Special advancing towards him. He side-stepped and continued on his way to "D" Company, where arrangements were made to deal with this tank on its return from reconnaissance. Everyone waited in some suspense for its appearance. Eventually it was seen moving confidently over ground which its commander considered safe and was knocked out at eleven hundred yards by the third shot from one of Keith Eggleston's guns. One other Mark IV Special poked its nose over the ridge and was dealt with in the same way. After that the German tanks kept well on their side of the boundary.

On Easter Monday evening a further night attack was ordered to occupy what was known as the White House feature. This involved an advance of two thousand yards over unreconnoitred country. Before the attack the Argoub el Megas was handed over to the 1st Battalion 60th Rifles. The anti-tank guns were to follow close behind the infantry. But there was only one route by which the 6-pounders could be got up to the new position. The leading guns were travelling up this track just before first light when they came face to face with six German Tiger tanks blocking a defile at two hundred yards' range and protected by an infantry company. Sergeant Barrett, who was in command of the guns, immediately went into action and exchanged shot for shot with the Tigers every time a flare was put up. Even at this short range the 6-pounder shells could not penetrate the front plates of the Tigers. The two guns were most gallantly handled by their crews, but inevitably both were knocked out by direct hits. Sergeant Barrett was twice wounded and evacuated only by the efforts of Rifleman Webb. The way of the supporting weapons to the new position was effectively blocked. There was nothing for it but to withdraw the whole party through the 60th's position into Brigade reserve.

The next day General Sir John Crocker, Commander of IX Corps, visited the Battalion and discussed the short night battle with the Tigers. He suggested that the Piat might have been used. This infantry anti-tank weapon was quite unknown to the Eighth Army. The Corps Commander therefore sent for one and offered to demonstrate its use against a derelict Tiger which

NORTH AFRICA—DJEBEL KOURNINE
A salt lake or chott in the foreground

[*Official Photo: Crown Copyright Reserved*

Lieutenant-Colonel (later Brigadier) Adrian Gore, Brian Shepherd and Dick Fyffe, near Goubellat

Official Photo: Crown Copyright Reserved]

North Africa—the 10th Battalion
Some of Corporal Thomson's section —and pig

stood near the Battalion's area. Results were, to say the least, spectacular, since the weapon set a neighbouring cornfield on fire and sent its spring flying in such an unorthodox direction that it wounded the Corps Commander sufficiently badly to necessitate his evacuation to hospital.

The whole forward area was still dominated by Djebel Kournine when the 7th Battalion again took over the Argoub el Megas on the 30th of April from the 60th Rifles. Mortaring and sniping cost the Battalion various casualties. There were many night patrols. On one of these on the 3rd of May Henry Beckwith was killed and Ken Rogers was taken prisoner. Sergeant Perrin, too, of "D" Company, was killed when trying to worm his way to a better position of observation from which to shoot his mortars. He had just dropped a bomb directly on top of a Mark III tank and this success had, perhaps, inspired him to take one risk too many. The enemy made one attempt to penetrate the position in a night attack which was driven off with the loss to them of two prisoners of the Hermann Goering Division. The fluctuating value of prisoners of war is always difficult to explain to the uninitiated; but these two, captured as they were before the last offensive began, were doubtless of value to the Intelligence Staff in identifying the position of one German division. Yet within a fortnight prisoners were to be counted in thousands.

Since the arrival of the 1st Armoured Division in the Bou Arada area there had been three battalions of the Regiment all fighting within the orbit of Djebel Kournine. Now for the final round the 7th Armoured Division, bringing with it the 1st Battalion, was moved northwards to the First Army. The route was across the carpet of wild flowers in the plains, through Kairouan, up steep, dusty roads, into the mountains, through Pichon, where there were French soldiers and—more remarkable to a desert eye—roses, within range of Bou Arada, and into a concentration area between Le Krib and Medjez-el-Bab, perhaps the most famous of First Army names.

Already by May the position of the Germans was hopeless. But they could not evacuate their soldiers across the Mediterranean in the face of the Navy and they would not, yet, surrender. There were still large forces, if the Italians are included, very large forces, in existence and as yet unbeaten. A full-scale battle was required by combined resources of the Allies to break through this last crust into Tunis. The plan was for a narrow wedge to be driven into the defences by the 4th British Division of the First Army and the 4th Indian Division from the Eighth Army. The direction of this attack was to be along the main road, the Route Nationale, into Tunis. As soon as the guns and Air Force, and in the last resort as always the infantry, had made a hole in the defences the 6th Armoured Division behind the 4th British Division, and the 7th Armoured Division behind the 4th Indian Division were to burst out and advance from ridge to ridge of this country of rolling cornfields which led to the Mediterranean. The 1st Armoured Division were to follow up on the right for exploitation after the initial break-through.

For a few days the four battalions waited in their concentration area. There was much coming and going between them, and, although the presence of Djebel Kournine restricted the social activities of the 2nd and 7th, officers of the 1st Battalion, as the newest arrivals in this cultivated land, visited the forward battalions and had as much of a look at the country over which they would fight as the enemy and security measures would permit. From the Irish Guards' area they saw the high hills which the 78th Division were to attack and gazed at the legendary outline of Longstop Hill. On all sides the cry was that the easy ways of the desert were over, that real fighting in semi-European country against the best Germans would mark every step of the advance to Tunis. The last round would be a hard fight.

It would be nice to record that the Regiment, which had played so prominent a part in all the phases of the African war, had a decisive role in the final advance. In the event it was not required to do so, for such was the success of the infantry divisions, following up an air and artillery bombardment on a new scale, that enemy resistance collapsed on both sides of the main road. When the armoured divisions were released the battle was practically won. There remained the pursuit to Tunis, the sealing off of the base of the Cap Bon Peninsula, and the rounding-up of the Axis forces. Although there were no spectacular actions, no Sidi Salehs and no Snipes for any of the battalions, the closing stages of the war in Africa were full of incident for everyone who took part and will be remembered as among the most exciting of the war.

The 1st Battalion was the most northerly of the four. On the evening of the 5th of May the motor companies joined their armoured regiments and moved up ready to pass through the gap to be made by the 4th Indian Division. At three o'clock in the morning of the 6th of May the barrage opened up. It was concentrated on a narrow front and by nine o'clock three hundred and fifty guns had fired two hundred and fifty rounds each. The Royal Air Force, too, put in an appearance in the greatest strength that we had yet seen. From earliest light there was hardly a moment when medium bombers and fighters were not passing over us. The Indians, known first to the 2nd Battalion at Sidi Barrani, famous at Keren and in all the recent victories in the desert, whose silent night attack had driven the enemy from the hills at Akarit, reached their objective this time by nine o'clock in the morning. Soon the Gurkhas were running about the enemy positions busily polishing off with their kukris any miserable Germans who remained. The 7th Armoured Division had a clean break, hardly hampered even by minefields. All the morning they advanced, meeting isolated tanks or self-propelled guns and small parties of infantry. By two o'clock a thousand prisoners had been taken and we were half-way to Tunis. Progress would have been even faster but for a curious feeling that the situation was too good to be true. We had been prepared for desperate fighting: the realization of the extent of our success took all that day to sink in. While the leading regiments with their companies were cruising forward there were continual cries from the rear to be ready for a German counter-attack from the north, and all day we looked towards the distant hills beyond the Medjerda River, half expecting the Hermann Goering Division to appear. But for the existence of this threat, which put a brake on our progress, we might even have reached Tunis that night. As it was, the Battalion leaguered —or perhaps, in Tunisia, harboured—at St. Cyprien, twelve miles short of Tunis.

On the 7th of May the advance was resumed and by shortly after nine o'clock we were in the suburbs of Tunis. On the other side of the main road the 6th Armoured Division (and the 10th Battalion) made parallel progress. The enemy forces were thus cut in half. Their only chance of delaying the end was to fall back into the Cap Bon Peninsula. To prevent the divisions facing the Eighth Army at Enfidaville from doing this, the 6th Armoured Division were switched to the south and directed on the base of the Cap Bon Peninsula, so that the 10th Battalion, in sight of their own particular objective for the past six months, since Bladeforce had almost reached it, were not concerned in its actual capture. It was the 1st Battalion, led by "I" Company with the 1st Royal Tanks, who entered the city. A troop of the 11th Hussars had driven right through the town to the docks before the Germans had realized what was happening. They were now besieged by crowds of French and Arabs and sniped at by Germans from the houses near by. At about four o'clock "I" Company started to enter the town proper. The way was blocked by cheering crowds of French men and women, greeting the Riflemen with flowers and fruit, wine and kisses. At the same time individual Germans would wake up to the presence of our troops in the town and, being good soldiers, would reach for their rifles and begin to shoot. The confusion was unbelievable—at one moment cheers and laughter, the next rifle fire from the buildings, and tanks firing at point-blank range into houses across the street. German vehicles would drive out of side-streets at high speed into the stream of traffic, firing all their weapons or hoping to slip by unobserved. The usual crowd of sightseers was well to the fore, Press reporters, conducting officers, men to reserve buildings for headquarters, sailors to examine the docks, military government officials, Frenchmen, liaison officers, souvenir hunters, and the stragglers of the 6th Armoured Division who had driven straight on. Colonel Freddie Stephens and the Adjutant, Francis Dorrien-Smith, in the middle of this mêlée, were sharply sniped at from the windows, and Francis replied in kind. At last light the 22nd Armoured Brigade (except for "I" Company) were withdrawn to the hills outside the town and slept in comparative comfort out of range of the shots and shouting and fires, which continued until three o'clock. By that time Bill Apsey had collected five thousand prisoners and more were coming in.

At first light the Battalion sent a liaison officer into the town with orders to contact the French civilian authorities. It was a memorable drive. The inhabitants of the suburbs rushed out to greet the vehicle—cheers, flowers and kisses. As it passed into an Arab district the atmosphere changed. Hundreds of Arabs stood crowded thickly together in the street and watched the jeep drive between them in absolute silence, every eye turned on the British officer and not a syllable uttered. Two streets beyond that the French and Jews thronged the roadway in such numbers that it was hardly possible to pass; their enthusiasm and excitement knew no bounds. The French mayor had been kidnapped by the Germans, but the advance elements of Allied Military Government were already installed in office.

The 1st Battalion then turned north to the River Medjerda. There were two hundred thousand prisoners to be collected. The booty far exceeded anything we had seen before or would see again. Whole regiments of artillery, whole parks of vehicles, infantry brigades, workshops, stores, and the administrative machinery of the German and Italian Armies were laid out for the taking. The Air Force hammered at the enemy all the morning of the 8th; but there was no longer the power or the will to resist. Only some senior officers, a few generals and some of the staff, had slipped quietly away by air.

The 1st Battalion in their battered vehicles set about the sorting and collection of this defeated army. It had been in contact with the enemy, except for a short rest at Mrassas and a week at Tripoli, since December, 1941, covering an immense mileage and taking its part in every battle, every withdrawal, every advance. It had retreated from Agheila to Gazala and by a more protracted process from Gazala to Alamein; it had advanced from Alamein to Tunis.

The 10th Battalion had lined up, too, on the evening of the 5th of May behind the 4th Division. The infantry break-through was complete. The Battalion soon found itself passing derelict gun positions and abandoned dumps. By the late afternoon the village of Massicault—red roofs and orchards—had been cleared of enemy: only a few 88-mm. guns and single tanks were encountered. The next day, just as the armoured regiments were bumping the anti-tank screen in the suburbs of Tunis, the Division was switched south to cut off the Cap Bon Peninsula from the south. The Arabs reported that many Germans had already moved north, driving herds of cattle before them to provide subsistence in the coming siege. The 26th Armoured Brigade was directed on Hammanlif, a small town on the shores of the Gulf of Tunis and standing in a narrow gap half a mile wide between steep mountains and the sea. Since its position commanded access to the Cap Bon Peninsula from the north, the town had been made into a strong-point by the Germans. The armoured regiments emerging from the thickly cultivated, prosperous farmland round Morgnania, were met by heavy antitank-gun fire on the outskirts of the town. "B" Company were ordered to try to deal with these guns. Their advance into the town was met by shelling and heavy machine-gun fire: Peter Frewen was killed, and the platoons were held up. It was clear that the task was beyond one company. The Guards Brigade was ordered to clear the town. But while preparations were in progress for this attack the Lothians and Border Horse forced their way along the sea-shore and broke through the anti-tank defences in an area where the Germans were confident that their position was virtually impregnable. This action, one of the most remarkable of the war in Tunisia, opened up the way into the town. The Battalion swept aside the French inhabitants, wild in their enthusiasm, and advanced on the blue-and-white painted palace of the Bey of Tunis, whose Ruritanian guard "laid down their 1914 rifles" without protest.

Prisoners were by now coming in in their thousands. The carrier platoons, reconnoitring through the olive groves for the armour, were overloaded by offers to surrender. At this stage bold action might result in capturing enemy parties far superior in numbers and armament to ourselves. John Bodley, by resolute and immediate action, caused a hundred and fifty well-armed Germans (and one Italian!) to surrender to a carrier section. Organized resistance seemed at an end. One enemy block remained—the German 90th Light Division and the Italian Ariete and Young Fascist Divisions—sandwiched between the 6th Armoured Division and the Eighth Army. They were not yet ready to surrender. The German general, Graf von Sponek, in command of this force had announced that he would fight to the last. There was great difficulty in persuading any prisoner to approach this officer with a request to surrender or be bombed—for none would face his wrath. The Brigade advanced slowly southward. The Air Force dropped bombs: the guns fired heavy concentrations. It seemed that there was no alternative but to attack. On the 12th of May, after a heavy bombardment, the hillside suddenly sprouted white flags and Graf von Sponek, who had finally ordered the "Cease fire," dressed immaculately in green uniform and greatcoat with scarlet facings and lining, drove in to surrender to Generals Freyberg and Keightley.

The campaign had ended for the 10th Battalion. It was six

months exactly since it had left Scotland. As the history of the Eighth Army's advance could be read in the War Diary of the 1st Battalion so the history of the First Army is traced by the 10th. It had had a hand in every phase of the campaign. Its casualties from first to last were five officers and forty-one riflemen killed, six officers and one hundred and fifty-two riflemen wounded, and one officer and thirty-eight riflemen prisoners of war. The price was mercifully small when one considers the hard fighting and the strange, difficult country and the number of days in contact with the enemy.

The battalions in the 7th Motor Brigade were not engaged in the main break-out battle along the Medjez road. But when the enemy cracked they took part in the chase across the Goubellat Plain towards the Cap Bon Peninsula. The 1st Armoured Division was directed on Creteville, where a narrow pass connected the Enfidaville position with the peninsula. The 2nd and 7th Battalions climbed the heights on either side of this pass to establish observation posts on the spurs and woods overlooking the road, with the result that the armour was able to pass through and accurate fire could be directed on to the enemy's gun lines. The Hermann Goering and the 10th Panzer Divisions were holding this area and there was much speculation as to whether they would fight. Between the 10th and 12th of May many prisoners surrendered, but there was never any certainty that isolated parties of Germans would not decide to fight on. Officers would advance confidently and receive a hail of Spandau bullets round their ears; heavy bombardments with no apparent object would proclaim that the enemy were firing off their last remaining rounds. The 10th Panzer and the remnants of the Hermann Goering Division withdrew to a mountainous area south of the pass from which their armour made frequent and effective sallies. The 2nd Battalion were then directed to penetrate into this stronghold, having under command one squadron of the 10th Hussars and supported by the Divisional artillery. At first strong opposition from infantry and artillery was met in a narrow pass and only gradual progress was made along the tops of the hills. That night the German local commander surrendered with his staff and indications were that General von Brausch, commanding the 10th Panzer Division, was himself prepared to surrender. We sent a carrier platoon and the Colonel's car through the outer defences and the divisional headquarters were duly located, General von Brausch surrendering to Colonel Tom Pearson on the morning of the 12th of May. The collapse was complete. Amid scenes far more remarkable than those that attended the end of the war in Europe the Afrika Korps, the German Tunisian Army and the whole of the Italian armies in Africa, with all their equipment, their dumps, their supplies and their administrative base, fell at one sudden, dramatic blow into our hands.

The 7th Battalion had reached the desert in the bad days before the situation at Alamein had been stabilized. They had seen much fighting since their first desperate experiences, when thrown into the battle straight from the ship in July, 1942. Their casualties at Alamein and Akarit had been heavy, and there had been a steady drain of killed and wounded all through the campaign. But their contribution to the successes of the Army had been substantial, and at Akarit their action had very nearly been decisive. In contrast to the 1st, 2nd and 9th Battalions, they had never been involved in a retreat.

The 2nd Battalion were the oldest of all desert fighters. They had known good times and bad. When they had first driven to the desert in June, 1940, there had hardly been two divisions in the Western Desert Force. Their two short rests in the Delta had spared them the most rapid retreats; they had not taken part in the advance on Tripoli. In every other battle, in every action, in advances and retreats, in long, dull periods of static warfare, the 2nd Battalion had been in contact with the enemy, often with the most decisive effect, throughout the entire period of the desert war. The high-lights in their long experience were Sidi Saleh, when they stood between the Italian army and the escape to Tripoli, Sidi Rezegh, gallant but indecisive, and the Snipe position at Alamein. It cannot be often in the whole history of the British Army that one battalion has twice in one series of campaigns made such an individual contribution to the success of the whole Army as did the 2nd Battalion at Sidi Saleh and Snipe.

When they ended their African war guarding their old—and almost their respected—opponents the 90th Light Division, there were few of the original members who had left the Citadel in 1940 still serving with the Battalion. True, it was commanded by Tom Pearson, who had won his first D.S.O. at Sidi Saleh and his second at Alamein. He, like many others, had been away

THE FALL OF TUNIS

from the Battalion on the staff. It would be invidious to single out individuals for special mention at the end of this long story. But one debt should be remembered—to Callum Renton, who had trained us in the earliest days and laid the foundations of our subsequent success. There were, too, few present at Creteville who did not wish that Hugo Garmoyle had survived to see the campaigns in which he had done so much culminate in complete victory. He was, perhaps, the greatest of all our desert soldiers to be classed with Strafer Gott and Jock Campbell, who had done so much with so little and had died before the resources were available to drive the Germans from Africa. The story of the 2nd Battalion in the desert would not be complete without reference to Ned Pinnock, who missed hardly a day and not one battle, first as Regimental Sergeant-Major—standing imperturbable at Battalion Headquarters at Sidi Saleh regarding an Italian tank at twenty yards' range and with obvious disfavour—and for the last years as Quartermaster. He was faced now with his biggest problem, to provide not only for his own battalion but for much of the 90th Light Division.

On the 16th of May a dinner was held in Tunis, at the instigation of Brigadier Jimmy Bosvile, which was attended by sixty-four officers drawn from the four battalions. It was a unique occasion in the history of the Regiment, and with champagne at 2s. 6d. a bottle was celebrated in a suitable fashion. For the best part of two years the 9th Battalion, also, had fought in the desert. Five battalions were thus involved for varying periods in the fighting in Africa—a sufficient indication, if any is needed, of the part played by Riflemen in defending Egypt, in driving the enemy out of Cyrenaica, Tripolitania and Tunisia, in destroying the Italian armies and defeating the Afrika Korps.

CHAPTER XVII

AFTER THE DESERT

It is easy to read history backwards. The next step after Tunis is clear enough to us now, but to the four battalions on guard over the 90th Light and the 15th Panzer Divisions, the Hermann Goering, the 21st Panzers and the Young Fascists, it was far from certain what new developments would now unfold. The desert had absorbed four battalions and Northern Tunisia a fifth. Now that there were no Germans or Italians at liberty in Africa we waited for a new theatre of war to be chosen where greater armies, fighting in European country, would dwarf the individuality of regiments and battalions. In the desert and in the early days in Tunisia the Regiment had had more than its share of the limelight. The story of the campaigns is the story of the battalions, for Riflemen were concerned in—and often decisively affected—all the stages of the fighting. Hardly a day had passed for three years without some of us being in contact with the enemy, and periods of rest, training and refitting had been few and generally short.

For four months in the summer of 1943 no battalion of the Regiment was involved in the fighting. Then, on the 22nd of September, the 1st Battalion landed in Italy, to be withdrawn after three months and shipped to England to prepare for the invasion of North-West Europe. The remaining three battalions waited in Africa or the Middle East until they were gradually drawn into the war in Italy. The 10th Battalion remained in Tunisia until, in March, 1944, it embarked for a year's fighting in Italy. The 7th Battalion, after a spell of heat and sand in Tripolitania, moved back to the Nile Delta, where various camps were visited, until, in April, 1944, it, too, embarked for Italy. The 2nd Battalion had an even more varied existence, since it moved first to Tripoli, thence after an interval to the Delta, to Syria, Palestine, the Delta, Syria again, the Delta, and finally embarked with the 7th Battalion for Italy in April.

This narrative has so far confined itself to operations, and the long periods out of battle, which were now enjoyed by all the battalions, must be passed over briefly. Mention must be made of what might be called the period of rejoicing, although for the staffs this was also a period of feverish planning. There was a Victory March through Tunis in which the 2nd, 7th and 10th Battalions were represented, the 1st having started that day on the return drive to Homs. The Motor Brigade left for Tripoli at the end of May, so that only the 10th was inspected on the 2nd of June by the Prime Minister. But when His Majesty came out he inspected all the battalions in turn, the 10th in Tunisia on the 17th of June and the other three as they lined the main road into Tripoli on the 21st. But when these celebrations were over the battalions rested and trained in an atmosphere of anti-climax during a hot summer, the Motor Brigade in sandy discomfort at Suani Ben Adem, inland from Tripoli, the 1st Battalion by the sea at Homs between the glaring white sands and the tall palms, and the 10th in the more congenial atmosphere of Bou Ficha and Hammamlif, within range of Carthage, Bizerta and Tunis—at least not in the desert. Training and refitting were much needed. But there were less useful intervals, such as that when the 7th Battalion carried out guard duties in Tripoli.

In July the invasion of Sicily disclosed the direction of the Allies' next offensive. In this campaign, for once, no motor battalion was employed in the bare, rocky island which was more suited to infantry on foot. The 1st Battalion made preparations for a move to Italy in the autumn and drew equipment on a scale previously unknown. On the 22nd of September they landed at Salerno to take part in fighting which will be described later. At the end of July the 2nd Battalion had moved, mainly by sea, from Tripoli to the Delta, and on the Regimental Birthday entertained General Jumbo Wilson near Alexandria. Early in September they set off to join the 10th Armoured Division in Syria. They remained there, first at Slenffe, and then in Palestine at Tulkarm, where they had last been in 1939, until they returned to the Delta at the end of September. Here Christopher Sinclair assumed command instead of Colonel Tom Pearson, who had led them from Alamein to Tunis. After more training, many courses, and some dabbling in combined operations, the Battalion were off again to Beirut, in Syria, in the middle of November. They were back again in the Delta in mid-December, where they moved from one camp to another until the Greek mutiny caused them to hurry to Alexandria on the 8th of April.

The 7th Battalion moved back to the Delta in mid-September. While for the next six months they had frequent moves, these centred round the Delta and the Suez Canal and interfered with training and comfort—without affording a view of new and more interesting scenery. In October the Battalion entertained Mr. Anthony Eden and on the 1st of November General Jumbo Wilson. They were involved in guarding the great and famous personages who gathered for the conference at Mena House in December—the only guard duties which could ever be described as interesting, involving as they did the possibility of a view of Mr. Churchill or President Roosevelt or General Chiang Kai-shek. Having spent these long months away from the battle and tasted the delights of Cairo almost to excess, the Battalion moved to Alexandria and were there on the 6th of April when the Greek mutiny flared up.

It is a traditional role of the British Army to become involved in other people's quarrels. We generally appear in the role of peace-maker and almost always succeed in achieving the enmity of both sides. This Greek mutiny was a particularly unfortunate occasion. It was sad that the Greeks, who had shown the will and the ability to fight, should have dissipated their energies in attacking one another. It was, perhaps, a foretaste of events in that country after the war. At any rate, the 2nd Battalion was rushed to Alexandria to deal with the insurrection, which was largely the concern of the Navy, to arrest ringleaders and to keep the peace. The 7th Battalion was already there and was immediately employed in picqueting the Greek camps. These duties were neither particularly exciting nor spectacular. But they lasted for over a fortnight and on the 23rd of April the 2nd Battalion was engaged in a successful attempt to disarm Greek troops in fighting which resulted in John Copeland, commanding "A" Company, being killed. The Greeks asked for an armistice the next day; but it was intolerable to have lost an officer in such a way by the hand of our allies, one, too, who had first been wounded at Sidi Rezegh and had survived many a desert battle against our avowed enemies in the past two years.

The 10th Battalion had spent the summer and winter training in Tunisia, less often uprooted for far-reaching moves. On the 21st of December "A" Company had been detached to help guard the Prime Minister during his illness at Sidi Bou Zaid. On the 18th of February Colonel Adrian Gore, to whom the Battalion owed so much in its first campaign, was promoted brigadier, and Dick Fyffe, who had commanded "C" Company for some time, took over temporarily. These months passed without any other important incidents, and on the 6th of March the advance party embarked at Bizerta for Italy.

In a few pages the story of three battalions for almost a year has been dismissed. Though there were no operations—and this is the history of the Regiment in war—during this time many Riflemen will remember this period as vividly as any in their war. Parties in Cairo or Tripoli, Tunis or Beirut, expeditions to Carthage or Leptis Magna, Lebanon or the Pyramids, curious meetings with French or Syrians, Egyptians or Arabs, life as a company or as a battalion after months of the individual existence of vehicle crews, central cooking, training in the light of experience of war, served to pass what may seem a long period of intense boredom. But a rest after fighting is never too long, especially when at any moment it may be ended by a return to war. As the news of the fighting in Italy spread, it was apparent that this new theatre offered desperate battles in great heat or intense cold, in mountains, in river crossings, on narrow, steep, rocky roads, mud in winter, dust-clouds in summer—a different and more uncomfortable war than that which had been fought so long and, in the end, so overwhelmingly successfully throughout the desert years. It was a war, too, in which the Italians were no longer our enemies.

* * *

Whatever may have been the problems of war in the desert, at least a sea crossing was not one of them. Now, as the 1st Battalion sat on the sand or under the palms at Homs, it was obvious that they would have to consider some of the aspects of "combined operations" if they were ever to play a part in the Italian war. In July the landings in Sicily took place. The officers went to the Roman amphitheatre in Leptis Magna, where the Corps Commander, General Horrocks, told the story of the start of this invasion. It began to be generally accepted that, as soon as Sicily had been cleared, the 7th Armoured Division was likely to be involved in the next phase—the invasion of Italy.

Very soon after the capture of Tunis Colonel Freddie Stephens left the Battalion, which he had commanded since the days when the Germans still seemed certain to reach Cairo. He had been in contact with the enemy almost the whole of this time: apart from Alamein and Djebel Saikhra, his period of command had been singularly free of heavy casualties. After a short interregnum Victor Paley arrived to take over a command he was to hold until the Battalion was about to cross the Weser, well within the borders of Germany.

One of the advantages of being a motor battalion is that it is not likely to have to be the first troops to land ashore in an enemy country. For the invasion of Italy the Battalion was ready to embark on the 16th of September, thirteen days after the Eighth Army had crossed the Straits of Messina and four days after the first landings at Salerno. It was known by that time that enemy reactions to this left hook were violent, that the assault divisions, American and British, were having the greatest difficulty in establishing themselves, and that, far from an immediate advance to Rome hard on the heels of the Italian surrender, it was not yet certain that we would not be driven back into the sea. The Eighth Army from the south was hurrying north against light opposition, but hampered by fiendishly ingenious demolitions in the mountain roads.

It was with this background that the Battalion drove to Tripoli to embark. It was known by that time that the beaches were such that vehicles could run directly ashore from tank-landing ships. It was not, therefore, necessary either to divide the men from their vehicles or to carry out the troublesome arrangements which had been carefully rehearsed for making the vehicles waterproof. The main part of the Battalion was, in fact, to be embarked in six tank-landing ships, all the riflemen being with their vehicles in the crowded space below decks. After two days in the hands of Movement Control they eventually embarked on the 18th of September in ships manned, as it happened, by the United States Navy. That night the convoy sailed on a glassy-calm sea. The route was to the east of Sicily, under the eyes of Etna and past the ruins of the town of Messina, well bombed by the Royal Air Force. On the morning of the 22nd the convoy sailed into the Gulf of Salerno.

The 7th Armoured Division was part of the British X Corps, which was to serve in the American Fifth Army. By the 22nd this army was firmly established, the counter-attacks which had, particularly on the American front, been so near to success had been finally repulsed, the port of Salerno was in our hands, and the British 46th and 56th Divisions had made some progress inland, although the Germans still had good observation of the beaches. The Eighth Army, who advanced three hundred miles in three weeks, was about to join up with us to the south.

Although the Germans must have had good observation of the beaches and the sea approaches, no attempt was made to interfere with our landing. Within four hours of grounding, all ships in the convoy had been unloaded. The Battalion in its vehicles drove off to its dispersal area some four miles inland near what were now the ruins of the village of Battipaglia. The aspect of this village was convincing proof of the damage which the Royal Air Force could do in European country; for not a house was intact, not a road was passable, when we arrived. The destruction made a great impression on the Riflemen, fresh from a desert, where the power of the air was limited to the destruction of vehicles. The Battalion had a week to wait while the rest of the Division completed its concentration. Its area was on low-lying ground, much of which had been reclaimed from the marshes of this coastal strip. Beyond them rose the foothills and then the mountains, dominated to the north by Vesuvius. The Riflemen were soon brought face to face with a new problem for them, the prevention of malaria. As the mosquitoes rose in clouds from the swamps, great efforts were made to enforce the simple but irritating regulations to prevent an epidemic of malaria, sleeping under nets, covering arms and knees at dusk, smearing exposed parts of the body with grease and, most important of all, swallowing the small, revolting, yellow mepochrine pills, which had already acquired a reputation, quite unfounded and based entirely on rumour, of making one tired, ill and impotent. In the Battalion these precautions were enforced so successfully that only seven confirmed cases of malaria occurred while in Italy.

During this interval the Riflemen had a chance to look round at this new, strange, non-desert country where they were now to fight. There were large villages with narrow, winding, cobbled streets whose inhabitants swarmed in astonishing numbers under the hot, dry, September sun. There were vineyards, orchards and maize fields, now burned up and dusty, but when the rains reached the Neapolitan Plain capable of becoming a sea of mud. There were stretches of meadowland not unlike the South-West of England, and bare, boggy fields like Sedgmoor, particularly in the lands bordering the Volturno and Garigliano Rivers. Always to the east, on the right, the mountains rose at varying distances, giving views of grandeur, perhaps of picture-postcard beauty, promising hard and difficult fighting, unsuitable for armour, steep, rocky slopes and hairpin bends on roads. In this first harbour area Vesuvius and the range to its east dominated the plain and spilt black, dirty soil, composed of lava, down its side. This lava was fertile. All kinds of fruit were grown in it. Since the Italians were no longer enemies, olives, grapes, pears, figs, melons, tomatoes and sweet corn were for the moment in abundance. This September Italy, with its dark, hard-working, poverty-stricken inhabitants, was surprisingly Southern in aspect. It was not a smiling land, for everywhere there were signs of wanton damage and vicious, deliberate destruction, the Germans, who could be so correct in their behaviour if they were told to be, now showing their true feelings for those allies who had joined them in success and deserted them at the first sign of failure. In Sicily the inhabitants, though still officially enemies, had given a great welcome to the Allies. In Italy the worse the behaviour of the Germans the more delighted the villagers were to see us. The consumption of "vino" became a recognized part of the daily routine: it was just better than plain water, but only just. For the move from Tripoli some attempt had been made to lighten the burdens of the trucks, and an attack on the accumulated livestock of the years of desert war succeeded in thinning out the fowls and some of the less attractive dogs. Before the Battalion had left Battipaglia chicken farming by some curious process had again begun.

The rest of X Corps were engaged in forcing the passes that led north to Naples. Opposition was light. But progress was slow owing to the difficult going on rocky, terraced hillsides. Eventually the Division was drawn into the battle; but at first the infantry brigade led and it was not until the 2nd of October that the Battalion, with the armour, passed through the infantry to take up the running. The 22nd Armoured Brigade drove through San Giuseppe Vesuviano, Octaviano and Somma Vesuviano, and advanced on two parallel routes, "C" Company, commanded by Desmond Prittie, and a platoon of anti-tank

MR. ANTHONY EDEN VISITS THE 7th BATTALION IN EGYPT, AUTUMN, 1943

General Jumbo Wilson (Field-Marshal The Lord Wilson of Libya), Mr. Anthony Eden, Colonel Douglas Darling. The Member for Windsor, Charles Mott-Radclyffe, has his back to the photographer

[*Official Photo: Crown Copyright Reserved*

ITALY—THE 1st BATTALION

A section during the capture of Sparanise

Face page 245]

guns from "B" Company being on the right, with the 1st Royal Tanks and "A" Company, under Ed Garnier, and another platoon of "B" Company's anti-tank guns on the left with the 4th County of London Yeomanry. This left Battalion Headquarters with "I" Company and half the anti-tank company to trail along behind with Brigade Headquarters.

That day progress was slow, not so much because of heavy enemy opposition but owing to demolitions, difficult going, wet weather and small enemy rearguard actions, cunningly fought, so that by nightfall the 1st Royal Tanks had got only as far as Afragola. Whilst in the column the platoon of "B" Company was shelled and lost one gun crew.

The next day, the 3rd of October, the advance was held up at the village of Cardito, where enemy anti-tank guns, well concealed in vineyards and maize fields outside the village, held their fire until we were within a hundred and fifty yards. "C" Company's two motor platoons tried to advance astride the main road leading into the village. Just as they were forming up to cross the start line they came under heavy shell and mortar fire, possibly directed by an unseen observation post near at hand. In three minutes they lost fourteen casualties—a third of their strength—and among them one of the two officers and both platoon sergeants. It was clear that the line of the main road was not a profitable approach. Colonel Victor Paley was sent for and made a plan to attack with "I" Company under Bill Apsey. The Colonel did a reconnaissance and chose for the attack a stretch of close country, with the main road on the left and a light electric railway on the right, both of which converged on the village. Bill Apsey decided to work on a one-platoon front up to the village, moving on foot and keeping to the thickest part of his area. Bryan Wyldbore-Smith, commanding the battery of the 5th Royal Horse Artillery, in support, managed somehow to obtain observation of the enemy's area and from what he saw and from the map a regimental barrage was laid on. Two troops of tanks on each flank moved forward to give support.

If Djebel Saikhra had been "I" Company's—and possibly the Battalion's—most successful battle in Tunisia, the capture of Cardito was their outstanding feat in Italy. The company's attack on its narrow front was completely successful, despite considerable opposition. John Foreshew's platoon first came up against an enemy post. He led them against it and was wounded by a grenade. But the post was captured. Paddy Biddell's platoon then took the lead and forced their way into the village. In face of this penetration of their position the remainder of the enemy slipped away into the close country to the flanks, an action which we were too thin on the ground to prevent. The enemy had clearly intended to remain where they were, at least until nightfall, and there now followed an anxious time, during which they seemed likely to put in a counter-attack; for they brought down heavy artillery concentrations on the village at hourly intervals. The situation gradually improved when the tanks from the left were brought into the village, though an obstacle prevented those on the right from joining them. At dusk the Gunners managed to locate the enemy guns by their flashes and a shoot by a Corps artillery group of heavy, medium and field guns more or less silenced the enemy for good. The village was a large one—some seven hundred yards long and two hundred wide—so that "I" Company, reinforced by the remnants of "C" Company's two motor platoons, merged into one and ten Sherman tanks crowded into the southern part of it for what was expected to be an alarming night. It passed, however, without any enemy counter-attack. During the action "I" Company had lost one officer wounded, Sergeants Jillings and Parker and one rifleman killed, and eight wounded.

The next day the 1st Royal Tanks resumed their advance, using "C" Company to clear up snipers in the outskirts of Aversa, and finally halted on the line of the Regilagni Canal, south of the River Volturno. When this and the two ditches on either side had been filled in by bulldozers the advance was resumed to the Volturno. Here "C" Company were soon engaged in patrolling along the banks of the river.

On the left route the 4th County of London Yeomanry and "A" Company had been much delayed by bad going, so that they reached the Regilagni Canal a day later than the 1st Royal Tanks. "A" Company established a bridgehead while the bridge was being built and experienced three days of heavy shelling, luckily without loss, before continuing to the river. Throughout the advance on both routes the German Air Force had been almost entirely absent.

The Battalion was then withdrawn to Aversa, where it spent ten days. Although only some ten miles from the fighting,

Desmond Prittie, aided by a Czech, Lieutenant-Colonel Karel Lukas,* who was attached to the Battalion, collected an opera company from Naples and held a concert in the village hall. This period of rest was interrupted by an order to move at short notice to the Volturno, near Cancello, where the right of the 46th Division had crossed the river, but, getting too far ahead of their supporting weapons, had been overrun by a counter-attack. After only two days spent in pouring rain in covering the left of the 7th Armoured Division, the Battalion returned to Aversa.

On the 21st of October there was another move, since the Division had been ordered to cover the left of the 56th Division, which was moving in the mountains north-west of Capua. After an early morning drive the Battalion lay up for the day and at dusk took over an area astride the more westerly of the roads to Rome, wisely avoiding the identical positions occupied by its predecessors. When it grew light it was seen that the Germans could overlook the whole area from above Francolise, four kilometres to the front, and from the high ground above Sparanise the same distance to the right. There was therefore incessant shelling and mortar fire, directed mainly at the old positions, so that we escaped unscathed. It was an exhausting time for everyone. Not only was there shelling by day, but a heavy programme of night patrolling kept officers and non-commissioned officers at full stretch.

It soon appeared that the Germans were not actually holding Sparanise below the left of the 56th Division's objective. After two days "I" Company were therefore ordered to occupy it and to try to work higher up the mountain without actually getting deeply committed. It was an unenviable task—a steep, bare hill six hundred feet high towering over the village. There was, however, a good deal of cover in the re-entrant and Paddy Biddell's platoon set off up this. About a third of the way up they came on a German post, attacked it, killed two of its occupants and took eight prisoners. But the route beyond that became too exposed for further progress. Soon afterwards, while the Colonel, Bill Apsey and the Gunner observation-post officer were up in a church tower, a single shell burst at the bottom, killing several civilians and seriously wounding Paddy Biddell, who at that

---
*This good friend to the Battalion was recently reported as killed during a "purge" of the Czechoslovakian Army.

moment was coming in to report on his patrol. Already in the desert and in Italy he had distinguished himself at the head of his platoon, now in comparative safety to be hit by a single, random shell.

In the afternoon Chris Christian, with his platoon, worked his way right to the top of the mountain and saw well-dug and well-concealed German positions on the reverse slope before returning according to orders. By the next day the attacks of the 56th Division were gradually gaining ground and a squadron of the 5th Royal Tanks made their way up by another re-entrant to the top. "I" Company then took over until relieved by the 56th Division. On the left the remainder of the 5th Royal Tanks had advanced as far as the Francolise feature, the top of which was too steep and too thickly cultivated for their tanks. The Battalion was therefore ordered to take it. "A" and "C" Companies quickly succeeded in this task, patrolling forward to the River Savone, where no enemy were found, though heavy shelling soon caused casualties to the main company position.

Two days later, on the evening of the 26th, the Battalion was relieved and moved to the coast to the line of the Aqena Nuova Canal, taking over from two battalions of the Hampshire Regiment. The 46th Division had attacked the day before we arrived and had gained a footing on the far bank. The Battalion, finding little opposition apart from shelling and mortaring, developed this foothold into a bridgehead, rather to the surprise of the Higher Command. This success was not achieved without casualties, for Mark Bond, whilst on a daylight reconnaissance in thick country among high reeds, was surrounded, with the result that he and his patrol were captured.

The Division exploited the Battalion's bridgehead, the lorried infantry brigade and the 1st Royal Tanks passing through to capture Mondragone. The Battalion, with the 1st Royal Tanks, then took up the advance up to the River Garigliano. For a fortnight the 11th Hussars watched the river line by day while we took over as soon as it got dark. As on the River Savone, there was at first no opposition, but later, as at Francolise, the Germans, finding that we were not regaining contact, decided that they themselves would have to do so. This resulted in night patrols becoming more and more exacting and on one of them Eric Haywood-Farmer, who had swum the river, was drowned on his way back, a sad ending to what had been a brilliant patrol.

On the 14th of November the Battalion was relieved and returned once again to Aversa. Here all vehicles and much equipment were handed over, and a move was made to billets in Sorrento. At last the preparations for the invasion of North-West Europe were nearing completion and it had been decided that three experienced divisions would sail to take their place in the great army now in training in England. No armoured division had had a longer experience of fighting than the 7th Armoured, and none had been longer abroad. So for a month the Battalion sat about with little equipment and practically no vehicles in Sorrento, waiting for orders to embark with nothing to do except to wonder at the cold and wet of an Italian winter. For the officers there was some duck shooting but none so good as that in the flooded marshes of the Garigliano, where, while still in contact with the enemy, Colonel Victor Paley and nine others during one early morning flight had shot some eighty-five duck, mostly teal, and seventeen snipe. The guns were Brigadier Hinde, two officers of the 11th Hussars, seven officers of the Battalion, and Sergeant Cubitt, who was also in charge of the evening patrol.

The Battalion in its stay in Italy had been engaged in no spectacular battles or in the capture of any famous city, but it had been in contact with the enemy for most of those two months. It had learnt something of how to fight in close country, so different from the desert, so much more difficult for armoured forces than for infantry; it had met demolitions on narrow roads, blown up bridges and impassable mud. When it was next to fight, in France, the transition would not be as strange as it would have been if there had been no Italian fighting to bridge the gap between sand and bocage. Quite apart from its value as a link in the experience of this now-veteran battalion, it could be proud of the model battle for Cardito and the exploitation of the bridgehead across the Aqena Nuova Canal. In those few months from September to December the Riflemen had watched the Italian countryside change its appearance from the dry, baked, dusty southern land of the end of summer to the sea of mud which swamped the Neapolitan Plain in winter, an unexpected development to those Englishmen who looked on Italy as a country of eternal sunshine, a refuge from the damp fogs of England.

On the 20th of December, 1943, the 1st Battalion embarked at Naples in the *Cameronia*. On the 25th of September, 1941, they had left England in the *Strathaird*. Since then they had fought from Agheila back to Alamein, from Alamein to Tunis, and now from Salerno to the Garigliano. They were returning to England, not for a rest from the war but to take their part as veterans in the reconquest of France, to drive the Germans from Normandy, and to free the Channel ports from where Hitler pointed a pistol at England, particularly Calais, the graveyard already of the Regular battalion, from whose ashes this new one had arisen.

CHAPTER XVIII

NO GENTLEMAN'S WAR—ITALY AND THE FORMATION OF THE 61st INFANTRY BRIGADE

"TUNISIA was a gentleman's war, and everybody packed up when the sun went down; not so in this infernal country. . . . I expect you can guess that our feelings about this campaign are different from the Tunisian battles, which really were exciting and, in a way, enjoyable. This business is just infantry slogging away in pretty foul conditions and in country ideal for the enemy. The only thing in favour of the war here is the fact that there are far more buildings than in Africa, so that one generally gets a roof (or part of one) over one's head at night, and somewhere to eat under cover. . . ." It is true that those extracts are from letters written in October and November, 1944, when the 10th Battalion had been fighting continuously since the spring; and one of memory's familiar tricks is to retain the pleasant and obscure to some extent the unpleasant. There are times now when most of us remember with some feeling of nostalgia the less unbearable periods of the war. But certainly the fighting in Italy had features more horrible than any that had been met with in North Africa. The nature of the country was all in favour of the defenders, for the Apennine Mountains occupied almost the whole width of Italy. Where there were narrow areas of low ground by the coast the "plains" were intersected by rivers, canals and irrigation ditches. In rocky, mountainous country armoured vehicles are at a disadvantage, artillery is often less effective than on more level ground, and the air arm, though able to affect vitally movement along roads, cannot play a decisive part against the ground forces, dug in or blasted in on steep hillsides or in deep valleys. It is the infantryman, the individual with his weapon, on whom the burden falls; and he cannot be supported without the aid of the sapper.

The Germans employed some of their best formations in Italy. Their infantry, particularly parachutists, fought with great skill and gallantry; their sappers brought the business of demolition to a fine art. As they had no offensive intentions whatever—their counter-attacks were a form of defence—they could concentrate on defence, with the one proviso that they must not allow any large proportion of their forces to be cut off. They hoped, no doubt, to be able to contain the Allies in this favourable country with small forces, and it was only because the Fifth and Eighth Armies kept them constantly on the stretch that they were not able to withdraw significant numbers of divisions to other fronts.

In this business of slogging up Italy, always attacking somewhere and never, owing to the nature of the country, being able to deploy really overwhelming forces at one point, our armies suffered many casualties. The battalions of the Regiment were not spared. In the desert and in Tunisia there were frequent, long periods between the great battles when losses had been negligible. One whole campaign had resulted in the eclipse of the Italian armies without the 2nd Battalion losing one officer killed. As soon as the battalions began fighting in Italy they sustained a steady flow of casualties. To take two months at random during the advances of the summer of 1944, the 10th Battalion lost seven officers and seventy riflemen in June, and six officers and seventy-nine riflemen in July. Even during the more static periods of winter there were always those who trod on mines or were hit by mortar bombs or did not return from patrols. And in the main battles, such as that of the 2nd Battalion's at Tossignano, losses could be on a larger scale. The battalions were engaged practically continuously for a year without a break and over these months the losses mounted up, though they were never comparable to those in the war of 1914-18.

Mountains, mines and casualties were not the only unpleasant features of this new theatre of war. One is apt to imagine Italy as a country of sunshine throughout the year. The Riflemen soon found that rain could fall as heavily in Italy as in England, and from December onwards there was snow above a certain height on the mountains. There is something incongruous to an Englishman in the idea of wearing white snow suits within a comparatively few miles of Rome and sticking in snow-drifts in a country more usually associated with dust. There was dust in plenty in summer, though north of Naples the heat could seldom be described as intense. In fact, throughout the Italian summer one finds frequent references to the lovely weather, which made up for some of the discomforts, such as the smell of dead horses decomposing gradually in the sun.

As the armies made their painful progress north, and particularly after the beginning of the Second Front in France, there grew up a feeling that this theatre was of secondary importance, and was almost forgotten in face of more fashionable events in other countries. There was, of course, no real foundation for these ideas, although reinforcements were sufficiently few to impose extra strain on the experienced veterans who came back time and again from hospital to the front. The authorities were alive to this psychological danger to morale. None of their efforts to dispel these clouds was more successful than the visit of His Majesty to Italy in June.

Yet the Italian campaign had its moments of relief. It took place in country of great beauty, of wonderfully clear visibility, presenting some of the most famous views in Europe, particularly in the autumn, when the first rains restore greenness to the burnt-up countryside or on clear days in winter "with the snow pink in the sunlight." It took place, after all, among towns of exquisite architecture which tourists in peace time visit at vast expense. No one could fail to be stirred at the prospect of capturing Rome, or Florence, or Venice. Even the lesser towns —the Capuas, the Paduas, the Ferraras—had names steeped in history, full of associations with a famous past. It was something to be fighting to reach Lake Trasimene, the Po, the Arno, the Brenner Pass: a quality was added, at least for the romantic, which had been quite lacking in the desert, where an advance of two hundred miles would bring one to a few mud houses bearing a name unheard of in the Western world. If the Riflemen were impressed by the dirt and squalor of Naples and the southern towns there must have been much to remember in a visit to Rome or Florence in the short intervals between advances. Unfortunately the Regiment did not happen to be represented in the capture of Rome, bypassing it by some ten miles on the way to Perugia.

After the departure of the 1st Battalion for England there was a period of three months during which no battalion of the Regiment was engaged in an operational theatre of war. It was not until the spring that the main armoured forces were moved

S

to Italy and our fortunes were still linked up with theirs. During this time the Fifth Army to the west of the Apennines and the Eighth Army to their east continued their advances northward. General Montgomery went home: there was talk of going into winter quarters. The landings at Anzio gave temporary promise of a speed-up in the tempo of the advance. Although after the spectacular wind-up of the North African war and the early promise of the Italian campaign results had, perhaps, been disappointing, the whole of the south had been cleared of enemy: the Foggia airfields were ours and possession of Taranto made our position secure in the Mediterranean. There had been great achievements already: everyone now looked forward to a spring campaign for the capture of Rome.

The 10th Battalion, still with the 6th Armoured Division, was the first to embark for Italy. The advance party sailed from Bizerta on the 6th of March; but the main party embarked at Bone on the 12th of March from the same dock where they had landed in Africa fifteen months before. They reached Naples on the 14th of March, going ashore over the upturned Italian hospital ship which had been scuttled by the Germans when they had abandoned the port. The Division concentrated at Piedmonte d'Alife, and by the 27th of March the whole Battalion had been collected there. On the 21st of March Colonel Dick Southby arrived to take over from Dick Fyffe, who had been commanding in the interval, and who was to leave in May to command a battalion of the Royal West Kent Regiment.

On the 7th of April the Battalion was sent up to hold a piece of the line opposite San Angelo, just south of Cassino, and on arrival came under the 2nd Parachute Brigade. Little was known of the ground between our positions and the river and we were soon employed in patrolling. Almost at once an officer, Angus McNaughton, was wounded by a Schuh mine while on patrol; but "C" Company managed to ambush an enemy patrol, causing casualties to them and taking three prisoners. The Battalion was used in an entirely infantry role, remaining in their positions without movement by day. At intervals there was heavy enemy artillery fire on or near these positions and the presence of nebelwerfers—multi-barrelled mortars—firing in salvos of six and making an exceptionally disturbing noise, perhaps the most unpleasant of German developments, soon made itself felt. On the 17th of April, after ten days in the line, the 8th Indian Division took over and a return was made to Piedmonte d'Alife, where it was hoped by intensive training to profit by the lessons learnt from this short acquaintance with conditions in Italy.

The weather was now expected to be suitable for a major offensive. The Eighth Army had been brought across from the Adriatic. Plans were made for a break-through by XIII Corps up the Liri Valley below Cassino, while the Poles and French were to clear the high ground on either side. The 26th Armoured Brigade, under whose command the 10th Battalion had up to now remained, was to support the infantry divisions initially and to return to the 6th Armoured Division when sufficient progress had been made to exploit the break-through. It would clearly take some little time to concentrate the Division and pass it through to take up the running. An armoured reconnaissance group, to make what ground it could while this concentration was in progress, was formed of the Derbyshire Yeomanry, equipped with Shermans and sawn-off Honey tanks, and the 10th Battalion. In April it may have seemed premature to talk about exploitation, for the Germans considered Highway 6 through Cassino to be the main road to Rome and had prepared to defend it with the 1st Parachute Division, the 15th Panzer Grenadier, the 90th Panzer Grenadier, the 26th Panzer and some good infantry divisions. The 15th and 90th had been re-formed after the capture of the original panzer divisions of those numbers in North Africa, and were now called panzer grenadiers, a title which laid as much emphasis on infantry as on armour—perhaps an unconscious tribute to the efficacy of the motor battalions who had faced them so often in the desert.

On the 11th of May the assault began with a barrage of a thousand guns to help the infantry across the Rapido. Although the bridgehead was only eight hundred yards in depth the 10th Battalion began to prepare to cross on the 13th. Only the scout platoons were able to get across during the next two days. The main part of the Battalion was not engaged, although Regimental Sergeant-Major Crocker was blown up on a mine, and there was much shell fire all along the south bank. It was apparent by now that the Germans were determined to fight it out, having already repulsed the Polish attacks on the monastery at Cassino. However, the Derbyshire Yeomanry and the scout platoons managed to make slight progress in the bridgehead. As the Germans were gradually forced back, a gap appeared between the

78th Division on the right and the Canadians on the left. On the 16th the Battalion were put in to fill this gap.

This entailed carrying out an attack on the enemy position at Point 83, which commanded the road to Aquino. Reconnaissance was almost impossible, although the scout platoons, particularly John Bodley's, managed to secure some valuable information and definitely confirmed that the enemy had not departed. The approaches were choked by transport of the 8th Indian Division withdrawing and the Canadian Corps advancing: the bridges were still under fire. It was not until last light that the motor companies were able to form up and then "A" Company had lost some riflemen through shelling at the crossing. As darkness fell "A" Company, commanded by Jim Lonsdale, on the right and "B" Company, under Teddy Goschen, on the left went in to the attack over unreconnoitred, difficult ground. Their first attempts to reach their objectives failed. Bert Westnedge was killed at the head of his platoon. The companies withdrew temporarily and then at dawn, with a fresh plan and increased artillery support, went in and drove the enemy out with considerable loss to the Germans, who were caught by a concentration as they were leaving their trenches to withdraw.

The enemy were now on the run. There were still snipers and bazookas to hold up the advance. But news came that the enemy had evacuated the monastery and Cassino under cover of a sharp air raid. The Battalion was able to press on up the valley, capturing prisoners from a varied assortment of divisions, a sure sign that German resistance was breaking up. What was, perhaps, the most maddening aspect of the Italian campaign soon emerged. Having taken one apparently commanding feature with great trouble and at the cost of casualties, another natural defence line, equally obvious and equally difficult to deal with, would appear on the line of advance. From Cassino to the Po there existed a succession of natural defensive positions on high ground which could not be outflanked, each overlooking the approaches along which we had, of necessity, to advance. Now, having broken through one great enemy defence line on the 18th of May, the leading vehicles of the reconnaissance group came up against the Hitler Line.

There were signs that the line was not held in strength. Such reports were to become a commonplace. Since the enemy was fighting a delaying battle there was always the possibility, often the likelihood, that he would pull back. One of the most difficult operations in war is to discover when the enemy opposite have, in fact, withdrawn. Rumours from the rear are frequent that their headquarters have moved back; the leading troops are unable to detect any movement or draw fire from the positions they believe to be occupied. The order is given to "find out if they have gone." More often than not a patrol of a few riflemen under an officer had then to go forward on foot or in carriers to draw the fire of the enemy, to go forward until they were shot at or until one of them stepped on a mine. It is a gruesome experience to be told to "find out if they've gone."

This time, at dawn on the 19th of May, Ralph Stewart-Wilson, with "B" Company's carrier platoon, was ordered to carry out a detailed reconnaissance of the defences of Aquino. One section soon found that a road-block on the outskirts of the village was covered by machine-gun fire and was held up. The platoon commander, with the other section, met a German anti-tank gun at thirty yards' range. They destroyed the tractor and the gun and killed the crew. This action drew heavy fire from mortars and machine guns. Stewart-Wilson's carrier was knocked out and the wireless set destroyed. The whole platoon came under such fire that they suffered casualties; all the carriers were knocked out and the remainder were told to withdraw under the platoon sergeant. Ralph himself remained out alone for a further six hours, at first moving about from point to point, sometimes within a hundred yards of the enemy, and frequently coming under fire, until he had got a really good picture of the enemy's dispositions, and finally hiding in what turned out to be a German latrine. He then returned with this valuable information. It was clear that the task of capturing Aquino was beyond the resources of the Battalion, who were relieved by a brigade of the 78th Division prepared for an attack based on Ralph Stewart-Wilson's information.

The Battalion had four days' rest out of the line, but on the 25th of May was on the move again, passing through the Hitler Line by a gap made by the Canadians and directed on the River Melfa and the town of Arce beyond. The leading tanks found a bridge across the river intact and got across it. But one tank was knocked out on the bridge itself so that it completely blocked the road. At the same time, the area of the bridge came under heavy fire, preventing "B" Company from crossing and causing casualties, among whom was Roger Parker, wounded. During the night German aeroplanes, seldom seen in daylight, bombed both ourselves and the Germans despite a remarkable display of Very lights, sent up in protest by the enemy. During the night reconnaissances were made up and down the bank, looking for an alternative crossing. At first light an attempt to cross drew fire; but an hour later Victor Hannay waded over to find that the only remaining enemy were a few deserters. The Battalion having established a bridgehead on the far side, the 1st Guards Brigade passed through.

After forty-eight hours of rest the Battalion moved up again on the left of the Guards Brigade. On the 29th of May the enemy fell back once more, allowing the Lothians to advance up Route 6 and enter Arce. That evening the Battalion was ordered to cross the river and capture Fontana Liri. The bridge had been blown and the river was too deep to wade. This was, perhaps, a blessing in disguise, since by the time a long detour had been made it was dark and the enemy had withdrawn. They had left a particularly unpleasant selection of booby-traps behind, one of which, situated in a house, went off, killing several men, and when Dicky Bomford, the platoon commander, rushed in to extricate the wounded another explosion killed him. What with mortars and booby-traps, an unpleasant night was spent and the town was handed over to the 10th Indian Division with the utmost relief, the Battalion moving back to an area south of Arce. In the short spell of fighting since the 11th of May they had lost two officers killed and four wounded, and eighteen riflemen killed and sixty-eight wounded.

The story of the advance of the 10th Battalion up the Liri Valley should give some indication of the nature of the Italian war. This fortnight had seen a comparatively fluid battle, resulting in important progress. Yet the distance covered was no more than a long night patrol in the desert might have involved. The capture of one vital piece of ground had merely disclosed another equally vital a little farther on. Before the 6th Armoured Division was well clear of one bridgehead its leading units had reached another river, which had in its turn to be crossed. The high-sounding names of the highways, the main roads to Rome, contrasted with the difficulty of moving across country or along the lesser-known routes. It was clear that in this mountainous country there would seldom be an opportunity for great armoured sweeps deep into the enemy's country. The need would be for more and ever more infantry, who even in an armoured division were more often than not the dominant arm, requiring the support of the tanks. Yet with the enemy falling steadily back there was reason in the early summer of 1944 to hope for the avoidance of another period of static, infantry warfare such as had occurred at Cassino.

It was because of the nature of the country that the 6th Armoured Division was reorganized to include a second infantry brigade. There was hope that this brigade would not always be required to operate at foot pace and therefore it was to include one motor battalion and two battalions on an establishment resembling that of lorried infantry. If there was again to be a hold-up in the hills of Italy it was hard to justify retaining a motor battalion; its vehicles would become a handicap instead of an asset and it could with difficulty find five hundred men to take part in an infantry attack. Yet infantry trained for a normal infantry role could hardly be expected to join effectively in an armoured pursuit, and an armoured brigade without a motor battalion is so vulnerable at night that it must either risk having inadequate defence or rapidly exhaust itself by keeping everyone awake and alert. The constitution of this new brigade was to be a compromise.

The 2nd and 7th Battalions had disembarked at Taranto on the 4th of May. They were still organized as motor battalions, but the 7th were immediately divorced from the 9th Armoured Brigade, with whom they had spent some time training, and sent to take over a part of the line near Cassino. The 2nd Battalion was due for a similar role. But after a few days near Fulignano, spent partly in learning how to load up mules, the plan was changed. On the 23rd of May orders were received that both battalions were to be reorganized and were to join a new brigade to be commanded by Brigadier Adrian Gore and to consist of themselves and the 10th Battalion. This decision, for which the efforts of General Jumbo Wilson were mainly responsible, meant that for the first time in its history three battalions of the Regiment were to be brigaded together. In the desert the 7th Motor Brigade had consisted of three motor battalions, our 2nd and 7th and the 1st Battalion 60th Rifles. It had been a brigade group with its own gunners, the 4th Royal Horse Artillery, sappers and services: it had operated almost always as a formation and battalions had comparatively seldom been detached. It had been a desert formation. This new brigade, now forming in haste at the very beginning of a great and successful offensive, soon to reach Rome and with, it seemed, every chance of continuing to the Alps, was very definitely a formation intended for the Italian war, so different in its nature from that in Africa.

The changes in organization of the 2nd and 7th Battalions consisted briefly in replacing the vehicles which carried the motor platoons by troop-carrying, three-ton vehicles driven by Royal Army Service Corps drivers. This entailed a fundamental change in outlook. Many mechanics and drivers and other skilled tradesmen were faced with the fact that their talents would no longer be put to the use for which they had for so long been trained. There is no doubt that it is a less attractive prospect to walk than to drive, and the comforts of war-time life, from "brews" and bedding to the hardly legitimate acquisition of poultry, come less readily to the lorried infantry than to the motor battalions. It had at first been intended by the authorities that the battalions should be organized exactly as normal infantry. It was only through the determined efforts of Colonel Douglas Darling, who was acting as Brigadier until Brigadier Adrian Gore should arrive from Anzio, that some extra vehicles were retained. These troop-carrying lorries gave promise that not all the road from Arce to the Alps was to be travelled on foot, not that such a prospect should have deterred a true Rifleman. Above all, the battalions retained a large number of wireless sets, which enabled them to work effectively with the armour and to continue to exploit those qualities of quick thinking and urgent action which distinguished the Riflemen of the desert no less than those of the Peninsular War.

The Brigade was named the 61st Infantry Brigade. Brigadier Adrian Gore, who had commanded the 10th Battalion from first to last in Tunisia, gave up his brigade in the Anzio beach-head and arrived to take over command. Hugo Baring, who had been Adjutant of the 1st Battalion for much of its fighting in the desert and on the staff of the 7th Motor Brigade afterwards, became Brigade Major. On the 29th of May the Brigade moved from Villa Volturno to catch up its third battalion in the Liri Valley and that evening the 2nd Battalion was given the task of picqueting the hills east of Arce to prevent the enemy infiltrating on to the main axis of XIII Corps.

THE 7th BATTALION IN ITALY
Flush a prisoner in an orchard—

—and search some more

From now on until the end of the war the story of the Regiment in Italy is in the main the story of the 61st Infantry Brigade and will be told as such, except on the occasions when one battalion or another was detached to work with one of the armoured regiments independently of the Brigade. In the cosmopolitan forces of the Allies in Italy there were many transfers of formations between the Fifth and Eighth Armies, and I have not always mentioned what might be considered an important change of command for the Brigade from one army to another. But such was the extent of the integration of the various nations and formations under General Alexander's guidance that an officer could write: "It does not much matter out here now which army you are in. . . ."

CHAPTER XIX

ADVANCE ON ROME

WHILE the 61st Infantry Brigade was concentrating at Coldragone—and the 10th Battalion was having a brief rest—what may fairly be described as the decisive battle of this campaign was being fought by the Americans in their break-out from the Anzio beach-head which threatened the rear of the enemy opposing the Eighth Army and was beginning to alter the whole complexion of the battle. The enemy in the Liri Valley had for three weeks been steadily pushed back by our superior fire power and constant determination, but their command could congratulate themselves that at least coherent resistance continued, and that heavy casualties had been inflicted as well as suffered. Now they were beginning to realize that unless a hasty but skilfully executed withdrawal was carried out the Allies might well encircle and destroy a large part of their forces opposite the Eighth Army. On the 31st of May American troops reached Route 6 near Valmontone, and the Allied air forces did great damage to the Hermann Goering Panzer Division, the enemy's last available reserve, which was moving from north of Rome to try to restore the situation. The left hook from the Anzio beach-head was at last able to come into effective operation.

The enemy was now faced with the need for a major withdrawal and it was generally anticipated that there would be no real stand again until the Gothic Line was reached. Defences were known to have been prepared and worked on since August, 1943, when we were still fighting in Sicily, in what was then commonly but inappropriately known as the Pisa—Rimini Line. The defences actually were considerably north of Pisa and considerably south of Rimini, and were sited where the approaches existed to the great mountain barrier of the Central Apennines which stretches from east to west right across Italy except for a narrow strip on the east coast. The task of the enemy was to get his forces back as nearly as possible intact to this line, a task he succeeded in achieving, even though in practice he soon abandoned the constructed defences and held the other side, the exits instead of the entrances to the mountains, to give us instead of himself the mountain passes as lines of communication, thereby coming to the same decision in action as to how to defend a mountain range as had Clausewitz on paper.

For this withdrawal he had the advantage that the terrain nearly everywhere favoured rearguards, who could sit on high ground and overlook the roads and then withdraw before an attack could be launched: he also had the advantage of possessing a number of troops with experience and skill at rearguards. The one real danger was the greater mobility of the Allies coupled with their large numerical superiority in tanks. The Allies were attacking northwards on a line stretching across from the west coast to Central Italy; only farther east were they, at this stage, simply following up any withdrawal. Near the west coast, particularly north of Rome, the ground was comparatively flat and this, combined with the fact that the enemy had inferior troops there, caused large numbers of prisoners to fall into the hands of the Fifth Army. Down the spine of Central Italy the enemy was always able to meet us on terms favourable to himself. The 6th Armoured Division was almost always throughout the next phase on the right flank of the pursuit, that is in the Apennines, and this meant that enemy rearguards were frequently able to observe the axis. This finally caused the whole advance to bog down south of Arezzo until sufficient infantry could be brought up to clear the hills on the right flank. One other feature that was important throughout this phase must also be mentioned here: there is a saying that all roads lead to Rome, and in this part of Italy this saying had a good deal of truth in it. This helps to account for the way in which both the Fifth and Eighth Armies converged on Rome and then diverged outwards afterwards.

On the 2nd of June the Brigade moved off to a new concentration area some fifteen miles farther up what was known as Route 6. It was a nightmare move of a type possible only when it was virtually certain that no German aircraft would interfere. That same evening the move was continued, bypassing Frosinone and harbouring for the remainder of the night in the woods west of the road two miles south of Alatri.

At dawn a 7th Battalion group was to continue up the road

as an advance guard until they met the enemy, who were that evening still being cleared from the village—so far as we could tell from the limited information available. The initial objective was the road junction four or five miles to the north where the Divisional axis forked left, but whatever happened they were to get on as far as possible. The other two battalions were to remain in the harbour area until further notice.

The advance was led by the 7th Battalion's carrier platoon, commanded by Arthur Thrift. Alatri, like most villages of this part of Italy, lies at the top of a hill overlooking the road. Troops of the 78th Division had confirmed it as held, but there was little information to suggest how far back the enemy might now have gone. It seemed common sense to suggest that he would still be defending the "T" junction some five miles to the north, thereby holding an escape route open for his troops retreating by the minor roads running north. Quite soon after Alatri our leading troops were held up for a while by a tank of the Royal Wiltshire Yeomanry which had to be pushed by a bulldozer off the road. A mile farther on, a bridge was found fully prepared for demolition. The charges were swiftly removed and the carriers then felt their way cautiously forward until, as they rounded a bend in the road, they were greeted by a volley of small-arms fire. The leading carriers withdrew to cover and the platoon dismounted and split into two parties for a close reconnaissance, Arthur Thrift and Larry Lowrison taking the right and left of the road respectively. The result was to locate two 88-mm. guns and about a platoon of infantry covering the road from the area of a group of houses. Larry Lowrison, having spotted a Spandau, opened fire on it with a Bren. A second, unobserved, Spandau fired a burst and he was killed outright.

The remainder of the column meanwhile had halted and the Colonel did a reconnaissance. He decided that "A" Company should attack from the left and clear the opposition. The 2nd Royal Horse Artillery opened fire on the position and some enemy were seen to leave the houses, but the attack went in quickly enough to prevent the enemy getting away as they had intended. "A" Company, under Peter Shepherd-Cross, put in their attack with supporting fire from the 2nd Royal Horse Artillery and the Battalion 3-inch mortars, and quickly cleared the area, taking twelve prisoners and claiming half a dozen dead. They exploited forward as far as the "T" junction and consolidated. Some of the enemy, however, had got away to the hills to the north-east, and to make the road open for vehicles without being dominated by the enemy a further attack was required. "B" Company, under Charles Mott-Radclyffe, moved up a small valley on the right of the road and advanced about half a mile beyond and to the east of "A" Company against some scattered opposition. By this time they were in the foothills of the dominating feature La Monna, one thousand nine hundred and fifty-one metres high. Here strong opposition was met from fifty to sixty enemy in good defensive positions, and "Scruffy" Downing was killed leading his platoon up the hillside. There were also fifteen other casualties, but against that a further twenty prisoners were added to the day's bag, some progress was made and the gains consolidated.

We were now told that troops from the 8th Indian Division were coming up on our right and would take over the ground won by the 7th Battalion east of the road. On our left a column of the 2nd Coldstream Guards and the Lothians and Border Horse was meeting bad going but no opposition from the enemy. The advance was therefore resumed with the carriers of "C" Company leading down the left fork road towards Trivigliano. After a mile the road was blown a bare fifty yards in front of the leading carrier, wounding the crew. It was now late afternoon and the next important task was for the 627th Field Squadron, R.E., to get the road open while the 7th Battalion protected them and seized and held the high ground to the north of the road. It had been a very successful day, marred by the loss of two officers killed, the other casualties being about twenty in all. One 105-mm. and two 88-mm. guns and thirty-three prisoners were captured. The latter were all from the 4th Alpine Battalion, an independent unit of mountain troops who had fought with skill but in many cases with a lack of final determination, which may be attributed to their Austrian nationality. It was also a satisfactory day for the 7th Battalion because operations, as so seldom happens, had been much on the lines of previous training. It was almost a téxtbook advance guard of a mixed column of all arms advancing to make contact with the enemy, to deal with them as rapidly as possible and then resume the advance. Such operations had been carried out as exercises in Egypt the previous winter, and the Battalion now used that training to good effect.

It had been intended on the next day, the 4th of June, that the 2nd Battalion should continue the advance operating on the same sort of lines as the 7th Battalion had done. They moved up at dusk to an area immediately behind the 7th Battalion, and were again to be a battalion group. The fluid and widespread nature of the campaign made information of the "big picture" scarce and it was only late that night that the Divisional Commander, General Vyvyan Evelegh, had sufficient news of the rapid withdrawal of the enemy on our left to cause him to decide that the moment had come to put the 26th Armoured Brigade in the lead, and the 17th/21st Lancers reverted to their command. Accordingly the 2nd Battalion's task became the rather different one of mopping up behind the armour. This was generally to mean clearing the villages on the high ground at intervals of two or three miles on the right (or north) of the axis. Fortunately this did not entail any fundamental change in the first part of the plan for the 2nd Battalion and "B" Company, commanded by John Reader-Harris, set out, directed on the village of Trivigliano, followed by "A" Company, under Dick Flower, clearing the axis and directed on the next and larger village of Fiuggi. "B" Company was greeted by Spandau fire as it approached Trivigliano, but the enemy was evidently in no mood to linger and the place was finally cleared soon after first light. "A" Company had meanwhile got on two or three miles without meeting any opposition and the tanks of the 16th/5th Lancers were racing up the road overtaking them. They paused for some breakfast while the troop-carrying vehicles came up and then drove to the outskirts of Fiuggi, which was soon cleared after slight opposition. Some thirty prisoners were taken, including a number rounded up by the military police and the field security section who were with the leading troops entering the village.

The role of mopping up behind the armour now became steadily more difficult owing to the amount of traffic on the narrow and cratered road. Some of "S" Company, under George Emerson-Baker, in the afternoon had some clearing to do in the village of Piglio, where eight prisoners were taken and the total for the day was about fifty, though this figure included many entirely voluntary surrenders. The enemy opposing us were again Austrians, this time from the 44th Division who did not on the whole fight with much determination. Unfortunately in one way they were in a strong position, for as they withdrew north they held the high ground overlooking the road and the enemy observation posts must have been embarrassed only by their limited resources in ammunition for dealing with the tempting array of targets, as half the Division was spread along the road or harboured off it. The 2nd Battalion's transport and reserve company attracted the attention of an enemy observation post and they suffered two spells of very accurate shelling which cost them some twenty-five casualties, including five officers wounded. This misfortune occurred at a time when our leading tanks were some twenty miles ahead and one was understandably lulled into a false sense of security.

The 10th Battalion was passed to the command of the 26th Armoured Brigade and was called forward to take over after dark. The 16th/5th had advanced twenty-five miles in the course of the day and it was a terrible struggle to get to the head with a mass of traffic and several diversions round blows in the road which were not fit for wheeled traffic. Yet another impediment on the road was a series of German Mark V tanks (Panthers) still burning by the roadside: there were about eight of these, presumably abandoned by the enemy for lack of petrol.

"A" Company (Jim Lonsdale) and "C" Company (David Basset) had to set out at midnight on a four-mile cross-country march to seize Monte Morrone, which overlooked the blown bridge at which the armour had been held up. This was achieved without opposition and the advance was resumed, with the Lothians leading. By six in the evening of the 5th of June the Lothians had met their first check (other than blows) at a bridge across the Tiber. For, on the 5th of June, Rome had fallen, twenty-four days after the offensive across the Rapido had begun; and, while the battalions of the 61st Infantry Brigade realized with more than a twinge of disappointment that they would bypass Rome, as the 10th Battalion in Africa had once turned aside from Tunis, the 1st and 8th Battalions poised on the eve of the invasion of France received the news as a good omen for their own adventure.

For the 61st Brigade, however, the greater part of the day was spent sitting in vehicles on the roadside in what seemed an endless queue that never moved. One or two spells of shelling must fortunately have been unobserved, as it was inaccurate and did not persist. There were reports of enemy not far to the north of the axis which may have been partly true, though investigation led to nothing and the enemy was preoccupied with getting away, not with interfering with us. To add to the delays caused by traffic congestion, as the Fifth and Eighth Armies converged on the outskirts of Rome there was some unseasonable rain which washed away a diversion at Cave so that nobody could move for a couple of hours while it was rebuilt. The final result was that the whole Brigade had to move nearly all night. The 7th Battalion was in front and its leading company was put under command of the 26th Armoured Brigade on arrival. It was already daylight by the time most of the Brigade harboured, but by midday the 10th Battalion was on the move again.

That day we heard the news that the Second Front had begun, a tonic to minds and bodies tired by yet another all-night drive. We did not yet know what part the 1st and 8th Battalions would play in this campaign, but it was certain that they would both be engaged and that soon there would be five battalions of the Regiment in action at the same time against the enemy.

The Divisional axis of advance was now Route 4 up the Tiber Valley, and the 26th Armoured Brigade were soon meeting resistance from strong enemy rearguards. The 61st Brigade were ordered to come up on their right where the ground was more hilly but still fairly open, with grassland and wheat fields. The 10th Battalion and "B" Squadron of the Derbyshire Yeomanry were given this task and, on the 7th of June, advanced up the road to Mentana. When about three-quarters of a mile short of the village "B" Squadron ran into a minefield and were engaged by machine guns and small arms when trying to clear a way through. The 10th Battalion tried to find a way round, but they also ran into mines and were brought to a halt by machine-gun and mortar fire. There was also a Panther or some large tank in the neighbourhood and for a time some quite heavy shelling. Patrols in the night found the enemy withdrawing once more, and at six o'clock in the morning the liberated population of Mentana were pressing flowers and vino on the liberators. We pushed on to Monterotondo, which had, however, already been liberated from the other side by the Lothians. The rest of the day was spent in fighting patrols by the 10th Battalion which produced six prisoners, two of them wounded; but they were unable to find the cave in which some enemy were hiding, according to a report by escaped South African prisoners, several of whom were now coming in. The Derbyshire Yeomanry were able to get some good observation posts and assist the Armoured Brigade in their battle. But, above all, it was a day's work for the Sappers. The whole area was liberally strewn with mines and one troop alone picked up just on five hundred in the course of the day.

The next day the Brigade was concentrated near Monterotondo and given a short rest. Rome was still in sight, but visits were as yet forbidden. There was plenty to do, with some reinforcements to be absorbed and maps to get ready for the next phase, not to mention catching up with sleep and washing, which get into heavy arrears in these mobile operations. The Guards Brigade, with the 17th/21st Lancers under command, had taken over the lead and had found the enemy holding out strongly by day but withdrawing at night. It was hoped that resistance would now, if anything, diminish, since the 6th South African Armoured Division had got well ahead on the west bank of the Tiber. All the bridges across the river had been blown, but the enemy could not expect to have an unimpeded withdrawal along the east bank for much longer. In practice they evidently felt that they must take this risk for one day longer in order to safeguard the withdrawal of their troops farther east. Later evidence shows that many of their best troops were withdrawn via Rieti and Terni. The Guards on the 9th already had a bridgehead over the River Farfa, and on the night of the 9th/10th they were to get across the Galantino some three miles farther on. A 7th Battalion group, similar to the previous one, with the Derbyshire Yeomanry substituted for the 17th/21st, was to pass through and advance north while the Armoured Brigade swung left to remain on the west bank of the Tiber.

The 2nd Coldstream Guards had a fair amount of shelling on the 9th, but it quietened down in the evening and it was thought the enemy would make his usual nightly withdrawal. Unfortunately they were held up in the night by infantry positions at Poggio Mirteto station, where there was a defile, with the hills coming down almost to the bank of the Tiber, and the news that they were held up did not get back to us until too late. It must be admitted that the real trouble was that everyone was, as so often on these occasions, in too optimistic a frame of mind. When the 7th Battalion group arrived at the Farfa just after first light they harboured close to the road and thought they had only to await the completion of a diversion by the Sappers. All was quiet for an hour or more and then heavy and accurate shelling began, soon causing a number of casualties. It was obvious that the position was overlooked and the Colonel decided to pull back behind the crest. This alleviated but did not put a stop to the trouble and by the end of a most unlucky day the 7th Battalion had had nearly fifty casualties, of whom eight other ranks, including two sergeants, were killed and three officers were wounded. One of these was Peter Shepherd-Cross. Most of the Guards Brigade had a bad day also and it was a shock to those who thought the enemy were disorganized and short of ammunition. He had evidently achieved his purpose and that night the Grenadiers and Welsh Guards advanced right through to beyond the Galantino.

As soon as news of this was received at about three in the morning the 2nd Battalion set off to pass through. Before long they were forced by demolitions to leave their vehicles; but they continued to make rapid progress on foot in the face of scattered opposition. Several times a Spandau opened up, but by the time our troops got to the position it had disappeared. One post was rounded up, however, at their objective, Cantalupo, resulting in the capture of six prisoners. An uncomfortable day was spent there, with mines round the approaches and spasmodic shelling and nebelwerfer fire on the area. The next night they were relieved by troops from the 8th Indian Division, and on the next day they joined in on the tail of the Brigade, which was following the Armoured Brigade up the east bank of the Tiber once again. The 7th Battalion was placed under command of the 26th Armoured Brigade, and from this point to Perugia the Armoured Brigade was always leading and always had one battalion from the Brigade under command.

With the exception of the 7th Battalion the Brigade was now left behind. This Battalion, with the Lothians, advanced up the west of the Tiber into hilly country. The first serious obstacle was a demolition a mile short of Narni. We managed to haul the majority of the vehicles across and moved into the town, one of the few up to that time to be captured practically undamaged. From here "B" Company, under Charles Mott-Radclyffe, were sent forward with all haste to try to secure the bridges at Terni. They arrived in time to see the main bridge blown almost under their noses but in such a hurry that an officer and fourteen other ranks of the enemy were left on the wrong side of the gap and were captured. "A" and "C" Companies took up a position on the heights overlooking the town. There was a pause while the Sappers built a bridge over the demolition. The Battalion was then directed on Todi and on the 15th of June it entered the town, led by Colonel Douglas Darling in his cut-down Honey tank, and took prisoner two officers and some twenty others. By this time the Battalion was well in front and on the 16th the rest of the Brigade had to drive fifty-three miles to catch up, the 10th Battalion then taking over night protection of the tanks. The Divisional axis now crossed to the west of the Tiber, and the 2nd Battalion was the next day passed to command of the Armoured Brigade to continue up the axis, while the 10th Battalion was almost literally stuck on the east bank, for it started to pour with rain. This gave the 2nd Battalion a most unpleasant night, but they managed to clear the village of Cerqueto, from which fire had been holding up the tanks in the afternoon, with no opposition, though they picked up a couple of stragglers.

The attractive town of Perugia could clearly be seen by the leading troops the next morning. That day showed resistance to be stiffening and several tanks were lost in an attempt to renew the advance, the close country favouring the enemy infantry with their "Faustpatronen"—the German version of the American bazooka. Furthermore, the armour had had a long spell and travelled over two hundred miles without a pause of longer than two days. For the first time, therefore, the Divisional Commander decided to employ both his infantry brigades simultaneously. The 1st Guards Brigade on the right was to clear Perugia and the ground to the north, and the 61st Brigade on the left to seize the high ground overlooking the town from the west and to open up Route 75 so that the advance could be resumed when the Armoured Brigade had done some maintenance.

CHAPTER XX

PERUGIA

THE Italian war offered few opportunities for individual distinction by regiments or even brigades. In the great battles such as those which had been fought at Cassino the size of the forces employed swamped the individuality of battalions. In between the great battles there were many company and battalion actions fought in difficult enough conditions with gallantry and often with remarkable success, to capture a village or a commanding feature, each in itself important and often costly to those who took part, but not sufficiently spectacular to excite the imagination of the Press or find its way into the history of the war. Few outside the 7th Armoured Division have heard of the 1st Battalion's capture of Cardito; the story of the 10th Battalion's advance towards Aquino up the Liri Valley is unknown outside the 6th Armoured Division. Yet if the capture of Perugia had not followed so soon after the political excitement of the fall of Rome and had not coincided with the most critical days of the invasion of France, the fame of the 61st Brigade's capture of the hills to the north-west of the town must have reached a larger public. Certainly within the Army these operations were regarded as a remarkable achievement.

The path of the Brigade's advance had veered towards the centre of Italy since leaving Rome. They were now directed on to the high ground, the mountains to the north-west of Perugia, between the town and Lake Trasimene. Perugia's military and no doubt economic importance lay in its position as a centre of communications, a meeting place for roads from every direction. The seizure of these hills would make it almost impossible for the enemy to remain in the town of Perugia and would open a route for the continuance of the advance to the north of Lake Trasimene.

The pattern of the battle is typical of this campaign. There were four successive night attacks, carried out in difficult, moun-

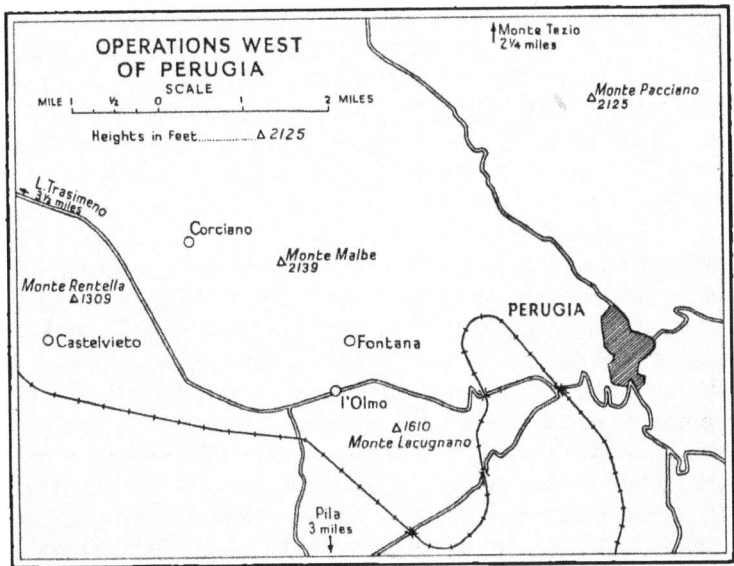

tainous country. Some enemy who were passed over in the night generally appeared at daylight behind the leading companies. There were sharp engagements on a company scale for single buildings or the summit of locally commanding hills. Few tanks on either side could operate effectively. But the mortar and the Schuh mine came into their own. Above all, the counter-attacks by the German infantry were carried out with such swiftness and determination and in such well-chosen country that their repulse was often more difficult than the capture of the ground in the first place.

The first of this series of operations was on the night of the 18th/19th of June and had the object of capturing Monte Lacugnano. The 10th Battalion was involved in a major attack and the 2nd in an important but subsidiary role. The 10th Battalion was given as objective the mountains overlooking Route 75, two to three miles west of Perugia, while the 2nd Battalion to their south were to move forward to cover the 627th Field Squadron constructing bridges required to open a route which did not pass through Perugia, and up which it was hoped to send the Lothians. The weather remained bad, a dark night with steady rain, and this naturally proved a serious handicap to the Sappers so that the first bridge was finished only just after dawn. An attempt by the 2nd Battalion after crossing to move on to the next bridge in daylight met small-arms and mortar fire and had to be abandoned. They also had considerable shelling later in the morning, and this part of the operations ended in the evening when the enemy withdrew, probably owing to the progress of our advance elsewhere.

Meanwhile "A" and "B" Companies of the 10th Battalion had been forced by weather and darkness to do a long night compass march. They reached their objectives successfully; but when first light came in the morning the situation was confused, as many enemy had been bypassed in the dark and started sniping well behind the leading troops. Others, obviously completely surprised, were in full view of Teddy Goschen's "B" Company. Amongst the latter in position just by the main road was a Mark IV tank, and clearing this area resulted in the destruction of the tank, two trucks and a motor-cycle, and the capture of nine prisoners. A success had been achieved; but the situation was not entirely healthy and Colonel Dick Southby sent out a message on the wireless advising the Brigadier and others not to come and see him for the time being, as his headquarters were being sniped at. The enemy were even more uncomfortable, and the snipers were not men deliberately left behind but those who had been passed in the darkness. As the morning wore on, the reserve companies gradually cleaned up the area, and the total bag of prisoners for the day reached twenty-four, including two officers. By the afternoon things were fairly quiet, and there can be no doubt that the enemy had received a nasty surprise. The capture of this ground was probably the major factor that decided the Germans to withdraw that night from the town of Perugia, on the southern outskirts of which they had resisted the Guards with great tenacity for two days.

At five in the evening on the 19th Colonel Douglas Darling received orders that the 7th Battalion was to capture Monte Malbe that night. A reconnaissance was made from Monte Lacugnano, held by "B" Company of the 10th Battalion, from where a view could be obtained of some, though not all, of the objective. The outline plan was made and orders given out. The Battalion was sent for and debussed at Pila, where it was rejoined by the company commanders. It was now after dark, despite being midsummer, and further time was imperative so that orders could get down to the platoon and section commanders, and to allow the motor companies to complete the approach march from Pila to Monte Lacugnano. The actual start was not therefore made until one o'clock, and it was hoped to capture the objective in the dark while not giving the enemy an opportunity to counter-attack until daylight. It was again a dark night with some rain. A five-mile cross-country march followed to L'Olmo, the junction of the track up to the mountain with Route 75. "A" Company, commanded at this time by John Brooke, remained in the large, low, white house of L'Olmo, while "B" Company (Charles Mott-Radclyffe) continued to a small village a mile up the track named Fontana, where the route changes from a cart track to a steep path. Here the first enemy were encountered and three prisoners taken without a struggle. "D" Company (Norman Odgers) managed to reach the summit so quietly that they caught the enemy post there completely by surprise, and, creeping stealthily into the small farmhouse that lies almost at the top, they killed two and captured three, while the German field telephone continued to ring. Meanwhile "C" Company (Larry Fyffe) had set out after "D" Company by a route slightly to the left, and while on a track on the west slopes were astonished to see a horse-drawn gun which was finding the going very difficult. Even more astonished were the gun crew, and what proved to be a 150-mm. infantry gun was captured intact, together with a crew of twelve and some horses, one of which was unfortunately killed and continued to pollute the air in the neighbourhood for some time afterwards. "C" Company now joined "D" Company on the summit and dug in as best they could on the rocky ground, while "D" Company protected them until at dawn they withdrew to Fontana. On the south-west slopes protecting "C" Company's left flank was Arthur Thrift's carrier platoon on its feet, and the stage was now set for the almost inevitable counter-attack.

Monte Malbe is six hundred and fifty-two metres high, not very steep and with no very distinct summit. The small, red-roofed farmhouse near the top has already been mentioned. Behind this on the north side are two rows of trees, but otherwise the mountain is mainly bare and rocky. From the top an excellent view can be obtained for miles around: Perugia to the east, Lake Trasimene to the west and the roads to the town from the south. Our position in Perugia would have become impossible if the enemy had held this ground. But, though there is also something of a panorama to the north, this is not ideal for the purpose of military observation. In the first place, some of the features only a few miles away are higher, with Monte Tezio (nine hundred and sixty-one metres high) dominating the area, and, secondly, the ground in the dip between the hills is very broken and in places thicky wooded. From this description both the importance of the feature and its limitations as a defensive position can clearly be seen. A counter-attack was for the enemy both desirable and practicable.

In the morning there was some unpleasantly accurate shelling and mortaring, but the first signs of a counter-attack did not come until three in the afternoon, when the enemy tried to come in from the north-west. Some of them may have succeeded in establishing themselves in an unobserved position, though at first the attack was dealt with fairly easily. Not very long afterwards, at a moment when visibility was bad, a new attack developed with great speed and considerable force from north-east and north-west simultaneously. Fighting appeared to break out on all sides at once and by sheer speed some penetration was made on the east side and sniping at Battalion Headquarters at Fontana began to be accurate and troublesome. This penetration was sealed off and dealt with largely by an assortment of signallers and others not usually concerned in firing their weapons in anger, and after some confused fighting for a couple of hours the arrival of a squadron of the 17th/21st Lancers finally decided the few surviving enemy to surrender or make a getaway. The main part of the attack was dealt with by "C" Company's small-arms fire, and thanks are due to the 2nd Royal Horse Artillery's accurate defensive fire, which was finally brought down within fifty yards of our own positions, taking a heavy toll of enemy dead. The Germans at one point of penetration when visibility was at its worst had managed to reach "C" Company's headquarters in strength. Larry Fyffe collected all the riflemen he could lay hands on and drove the enemy out. Thirty was considered to be a conservative estimate of enemy dead, and the total of prisoners for this operation was brought up to one officer and thirty-two other ranks. Though mortaring and shelling of the position were to continue, the enemy never again tried to attack it, though he might well have persisted if he had not been taught such a thorough lesson at this first attempt.

The house on the top of the hill was such an obvious target that it attracted a great part of the enemy fire over the next ten days.

It was at this house, two days later on the 22nd of June, that Colonel Douglas Darling was hit in the shoulder by a shell splinter. He had already commanded since December, 1942, and it had seemed that it was beyond the power of the enemy to touch him with shot, mine or shell. He was to return long before the Germans had been driven from Italy. In the meantime Hugh Meldrum assumed temporary command until Colonel Dick Fyffe arrived from the Royal West Kent Regiment to take over.

Both the 10th Battalion's attack on Monte Lacugnano and the 7th's on Monte Malbe had been "laid on" at very short notice and executed with great speed after a quick reconnaissance of the ground without any elaborate planning. A silent attack at night which gave the enemy no warning of one's intentions had been very successful two nights running and it was obviously the 2nd Battalion's turn—but not necessarily the very next night. Fortunately Colonel Chris Sinclair did the necessary reconnaissance during the day and warning orders had been issued, though for various reasons the actual plan for the night was made only after dark. There were reasons to suggest that it would be better to push on hard before the enemy had recovered his equilibrium. On the other hand, there were indications that they had already done so and that we would therefore be wise to consolidate and build up before renewing the attack. It was the latter view which finally prevailed.

The Lothians had on the 20th met demolitions and anti-tank fire on Route 75 where it turns north about five miles from Lake Trasimene, and the first objective of the 2nd Battalion was to clear these positions and cover the 627th Field Squadron while they were getting the road open. By again achieving surprise, the enemy in position near the road were rounded up after only slight opposition, and nineteen prisoners were taken. The identifications were interesting, as the prisoners all came from the 15th Panzer Grenadier Division, while those of the previous day had all been of the 305th Infantry Division. This showed us fairly precisely where the divisional boundary was and also indicated that the Germans were holding the shorter line (provided by having Lake Trasimene in the middle) in some strength. Having made a late start and having had this first task to perform (it was the shortest night of the year), the 2nd Battalion had little chance of establishing themselves on their final objectives by dawn unless they were unopposed. This was not the case, and on the right of the road fire came from the church of Corciano, which lies on a small hill in front of the village, while on the left Spandaus opened up from the area of Monte Rentella to the north and the village of Castelvieto to the west. At dawn some close fighting was still going on, particularly on the left, and the Colonel ordered a slight withdrawal to get the position consolidated. More prisoners were taken, making thirty-three.

There followed a most unpleasant day, in the course of which any movement even on foot seemed to attract the enemy's attention and bring down a few shells or mortar bombs. The intermittent but quite heavy rain of the last day or two had made the ground very soft and some carriers were completely bogged so that they had temporarily to be abandoned, as they were evidently in full view of the enemy. It seemed essential to clear Corciano and Rentella, and it was almost impossible to use the 2nd Battalion, who were pinned to the ground. The Brigadier therefore decided to use the 10th, who had fallen back into reserve, as the Guards had passed through on the right and the 7th on the left.

The relief of the 2nd Battalion by the 10th went quite smoothly and did not appear to attract undue attention from the enemy. "A" Company took over on the right and patrolled on to find that Corciano church was still held. An attack was put in, and after a sharp fight the church and the hill on which it stood were cleared. A further patrol found that the village immediately in front of them was still strongly held and owing to lack of time they consolidated where they were, in a strong position overlooking the village. Early the next morning two Mark IV tanks and some infantry were seen on the edge of the village, were heavily engaged and withdrew northwards. This occurred at the same time as the counter-attack on Rentella and may have represented a design by the enemy to recapture the church feature, but more probably was just a diversion which caused some dispersion of our artillery fire.

Meanwhile on the left "C" Company had been established on Monte Rentella and "D" Company (Ian Blacker) on another small, unnamed feature four or five hundred yards to the east. Some enemy were known to be dug in on the west slopes of Rentella and others in the village of Castelvieto to the south-west, but the night passed more quietly than had been expected, some bursts of machine-gun fire from the latter being all that occurred. At about half past six in the morning, however, heavy and accurate mortar fire began on both positions, and under cover of this fire eighty to a hundred infantry advanced with great speed through the saddle between the hills, and then swung round to envelop them. The attack was carried out with great skill, and in particular with such speed that it was almost at once impossible for our artillery or mortars to fire without endangering our own troops. Hand-to-hand fighting took place with considerable casualties to both sides, and "D" Company was cut off. Ian Blacker, Pat Wilding and eight riflemen were killed after hand-to-hand fighting in a gallant attempt to hold their position, but by eight o'clock there could be no doubt that the enemy had prevailed, having captured "D" Company's feature and also the summit of Rentella. Some fearless work by the stretcher-bearers had resulted in the evacuation of about thirty wounded, but there were nearly seventy missing, being the balance of "D" Company. In fact, quite a number had evaded capture and returned to the Battalion the following night, though four officers and thirty-three riflemen, many of them wounded, were taken prisoner. "C" Company had meanwhile held their own except for the loss of the summit. By now they were in a thoroughly unhealthy position, and fire started coming down on them from three sides. They were withdrawn with the aid of "B" Company and the Support Company, and, though they continued to be harassed by fire from two or three tanks and self-propelled guns at close range from the north and west, the situation was successfully stabilized with virtually no further loss, while the Gunners were able to fire some accurate concentrations on to the enemy, who were overlooked. Teddy Goschen and James Booth gave a running commentary by wireless and their coolness not only saved the day but caused the enemy severe losses.

The Germans were overlooked from Monte Malbe and, more closely, from Corciano church. They made several attempts to drive "A" Company from the latter during the day, and two tanks and a self-propelled gun came in to very short range and tried to blast them out by fire. Some thick walls assisted and the position was never in serious danger, perhaps owing to the fact that the enemy had used all his available infantry in the earlier attacks on the other side of the road. Thus the position was that, though we had had a nasty knock so had the enemy and his success had been only partial. This accounts for the fact, surprising at first sight, that the following night (the 22nd/23rd of June) patrols of the 10th Battalion found the enemy withdrawing not only from Corciano village but also from Rentella and the other feature which they had won at considerable cost the previous morning. Ten prisoners were picked up, five on each side of the road, and the Germans may not finally have been satisfied that they had the best of the bargain in the Rentella operation, in which they undoubtedly scored an initial success.

It had generally been expected that the enemy would make no attempt to resist with more than rearguards between the fall of Rome and the Gothic Line. This expectation had already proved ill-founded, as all along the line enemy resistance had stiffened and identifications showed that the greater part of Kesselring's Army Group, including all his best divisions, were fully committed in holding us and putting in counter-attacks. What almost nobody then guessed correctly was that Kesselring put little faith in the constructed fortifications of the Gothic Line and preferred to take advantage of the natural lines of defence provided by the Italian terrain in a seemingly never-ending series. What was clear, however, was that we had come up against a line that needed a build-up of the Allied forces before the advance could be resumed. The unseasonably wet weather of the previous few days has already been mentioned, and it had a big influence on bringing the advance to a halt, for it had the dual effect of slowing down the Allies and of making it more difficult for the enemy to extricate his guns and equipment and therefore more determined to bring us to a halt.

The offensive operations of the Brigade were thus temporarily at an end, and with the arrival of the King's Dragoon Guards to clear and hold the area between the 10th Battalion and Lake Trasimene a good defensive position existed where we were. Some thinning out was possible and parties from the battalions were able to go each day to Perugia, where X Corps Welfare got cinemas and canteens going while the town was still under occasional shell fire. It was a charming town and seemed clean and civilized after what we had seen in South Italy, and it was some compensation for not having seen Rome.

The 1st Guards Brigade were given the task of clearing the

hills to a greater depth north of the town and the 7th Battalion extended to the right to enable them to do this. The area taken over proved to be the most unpleasant in our sector, as it was strewn with deeply buried "S" mines, which caused them several casualties, including Norman Odgers wounded. Shelling on the main features was regular but did little further harm. There was a short stretch of road near the station on the way from Brigade Headquarters to the battalions which had to be traversed as quickly as possible, as it had evidently been accurately registered, but, though there were several casualties there, the Brigade was lucky in avoiding any. Apart from regular patrols, we were called on for only one active operation during the week, which was to clear a feature named Monte San Croce on the right of the Divisional sector. A careful and detailed plan was made by Colonel Chris Sinclair and it was hoped to account for a platoon of Germans, but they evidently suspected what was in the air and withdrew a few hours before the 2nd Battalion attacked and occupied the hill unopposed.

On the 30th of June the 10th Indian Division started to take over the Divisional sector. The enemy chose this inconvenient moment to carry out a withdrawal, and the 10th Battalion had to spend a hot day busy on patrols to regain contact. This was achieved and by that night the whole Brigade was concentrated in an area four to five miles south of Lake Trasimene to have a short rest before resuming on the other side of the lake, a rest that was much needed if only because this period of severe fighting had caused a significant number of casualties. The 10th Battalion had lost the best part of "D" Company and on Monte Malbe four officers of the 7th Battalion, including Johnnie Persse, had been killed by mines or shelling after the position had been captured. For a time this Battalion had to be reorganized on a basis of two rifle companies and a support company. But, as the Brigade rested for these few days, securely established in the centre of Italy, they could look back with satisfaction on their achievements in these rocky mountains where they had struck a shrewd blow at the Germans not only in forcing them to give up this vital ground but in inflicting heavy casualties during the counter-attacks of their infantry, a satisfaction tempered by remembrance of the loss of Ian Blacker and so many good, young officers, stalwart non-commissioned officers and brave riflemen, who in Italy could never be replaced.

CHAPTER XXI

THE ARNO VALLEY AND THE GOTHIC LINE

The first month of existence of the 61st Infantry Brigade had been very successful and justified the confidence we had all felt at the time of its creation. Over two hundred prisoners had been taken, of whom not more than two or three could be regarded as deserters, while Rentella was the only place at which the Brigade had lost a prisoner and the enemy had still not identified the 2nd or 7th Battalion in Italy. For producing concrete results, subsequent months were to be much less satisfactory, chiefly because the Brigade was not again called on in the mobile role for which it was best suited until the last month of the war. Throughout this period there was never a big bag of prisoners. It is a tale of the enemy constantly choosing his ground to fight on and withdrawing before we had a chance to develop our plans to deal with him. This was not true of the 61st Brigade only, but of the way the campaign in Italy as a whole was going at this time. One good haul of prisoners by the Poles in the Ancona area was the only major victory during the months of July and August, while a large part of the Allied forces in the country were preparing for the invasion of the South of France, to be followed by the fierce attempts to finish off the enemy in Italy in September.

Theoretically the month of July started with a three-day rest period which was a useful chance to catch up with letter writing, washing and sleeping, or, for the unlucky, such things as the "bumph," censoring letters or writing the War Diary. They seemed to be the three hottest days of the year, and we were unlucky to be in an area with few houses and lacking in shade. Lake Trasimene was rather too far, and when one got there one found the southern shore not much good for bathing owing to reeds and slimy mud. Even the war did not leave us alone: the Luftwaffe put in one of its already rare appearances and dropped some butterfly bombs one moonlight night. It is true that no damage was done, but they caused some alarm to an open-air cinema show.

When we had left the east side there was an enemy withdrawal in progress; at the same time something similar started on the west side. Enemy resistance, which had been fierce for over a week, was weakening and rearguards were evidently covering a thinning out followed by a withdrawal. Once again the usual appreciation was that there would be no further serious resistance until the Gothic Line was reached, and the plans now made envisaged another pursuit, with Pontassieve as the objective. It was to be nearly two months before it was reached. The original plan was for the 61st Brigade to take the lead with the 16th/5th Lancers under command: a regimental group of the latter with the 10th Battalion was formed for this purpose, and this group did in fact set forth on the 3rd of July. As so often, the enemy had chosen the highly inconvenient time of a relief to make a withdrawal, and when the 10th Battalion took over after dark from the 36th Brigade the first task was to discover where the enemy had got to. A motor platoon was told to see how far it could get by midnight and then report. It got over three miles without making contact. The Sappers reported at the same time that a demolition on the road could quickly be made fit for tracked vehicles but would need a bridge for wheels.

The Divisional Commander therefore decided that the 26th Armoured Brigade should take charge of the battle from first light in the morning, still with the 16th/5th Lancers, and the 10th Battalion in the lead. The next day an advance of eleven miles was made in the face of considerable demolitions and mines, but only slight shelling and no contact. Patrols of the 10th Battalion made contact that night some five miles south of Arezzo. The night was remarkable for torrential rain, which may have been as much the cause of the check that now came as were the enemy.

The Divisional axis was now Route 71, which runs to Arezzo up the right edge of the Chiana Valley. The valley was thickly cultivated with vines and orchards and cut up by dykes and irrigation ditches. The left flank was a canal, while the right flank was (as usual) mountainous, and the main road runs right at the foot of these mountains. The rain made the many demolitions more difficult and interfered with cross-country movement. Where the 10th Battalion had made contact with the enemy the previous night proved to be as far as the tanks could get, and so the greater part of the Division was strung out along the valley, with the enemy overlooking us on the hills to the right. His anti-tank guns covered demolitions in front; there was no possibility of working round to the left owing to the canal and a further anti-tank gun, and the only thing to do was to set about clearing the right flank in the mountains. This was a formidable task and already the 7th Battalion had been involved miles farther south in several fruitless expeditions into the hills. The Partisans of Cortona took over protection of their area farther south and "F" Reconnaissance Squadron (a group of former Italian paratroops) came under command of the Brigade and patrolled into the hills to the east of Castiglion Fiorentino. This did something to make the task manageable, but to put a stop to the shelling of increasing volume and accuracy and to enable the advance on Arezzo to be resumed two, if not three, features had to be cleared of enemy. To the south was Monte Castiglion Maggio (Monte Maggio henceforth), and four miles to the north Monte Lignano; in between the ground rose less steeply, but, though more remote, Monte Camurcino, towards which these slopes rose, also overlooked the road and might also subsequently have to be cleared. It should, too, be mentioned here that the features are large and complicated, with no clearly defined summits, covered with scrub and in parts with trees.

The first attempt to clear the area was made by the 10th Battalion, under command of the 26th Armoured Brigade, on the evening of the 5th of July. "C" Company gained a foothold near the top of Lignano, but found the enemy dug in on the summit and reverse slopes. "B" Company were in much the same position on Maggio, and an attempt to clear the summit cost a number of casualties, including Eric Clark, who was killed, and Charles Morpeth wounded. "A" Company were sent to relieve them the next morning, and the 2nd Battalion was sent to assist "C" Company and to take over the ground in between. They were originally all under command of the 26th Armoured Brigade, but that evening another reshuffle took place. "B" Company of the 7th Battalion passed to command of the 26th Armoured Brigade to take over night protection and patrolling on the sector astride the main road, and the remainder reverted to command of the 61st Brigade. The 2nd Battalion took over on Monte Lignano and the 7th, less "B" Company, passed through "A" Company of the 10th to clear Maggio. "C" Company of the 7th reached the top at three in the morning and took two prisoners of the 194th Artillery Regiment (the artillery observation post), but the enemy were dug in on the reverse slopes, some of them within hand-grenade range, and a sharp exchange took place. The essential was to get dug in before first light, and while a covering party continued this duel the remainder dug positions thirty yards down on our side, with "A" Company on the right and "C" Company on the left.

This action had caused some improvement in the situation, as the enemy had lost his observation post; but the position was still in the nature of a stalemate, with the enemy and ourselves on the respective reverse slopes on both features, and the enemy probably still having observation from Lignano. A full company of the 2nd Battalion was required for portage, involving a two-and-a-half-hour climb to keep the forward troops supplied, and the fourth company of the 7th, though having a less lengthy walk, was also fully committed, being already in a depleted state. "B" and "C" Companies of the 10th Battalion were the only reserve and they had only just come out of the battle. The next night's activities were therefore to be confined to fighting patrols. The enemy proved to have other views. A civilian warning of an enemy attack on Lignano proved to be accurate. They were given a hot reception before the attack could develop, and suffered a number of casualties with none to ourselves. An unexpected counter-attack on Maggio was unfortunately more successful. In the dark before the moon rose the enemy came round both sides of the summit as the 7th Battalion was just preparing to send two strong fighting patrols in the opposite direction. Owing to these preparations and the darkness, the enemy got to within fifty yards of our positions before being spotted. Confused hand-to-hand fighting (in places quite literally) took place, and after receiving and inflicting a number of casualties the two companies withdrew five hundred yards. They then reorganized without further interference in the area of "A" Company of the 10th Battalion.

The stretcher-bearers of the 7th Battalion were permitted by the enemy to recover our own wounded, but naturally not to move the German dead, of whom there were several in the area. All but two of the riflemen were accounted for. One pair of stretcher-bearers, continuing the search under the Red Cross flag, walked into a German Spandau post, where after exchanging cigarettes, they were told that the missing two had been taken prisoner the night before. It is surprising to record that the Germans allowed these two stretcher-bearers to return to our lines. Thereafter it was a comparatively quiet day with some vigorous patrolling by the 2nd Battalion, who gained some useful information of positions on Lignano and Camurcino. That night the 1st Battalion 60th Rifles came under command and relieved the 2nd Battalion, a long process owing to the distance that they had to walk and one which caused them casualties from the mortar fire that came down on the way. The following night, the 9th/10th of July, the 1st Argylls took over from the 7th Battalion and the Brigade passed to reserve with, at first, no operational tasks. A few small commitments were undertaken a day or two later, and the 2nd Battalion had to provide one and later two companies as a firm base for the subsequent attack of the 1st Guards Brigade.

The day the Brigade was relieved Brigade Headquarters moved two or three miles out of the gun area and to get into a house. All the vehicles of Brigade Headquarters had just driven up the road and turned into the yard of the house when a loud explosion was heard. Major Harris, commanding the 627th Field Squadron, R.E., had been in a jeep on his way to visit the Brigadier and was within a hundred and fifty yards of the house when what must have been a large and very deeply buried mine exploded. "Harry" was instantly killed and his driver badly wounded. The Brigadier was also in a jeep and was just pulling out to overtake when this happened. He appeared to be badly injured, being covered with blood on his face, arms and legs. Fortunately, though large numbers of fragments had caused scratches from head to foot, there was no serious wound.

On the 15th the 2nd New Zealand Division attacked the main features on the right and the 1st Guards Brigade the high ground astride the main road. The attack was successful and the enemy did not linger to see the later stages develop. On the morning of the 16th the 26th Armoured Brigade, with the 10th Battalion under command, entered Arezzo. Not pausing, they raced hard for the bridges across the Arno, five or six miles to the north and west. "A" Company, with the 2nd Lothians, captured the bridge at Buriano intact; but "B" Company, with the 16th/5th Lancers, had the disappointment of seeing the more important road bridge on the left go up when they were within a hundred yards of it. There were a lot of enemy still in the neighbourhood and the 7th Battalion was sent up in the evening to assist in holding the bridgehead and protect the armour. The enemy did not, in fact, appear that night to have the aggressive intentions some people had anticipated, and the several small parties encountered in the dark seemed to be lost or trying to withdraw, having been left behind by the speed of our advance. Four prisoners were taken and one German was killed from these parties.

The Divisional axis now turned west, following the Arno and directed on Pontassieve. Although the 10th Battalion entered Arezzo on the 16th of July, it was not until the 30th of August that the leading elements of the 26th Armoured Brigade reached Pontassieve, an event which coincided with the fall of Florence. For all this time, all three battalions of the 61st Brigade were more or less continuously engaged. German opposition was always intense: their 1st Parachute Division, about the best troops in their Italian armies, seemed often to be on our front. They did not always come off best, as the sharp battle which the 10th Battalion, temporarily commanded by Bobby Selway, and the 17th/21st Lancers fought for Renacci was to show. Daily casualties in the Brigade mounted steadily, until by the 26th of August the motor companies were down to a strength of fifty and the total casualties in the Brigade were over a hundred officers and men. Among them no loss was greater than that of John Bodley, who was killed when his carrier went over a mine, one of the best carrier commanders, who had only just returned, much sooner than he should have, from the hospital where he had been recovering from an earlier wound. It was during this time, too, that Charles Calistan was killed. He had won the Military Medal with the 2nd Battalion early in the desert war; he had been recommended for the Victoria Cross after the Snipe action at Alamein and been awarded instead a Distinguished Conduct Medal. He was commissioned in the Regiment and served as an officer in the 7th Battalion, until his luck at last forsook him in the fighting just short of Faella.

It was difficult to see at times what corresponding results could be set against these losses. But those who have fought the Germans know well enough that they must never be allowed a respite. In addition it was necessary to keep them occupied while the Eighth Army were building up for their next operations. For lack of space over a month has been dismissed in a few pages, six weeks of desperate fighting in really hot, unpleasant weather. While the 21st Army Group had stolen the limelight and hopes of a swift advance had been dashed by the endless succession of excellent defensive positions which the country presented to the Germans, there was a disposition among the soldiers in Italy to feel that their efforts were forgotten. The visit of the King to Italy did much to dispel this feeling. On the 26th of July the Brigade had sent five hundred men under Colonel Dick Fyffe to line the route south of Arezzo and cheer the King as he passed.

On the same day General Evelegh had handed over to General Templer. The new Divisional Commander had the misfortune to be wounded by a mine explosion only just over a fortnight later, and his successor at the end of August was General H. Murray, who remained in command of the Division to the extreme satisfaction of the Brigade until the end of the war.

Colonel Douglas Darling returned recovered from his wound on the 30th of August and resumed command of the 7th Battalion. Colonel Dick Fyffe moved to take over the 10th Battalion from Bobby Selway, who had again been in temporary command, Colonel Dick Southby having a recurrence of stomach trouble and now being declared definitely unfit. Colonel Dick Fyffe was taking over his third battalion in a few months, and may claim to have established a further record, as the battalion he commanded was, in March, 1945, christened the 2nd Battalion, though it will be seen that this was largely only a change of name.

Taking over in the Sieve Valley from the Armoured Brigade we might almost have thought we were back in the Arno Valley once more. There were one or two differences, of course, and in particular the fact that the dominating ground now lay on our left instead of the usual right flank. Monte Giovi was the important feature commanding the Sieve Valley, and until this had been cleared by the 8th Indian Division our operations were inevitably limited in scale. Once again the 2nd Battalion was on the flank, this time the left, patrolling into the hills ahead, while the 7th and 10th Battalions alternated on the main axis in the Sieve Valley supported by the 17th/21st Lancers. The weather began to break with one or two thunderstorms which were a relief in that the worst heat was over, though the rain was soon to become too much of a good thing, and by the end of this period became a really serious handicap to operations, particularly in combination with the cold of the mountains.

Opposition was on the whole less strong than it had been in the Arno Valley, but there was some heavy shelling of the road demolitions, resulting in a number of casualties, mainly to the 626th Field Squadron, R.E., in their bridge-building work. There were also some sharp patrol clashes, causing casualties to the enemy but to us too, the 10th Battalion again being unlucky in losing Duncan Gray and Jimmy Stevens. The 7th Battalion was called on for one rather bigger operation when resistance was met at Rugiano. "B" Company put in an early morning attack after a heavy barrage: it might almost be used to illustrate the advantages and limitations of this type of attack, on the whole not used by the 61st Brigade, to whom the silent attack with artillery on quick call was normally better suited. Colonel Reggie Green, commanding the 57th Field Regiment, R.A., then supporting the Brigade, arranged the barrage of nearly three thousand shells on a target of a tiny village on a hill and the reverse slopes, and "B" Company, following the barrage in, rounded up eleven prisoners without opposition from the dazed men of the 715th Fusilier Battalion. Despite the accuracy of the barrage, so far as could be discovered not one single casualty was inflicted by it. "A" Company (now under Tim Dewhurst) worked round the flank to prevent any enemy getting away, though they were handicapped by a heavy mist. However, interrogation of prisoners showed that only three had made good their escape, of whom two were rounded up later in the day. A more difficult proposition was Villa Peruzzi, on the left of Rugiano, and "C" Company had two killed and five wounded in an attempt to clear this fortress-like building, the only approach to which was across an open, mined terrace. The enemy did not wait for our second attempt, though one German overslept so badly that he was put in the bag.

On the night of the 8th/9th of September the enemy made off and we started pushing forward against no opposition until, on the 10th, the 1st Guards Brigade passed through, and we were left with only a minor commitment on the right flank and with having to find parties to work for the Sappers. This gave most officers and a good many riflemen a chance to see Florence for the first time. It was a brief period and by the 16th the Brigade was almost fully committed again. The following day the 1st Guards Brigade started to move away, the Division having been called on to send a brigade to take over a large but inactive sector from the 10th Indian Division under X Corps. The Eighth Army's attack on the Gothic Line on the Adriatic coast was making good progress, but it had been at considerable cost and there was a demand for fresh troops to keep the impetus of the attack going against the troops being reinforced with remarkable rapidity by Kesselring. We ourselves were now in the Fifth Army, XIII Corps providing right-flank protection to the American attack over the mountains towards Bologna, and taking over ground won by them to enable them to continue their attack on a fairly narrow front. The Gothic Line as we had thought of it was already penetrated by both armies, and, though nobody thought our troubles were at an end, it was commonly believed that we could force a steady withdrawal on the enemy. Events on the Western Front led many of us in Italy, as elsewhere, to suppose that the war would be finished in a month or two.

On the front that we took over at this time the constructed defences of the Gothic Line were in our hands, the Germans having made no attempt to hold them. But the main hills overlooking those defences were still held in some strength by the 1028th Regiment of the 715th Division. This was the worst regiment of a poor division by the standards of the German Army in Italy, and in fact they did provide a number of deserters for the bag of the next few days. But even poor troops can do a lot of damage with a Spandau, as they had the advantage of well-prepared positions in close country. As so often with such troops, their officers and most of the non-commissioned officers were able to keep them fighting so that they were only likely to collapse when left on their own. Perhaps it was partly due to this fact that they concentrated a whole battalion to hold the most important feature, named Monte Peschiena. This was a mountain of one thousand one hundred and ninety-eight metres (six thousand five hundred feet), difficult to approach except by a stiff climb on foot and which necessitated our first acquaintance with the animal we were to meet all through the winter—the mule. The transition from a motor battalion to infantry pure and simple was now complete when supply depended on mule transport.

The 2nd Battalion took over this feature from the 3rd Battalion Grenadier Guards on the 16th and found themselves in the all-too-familiar situation of holding the reverse slopes while the enemy were on the summit and strongly dug in on the slopes on their side. In view of the supply trouble and the thick, difficult nature of the ground, it was essential to spend a day or two on patrolling before an effective attack could be mounted. On one of these patrols Roger Kingsley was killed. Others were luckier and more successful and two troublesome machine-gun posts were eliminated by small raids of fighting patrols, resulting in the capture of four prisoners and at least two enemy being killed. This cleared the way for the main attack, which was to take place on the 21st at first light. A suspicion arose that the enemy had withdrawn in the night; so the artillery support was called off and a fighting patrol was sent out first which discovered that the enemy had indeed got away in the nick of time.

The 10th Battalion meanwhile were on the right of the 2nd astride Route 67, "A" and "B" Companies suffering from some accurate mortar fire in the area of Castagneto, whence they were patrolling to find routes to assist some ambitious projects for releasing the armour into the hills. On the night of the 20th of August they were to assist the 2nd Battalion by a preliminary operation, the capture of Monte Erbolini on the right of Peschiena. It was a dark night and many wire obstacles and some enemy, who hastily fled, were met on the way there. The operation fell rather behind schedule, but at first light two platoons of "B" Company were digging in on the hill in a heavy mist. A burst of Spandau fire revealed that the enemy still had an outpost on the summit, but this soon withdrew. "D" Company, under Jim Wilson, passed through and climbed steadily on in face of some harassing fire, to establish themselves that night on the top of the Muraglione Pass. A reconnaissance patrol of a section, with an officer of the 626th Field Squadron, was ambushed the next night and taken prisoner except for one man; but a further patrol directed fire on to the enemy, and, returning by the road, found no "blows" on the downward path from the pass.

The absence of "blows" on the road down from the Muraglione Pass was good news for the Sappers, who were faced with a formidable task on the road up to the top. Several Bailey bridges were required, and demolitions on the pass entailed constructing a new road out of the side of the cliff for several stretches. This work was completed in amazingly quick time and was open to one-way traffic on the morning of the 25th of September. There was no need for the infantry to wait for the road to be opened and the 7th Battalion was called on to pass through on the night of the 23rd/24th. They had had a fortnight in reserve, but during that time had hardly been idle, for they had provided regular work parties for the Sappers and had often been working under shell fire. On the morning of the 24th the Colonel, accompanied only by Tactical Headquarters and one platoon from "D" Company, set forth for a nine-mile "swan" on foot. Shortly after midday this party entered San Benedetto, which they found completely deserted and two bridges a little farther on intact. The rest of "D" Company came up to join them and a platoon was allotted to each bridge. The 2nd Medium Regiment, R.A., had an observation-post officer with the party and his guns could with difficulty give them some support, while the 25-pounders were well out of range twelve miles back.

Fortunately no counter-attack came in, but in the night a small party of enemy with a mule approached, presumably to blow the bridges. There was a brief exchange of fire and the enemy made off. An explanation of the enemy's lack of enterprise and failure to blow several bridges can be given without detracting from the credit due to the 7th Battalion for the dash they showed. While our line of advance lay north-east up Route 67, the German line of withdrawal lay north or even north-west and therefore the 715th Division moved off to Marradi and the division previously opposite our right, the 305th Division, came up to block Route 67. This left something of a hiatus which they no doubt thought would be adequately covered by the numerous demolitions left behind by them. By the next day the enemy, a few miles farther back, had time to get himself organized in country of which it is more than ever true to say that it was "ideal for defence." It was full of high peaks, usually scalable only from one side and cut by deep, narrow ravines.

On the 25th further progress was made down the road, but four casualties were suffered getting over a "blow" with the rubble liberally sown with Schuh mines. At the next village down the road, Bocconi, five miles beyond San Benedetto, an enemy outpost was surprised and two prisoners taken. Heavy fire in the village prevented further progress and a sergeant was killed.

An attempt was made the next day by the carrier platoon, after a short shoot by the 2nd Medium Regiment, to charge through the village. This achieved some success, but they were heavily shelled in the east end, and infantry began to emerge from the cellars with grenades; so the Colonel ordered them to withdraw after two carriers had been knocked out and all the crews killed or wounded. Enemy resistance, particularly shelling, was on the increase and it was evident that it was useless to try to get farther until more forces had been deployed and the hills astride the road occupied to get observation. This was done and a wonderful panoramic view could be obtained from the summits, Forli and the Lombardy Plain stretching away in the distance, and it may be true, as was claimed by the inhabitants, that on a clear day Ravenna could also be seen, over fifty miles away. Though a good deal of the road could be seen, the country was so cut up that in most cases this did not mean that we overlooked the enemy positions, and he could still see much of the main road behind our forward positions as it wound up the valley. The stage seemed set for further developments; but, though some further progress was made, nothing very spectacular was achieved, for two main reasons.

The first was the weather, which seemed to do everything we did not want it to do. Torrents of rain were the worst feature, washing away some of the Sappers' work and turning the few areas in which it might have been possible to put guns or harbour vehicles off the road into quagmires. This, combined with cold at night, which in the mountains was already intense at times, made life in a slit trench quite unbearable. On the night of the 28th/29th of September the weather was so bad that a rifleman on Monte Fuso died of exposure, a tragic example of what was to be expected unless cover could be found or frequent reliefs carried out. The latter was not altogether possible as long as we were still on the offensive: the 1st Guards Brigade was not with the Division, and in any case the state of the road restricted movement to the area and shortage of supply mules limited the number of troops who could be maintained and relieved on the hills.

The second was the fact that, rather than be content with a nibble at the enemy with the 61st Brigade, the Divisional Commander decided to try for a bigger bite with the Armoured Brigade. He had an armoured brigade complete at his disposal and comparatively fresh, and air photographs showed that the country a little farther on was rather more suitable for tanks. Further, if a break-through could be achieved the enemy opposite the Eighth Army would be threatened in the rear. Route 9 was the life-line of the German Tenth Army, and it was only the existence of this broad, straight highway, with its network of minor roads, that enabled them to switch forces from one sector to another with such rapidity, despite our overwhelming air superiority. The enemy had just lost Rimini, but was now able to use the series of rivers flowing from the mountains to Lake Comacchio to fight a number of delaying actions. This could be done with a much smaller force than the ten divisions that he had assembled on the Adriatic sector against an army on whom he had inflicted heavy losses. Now the threat was coming from the Americans heading towards Bologna and as much as possible of the force must be switched back to the central sector, which had been dangerously thinned out in order to provide this concentration on the east coast. There was, then, for us a big prize to gain and almost nothing to lose. But once again the weather was a decisive factor. It was, to quote a phrase from an account of the 26th Armoured Brigade, "a period of many alarms and few excursions, when hopes of a break-through were washed away by torrential rainstorms."

On the 27th of September the 10th Battalion passed to the command of the 26th Armoured Brigade, and as there was no possible harbour area they were stretched nose to tail behind the 17th/21st Lancers down the road, waiting for the chance to dash forward. After three days of this all the Battalion, except "C" Company, moved back again. Meanwhile the 2nd Battalion came up, took over the 7th Battalion's positions on the right of the road, and started pushing on to work their way round the right flank. They were slowed up by the maintenance problem and many men were employed on making jeep tracks to ease the shortage of mules.

The 7th Battalion continued to be responsible for the high ground to the left of the road, and their next operation was to clear an enemy outpost covering a blown bridge less than a mile beyond Bocconi. Although this was defended by only one enemy platoon, a detailed study of the ground revealed what a difficult operation it was likely to be. The only approach was by a long detour to the left, involving a march along a narrow and precipitous mountain ledge, finally coming on the position from the rear. To protect this route "C" Company of the 7th Battalion had first to capture Monte Freddo; it was occupied without opposition on a bitterly cold night in a heavy storm. However, fire of all kinds came down on it, the mortaring being particularly accurate and causing nearly a whole platoon of ex-Ulster Rifles to be casualties. The position was held and the next night "A" Company, with a platoon of "B" Company under command, made the detour and came down to the road behind the "blow." The enemy had guessed what we were doing and had ordered his outpost to withdraw; but one section had been left behind and after a brief resistance one was killed and four taken prisoner.

The Sappers now had a difficult bridge of a hundred and thirty feet to build. The task was made more difficult by the accurate fire the enemy put down by day, while rain and darkness made work at night almost impossible. Aided by a temporary improvement in the weather, it was completed by the 6th, and we were ready for Operation Two. With a bit of luck and better weather, however, we might have been at this stage a week earlier. By now the chief element of surprise had almost certainly been lost. It had been hoped that the enemy would be completely surprised by the speed with which the Sappers had opened the road over the pass and that they would not have calculated on the possibility of our tanks and guns having got over. Now we had been forced to disclose some of our gun positions, and the passage of time would have allowed the enemy to prepare his positions and at least to consider the possibility of tanks appearing.

Only a mile farther down the road there was another "blow," but this one was of modest dimensions and it was planned to get over by using a scissors bridge, and sweep on before the enemy recovered from his surprise. This expedient achieved considerable success, the 17th/21st Lancers getting through to the outskirts of Portico, three miles farther down the road; but strong resistance came from inside the small town, a bridge was blown just in time from the German point of view, and the advance was brought to a halt once more, although "C" Company of the 10th Battalion held positions overlooking the enemy to the west of the road. Some progress was also made up the lateral road to the left and ten prisoners were taken. The 10th Battalion came up and took over the ground won by the 17th/21st Lancers.

Meanwhile the 2nd Battalion was struggling to clear the hills on the right of the road. Originally their difficulties were entirely those of maintenance and of finding shelter from the appalling weather. A route was found, Monte Roncole occupied with one casualty to the enemy, and the lateral track to the village of Premilcuore opened. The next task was to clear Monte Orlando, where Charles Allford was killed on a patrol to locate enemy positions. It was an extremely difficult feature to tackle, as there was only one practicable line of approach to the top, and once on the summit the companies were again overlooked from Monte della Serra behind it. Aided by the close country, positions were established on the lower slopes of Orlando. It seemed necessary to tackle both features the same night. The first attempt was made on the night of the 7th/8th of October and was intended further to clear the way for the dash of the 17th/21st Lancers the next morning. It was rather a rush job and Colonel Chris Sinclair would have preferred at least one more day for reconnaissance and the maintenance side of the operation. However, every day was important and the attack started under a handicap. "C" Company had to come up in the night, as it was impossible to get them to a forward concentration area: "B" Company did the attack, which was necessarily on a narrow front, and as they neared the summit they were heavily fired on by six Spandaus and some mortars. They had one killed and eight wounded and, initially, ten missing, but six of the latter returned the next day. "C" Company, under Riggy Wrigglesworth, had a terrible struggle in getting even jeeps forward and were never committed, though it had been hoped to pass them through "B" Company. The strength of the resistance on Orlando was a good deal greater than had been anticipated and it seems that the enemy were expecting the attack.

Further patrols were subsequently made to Orlando by the 2nd Battalion and some casualties were inflicted, including four prisoners taken. The enemy eventually abandoned the summit; but the approach to Monte della Serra from this side was strewn with mines and covered by machine guns. Attempts were also made to get at the feature from the other side (the side facing the road). This also was opposed, and operations were still continuing when we were moved away. It was unfortunately a tale of frustration, since we could always give as good as we received, and usually better so long as the *status quo* existed, but an attack was bound to cause considerable casualties unless some surprise could be achieved.

The last week in this sector saw a great increase in enemy shelling, mainly directed on the village of Bocconi, which luckily was very difficult to hit, and on the road. We were on the whole fortunate, while the 26th Armoured Brigade, particularly the 17th/21st Lancers, had some serious misfortune. The sector was otherwise becoming uneventful apart from patrols. The 10th Battalion did some enterprising patrols into Portico and to the north, while on the 7th's front the enemy began doing patrols, causing themselves several casualties for their pains, one of which was inflicted by a party taking up rations at night to Monte Freddo. Things seemed to be settling down when, on the 15th of October at midday, there was the first warning that a 26th Armoured Brigade group was to take over and the 61st Brigade was to move to a new sector in the hills north of Castel del Rio. By the night of the 16th/17th the whole Brigade had been relieved and only two nights later the relief of the 38th Irish Infantry Brigade had been completed in a sector which, though not very far as the crow flies, involved two lengthy journeys over the mountains on bad and congested roads. So far from being disheartened by this tiresome change-over with no rest between the two, it will be seen that both the 2nd and 10th Battalions were causing the enemy discomfiture right from the beginning.

A good deal has already been said about the discomfort of the period covered by this chapter, but one noticeable feature has not been mentioned. Just beyond San Benedetto there was a large building that had once been a sanatorium. In this building on the evening of the 24th of September the Colonel of the 7th Battalion set up a small Tactical Headquarters, together with "D" Company headquarters and the reserve platoon. Two days later there was a reserve company there, the next day two more rooms were found for a Brigade Tactical Headquarters, and before long a 26th Armoured Brigade and 17th/21st Lancers Tactical Headquarters joined them, and finally Divisional Tactical Headquarters. On the road outside there was a long line of tanks and vehicles nose to tail, and whichever direction one went in by road one had to take care not to drive almost up the muzzle of a gun that would probably choose that moment to fire. When an advance was made some tenants moved out, but there was always a waiting list, so that more would move in, and it was never safe to walk through any room or passage at night without a torch, as one was sure to tread on some unfortunate Rifleman trying to get some sleep.

CHAPTER XXII

WINTER IN THE APENNINES

By the beginning of October it was clear that, as far as the Italian campaign was concerned, winter had come to the rescue of the Germans. In North-West Europe the narrow failure at Arnhem meant that the war would continue probably until the spring. It was not that the Allied armies had ceased to be successful: they were indeed still advancing, though less rapidly, on all fronts. But the recuperative powers of the German armies, the fighting qualities of those stubborn individuals who manned their Spandaus behind bushes without hope, but without thought of surrender, the resilience of the paratroopers, who would attack again and again over the bodies of their comrades, the skill of such professional soldiers as von Rundstedt and von Kesselring, all these contrived to make it possible for the Germans to hold on for one more winter and to complete the overthrow of European economy for a time not yet measured by man.

The Allies did not go into winter quarters. The 1st and 8th Battalions were busily engaged in operations in the Low Countries. The Higher Command in Italy did not at once forgo its offensive intentions. From the end of October the 61st Brigade was several times engaged in spasmodic advances, generally following up voluntary withdrawals on the part of the enemy. In December the 2nd Battalion undertook the disastrous attack on Tossignano. But on the whole it was, compared with the summer, a static period, when the cold became almost as formidable an enemy as the Germans. From the New Year until March the armies on the front where the 61st Brigade was engaged gave up any serious thoughts of advancing and settled down to prepare for the final efforts of the spring.

The weather and the ground have received the chief blame for bringing operations to a halt and are, therefore, worth describing in detail. Generalizations about the weather experienced over a period of as long as four and a half months are apt to be inaccurate, but for this particular period they give a reasonably true picture. The weather for the first month in the Santerno Valley was as bad as it had been in San Benedetto: torrents of rain caused landslides and washed away tracks, leaving such seas of mud that for a time even mules could not get to our forward positions on the right, and the supply and maintenance problem caused many headaches. Work on tracks was continuously required and, though much valuable assistance was given by "Shelldrake Sappers" (anti-aircraft and anti-tank gunners for whom there was no operational role and who were working for the Sappers), the unfortunate Rifleman was also often needed for work when he thought he had got a spell in reserve. The "Q" branch from Brigade Headquarters down to the riflemen in "A2" Echelon had the arduous task of keeping the battalions supplied with necessaries, and at the same time struggling to provide extra "luxuries," such as a change of clothing and dry blankets to men who were soaking. Much was achieved as a result of long hours of toil, but nothing can alter the fact that it was a thoroughly unpleasant period for all concerned. Yet it was during this time that the most successful patrolling took place.

The first fall of snow was on the night of the 9th/10th of November, but this was soon washed away by further rain. By a week or so later, however, the rain was at any rate becoming less heavy and colder weather with some bright days made conditions a little easier. The first fall of snow to remain lying was on the 22nd of December so that we had a white Christmas. The Divisional Commander came to dinner at Brigade Headquarters on Christmas Eve, and, rather like a Father Christmas, a 7th Battalion rifleman was produced for inspection dressed in a snow-camouflage suit, of which the first issue had just been made. It was a great success and became the universal wear of patrols and those in forward positions for several weeks thereafter. Some form of camouflage for weapons, which were apt to stand out black against the snow, was also needed. Further snow and intense cold persisted until the middle of January, but the rest of the winter almost restored the reputation of "Sunny Italy." It is true that the nights were unpleasantly cold for those on sentry, but the succession of bright, sunny days with not more than a pleasant bite in the air was a great compensation for the

[*Official Photo: Crown Copyright Reserved*

THE 7th BATTALION

Their mules, led by Italian soldiers, cross a repaired demolition on the Portico road, two miles beyond San Benedetto

[*Official Photo: Crown Copyright Reserved*

SNOW IN ITALY

A patrol of Riflemen returning in the snow near Monteloro

hardships of earlier days. The winter ended unusually early, and before we left this sector at the beginning of March the snow persisted only in sheltered hollows on the mountains. So much has been written, and even more said, about the way the weather in Italy seemed always to be against the Allies that it is only fair to mention that it could hardly have been more favourable than in the last months, and if the weather in February and March, 1945, had been even normal it is difficult to see how the final offensive in Italy could have achieved such a quick success in April. It would probably not even have started until at least a month later; yet it is none the less true that the weather was one of the main causes of the failure to finish off the campaign in Italy in September or October, 1944.

Any description of the country in which we spent the winter must start with a mention of Monte Battaglia, even though none of the Brigade ever occupied it. Not only was it the highest point in the area but the impression conveyed from any viewpoint round about was of a series of mountainous features, all dominated by this sinister-looking mountain crowned with a ruined castle. Though the country is broken by ravines and watersheds, there seemed to be a pattern radiating from this summit. To the east there is a steep descent to the Senio Valley, to the west and north a rather less steep drop to the Santerno Valley, while between the two to the north-east there is a constant succession of broken ridges of decreasing height until after about fifteen miles there lies the plain, green and fertile and thickly populated, in contrast to the empty spaces of the bare, rugged mountains. Even the valleys of the Senio and Santerno have little green in the winter, for they both, particularly the latter, consist mainly of orchard country and the trees seemed very bare. The 1st Guards Brigade took over Monte Battaglia from the Americans a fortnight before we came into the sector on their left, and the Germans showed the importance they attached to its recapture on several occasions, finishing with a large-scale, but fortunately ill-planned, attack on the night of the 11th/12th of October which resulted in a defensive triumph for the Guards and the capture of one officer and seventy-five other ranks.

The line originally taken over was on the left of the 1st Guards Brigade, who were having a relatively quiet time on Battaglia by then. Monte Capello was taken over by the 10th Battalion and was a feature of equal importance in appearing to dominate the Santerno Valley. A ravine provided a natural no-man's-land nearer the valley, cutting the road just short of Gaggio, where the Santerno and the whole valley bend. The enemy soon pulled back from this line to conform with events on our left, where the 78th Division made some gains, and this time used Monte Roncosole and Monte Taverna as the bastions of the defence between the two valleys, while in the Santerno Valley there was again a ravine (in fact, there were two within a hundred yards) on the edge of the large village or small town of Fontanelice. During this period the 1st Guards Brigade came round and were henceforth on our left, while, until we took over, a brigade of the 8th Indian Division was on our right. This line was a fairly strong one for the enemy, but needed more troops to hold than the next line back. It is difficult to offer an explanation of why he held it for more than a month or of why he gave it up when he did, unless he anticipated an attack on Taverna which, if successful, would turn the rest of the line. The line he then went back to was the Vena del Gesso.

The Vena del Gesso (the Vein of Chalk) is a curious geological phenomenon that we might almost have believed to have been constructed by German engineers rather than by Nature. It is most clearly defined between the Senio and Santerno Valleys, where it runs north-east to south-west for six miles. It continues on the far side of the two valleys, but to the south-east it soon blends with the rugged hills and becomes ill-defined, while on the left of the Santerno there is a change of direction and it runs south-east or parallel to the river and is clearly defined as far as Monte Penzola, and after that in patches such as Monte Acqua Salata. Throughout its length it is a cliff, almost sheer on one side and with comparatively gentle slopes on the other. Between the two valleys this cliff faced us as an obstacle, only in two or three places scalable at all, and then only by a steep and tortuous path. On the left of the Santerno it is equally an obstacle on the side facing the valley, but we started with the advantage of being, as it were, already on the top. This big advantage was partly offset by the fact that the far side of the Penzola Ridge, though much less steep, descended steadily to the narrow valley of the Mescola, on the far side of which the ground rose steeply again to the Croara Ridge, and from there the enemy had a good view of any movement on the summit of Penzola and the whole ridge. This meant that the attack by the

Coldstream Guards had to be by night and all supply thereafter also in darkness, which for those on the sharp, rocky peak was a formidable task.

This cliff obstacle was such that the whole plan of attack by the II American Corps in the autumn was made on the assumption that it was more practicable to continue pressing north through the mountains to Bologna than to turn towards the plain, even after the capture of Battaglia, when at first glance it might have appeared an obvious short cut. This was the obstacle that the 2nd Battalion were invited to tackle when ordered to capture Tossignano; such a bare statement is, in fact, misleading and does ill justice to our Higher Command unless qualified in various ways. The enemy was so convinced of the strength of the position and could so easily perceive the direction of the American advance (and also of the Eighth Army) that he had left this sector much more lightly held, and it was hoped that an attack from this direction might achieve complete surprise.

A little more must be said of the part of the Santerno Valley that bisects the Vena del Gesso which we christened the Borgo Gap. The river does another loop round the small town whose full name is Borgo Tossignano, and bridges carry the road and single-line railway across the river on the north of the town. From the point of view of further military progress this means that the best place to break through the gap is on the river's left bank. This obviates the necessity of having to cross the river, while at once rejoining the road to Imola, the goal of an advance down this valley. It is true that the Mescola flows into the Santerno on this side and presents an obstacle, but it is not very broad; nevertheless, there are two much more serious objections. In the first place the gap from the foot of the cliff to the river is little more than a hundred yards wide and was liberally sown with mines by the enemy, and, secondly, there is no approach to the gap this side except on foot. On the right bank the gap is at any rate a little broader, even though it is a bottle-neck, and the road leads up to Borgo, and from there another road climbs to Tossignano, less than a mile away up some hairpin bends. On one of these bends lies Casa Frascoleto, and at the top of the road at the north-west end of the town Casa Colombaia lies isolated from the other buildings amongst which the road disappears from view.

More will be said later of the geography of Tossignano and its approaches. But something must be said of the "casas," a subject of the greatest importance to the Brigade in the winter campaign. One of the reasons why most of the riflemen of the 10th Battalion preferred twenty-three days in the Casola Valsenio sector to fourteen days in the Tossignano sector followed by seven days in Grassina, near Florence, was because the houses in the former area were more plentiful and more comfortable. Even in the latter sector nearly all the men had shelter of a sort by day, and to a less extent by night, though the houses were small, dirty farmhouses and were icy-cold inside. There was a marked contrast also between the small towns lying behind the forward area in the two sectors. Fontanelice was a cramped and congested town which had suffered much damage even before we occupied it, and yet, despite the shelling it attracted, such was the shortage of shelter that every little dwelling that offered a pretence of indoor life was occupied by soldiers or the few remaining civilians of the little town which was unfortunate enough to remain within shelling distance of one or other of the contestants for over six months. Casola Valsenio, on the other hand, was a pleasant market town that had an air of quiet, modest prosperity: though the normal population of the two places must have been much the same, Casola covered about three times the area, and, having plenty of good houses and many fewer troops, everybody got himself shelter and something approaching comfort. On the whole, the area of the Guards Brigade was far worse, being almost totally lacking in "casas," and battalions of the Brigade had a taste of their area under the later system of reliefs. They were compensated by more frequent spells in the rest area, where comfort was the first consideration and there was a chance of really returning to the joys of civilization in the beautiful town of Florence. Whether it is better to put up with acute discomfort for a week followed by a week of comfort, or to have moderate discomfort for a fortnight for the same amount of relief is a question that every individual must answer for himself—and every Rifleman did.

The 10th Battalion set the ball in motion. On the 20th of October the enemy was known to have withdrawn and was believed to be in the area of Monteloro, and an advance was being planned for that night. Two things were required, the first being a study of the route across a difficult ravine that intervened, and the second being a rather more accurate idea of what opposition was likely to be met that night. A reconnaissance patrol of Sergeant Martin and two riflemen was sent out for this purpose, leaving after lunch. Having found a route fit for human beings and mules, they climbed up the path on the other side and made acquaintance with a civilian who volunteered the information that he had that morning seen nine Germans with a Spandau in slit trenches covering the house at Trida. Sergeant Martin thought this was worth investigating and, aided by a good covered approach, the patrol worked its way forward. The sound of voices was heard and there, a bare twenty yards away, they saw two Germans sitting in a slit trench chatting together apparently without a care in the world. One of the patrol was left covering these while the other two crept forward and tapped the startled "Krauts" on the shoulder. As they started to lead their prize away a third enemy popped his head up from another trench and fired; a burst from a tommy-gun kept him quiet and he was either killed or wounded. But the alarm had now been given and the patrol hustled their prisoners away and returned to our lines at some speed and without further incident.

This brief account is given because it was an excellent patrol and because it was the first haul on this sector, but not as being a typical patrol, for it had two unusual features. In the first place, it had been very rare in the Regiment to send out a patrol without an officer, and, secondly, daylight patrols were the exception and all the other patrols referred to in this chapter were night patrols.

This first success was followed by a series of hauls by Charles Morpeth in the area of Monteloro. He surprised an enemy outpost of six men on the summit of the hill, which was always easy to pick out on account of the lone, umbrella-like tree. The next night the enemy sent six men apparently to relieve the outpost, and of these three were captured and one wounded. Two nights later a reconnaissance patrol of the 10th Battalion, again under Charles Morpeth, found a German non-commissioned officer wandering on his own and brought him back to company headquarters, where he was questioned by Teddy Goschen. He said that he had been picked up when on his way to his company headquarters, as he felt the need of further orders. He and his section of four men had been ordered to occupy a house in the little village of San Margherita and had been there a couple of days without any real idea of what they were meant to be doing. A few mortar bombs on the village coming from the German side had made the section commander think it was time they moved elsewhere. Our patrols had been in the village several times and had never drawn enemy fire and therefore at first the tale sounded unlikely, but the non-commissioned officer said that his men were of poor morale and interested in lying low rather than interfering with British patrols. Questioned further, he did not think the men would desert, but that they would surrender to a show of force. He was therefore invited to go with a patrol of ours and inform his men that they were surrounded: the invitation was accepted without duress and four more were in the bag, while the defences of Monteloro were thickened up by another Spandau and ammunition.

Meanwhile the 2nd Battalion was busy patrolling on the left and inflicted several casualties, but the enemy seemed far more alert in this sector, which was at this time held by the battalion later to hold Tossignano, the 1st Battalion 755th Regiment of the 334th Division. Our patrols were also handicapped by mines, which caused casualties. But the bag was swelled by the damage inflicted on the enemy patrols which came with the greatest regularity nightly to one or the other of the 2nd Battalion's forward positions, Casa Collina being perhaps the favourite. We heard from prisoners that their patrols had been told that it was of great importance to secure an identification and the maximum information, for the enemy were anxious to hold this sector as thinly as possible to spare more troops for other dangerous sectors. The enemy did not get an identification, but provided us with a regular flow which enabled us to follow his regrouping with considerable accuracy. Eventually the 2nd Battalion 735th Regiment took over this sector, one battalion of the same regiment of the 715th Division being opposite our right, and this facilitated the resumption of fighting patrols by our 2nd Battalion. This regiment had recently been re-formed mainly by a comb-out of the echelons and base units in North Italy. They were better troops than the other two regiments of the division, for they were almost a hundred per cent. German, in contrast to the others, who had a very high percentage of Poles and Alsatians. At first glance the many prisoners we took from this regiment might have seemed to be the cream of the German Army, for they were nearly all of good physique and at least average intelligence. Yet their morale can only be described as low, for they fought with less skill and less obstinacy than one normally expected from the Germans, even at this stage of the war. The reason appears to have been that they were disgruntled at their change of fortune in leaving a safer and more comfortable job, and after a very short training finding themselves in the front line.

One particular patrol is worth a further mention in this second phase. Enemy patrols had almost ceased and the 2nd Battalion had taken the initiative, but there was a rather limited number of places held by the enemy that it was practicable to visit. One of these was Villa Mengoni, where the enemy maintained an outpost of about six men. On the night of the 6th of November a patrol managed to abduct the sentry from outside the house, and on the 10th it was decided to repeat the performance. This time the enemy was more alert, but the sentry was shot at close range and after a short exchange of fire the patrol made its way back to a collecting point, where it waited some time but had to return to report Riflemen Doherty and Aldridge missing. These two riflemen had in fact found a Spandau covering their line of withdrawal and had taken cover in an out-house. While waiting there they had seen four men approaching who they at first thought were other members of the patrol, but close inspection showed they were Germans. A burst from their tommy-guns killed the leading two, and the other two made off, one certainly being wounded. Probably bearing in mind the doubting spirit of intelligence officers, they then removed the pay-books from the pockets of the dead Germans, one being well soaked in blood and the other neatly perforated by a tommy-gun bullet. Their blood was now up, and instead of returning after this achievement they decided to wait and see what happened next. Sure enough after another interval a party of five or six Germans came to investigate, and were just approaching the dead bodies of their comrades when they also were scattered by some rapid fire, and they are believed to have had another two casualties. By this time the ammunition was running low, and the two enterprising riflemen returned to our lines.

The 7th Battalion were the last to arrive in the sector, but they were soon trying to catch up with the bag of the other two battalions.

The worst of the positions they had to hold was Orsara, a squalid, little place on the top of a hill but overlooked from Monte Taverna, only a few hundred yards away. It was an important place to hold, however, both as an observation post and a starting point for an attack on Monte Taverna. An early misfortune came as a result of some heavy and accurate mortaring just as the platoon there was standing-to, as a raid appeared likely to materialize: the heavy casualties of three killed and twenty-two wounded in this incident were a great blow and it looked as though the position would have to be abandoned for fear of a repetition of such a disaster. The Colonel decided, however, to make the place into a miniature fortress, the garrison of which was reduced to one officer and ten riflemen. From this time onwards raids and mortaring were frequent, but we never had a serious casualty. Two of the strongest raids were when Ted Eakins was in charge and cost the enemy no fewer than six casualties.

It was at Orsara also that an original plan of defence was introduced. It was found from experience that small parties of enemy on dark nights could get so close to the house unobserved that they were not touched by the artillery defensive fire and were difficult to deal with by the garrison of the house, who had limited observation. This was overcome by a new kind of defensive fire by the machine guns, which were at night laid on a fixed line to fire on the house itself. This fire spattered against the wall of the house, harmlessly to those inside but to the discomfiture of a patrol trying to creep round the house or to use a faustpatrone to knock a hole in it. This type of defensive fire became quite fashionable later in the winter, but it is believed to have been first used at Orsara. Several more attempts were made by enemy fighting patrols against the hamlet (one church and two houses), none of which achieved any success, while on one occasion the enemy left three dead behind. A similar raid was made one night against the "Barn" (as a small, barn-like cottage near San Margherita was called), where a section of the 2nd Battalion repelled a party under a German officer, and at least twelve enemy casualties resulted. There were to be many such affairs in the winter, Casa Cogalina being the enemy's favourite. But it must suffice to say that these raids never achieved any substantial results for the enemy and frequently cost him casualties. Much of the credit must go to the 104th

Royal Horse Artillery, by this time the gunners supporting the Brigade, who at any time of night would bring down the necessary defensive fire to the discomfiture of the enemy fighting patrols.

Returning to the exploits of our own patrols, an instance of a 7th Battalion patrol of this period can be given very briefly, for it is a short story. Oliver Montgomery was ordered to take a fighting patrol to Monte Taverna on the night of the 29th/30th of October. The weather could hardly have been more unpleasant, but this fact was used to good advantage by the patrol. On the summit of Taverna there were about six slit trenches, the first of which was unoccupied, while the second was covered with a cape. Oliver removed the cape and despite the darkness and his short-sightedness he had no difficulty in recognizing the contents to be two Germans and one Spandau. Picking up the latter he invited the men to surrender, who from surprise, sleepiness and possibly knowledge that their comrades were very near, seemed disposed to refuse this invitation and were killed at point-blank range. A third German popped up from another trench and was given a burst at close range, and the patrol then made a rapid withdrawal.

Only a few instances have been given, chosen largely for the success achieved, and it seems only fair to mention that such stories do not give a full idea of the difficulties. Yet the total results of the Brigades' activities in patrolling and dealing with the enemy patrols in the first month in this sector make impressive reading and do credit to all concerned, and above all to the platoon commander, who bore the greatest burden. In this one month a conservative estimate of the casualties inflicted on the enemy by infantry action was seventy, of whom thirty-seven were prisoners and twelve more definitely established as killed. Our casualties for this period from infantry action were four wounded, none of them seriously. We did not lose a prisoner despite the determination of the enemy to get an identification. Later patrolling in the static period did not achieve the same results, but it still remained true that we always gave better than we got. The strain of a night patrol followed by several nights in a position to which an enemy patrol may at any time come may be overlooked or soon forgotten by all those who did not actually take part. Nothing has been said of the many reconnaissance patrols that were required, particularly in the period when preparations for a second attack on Tossignano were being made, and one patrol lay for three hours in the snow to discover which of a particular group of houses was occupied by the enemy, while another explored a route which was dangerous enough even if there had been no enemy within miles. All that is what one reads of in the official communiqué as "patrol activity," and one then passes on to something more interesting in the newspaper, saying: "There's nothing happening in Italy."

ITALY

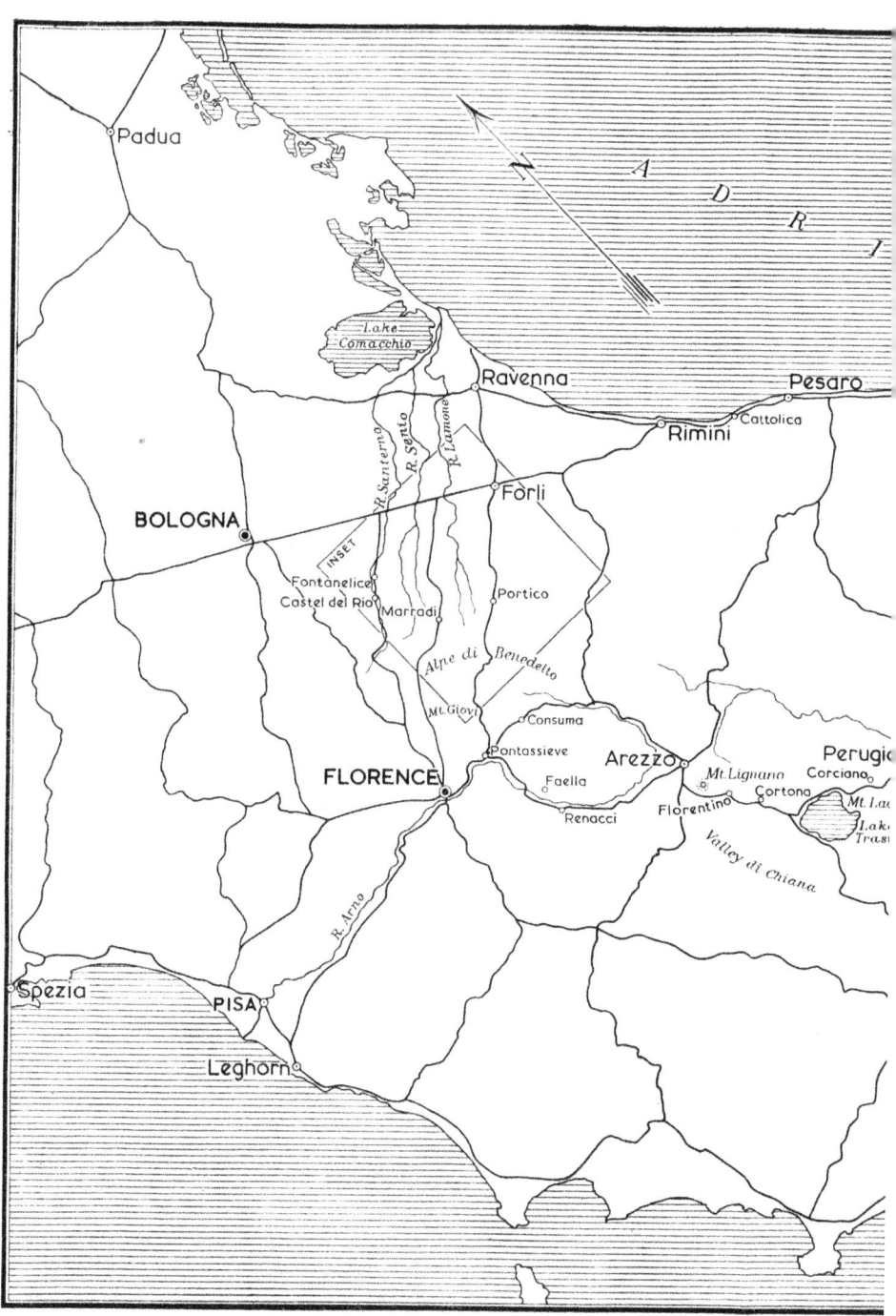

ITALY

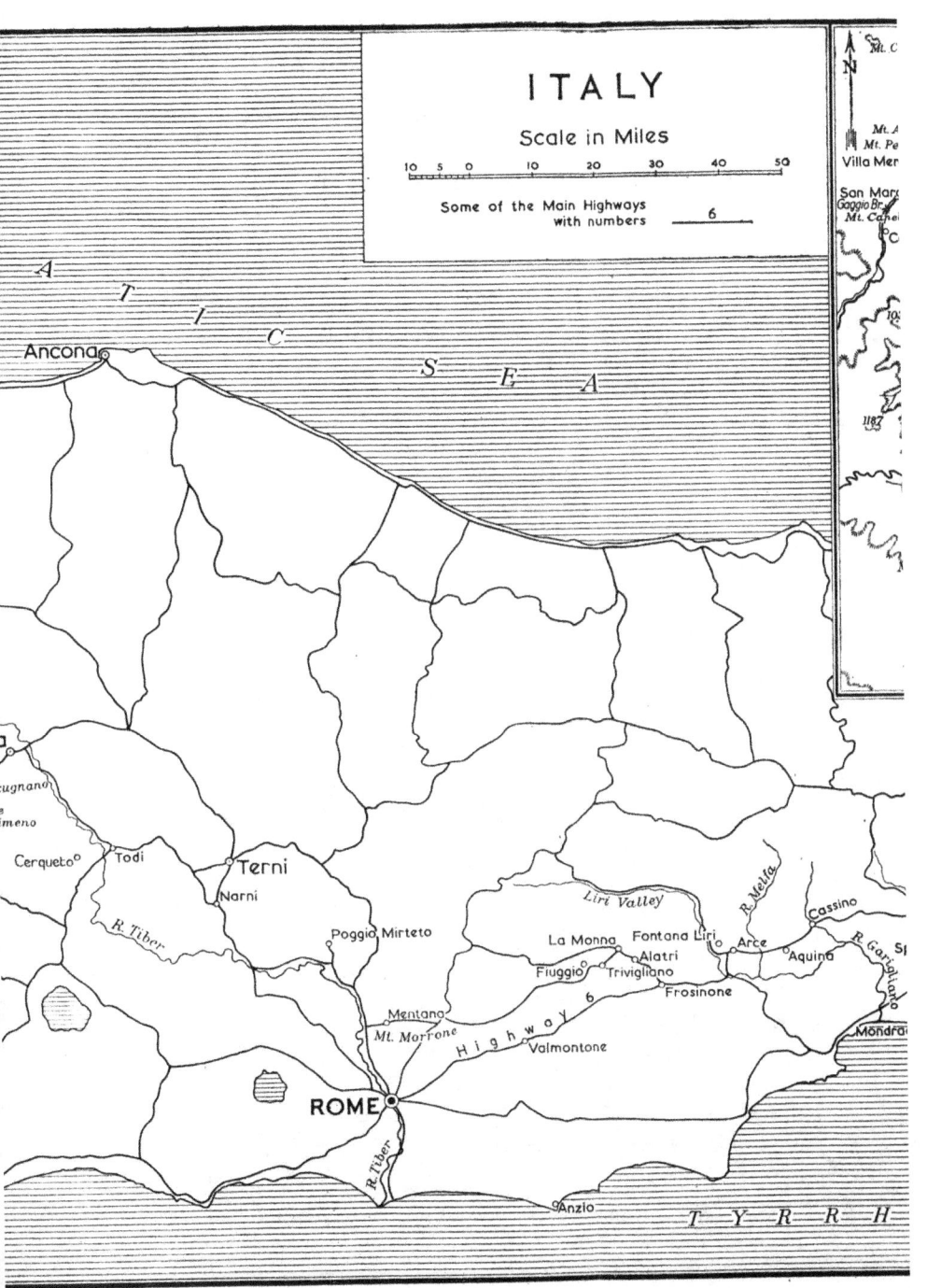

ITALY

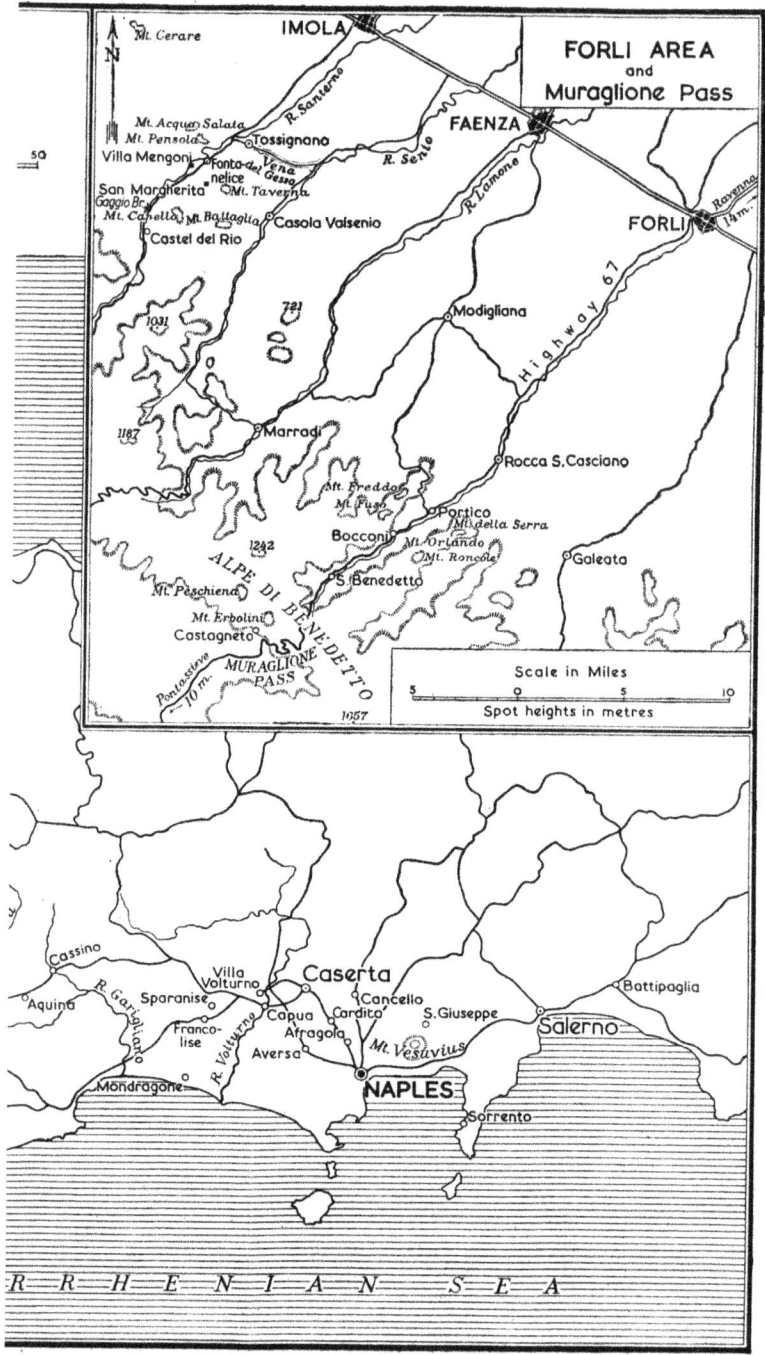

CHAPTER XXIII

TOSSIGNANO: ATTACK AND DEFENCE

If the successes of the Regiment have been described in full, so the unfortunate Battle of Tossignano must be too. In the early stages of the war the Regiment was no stranger to defeat. No greater blow could have befallen anyone than the loss of one Regular battalion in the defence of Calais. In the desert the battalions had all known withdrawals and learnt the lessons of adversity. As recently as June, 1944, the 1st Battalion had lost almost a company outside Villers Bocage. The reason that the failure of the attack on Tossignano created such an impression was that it occurred at a time when successes had become commonplace, when it seemed, even in Italy, that the process of advancing had become almost automatic.

The difficulty of the task of the 2nd Battalion should not be underrated; for the enemy's positions at Tossignano possessed great natural strength. In order to understand why it was considered necessary to attack the town and what was to be gained of decisive importance, if all went well, and to gauge what value the Germans set on holding this almost impregnable position, the whole aspect of the war in Italy must be considered.

The position of the Allies in Italy at this time was disappointing. It is true that much had been achieved and that the Prime Minister himself had drawn attention several times to the importance of the campaign in holding down twenty-seven German divisions, including some of the best, which might well have turned the scale against the Allies on the Eastern and Western Fronts. But it cannot be denied that a feeling of frustration was common, encouraged by a campaign in one or two newspapers. The Eighth Army had breached the Gothic Line in September, inflicting heavy casualties but at considerable cost, only to find that when Rimini and the plain was reached there was no breakthrough such as many people had anticipated, but instead a series of river lines, at each of which the enemy put up a clever defence for a few weeks and then withdrew in time to prevent anything decisive being achieved. The Fifth Army, on the left of the Eighth Army, had fought its way across the Apennines, also at heavy cost in men, only to find that the last barrier to Bologna and beyond was the most strongly held. They needed time to build up their strength once again, but were preparing for a final assault which would carry them on to the plain where there were no rivers to cross until the Po was reached. In short, one more attempt was to be made to achieve decisive victory in Italy before the full rigours of winter set in.

The general plan was not unlike that adopted the following April. The principal difference was that this time XIII Corps, the British troops on the right flank of the Fifth Army, was to open the offensive by creating a strong threat on the rear of the enemy opposite the Eighth Army. This might not only draw off troops from the other fronts but might well persuade the enemy to give up two river lines, the Senio and Santerno, rather than invite disaster by remaining where he was. The Eighth Army opened their offensive against the line of the River Lamone on the 10th/11th of December. The XIII Corps' attack was intended to persuade the enemy to be driven from that river and also to cause confusion well to the rear, at the worst to give the Eighth Army two rivers and several canals the fewer to fight their way across in the spring.

The XIII Corps' offensive was limited by the nature of the ground and the forces at their disposal to an attack down the Santerno Valley towards Imola. The capture of Monte Penzola by the 1st Guards Brigade was an important and essential preliminary, and was to be followed by the capture of Tossignano by the 61st Brigade and of Croara by a battalion of the 78th Division. Meanwhile the Eighth Army's offensive would continue and, the enemy's last reserves having been drawn off, the Fifth Army would attack and crash through to the plain, bypassing Bologna to the west. The attack on Croara took place the night after that on Tossignano while the struggle there still continued, and it met with no success largely owing to a long and arduous approach march. The Eighth Army's offensive reached the Senio; there was a pause and then finally, on the last day of the year, it was revealed to officers that offensive operations were off until the spring. Not only was there snow over the whole battlefield but, what was more important, the

Eighth Army had had its strength greatly depleted by events in Greece and then by an order to send I Canadian Corps to North-West Europe. The 2nd Battalion's action should therefore be regarded not as an isolated, unsuccessful attack but as one of a series of operations by the Allied armies, none of which completely succeeded.

When the Brigade first took over from the Irish Brigade there was a rather miscellaneous collection of German units opposite us, but their first withdrawal took them to a shorter and stronger line, enabling them to sort themselves out. Until that sort-out was complete, astride the Imola road in the valley was the 1st Battalion 755th Regiment of the 334th Division, which was described in a British Army intelligence summary as the best German infantry division in Italy. Presumably in this description the parachute divisions were not included as infantry, and our past experience of the division had given us the impression that they were what might be called "good ordinary soldiers." Deserters were not unknown owing to there being a fair sprinkling of foreigners, particularly Poles. When the enemy appeared to have settled down on the Monte Taverna—Fontanelice Line this battalion was replaced by the 2nd Battalion 735th Regiment, of whom something has already been said. The second enemy withdrawal at the end of November did not cause us to think that there was any change in the lay-out, and an identification of the 1st Battalion 735th Regiment by the 2nd Battalion as still opposite our right only a few days before the attack on Tossignano seemed to confirm this. However, on the night of the 11th/12th of December, the night before the attack was due, a patrol took a prisoner from the 1st Battalion 755th Regiment, and seven deserters from the 334th Fusilier Battalion picked up by the 7th Battalion stated that they were being relieved that night and had been there only to fill in a hiatus. This meant that the defenders of Tossignano were definitely from the 1st Battalion 755th Regiment, and though this probably reduced rather than increased the numbers of the garrison compared with what we had anticipated, it certainly increased the quality of the troops. Above all, they had leaders of exceptional skill and the kernel of this particular battalion seems to have been first class. What was more important was that they had in the past had their battalion headquarters and reserve company back in the Tossignano area, and, no doubt realizing that the Vena del Gesso was the line on which they would fall back for the winter, their comanding officer, Captain Pfeiffer, would, even before we arrived in this sector, have concentrated much of his time on plans and preparations for the defence of the town. It was at first thought that the 2nd Battalion might benefit by the fact that their opponents had taken over only the night before and might not be properly orientated; but this was to overlook their previous residence in the area, and, in fact, they may even have been ordered to take over defence of the town expressly because the German Higher Command realized that an attack was imminent, and therefore decided that they had better put back the battalion of good quality which had originally been earmarked for the task.

The attack of the 2nd Battalion was at one time planned for the night of the 11th/12th of December, the very night of the enemy relief, but it was postponed for twenty-four hours to give a little more time for reconnaissance. It is idle to speculate on what might have happened on the night originally planned. It would certainly have made things simpler initially, though it would have made it easier for the enemy to launch a counter-attack if the town had been captured. On the night of the 12th/13th, when the attack in fact took place, the enemy garrison was laid out as follows: 2 Company, with a platoon of 3 Company, were responsible for the town itself; the rest of 3 Company were in the Borgo gap and the machine guns and mortars of 4 Company were deployed in support of both. The whereabouts of 1 Company were not known, but it was believed to be in reserve in the area of Laguna, a couple of miles to the north-east. The battalion were well below strength, but they had the advantage, not often given to German troops at this stage of the war, of being fresh from a rest out of the line. They could call on an exceptionally large number of guns for support, about a hundred being theoretically in range and fifty to sixty, including a few self-propelled guns, in practice ready to support. Their mortars were also likely to be troublesome at first, for they had not fired at all since moving back, either because of reliefs or expressly to prevent our counter-mortar organization discovering their positions.

Tossignano has been likened by many who saw it to Cassino, which is a tempting parallel to draw but hardly a fair one. For one thing, the town is only a fraction of the size of Cassino and lies on the forward slopes of the hill, whereas to provide a parallel it would have to lie in the Borgo gap, leaving one large building on the top of the hill as the equivalent of the famous monastery. Comparison of the two derives from the way in which we were forced to sit and look at the place where the enemy had caused us a reverse by fighting with the utmost skill and tenacity in a position of great natural strength. It is difficult to know whether to feel disappointed or thankful that the Brigade was never permitted to have a second attempt: one felt disappointed that for nearly three months the Brigade remained opposite an enemy who made it obvious that he felt that he had scored a success and such revenge as we could take was petty and left one frustrated. Yet a mistake that the Brigade never made about the attack on Tossignano was to under-estimate its difficulty and therefore one felt thankful that further casualties were not incurred, knowing that they would be inflicted however successful the operation.

The Vena del Gesso has already been described, and the cliff on which Tossignano lies is clearly a part of this "Vein of Chalk," though it is divided from it and can almost be regarded as a separate feature. On the east side is the Rio Sgarba, cutting Tossignano off from the rest of the Vena, and the cliff is precipitous on both sides of this river bed, which runs as a sort of dry tributary of the Santerno, increasing in breadth and the height of its banks until its mouth through the Vena, where the banks are both some three to four hundred feet. This meant that there was no possible approach to Tossignano on the right, and the enemy was reported to have made doubly sure by strewing the entrance with mines. It must be added, however, that this isolation of the town from the east part of the Vena, though adding to the difficulties of the attack, was what made it a practicable military proposition, since it would be inconceivable to maintain, apart from capturing, a foothold on the cliff-top with the enemy on both sides unless there was some natural feature to hold with a good line of approach.

On the south and south-west side the cliff is steep but not precipitous, and it is on the upper part of this side that the small town is built. Like many such places in Italy, it should really be called a village from the point of view of size, but it was generally referred to as a town, partly because of its lay-out and partly because it was common to refer to little groups of half a dozen houses as villages. The lower part of this side of the cliff is bare and rocky, while the upper part is terraced to divide the town into three parts. The lower part contains many small houses tightly packed together, the middle the town square surrounded by the largest buildings, and the top has the church and one or two scattered houses with gardens and a line of trees. This description, of course, errs on the side of over-simplicity—for instance, there proved to be terracing within the lower part of the town. Patrols found that there were two entrances to the town from this side, one via Point 222 leading into the bottom of the town at the south-west corner, and the other via Point 282 which led to the middle of the town—that is, the south—where only a few houses barred the way to the square. There exists also a third way in from the west-north-west via Casa Frascoleto, of which something has already been said in the brief description of the Borgo gap. This in many ways would be the easiest entrance; but there were serious objections, chiefly owing to the fact that troops attacking from that direction would have to turn their backs on the enemy on the other side of the Santerno and they would also have to put down a strong force to safeguard the left flank. In any case, for the attack of the 2nd Battalion this approach could not really even be considered without postponing the whole operation for some days, for the essential preliminaries entailed getting bridges built on the main road and occupying Borgo. By the time the "blows" were cleared of enemy covering parties there was only one night before the attack and it was thought better not to build bridges in order that the enemy, observing the lack of activity, would be taken by surprise.

One other point should be mentioned in connection with this description of the town: when the 2nd Battalion attacked they were well supplied with air photographs of the area which gave a very good idea of the approaches, but something more was needed of the town itself. An attempt was made to fly a sortie for this purpose, but when it was flown after several days of bad weather the results were far from satisfactory. This might not have mattered very much, as so good a view of the town can be obtained from several angles, but between our capture of the points of observation and the attack there was a spell of heavy mist. Owain Foster, who had been acting Commanding Officer of the 2nd Battalion since the beginning of November when

A PATROL OF THE 10th BATTALION
Crossing a shallow tributary of the River Arno

TOSSIGNANO

Colonel Chris Sinclair had gone home, was forced to waste a lot of time sitting on a hill-top waiting for the mist to clear and, though he and the company commanders saw all that they required in the end, the majority of the 2nd Battalion never saw the place before the attack. As luck would have it, a few days later there was a spate of excellent air photographs and a spell of fine, clear weather enabled a view of the town to be obtained by anyone who cared to take a walk.

The plan was necessarily a simple one in its main outline: there were two possible entrances and an attempt would be made to force both and exploit success at either. Obviously the more promising of the two was that via Point 282 which would get the attackers half-way to their objective before they were involved in street fighting, whereas an attack via Point 222 meant fighting from the bottom to the top of the town. But both entrances were narrow and with steep approaches, and there was no way of deploying more than a platoon to force either entrance, so equal weight had to be given to both possibilities. The 7th Battalion was to occupy Borgo and stage a diversionary attack against Casa Frascoleto. Since a good deal of faith was being put in gaining a measure of surprise, a silent attack was considered, but it was rejected on the grounds that both entrances were so difficult that there was no hope of getting in unless the enemy were stunned by a barrage, and, though this would destroy the element of surprise, once it started, it was hoped to put down sufficient concentrations on the reverse slopes and enemy routes to Tossignano to make it impossible for him to do any last-minute reinforcement or adjustment of his position. The other question that caused a great deal of thought when making the plan was the assembly and start line of the attackers: it was an alternative between starting from a fairly well-concealed position with the men in houses, which involved a cross-country march before the start line was reached (not a very great distance, but over difficult country at night and with ammunition and weapons to carry), or to move up the night before to the start line, dig in and lie up in order to have only the arduous climb and assault on the night of the attack. The former was chosen because the latter might so easily defeat its own purpose, in the event of bad weather, by getting the men cold and wet before the attack started, and there was also the risk of being observed and losing surprise.

So much has now been said regarding the setting and circumstances of the attack on Tossignano that the narrative of what happened must seem disproportionately brief. This is due to the fact that the setting must be somewhat elaborate to make even an outline narrative intelligible.

When the 2nd Battalion took over the right of the Brigade sector from the 10th on the 2nd of December the enemy still had a rearguard of platoon strength in the area of Casas Monteleto and Poggiolo. "A" Company, under Dick Flower, were given the task of clearing resistance from there and the approaches to Tossignano, forming a firm base for the attack. The first area was cleared on the 5th, but the enemy still showed no intention of leaving the way to the Vena del Gesso clear and himself put in a strong raid against the positions he had just given up, as well as leaving small outposts in the one or two houses on the approaches. Similarly, the 7th Battalion on the left had to deal with a series of small rearguards astride the valley, while to the left again, even after the capture of Monte Penzola, the enemy retained a foothold on the cliff farther back for a few days, making any move forward in the valley by day impossible. To this must be added the delays caused by mines, booby-trapping of houses and demolitions on the road: the consequence was that the way was not clear for even the final preparations until the 10th, and the attack was scheduled for the night of the 12th/13th of December, which was the earliest possible under the circumstances.

The outline plan has already been given: "B" Company, under John Reader-Harris, was given the right-hand entrance via Point 282 and "C" Company, under John Brown, the left-hand via Point 222. In addition, the 21st Indian Brigade on the right and the 1st Guards Brigade on the left were to stage demonstrations to divert the enemy's attention and fire. The move forward of the 7th Battalion into Borgo and the artillery plan were timed to start at eleven o'clock at night, and the attack of the 2nd Battalion with close support from 25-pounders at two o'clock in the morning of the 13th of December. Success at either entrance was to be exploited; but the right hand was the more likely to be decisive, and in the unlikely event of both being successful the build-up was to be on the right. The reserve was "S" Company, under Basil Naumann, only two platoons strong, and the carrier platoon, under John Wood, on their feet.

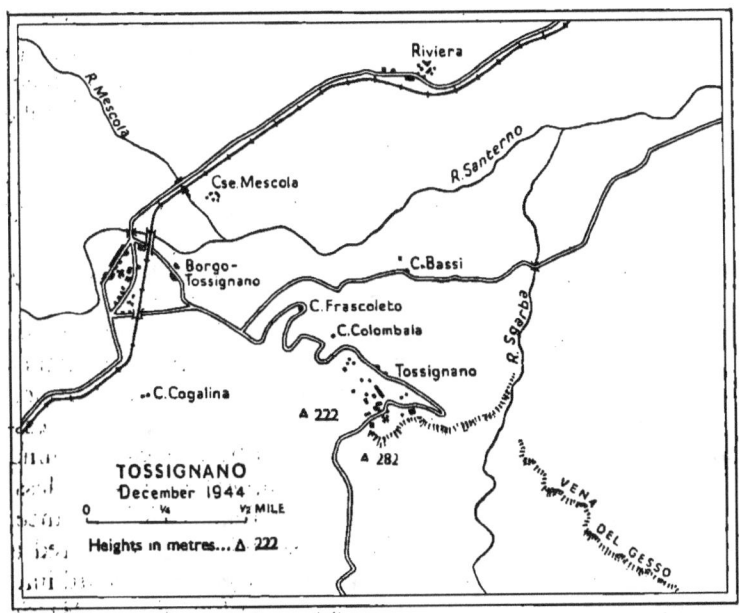

TOSSIGNANO December 1944

The feint attacks of the 1st Guards Brigade and the 8th Indian Division were successful in inducing the enemy to disperse his defensive fire. The feint attack by the 7th Battalion was in a sense too successful: it certainly drew the enemy's attention, but it drew it too soon and too thoroughly, and the main weight of the enemy's fire came down all round Borgo as soon as "C" Company occupied it, and casualties were caused when an attempt was made to form up on the start line for the attack on Casa Frascoleto. The attack was finally made in less strength and later than had been planned, and it was not successful, as the enemy was thoroughly alert and swept the open ground with Spandau fire. In addition, a self-propelled gun came right up close to the north bank of the river in the area of Casa Mescola and shelled the road from Fontanelice to Borgo with great persistence and accuracy, and prevented any build-up of men and supplies in Borgo. The latter and its approaches were heavily mined, further casualties being caused to the 7th Battalion, while it was here that Charles Morpeth was badly wounded a few days later when the 10th Battalion had taken over.

The attack of the 2nd Battalion could hardly have started more unluckily, the troops being heavily shelled on their way to the start line. This caused nearly twenty casualties, among them two or three riflemen who were carrying phosphorous smoke grenades which went on fire and burnt the men themselves. It also caused a certain amount of delay. Some of the shelling was thought to come from our own guns, and there were so many batteries firing in support that it was quite impossible in the middle of a barrage to discover who was the culprit: eventually the position was eased by an order for all the 25-pounders to lift their fire by four hundred yards, but this resulted in the greater part of the barrage going right over the top. The Germans knew our barrages so well that, though they were still stunned and dazed by them, they could tell how the attack was progressing and it was essential for our troops to be very close behind the barrage. This was now more or less impossible. Nevertheless, at half past three a success signal went up from the left entrance, though at the right entrance Spandaus and mortars covered a block across the track. John Brown at once moved forward into the town with the rest of "C" Company, and John Reader-Harris followed with the two platoons of "B" Company not previously committed, so that they managed to get in just before dawn.

It first became light at about half past six and this was the one moment in the whole operation when things really looked quite healthy, and optimism prevailed. John Brown himself, one could tell by the sound of his voice on the wireless, felt confident and indeed with reason: despite the misfortunes of the night, the left entrance had been forced with only slight opposition, and five prisoners were taken. Now he had five platoons in the town and had made some progress, having got one position in a house in the middle of the town from which the square could be observed. The riflemen were tired and some reorganization was needed, but before long he would start moving forward again in short bounds, systematically cleaning up.

The next hour saw the reverses that were to prove decisive: some accurate mortaring of the area occupied by our troops caused John Brown and two of his platoon commanders to be wounded and also drove the troops to cover in the buildings. "C" Company had no officer in the battle by now, for Harry Huntsman had been wounded early in the assault, though he had carried on to gain the initial success before he was ordered to be evacuated. "B" Company were better off in this respect, but they had arrived later and were in any case less well orientated, having made their plans for the other entrance. Furthermore, John Reader-Harris had gone forward to get in touch with John Brown and was himself pinned down in the forefront of the battle, and though platoons were equipped with No. 38 sets these proved useless amongst the buildings and there was therefore no intercommunication amongst the forces in the town. The Gunner observation posts were in another house and, though, like the company commander, they had communications rearwards, they were not in touch with any of the infantry in the town. In the course of the morning they reported that a portion of the force was on the offensive and had reached the square where a fire-fight was taking place. But this effort was on a junior commander's initiative and by the afternoon it was the enemy who were doing the attacking. They used 1 Company and the regimental pioneer platoon of the 755th Regiment, and with petrol bombs and grenades they assaulted the houses held by our troops. John Reader-Harris reported that by dusk the garrison of the house occupied by himself had successfully warded off five attacks; what actual success the enemy achieved elsewhere is hard to gauge, but it appeared to be negligible in so far as our troops drove off the attacks and held the positions. What was to be serious, however, was that the enemy managed to infiltrate into positions in houses covering the entrance.

The following night the greatest need was to get supplies into the town, for they were running short of ammunition, and the second need was to get in more troops to pass through and continue clearing the houses. Any attempt to supply or reinforce in daylight was out of the question, the bare approaches being not only under shell and mortar fire, but any move forward of Point 222 brought a hail of aimed machine-gun fire. Owain Foster himself concentrated his small remaining reserve at Point 222 after dark and made an attempt to get supplies in. But it was evident that even the entrance was now again held by the enemy and there was nothing he could do but wait for the reinforcements from the 10th Battalion, who, it was hoped, would arrive at eleven o'clock. They did not, in fact, arrive until nearly one o'clock and were then in need of a rest, having had a six-hour march. It had been intended by the Brigadier to accelerate their arrival by arranging that they went in their transport to within little more than a mile of Borgo and thence across country to Point 222, thus saving an enormous detour, all of which would have to be on foot via Monteleto. Unfortunately the short cut was by a difficult path, which was the only way across a ravine, and the guide himself had done the journey only once before, when on patrol, and failed, as so often happens in moments of crisis, to find the way.

This further misfortune meant that the attack by "D" Company of the 10th Battalion could not commence until three o'clock, while "C" Company did not get used at all that night. Jim Wilson's company were greeted by Spandau and rifle fire as they climbed the hill and by grenades as they neared the houses, but by great determination and after several casualties the leading platoon forced an entry aided by covering fire from the others. They made contact with some of the troops in the town, though not with company headquarters. The other two platoons were pinned down amongst the rocks under the cliff and they had to be extricated after first light with the aid of smoke.

Communication with John Reader-Harris the next day, the 14th, was spasmodic and he was last heard on the wireless at about two o'clock in the afternoon. It was fully realized that the situation was serious, though some, and probably most, of our troops were still holding out, and the lack of communications was initially due to wireless batteries running out. But by this time there was only one officer left unwounded, and what was even more serious ammunition had completely run out. Captain Gwynn, the Medical Officer of the 2nd Battalion, had twice been into the town, but was unfortunately now missing (he later got out slightly wounded). It was realized that it was now a question of relieving rather than reinforcing the Battalion, and this was to be the object of further attacks by "C" Company of the 10th Battalion under Bob Fairweather. Three separate attacks were made that night, all of which got to close grips with the enemy. No support was given by artillery fire on the assumption that the garrison in the town was still holding out, but the attackers, after gaining some success, were called back, as it was evident that there was no organized resistance within the town. The enemy had renewed his counter-attacks at midday. At first there had been strong resistance and then as each section in turn had run out of ammunition the Germans steadily got the upper hand and by the evening had dealt with the last opposition.

General Murray, the Divisional Commander, concludes his account of the Tossignano battle with the following words: "The fighting qualities of the 61st Infantry Brigade in this operation were abundantly proved. They put up a first-class performance in extremely difficult circumstances and their failure was a magnificent failure." It has been the intention of the rather lengthy introduction of the actual narrative of this operation to show that the chief cause of the failure was the intrinsic difficulty of the operation, and the narrative shows that there were also one or two strokes of misfortune. It is not intended to claim that no mistakes were made. The difficulty of forcing an entrance to the town was fully appreciated, but it was thought that once an entrance had been made the next really difficult operation would be capturing the summit: the past experience of the Brigade was a handicap rather than a benefit, and too much thought was paid to the old question of forward and reverse slopes and not enough to street fighting and how to clear the town. This tendency was accentuated by the comparatively short time for reconnaissance and planning, by lack of experience in street fighting and finally by the early loss of those who had thought the matter out most carefully, particularly John Brown.

The lesson was learnt and the plans for the next attack could hardly have been more detailed and thorough. Aircraft and heavy guns were called in to assist by knocking down houses that interfered, hundreds of copies of a town plan were made with all the houses numbered, and, most important of all, the 10th Battalion patrolled into the town every night discovering ever more detailed information and keeping the enemy on tenterhooks. The plan is not described, as it was never put into effect; after two short postponements the order was received on the last day of the year to go over to the defensive and to take over the Casola Valsenio sector, a responsibility which involved our being thinner on the ground. Thus Tossignano remained in German hands until April.

The armies in Italy had been living on their fat since the opening of the Second Front. Such losses as were sustained by the 61st Brigade in the operation at Tossignano could not easily be replaced. These totalled thirteen officers and two hundred and seven riflemen, of whom seven officers and a hundred and forty-seven other ranks were missing. A large proportion of those not accounted for were later reported to be prisoners of war, many of them also being wounded. Soon afterwards the "Python" scheme for the return to England of men who had been abroad for a long time claimed some eighty more from the 2nd Battalion, many of them being non-commissioned officers, whom there was no possibility of replacing. The 2nd Battalion had, therefore, to work on a basis of two rifle companies, while the other two battalions were down to three companies each.

In such circumstances it was clear that two battalions would have to be made up to strength at the expense of the remaining one. While it was, in fact, the 2nd Battalion which needed almost completely re-forming, the 10th, as the one with the highest number, was the most likely to be offered for sacrifice. It would, indeed, have been sad if the name of the 2nd Battalion, famous for its exploits from Sidi Saleh to Alamein, to Tunis and in Italy, had ceased to exist while there were still Germans at war. In 1945 none could have forecast that within a few years of the end of the war the authorities would destroy the Battalion more effectively by a stroke of the pen in a Whitehall office than even the Germans at Tossignano had succeeded in doing. The 10th Battalion had, too, a proud history in North Africa and in Italy. No Territorial—or Regular—battalion could claim a more consistently successful record. Whether at Thala or Medjez, advancing up the Liri Valley or on Monte Rentella, it had been a credit to the Regiment and to the Tower Hamlets. But it was clear that one battalion would soon have to go. However, for the rest of the winter the Brigade limped on at reduced strength.

The Brigade was not yet to leave this sector of the line. It remained in the same positions opposite the Germans until March. It was a period of patrolling and of heavy, intermittent shelling.

The enemy opposite us was full of enterprise, and did not appear to be short of ammunition, nor on the whole did his morale appear to have suffered from the news from the other fronts. So we had to remain alert and active in order to ensure that he did not get too much above himself. For the first two months of 1945 the only task was to hold the enemy where he was, and this meant having constantly to try to beat him at his own game. The advantage of our normal vast superiority in artillery was temporarily denied to us by a rationing scheme to build up supplies for the spring offensive, and we had no numerical superiority of troops on the ground. On the other hand, we did have one advantage rarely granted to us in Italy, and that was that we did for once overlook the enemy. Even this was largely outweighed by the fact that he was able to observe a great part of the main road from right back at Gaggio to Borgo. It was on the road that he concentrated the greater part of his shelling. The mule train was several times put to rout by shells panicking, if not killing, some of the mules, and on at least one occasion, during a relief, several casualties were caused to men just waiting to drive away to their rest area.

The battalions derived a little illegitimate amusement from the frequency with which Brigade Headquarters was shelled; its most serious misfortune was when the enemy scored an absolute direct hit on the officers' latrine, fortunately at three o'clock in the afternoon.

The Germans had quite an assortment of projectiles besides shells. Mortars and nebelwerfers occasionally added to the unpleasantness of life in forward positions, and there were one or more unpleasant rocket-firing weapons that could be recognized by the peculiar winding-up noise they made when firing, and even more by the loudness of the bang that they made at the receiving end. The noise of the explosions was so great as to be quite stunning, but the fragmentation of the missiles was negligible, and it is believed that they did not cause a single casualty despite the persistence with which they were used against our forward positions. A more pleasant missile to receive was that containing propaganda. Apart from relief at receiving a shower of paper instead of hot metal, there was sure to be a suitable contribution to the mantelpiece or to the fire: it might be a rather old-fashioned Christmas card reminding one of how delightful it would be to have Christmas at home, or an amusing bit of obscenity intended to be anti-Russian or anti-American, or, much the most clever, a pamphlet got up to look like a packet of book matches, entitled "How to Fool the M.O.," the only snag to which was that the wider the circulation the more it defeated its purpose; for every medical officer was sure to have his own copy to assist him if he had ever been so stupid as to require it. A more useful contribution to the Brigade was a leaflet, "To the Boys of 61 Infantry Brigade," giving the names of all those taken prisoner at Tossignano. The real mistake of German propaganda as addressed to Riflemen was that where it was relevant it was superfluous; if there was anything to grumble about then the Rifleman could do it for himself without any suggestions from the heavy-humoured Hun, and yet the grumbles in no way interfered with duty or even with a fundamental cheerfulness and confidence.

There was a far more effective type of propaganda, largely unintentional. This was the signs that the enemy's morale was high despite the obvious blackness of the world situation. The ringing of the church bells of Tossignano on Christmas Eve, the fantastic display of pyrotechnics to usher in 1945, the attempt of some prisoners to fool their interrogators, the daring penetration of patrols led by a speaker of English—all this had the irritating effect of making one feel that the enemy opposite us did not even yet see defeat staring them in the face. There may have been elements of hysteria and bravado about this, however, and in the end one could see symptoms of nervousness, possibly even of "the jitters." At half past three one morning late in February the enemy staged an exhibition for which no explanation except bad nerves can be offered: in the course of an hour and a half over five hundred missiles, including many rockets, were fired in the area of Borgo and its environs, many thousands of rounds of machine-gun ammunition were fired, and even Schmeisers, the German tommy-gun, joined in, and yet nothing else happened. It seems that the enemy for some unknown reason thought that we were attacking Tossignano. This colossal expenditure of ammunition did not cost us a single casualty.

No account of the Brigade's winter campaign is complete without a reference to the pleasant contrast offered by rest areas south of Florence. At the end of a fortnight in the line there was a six-hour journey in a three-ton lorry, uncomfortable and usually bitterly cold, and there was the same journey back at the end, so that the week's rest was really little better than five days; but this was absolutely necessary and considered well worth while for the sake of the comfort at the end of the journey and for the proximity to Florence. Officers were particularly fortunate to have frequent opportunities to spend a day or two at the

Villa Capponi, run by Teddy Voules on the lines of the sort of pre-war country house in England to which one always hopes to be asked for the week-end. People could not quite forget the "sharp end" and sang a skit of a popular Italian song, the Rifle Brigade version running: "Up, up to Cogalina," the latter being about the most unpleasant place to which to be returning. At the beginning of March the whole Brigade assembled for the first time simultaneously in the area, and spent a few carefree days "celebrating life in general, and the wedding of Vivian Street in particular." It was a sad day for many of us when we had a last view of Florence, which stood for the happier days of the winter as a contrast to the discomfort and danger of the mountains, and which an early spring was making more lovely than ever.

CHAPTER XXIV

THE LAST CAMPAIGN IN ITALY

THE necessity for reorganization has already been foreshadowed, for two problems of major importance had been lurking in the background ever since the Brigade was formed: the first was the lack of Rifle Brigade reinforcements, initially overcome by taking reinforcements from other regiments until the flow from this source seemed also to dry up; and the second was that the war establishment of units, so far as it can be said to have existed at all, was unsuitable for any of the types of warfare in which we had been or were likely to be engaged. The Brigade had been formed in haste, and the 2nd and 7th Battalions had had to convert themselves into something resembling infantry battalions, while the 10th had never been reorganized at all and so remained nominally a motor battalion. In one main principle this had given us what we wanted: that is to say, we had a motor battalion to operate with the Armoured Brigade but were still able to function as an infantry brigade. And yet if the 10th Battalion had had to bear the whole burden in the summer and the 2nd and 7th Battalions in the winter, the point would have been lost. In practice both the 2nd and 7th had at times operated as motor battalions, and the 10th had taken their full share of normal infantry roles. Thanks to good improvisation by all concerned, this had worked reasonably well, but it involved constant minor but detailed reorganizations, and much labour which it was hoped and believed was unnecessary.

To the lack of reinforcements there was really only one answer; in fact, it was clear enough to cause some people to start doing some not entirely inaccurate guessing. As far back as November, 1944, the Brigadier quashed all rumours by letting everyone know the facts as known to himself. The 10th Battalion was to be broken up, but the date for this was not known: on the other hand, as far as possible officers would be transferred complete with their platoons to one of the other two battalions. The time had now come in March, 1945; but the effect of the losses at Tossignano was such that it really became more a break-up of the old 2nd Battalion; the latter was still losing men steadily as they went home to England on the "Python" repatriation scheme, and was far the weakest battalion in numbers. It was really little more than the name that could be preserved. It was a sad day for both battalions but with some consolation for both. For the 2nd Battalion it was the final dissolution of the body of men who had a proud record that included the most decisive victory of an individual unit in the Battle of Alamein, but the name was to be preserved by a battalion worthy of its best traditions. For the 10th Battalion it was the end of a battalion that had retained a nucleus of the 2nd Battalion Tower Hamlets Rifles from pre-war Territorial days, and had had a fine record of success in two and a half years' fighting in Tunisia and Italy. They had the consolation that large numbers of old comrades would remain together.

The first task of reorganization, therefore, was the break-up of one of the three battalions and the amalgamation into two. It seemed at one time as though there would be almost no surplus men, for after forming the new 2nd Battalion and providing reinforcements for the 7th Battalion there remained also the task of creating the 2nd Heavy Support Company of two platoons of medium machine guns and two of 4.2-inch mortars, which were to be under James Booth, consisting in all of about two hundred and thirty men. It was a last-minute change in the organization that caused a surplus of riflemen enough to justify the creation of a reinforcement company under John Mansel which was put under the Guards Battalion at the Infantry Reinforcement Depot at Fano. Perhaps the most remarkable change in the composition of the 2nd Battalion was that it now lacked Ned Pinnock, an essential part of its make-up as Regimental Sergeant-Major or Quartermaster since the earliest days. He had at last been persuaded to go home to the Motor Training Battalion at Ranby.

Replacing the third battalion in the Brigade was the 1st Battalion The King's Royal Rifle Corps, commanded by Colonel John Hope. It was the natural and proper choice, for it meant that the wholly Rifle Brigade constitution of the 61st Brigade was replaced by one wholly Greenjacket, a change of atmosphere so slight that there was no feeling of a break in continuity.

Furthermore, there were so many old friendships renewed that there was no need for the usual business of "getting to know the new battalion." The 1st Battalion 60th Rifles were organized much as the 10th Battalion had been, in that they were on the establishment of a motor battalion but had spent the winter in a purely infantry role, involving improvised internal reorganization. They also therefore were to reorganize on a new war establishment.

After much discussion and various changes of front by the authorities, the Brigade was reorganized with a pool of White scout cars sufficient in numbers to lift two battalions at once. These half-armoured vehicles were to be driven by Royal Army Service Corps drivers. In practice the pool was used to carry two of the three companies which were now all that was left to each battalion. The third company was carried in ordinary troop-carrying three-tonners. This method was adopted to suit the peculiar needs of the short, mobile campaign which was now expected to ensue, all three battalions being employed at the same time, widely separated from each other for most of its duration. This organization marked a return some of the way towards the earlier conception of a motor battalion, apart from the important fact that the vehicles were not driven by riflemen. The change from four companies to three entailed inevitably a surplus of riflemen, bringing disappointment to those individuals who had to leave their battalions.

The Brigade spent exactly a month at Cattolica, thus finding itself for the first time on the Adriatic coast. The unattractiveness of the town was more than outweighed by the persistence of the fine weather and a varied countryside where even the dull plain seemed pleasant enough to those who had recently seen too much of mountains. There was a fair degree of comfort and, more important than one might think, the advantage of having the whole Brigade concentrated at such a time made life easier and more convenient, so that all the complications of the reorganization were got over with speed and efficiency, and there were still two to three weeks for training. Never before had the Brigade as a whole had an opportunity to do any training, and the chances for battalions to get some training done on their own had been brief and rare. Shooting was the biggest item on the programme and included every weapon we possessed from rifles to 4.2-inch mortars, and shots and explosions could be heard at any time of day or night. The ruins of the unhappy village of Gemmano, the scene of bitter fighting six months before, were further shattered by training in street fighting and by trial of the horrible toy now allotted to us, the flame-thrower.

What was to be most important in the training carried out in this period was co-operation with tanks, not just with tanks but with regiments of the 26th Armoured Brigade training in the particular operations that it was anticipated would be required in the next campaign. Already there were plans made for the employment of the 6th Armoured Division, and the Divisional Commander indicated how he was likely to employ his force. The point most to concern us was the idea of using regimental groups. A happy and fruitful partnership was founded between the 2nd Battalion and the Lothians and Border Horse. At this time it was thought that the 7th Battalion would probably be the battalion carried in three-tonners and would be required for a more normal infantry role, while the 17th/21st Lancers were training mainly with the 1st Guards Brigade. But the 7th Battalion also did the complete training with the Lothians, and, though they had not actually trained with the 17th/21st Lancers, they were later to have time to get together and talk it over.

It was a busy month and a happy one. Despite the amount of work that was done there was time for recreation, sport and parties. There can be no denying that it was a useful month, for at the end of it everybody was full of confidence and seemed to be on the top of their form. We were told that this was to be the last battle in Italy. It was to involve the final defeat of the German Army Group South, and instead of having the normal soldierly reaction of saying that we had heard that one before, this time we knew it was true.

On the 8th of April, 1945, the Brigade moved to the area of Forlimpopoli and the following day the final offensive in Italy began. The 6th Armoured Division was in Eighth Army reserve, and the Army Commander had stated his intention not to use the Division, almost his total reserve, until he "saw daylight"—that is until the moment came when weakening of enemy resistance might be exploited and a break-through achieved. The enemy's lack of mobility was certain then to lead to disaster. This break-through was not merely intended to be a prelude to a long pursuit of the enemy, in which case sufficient forces would almost inevitably have escaped to man the Inner Redoubt while our troops were held up by the Po, an obstacle not less than twelve hundred feet wide. It was intended rather to encircle and destroy the enemy where he was; in other words, to defeat him south of the Po, which was little more than thirty miles from where the offensive began.

There were several places in which we might have to operate when the infantry divisions had broken through what was known as the Senio Line. Our object was in any case to reach the Po to the north and west of Ferrara. The axis of advance might be to the north of, and parallel to, Route 9 until the Idice was crossed and then northwards, or up Route 16 through the Argenta Gap and thence north-west. Of these the latter was likely to be the more decisive, and perhaps as a consequence of the pessimism that comes in the sixth year of war the former was at first considered to be the one that we were the more likely to employ.

After a week of waiting and constantly getting much information of how the battle was going, and studying and planning accordingly, the Division moved to the area of Bagnacavallo to get into a more forward concentration area and to arrange itself into groups ready for battle at short notice. The 1st Battalion 60th Rifles and the 2nd Battalion joined their respective regimental groups and passed to command of the 26th Armoured Brigade, while the 17th/21st Lancers came to join a 61st Brigade group. It was still not clear by which route we were to go: although the offensive was going well on all sides, there was bitter fighting and certainly no sign yet of an enemy collapse. However, by the morning of the 18th the town of Argenta had been cleared by troops of the 78th Division and the gap had definitely been breached. The 6th Armoured Division passed to command of V Corps, and by the next day the two regimental groups were in contact with the enemy. The following day, the 20th of April, a third regimental group was formed of the 17th/21st Lancers and the 7th Battalion and was placed under command of the 26th Armoured Brigade. All three battalions were now committed.

The outline plan for the advance was comparatively simple. The Division was to advance west and north-west as far as the River Panaro, up the far or west bank of which the Fifth Army troops would soon be advancing, having on the 19th after three days' furious fighting reached the plain. The junction of the two armies was to be effected by a strong thrust northwards from west of Bologna by the Fifth Army, while the Eighth Army thrust north-west with the 6th Armoured Division now on the right of this drive. If the Division could advance rapidly enough they would cut off the line of withdrawal of the 1st Parachute Corps, containing the best German troops in Italy. What in fact happened was that the 1st Parachute Corps did find their line of withdrawal cut; they made a desperate effort to swing away to the north-west, using the 278th Division as a pivot to ensure the safety of the 1st and 4th Parachute Divisions. This achieved a partial success but at an enormous cost, for not only was the 278th Division sacrificed but the parachute divisions were caught in the open by the air and ground forces trying to get away and suffered heavy losses in men as well as abandoning most of their equipment.

On the morning of the 19th of April the 2nd Battalion moved forward with the Lothians and Border Horse for its first battle in its new form. "A" and "B" Companies, each under command of the corresponding squadron of the Lothians, were to attempt to secure a crossing of the Po Morto di Primaro, south of the village of San Nicoso Ferrarese. For the first time in Italy companies and squadrons were able to move freely in a manner reminiscent of North Africa, relatively unfettered by the going. Progress at first was good and yielded a fair number of prisoners. Towards nightfall and about a mile and a half short of the obstacle, resistance stiffened, the Lothians losing four tanks to a well-sited anti-tank gun. The motor companies came up to protect the leaguer and strong fighting patrols from "A" and "B" Companies were soon going forward, one of them, under Roger Parker, reaching the river to find it held in strength by something like a company of infantry supported by a troop of tanks. Harassing of the bridges by our guns failed to prevent them being blown.

A plan was made for "A" Company, under Jim Lonsdale, with "A" Squadron of the Lothians, to secure the village of San Nicoso in daylight, after which "B" Company and "B" Squadron were to pass through and exploit the bridgehead. The attack was successful and the village was cleared despite considerable shelling and the unorthodox approach of a German colour-sergeant and his clerk, who appeared sitting on top of a pile of baggage in a horse and cart and charged wildly down the street

z

until they were shot-up at close range. "B" Company and their squadron passsed through and made some progress on the far bank, the leading platoon, Ian Mitchell's, advancing some one thousand yards through the town, despite shelling, mortaring and attacks by bazookamen. Opposition continued all day and when, towards nightfall, the Lothians began to lose more tanks it was decided to hold on to what bridgehead had been secured and to bring "C" Company up into the village for the night. To everyone's surprise, no counter-attack materialized.

The 7th Battalion and the 17th/21st Lancers started off at four in the morning on the 20th of April, "C" Company, under Peter Shepherd-Cross, travelling on the tanks of the reserve squadron. After a day more remarkable for discomfort than danger, the leading tanks reached the ditch—Fossa Cembalina —at Segni, where the bridge had been blown. "C" Company waded across and on the other side found about forty Germans, who were completely surprised and rapidly surrendered. A few moments later a staff car bearing their officer coming to give them orders was destroyed. The rest of the Battalion were still many miles behind and were marching nearly all night—but not marching on their feet, for the Colonel had impressed every tracked vehicle that was going in the right direction to carry his riflemen. Even the Arks* of the Assault Regiment, R.E., were not exempt from troop-carrying, probably the only time these vehicles have ever been used for such a purpose.

While the bridgehead over the Fossa was a useful first step, it did not open the way to a further advance across the Reno, for it led on to what was almost an island with a narrow exit between the Reno on the left and a canal on the right, this exit being blocked by a high bank. An operation was therefore required to clear this obstacle. At two in the afternoon the 17th/21st Lancers, with "A" and "C" Companies, and aided by a part of the Assault Regiment, R.E., began to advance under a barrage. For nearly three hours progress was slow. Then the tanks reported that they had captured a bridge intact where the canal is crossed by Route 64, the main road from Bologna to Ferrara. This success—described on the wireless by the Brigade Major as "the scoop of a lifetime"—opened up the most dramatic possibilities. There followed a mad chase along the corridor

---

*Churchill tanks carrying explosives for use by Royal Engineer assault regiments against fortifications.

between the Reno and the canal for four miles to cut Route 64 and then on for another five miles to the outskirts of Poggio Renatico to get into the heart of the enemy's supply base, not yet evacuated northwards. The carriers of the Battalion joined in the chase, with most of "A" Company hanging on as best they could. When the town was reached at dusk it was found to be held by a force of well-organized enemy, in contrast to the parties of stragglers, horses and vehicles which had been met during the evening. It was too dark to attempt to clear the town immediately. The group therefore stopped in the outskirts, blocking the exits to south and east.

It was clearly essential to get at least a foothold in Poggio, possession of which put the enemy in an extremely strong position in daylight, as the surrounding country was bare and open. The plan made during the night was, according to an account written by the 17th/21st Lancers, "received rather glumly by all except Colonel Douglas Darling, who appeared quite enthusiastic about clearing some twenty houses with only about fifty men in pitch darkness." "A" Company, commanded by Tim Dewhurst, played the principal part in this attack. Going in at four o'clock while it was still dark, they rapidly cleared their corner of the town, capturing some forty prisoners. The rest of the Battalion then took a hand and gradually made good the rest of the town, so that by 9 a.m. the total of prisoners had risen to two hundred and fifty. Although they fired many shells into the buildings, the enemy produced no counter-attack and the next morning contact was made with the New Zealanders moving up south of the Reno. The forcing of the obstacle at Segni and its exploitation to Poggio Renatico was undoubtedly the decisive action of this brief but exciting campaign.

The 7th Battalion moved on to San Agostino, near which place they met tanks of the American armoured division advancing from the south, clear proof that enemy resistance south of the Po had collapsed. Their operations had much to do with the weakening of the enemy opposition farther east. The 2nd Battalion had moved up on the 22nd behind the armoured regiments, past abandoned German guns and overturned vehicles, as convincing evidence of German disorganization as were the lines of prisoners walking back under the escort of grinning riflemen. The Battalion and the Lothians were directed on the bridge over the Panaro at Bondeno, about four miles south of the Po itself, the capture of which would seal one of the few exits from the area between the Po and the Apennines. "C" Company, commanded by Jim Wilson, and "C" Squadron led the advance. They met opposition from two Mark VI tanks and numbers of men with bazookas. "C" Squadron lost eleven tanks, but succeeded in getting one tank across the bridge before it was blown up in their faces. "A" Company cleared a village east of Bondeno, while "B" Company, also directed on the bridge, found a site on an embankment from which they had a good shoot at the Germans as they withdrew.

The Battalion had moved with enough speed to have made the Germans blow their bridge before they had meant to. The Colonel therefore decided to hold the bridge site with three company groups supported by tanks, more to prevent enemy from the south rejoining the main forces than against a possible counter-attack from the north. This regrouping was effected by midnight of the 22nd/23rd of April. On "A" Company's front a Mark IV tank, an 88-mm. gun and some infantry materialized at about four o'clock. The tank was destroyed at point-blank range by the Lothians—and our own 6-pounders—while the infantry vanished into the mist. Opposite "B" Company near the bridge itself enemy infantry appeared and all unaware began to dig in within a hundred yards of our platoons across the river. They were engaged by "B" Company and Ralph Stewart-Wilson's 3-inch mortars, firing with a quarter charge at two hundred and fifty yards' range, to such effect that the Germans retired in some disorder. "C" Company collected a number of unsuspecting enemy lorries on whose line of withdrawal they were sited. The next morning the Lothians moved forward to the Po itself.

No goal in war, however fabulous, however long-looked-forward-to is final until the complete surrender of the enemy. Now that the Po was reached, so confidently regarded as the limit of our troubles, that river surrounded, we had thought, by flat country, almost unimaginable in the high mountains of the Italian winter, the battalions were pulled back out of the battle, not to rest so much as to prepare to follow up the immediate crossing, which was already being planned. It had been a short, decisive campaign, lasting for the Brigade only four days, and yielding large numbers of prisoners and great quantities of booty. If more Germans had escaped than had, perhaps, been hoped, they had been forced to struggle over the congested ferries south of Ferrara in complete confusion, at the expense of most of the tanks, guns and heavy equipment which were left abandoned along every road. There were hardly enough troops to hold the Po against an Allied assault. The last hope of the German armies was to draw back a small, *élite* force, the few survivors of their best divisions, into the Inner Redoubt, there to join the Fuehrer in a death-bed scene more suited to Wagnerian opera than to the hard logic of modern wars. In his plans for this, the German commander, Vietinghof, had reckoned without the Partisans in Northern Italy and the speed with which the Allied armies were able to develop their crossing of the river and surge northward to the Alps.

For these few days the battalions waited to be launched on what must now surely be the last of all armoured advances, conscious of the success of their latest battles, marred only by the death of the Colonel of the 1st Battalion 60th Rifles, John Hope, well known to the Regiment since the early days in the desert, and the serious wound to Tony Palmer, recently arrived as Second-in-Command of the 2nd Battalion and hit by a shell from a German self-propelled gun which had recrossed the Po to fire some fifty random rounds. It was his fourth wound in four years—or fifth, if one counts a small splinter of anti-aircraft metal which lodged in his bottom on one of the earlier entries into Benghazi.

It was now almost the end of April in the last year of the war. The Allied armies, and with them the 1st and 8th Battalions, had already penetrated deep into the heart of Germany. It was evident that even the parachutists would be unable to continue the struggle much longer. But those who had been fighting the German Army for five years knew too well that the slightest let-up on our part, the shortest pause, would enable our enemies to scrape together some organized resistance, soldiers fighting on without hope at the orders of fanatical officers. Though there was relatively little fighting after the crossing of the Po, it was the speed of the advance which made certain that no breathing space was given long enough to allow anyone who still wanted to resist to be able to do so. The story of the battalions is mainly one of quick moves. The count of prisoners was vast enough to give the impression that all opposition had ended. But those who advanced on the masses of enemy drawn up across our path could not tell beforehand that they would surrender. There was still room for treachery, as James Keith found to his cost. The picture of this last advance is of the battalions motoring furiously northward, intoxicated with success and the knowledge that the war really was at an end, meeting occasionally with fierce opposition, as at Cavanazza, thrusting aside refugees, prisoners, and the transport of other formations in the anxiety to get on to the borders of the Reich. The two battalions pursued their own individual courses which must be described separately.

On the 26th of April the 2nd Battalion crossed the Po by a pontoon bridge. Its role was to protect the right flank of the New Zealand Division, who were forming up to cross the Adige. Moving on their right, the Battalion was directed on Lusia, with the object of cutting off the Germans remaining between the Po and the Adige. "A" Company cleared the village of Saguedo. "B" Company then went forward five miles on foot in the darkness to capture Cavanazza. Here a sharp battle took place. Ian Mitchell's platoon advancing ahead of the rest of the company reached the cross-roads at the centre of the village without trouble. Before they had well settled in about sixty Germans launched a determined counter-attack, causing nine casualties to the platoon and forcing them to pull back into a house dominating the cross-roads. This was a difficult operation, made possible only by some excellent work on the part of Sergeant Thompson, by whose efforts our wounded were recovered. Their new position was, however, a commanding one, for they managed to cause casualties to the enemy—seven killed to Sergeant Thompson's own gun—and to hold on, though surrounded, until the remainder of the company, supported by a troop of tanks from the 7th Hussars and Ralph Stewart-Wilson's mortars, arrived to clear the rest of the village. The enemy were still determined enough—even ten days before the end of all resistance—to counter-attack more than once and to try to infiltrate into the buildings. These attacks were beaten off with the aid of a carrier fitted as a flame-thrower. In the afternoon the 1st Battalion The Welch Regiment arrived to take over the position.

The Battalion had a short night's rest, being joined by that familiar figure of desert days Tim Marten, the Adjutant at Snipe and now to be Second-in-Command. After crossing the Adige the role was still right-flank protection to the New Zealanders.

The Last Campaign in Italy

By now events were moving quickly and the 29th was a day of fast motoring and surrendering Germans. Monselice, about fifteen miles south of Padua, was entered, a New Zealand tank with a bulldozer leading the advance, while immediately behind followed a section of the 2nd Battalion's carriers and then the bulldog figure of General Freyberg in his jeep. The Battalion followed up the Germans for three or four miles beyond the town before the chase was called off. Everyone was by now much in need of sleep.

The orders were that no move would occur for two days. The Battalion remained in harbour near Monselice with the rest of the 61st Brigade. It came as no surprise, however, when at two in the morning of the 1st of May the whole Brigade was on the move directed on Padua and Trevisio. The 2nd Battalion were now to work with the 27th Lancers, who were an armoured reconnaissance regiment. With them they reached Trevisio without meeting opposition. On the 2nd of May a rapid advance by "A" Company and "C" Squadron, 27th Lancers, towards Belluno, that nineteenth-century fortress fought for by Austrians and Piedmontese, led to the surrender of the whole of the German 65th Infantry Division. The next day Colonel Dick Fyffe went blindfolded behind the German lines to the opposing corps headquarters and negotiated the surrender of a further six thousand of the enemy, including the complete divisional artillery of the 715th Infantry Division, whose guns had harassed the Battalion to some purpose during the past winter at Fontanelice. Collapse was now general. A whole army corps surrendered to Field-Marshal Alexander. Prisoners appeared in embarrassing quantities, far outnumbering the riflemen, and accompanied by a steady stream of armoured cars, guns and assorted vehicles.

On the 4th of May the Battalion was ordered to make for Austria at full speed by way of the Isonzo Valley and the Predil Pass. Force was not to be used except in self-defence, but every effort was to be made to get the road open as soon as possible. "B" Company, leading the Battalion, reached Plezzo that evening. There followed several days of patrolling, bridge building and parleying. The Colonel and Regimental Sergeant-Major Crocker went, blindfolded, to the German divisional headquarters; Battalion Headquarters at Mittel Brett received a circus of enemy negotiators and conversed with them through the medium of Tim Marten's fluent German. Roger Parker walked from Plezzo to Cave del Predil, sixteen miles and four thousand feet up, to try to arrange a "Cease fire," while David Pontifex took his scout platoon by a roundabout route in an attempt to find a way into Austria by way of Yugoslavia, only to find the route blocked by four feet of snowdrift. Eventually contact was made with the commander of the German 97th Corps, who was empowered to arrange for the final surrender of the whole Army Group South-East.

The 2nd Battalion moved up to Trevisio and on the 8th of May crossed the frontier into Austria. It was five years and one week since it had set out from the Citadel along the Mena Road with the bougainvilleas in bloom against the white walls of the houses and turned off before reaching the Pyramids for its first introduction to the desert.

The 7th Battalion had followed across the Po and the Adige, hard on the heels of the New Zealand Division. After one night at Casa Odo news came that the 6th Armoured Division would take no further part in the pursuit. The Battalion had no time to celebrate the end of their war before orders were received to move at once with a part of the 27th Lancers to Udine.

Passing through Padua at dead of night the Battalion made for Trevisio, where contact was made with an American combat team. Pushing on, they made for the Piave, only to find the eastern bridges destroyed and no possible way round. At this time the Battalion was leading the advance of the Eighth Army and it seemed that these demolitions would put it out of the hunt and enable others far behind to draw ahead on the more northerly route, where the bridges were believed to be intact. Colonel Douglas Darling was not to be outdone so easily; so, waving on the American combat team, who had been jostling for the lead for the past hour, he turned the Battalion about and flew with all speed back to Trevisio and thence on to the northerly route before anyone realized what had happened.

With a squadron of the 27th Lancers the Battalion swept on over the Piave and headed for the next great river, the Tagliamento. The advance had now become a triumphal procession, for every man, woman and child in the villages and hamlets they drove through lined the way, singing, cheering and showering the riflemen with flowers. As each new village was passed the church bells rang out to warn the next of their approach.

The Last Campaign in Italy 341

And so the advance continued in perfect spring weather with a feeling of victory in the air.

Just short of St. Vito, near the Tagliamento, scattered remnants of the German Army were encountered. They slipped away in the darkness, but at dawn they were pursued past St. Vito and in a short skirmish on the Tagliamento several hundred superfluous prisoners and several tanks were captured.

By this time the Battalion was many miles ahead of anyone else in the Army, the New Zealanders having turned off along the coast towards Trieste, where it was reported, on the authority only of rumour, that their divisional commander had spent his honeymoon. All contact by wireless had been lost with Division and Brigade; the Colonel characteristically decided to push on to Udine. Using the causeway over the Tagliamento, the Battalion sailed down the highway into Udine at a steady forty miles an hour. Here the scene was beyond description. Some twenty thousand people had gathered to welcome the Riflemen with cheers, flowers and wine, while several hundred Partisans, armed to the teeth, saluted their entry with repeated volleys from their weapons. Slowly a way was made through the dense and clamorous crowds to the farther exits of the town, where road-blocks were established to north, east and south. It was now the evening of the 1st of May.

Shortly after arriving in Udine contact was made with a small party of German tanks to the north of the town. These had every appearance of being on the verge of surrender. But when James Keith went forward on foot to meet the leading tank commander a German officer in the tank shot at him with a pistol and wounded him seriously. A general skirmish ensued in which several riflemen were wounded, one of whom died later. Geoffrey Merrick soon got his anti-tank guns into action and knocked out one tank—the last of many tanks destroyed by the Battalion during the war. The remainder of the Germans slipped away in the failing light, taking James Keith and several other prisoners with them, who were not recaptured until the following day.

This was the last action fought by the 7th Battalion. After twenty-four hours at Udine the Battalion went off eastwards to prevent a junction between the Chetniks and Marshal Tito's forces. Some twenty thousand Chetniks were encountered at Cormons and an arrangement was made by which they would withdraw through the Battalion to concentrate at Palmanova. Tito's forces were intent on following up and clearly intended battle. No force could be used to prevent this. The only course was physically to block the roads to allow the Chetniks time to withdraw. These tactics were successful, though Tito's forces reached Cormons only a few minutes after the last of the Chetniks had been evacuated. Thus early, before the war with the Germans was formally ended, did the 7th Battalion have a foretaste of the problems which were to complicate the peace.

Moving back to Udine and thence to the Tarvisio Pass, the Battalion was ready at 8 a.m. on the 8th of May to cross the frontier into Austria. There has been much argument as to who were the first to enter the Greater Reich. The 2nd Battalion provided the carrier escort for General Murray when he met the German commander on the border, and these Riflemen were the first British troops to cross the frontier. But it was the 7th Battalion who led the Eighth Army in their progress to Klagenfurt, an advance of far-reaching importance, since it was only the speed of their move—and the various subterfuges by which our Eastern allies were hampered—which forestalled Tito's forces by a bare four hours in the occupation of the town—four hours of the deepest political consequence. The Battalion was led into Austria by the formidable figure of Douglas Darling, who had first taken command in the Djebel Akdar in December, 1942, and had continued for two and a half years, broken only by a short absence through wounds. He had led the Battalion from Tmimi to Tunis and for the greater part of the Italian campaign, from the Liri Valley to the Gothic Line, from Cattolica to the Po, and now, in the final race across the battlefields of General Bonaparte, Louis Napoleon and Marshal Radetsky, from the Adige to the Austrian frontier.

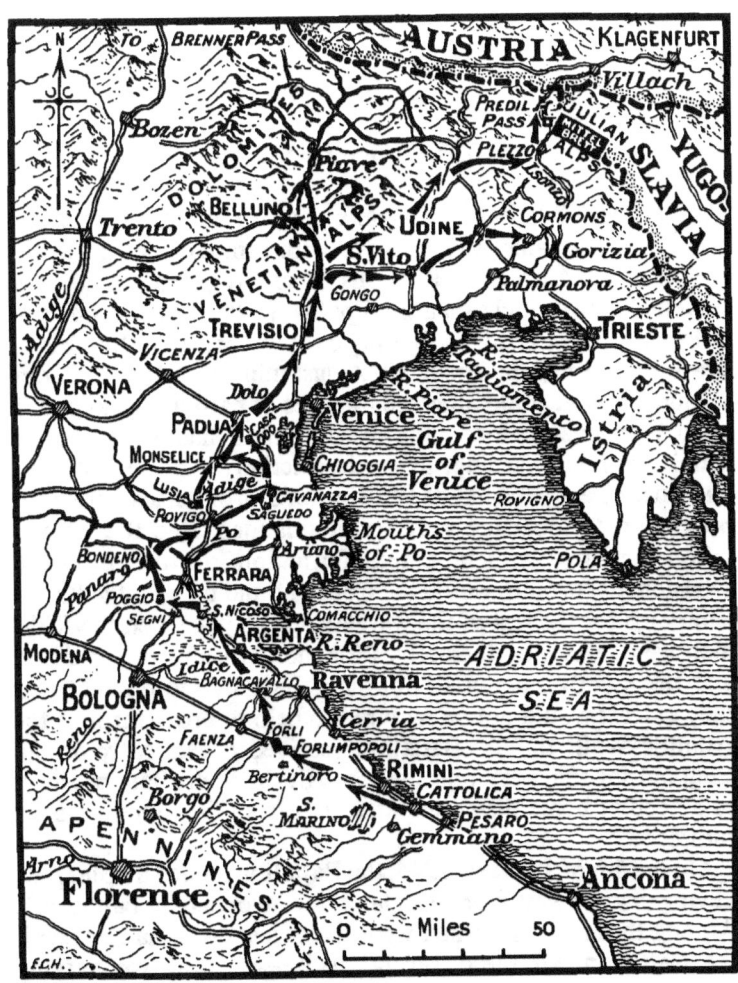

Advance into Austria

CHAPTER XXV

THE SECOND FRONT

THE 1st and 8th Battalions were cast for the same role and trained in the same way to work with armour. Yet up to the spring of 1944 no two battalions of one regiment could have travelled more widely separated paths. In this last war one was either involved in endless fighting overseas or, after Dunkirk, in years of training in England. A last-minute order, a sudden change of plan, could alter the fortunes of battalions more radically than ever before. The 1st Battalion had been sent to Calais, without warning, to its destruction: the 8th Battalion had once already loaded its vehicles for North Africa before the orders for its departure were countermanded. Had the 1st Battalion remained with its parent formation, the 1st Armoured Division, its fortunes would have been bound up with the Italian campaign for the rest of the war. As it was, just when the Riflemen were consoling themselves for the hardships of the desert and the muddy squalor of Southern Italy by the thought that they at least would not be required to help to break through the Atlantic Wall, the 1st Battalion received orders to return to England for that very purpose, though the immediate prospect of a spell at home distracted attention from the more ominous future.

On the 5th of January, 1944, the Battalion landed at Glasgow, having been away from England for two and a half years. Among those who returned were ten officers who had left with the Battalion. Of these, several had been away for varying periods on staff appointments and the like. The whole party went off to a camp near Brandon, in Norfolk, where they prepared to face the exigencies of an English winter and to discover the shortcomings of war-time military dwellings. But, although huts in the dripping woods of Norfolk bore little relation to peace-time comfort as the Riflemen remembered it, their feet were at least half under the table and this brief rest from war would make it all the more difficult to start off again in the spring.

The 8th Battalion knew all about hutted camps. While they had been spared the casualties and extreme hardships of active service, they had passed through every stage of frustration. It was easy for the first few years to sustain an enthusiasm for training and to feel that all this disruption of a normal existence was leading towards some great enterprise. The forces which remained in England for those four years did not have it all their own way. The minor discomforts irked the more because they seemed to have no object: there was a vociferous school of civilian opinion who held that the soldiers in England did everything but fight. Above all, there must have been a fear that the Battalion would be broken up, as the 8th Battalion 60th Rifles was later to be broken up, and its officers and riflemen scattered in every direction so that each man would have to start again to form the friendships and associations, to assume the habits and take on the traditions of a strange battalion or unit. Whatever may be said in Whitehall of the regimental or the battalion spirit, every Rifleman knows the dread that his company or, worse, battalion may be split up to form reinforcements for others. I am not claiming for the battalion at home that it was not lucky compared with those who fought continuously overseas. But even in this cynical age there is left some pride of achievement, some consciousness of making a contribution to ending the war, which the soldier in action still feels, if only perhaps because it provides him with the chance to be able to say—and that afterwards—that he "has marched and fought with the Eighth Army."

The 8th Battalion, now commanded by Colonel Michael Treneer-Michell, formed part of the 11th Armoured Division. It acted as the motor battalion of the 29th Armoured Brigade, whose Brigadier, Roscoe Harvey, had known the 1st Battalion when he commanded the 10th Hussars. The 11th Armoured Division, who had not yet seen action as a formation, were commanded in the spring of 1944 by General Pip Roberts, an experienced desert commander who had already had the 1st and 10th Battalions in his armoured brigades and was well known to the 2nd Battalion from the earliest days. The Regiment was always happy under his command. Many of these appointments had resulted from the return of General Montgomery to take over the 21st Army Group, and whatever may have been his impact on the Army in England there was no doubt that his presence was a source of confidence to the 1st Battalion and to all those who had served under him in battle.

As motor battalions it was clear that we should not have to assault the beaches of whatever country was chosen for the invasion. But there was every likelihood of having to drive vehicles through deep water before they landed and "waterproofing" became one of the main preoccupations of the battalions. The 1st Battalion had great preparations to make, and hardly time to absorb reinforcements and make up for the deficiencies in individual training which resulted from a prolonged spell of almost continuous warfare. The 8th Battalion had to go through again the same preparations that had already occupied four years, this time with a real expectation of action.

May, 1944, was a month of clear, blue skies and fruit blossom. It seemed to those returned from abroad as if the English spring put on its best beauty for this one year. As the time for the invasion approached—a time no one in the battalions knew—day after day was warm and rainless, yet with the clear atmosphere and fine visibility which Italy and Africa could not match. All through May the seas were calm. When towards the end of the month the battalions were sealed off in their camps to be ready to be marshalled for embarkation, the weather was still as perfect as anyone had known.

The Riflemen were confined to camp. The destination and the role of the divisions became known. The 1st Battalion, with the 7th Armoured Division, was to land in XXX Corps on the beaches to be captured by the 50th Division, almost as soon as they were clear. The plan was for a quick thrust inland through Bayeux and to the south into the bocage country of Normandy on the right of the British forces. Already the name "Villers Bocage" had made its ominous appearance. The 8th Battalion was to be in VIII Corps and was to land a few days later than the 1st Battalion in the area north of Caen and to be employed in a great armoured break-out to the south. The weather and the rough seas, the nature of the Norman countryside, and the tenacity of the Germans were to control the dates of landing and the progress of the battle itself.

In the middle of May the 1st Battalion left Norfolk for a marshalling area near Brentwood. From there they were split up into smaller parties, one going to the Stadium at West Ham and another back to Norfolk for a time. The Battalion was delivered entirely into the hands of Movement Control, who from now on ordered all moves and controlled practically all activities. At the end of the month the vehicles were embarked in motor transport ships and in the first days of June the companies moved down to the docks in Royal Army Service Corps transport. For the voyage the Battalion was divided into three main parties: the first, of two hundred men and fifty-eight vehicles, scattered amongst some seven motor transport ships and with sixty men in one personnel ship went on board at the West Indies and Victoria and Albert Docks on the Thames; the second and main party of five hundred men and a hundred and thirty vehicles embarked in two motor transport ships from Tilbury; and the third party was to leave from London a week later and consisted of fifteen vehicles and twenty-five men. Each party had the same story of crowded ships, crowded even as the word applies to troopships.

The Battalion's ships moved out into the Thames Estuary behind the fleets which carried the assault divisions. No one who saw it will forget the sight of the invasion fleet stretching to the horizon in every direction. During the voyage one vessel in the convoy was hit by gun fire from Calais. The first party arrived off the coast of Arromanches ahead of time at eight in the morning of D plus one. Arromanches looked unexpectedly peaceful from the boat and the only warlike sound was of gun fire from far inland. This was as well; for nothing went ashore until the evening and it took thirty-six hours before this first party was disembarked, complete except for one personnel ship which carried the crews of all the carriers and was diverted by some error to Cowes, where it remained for five days. The main party landed on D plus four and the third party two days later on the 12th of June.

Much time had been spent and much attention devoted to the waterproofing of vehicles. But most people's hearts were in their mouths as they took to the water to drive ashore; for the prospect of losing one's vehicle and all one's belongings was by no means attractive. Those landing on the high tide were lucky, their landing being almost dryshod. Those at half or low tide had a longer and deeper drive and occasionally disappeared completely from view through driving into holes up to eighteen feet deep made by ships which had beached on previous tides. In such cases the driver and crew would have to bale out and make a sad and ignominious progress to the beach. On the whole there were remarkably few cases of "drowned" vehicles in the Battalion and such as there were were for the most part quickly rescued by the Royal Electrical and Mechanical Engineers' beach recovery detachments working with specially waterproofed bulldozers. The Battalion's short acquaintance with the beach was sufficient to make them thankful that they had not arrived with the assault.

The Battalion concentrated inland a few miles short of Bayeux, that grey-gabled Norman town of narrow, cobbled streets and ancient buildings, market centre of a farming countryside, with old-fashioned inns and scent shops and elementary sanitation, strangely untouched by the war. The advance started on the 10th of June. But "C" Company (Bill Jepson-Turner) and the Support Company, "B" Company (John Witt), were still far from complete. Nevertheless, "A" Company (James Wright) and "I" Company (Bill Apsey), each with an anti-tank platoon under command, were ready to join the 4th County of London Yeomanry and the 5th Royal Tanks, the armoured regiments with whom they usually worked.

The advance was directed south from Bayeux towards Tilly-sur-Seulles. The road is straight enough to have dated from Roman times, undulating and lined on each side by an avenue of trees. To say to a soldier of Burma that the bocage country is thick is to invite derision. But it does consist of small fields intersected by high, thick hedges on banks such as you might find in Devonshire. There are orchards and copses where the trees grow naturally, thickly and at random, not man-planted as in the spinneys of Belgium and Flanders. This June the country was green and lush, every tree and hedge in leaf and the corn high in the fields. When one entered a field it was practically impossible to tell what Spandau or anti-tank gun or even Tiger tank might not be pointing its nose at one from the other hedge. The armour was particularly handicapped by inability to see farther than one field. Some of the banks were obstacles to tanks; houses were suitable cover for bazookamen. Almost at once the companies were engaged in clearing clusters of houses, in making hedges good, and in protecting the tanks from infantry who might be lying up anywhere. When the houses were cleared there was no knowing how soon the Germans might creep back in again. "I" Company found themselves clearing one small set of houses no fewer than three times in the day, since small parties of enemy kept filtering back. While doing so they lost Sergeant Hines, whose distinguished record in the 9th Battalion and later in the 1st included the award of a Military Medal and bar. This type of country uses up infantry with astonishing rapidity and each little operation results in a few casualties. If the bane of Italy was "finding out if they've gone," the curse of Normandy was the order to "go and clear those houses for the tanks."

It soon appeared from the slow progress of the armour along the Tilly road that the rapid dash across country for which the Battalion had been briefed, the capture of Villers Bocage and the thrust to Mount Pincon could hardly yet materialize. Those few days of imperceptible progress served only to give everyone experience of the country where this war was to be fought. On the 12th of June the decision was made to switch the Armoured Brigade to the right by small side-roads to pass through the Americans and to approach Villers Bocage from the west with the object of capturing the high ground to the south and east of the town. Speed was to be the essence of the operation.

The move started at four in the afternoon, the 8th Hussars moving ahead and to the flanks. "A" Company followed with the 4th County of London Yeomanry and had Roger Butler's platoon of 6-pounders from "B" Company under command. The first opposition came near Livry, where the Riflemen were used to clear what was described as parkland. But subsequently some progress was made and the group leaguered at La Paumerie. The next morning, the 13th of June, Bruce Campbell's platoon reported the centre line clear for half a mile. The armoured regimental group moved off in an order typical of such operations. "B" Squadron and one section of 5 Platoon led. Then came Regimental Headquarters, "A" Company headquarters with the company commander, James Wright, the three motor platoons, the mortar detachment and such of the scout platoon as had up to that time arrived from the beaches. The rest of the armoured regiment and the battery of the 5th Royal Horse Artillery followed. The 1st Battalion, less "A" Company, were farther back in the Brigade column, the companies being with their armoured regiments.

The route taken by the Brigade led them well behind the lines of the enemy who were facing the rest of the Second Army. They approached the village of Villers Bocage from the south-west along the main road from Avranches to Caen. The road twists uphill as it enters the village and then runs straight on a long, gradual slope between the houses and up to the high ground a mile and a half towards Caen. To the south-west Mont Pincon and its surrounding hills could clearly be seen. The country is true bocage, hilly and leafy and thick; small fields and orchards and high banks make fields of fire short. High features are not commanding: there is no such thing as a good observation post.

There was some delay in getting the column started because the reconnaissance to be sent right and left of the road had to cross the main line of the advance. When they had finally shaken out there was further delay, near La Masure, while an enemy armoured car—ominous sign—was disposed of. But the village seemed free of enemy: the inhabitants came out to cheer: there were no snipers. It seemed that the enemy had been caught off their balance and that all that remained was to occupy the vital ground a mile and a half north of the village. The platoon commanders were called forward to the head of the column to receive orders for occupation of this new position with the County of London Yeomanry. By nine o'clock the head of the column had reached its objective and the motor platoons, without their officers, were being exhorted by those behind to close up head to tail at the side of the road. Visibility to a flank was not more than two hundred and fifty yards and the riflemen had jumped out of their half-tracks to stretch their legs and put out sentries.

At about a quarter past nine Sergeant O'Connor, of Bruce Campbell's platoon, suddenly reported two or three Tiger tanks moving parallel to the column about two hundred and fifty yards away. Someone opened fire on them. They swung north and engaged the vehicles standing in the road. The last tank of "B" Squadron was hit and set on fire; another tank went up and then it was the turn of "A" Company's half-tracks, which were set on fire one by one. Two more Tigers started firing from due south near the outskirts of the town and two or three more of our tanks were destroyed. The four tanks of Regimental Headquarters were hit, the first to be knocked out being the only one

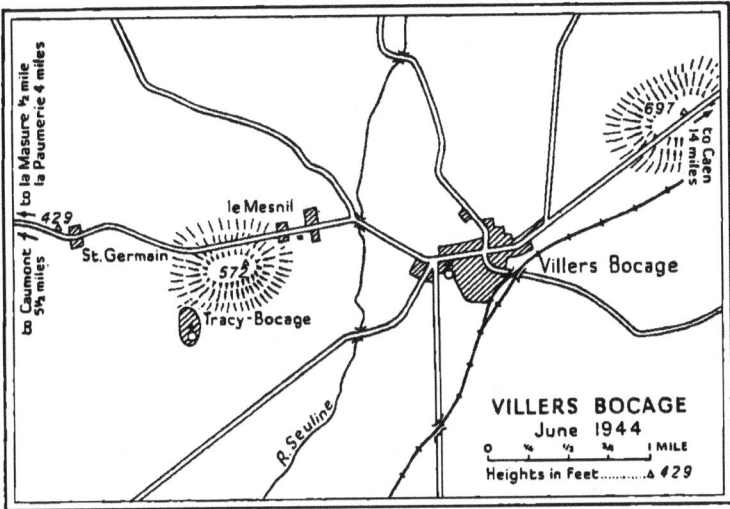

of the four which carried a 17-pounder and therefore capable of dealing with a Tiger.

Thus, within a few minutes, the leading part of "B" Squadron and all the officers of "A" Company had been cut off from the rest of the Brigade. Regimental Headquarters of the County of London Yeomanry, the rear tanks of "B" Squadron and the half-tracks of "A" Company were in flames along the road. The riflemen were on their feet and without officers, and had already sustained casualties. Sergeant Bray had managed to get one 6-pounder into action and he claimed to have hit two half-tracks and one armoured car before a tank had knocked his gun out and then driven down the road machine-gunning the ditches.

The armoured thrust had been effectively halted. Whether the Germans had watched the leading tanks advance through the village and then pounced on them from behind or whether a German panzer division had happened to drive in from the south at the moment when the 4th County of London Yeomanry were half-way through the village is anyone's guess. It is sometimes the fashion to attribute devilish ingenuity to the Germans —or any other enemy, except perhaps the Italians. The Battle of Villers Bocage might seem a model ambush. But there are indications that the Germans were not as completely in control of the situation as might at first have appeared. There is a theory that the first enemy to enter Villers Bocage were the headquarters of the Adolf Hitler Panzer Division and that is what explains the pause in operations that now ensued. At any rate, for some hours no attack was made on the isolated party on Point 697, north-east of the village. Any movement attracted fire: an attempt to investigate a side-road resulted in a Sherman tank being destroyed by a Tiger. It was not until half past one that eight Tiger tanks supported by a few infantry made their appearance. The remaining Shermans were soon disposed of and the tanks moved slowly up the road machine-gunning the ditches. The squadron leader of "B" Squadron was killed, many others were wounded and the remainder of the party were gradually rounded up. James Wright and the Colonel of the 4th County of London Yeomanry were among those taken prisoner. About thirty Riflemen, including Chris Milner, made their way back by stages to rejoin the Brigade. But we suffered some eighty casualties, including three officers killed, and "A" Company ceased for the moment to exist.

The rest of the Brigade, when their efforts to join the leading squadron had finally proved unsuccessful, were withdrawn to the high ground two miles west of Villers Bocage. Augmented by two infantry battalions and with the 1st Battalion plugging the holes in the defences, the force dug in to await the counter-attack. The leading armoured regiment, or what was left of it, was withdrawn within this perimeter that evening. The area was constricted: shells could hardly fail to land near some vehicle. Throughout the 14th the enemy brought down concentrations, one of which landed in "I" Company's area, the first shells killing Geoffrey May and Company Sergeant-Major Jefford, and wounding Gerald Pritty.

The afternoon was ominously quiet. At about eight in the evening the Germans put in their attack, which included "I" Company's area in its scope. The enemy had quite appreciable artillery support and the infantry were supported by Tiger tanks. This time, unlike the previous afternoon, it was we who were sitting still and the German tanks who were moving. After a little while several of them were "brewed up" by the Divisional anti-tank regiment, the Norfolk Yeomanry, and after that the infantry rather lost heart. "I" Company had some stiff fighting, particularly when an unexpected gap appeared in the defences. The Royal Horse Artillery had to engage the enemy over open sights at four or five hundred yards' range. Dennis Matthews's platoon took a hand and he himself was badly wounded; our tanks sprayed the area with machine-gun fire and finally the American gunner liaison officer called down a concentration of really remarkable proportions. This special concentration landed on a wood where the Germans were known to have collected and two prisoners who surrendered said that arms and legs were flying in every direction and put the casualties at eight hundred—no doubt a gross exaggeration. Whatever its effect, the Germans did not attack again that evening.

The position which had been held so successfully was well behind the German lines to the east. It was, however, isolated and the lines of communication highly vulnerable to the enemy. If fresh troops had been available to secure the rear areas and exploit behind the Germans results might have been permanently effective. The assault divisions had by this time had enough casualties to prevent them taking part in this venture: all eyes were turned in the direction of Caen. It was therefore decided to withdraw during the night. A raid of a hundred Lancaster bombers on the village was arranged to distract the attention of the Germans. After dark the whole Brigade went off nose to tail down one road and arrived in a more secure area at daybreak, the enemy making little attempt to interfere, though one of the few shells they did fire landed on John Foreshew's carrier, killing him and his crew instantly.

While the armoured regiments rested, the 1st Battalion went off to hold some two thousand five hundred yards of front near Le Pont Mulot, four miles from Caumont. Being thoroughly stretched on this front, much patrolling and harassing by 3-inch mortars had to be done. Everyone stood-to at a quarter past four in the morning and at a quarter past ten at night, in each case for an hour. What remained of the night was frequently disturbed by shelling or machine-gun fire, and the days by hordes of unnecessary visitors. When eleven days of this had passed there were few men in the Battalion who were not crying out for sleep, and only Sergeant Barrett can have pleasant memories of Le Pont Mulot, where his 3-inch mortars had some particularly good shoots.

While the Battalion was holding this part of the line the process of re-forming "A" Company in the "B" Echelon area had begun. This was some eight miles behind the lines, a safe enough area to choose for such a purpose. Here they received a most useful draft from the 8th Battalion 60th Rifles. Francis Dorrien-Smith, who had commanded a carrier platoon in the desert and been Adjutant afterwards, was sent back to command the company. While he and James Caesar, just arrived from England, were in this area the enemy indulged in some long-range shelling, rare for him, and immediately killed both of them. A few minutes later Gilbert Talbot, commanding H.Q. Company, was killed too. It was bad enough in the heat of the battle to have lost most of "A" Company at Villers Bocage, but now in the comparative security of "B" Echelon to lose by pure mischance three such officers seemed an unbearable blow.

By the 22nd of June, a fortnight and a day after the first Rifleman had landed in Normandy, the 1st Battalion had lost fourteen officers and a hundred and sixty-three other ranks. The bocage exacted a high price from those who fought in it. No one suffered more heavily than the armoured formations, blind among the green, leafy hedges and high banks. The advance to Villers Bocage had come near to being a striking and spectacular success. It had penetrated far into enemy country, farther than we were to get for some weeks yet of hard fighting. If the enemy had appeared an hour later the 4th County of London Yeomanry and "A" Company would have been established on Point 697 astride the main lateral road from Caen to Avranches, miles behind the enemy line at Hottot and Juvigny. If the 7th Armoured Division had been able to maintain itself with secure lines of communication and fresh troops had been available to exploit this more than local success the battle for Caen and the struggles to cross the Orne and the Odon, the break-out from the bridgehead, would have cost less heavy a price. As it was, the thrust to Villers represented a remarkable gain at a time when elbow-room was vitally needed.

CHAPTER XXVI

THE DOG-FIGHT

THE Battle of Villers Bocage can fairly be described as belonging to the early stages of the invasion. There was still a hope of breaking through into the interior of France: quite large gains could be made by opportunist action. The nature of the fighting in Normandy was not yet understood, and while the leading tanks were engaging the enemy the remnants of troops or platoons or sections would drive up straight from the beaches, where chance or weather or the Build-up Control had deposited them some time behind schedule. The assaulting divisions continued to try to keep the battle fluid. Efforts were made to push forward into Caen, but by the third week in June everyone knew that these struggles, important as they were to those who took part in them, were side-shows. The enemy had reacted to the shock of the initial invasion. He had lost ground, but he had not given way. It depended now on how quickly we could build up our forces across the Channel and how effectively the Air Force could prevent the enemy's concentration by road. It was against this background that VIII Corps began to assemble.

The 8th Battalion left Aldershot on the 8th of June, embarked on the 10th, and lay in the Thames Estuary until the 12th. On Tuesday, the 13th, the convoy anchored off Normandy and began to unload by landing craft. Most of the Battalion disembarked on the next day at Craye-sur-Mer, near Arromanches, and at Courseulles, having on the whole as dry a landing as anyone could have wished for. There followed ten days near Cully while the vehicles were dewaterproofed and the rest of the Corps assembled. The Riflemen became accustomed to the sights and sounds of the Normandy beach-head. There were dead cows and wrecked buildings. The grey villages reminded some of the Cotswolds, though advertisements on the walls for Byrrh or Cinzano were clearly out of keeping with Stow-on-the-Wold or Cirencester. The inhabitants, with their dead stock lying legs upward in the fields and the Germans only three miles away, were naturally cautious of welcoming the liberators openly. They had been left comparatively undisturbed by the Germans and transport difficulties had prevented the export of all their agricultural produce. Butter, cheese and eggs could be purchased. There was abundant Calvados, a drink, it was said, that "one buys when it is the only one sold." Every night the anti-aircraft barrage from the beaches and the sound of falling bombs were reminders that the war was near.

The strategic object of the attempts to capture Caen and push on to Falaise, to strike at the hinge of the German position, was largely to draw the enemy's armour away from the American front. The Battalion was not concerned with strategy. It was, however, intimately concerned in the plan to cross the Odon west of Caen and establish VIII Corps on the high ground between that river and the Orne. From such a position the possibilities of exploitation must have appeared limitless. The 15th (Scottish) Division was to break into the enemy position west of Carpiquet aerodrome in the area of Cheux—St. Mauvieux. The 11th Armoured Division was then to pass through, cross the Odon, establish itself on the high ground beyond, particularly on two features known as Hill 112 and Hill 113, and cut the main road running south-west from Caen, with a view to a much more ambitious advance to the other side of the Orne. The operation was to be known as "Epsom." The formations taking part, except the 4th Armoured Brigade, were new to active service. It was only later in the light of experience of fighting in the bridgehead that the ambitious scope of this task became clear.

For the battle the motor companies went out to their armoured regiments, "F" Company, under Foster Cunliffe, to the Fife and Forfar Yeomanry, "G" Company, under Mickey McCrae, to the 3rd Royal Tanks, and "H" Company, under Kenneth Mackenzie, to the 23rd Hussars. The Support Company ("E"), under Tony Rowan, was split up among the armoured regimental groups.

On the 26th of June the 29th Armoured Brigade moved forward. At first they followed up the 15th (Scottish) Division, passing through Bretteville L'Orgueilleuse and Cheux, where dead Canadians, mined houses and the smell of decay showed signs of earlier fighting. Before they entered Cheux one of "F"

Company's half-tracks received a direct hit, resulting in ten men being killed. When they came out on the forward slopes south of Cheux the enemy 88-mm. guns opened up effectively on the Brigade. Rain did not make things any more pleasant; and as it grew dark there was much groping to find the harbours where the Riflemen would protect the tanks for the night. Smouldering houses gave the only light.

The next day, the 27th of June, the tanks found a way through Tourville, across the main road from Caen to Villers Bocage and on to the narrow, flat plain on the other side of which was the Odon. Although Colonel Perry Harding, of the 23rd Hussars, had his tank shot under him, he ordered the two leading squadrons, followed by "H" Company, to cross the bridge—still intact—and climb the steep ridge beyond. This was done successfully. The woods were found to be clear of enemy. By midnight the 23rd Hussars and "H" Company had leaguered for what little remained of the night. The rest of the Battalion followed up, "F" Company having spent an unpleasant time under shell fire in Baron.

The next morning as soon as it grew light it was obvious that the wood on Hill 112 dominated the whole surrounding area. "H" Company was ordered to clear it, concentrating first in a wood at the east end of Baron. At first all went well. Two German officers were taken prisoner before the objective was reached: the motor platoons advanced through the wood successfully, with Sergeants Bowden's and Macaree's carrier sections on each flank. But at the end of the wood German tanks counter-attacked. In the confusion a whole section was shot-up in error by one of our own tanks. The company and supporting tanks had many casualties and in the early afternoon were ordered to withdraw. The enemy were by now able to concentrate fire from three directions on to Hill 112. Their guns fired from Carpiquet to the north; there was heavy mortaring from Esquay; Tigers and 88-mm. guns were picking off our tanks on all sides. A plan was made to launch a Battalion attack on the wood during the night, though by the time the companies were concentrated this project was cancelled. The rest of the day and the early part of the night were spent under intense fire and casualties were heavy. During the night Donald Sudlow and Corporal Hone's section of 15 Platoon patrolled down into Esquay and confirmed the presence of Tigers there.

Once again in the early morning of the 29th of June it was decided to clear the wood on Hill 112. "H" Company, with one platoon of "G" Company, went in to the attack supported by the armour at eight in the morning. The wood itself was not occupied; but heavy shell and mortar fire came down on it, causing many casualties, among them the company commander, Kenneth Mackenzie, who was wounded. Positions on the far edge of the wood were secured and a further platoon of "G" Company, with some anti-tank guns and machine guns of "E" Company, came up to help in consolidation. This party remained there throughout the rest of the day. The Colonel visited them despite the mortar fire which pinned everyone to their trenches, and warned them that a withdrawal was likely. A German patrol to the wood was driven off. But soon after midnight the order was received for the Brigade to withdraw to the other side of the Odon. By dawn the whole Battalion had passed back across the narrow bridge and the VIII Corps' offensive was ended.

Hill 112 was for the 8th Battalion its first experience of war. The operation combined the worst features of the fighting at this time. While the Germans could not maintain their position on the hill, they could bring very heavy fire to bear on anyone who turned them off it. Most of the Riflemen were subjected to shelling and mortaring without ever seeing a German, and our tanks were picked off by an enemy whose better armament and skill in concealment gave him an advantage over our troops who were advancing across the open. The thick, wooded, leafy bocage country handicapped our Gunner observation posts as well as the armoured regiments; and as vehicles burnt and bombs and shells exploded in the cramped area of Hill 112 the air became loaded with a fine, grey powder, covering men and vehicles and the bodies of cows so that the wounded looked even more ghastly than usual, lying among the smouldering shell-holes and splintered trunks of trees. Casualties in this first battle had been heavy, amounting to three officers and thirty-four non-commissioned officers and riflemen in "G" Company alone. Already two company commanders had been wounded.

The defeat of the VIII Corps' thrust across the Odon was but one of a series of disappointments at this time. Hill 112 was to be fought for by other formations until the days of the Falaise pocket. Its summit was untenable by Germans or ourselves. While there was fighting all along the front and Caen itself was being captured and cleared, the 8th Battalion remained in reserve, first at Norrey-en-Bessin and Bretteville, then in a counter-attack role north of Cheux. Colonel Michael Treneer-Michell left and his place was taken by Tony Hunter (60th Rifles), an officer with a long experience of war in the Middle East, where, as a company commander in the 60th, he had been well known to the 2nd Battalion. This was the first and only occasion when a battalion of the Regiment was commanded by an officer who was not of The Rifle Brigade. Within three months we were to provide two colonels for battalions of the 60th. Colonel Tony Hunter commanded until after the end of the war with the greatest success. To no one outside the Regiment—if a 60th Rifleman can really be regarded as such—do we owe a greater debt.

Until the middle of July the 8th Battalion remained out of the line while more and more guns arrived in their area to fire off five rounds gunfire at the most unexpected moments of day or night and always when one had just dropped off to sleep. The 1st Battalion, too, spent a period out of the line, first at St. Honorine de Ducy and later at Ellon, some four miles south of Bayeux. Life was comparatively pleasant despite the arrival of medium guns in ever-increasing numbers. It was certain that the activities of these guns would earn the attention of the enemy counter-battery organization. On the last night before the Battalion moved they fired the heaviest concentration so far encountered. They landed between two hundred and forty and four hundred shells in the Brigade area, mainly from 150-mm. guns, causing four or five casualties to "A" Company and destroyed a fighter on the landing strip, which had been completed only that day. Twenty minutes later we replied with two thousand four hundred shells from medium and heavy artillery.

When one's battalion has a period of rest in war delight in washing and sleeping, in drinking, perhaps, Calvados, and in buying eggs and butter, is tempered by the realization that this respite does not spring from the altruistic motives of the Higher Command, but that you are simply being fattened up, like pheasants in pre-war Septembers, for a particularly important occasion. Caen had been captured; no further progress had been made west of the Orne. The new plan was distinctly ambitious. The next thrust was to be aimed east of the Orne, in an area popularly supposed to consist of good tank country, rolling cornfields and compact villages, to be heralded by an air bombardment on a hitherto unprecedented scale, to be carried out by no fewer than three armoured divisions. The adjectives used to describe the numbers of aeroplanes and tanks employed might have been borrowed from Hollywood. Operation "Goodwood" was in many ways—and not least in the traffic congestion it produced—one of the most remarkable of the war.

It concerned the 8th Battalion as part of the 11th Armoured Division and the 1st Battalion as part of the 7th Armoured Division. The third armoured division involved was the Guards. The appearance of this mass of armour hard on the heels of the Royal Air Force's bombs was expected to lead to decisive results —at least a substantial advance towards, if not right up to, Falaise. The preparations involved the most complicated staff work and in two days and nights the 1st and 8th Battalions, exhorted by camouflage experts and egged on by Movement Control, moved round north of Caen to be ready to follow up the bombardment.

On the 18th of July, with the 11th Armoured Division in the lead, the battle began. The heavy bombers appeared in unbelievable force. It was impossible to imagine that anyone could survive such an onslaught of bombs, and when one or two sticks fell short among our own troops the explosions gave us only a little idea of what must have been happening to the Germans. Some of the vast number of guns now collected in the bridgehead joined in the bombardment.

The whole operation was led by the 3rd Royal Tanks and "G" Company. The battle formation employed was two squadrons of tanks in line abreast, followed by a line of flail tanks and the carriers of 9 Platoon. After them came the Headquarters vehicles of the group, Noel Bell's command vehicle alongside Colonel Silvertop's tank, and the assault engineers' Churchill tanks. The last line consisted of the remainder of the company and the Royal Horse Artillery's self-propelled guns. The whole formed a square with the third squadron of tanks split into two, one half being on each flank of the square. The vehicles were camouflaged with bundles of corn tied all over them—at the

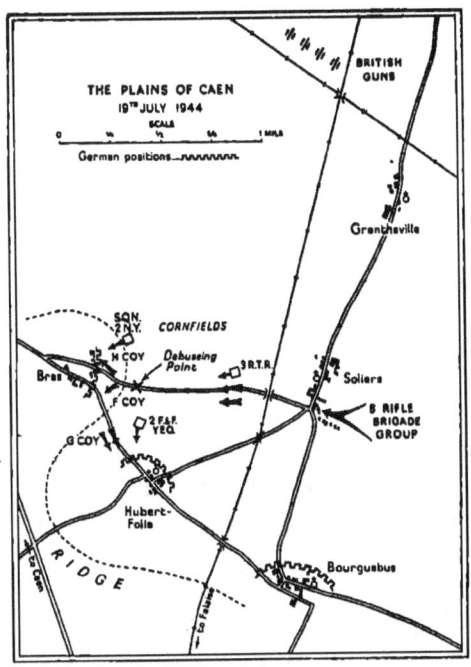

risk of an incendiary bullet setting the sheaves alight and the vehicle on fire as well.

The 9th of July was a lovely, sunny, summer's day. With morale lifted by the sight of the Royal Air Force to the highest degree of confidence, the 3rd Royal Tanks group and "G" Company led the advance of the Second Army across the rolling cornfields, now cratered with huge bomb-holes. At first all went well. For five miles the only Germans who showed themselves were dead or too dazed by the bombing to resist. At Grentheville a nebelwerfer opened up just in front of the leading troops. Half a dozen Shermans immediately blew it and its crew to pieces. By the time Hubert Folie and Bras had been reached the enemy were recovering. While "G" Company sat on the outskirts of Hubert Folie and the main advance struck opposition at Bras, enemy anti-tank guns and then Panther tanks began to fire at us. It was soon obvious that an anti-tank defensive line of considerable strength had been met. For the rest of the day the 29th Armoured Brigade fought to get forward along the line of the railway from Caen to Argentan. By nightfall they had lost a hundred and fifteen tanks; the Northamptonshire Yeomanry had practically ceased to exist; the armoured regiments averaged less than twenty tanks each. The motor companies spread out among these regiments had their share of casualties from shelling and mortar bombs.

That night as the Battalion protected the tanks with every prospect of more desperate fighting the next day many must have wondered how it was that the German anti-tank screen had suddenly sprung to life five miles behind the original front line after such a promising start to this great operation had been made.

The next day the tanks were still unable to make much progress. The 1st Battalion made their way through craters and traffic blocks to take over Grentheville from "F" Company of the 8th Battalion, who had spent an exceptionally unpleasant time there under intense shell and mortar fire, apparently well observed. The three companies reverted to the command of Colonel Tony Hunter for the capture of Bras and Hubert Folie. By three in the afternoon the Battalion had concentrated just west of the Caen—Falaise railway. The reconnaissance was done from the embankment and the Colonel gave out his orders there. At four o'clock the Battalion advanced in its vehicles round the right flank, having difficulty in negotiating the railway which runs from Caen to Vimont. By twenty-five past four the companies had made contact with the remnants of the 2nd Northamptonshire Yeomanry on the right, and with the 3rd Royal Tanks began to advance on the village. "H" Company were on the right, "F" Company on the left, followed by the Support Company ("E") and "G" Company, who were already earmarked for a further attack on Hubert Folie. The motor platoons were in their half-tracks until the village was reached and the carriers, thrashing through the corn like destroyers, rounded up many prisoners on the way in. The leading companies reached the village just behind the 3rd Royal Tanks. They jumped out of their vehicles and set about clearing the houses. There was much opposition. Germans with panzerfausts appeared everywhere; several anti-tank guns opened up. By really resolute action Phillip Sedgwick's platoon was got through to the far end of the village by twenty past five, and in another twenty minutes the village was more or less clear. "F" Company had a good shoot at fifty enemy who tried to slip away, causing many casualties and bringing in most of the rest as prisoners. By six o'clock the 3rd Battalion The Monmouthshire Regiment began to arrive to take over the village. The Battalion was ready to go on to the next objective. The attacking companies had had comparatively light casualties; well over three hundred German prisoners had been captured, all from the 1st S.S. Panzer Division (the Adolf Hitler), the formation which had driven into Villers Bocage to meet the 1st Battalion a month before and whose quality as fighting soldiers was as high as any we were to meet.

"G" Company had been the reserve company for the attack on Bras. Apart from a call to deal with some enemy in the corn, they had not been seriously engaged. They were therefore ready to take on Hubert Folie with the 2nd Fife and Forfar Yeomanry. This regiment was now down to two squadrons each of eleven tanks, with two tanks in regimental headquarters. An attempt by the Northamptonshire Yeomanry to get into the village having failed with casualties, the Fifes and "G" Company were ordered at a quarter to seven to capture it. A quick plan was made for the high ground south of Bras to be smoked off and for supporting fire to be brought down by two field regiments and a medium regiment on to the orchards on the north edge of Hubert Folie, subsequently lifting on to the centre of the village. The attack was to go in from the north-west of Bras, directed almost due south on to Hubert Folie. It started at eight o'clock. The leading squadron arrived on the edge of the village before the barrage had finished: "G" Company were right behind the tanks and out of their half-tracks like lightning. In a very short time some eighty S.S. prisoners had been rounded up. The rest of the village presented little trouble, except for fire from a Sherman tank which came down on the carriers, killing Corporal Isard and wounding several riflemen. There was much recrimination between the company and the tanks until it was discovered that the Sherman was one which had been captured by the Germans the previous day and was now manned by an S.S. machine gunner. Once identified it was soon knocked out. By nine o'clock "G" Company were through the village and by nine-fifteen the battle was over. The 4th Battalion The King's Shropshire Light Infantry came up the hill and took over the area and the whole of the 8th Battalion withdrew to harbour for the night, just after a concentration of our own medium artillery had fallen with some suddenness and in error on the village.

The London Rifle Brigade can, indeed, be proud of the efforts of the 8th Battalion on those two days, the 18th and 19th of July. Between three o'clock in the afternoon and nine at night they had taken part in two major attacks, cleared two villages of the enemy, captured about four hundred S.S. troopers of the Adolf Hitler Division and killed a large number in addition.

Their own casualties had been light. It was because the Battalion had concentrated quickly, because the Colonel had made a quick plan, and because it had been executed with speed and determination that such results had been achieved. Quickness of thought and action has always been the quality sought by Riflemen. In this operation the motor battalion was put through all its paces. It was asked all the questions which by its constitution it was designed to answer, except to deal with a tank counter-attack. And it proved effective.

The 11th Armoured Division had shot its bolt for the moment. Its tank casualties had reached too high a figure to allow of immediate replacement of Shermans or crews. On the 30th of June the Division, and the 8th Battalion with it, was withdrawn from the battle of refit.

The 7th Armoured Division was the last of the three armoured divisions in the order of march and as such had the worst of the going and the longest waits in the traffic blocks. The 1st Battalion was not seriously engaged for the first forty-eight hours, although "I" Company were soundly shelled in Grentheville and "C" Company had to clear some woods near Giberville. By the time the 22nd Armoured Brigade did get a clear run, the chances of a complete break had probably gone. "I" Company, with some artillery support, were put in to clear Soliers, which they succeeded in doing, only to have Bill Apsey, the company commander, badly wounded by a mortar bomb. "C" Company occupied Fours and "I" Company moved on to Bourgebus.

"A" Company were engaged south-west of Ifs, where some infantry who apparently had been ready to surrender to the tanks came very much to life when Alan Mather's scout platoon arrived to collect them. In confused fighting Austin Dore was killed and nine or ten others became casualties before the task was handed over to the Canadians, who attacked with two battalions and secured some two hundred prisoners.

There then followed a distinctly trying period during which infantry held the front and masses of armour and other vehicles remained close behind them in the cramped space between the front and the Orne. It was the old story of being shelled in what resembled a race-course car park by guns only six thousand yards away whose observation posts could overlook the whole area from Troan at four thousand yards' range. The Battalion could only drive or walk about in a quagmire of ground churned up by tanks and in pouring rain. Fortunately the Germans seemed to prefer to shell a few places often rather than try new ones, a characteristic reminiscent of their reputed habits of 1914-1918. The first salvo of these concentrations, seldom more than sixty shells at a time, nearly always hit someone: after that everyone took to their slit trenches and little damage was done. All the same, twenty-five or more riflemen were hit by shell splinters in those four inactive days.

The general axis of the attack was changed and the Division came under the Canadians for an attempt to advance west of the road to Falaise. The Battalion was brought close up behind the Canadians. There were great hopes of a break-through this time. But the Canadians never managed to capture their objective and the Battalion was left on a forward slope within three thousand yards of the enemy waiting for the morning mist to lift. The vehicles were got back on a reverse slope and a further period of mud and congestion set in, leaving a hopeless feeling of claustrophobia and frustration in the Battalion. Two more officers were wounded and then Robin Birch was killed by a solitary shell from an 88-mm. gun, a weapon which at the shorter ranges propels its missile faster than the speed of sound, so that one does not hear the shell coming and its noise through the air is often heard after it has arrived. He was the twenty-fourth officer casualty since the landing.

On the 30th of July the Battalion was relieved and moved back through Caen, being much impressed by the extent of the destruction of the town. In twelve days the drain of casualties had been continuous, while the Riflemen had had no chance to get to grips with the enemy or indeed to do anything except exist in mud and slush and overcrowded areas. It must have seemed that the battles to break out of the bridgehead would be unending and few could realize at the time that the strength of the opposition south of Caen was a pointer to its weakness farther west. Containing the enemy can be an expensive and disheartening business for those who take part in it.

CHAPTER XXVII

THE BREAK-OUT AND THE "SWAN"

THE first six weeks of fighting had brought heavy losses to the two battalions. There was little substantial result to show for these efforts. The Army had still failed to break out of the bridgehead; each succeeding offensive had been halted. Yet the concentration of German forces in the area south of Caen which had been required to hold off our attacks had made possible the American success at St. Lo, the implications of which had, by the end of July, hardly been fully appreciated. The battalions themselves, while they had been much weakened by their experiences at Villers Bocage and Hill 112, could look back with satisfaction on the repulse of the German counter-attack north of Villers Bocage and the brilliant capture of Bras and Hubert Folie. There was no doubt that from a count of prisoners captured and casualties inflicted the Riflemen had given better than they had got.

Though no one could know it, the end of July had seen the last of the failures. The opportunity of the armoured divisions had arrived. Yet it is a fair commentary on the state of feeling at the time that before the 11th Armoured Division moved into battle south of Caumont an officer from another formation lectured on the nature of the fighting in the bocage. In that blind country there was much emphasis on snipers, though the shots which frequently disturbed an otherwise peaceful scene at unexpected moments were fired by Germans armed with rifles rather than trained snipers deliberately left behind. It was as well for us that this was so. Sniping was not confined to small arms, for single tanks and self-propelled guns were often used effectively by the Germans to pop out from behind a house or peer over a hedge and destroy the leading vehicle before retiring. Our tanks were always in danger from bazookamen.

In the break-out and the great advance into Belgium the 8th Battalion had a more spectacular role than the 1st, partly because its axis of advance lay farther south and in more suitable country. It belonged to a division which, particularly after the Seine, was given every encouragement to make remarkable progress. While the 11th Armoured Division played the lead, the 7th Armoured Division often in a secondary role had an equally arduous time, rewarded by less obvious results. I shall therefore describe the experiences of the 8th Battalion first, though the general background of the story applies equally to both the 1st and the 8th.

It was on the 29th of July that the 8th Battalion was switched to the area south of Caumont. This was immediately on the left of the American advance. After arriving in Sept Vents just after the last unwounded German had left, the Battalion reached the important centre of communications of St. Martin de Besaces. By the time the village was reached "H" Company and a squadron of the 3rd Royal Tanks were in the lead. There were signs that the village was held and 14 Platoon went forward to reconnoitre, only to be fired on by a tank tucked away on the road under a steep bank. Deciding that the village was certainly held, the platoon withdrew, but not before Corporal Fulton had considerably shaken the occupants of the tank by a well-aimed grenade which caused its driver to depart rapidly towards the village. The rest of the company then went firm for the night behind the railway embankment.

On the next morning "H" and "G" Companies put in attacks on the village. The embankment prevented the tanks giving close support to the infantry: there was more opposition than had been expected. The two leading platoons were pinned down and suffered heavy casualties, among them David Stileman, wounded. But Eric Yetman and 12 Platoon managed to work round to their objective, although losing a complete section from machine-gun fire. Having got there, they succeeded in holding on, although the platoon commander was wounded, and they remained in position until a joint attack by the 159th Brigade, and a battalion of the 15th (Scottish) Division eventually cleared the houses. One never knew when one attacked these villages that a minor action might not develop into a considerable operation. This particular battle cost almost a whole platoon of "G" Company, while it was also the first of the three occasions on which John Straker was wounded.

After St. Martin de Besaces more rapid progress was made

through the beautiful country of the Forêt d'Eveque to Ferrieres. An American tank column was met travelling in the opposite direction during the night, "causing," it was said, "many drivers to think that their last hour had come." There is also a curious story of another American column being met, running parallel with the Battalion, and the unusual spectacle was witnessed "of Riflemen plying the marching Yanks with Army biscuits, for which they appeared most grateful!" As the advance gathered speed and the issue of the fighting began to be clear, the French civilians declared themselves openly and with the wildest enthusiasm, greeting the Riflemen with "a mixture of eggs and kisses." No one who "liberated" a French village will ever forget the Gallic abandon with which they were met. Apart from material rewards in the form of Calvados and cider, Camembert and chickens, and an occasional glass of brandy, the inhabitants were a great assistance to us as we advanced. For one thing, they acted as effective mine detectors. If there were flags on the houses it was a sure sign that the enemy had gone. If one entered a village in silence, with no flags, no welcoming cheers, no children, only eyes watching silently from windows, stray dogs, a cart, perhaps overturned, then one could expect to meet the Germans round the corner. During the advance there were unfortunately all too many occasions when we passed through scenes of passionate excitement and wildly waving flags, and no sooner had we gone than the Germans appeared while the demonstrations of joy at their departure were still in progress.

The Battalion passed through the thickly wooded country to Le Beny Bocage with little opposition. The advance continued for a further ten miles south-west. The Battalion worked with the 23rd Hussars, a connection which was to last, with various short periods of separation, until the end of the war. No armoured regimental group could have worked together with more harmony or more effectively. Squadrons and companies, troops and platoons, came to know each other perfectly. When the armour was the dominant arm Colonel Perry Harding commanded: as soon as the tanks were held up, Colonel Tony Hunter automatically took over. It was because of the mutual confidence established between the two that joint operations could be laid on quickly with hardly any need for the pauses and waits and order groups and preparations, which can so readily devour the hours of daylight in the face of the enemy.

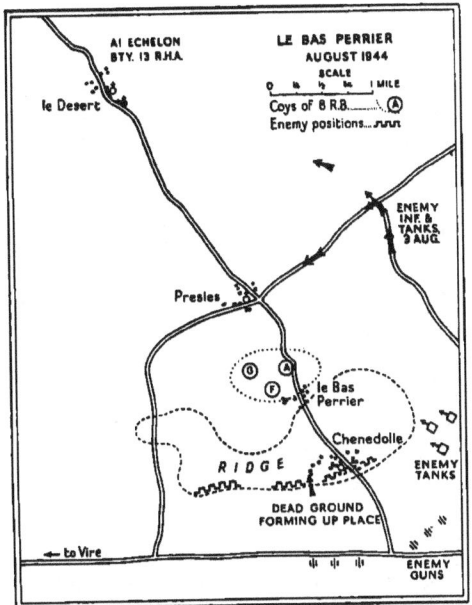

The Bas Perier operation was a test of this co-operation. "H" Company and "B" Squadron, directed on Chenedolle, passed through the attractive village of Presles amidst great rejoicing by the inhabitants. This rapid advance had left a long, open left flank and after passing through the village the leading group was ambushed at Le Bas Perier, the first six tanks being "brewed" up. In consequence they were forced to go firm for the night in a place not at all to their liking, on a forward slope with the Germans on the ridge above from which there was every anticipation of a counter-attack. "F" Company had a successful battle on the left, destroying some machine-gun posts, and in Chenedolle Sergeant Triggs, of "H" Company, succeeded in hitting a tank with his Piat. The next day, the 3rd of August, the German infantry were seen to be streaming back into Presles behind the companies, thus cutting the centre line and all communication to the rear. Soon afterwards tanks, nebelwerfers, mortars and guns began to plaster the Battalion's area with shells, to such effect that many casualties to vehicles and men were caused in the congested area. Elements of the two S.S. panzer divisions put in various uncoordinated attacks on the position without making any impression. But the situation was decidedly unpleasant, particularly as the wounded could not be evacuated. It was here that Michael Wilcox, the Battalion doctor, was invaluable, and with the 23rd Hussars' doctor and the Padre, Jeff Taylor, did really magnificent work. During the night the 2nd Battalion The Royal Warwickshire Regiment attacked Presles and found it empty, moving on to relieve the 8th Battalion at Bas Perier on the 4th of August. The companies moved back on foot to Presles, the vehicles under Brian Adams following, not without difficulty, after dark. It was a very different place from the Presles which had been liberated two days before, where the church bells had been rung in our honour and where there was more wine than even the thirstiest Rifleman could drink. From the 5th of August five dangerous days were spent there under incessant shelling and mortar fire. On the 10th of August the Battalion was pulled back to Le Beny Bocage.

The thrust to Le Bas Perier had been a successful operation for the Division, since a risk taken had paid a satisfactory dividend. For the Riflemen who had sat on the hill for two days under intense fire, cut off so that even ambulances could not drive back, and for another five days among the ruins and shelling at Presles, the battle had been less satisfactory, for they had had little opportunity to retaliate.

Only two days were spent in reserve. But during this time a complete company of the 8th Battalion 60th Rifles joined the Battalion. It was merged by platoons into the existing organization; Peter Bradford took over command of "H" Company. At the time of their arrival these reinforcements were sorely needed to replace the casualties already sustained. In a few weeks they had become so much a part of the Battalion and the Regiment that it was hard to believe that they had not been with us all the time, while their value as fighting riflemen gave a good indication of what a good battalion theirs would have been had it been able, after so many years of training, to go to war in its entirety.

On the 18th of August the Battalion moved up by night to take over a defensive position near Estry from the 15th (Scottish) Division. Muddy lanes and traffic diversions made the move chaotic. After two days the advance was resumed. Since this was still close country and the opposition was at times determined, the Battalion worked with the 23rd Hussars as an armoured regimental group. After the Seine crossing, when speed against less co-ordinated opposition in more open country was what was required, the companies worked with their armoured regiments. Such was the value of serving under a divisional commander whose knowledge and experience had taught how a motor battalion should be used. Although the rate of advance was as much as twenty miles a day, as it led through

The Break-out and the "Swan"

Flers and Vassy, to the Orne at Putanges and thence to the Seine, opposition might at any moment be encountered. All three carriers of the leading section of "F" Company were hit by fire from two Panther tanks as they crossed the main Falaise—Argentan road; while the bridgehead at Putanges was being formed all Sergeant Kitson's carrier section, except the drivers, were wounded: James Ramsden and Sergeant Kisby, of "G" Company, narrowly escaped the same fate north of Vassy. The carriers came in for this treatment partly because the advance was generally led by a vanguard of a section of carriers, a troop of tanks and a motor platoon. This method was effective enough as the Division pushed steadily on at the southern edge of the Falaise pocket and thence towards the Seine.

Progress was fast enough to surprise the Germans. On the 20th of August, as Michael Anderson and 12 Platoon of "G" Company were moving into Bailleul on foot, an old lady rushed up to them and told them that there were some Germans in a farmhouse. On closer investigation a general was seen at a window and in a short time the whole divisional headquarters of the 271st Infantry Division was captured complete, staff officers, clerks, signallers, orderlies and the commander, General Kurt Badinsky. At this point a difficulty arose because the general was particularly anxious to surrender to an officer. He refused to believe that Michael Anderson was one, brushed aside Noel Bell as a non-commissioned officer and took a great deal of convincing that Colonel Tony Hunter held the King's commission. It has always been difficult to make foreign generals understand that the dress of British officers in action is almost identical with that of their men and that in war, though only in war, age is not the first consideration for promotion.

On the 22nd of August, after rain and mines and a blown bridge had delayed matters, the Battalion halted near L'Aigle. Here the reception from the villagers of Rai-sur-Rile surpassed anything that had yet been met with, one further indication of how much more pleased the people were as we went east than the farmers of Calvados had been—who, after all, did have to endure the chaos and destruction of war for weeks, while these luckier Frenchmen could hope to wave once to a column, hear a few shells and then return in peace to their farms.

At Rai there was a pause for five days, in beautiful weather, while the infantry divisions crossed the Seine at Vernon. Reinforcements caught up with the Battalion; Mickey McCrea, one of the earliest casualties of Hill 112, returned to resume command of "G" Company. Much time was devoted to maintaining the vehicles which were to carry us forward for the next advance. News of American progress in the south was beyond all expectation. Not only was the success of the Second Front assured; the end of the war seemed in sight. Yet those who paused to think expected stiff opposition on the Seine, on the Somme and all across the plains of Northern France, the traditional battlegrounds of Europe.

On the 28th of August the move up to the Seine began. The river was crossed in the evening, preparations were made to break out of the 43rd Division's bridgehead, and on the 30th of August the advance commenced. "F" Company had to mount a full-scale attack supported by their mortars and the Fife and Forfar Yeomanry to capture Etrepagny; a night patrol by Kenneth Chabot discovered that Amecourt was held by some four hundred Germans. In the ensuing battle before "G" Company handed over to the 159th Brigade their command vehicle was hit by a shell. All the occupants, including the company commander, were killed or wounded except Corporal Kingsmill, who continued to operate the wireless unperturbed. So as the company started off on the most sensational march of the war in France, Mickey McCrea, for the second time, was evacuated, wounded, to England.

While "G" Company and the 3rd Royal Tanks were held up at Amecourt, "H" Company and the 23rd Hussars established a long lead. It was soon clear that quite remarkable possibilities were opening up. There was hardly any organized opposition, though parties of Germans of varying sizes and with varying degrees of morale kept appearing in every direction, on the main axis or down side-roads, from the rear and suddenly for no apparent reason in the middle of the column. No one stopped to collect prisoners: the only object was to get forward. The crew of any vehicle which broke down or otherwise dropped out was bound to experience the most memorable adventures, as Germans and French Maquis and Americans and British followed up in nonsensical order. Encouraged by the palpable rout of the German forces, the French set to work on the collaborators, shaving women's heads, making men wash Nazi slogans from the streets and walls, and, no doubt, paying off such individual

BATTALION HEADQUARTERS OF THE 1st BATTALION IN A CORNFIELD BEFORE CROSSING THE SOMME

Colonels Vic Turner and Victor Paley with the 1st Battalion

Three Sergeants and a Cat

Sergeants Barton, M.M., Cooper, M.M., and Bonner, of the 8th Battalion, wait to cross the Rhine

scores as each man owed his neighbour. In the general excitement crowds in the streets were often the greatest obstacle to progress.

At Marseilles-en-Beauvais the 3rd Royal Tanks and "G" Company passed through into the lead. The advance continued through Crevecoeur-le-Grand, thence through a wooded valley, almost a ravine, with sides rising steeply, where a certain amount of caution was necessary. As it grew dark the leaders halted at Croissy-sur-Selle, ready to settle down for the night. It was then that General Horrocks, commanding XXX Corps—a man well cast for the role of pursuit—issued his famous order to drive through the night to Amiens and to rush the next defence line of the German armies. "It is moonlight tonight," the order began; and instead of settling down comfortably in Croissy village "G" Company and the 3rd Royal Tanks, followed by the rest of the Brigade, started off to drive the forty-odd miles against unknown opposition along strange roads and in pouring rain which effectually obscured the moon.

No organized enemy were met with and the various stray parties of Germans who appeared in our path were brushed aside. At dawn on the 31st of August there was a short halt for reorganization, during which we heard the B.B.C. announce on the wireless that British forces were still thirty miles short of Amiens, and then the three regimental groups set off to drive into the town. There is no more thrilling expedition than one to capture a bridge intact: the excitement of the moment did something to make up for lack of sleep. The Fife and Forfar Yeomanry, with whom "F" Company moved, captured the commander of the German Seventh Army, who had stopped unwisely to have his breakfast by the road. Civilians reported that there were some five thousand German troops in Amiens. But they could hardly expect the Second Army yet.

"G" and "H" Companies entered the town with their armoured regiments soon after eight in the morning and at once fighting developed in a series of individual platoon actions. Donald Sudlow's platoon managed to cut one route by which the Germans were retreating and destroyed a number of lorries, killed many Germans and captured some fifty prisoners. 11 Platoon reached the Somme to find the bridge blown in their faces; but at about the same time Sergeant Triggs, of "H" Company's carriers, got to within striking distance of another bridge. It was certainly held: any attempt to approach was met by small-arms fire. It seemed only a matter of seconds before the bridge would be blown sky-high. Sergeant Triggs, quite undeterred by the prospect of going up with it, worked his carriers close up to the defenders and then made a dash for it. The German infantry made off, and the 8th Battalion had captured intact the principal crossing of the Somme, the last line on which the Germans could stand if they were not to abandon France.

On the 1st of September the advance continued to Arras, across the plains of Flanders, that dull, muddy country where every signpost bore a name redolent with memories of the First World War. When we had passed through, the inhabitants set about looting the food dumps of Amiens, for Frenchmen in towns knew real hardship during the occupation. Meanwhile small parties and single vehicles which had been left behind in the rapid moves of the past two days began to catch up, each with their stories of individual adventures, of German half-tracks met unexpectedly round corners, of villages with no flags where enemy suddenly appeared well behind the advance, of Sergeant Fruin's rout of a whole supply column with a bag of twenty-three prisoners and various vehicles on fire.

But the enemy resistance was not entirely broken. At midnight on the 2nd of September, 12 Platoon were holding for the night a bridge over the canal near Anneullin when a large force of Germans attacked them hard on the heels of a mortar bombardment. Michael Anderson and Sergeant Macaulay were killed. Corporal Shutz took over command and managed to maintain the position, although some few Germans crossed the bridge. It took the rest of the company and a troop of tanks to restore the situation at dawn, but not before three carriers had been lost.

The tempo of the advance continued. Skirting Lille, the Battalion reached Willems, and the next day, the 3rd of September, crossed the frontier into Belgium. The Belgians at once gave them a tremendous welcome. The simple, hard-working people of the Low Countries, speaking their own dialects, hardly understanding the inhabitants of the next village, were almost universally kind to the Riflemen and there was no end to the hospitality of Belgian farms.

The rate of progress had been so rapid that the bridges over the innumerable canals and water courses had not been blown. The route was through Tournai, Renaix, Ophasselt and Ninove.

As the 10th Battalion had been turned away from Tunis and the 61st Brigade from Rome, the 8th was denied the opportunity of entering Brussels. After an advance of eighty-five miles they halted for the night level with Brussels, which was entered by the Guards Armoured Division. On the 4th the whole 11th Armoured Division rushed on towards Antwerp, moving double-banked along the wide main road. There was no opposition until the suburbs were reached, where a few surprised Germans lobbed grenades from the windows. There was some mortaring, an occasional anti-tank gun fired, the largest crowds yet encountered blocked the streets and in a surprisingly short time the banks of the Scheldt were reached. There were still Germans to clear from the houses; the main bridge had been blown. But none the less Antwerp had been captured and half of Belgium was free. Even while the Belgians were showering hospitality on any Englishman they could find, Sergeant Fruin's mortars were having a most successful shoot at packed German transport on the other side of the Scheldt, using the sixth floor of a factory as an observation post and going up and down in the lift.

The speed of the 11th Armoured Division's advance had surprised themselves as much as the Germans. In those few days since they had left the Seine the steady withdrawal of the enemy had been turned into a rout. The Riflemen could be forgiven for thinking that the end of the war was at hand.

The 1st Battalion had played their part in this transformation, though they had not been engaged in such rapid advances, nor were they so continuously in action. We had left them at the end of July resting for a few days at Ellon. On the 1st of August the 7th Armoured Division returned to the front in the area of Villers Bocage and Aunay-sur-Odon. The 5th Dragoon Guards had replaced the 4th County of London Yeomanry in the 22nd Armoured Brigade. At this time the Battalion suffered a personal blow in the departure not only of Brigadier Hinde, who had commanded since North African days, but also of General Bobbie Erskine, two friends and commanders whose loss was much lamented. For two days the motor companies, with their armoured regiments, were fully, and not very profitably, occupied in pushing forward against determined enemy rearguards. It was difficult country, still thick and hilly. Aunay itself had been bombed flat, with the sole exception of the church tower, which still stood an erect and gloomy sentinel over the devastation. One of the high-lights of this time was a really remarkable patrol near Breuil by Sergeant Lee, who, while on a reconnaissance with three riflemen, succeeded in surprising the enemy and capturing some seventeen prisoners. But on the 5th of August Alan Mather was killed when his carrier drove over a mine. After two or three days in this area the 7th Armoured Division was withdrawn from Aunay and came under command of the I British Corps of the First Canadian Army.

The Battalion was therefore engaged in the operations west of the main road from Caen to Falaise and took over a small bridgehead near Livarot. There was, as was only too usual in that part of France, another river obstacle a few miles ahead. On the 19th of August the Battalion was ordered to seize the one bridge, which was supposed still to be intact, at Fervaques. On the 20th of August, in the failing light, "I" Company were hastily mounted on the tanks of the 5th Royal Tanks and succeeded in rushing and capturing the bridge intact. Just beyond it the enemy were still using the lateral road running through the village, and a good harvest of their vehicles and of prisoners was gathered in during the night, of which the most satisfactory prize was the capture of a cook's lorry with a hot breakfast intended for the German garrison.

The enemy were not prepared to give up Fervaques without a struggle and in the evening a vigorous counter-attack was put in. "A," "B" and "I" company commanders had all taken up their headquarters in the local château, a splendidly constructed building whose walls, at least five feet thick, were an adequate protection against shelling and small arms. After a great deal of firing on both sides some well-directed defensive fire from the Gunners, the generous use of the Browning guns recently acquired by "I" Company's scout platoon, and some effective shoots by "B" Company's machine guns, the enemy were beaten off. Among our casualties was Tony Clarke, who was killed. But the enemy had suffered heavily, as was learnt from the fifty prisoners who were captured from the panzer grenadier regiment of the 21st Panzer Division, a formation which had travelled a long way from Agheila, Tobruk and Alamein, though no farther —and much less successfully—than had the 1st Battalion in these same three years.

The Battalion moved on, on the 24th, passing in sight of the new cathedral of Lisieux, where William the Conqueror and some earlier Montgomerys were born. The intention was to force the enemy into the big loop of the Seine south-west of Rouen. In this lush country there was much clearing of woods and orchards to be done by the motor battalion. It was an area of large woods, such as the Forêt de Montfort, and, partly because of this, many enemy escaped across the Seine, though the bag of prisoners was considerable and our own casualties light. Although the rapid advances farther south created a greater impression on the inhabitants, the 1st Battalion's progress was attended by similar scenes of rejoicing and recrimination.

On the 31st of August the 1st Battalion crossed the Seine and by last light was well on the way to the Somme. Opposition was disorganized and on the 2nd of September the Somme was crossed. By that time we had run off almost all the maps and navigation was mainly by signpost and by courtesy of the French, who in this part of France were wildly enthusiastic, so much so that they often held up the progress of the advance. On the 3rd of September it was information from the Maquis at Caunchy which enabled Sergeant Meyer and a section of "I" Company's carriers to creep up on three German 105-mm. guns, drive off the crews, destroy the guns themselves and their ammunition lorries, and kill an officer who tried to make off in an Opel car. As the war went on a German officer became every day a more valuable prize. It was on the 3rd of September, too, that Lillers was occupied after some street fighting in which two officers and seven riflemen were casualties. The Germans kept on trying to filter back into the town and it was unfortunate that the Battalion had to move on before they had all been dealt with, leaving to the Maquis the task of defending their homes.

That same evening the Battalion pushed on to the La Bassée Canal near Béthune and then to Mazingarbe, near Lens. Large numbers of prisoners kept coming in—three hundred in three days—but there was a constant drain of casualties in ones and twos with, as always, a high proportion of officers. The Battalion rested in this area for a few days, except for "A" Company, who went on into Belgium with the armour directed on Ghent.

It was while the Battalion was at Mazingarbe, a mining village between Béthune and Lens, that members of the French and Belgian Resistance Movements began to volunteer for service.

They came at a time when the Battalion was under strength and so were particularly welcome, remaining with us for nearly ten months. By early September the tide had turned very definitely in favour of the Allies: all the inhabitants came out to cheer and welcome the liberators in every town and village: the regular forces of France were expanding too suddenly to accept all volunteers immediately and the Belgians had to start practically from scratch. It was natural that there were young Frenchmen and Belgians who saw their best opportunity to strike a blow at the Germans in joining the first British unit which would take them and in doing so they followed the example of a number of Spaniards who, in 1813, enlisted in the Regiment in the Peninsula and also "made excellent Riflemen and were distinguished for their bravery."

The first Frenchman to join was Yves Dumy, who was recruited by Charles Steer, then commanding a motor platoon in "I" Company. He was immediately nicknamed "Ifs and Buts" by the riflemen. Noel Paniez was, perhaps inevitably, called "Christmas Basket," which gave pleasure to all. By the 7th of September the numbers had risen to seventeen, divided more or less evenly between "C" and "I" Companies, and scattered among the various platoons and sections, where their local knowledge of languages was found to be very useful. Practically none of them spoke English at all. A few days later we were joined by a Belgian, Dennis Vanoystaeyen, who spoke perfect English and whose brother also came in November.

At first when they joined they wore rather nondescript uniform, composed mainly of a battledress blouse and civilian trousers with a pair of German jackboots to complete the picture. Alan Parker, the Adjutant, was rather taken aback— and the Regimental Sergeant-Major still farther—when inspecting some men one day to find one of the parade wearing check trousers. It was a very broad check and visible a good way off. Later, however, they were all issued with Army kit and went about looking extremely smart, most of them with a large "France" written on their shoulders for all to see.

Giving them leave to go home was quite easy and they seemed never to have any trouble lorry-hopping to their destination or in getting back to us, even though we had moved, as on one occasion, seventy miles across the front. They spoke little or no English, and in spite of their uncertain and erratic method of travelling, they always seemed to get back at about the right time, even when we were on the Dutch-German border, usually loaded with parcels of cakes and presents for their friends.

Their pay was a much more difficult matter. The British Treasury was clearly unwilling to take on any extra commitments if they could be avoided, and for a long time they existed with the support of company and regimental funds: their brother-Riflemen always kept them supplied with cigarettes. After more than two months of haggling and rude letters, and after several visits from the French Army liaison staff, who naturally pointed out how much easier it would be if they were transferred to the French Army, we finally managed to get them paid by the French authorities on French Army rates of pay, which worked out almost the same as ours. Moreover, their time with us was allowed to count as part of their French Army service.

Two of their number were killed in action. They also had their share of wounded, all of whom made a good recovery. Gilbert Cleret was even evacuated to England, which must have made hay with the hospital records.

They fought very well, and rapidly fell into our way of doing things. Two of them were awarded the Croix de Guerre on the report of them sent to the French Army authorities by the Colonel. They showed the spirit of resistance at its best.

On the 8th of September the Battalion crossed the frontier into Belgium and made its way unopposed amid scenes of welcome and rejoicing to St. Nicolas, about ten miles from Antwerp, where "A" Company rejoined them. Here they settled down, despite some shelling from the north, to share in the Belgians' joy at the disappearance of the "Moffe," the Flemish word for "German," and were more than sorry to be moved off to an area about five miles north of Malines. It was clear by the 12th of September that the period of swift advances was, at any rate temporarily, at an end and, though they shared in the delusion that the war was nearly over, it is unlikely that the Riflemen of the 1st Battalion were as intoxicated with success as were those of the 8th. For one thing, their progress had been less dramatic and their casualties had been sufficient in number to sober the more unreasonable optimists. For another, it was not for the 1st Battalion a new experience to advance far into a liberated country; and, if long acquaintance with war as it was fought with the pendulum strokes of the armies in the desert makes one discount the worst symptoms of defeat, so it was unlikely that these veterans would be over-easily persuaded of the imminence of victory now. Yet in September, 1944, the final victory really did seem near.

FRANCE 1944

Face page 380

FRANCE 1944

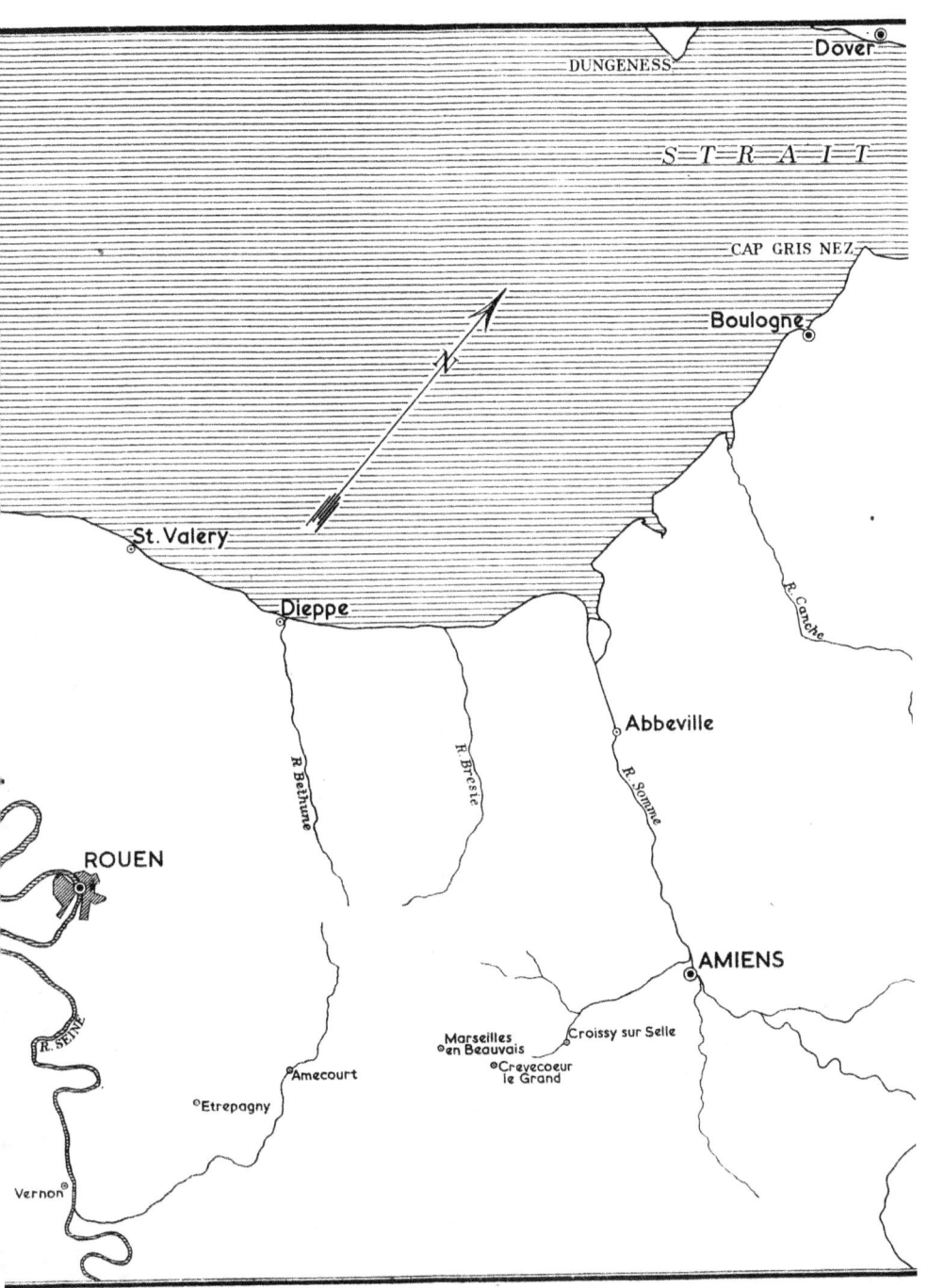

FRANCE 1944

THE MAAS AT MAASTRICHT
The River so well known to the 1st and 8th Battalions

A HALF-TRACK IN THE SNOW

CHAPTER XXVIII

THE LOW COUNTRIES

THERE is a melancholy atmosphere about the Low Countries in winter. The flat, wet, featureless countryside, crossed and re-crossed by canals and rivers, dotted with red houses and bright, new barns, has few attractions to the casual eye. Most of the houses in Southern Holland seem not to have been built for beauty: the church towers, square and squat, or tall enough to dominate the countryside, are planted deliberately in an attitude that admits of no compromise. Muddy roads and wet fields make movement difficult, though there are occasional stretches of heathland where heather and birch trees remind one of Chobham Ridges, a resemblance which is belied by the presence of a few small packs of blackgame which can often be seen but seldom shot. The country provides a fair selection of game, some partridges, duck and snipe on the marshes, and wild pheasants in the dank osier beds.

It is a land which takes its pleasures seriously, more often than not under the direction of the priest; for, if the North of Holland was the cradle of Protestantism, south of the Maas all the country people are Roman Catholics who attend Mass with regularity twice or three times a day. The attitude of the village priest had a great bearing on the comfort and recreation of the Riflemen, for he could forbid the people to open their houses to the soldiers, stop the girls from attending dances, discourage football matches, keep his community entirely separate from the invaders or open the doors of every household to the liberating armies of the Allies. Not that there was room in most houses for outsiders. In the Low Countries the cattle are brought for the winter into the barns, most of which were built on to the farmhouses and connected to them by a door. It was in these byres among the straw, often in between the beasts, that the Riflemen would sleep, and no one who fought in the winter of 1944-45 in the Low Countries will forget the smell, compound of sour milk and dung, associated with barns in Holland which greeted them morning and evening. Yet there were mornings when the sun shone on the willows or the silver birches, or set over the marshes, with wild duck circling in the sky, which relieved the sombre background of this time.

In the field of operations there was a feeling of anti-climax after the rapid advances of August and early September. The story of the German revival is a clear example of the importance of morale in war. Whatever inventions the leaders were breeding, the German soldier had nothing to sustain him but his will. On the framework of the water obstacles and muddy ground presented by the Low Countries the Germans somehow managed to construct a defence. In the first attempt to break through these natural barriers, to cross at one blow the Meuse and the two arms of the Rhine, the Arnhem operation, neither battalion was directly engaged. The Guards Armoured Division was chosen to lead the follow-up forces which were to link up with the airborne troops. The 7th and 11th Armoured Divisions were used to advance on either flank of the main axis and to broaden the base of the offensive. When it was clear that the ambitious objectives of the Arnhem operation could not be reached and that the pencil thrust into Germany would not be an immediate result of the airborne assault, the two divisions were engaged up to Christmas in clearing Holland as far north as the Maas of those tenacious German forces who remained in position without visible hope for the future until they were physically removed. As it happened, the 7th Armoured Division and the 1st Battalion were employed on the left of the main advance and the 11th Armoured Division and the 8th Battalion on the right. This allocation of tasks entailed for the 8th Battalion some of the heaviest fighting of the campaign. The 1st Battalion was luckier.

There is another reason why the emphasis in North-West Europe is more often on the 8th Battalion than the 1st. The methods of fighting of the two divisions were not identical. For long periods the 8th Battalion and the 23rd Hussars, working together as one armoured regimental group in a division organized in four such groups, would carry out operations on their own axis. In the 7th Armoured Division the advance was more often led by an armoured regiment with one or two companies under command, while the Armoured Brigade had an extra infantry battalion allocated to it from the Lorried Infantry Brigade. But when the advance was halted in a period of static war the 1st Battalion would often take over the whole Brigade's front. While, from the Rifleman's point of view, each method involved for him something like equal periods in contact with the enemy, the same number of fearsome patrols and frozen nights on guard, the 8th Battalion had more to show for their efforts—or results which can more easily be described. In any case, the 11th Armoured Division was allotted by chance or the General Staff more mobile and more interesting roles.

On the 7th of September the 8th Battalion set off from Antwerp directed on Rotterdam. After the exaggerated successes of the advance across France even this seemed possible. However, the task was soon narrowed down to one of crossing the Albert Canal behind the Guards Armoured Division at Beeringen and pushing out to their right. The Battalion was grouped with the 23rd Hussars as an armoured regimental group. On the 10th of September this force reached Helchteren, a village much like any other on the borders of Holland and Belgium, in flat, wet country, where tree-lined, cobbled roads joined at a cross-roads in the centre of the village. From the south-east the meadows and ditches hampered movement of tanks; to the north-west, beyond the village, some heathland and scrub provided good cover for infantry. The village was held by a considerable number of German paratroopers, lightly armed and ill-organized, but ready to fight fanatically, to shoot themselves rather than be taken prisoner. In no battle fought by the Battalion was opposition so unreasonably determined; and in no battle was there more positive evidence of a large number of German dead.

"H" Company and "C" Squadron advanced first and succeeded with little trouble in getting as far as the church. In fact, 14 Platoon took up a position four hundred yards beyond it. The enemy then began to mortar the area in earnest. Each platoon in turn took part in attacks to clear groups of houses or hedges. Angus Dixon was wounded and Sergeant Read was killed. Corporal Pratt took command of his platoon and succeeded in reaching his objective. The remainder of the company began systematically to clear the rest of the village. Meanwhile, "G" Company had been moved round to the left. They took one party of enemy completely by surprise and put out of action a 75-mm. gun and its crew. But they soon met determined opposition and in the ensuing fighting Donald Howarth was killed. "F" Company had gone round to the right and soon made their presence felt from this new direction. The whole Battalion was by this time involved; and by dusk, after nine hours' heavy fighting, resistance in the now-ruined village of Helchteren and in the fields beyond it had finally ceased.

After the heavy fighting at Helchteren—"'H' Company's battle"—the advance continued, with much less opposition, to Petit Brogel, about five miles south of the Meuse—Escaut Canal. Four days were spent in comparative quiet, though "G" Company were rudely awakened by a German patrol which penetrated to company headquarters. On the 16th of September a move was made to Grand Brogel, a few miles nearer the battle. Here, on the 17th, a German patrol in the morning mist walked right into the village. But a civilian gave warning of its approach and two enemy non-commissioned officers were casualties before the rest scattered and were lost.

On the 20th of September the Battalion crossed the Meuse—Escaut Canal at Lille St. Hubert and entered Holland. The Guards Armoured Division were pushing on towards Arnhem, and the 11th Armoured's role was to protect the right flank in their advance. The country was dead flat, either wet meadowland or heathland covered with small trees and heather. There was no opposition along the wide road into Heeze. At Geldrop contact was made with American paratroopers. But at Gerwen Sergeant Triggs's carrier section was told by a civilian that German tanks were advancing down the road behind them. Two tanks armed with 17-pounder guns of the 23rd Hussars waited for these, and as soon as they appeared knocked them both out. It was the first time that German tanks had been met since the beginning of the "swan" in Normandy; and the destruction of two Panthers was greeted with no little satisfaction. In the fading light a sharp battle was fought with the remaining Panthers, who were evidently attempting to cut the main supply route towards Arnhem and had been rudely interrupted in the process.

On the 23rd the Battalion crossed the Le Duc Canal over the bridge at Zomeren, captured at some cost by the Herefords. The enemy were caught up at Ommel. "G" Company had three half-tracks destroyed and one of the 23rd Hussars' tanks was hit.

At this moment Jeff Taylor, the Padre, came up to try to find some wounded Dutch children, helpless in the middle of the battle. He was hit by a bomb from a nebelwerfer and died soon afterwards, a loss felt by all the Battalion and particularly by those who had seen him at Le Bas Perier among the wounded who could not be evacuated while the centre line was cut. "H" Company passed through, lost their leading carrier and patrolled towards the village of Vlierden. No further action was taken that night. On the 24th the leading platoon of "H" Company were fired on by bazookas at close range and lost, among others, Corporals Clarke and Hone killed, and Jeffery Coryton and Sergeant Killick wounded, before "F" Company, who had made a detour in thick, wooded country, were able to clear the village. This was one of the earlier occasions when a broadcast apparatus was used to try to persuade the Germans to surrender. However much the foreigners and the less-strong-minded might wish to abandon the struggle, which to them must already have seemed hopeless, fear of officers and non-commissioned officers armed with the power to shoot deserters was too strong for mass surrenders to result.

When Deurne was reached on the 25th of September the task of the 11th Armoured Division as the right-flank protection of the main offensive had been completed; for the news from Arnhem was bad; the pencil thrust into Germany had been halted on the most northerly of the three rivers. While the fighting north of Nijmegen continued to take the public eye, the 8th Battalion settled down at De Rips to some three weeks of static warfare in the dampest and most unpleasant piece of Holland that they had yet encountered. Windmills and church steeples were the only landmarks. As such they were frequent targets for the gunners of both sides. It became no unusual experience to walk up fifty or more steps to the top of a steeple, crowded with Gunner observers of every type and description, and hear the armour-piercing shells of the Germans whistle past in the wind. For those at De Rips there was comparative quiet under a roof, with friendly, if inarticulate, farmers always ready to supply eggs and milk. But the company detached at Meijel had a very different experience. The Germans patrolled nightly: our platoons were widely separated. Once the enemy penetrated to the gun lines and two officers were killed. More often they laid mines in unexpected places. It was clear that Meijel, that battered village among the mud-flats and the water meadows, was an object of interest to the Germans. It was much to the relief of the whole Battalion that the American 7th Armoured Division arrived to take over, led, it was said, by a jeep, "the driver of which, smoking the usual cigar, fingered the wheel and worked the clutch while the commander, with feet over the windscreen, chewed his gum and worked the gears." Whatever the misfortunes of this division at Meijel, its exploits in the Ardennes were soon to be famous throughout the Army.

On the left of the main line of advance the enemy were on the whole less active. For one thing, progress westwards was not so direct a threat to the Reich. At first the 1st Battalion assisted the 131st Lorried Infantry Brigade to hold a stretch of some twenty miles of the Albert Canal. Though the companies were well spaced out, the canal was between us and the enemy and on the whole things were reasonably quiet. For a time after this "A" Company and the 5th Dragoon Guards went off to join the 53rd Division, and "I" Company and the 5th Royal Tanks to the 15th (Scottish) Division. The rest of the Battalion moved up to line the Meuse—Escaut Canal, north of Moll. Such was the shortage of infantry that the anti-tank platoons of the Support Company ("B") parked their guns and with the machine gunners took over as normal riflemen the defence of a large factory area on the banks of the canal. When the Germans did pull back, Michael King and some of his platoon, accompanied by a Belgian officer, commandeered some bicycles from the onlookers, who were reluctant to part with such valuable articles, were ferried across the canal and bicycled to Rethy, four miles away to the north. From this village civilians covered the surrounding area by bicycle and telephone, so that much useful, if negative, information was obtained.

When the Arnhem operation began the 1st Battalion tailed along on the left flank of the main axis, at first well behind the leading troops. On the 24th of September they crossed the frontier into Holland, moved up to the large town of Eindhoven and then to St. Oudenrode. A German attempt to cut the centre line to the north did not seriously affect the Battalion's position and the advance continued to Dinther and Reeswijz, where "A" and "I" Companies rejoined. Here we were in contact with the enemy, who were unpleasantly accurate with their mortars.

The Battalion then took over a defensive line near Heesch with the 11th Hussars on the right around Oss. The positions faced towards s'Hertogenbosch, some eight miles farther west. In this flat country there was little activity in the day: church steeples took on an exaggerated importance. The Germans thought that Geffen church tower was the one and only observation post which gave a view of their positions, although there were in fact other less obvious landmarks equally effective as viewpoints. The Germans were, however, obsessed with this particular church. Three times they attacked it by night. The first time there was only an officer's patrol near the church. This was forced to withdraw and the enemy succeeded in blowing up part of the tower. George Burder's platoon then took over the position and foiled the next attempt, again at night, to complete its destruction. The force was then increased to two motor platoons, a section of "A" Company's carriers and one troop of tanks of the 5th Dragoon Guards, all under the command of George Burder. On the night of the 10th/11th of October the Germans attacked again, this time in battalion strength supported by artillery and mortars. A first attempt was driven back fairly easily. But they came in again from another direction under a barrage. A shell landed directly on top of a half-track, setting it on fire. Though it was loaded with ammunition and surrounded by mortar and Piat bombs, Sergeant Langenscheid and Rifleman Jordan promptly ran to the courtyard where their vehicles were parked and drove them to safety, returning in time to take part in the final repulse of the attack, which resulted in considerable losses to the enemy, many of them caused by the 5th Royal Horse Artillery's defensive fire. When the Battalion left Heesch on the 20th of October the church spire at Geffen was still standing.

During the operations to capture s'Hertogenbosch the Battalion was engaged only in flank protection. They had little fighting, although John Poole's machine guns had one good indirect shoot. The Armoured Brigade was then directed westwards to cut the roads north of Tilburg. Working with their armoured regiments, the companies at first did useful work patrolling and clearing woods in what is best described as "Bagshot country." But just beyond Udenhout there was a strongly defended position in front of some woods at the crosstracks near De Heidenbloom. After a heavy artillery concentration and support from the Vickers guns, "I" Company went in to the attack riding on the backs of the tanks of the 5th Dragoon Guards. Before they could get close enough to assault, several tanks were bogged, one went up on a mine, and another was "brewed up" by an anti-tank gun. The attack came to a temporary halt in a small wood. Meanwhile "C" Company and the 1st Royal Tanks, under a new and inspired Colonel, Pat Hobart, who were working on a parallel route through the trees and heather, had made rapid progress and swung in so that they came out at a position from which they dominated the village effectively. It was as a result of this manœuvre that "A" and "I" Companies were able to go in from a different direction on sounder going, clear the area of enemy and collect the satisfactory bag of a hundred and twenty prisoners.

The Battalion had two days' rest and then moved off to take over the town of Ramsdoncksveer from the 51st (Highland) Division. Here they were only a thousand yards from the Maas and separated from the Germans in Gertruidenberg by a canal. After a few days of mutual shelling and mortaring, the Poles took Gertruidenberg from the south. Most of Holland south of the Maas on the west of the British armies was now clear of the enemy, so that the 7th Armoured Division could be released to take part in operations farther east.

On the 13th of November the 1st Battalion arrived at Neeroeteren, a small village a few miles from the Maas, just opposite the narrowest point of the Maastricht Appendix. With no operational commitments there was a fortnight for rest and maintenance, a chance to unload vehicles, to cut hair, to darn clothes, to write letters, to chase the partridges and pheasants and wait in the evening for the duck, and to prepare the outline of a training programme.

On the 15th of October the 8th Battalion left De Rips to take part in a drive towards Venray, part of the process of clearing Eastern Holland up to the Maas. There was some heavy fighting and heavier rain on the 17th near the Deurne—Venray road. "G" Company picked their way through a mined area to the village of Haag; "F" Company had some casualties from shelling near Melderslo, but "H" Company met heavy opposition beyond Haag. John Straker and others in the carrier platoon were wounded at once, and in clearing some woodland Gerald Ryan was killed when almost a whole section of his platoon became casualties from the fire of a Spandau, which was later discovered to have been perched in an observation tower hidden among the trees. The enemy withdrew at night, and when Heide was reached the next day a large quantity of enemy equipment was found abandoned.

For the next two months the 8th Battalion was employed in a holding role. At first the area of Leunen and Schei was the responsibility of the Battalion. No part of Holland was more marshy, flatter, duller, or less well served by roads. The role was static: in some positions companies had to leave their vehicles well behind. We were thin on the ground, so that great use had to be made of such devices as trip flares, for the enemy patrolled actively. In the desert when the fortunes of war ran heavily in their favour the Germans had left patrolling at night to us; now, in time of adversity, they in turn became particularly aggressive at night. Instead of divisions and more orthodox formations, various battle groups had been formed, generally named after their commander, whom one could picture as some horrible thug unfortunately imbued with some of the spirit of a Jock Campbell or a Wingate. One's nights were always disturbed if Regiment Hübner or Regiment Hardegg happened to be opposite your sector. For the rest of October and November the companies spent their time pitting their brains in daylight against German observation posts and at night against their patrols, while day and night the struggle continued with the mud. There were rest areas at Usselstein and later at Hatert, but they were only fairly restful, since patrols were still active on both sides.

By the 29th of November the whole area up to the Maas had been cleared. The Battalion was moved up to the river and between that date and the 16th of December held sectors of the river line at Swolgen and later at Grubbenvorst. Those who know the Meuse where it flows through the Ardennes, a countryside unequalled for beauty in North-West Europe, would hardly recognize it under its Dutch name in the flat fields and damp woodlands of this part of Holland. No river could be more uninteresting. The Maas Valley has its own climate, dark and misty and wet in the autumn, even when there is bright sunlight farther to its east and west. Although the time spent watching the banks of this melancholy stretch of river was not among the most strenuous of the war, there were constant guard duty, frequent enemy shelling, incessant patrolling, difficult maintenance in the floods, false alarms and sufficient activity often to interfere with sleep. The 3-inch mortars fired many bombs, taking a particular liking to a village called Loom on the opposite bank. "H" Company lived at one time within the thick, shell-proof walls of the "Kasteel" at Brockhuizenvorst, surrounded by floods, a more effective barrier than the moat which normally encircled it; and while this static warfare continued, leave parties began to go off to Brussels, that city of cobbled streets and hills and ancient buildings which Army Welfare and the traditional hospitality of the Belgians made into as excellent a leave centre for a holiday as any organization could make it.

On the 16th of December the Battalion moved back to Belgium for a rest and a refit, while the Armoured Brigade were equipped with new tanks. On the 17th they arrived in the neighbourhood of Poperinghe, on the borders of France and Belgium, a town which needs no introduction to Riflemen of the First World War.

The Battalion was to rest for the first time since landing in France. The unloading of vehicles disclosed a most remarkable assortment of equipment and baggage. By the 19th of December practically everyone's belongings and all equipment lay spread upon the ground in an apparently inextricable muddle. The armoured regiments had already handed in their Sherman tanks and were waiting to be issued with Comets. Those who had for the past six months been ready to go anywhere at a moment's notice at any hour of the day or night had become in forty-eight hours of relaxation practically non-operational. At eight o'clock in the morning of the 20th of December the order was given to move in four hours' time to the front.

It is difficult now to recall the excitement, amounting almost to panic, caused by the "von Rundstedt offensive." For four months we had been doing the attacking: the Germans were clearly on the run, struggling for survival. This sudden advance into the Ardennes, reviving memories of 1870, of 1914 and of 1940, temporarily restored to the Germans their reputation of infallibility. All the bogies, the phobias, of 1940 returned. The civilians were more affected than anyone. Rumours spread of vast numbers of tanks, of new aircraft and of phenomenal advances: people in Flanders would turn their heads to the east as if expecting hourly to see the German armour appear on the horizon.

In this tense atmosphere the 8th Battalion set off along the road to Brussels. The armoured regiments were to follow when they had redrawn the Sherman tanks which they had only just finished handing in. The route skirted Brussels and by nightfall the village of Overische had been reached. The inhabitants, peering furtively down the road to Charleroi, welcomed the Riflemen cautiously and continued unabated to spread rumours of the speed of the German advance. In the early hours of the morning several shells landed in the village. It seemed that the Germans had crossed the Meuse already, that the panzer divisions would soon be in Brussels. There was no more firing, no definite news of the approach of the Germans. The arrival of those shells has never been satisfactorily explained, for the main German forces were still well east of the Meuse. The mystery is usually accounted for by a story of a German armoured car which fired at random into the village to increase the general confusion in the rear areas. But no one ever saw it nor could anyone explain how it got there.

The next day the Battalion drove on to the Meuse. "F" Company was employed on guard duties in Namur, "H" Company became responsible for the bridge over the river at Givet, and "G" Company for that at Dinant, while Battalion Headquarters were established at Meltet. It was a very different river from the Maas at Venlo, for no one can fail to be enchanted by the beauty of the Ardennes. There were various non-combatant American units in the area and a nondescript party mainly composed of Sappers called "R" Force had just arrived to guard the bridges. Refugees, with the same despair in their faces as they had had in 1940 were streaming west. There were fantastic rumours of spies and of parachutists: German S.S. men were expected in every guise, from American uniform to that of bearded monks. In this hectic atmosphere the companies took charge of their bridges.

"G" Company at Dinant had, perhaps, the key position. Noel Bell was bombarded with questions and visitors of every sort. Not the least important was an American colonel from S.H.A.E.F. who insisted that Noel was Field-Marshal Montgomery's personal representative and as such entirely responsible for defending the bridge or blowing it up if need be. There is no more awkward responsibility than that for the defence of a bridge. If you blow too soon or if you blow too late you head equally certainly for court-martial. When the 3rd Royal Tanks arrived in their Shermans the position of the company became more secure, but their duties on the bridge were not lessened. American traffic was moving freely across it: refugees clamoured for right of way. Rumour brought the Germans hourly closer. On the third night an incident occurred which did nothing to soothe the nerves. On the far bank was a road running alongside the river, at one point passing through a hole carved in the rock, just wide enough to take a Sherman tank. "G" Company had a post at this rock manned by Sergeant Baldwin's carrier section, whose task was to stop all passers-by and examine their papers. The sentries who were doing the checking had a Very-light pistol which they were to fire if any vehicle failed to stop. Sergeant Baldwin would then pull a string of mines across the road at the exit to the hole in the rock. At midnight the Very light went up. The mines were pulled across. There was a deafening explosion. When the smoke had cleared, the remains of a jeep were disclosed, containing three dead Germans wearing American greatcoats over their S.S. uniforms and carrying in their pockets detailed plans of our defences.

Every day the weather had been getting colder. It was an ordeal to do guard duty at night. The next day—it was Christmas Eve—was as cold as ever. As the patrols of the 3rd Royal Tanks moved out to their day positions they made contact with German tanks near Foy-Notre-Dame. The machine-gun platoon advancing to its usual posts from Boisselles met a six-wheeled armoured car, retired hastily and was for a time cut off until extricated by a squadron of the 3rd Royal Tanks.

The German armour was certainly heading for Dinant. We had made contact with the leading tanks. Yet all through the 24th of December the enemy made no move: no shot was fired. Refugees continued to stream down the roads. "G" Company were issued with ten carrier pigeons for dispatch in dire emergency to Headquarters, 21st Army Group, and handed a pamphlet couched in military terms about their maintenance. But even this remarkable evidence of the critical situation in which higher authority considered us to be was not enough to make the Germans move.

During the night orders were received to turn over the next morning to the offensive. At a moment when a further German advance by night was hourly expected, when paratroopers might drop at any moment on the bridges, such orders were a great fillip to morale. Unlike so many similar instructions, it proved possible to put them into effect. Christmas Day was the sort of bright, clear day, with a cloudless sky (no wind and a white frost everywhere), that the Air Force delight in. As two columns moved out, each consisting of a squadron of tanks and a motor platoon, directed on Sorinne and Boisselles, the air attack on the Germans began in earnest. Sorinne was clear; but 12 Platoon had to put in an attack on Boisselles supported by the tanks which resulted in the capture of thirty prisoners. From then on the 2nd American Armoured Division took over. "G" Company watched Lightning aircraft put in successive attacks on the Ferme de Mahenne and Foy-Notre-Dame to be followed up by fifty Sherman tanks in perfect formation. As it was getting dark 11 Platoon and a troop of tanks were put in to clear a part of the village which the Americans had not touched. It was found to be full of German vehicles and equipment, the debris, perhaps, of a headquarters, and after much searching of houses forty more prisoners were taken, one being fetched down from the top of the church steeple, where he was hiding.

The German offensive had been halted. It was now a question of driving the Germans back into the Reich, a task which was mainly to fall on the Americans. Once again a German armoured thrust had petered out when apparently at the height of its success. At Alam Halfa and again at Thala, battalions of the Regiment had faced the enemy fully expecting them to carry on with their advance: once again there was nothing to show on the 24th of December that the Germans had shot their bolt. Now the 8th Battalion, under command of the 6th Airborne Division, followed up gradually as the Germans were pushed back, not being seriously engaged in the fighting. The weather grew even colder: much snow fell. All were struck by the beauty of the Ardennes, the hills covered with snow, winter sunlight and blue skies. Colonel Tony Hunter failed in several organized expeditions to shoot a wild boar, but Donald Sudlow and Eric Yetman on an afternoon stroll met at a few yards' range one of the largest boars in Belgium and killed it with their pistols. "F" and "G" Companies were obliged to occupy in turn a high, snow-covered feature called Chapel Hill which overlooked the Germans in Bure who were being attacked by the Airborne Division, and suffered occasional casualties from shelling and considerable discomfort from the cold. On the 12th of January this brief, exciting interlude came to an end and the Battalion moved back to the small village of Bree in the canal country near the Maas, where the rest and refit so long and persistently promised eventually came to pass.

The 8th Battalion remained for a month at Bree, extracting from this solemn, cobbled town more rest, relaxation and enjoyment than any had at first imagined to be possible. On the 17th of February they moved to Rosendaal and then to Tilburg, to the oyster country, where the oyster beds at Bergen-op-Zoom provided a great many dozen at a fairly reasonable cost. Early in March a move was made to take over a sector on the Waal near Wamel, on what was known as "the Island," the neck of land between the Maas and the Waal. Here the difficulties of maintenance by road were so great that Harry Townsend was often seen leading an echelon of Dukws up the canal to the rear of the company positions. It was from here, too, that "H" Company were detached to join "Brockforce" in the task of guarding Nijmegen bridge against saboteurs and "frogmen" who might swim up the Waal. A great deal of ammunition was expended on various bits of flotsam.

The enemy opposite the Battalion were Dutch S.S. and they patrolled occasionally across the river. The Battalion was under command of the 49th Division, who ordered a patrol to cross the river and capture a prisoner. The Waal here is a good five hundred yards wide and fast-flowing, so that it is a considerable feat to cross it in a small boat. Two successful reconnaissance crossings were made by "F" Company: an air reconnaissance was flown to decide on the exact location of the raid. On the 10th of March, on the final ground reconnaissance, the craft were carried too far down-stream and landed right on top of the enemy under heavy fire. Phillip Sedgewick was killed and Tubby Mason wounded, and Sergeant Elkington did well to evacuate the rest. After the war had moved on, Phillip Sedgewick's grave was found near Tiel; it was the grave of as good a platoon commander as the 8th Battalion were to know. On the 12th of March, before a new raid could be planned, the Battalion moved off to rejoin the 11th Armoured Division near Louvain, to complete preparations for the final battles of the European war.

There was no doubt that between August and December the 7th Armoured Division had been to a certain extent out of the limelight. The 1st Battalion had had a less interesting though hardly a less costly role than the 8th. Nor was it less exhausting. The rest at Neeroeteren was much needed and was put to good use. In October command of the 22nd Armoured Brigade had been given to Brigadier Tony Wingfield, the son of a Rifleman and well known to the Battalion from Tidworth days and with the 10th Hussars in the desert. General Lyne shortly afterwards assumed command of the Division. Reinforcements arrived for the 1st Battalion, and the Lorried Infantry Brigade was reconstituted. After the rest and refit, and under new command, the Division came straight back into form and for the rest of the war played a part reminiscent of earlier days.

On the 1st of December the Battalion took over an area to the north of Sittard. For the first five days it was under command of the 5th Guards Armoured Brigade, who proved to be most excellent hosts. The frontage in this new area was some three thousand yards, held with two companies up and one back. The position is described by the Colonel:

"On the right was Nieustadt, a large but compact village only three hundred yards from the Vloed Beek, a deep, fast-flowing channel between high banks about thirty feet wide, beyond which the Germans were in strength over the German-Dutch frontier at Isenbruch. It was held by us with a company together with a machine-gun platoon and an anti-tank platoon. This force also had to cover the main road from Maastricht and Sittard northwards to Schilbracht, Roermond and Nijmegen, which ran past but not through the village, though we knew that the bridges over the Vloed Beek and over two other streams were also blown and so we were never unduly perturbed about the dangers of a German attack in the area, which was low-lying and much cut up by streams. All the same, it was pretty unpleasant at first, as the Germans had rather better observation than we did and used to do a lot of shelling: one early morning concentration included over a hundred and fifty shells and mortar bombs, mostly around Paddy Boden, the Second-in-Command, who had gone up to visit the company. But the 5th Royal Horse Artillery strictly enforced the ten-for-one retaliation rule and a little time later all the Corps artilery, reinforced by super-heavies and many anti-aircraft guns in a ground role, spent a complete day on every known hostile battery. After this we had very little trouble. About ten to fifteen rounds were the average and throughout the whole month we had under half a dozen casualties there.

"Between Nieustadt and Holtum on the left was a very big gap more or less uncovered. At Holtum we had another company, at times relieved by a number of dismounted tank crews. The shelling had never been so serious here and the average was only from six to twelve shells or mortar bombs. During the month we had only one casualty on this flank. As at Nieustadt, platoons were out in their slit trenches all night and got what rest they could in the houses by day. Those at Holtum had electric light and windows, whereas Nieustadt had cellars, and needed them, especially after an air raid on the eve of the German Ardennes offensive had burnt part of the village.

"It was a long and rather exasperating month. We had not really got enough men to hold the villages and put out as many patrols as we would have liked. The Germans were very active at night, and, being closer to the Vloed Beek, which was the dividing line in daylight, were always able to forestall us there at dusk. They had, in fact, dug tunnels into the bank, making themselves practically impervious to shelling. Many and varied were the traps we laid to get a prisoner, but we never brought it off. Those nights when we lay out they did not come, whilst on other occasions they came right up to our positions but were warned by their patrol dogs; and at times they tried to ambush us, but with equal lack of success. Once we had much pleasure in seeing the Germans put in a sharp attack at midnight on a wood five hundred yards in front where we had waited the night before. We brought down a good defensive artillery concentration on it too. Once again the 5th Royal Horse Artillery were in great form. On many other occasions our listening patrols were able to direct satisfactory artillery shoots; but we never actually 'gathered' any of the enemy wounded. Once or twice our snipers had a good day, but in general neither side could move about much in front of their positions without being seen.

"As the month went on it got firmer and drier and then colder and colder, with some snow and much frost, and enemy activity tended to decrease. Before Christmas we were regaled with a good assortment of propaganda pamphlets from the enemy artillery. It was shockingly bad luck that a 105-mm. shell case

ATTACK AT ST. JOOST
"I" Company, 1st Battalion, supported by flame-throwing tanks

A CARRIER (Not on Patrol!)

should go through two inches of concrete into a cellar and land on Gilbert Williams's lap, killing him instantly. He was just going to take over 'C' Company, as Cyril Suter had gone sick. This necessitated a general change-round of company commanders, Eric Sergeant going to 'C' Company and Chris Milner taking over 'A,' whilst Peter Luke and John Witt remained in command of 'I' and 'B' (Support) Companies respectively.

"Meanwhile Battalion Headquarters and whichever company or companies were resting were in the large village of Born, in pretty good comfort, even though within four thousand yards of the enemy. The village was fully occupied by its normal civilian population—unlike Nieustadt, which was much battered and empty before we arrived, and Holtum, which was more or less intact but evacuated of civilians during the month. There were also other troops in the village, including 'K' Battery, 5th R.H.A., some of the Norfolk Yeomanry (65th Anti-Tank Regiment, R.A.) and later our own Brigade Headquarters."

As December passed, the weather grew colder and colder. In the forward companies half the Riflemen had to stand-to all night in temperatures of up to 26 degrees of frost. After a short rest at Geleen, just south of Sittard, where those who could skated along the canals, the Battalion returned again to the line for the operation known as "Blackcock." XII Corps was given the task of clearing the enemy from the triangle formed by the Rivers Roer, Wurm and Meuse. The 7th Armoured Division was to remain on the left of the Corps, the 131st Brigade attacking northwards to secure Echt, Schilberg and Süsteren. The ultimate task of the 22nd Armoured Brigade, of which the 1st Battalion remained a part, would be to break through northwards to Montfort and St. Odilienberg. In this low-lying country of deep ditches, canals and water meadows, such an operation was feasible only in frost. The hard ground held only just long enough for the deliberate operations to be completed, planned to be deliberate, because of the nature of the ground and the climate and the desperation with which the Germans were expected to resist on the borders of the Reich.

On the 16th of January in the evening covering parties from "I" Company moved out to protect the Churchill tank bridge-layers who were to span the two small streams south of the Vloed Beek. A German mobile patrol had to be brushed aside

2D

and a standing patrol cleared from a house. The bridging was completed before dawn and soon afterwards "I" Company found that the enemy had withdrawn from the Vloed Beek. At about ten o'clock "I" Company were told to link up with the 2nd Battalion The Devonshire Regiment in Süsteren. In doing this Peter Mitchell's platoon took seventeen prisoners from one house. The Battalion was then left to garrison Nieustadt and the three bridges. Night patrols were carried out across the Vloed Beek and on one of the best of these Peter Bickersteth was wounded.

The 131st Brigade had taken Schilberg and Echt, but owing to a sharp thaw had not yet reached St. Joost. A plan was made for "I" Company to attack the village with a squadron of the 8th Hussars in tanks and a troop of Crocodiles (flame-throwing tanks) in support. Peter Luke, commanding "I" Company, was therefore to be supported by his fag-master at Eton, Henry Huth, who commanded the squadron of 8th Hussars. It was estimated that the village was held by a company of enemy. Owing to delay in the arrival of the crocodiles the attack did not start until three o'clock. Before it began the enemy brought down a concentration on the start line, hitting a half-track, killing two riflemen and wounding Sergeant Hart. Within fifteen minutes of starting seven prisoners had been taken—no ordinary prisoners, but members of the Parachute Regiment Hübner, than whom no German troops were tougher. What was even more ominous was their story that the village was held not by a company but by a battalion supported by self-propelled guns. Gerald Lascelles's platoon on the right managed to make fair progress in bitter house-to-house fighting, assisted by the flame-throwers and their own 2-inch mortar smoke. But when he reached the first bound an accurate artillery concentration caused two complete sections to become casualties. Peter Apsey, on the left, also made gradual progress, although his platoon sergeant, Sergeant Hutchinson, was wounded early on. One Crocodile went up on a mine, and two Honeys (light tanks) were knocked out. The reserve platoon, Peter Mitchell's, then went through and got most of the way towards the second bound. By now it was dark, except for the light thrown by the flames of the burning houses set on fire by the flame-throwers and phosphorous grenades. The leading platoon was halted, and in this pause Paddy Boden, commanding the Battalion in the absence on leave of Colonel Victor Paley, called off the attack, as it had been decided to pass the Durham Light Infantry through at first light to complete the capture of the village. By this time forty-three paratroopers had been taken prisoner by "I" Company and at least twenty Germans had been killed, two personally by Corporal Cable, one by a Piat and the other by a grenade. For the rest of the night 14 Platoon lobbed grenades over a garden wall at the Germans, who then did likewise. Twice riflemen went in through the wrong door or window to find that they were in an enemy house, and escaped back to their own in the confusion. "I" Company's casualties were three killed and twenty-three wounded, including one platoon sergeant killed and the other platoon sergeants wounded. It was to take another battalion the whole day and four separate attacks to clear the rest of the village.

"A" Company took a successful part in the closing stages of the St. Joost operation and on the 22nd of January the 5th Dragoon Guards, with "C" Company, who were commanded by Dawson Bates in Eric Sergeant's temporary absence, set out for Montfort. The leading group, consisting of a troop of tanks, the scout platoon and a motor platoon, reached Aandenburg, just north of Montfort, where they spent a hectic twenty-four hours, the enemy reacting strongly to this intrusion. That they held out successfully until relieved by the Queen's and subsequently the Devons was largely due to Sergeants Murray and Skipper, the platoon commanders. On the 24th of January Montfort was entered and its defence assigned to the Battalion, less "A" Company, who went back for a short rest.

In the remaining operations to close right up to the Roer and to capture St. Odilienberg the Battalion's main activity was that of lifting mines; and it was while doing this that Ben Remnant was killed. On the 27th of January "A" Company were moved into the southern end of the town and were kept busy lifting mines and rounding up prisoners from the cellars. While there a German fighting patrol got close enough to score a direct hit on a section post, killing one rifleman and stunning the rest. After that the position, which overlooked the far bank of the Roer, was held by two companies.

The operation known as "Blackcock" was now ended and with it the series of operations to clear the Germans from Belgium and Holland south of the Maas. The success of "Blackcock" did much to revive the reputation of the 7th Armoured Division. It was a triumph over conditions of ground and climate as well as over German paratroopers in their most stubborn mood. No single action had been more successful than that of "I" Company in St. Joost.

Early in February the 1st Battalion was due to be relieved. But the thaw which now set in turned even tarmac roads into porridge. For a month the Sappers had gone about with black faces warning everyone of the dreadful consequences of a thaw. Their worst forebodings were borne out. But the Battalion managed to move out of the Roer salient on the 13th of February and settled at Maeseyck on the west bank of the Maas for rest and training. A pleasant, grey, cobbled, little town, full of Belgian hospitality, where you could buy a shotgun, engraved with pretty pictures, for £10, the Battalion were sorry to leave it for the barren neighbourhood of Zomeren in Holland. At this place, which had been blasted by the 11th Armoured Division in a battle to cross the canal, the Battalion awaited the Rhine crossing and final advance into Germany. Like the 8th Battalion, the 1st took no part in the battle for the Reichswald, between the Maas and the Rhine.

It was on the day that they were due to leave Maeseyck for Zomeren that General Sir John Burnett-Stuart, Colonel Commandant of the 1st Battalion since 1936 and now due to retire, came to visit them. He inspected the Battalion in barracks and then, for the last time as Colonel Commandant, saw them march past in their vehicles and took the salute by the side of the Zomeren road.

CHAPTER XXIX

INTO THE REICH

For years there had been much talk of the North German Plain. It was often described as suitable country for an armoured advance. But one had only to look at a map to see that frequent streams, canals, great rivers, and woodlands of varying sizes made it little better for tanks than the more open stretches of the bocage. While there are sandy areas, such as the Luneburger Heide, even these are broken by woodland and patches of bog. Those who held the idea that the armoured divisions could be launched on a great sweep across this plain were doomed to disappointment, even if the strength of the German resistance had not to be taken into account. It was expected by some that within the Reich the Germans would fight with Japanese tenacity. The civilians were expected to rise and slaughter small, isolated parties with whatever weapons they could lay hands on. There were, in fact, few instances of the inhabitants taking any active part against us. At one town the 8th Battalion had to compete with the Volksturm, not in uniform and inadequately armed, who certainly assisted the soldiers; occasionally there would be a report of a wire stretched across the road at the height of a motor-bicyclist's head. But on the whole the Germans in the towns and villages met us with black looks and despairing resignation rather than any definite appearance of hostility. Perhaps they feared the Russians so much more than they hated us.

The German soldiers continued to fight on. It was noticeable that the farther north one went the more desperate resistance was likely to be. The main reason for this was that the parachute armies were in the north. Thus the most rapid progress in the advance across Westphalia was made on the right, while on the extreme left hardly any gains could be made. Though the enemy still fought, there was discernible in their behaviour a disposition to surrender when they had put up a show of fierce resistance, to fire their panzerfaust at the leading tank at ten yards' range and then rise to their feet with their hands above their heads. The second vehicle in too many of our columns saw the one in front burst into flames at it rounded a corner and was greeted immediately afterwards by half a dozen white flags. Up to the very last day no one knew if the enemy they encountered would choose to fight or to surrender.

The 1st Battalion crossed the frontier into Germany on the 25th of March fully prepared for saboteurs and a hostile population. On the 27th of March the companies went out to their armoured regiments and with them crossed the Rhine. On the 28th they drove out of the infantry bridgehead and began the apparently unending process of clearing woods and villages. Each operation demanded a rapid appreciation and a fire plan, followed by an energetic assault by the motor platoons supported by tanks. Casualties were light when compared with those of the enemy. It was the loss of individual leaders that was hard to bear, the harder at this stage in the war. Peter Apsey was the first to be mortally wounded in one of these earlier actions.

Opposition was always fiercest on the left, the northern, flank. The 7th Armoured Division was directed northwards to cut the communications of the German parachute armies. Chris Milner and "A" Company had a particularly successful action at Stadtlohn against considerably superior numbers; "C" Company had to fight their way through Ramsdorf, blowing up houses for the tanks to roll over when the road was blocked; "I" Company had a fierce battle between Ahaus and Ochtrupp, where Mike Robinson was killed by a mine and Corporal Coward fought a gallant action on his own after being wounded in the throat. On this last occasion Peter Mitchell's platoon and a troop of the 5th Royal Tanks took on about four hundred paratroopers in some houses. The company and their tanks then drove them out into a wood and, according to a prisoner's account, inflicted over a hundred casualties.

The advance reached the Ems near Rheine. Here demolitions and stiff resistance brought about a halt. The Division moved south to cross the Ems—Dortmund Canal where the 11th Armoured Division had secured a crossing, though not a passage through the Teutoburger Wald, a tree-covered ridge rising sharply from the plain, to be crossed only by twisty roads running through defiles, the traditional barrier to invaders from the west. It was defended by the pupils of the Hanover School for Non-Commissioned Officers, probably the best collection of fighting men that remained at the disposal of the Reich. After an early failure to outflank Ibbenbüren the Battalion and the Brigade bypassed this formidable opposition and drove straight for the Weser. For the first time rapid progress was made, though not rapid enough to prevent the bridges over the river at Hoya being blown, despite a ten-mile advance by "C" Company with a patrol of the 11th Hussars in the dark.

The next move was to the north to cut the enemy route to Bremen. The motor companies were again heavily engaged. "A" Company had a successful action at Bassum, while "I" Company captured Barrien. Just north of that place they bumped an enemy position in a wood. Peter Mitchell's platoon was put in to clear up this opposition, and it was in the heavy fighting that ensued that he, too, was killed. It was the loss—at the eleventh hour—of an officer whose name has appeared with distinction in all the recent battles of "I" Company from St. Joost to Ochtrupp. The enemy showed signs of counter-attacking with tanks from west of Syke and even when these attempts were foiled, non-commissioned officers with bazookas tried to stalk our tanks and "C" Company chased one of these parties for three miles before capturing it complete. The Battalion then moved off east to Nienburg to prepare to cross the Rivers Weser and Aller.

It was here that Colonel Victor Paley, who had commanded ever since June, 1943, when he took over from Colonel Freddie Stephens, left the Battalion for the staff of VIII Corps. It was a far cry from the white sands of Homs or the Italian battle of Cardito, where the new Colonel had based his timings on pre-war Staff College exercises—and found that they worked out accurately—to the flat, wet meadows which lead to the Weser at Nienburg. Paddy Boden, who now took over, was the fourth Colonel of the Battalion since they had left England in 1941 to take part in the desert war.

On the 16th of April the Aller was crossed at Rethem. "A" and "C" Companies were with their armoured regiments directed on Lüneburg, a name soon to acquire a wider fame. There was much clearing of villages and woods, opposition coming mainly from marines and the cadets at a sapper school, who were particularly adept at demolishing bridges. Despite this, "A" Company cleared Walsrode so quickly and successfully that they captured the bridge intact. At Fallingbostel a large prisoner-of-war camp was librated, containing five Riflemen taken at Calais and one from the 9th Battalion captured at Derna in 1941. Soon after this George Burder was killed in a minor operation. He had defended Geffen twice against serious attacks and led his platoon ever since, now to be killed within three weeks of the end of the war.

The advance continued towards Hamburg. The Wasps (flame-throwers in carriers) were used for the first time in anger and with great effect; "A" Company had a fierce battle in Daersdorf. And then the Brigade found itself on the high ground looking across the Elbe to the great, burned city of Hamburg. It was the end of the fighting for the Battalion. While the Gunners—the 5th Royal Horse Artillery, whose association with the Battalion had lasted from the time of Alamein—spent their time shooting at ships in the river and trains travelling along on the far bank, the negotiations which were to lead to the surrender of the city had begun.

Meanwhile the Battalion was ordered to occupy the small town of Buxtehude, where the barracks were said still to be held by German troops. In a sense they were, for when the leading Riflemen reached the buildings they found several hundred German "Wrens" and one admiral. It was a matter of the utmost difficulty, requiring all the qualities of tact at the disposal of the Colonel, to clear these formidable women from the battlefield with no more serious damage than a bruised foot for Regimental Sergeant-Major Stacey, on whom one lady elected to drop the heaviest volume in the archives of the German Navy. Eventually the whole party was marched off, many in tears, the admiral taking the salute, to become one more problem of the occupation. Soon after they had gone, on the 3rd of May, the Battalion led the Brigade into Hamburg and "A" Company and the 8th Hussars crossed the Elbe into the heart of the city, into a scene of devastation such as none could have imagined.

After leaving Hamburg the Battalion drove without opposition across Schleswig-Holstein, and on the 8th of May (VE Day) came temporarily to rest north of the Kiel Canal near Bunsoh.

At times in this last campaign there had been fighting as bitter as any in Normandy or, for those with longer memories, as any at Calais or Gazala or Ruweisat, at Gebel Saikhra or in the

Plain of Naples. If results measured in casualties inflicted and prisoners taken were out of all proportion to those which we had suffered, satisfaction was tempered by the knowledge of the loss of so many of the best young officers and most experienced non-commissioned officers and riflemen in these last, wasteful days before the final surrender of the German armies.

The 8th Battalion had watched the Royal Air Force fly over for the Rhine assault. They waited, far back in Belgium, for the infantry battle to reach the stage when the armour could pass through into the open. On the 28th of March the Battalion moved straight from Louvain through Belgium into Holland, into Germany and across the Rhine at Wesel. There was a wait of one day while the transport of the advancing army was sorted out and on the 30th of March the Battalion's part in the battle began. That day the centre line of the advance was mapped out as far as the Elbe. The 11th Armoured Division was to move to the south of the 7th Armoured Division. It was never diverted to the north to the rear of the parachute armies.

The 29th Armoured Brigade was first directed on Horstmar. The atmosphere was one of optimism reminiscent of the beginning of the great drive to Antwerp. The motor companies were therefore sent off to work with their armoured regiments. But the Germans were still capable of resistance on a small scale, a few men with panzerfausts, enough snipers to make much work for the companies, and occasionally a whole battalion which had marched hurriedly from Denmark. "G" Company and the 3rd Royal Tanks reached Horstmar by nightfall, but "F" Company and later "H" Company on the left of the routes made slower progress through having to clear various woods and villages on the way. The Brigade had covered twenty-eight miles in the day. 11 Platoon of "G" Company were sent off to assist bridging operations at Burgsteinfurt and ambushed several parties of unsuspecting Germans under the walls of the medieval castle which was later to house the 2nd Battalion.

From now on the nature of the country and of the German resistance made it necessary to move as armoured regimental groups, the 8th Battalion being teamed, as usual, with the 23rd Hussars, "F" Company with "B" Squadron, "G" with "A" and "H" with "C," "E" Company being used to give support when required and for many odd jobs all the time. Our group was not in the lead on the 30th; but "H" Company had to put in an attack to capture an anti-aircraft-gun site from which the road was being shelled. They collected two hundred and fifty prisoners. On the 2nd of April the Battalion crossed the Dortmund—Ems Canal below the Teutoburger Wald where the 159th Brigade were meeting fierce opposition from the non-commissioned officers' school from Hanover, and turned to the right along the far bank, where the road runs close to the forest, the trees and blossom in the full beauty of an early spring. At Tecklenburg strong resistance was met. The black-and-white houses, some of great antiquity, and narrow streets, built in a hollow surrounded by tree-covered hills, were defended fiercely by German soldiers and civilians alike. It was the first and only town where active measures had to be taken against civilians, and it was not until many houses had been reduced to smoking ruins that resistance ceased. In the process Tubby Mason was killed while directing the fire of a tank, and a small party of Germans crept through the woods to attack the "A" Echelon vehicles at the rear of the column. "E" Company dealt with this intrusion.

During the night the Battalion moved on in pouring rain behind the 3rd Royal Tanks. The object now was to move fast enough to capture intact the bridges over the next water obstacle. The 3rd Royal Tanks group succeeded that night and the Battalion, led at first by "G" Company, passed through them directed on the bridges across the Ems—Weser Canal north-west of Osnabrück. There was spasmodic opposition and during one small action Sergeant Triggs was treacherously wounded by one of a party of Germans who seemed willing to give themselves up. The tanks, followed by Sergeant Connelly's carriers, pushed on and succeeded in capturing one bridge which the Germans made a feeble attempt to blow, and subsequently four others. This success was of some tactical importance at a stage in operations when available bridging material was barely enough to go round.

On the 5th of April the Battalion took up the lead in the race for the Weser. Brigadier Roscoe Harvey was quite determined that his brigade should reach the river before the Infantry Brigade. Spurred on by every sort of imprecation and encouragement, "F" Company's carriers forced their way through the town of Stolzenau up to the bridge. But it was not to be another

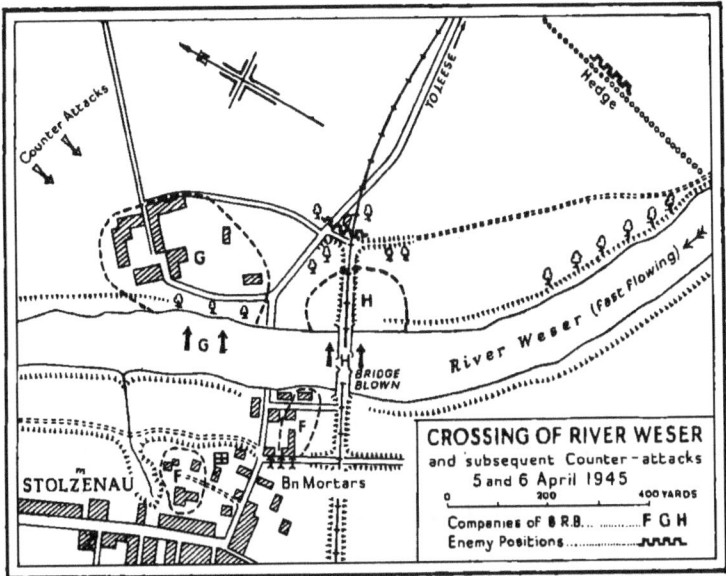

Amiens; the Germans blew it within a few hundred yards of the leading carrier, not a complete "blow" but serious enough to prevent a vehicle crossing. "F" Company then set about clearing the town. One of their earliest discoveries was a wine store containing very large quantities of Hock, stored in a house unpleasantly near to the bridge.

Since the bridge looked repairable within a reasonable time, it was decided to make a quick crossing before the Germans recovered from their surprise. Assault boats were soon on the spot. "H" Company were chosen to cross first, south of the bridge. At one o'clock the leading platoon, under Geordie Leslie-Melville, made a rapid crossing, despite the fast-flowing current, under cover of smoke from the Gunners. The other leading platoon tried to cross by the framework of the bridge, but, seeing that they were making slow progress, Peter Bradford called them back and told them to cross by boat. As they were launching the craft a Spandau opened up, killing Philip May and wounding Rifleman Hawkins, and at the same time a 20-mm. gun began to make things unpleasant. In view of this, the Colonel ordered "G" Company and the remainder of "H" to cross north of the bridge, which they succeeded in doing without casualties. Under cover of this bridgehead the Sappers began to work.

It was then that the Luftwaffe made its last significant appearance. No one had seen a Stuka since what now seemed the early days of the war. One of these now curiously old-fashioned-looking aircraft appeared at fifty feet over the bridge. Within an hour a remarkable assortment of aircraft of every type and date had arrived to bomb the bridge site, and "G" Company immediately had some casualties, among whom was Sergeant Wickham, who died. But the Sapper party on the bridge received a direct hit, sixteen being killed and as many wounded, and the work already done was hopelessly damaged. It was now raining, a factor which handicapped the Air Force, who had long distances to cover, much more than the Luftwaffe, whose airfields were close at hand. It was clear that the bridge would not be ready by the morning; it was more than unpleasantly wet, and there was every prospect of a counter-attack during the night.

The hours of darkness passed without incident. But before six, in the half-light, a party of some forty men rushed Corporal Stone's section, the right section of "H" Company, and succeeded in overrunning it. This put the enemy in the middle of the platoon's defensive system. At such close quarters neither side could move. Throughout the day 16 Platoon remained in position, picking off any German who appeared above ground, but in the process they lost first Sergeant Hancock, who died of his wounds, then Corporal Culnane, who was killed while looking over the top of his trench to observe the fire of his Piat, and then Tim Swanwick, the platoon commander, besides the wireless operator and various others. Sergeant Pratt took over, apparently unperturbed.

Meanwhile, at about nine o'clock, a large-scale infantry attack was put in across the open on "G" and "H" Companies. The Gunners and the Battalion's 3-inch mortars seized this chance and broke up the attack before it reached the companies, and then throughout the morning heavy concentrations were brought down on all attempts by the enemy to form up for an attack. Shelling, mortar and air attacks were causing a steady drain of casualties so that Michael Raymond's platoon of "G" Company had to be ferried across to join "H" Company, but before it had arrived a Commando battalion crossed the river directed on the village of Leese, about two thousand yards to our front. They were pinned down almost as soon as they had crossed. It was clearly too late to exploit the unpreparedness of the enemy: at least a brigade operation was required. During the night the rest of the Commando Brigade was ferried over the Weser to take over from "G" and "H" Companies, who were withdrawn to the west bank without further loss. This action had cost the two companies fifty casualties; but the bridgehead had been held and the 12th S.S. Regiment put in to drive them out had suffered much more heavily than they had.

By this time the Weser had been bridged to the south. The Division crossed there and pushed on for one day with little opposition. On the 9th the village of Steimbke was reached, where the remainder of the 12th S.S. Regiment had been withdrawn. "G" and "H" Companies met fierce opposition and it was not until almost every cottage in the village had been demolished that the advance could be continued. During the fighting Eric Yetman was among those fatally wounded, one more name to add to the list of platoon commanders killed in these last days. "F" Company and "B" Squadron bypassed the village and drove on to the Leine River at Nordrebber, where the leading carrier was hit by a bazooka and the houses had to be systematically cleared. After a four-day wait the Aller was crossed. The Battalion drove rapidly past Belsen, declared open territory by Himmler himself owing to the risk of typhus. All three companies had sharp engagements on the 16th and David Fyffe was killed by a mine. On the 17th the two leading tanks and one of "G" Company's carriers were "brewed up" by an 88-mm. gun. A squadron of Typhoon aircraft was called in to attack the enemy only a few hundred yards in front of "G" Company and left little for the motor platoons to clear up.

While this was going on the rest of the armoured regimental group was carrying out a "model operation" at Barum. The first attempt to get into the village failed across open ground: Sergeant Connelly was killed and two tanks were lost. It was clear that the position was held by well-organized enemy supported by artillery. "F" Company and "B" Squadron were sent round behind the village, where they did much destruction among the enemy trying to escape to the Elbe. All available guns, mortars and tanks, and every support weapon in range was brought to bear. Under cover of smoke "H" Company advanced in open formation. The tanks at first "shot them in" from the flanks.

Just before the houses were reached the tanks moved past the infantry and established themselves on the outskirts of the village, while the company cleared the houses and gardens. In a short time every house was on fire, two hundred and fifty prisoners had been taken, and three 88-mm., four 20-mm. and one 37-mm. guns had been captured. In the final assault "H" Company did not have one casualty.

The advance continued to the Elbe with no more serious engagements. "G" Company late in the evening fired at some vehicles hidden in a wood, went closer to investigate, discovered that they contained Belli's Circus, and were able to report over the wireless: "Two lions brewed up, two bears escaping, two elephants and the circus staff captured."

From the 19th to the 30th of April the Battalion rested to await the crossing of the Elbe. It was beautiful, sunny weather. The apple blossom was out on the trees which line the roads and surround the villages in this part of Germany. Colonel Tony Hunter caught a three-pound grayling, and someone discovered a trout hatchery. But the fighting was not yet entirely over. On the evening of the 30th the Battalion and the 23rd Hussars moved forward in appalling conditions of traffic congestion, starting and stopping at intervals all night, and in the early hours of the next morning passed through the forward elements of the 15th (Scottish) Division. At once in the dark two Tiger tanks were met and two of our tanks and one of "G" Company's carriers knocked out. As soon as it was light "G" Company attacked and captured the village of Sahms, taking sixty prisoners, one of whom was a German battalion commander, captured by Neil Hughes-Onslow while on a reconnaissance patrol. "F" Company lost a carrier on a mine, and "H" Company were quite heavily shelled. It seemed as if the familiar, desperate business of a slow, opposed advance would continue right up to the Baltic; but when the Battalion leaguered for the night in a bog on the evening of the 1st of May their part in the war was over, for the next day resistance was at an end. The advance continued at great speed up the wide autobahn from Hamburg to Lübeck, the copper domes of whose churches were green in the sunlight ahead. On all sides there were Germans waiting to give themselves up, our own released prisoners, displaced persons, refugees, and people of every race and description, all wanting food, orders, instructions and homes. The

Battalion drove through Lübeck; the houses, comparatively undamaged, were suddenly strangely northern in appearance after the black-and-white cottages and new brick farms of the advance. They passed through the city northwards, and as the Baltic came in sight at Travemünde the road began to be choked with refugees fleeing in desperate panic from the Russian armies to their east.

EPILOGUE

AT the end of the war in Europe there were two battalions of the Regiment between the Baltic and the North Sea and two in the heart of Austria. In these all the elements which go to make up The Rifle Brigade in war were represented. There were the Regulars; there were the Territorials of the London Rifle Brigade and of the Tower Hamlets Rifles; and there were, in great numbers, all those who had been called up from their ordinary jobs to fight in the war. In the 8th Battalion there was a fair proportion of 60th Riflemen, now absorbed in spirit as well as in uniform into the Regiment. In Austria both the 2nd and 7th Battalions contained numbers of men who had not started their military life as Riflemen but whose identities had, in the fighting, become indistinguishable from the rest of the Regiment.

All four battalions were immersed in the immense and immediate problems of the peace. The 1st Battalion was occupied in disarming and guarding the German armies from Denmark and in Schleswig-Holstein; the 8th Battalion was engaged in guard duties and in helping to solve the various problems on the fringe of military government; and the 2nd and 7th Battalions in Klagenfurt were overwhelmed with the business of helping out the administration in their areas. In Germany and Austria crowds of displaced persons of every conceivable shade of race and nationality clamoured for food, for housing, for transport and for instructions. The inhabitants stalked about, grey and watchful, immensely relieved at not being overrun by Russian armies, and prepared to be scornful of the English as soldiers, not to be treated as friends. There was one thing about which all Germans were clear: none of them, they said, had been Nazis.

The battalions grappled with these unusual situations. They released our prisoners and sent them home: they discovered the answers to innumerable and extraordinary questions. Battalion headquarters were remarkably overworked, and at Headquarters of the 61st Brigade Brigadier Adrian Gore, who had been continuously at war since November, 1942, commanding the 10th Battalion, commanding a brigade at Anzio, and forming and fighting the Greenjackets Brigade, awaited the break-up of his formation surrounded by diplomatic problems of every conceivable kind. Gradually the war-time structure fell away. The 7th Battalion went off to run down its strength in Egypt, and the 8th was to end its days in the schloss at Schleswig, owning some of the best race-horses of the occupation.

The Regiment had taken part in almost every phase of the war. Riflemen had defended Calais. They had fought through Wavell's campaign in the Western Desert, throughout the see-saw struggles of the early years in Libya, at Sidi Rezegh, at Alamein, and in the great advance to Tripoli, Mareth and Tunis. They had been represented in the First Army in North Africa, and in all the vicissitudes of that finally successful campaign. In Italy four battalions had played a part, three of them in one brigade, from the Liri Valley to Perugia, through the Apennines and in the advance to the Po, until in the final stages they had led the Eighth Army into Austria. In North-West Europe two battalions had made their way through the bocage and captured intact the bridge at Amiens, had swept into Antwerp, had held the river crossings at Dinant, and fought their way fiercely through Germany itself, across the Weser to the Elbe to end the war one in Hamburg and the other in the Baltic city of Lübeck. Only in Burma had they had no hand. Now in the summer of 1945 the 2nd Battalion returned home across Europe from Austria, to be re-formed as a light reconnaissance regiment for service in the Far East. A new and a young battalion was to be collected together to include many of those Regular soldiers released from imprisonment five years after the fall of Calais. But as the Battalion landed in England—the last time in its history that it would do so—to set about the preparations for this first venture against the Japanese, the news spread of a "Cease fire" in the Far East, and it gradually became apparent that the Regiment's part in the war against the Axis Powers had finally come to an end.

APPENDIX "A"

COPY OF A LEAFLET DROPPED BY GERMAN AIRCRAFT UPON THE DEFENDERS OF CALAIS

LA VILLE DE CALAIS
est sommée de se rendre immédiatement.

La garnison de la ville quittera la ville sans armes, les mains levées

dans le delai d'une heure, sur la route de Coquelles, dans la direction de Coquelles.

A tout résistance continuée sera répondu par de noveaux lancements de bombes et par un bombardement avec la plus lourde artillerie.

Le général Cdt. le corps d'armée.

Boulogne a capitulée
aujourd'hui a 11.30h.
C'est à vous de suivre.

APPENDIX "B"

MESSAGE FROM THE COLONEL-IN-CHIEF

THE following message to all Riflemen of The Rifle Brigade was received from Field-Marshal H.R.H. The Duke of Connaught, K.G., K.T., the Colonel-in-Chief:

"BAGSHOT PARK.
"2nd June, 1940.

"I am prouder than I can say of the manner in which the Battalion I once commanded acquitted themselves in the defence of Calais. In the glorious record of the Regiment there is little, if anything, that has been finer than the part they took in this action.

"The defence contributed enormously to the successful evacuation of the British Expeditionary Force from Dunkirk.

"The superb conduct of all ranks in an operation attended by the greatest difficulty was worthy of the highest traditions of the Regiment.

"England is proud of this magnificent action, and as an old commander of the Battalion I am equally proud. I am sure that this glorious passage in the history of the Regiment will live in the history of the Army.

"My sympathy goes out to all the relations and friends of those who fell.

"ARTHUR, *Colonel-in-Chief.*"

APPENDIX "C"

THE SNIPE ACTION

AFTER the action at Snipe Lieutenant-Colonel Vic Turner and Sergeant Calistan were recommended for the Victoria Cross.

Colonel Vic Turner's citation reads as follows:

"The King has been graciously pleased to approve the award of the Victoria Cross to Major (Temporary Lieutenant-Colonel) Victor Buller Turner, The Rifle Brigade (Prince Consort's Own) (Thatcham, Berks), for most conspicuous gallantry and devotion to duty on the 27th of October, 1942, in the Western Desert.

"Lieutenant-Colonel Turner led a battalion of The Rifle Brigade at night for four thousand yards through difficult country to their objective, where forty German prisoners were captured. He then organized the captured position for all-round defence; in this position he and his Battalion were continuously attacked from 5.30 a.m. to 7 p.m., unsupported and so isolated that replenishment of ammunition was impossible owing to the concentration of the enemy fire.

"During this time the Battalion was attacked by not less than ninety German tanks, which advanced in successive waves. All of these were repulsed with a loss to the enemy of thirty-five tanks.

"Throughout the action Lieutenant-Colonel Turner never ceased to go to each part of the front as it was threatened. Wherever the fire was heaviest there he was to be found. In one case, finding a solitary 6-pounder gun in action (the others being casualties) and manned only by another officer and a sergeant, he acted as loader and with these two destroyed five enemy tanks. While doing this he was wounded in the head, but he refused all aid.

"His personal gallantry and complete disregard of danger as he moved about encouraging his Battalion to resist to the last resulted in the infliction of a severe defeat on the enemy tanks. He set an example of leadership and bravery which inspired his whole Battalion."

Sergeant Calistan was awarded the Distinguished Conduct Medal. He had already been awarded a Military Medal for his conduct at Bir Hacheim in June, 1942.

The citation after the Snipe action was as follows:

"Sergeant Calistan was sergeant commander of a section of 6-pounder anti-tank guns, sited on the west flank of the Snipe position, on the 26th/27th of October, 1942. Sergeant Calistan's troop was engaged by enemy tanks both during the night and the following morning; by midday on the 27th of October all the other guns in his troop had been knocked out, and all the other members of his own gun crew but himself wounded and incapacitated; also the troop was almost out of ammunition.

"At about 1300 hours fifteen German tanks attacked his section. The Commanding Officer arrived at his position and acted as loader while he laid the gun and acted as No. 1.

"With the greatest courage and coolness he waited until the tanks were some three hundred yards away, and hit and set nine of them on fire. He then had no more ammunition left.

"Unperturbed, he waited while his troop commander fetched more ammunition and when it arrived he hit three more enemy tanks in as many shots and so broke and repelled the enemy attack.

"He continued to operate his gun for the rest of the day; after dark he received orders to close on to company headquarters and withdrew with the rest of his company. He set off to walk the quarter of a mile back under heavy machine-gun fire from three German tanks, carrying one of the wounded members of his crew; the wounded man was hit and killed in his arms. He immediately returned to his troop position to fetch the last remaining wounded men, whom he brought safely back; still under intense and accurate fire.

"Throughout the action the quality of his determination was such that when the last point of human endurance and ability to continue to fight had been reached Sergeant Calistan took a new lease of courage. This he communicated to all around him and with their help he saved the day, so enabling his Battalion to withdraw safely from a critical position after inflicting losses on the enemy of fifty-seven tanks burnt.

"During this action his superb gallantry was outstanding among many courageous acts performed."

Sergeant Calistan was later commissioned as an officer in the Regiment and was killed in action when serving with the 7th Battalion in Italy.

APPENDIX "D"

MESSAGE FROM H.R.H. THE DUKE OF GLOUCESTER TO ALL BATTALIONS OF THE REGIMENT AT THE END OF THE WAR

THE following is the text of the message sent by H.R.H. The Duke of Gloucester, Colonel-in-Chief of the Regiment, to all battalions of The Rifle Brigade at the end of the war:

"Now that the war in Europe is over I wish, as your Colonel-in-Chief, to send my warmest congratulations to all ranks. From the dark days of Calais through the Western Desert and then on to Tunisia where battalions from North Africa met those who had advanced from Egypt, through bad times and good, one thing has never varied. This is the spirit of the Regiment and its reputation for close co-operation with other arms for the purpose of defeating the enemy. Since those days you have fought in Italy and in North-West Europe from the start of that campaign until at the end you led the pursuit over the Rhine and into the heart of Germany. From my present appointment in Australia I have watched these closing scenes with admiration and pride. Whatever the future holds in store you can be certain that never in all the splendid history of the Regiment have your achievements been surpassed. I am proud to be your Colonel-in-Chief.

"HENRY, *Colonel-in-Chief.*"

APPENDIX "E"

THE 9TH BATTALION

The following extracts from a letter from Colonel Squeak Purdon, who commanded the 9th Battalion for a year and a half, though not fitting easily into the narrative, are reproduced here in the hope of filling out the necessarily meagre story of that battalion:

"The day after the unfortunate battle at Hasseiat (just after Christmas, 1941) I remember hearing cheering start amongst the troops, which was taken up by those nearer as a staff car approached. The car, it transpired, contained Jock Campbell. Comparatively few of the Riflemen of the 9th Battalion had served under Jock before; but they recognized him instantly, and in him someone who, they felt confident, would not allow them to get into those puzzling situations where apparent victory was suddenly turned to ignominious withdrawal. Anyway, it was the first and only time I heard spontaneous cheering of the sort in the desert. Immediately after that the 9th Battalion, under Jock, was formed into columns with the 2nd Royal Horse Artillery and the Northumberland Hussars, to renew friendships made with them in the 2nd Armoured Division, and to establish an operational harmony analogous to that of our 2nd Battalion with the 3rd and 4th Royal Horse Artillery. Many members of the 9th Battalion will remember names like Bill Blacker and Peter Worthington of 'H/1' Battery and Len Livingstone-Learmouth of 'L/N' Battery, 2nd Royal Horse Artillery—not to mention Linden Bolton of 'Lindencol' —and John Cookson, Dick Taylor, Hughie Northumberland, John Pumphrey and others, of the 102nd Royal Horse Artillery (Northumberland Hussars)."

It was only a month or two after this occurrence that Brigadier (by then Major-General) Jock Campbell was killed in a motor-car accident.

"During these kaleidoscopic switches the 9th Battalion served either 'under command' or 'in support' of practically every unit of both armoured divisions, whether armoured regiments, armoured cars, Gunners or Sappers. By doing so the Battalion extended the friendships and mutual respect established between battalions of The Rifle Brigade and other arms in what was to become the Eighth Army, and was to pay big dividends both then and later.

"At the time, about the only apparent advantage was that, in spite of frequent changes of call signs, Battalion Headquarters could identify the voices of wireless operators and commanders of other units with a facility which one hopes was not enjoyed by Axis intercepts. It also helped considerably, in tricky situations, to pass urgent messages over the air in the topical baby-talk often employed at that time, and which was often more 'secure' than the official signal procedure.

"It was this work on the air which could start a motor battalion or any of its components on anything from a 'swan' to an operation in a matter of moments, on information or orders so disguised as to call for speed of uptake by the recipient which would be the envy of a music-hall thought-reading act!"

APPENDICES

APPENDIX "F"

ROLL OF HONOUR

THE RIFLE BRIGADE

1939—1945

The following is a list of those who lost their lives while serving with the Regiment in the war. The list of names in Winchester Cathedral has been checked, as far as possible, with Records, The War Office. But I would hesitate to claim complete accuracy for any statistics compiled by hand or machine-made, and I would apologize in advance for any omissions or inaccuracies which may be found. I hope there are none.

R. H. W. S. H.

The following is an extract from the Book of Remembrance in Winchester Cathedral:

THIS PAGE IS DEDICATED TO

THE MEMORY OF

FIELD-MARSHAL HIS ROYAL HIGHNESS

THE DUKE OF CONNAUGHT

AND STRATHEARN

K.G., K.T., K.P., G.C.B., G.C.S.I., G.C.M.G., G.C.I.E.
G.C.V.O., G.B.E., V.D., T.D.

BORN 1st MAY, 1850

DIED 16th JANUARY, 1942

COMMANDED 1st BN. THE RIFLE BRIGADE
1876—1880

COLONEL-IN-CHIEF, THE RIFLE BRIGADE
1880—1942

OFFICERS

Name.	Date and Place.	
Lieut. Harold J. Adler	25/ 2/42	Middle East.
Lieut. Charles A. W. Allford	10/10/44	Italy.
Lieut. Michael C. Anderson	3/ 9/44	France.
Major Arthur J. Andrews	7/ 4/41	N. Africa.
Lieut. Peter C. Apsey, M.C.	29/ 3/45	Germany.
Capt. John E. A. Atkinson	12/12/40	E. Africa.
Lieut. John W. Bacon	31/ 3/43	N. Africa.
Lieut. St. John C. Bally	8/ 6/44	Italy.
Capt. Jack S. Bare	8/ 2/44	N.W. Europe.
Capt. Henry A. H. Beckwith	5/ 5/43	N. Africa.
Lieut. Robert M. Birch	28/ 7/44	France.

Name.	Date and Place.	
2/Lieut. Edward A. Bird	25/ 5/40	Calais.
Capt. David L. Birney	28/ 4/42	France.
Lieut. John R. M. Birnie	4/ 2/44	Italy.
Capt. Ian F. E. Blacker	22/ 6/44	Italy.
Lieut. John E. C. Bodley, M.C.	30/ 7/44	Italy.
Lieut. Richard L. Bomford	29/ 5/44	Italy.
Capt. Peter G. A. Borthwick	15/11/44	Holland.
Brig. Thomas J. B. Bosvile, C.B.E., D.S.O., M.C.	5/ 7/45	U.K.
2/Lieut. Peter H. Bradshaw, M.M.	19/12/41	U.K.
Lieut. Robin Brand	17/ 1/45	U.K.
Capt. Peter N. Brealy	4/ 6/44	Italy.
Major The Hon. Henry G. A. Browne	8/ 9/42	Middle East.
Lieut.-Colonel Edward G. Buckley, M.B.E.	21/ 1/43	U.K.
Capt. Frank G. Budd	2/ 7/43	At sea.
2/Lieut. Charles R. D. Budworth	27/11/41	Middle East.
Lieut. George C. Burder, M.C.	17/ 4/45	Germany.
Lieut. Roger M. Butler	13/ 6/44	France.
Lieut. James V. Caesar	20/ 6/44	France.
Lieut. Charles V. Calistan, D.C.M., M.M.	30/ 7/44	Italy.
Lieut.-Colonel Henry F. Campbell	18/ 3/43	U.K.
Lieut. Eric G. Clark	5/ 7/44	Italy.
Lieut. Anthony Clarke	21/ 8/44	France.
Lieut. Clive H. P. Clerihew	28/ 4/43	N. Africa.
Lieut. Peter O. Coop	13/ 6/44	France.
Major John R. Copeland	23/ 4/44	Middle East.
Lieut. William P. Coryton	22/ 7/42	Middle East.
Lieut. Alan P. L. Cowan	30/ 4/44	Italy.
Lieut. Timothy O. K. Cross	15/11/44	Holland.
Capt. Martin K. Crowder	17/12/42	Middle East.
2/Lieut. Peter R. S. Dalbiac	15/ 6/42	Middle East.
Capt. Kenneth B. J. Dale	8/ 1/45	Italy.
Lieut. Alfred P. de Pass	13/ 6/44	France.
Lieut.-Colonel Edward P. A. des Graz	6/ 6/42	Middle East.
Lieut. Norman J. Deveson	3/ 9/44	France.
2/Lieut. Richard A. Dewing	29/ 5/42	Middle East.
Lieut. Austin F. Dore	20/ 7/44	France.
Major Francis A. Dorrien-Smith	20/ 6/44	France.
Lieut. Sidney J. F. Downing	3/ 6/44	Italy.
Lieut. Jerome P. Duncanson	28/ 5/40	Calais.
Lieut. Ronald A. Dust	9/ 4/43	N. Africa.
Lieut. Patrick C. Edwards	17/ 8/43	Middle East.
Lieut. William B. M. Edwards	26/ 3/43	N. Africa.
Capt. Richard F. R. Elkington	19/ 1/43	N. Africa.
Capt. William A. R. Farmiloe	9/ 6/41	Middle East.
Capt. John R. L. Fellowes	8/12/45	U.K.
Capt. Kenneth J. Fish, M.C.	8/ 5/43	N. Africa.
Capt. Geoffrey E. Fletcher	27/ 3/43	N. Africa.
Lieut. Philip E. Flower	25/10/42	Middle East.
Lieut. Thomas J. Foreshew	15/ 6/44	France.
Capt. Anthony A. Franklyn	24/12/41	Middle East.
Lieut. Edward P. B. Frewen	9/ 5/43	N. Africa.
Capt. Harold L. Fry	18/ 4/43	At sea.
Lieut. David O. Fyffe	16/ 4/45	Germany.

APPENDICES

Name.	Date and Place.	
Brig. The Viscount Hugh W. J. Garmoyle, D.S.O.	3/ 7/42	Middle East.
Lieut. Alan W. D. George	21/ 2/43	U.K.
Capt. Edgar W. L. Gibbons	30/ 3/43	N. Africa.
Lieut. Duncan J. Gray	4/ 9/44	Italy.
Lieut. Frederick C. Hall	4/12/42	N. Africa.
Major Arthur G. L. Hamilton-Russell	27/ 5/40	Calais.
Lieut. Marcus H. Hawkins	27/ 8/44	Italy.
Lieut. Richard Haywarden	9/ 8/42	N. Africa.
Lieut. Eric C. Haywood-Farmer	11/11/43	Italy.
Lieut. John K. Hood	29/ 9/43	N. Africa.
Major John O. Hopper	30/ 7/44	France.
Capt. The Hon. Alexander H. P. Hore-Ruthven	24/12/42	N. Africa.
Lieut.-Colonel Chandos B. A. Hoskyns	18/ 6/40	U.K.
Lieut. Donald Howorth, M.C.	10/ 9/44	Belgium.
Lieut. Edward A. M. Humphery	25/ 5/40	Calais.
Lieut. Reginald C. Hurley, M.C.	4/ 9/44	Italy.
Capt. Quentin B. Hurst	7/ 4/41	Middle East.
Lieut. James B. D. Irwin, M.C.	26/ 4/43	N. Africa.
Lieut. David B. H. Jacobson	27/ 4/41	Middle East.
2/Lieut. John E. Jones	2/12/40	U.K.
Major Noel L. Kelly	27/ 3/43	N. Africa.
Major Mark G. Kerr	13/ 1/45	Italy.
Lieut. Adrian G. Kingsley	19/ 9/44	Italy.
Lieut. Michael Lane	1/ 7/44	U.K.
Capt. Thomas F. Lane	17/ 3/43	Middle East.
2/Lieut. John W. O. Lentaigne, M.C.	25/ 7/42	Middle East.
Lieut. Rodney W. B. Lloyd, M.C.	22/ 2/45	Germany.
Lieut. Timothy P. Lloyd	27/ 7/44	Italy.
Lieut. Francis J. Lowrison	3/ 6/44	Italy.
2/Lieut. David Marshall	25/12/41	Middle East.
Lieut. Francis C. W. Mason	2/ 4/45	Germany.
Lieut. Alan N. Mather	6/ 8/44	France.
Capt. Edward P. May, M.C.	5/ 4/45	Germany.
Lieut. Geoffrey T. May, M.C.	14/ 6/44	France.
Capt. James N. McGrigor	29/11/41	Middle East.
Lieut. Anthony N. Miall	27/10/42	Middle East.
Lieut. Gordon F. Mills	12/11/43	Italy.
Lieut. Peter A. N. Mitchell, M.C.	8/ 4/45	Germany.
2/Lieut. Merlin Montagu-Douglas-Scott	9/ 5/41	Middle East.
Capt. Michael H. Mosley, M.C.	2/11/42	Middle East.
Lieut. David L. Mostyn-Owen	17/ 1/45	U.K.
Lieut. Kenneth F. F. North	1/ 4/41	Middle East.
Lieut. Donald C. Oldham	9/ 9/42	Middle East.
Lieut. David E. Parry-Jones	3/ 8/44	France.
Lieut. Christopher G. Parsons	3/11/42	Middle East.
Major Jocelyn A. Persse	26/10/42	Middle East.
Lieut. John H. Persse	20/ 6/44	Italy.
Lieut. Richard J. M. Peters	8/ 2/45	Burma.
Lieut. Hugh G. Preston	18/ 3/42	Middle East.
Lieut. John R. Priestley	6/ 8/44	France.
Lieut. Gerald Ramacciotti	12/12/44	Italy.
Lieut. Thomas Redfern, M.C.	7/ 7/42	Middle East.

Name.	Date and Place.	
2/Lieut. John M. W. Reeve	21/ 6/42	Middle East.
Major Ralph R. Reeve	15/ 6/41	U.K.
Lieut. Bennett J. F. Remnant	26/ 1/45	Holland.
Lieut. Michael H. A. Robinson	1/ 4/45	Germany.
Lieut. Albert M. Rueff	8/ 4/41	Middle East.
Lieut. George A. Russell	2/11/42	Middle East.
Lieut. John B. Russell	28/ 4/43	N. Africa.
Lieut. Gerrard V. Ryan	17/10/44	France.
Capt. Hugo N. Salmon	27/10/42	Middle East.
Lieut. John N. Salt	19/ 4/43	N. Africa.
Lieut. Roy M. Salt	27/10/42	Middle East.
Lieut. James P. Sedgwick, M.C.	10/ 3/45	France.
Lieut. Hugh W. N. Seymour	14/ 6/42	Middle East.
Lieut. Christopher W. Sheepshanks	31/ 3/43	N. Africa.
Lieut. John E. Simeon	29/ 5/42	Middle East.
2/Lieut. David R. Sladen	25/ 5/40	Calais.
Lieut. Joseph R. F. Smalley	16/12/44	Germany.
Lieut. Gordon L. Stevens	11/ 9/44	Italy.
Lieut. Ronald W. Sturgess	24/ 4/43	N. Africa.
Lieut. Timothy K. Swanwick	6/ 4/45	Germany.
Capt. Gilbert S. W. Talbot	20/ 6/44	France.
Major James H. A. Tanner	30/ 7/44	France.
2/Lieut. George A. Thomas	26/ 5/40	Calais.
Lieut. Henry J. L. Toms	11/ 4/43	N. Africa.
2/Lieut. Anthony F. Trollope-Bellew	3/11/42	Middle East.
Capt. Eric B. Tuxford	2/ 2/43	Burma.
2/Lieut. Adrian J. B. Van de Weyer	26/ 5/40	Calais.
Lieut. John W. Verner	29/ 4/43	N. Africa.
Lieut. Derek F. Ware	5/ 6/44	Italy.
Lieut. William M. Welch	25/ 5/40	Calais.
Lieut. James W. D. West	31/ 3/43	N. Africa.
Lieut. Bertram J. Westnedge	16/ 5/44	Italy.
Lieut. Robin C. J. Whitehead	20/ 6/44	Italy.
Lieut. Henry T. Whiter	7/ 7/44	Italy.
Lieut. Patrick J. Wilding	22/ 6/44	Italy.
Major Gilbert C. Williams	23/12/44	Holland.
Major David O. Wilson	30/11/41	Middle East.
Lieut. James W. Wright	24/ 6/44	France.
2/Lieut. Peter A. L. Wright	21/11/41	Middle East.
Lieut. Eric R. Yetman, M.C.	9/ 4/45	Germany.

OTHER RANKS

6857015	Rfn. Joseph Abrahams	17/ 8/44	N.W. Europe.
6921174	Rfn. Michael Abrahams	14/11/42	At sea.
6922005	Rfn. Cyril H. Abram	23/10/42	Norway.
14220452	Rfn. Leslie C. Adams	22/ 6/44	Italy.
5908903	Clr.-Sgt. William L. Adams	24/ 6/43	S. Tunisia.
6924146	Cpl. John W. G. Akers	27/ 2/45	U.K.
6968054	Cpl. Douglas E. Allardyce	5/ 4/43	S. Tunisia.
1709185	Rfn. Maurice F. Allcorn	13/12/44	Italy.
6919133	Rfn. Joseph W. Allen	31/ 1/41	U.K.
14229096	Rfn. William Allen	28/ 8/44	Italy.

APPENDICES

Name.		Date and Place.	
6924148	Rfn. Bertram W. G. Allin	9/ 1/43	N. Africa.
5571014	Rfn. John T. Amer	1/ 5/45	N.W. Europe.
6918069	Rfn. Thomas G. Ames	23/10/42	Egypt.
4123883	Rfn. Ronald Anderson	12/ 6/42	Egypt.
4078073	Rfn. Wilfred Andrews	25/10/44	S. Africa.
6915018	Rfn. Frederick G. H. H. Archer	1/ 5/45	N.W. Europe.
6970024	Rfn. John V. Armstrong	3/ 9/44	N.W. Europe.
5555604	Cpl. Albert T. Arrowsmith	30/ 6/44	N.W. Europe.
7605590	Rfn. Leslie Ashford	9/ 9/44	Italy.
6917002	Rfn. Kenneth A. S. Atkins	21/11/41	Egypt.
6923194	Rfn. Charles S. Attfield	30/ 4/43	S. Tunisia.
14390959	Rfn. Rex. Austin	4/ 9/44	Italy.
6146031	L./Cpl. Eric W. Axam	8/ 5/43	S. Tunisia.
4131174	Rfn. Frederick R. Back	22/12/42	Egypt.
6914120	Rfn. Ernest B. Bacon	26/ 5/40	Calais.
6910651	Cpl. Reginald Bacon	3/ 4/41	U.K.
6922095	Rfn. Albert W. Bailey	1/ 1/43	N. Africa.
6968207	Rfn. Joseph Bailey	20/ 2/43	N. Africa.
6918075	Rfn. Leonard G. Bailey	1/ 9/42	Egypt.
6846909	Rfn. Phillip J. J. Bailey	6/ 4/45	N.W. Europe.
6916088	Rfn. Frederick Bainbridge	22/ 1/41	Egypt.
6348579	Sgt. Edward A. Baker	26/ 6/44	Italy.
6916924	Cpl. Reginald H. H. Baker	31/ 8/42	Egypt.
14410082	Rfn. Douglas W. H. Balaam	26/ 6/44	N.W. Europe.
D/39217	Rfn. Joseph Balbi	7/ 8/44	At sea.
14220469	L./Cpl. Robert J. Balchin	26/ 6/44	N.W. Europe.
6970028	Rfn. Edward J. Baldock	7/ 3/43	N. Africa.
6912180	L./Cpl. Edward P. Baldwin	3/ 6/42	Egypt.
6922019	L./Cpl. Anthony S. Ball	28/ 6/43	U.K.
14228228	Rfn. Bernard A. Ball	28/ 8/44	Italy.
6917714	Rfn. William H. Banks	31/ 5/42	Egypt.
6967465	Rfn. Thomas Bannister	11/ 3/42	Egypt.
5344046	Rfn. Alfred E. Barber	31/ 3/43	S. Tunisia.
6921747	Rfn. William G. Barber	22/10/44	Italy.
6924155	L./Cpl. William J. Barber	16/ 5/44	Italy.
6850096	Rfn. Harry Barleycorn	15/12/45	U.K.
6911598	R.S.M. Frederick W. Barlow	25/10/42	Egypt.
6921749	Rfn. Thomas J. Barnes	23/ 9/44	N.W. Europe.
6970504	Rfn. Jack E. Barnston	17/ 2/40	U.K.
6971182	L./Cpl. Peter C. Barrand	14/11/41	Egypt.
6921569	Rfn. William J. Barrett	11/ 9/41	U.K.
6913008	Sgt. Joseph Bartlett	16/ 6/42	Egypt.
14416730	Rfn. Wilson G. Bartlett	19/ 5/45	U.K.
6913941	Rfn. Frank E. Batt	29/10/42	Egypt.
6916097	Rfn. George H. Bayley	11/ 1/42	Egypt.
6969905	Rfn. John Beach	1/12/44	N. Africa.
6919554	Rfn. Albert H. Bears	26/ 6/44	N.W. Europe.
6918080	Rfn. John H. Beasley	8/ 9/42	Egypt.
6916079	Rfn. Louis Beavois	21/ 1/42	Egypt.
6924434	Rfn. Frederick D. B. Bedford	24/10/42	U.K.
6853280	Cpl. Charles J. Beer	17/ 4/45	N.W. Europe.
6920786	Rfn. Norman J. Benner	18/ 3/44	U.K.
6970132	Rfn. Bernard A. F. Bennett	10/ 6/44	Italy.
6916100	Rfn. Harold T. Bennett	12/ 6/42	Egypt.

The Rifle Brigade

Name.		Date and Place.	
6922107	Rfn. Thomas C. Berg	9/ 5/43	N. Africa.
6970133	Rfn. Alfred W. Bergstrom	18/ 7/44	Italy.
6916299	Rfn. Louis Berkovitch	22/ 2/45	Italy.
14435118	Rfn. George Berry	6/ 4/45	N.W. Europe.
6969162	Rfn. Gerald H. Berry	1/ 4/41	Egypt.
6850120	Rfn. Richard J. Bevan	4/ 6/44	Italy.
6969275	Rfn. Frank E. Beviss	26/ 6/44	N.W. Europe.
6915429	Rfn. James S. Bilham	19/ 6/41	Egypt.
6970134	Sgt. Frederick L. Billingham	9/ 4/43	N. Africa.
692383	Rfn. John E. Billingham	25/ 5/40	Calais.
6970384	Rfn. Eric T. G. Binstead	10/ 9/44	N.W. Europe.
6913393	Rfn. Douglas L. Bird	9/12/41	At sea.
6969450	Cpl. Reginald D. Bird	12/ 4/43	N. Africa.
6898762	Cpl. William Birleson	23/ 9/44	N.W. Europe.
6969796	Cpl. Peter G. Bisset	28/ 6/44	N.W. Europe.
14426879	Rfn. William J. Bissmire	4/ 7/44	N.W. Europe.
6911195	Rfn. Thomas Blackburn	26/10/40	U.K.
6846996	Rfn. Frederick B. J. Blackhall	20/ 1/45	N.W. Europe.
14427073	Rfn. John A. B. Blake	29/ 3/45	N.W. Europe.
6912156	Rfn. Robert H. Bland	23/ 5/40	Calais.
6916949	Cpl. Albert L. Block	17/ 5/44	Italy.
6208451	Rfn. Robert Blogg	2/ 2/43	Libya.
6921768	Rfn. Edward S. Bloomfield	21/10/44	N.W. Europe.
6969278	Rfn. Gordon L. Blyth	30/10/44	N.W. Europe.
6912597	Rfn. John E. Blythe	12/12/40	Calais.
6916103	Rfn. Thomas P. Blythe	13/ 8/42	Egypt.
6919567	Cpl. Joseph J. Bocking	1/ 2/45	N.W. Europe.
6921209	Rfn. John H. Boorman	31/10/43	Italy.
6915647	Rfn. Leopold W. H. Booth	8/11/44	N.W. Europe.
6971230	Rfn. Sam Borman	28/ 6/44	Italy.
6969280	Rfn. Albert A. Botfield	27/ 6/44	N.W. Europe.
6968254	Sgt. Eric H. Botting	25/10/42	Egypt.
6914776	Rfn. Alfred Boulden	7/ 4/41	Egypt.
6921212	Rfn. Frederick W. Bower	27/ 3/43	S. Tunisia.
6911829	Rfn. Patrick Bowler	9/12/41	At sea.
6913263	Rfn. Jack C. Bowley	26/ 5/40	Calais.
6918089	L./Sgt. Frederick O. Bowsher	29/ 5/42	Egypt.
6913264	Sgt. Graham C. Bradbury, M.M.	25/10/42	Egypt.
6918090	Rfn. Thomas W. Bradbury	1/ 6/43	Egypt.
6918091	L./Sgt. George F. M. Brand	20/ 2/43	Libya.
6918595	Cpl. Sidney A. Brandon	23/10/44	Italy.
6924044	Rfn. George Brannon	20/ 6/44	Italy.
6917730	Rfn. Edgar M. Bream	13/ 6/44	N.W. Europe.
6969114	Rfn. Michael D. Breen	11/ 7/43	S. Tunisia.
14420451	L./Cpl. Ernest G. F. Brewer	27/ 1/46	U.K.
6924045	Rfn. Leonard E. Brice	11/ 8/44	Italy.
7019149	Rfn. John Brien	9/ 9/44	Italy.
6913528	Rfn. William V. Brindley	22/ 2/41	Libya.
6561960	Sgt. Francis H. H. Brine	3/11/42	Egypt.
6968554	Sgt. Frederick W. Brittain	5/ 4/43	S. Tunisia.
7017973	Rfn. Victor C. Brondle	29/ 9/44	Italy.
14389952	Rfn. George W. Brooks	23/12/44	Italy.
6915897	Rfn. John Brooks	8/ 8/42	U.K.
6921785	Rfn. Timothy E. Brophy	26/ 6/44	N.W. Europe.

APPENDICES

Name.	Date and Place.	
6856384 Rfn. Cyril D. Brown	29/ 5/44	Italy.
6917733 Rfn. David W. Brown	12/11/42	Egypt.
6913230 Rfn. Ernest W. Brown	24/ 5/40	Calais.
6913630 Rfn. Henry Brown	26/12/40	Egypt.
6923225 Rfn. Henry E. Brown	27/ 9/44	Italy.
6917734 Rfn. Henry G. Brown	26/10/42	Egypt.
6914781 Rfn. Herbert G. R. Brown	12/ 7/41	S. Africa.
14324938 Rfn. Sidney W. Brown	8/ 9/43	U.K.
7017972 L./Cpl. William J. Brown	28/ 8/44	Italy.
6912447 L./Cpl. Omar A. Browne	21/11/41	Egypt.
6922411 Rfn. Reginald Browne	19/ 9/44	Italy.
6911962 Rfn. Mark Bryce	24/ 5/40	Calais.
5674468 Rfn. Kenneth S. Budd	9/11/41	U.K.
6916108 Sgt. William H. Bull	29/ 4/43	S. Tunisia.
5681684 Rfn. John W. J. Burborough	12/ 6/42	Egypt.
6922945 L./Cpl. Allen J. Burian	26/ 6/44	Italy.
6916439 Rfn. James W. Burleigh	14/ 4/43	S. Tunisia.
6968046 Rfn. Albert Burls	10/ 8/43	U.K.
6924867 L./Cpl. Frank E. Burn	26/ 6/44	Italy.
6921794 Rfn. Frederick J. Burn	2/11/42	Egypt.
692131 Rfn. Charles R. Burnham	24/10/42	Egypt.
14671526 Rfn. Frederick Busby	6/ 4/45	N.W. Europe.
6917741 Rfn. Frederick T. Butcher	28/ 2/43	S. Tunisia.
6924460 Rfn. John J. Butler	21/ 6/44	Italy.
6923233 Rfn. Albert P. Butterworth	22/ 6/44	Italy.
14590248 Rfn. Ernest Caddet	21/ 2/45	Italy.
6924461 L./Cpl. David Cahill	26/ 7/44	Italy.
6915903 Rfn. William P. Cahill	3/11/42	Egypt.
6970276 L./Cpl. Lionel R. Callow	20/ 7/44	Italy.
6968695 Rfn. Aubrey C. Calvert	14/ 6/42	Egypt.
6917743 Rfn. Frederick W. Campbell	20/10/42	Egypt.
6913818 Rfn. John R. Campbell	31/10/42	Egypt.
6968058 Cpl. Horace E. J. Cann, M.M.	10/ 6/44	Italy.
6922960 Rfn. Arthur J. Carneham	2/ 2/45	U.K.
6921648 Rfn. Felix Carpenter	1/ 4/41	Egypt.
14666076 Rfn. John A. Carpenter	4/ 9/44	N.W. Europe.
6918602 Rfn. William G. Carpenter	29/ 5/44	Italy.
6924464 Rfn. Bernard W. Carroll	21/ 9/44	Italy.
6915439 Rfn. Stanley J. Cart	7/ 4/41	Egypt.
6912999 Sgt. Cyril H. Carter	28/ 3/45	N.W. Europe.
6915270 Cpl. Royston Carter	7/ 4/41	Egypt.
3914834 Rfn. Reginald V. Cartledge	2/11/42	Egypt.
6911306 Rfn. Joseph E. Case	15/10/39	France.
4132950 Rfn. George Casey	18/ 3/44	Middle East.
6912978 Rfn. John W. Cave	4/10/39	U.K.
6968945 L./Cpl. Horace H. Chadwick	1/ 4/41	Middle East.
7018239 Cpl. Francis A. Chalk	20/ 6/44	Italy.
6914450 Rfn. James C. Chalmers	26/ 5/40	Calais.
6700386 Sgt. Robert T. Chambers	23/11/41	Egypt.
6354950 Rfn. Sydney J. Chambers	18/ 7/44	Italy.
6921811 Rfn. Richard W. Chandler	16/ 5/44	Italy.
6913616 Rfn. Arnold P. Chapman	13/ 9/40	Egypt.
7017985 L./Cpl. Herbert S. Chapman	6/ 7/44	Italy.
14424202 Rfn. Alfred Cherry	10/ 6/44	N.W. Europe.

Name.		Date and Place.	
6914270	Rfn. James E. Chipp	26/10/44	Italy.
6970206	Sgt. Leonard L. Chipperfield	16/ 5/44	Italy.
6913639	Rfn. William E. Chipperfield	22/11/41	Egypt.
6918109	Rfn. William E. Chivers	13/ 6/42	Egypt.
14431700	Rfn. Cyril J. Chugg	11/ 8/44	N.W. Europe.
6970040	Cpl. Albert J. Clapp	19/ 5/42	U.K.
6912943	Rfn. Alfred R. Clarey	9/ 4/43	S. Tunisia.
6898614	Cpl. William J. Clark	24/ 9/44	N.W. Europe.
6917750	Cpl. Charles T. Clarke	23/10/42	Egypt.
6968826	L./Cpl. Norman Clarke	7/ 4/41	Middle East.
6924884	Rfn. Ronald C. W. Clarke	11/ 9/44	N.W. Europe.
6912918	L./Cpl. Walter G. Clarke	3/11/42	Egypt.
6913669	Cpl. Walter L. H. Clarke	12/ 1/42	Egypt.
6910840	Rfn. George Clements	2/ 6/40	B.E.F.
6916813	Rfn. Gastone Clermont	23/ 9/44	N.W. Europe.
6920081	Rfn. James Clift	7/ 8/44	At sea.
6915907	Rfn. Alfred J. Clifton	3/11/42	Egypt.
6917753	Cpl. Gerrard H. Clinton	2/ 3/43	S. Tunisia.
6919813	Rfn. William G. Coates	29/ 7/44	N.W. Europe.
6914530	Rfn. William D. Cobbett	26/12/41	Italy.
D/41329	Rfn. Frederick W. Coe	20/12/42	U.K.
6404498	Rfn. Dennis Coffee	2/ 8/44	N.W. Europe.
6913792	Rfn. Albert Cohen	17/ 9/40	Egypt.
6970047	Rfn. William G. Coker	7/ 3/43	N. Africa.
6921826	Rfn. Frederick C. Cole	20/ 6/44	Italy.
6913899	Rfn. Frederick G. Cole	26/ 1/40	Egypt.
6914599	Rfn. Roy Cole	22/11/41	Egypt.
14427990	Rfn. Frank E. Coleman	13/ 6/44	N.W. Europe.
6911245	Rfn. Benjamin W. Collier	10/ 9/44	N.W. Europe.
6917758	Rfn. Charles F. Collier	29/ 5/42	Egypt.
6895621	Rfn. Henry C. Collier	17/10/44	N.W. Europe.
6969699	Cpl. Harold G. Collingwood	29/ 6/44	N.W. Europe.
6915909	Cpl. Albert H. Collins	16/ 6/44	Italy.
14421518	Rfn. George J. Collins	19/ 7/44	N.W. Europe.
14259995	L./Cpl. Reginald W. Collis	1/ 1/45	Greece.
6967526	Rfn. Harold J. Comer	16/ 5/44	Italy.
6967010	Sgt. George H. Conlan	4/ 6/44	Italy.
6969573	Sgt. Robert W. Connelly	17/ 4/45	N.W. Europe.
6968206	Sgt. Charles F. Conus	10/ 6/44	Italy.
6914802	Cpl. William Conway	20/ 5/42	At sea.
6911800	Sgt. George C. Cooper	20/ 5/42	At sea.
6914100	Rfn. Wilfred W. Cooper	26/ 5/40	Calais.
6970052	Rfn. William Cooper	21/ 2/45	Italy.
14425256	Rfn. Daniel F. Coopey	3/ 9/44	N.W. Europe.
6918118	Rfn. James C. Copley	10/ 5/42	At sea.
6919206	Rfn. Charles E. E. Cormeau	24/11/40	U.K.
6969527	Rfn. John W. Corsie	14/ 8/44	N.W. Europe.
6911801	Rfn. Jack W. Cottell	26/ 5/40	Calais.
6914806	Rfn. Robert Cottrell	23/ 2/41	Libya.
6918612	Cpl. Walter A. Coulthard	31/ 3/43	S. Tunisia.
6915916	Cpl. Ernest S. Coward	8/ 7/44	Italy.
6922991	Rfn. William E. Cowlard	9/ 4/43	N. Africa.
6917008	Rfn. William G. Cowling	18/12/45	N.W. Europe.
6920635	Rfn. Anthony F. Cox	18/ 7/43	Middle East.

Name.		Date and Place.
6969175 Cpl. Charles E. Cox	4/ 4/41	Middle East.
6921843 Rfn. Harry T. Cox	16/ 4/45	N.W. Europe.
6913651 Rfn. Leslie H. R. Cox	21/ 3/43	S. Tunisia.
6919598 L./Cpl. William L. Craggs	19/ 8/42	Dieppe.
6970053 Rfn. Ernest W. Crane	6/ 4/41	Cyrenaica.
6917768 Rfn. Herbert Cranfield	25/ 7/42	Egypt.
6914607 Rfn. Edward J. Crawford	27/ 3/43	S. Tunisia.
6916448 Rfn. Joseph Crawford	25/10/42	Egypt.
6970210 Rfn. Ronald C. H. Cregan	20/ 1/43	N. Africa.
6968176 Rfn. Philip D. Crimmins	20/ 3/40	U.K.
6921849 Rfn. Herbert G. Crisp	16/ 4/45	N.W. Europe.
6912077 L./Cpl. Gilbert D. Cross	24/ 5/40	Calais.
6925196 Rfn. John T. Crotch	5/ 6/44	Italy.
6925065 Rfn. William G. Crowhurst	29/ 5/44	Italy.
1781642 Rfn. Cyril Crump	13/12/44	Italy.
6969702 Cpl. Stephen R. Culnane	7/ 4/45	N.W. Europe.
6911461 Sgt. Leonard F. Cumbers	25/ 5/40	Calais.
6969405 Rfn. Charles E. Cummings	30/ 7/44	Italy.
6969870 Rfn. George A. Cummins	23/ 7/42	Egypt.
6912829 Sgt. Eddy Cunningham, M.M.	30/ 4/43	Tunisia.
6916844 Rfn. Ronald H. Currell	1/ 7/45	N.W. Europe.
6913296 L./Cpl. Leopold Curtain	9/12/41	At sea.
14260258 Rfn. Francis W. Curthoys	1/ 8/44	Italy.
6919604 Rfn. Frederick J. Curtis	7/ 8/44	At sea.
6916449 Rfn. Frank W. Cushion	21/ 6/44	Italy.
6922152 Rfn. William D. Daly	21/ 7/44	Italy.
14407942 Rfn. Denis J. Daniels	6/ 7/44	Italy.
6922153 Rfn. Charles R. Darvill	27/ 6/44	N.W. Europe.
6916846 Rfn. Henry J. Darville	19/ 1/42	At sea.
6924188 Rfn. James K. Dart	23/ 4/44	N. Africa.
3535359 Rfn. George Davenport	3/ 9/44	N.W. Europe.
6921856 Cpl. Aneurin Davies	28/ 7/44	Italy.
14224020 Rfn. David Davies	29/ 8/44	Italy.
1817045 Rfn. Elwyn Davies	3/10/44	Italy.
6919610 Rfn. William D. Davies	24/ 3/43	S. Tunisia.
4129726 Rfn. William H. Davies	12/ 5/44	Middle East.
6968344 Rfn. Ronald D. H. Davis	25/10/42	Egypt.
6912869 Cpl. William D. Davis	12/12/41	Egypt.
6923257 L./Cpl. Samuel G. Dawson	20/ 4/45	Italy.
6921278 Rfn. Leonard W. Day	28/ 6/44	N.W. Europe.
6912540 L./Cpl. Frederick A. Dean	23/ 1/41*	Egypt.
6915598 Rfn. Walter S. Dean	24/10/43	Italy.
6845396 Rfn. Arthur Dearman	10/ 9/44	N.W. Europe.
6347854 Rfn. Albert S. Denney	28/ 6/44	N.W. Europe.
6699342 L./Cpl. Edward Dennis	26/10/40	U.K.
6921281 Rfn. Albert S. Desmond	10/ 6/44	Italy.
6916453 Sgt. Edward N. Dicker	26/ 8/44	N.W. Europe.
6924904 Rfn. George F. Dickerson	26/ 7/44	Italy.
6348220 Rfn. Laurie E. A. Diplock	4/ 9/44	N.W. Europe.
6561934 Sgt. William F. Dix	18/ 5/42	U.K.
6912336 Rfn. Bryan D. V. Dixon	24/ 5/40	Calais.
6916864 Rfn. Herbert R. Dobson	21/11/41	Egypt.
6968791 Cpl. Leonard G. Doggett	2/11/42	Egypt.
6923021 Rfn. John P. Donnelly	29/ 5/44	Italy.

Name.	Date and Place.	
6914186 Rfn. Edward A. Donrick	9/ 4/42	Egypt.
6700569 Rfn. Albert J. Dormer	2/ 5/41	Palestine.
6916075 Rfn. John Dorrell	18/ 6/41	Egypt.
6918130 Rfn. Jock Douglas	11/ 6/44	Italy.
6924907 Cpl. Norman A. J. Dowsett	28/ 8/44	Italy.
6968239 Rfn. Albert Drew	6/ 6/42	Egypt.
7017098 Rfn. Joseph A. Driscoll	5/ 7/44	Italy.
14445874 Rfn. Thomas W. Driscoll	27/ 7/44	U.K.
6923030 Rfn. Eric L. Duer	7/ 8/44	N.W. Europe.
6913635 Rfn. Arthur A. J. Dullaway	19/12/41	Egypt.
6924085 Rfn. Albert F. Duncan	14/12/44	Italy.
6914006 Cpl. Albert W. Dunford	19/ 1/42	Middle East.
6912760 L./Cpl. Herbert J. Dungay	24/ 5/40	Calais.
6209427 Rfn. Henry J. Dutton	3/10/43	Italy.
6916877 Cpl. Harry A. Dyer	25/ 7/44	N.W. Europe.
6923263 Rfn. Stanley V. Dyer	8/11/42	Egypt.
6908637 P.S.M. James Easen	26/ 5/40	Calais.
14723014 Rfn. John B. Eaves	8/ 4/45	N.W. Europe.
6911677 Rfn. Albert Edgar	29/ 5/40	At sea.
6921292 Rfn. Harry Edmead	21/ 6/44	Italy.
6969185 L./Cpl. Percy J. Edmonds	7/ 4/41	Middle East.
6912872 Sgt. Stanley C. Edmonds	26/ 6/44	N.W. Europe.
14603917 Rfn. William L. Edmunds	11/ 7/44	N.W. Europe.
6911516 Sgt. Leonard A. N. Edwards	12/ 9/42	At sea.
13028546 Rfn. Stanley O. Edwards	26/ 7/44	Italy.
6214187 Rfn. Stanley W. C. Edwards	22/ 2/43	N. Africa.
6912680 Rfn. Thomas J. Edwards	9/ 5/45	N.W. Europe.
6913957 Rfn. George E. Eggby	28/ 6/44	Italy.
6912983 L./Cpl. Frank W. Eggs	25/11/40	U.K.
6920585 L./Cpl. Richard C. Elliott	23/ 7/42	Egypt.
6969754 Rfn. Joseph Ellis	27/ 4/43	N. Africa.
6916884 Sgt. Robert A. Ellis	2/ 3/45	Italy.
6913500 Rfn. Haydn Ellison	23/ 5/40	Calais.
6921293 Cpl. Edward V. Elsmere, M.M.	24/ 7/44	Italy.
6924503 Rfn. Sydney W. Elson	13/12/44	Italy.
6918704 Rfn. Reginald H. Elvy	19/ 3/41	U.K.
6913038 Rfn. William Elworthy	26/ 4/43	Middle East.
6917800 Cpl. Edwin R. Emes	27/ 6/44	N.W. Europe.
6911371 C.S.M. Alfred Endean, M.M.	24/ 1/42	At sea.
14338522 Rfn. Albert England	13/11/44	N.W. Europe.
6921884 Rfn. Harry England	29/ 4/43	S. Tunisia.
4030961 Rfn. John J. Evans	16/ 7/42	Egypt.
5255746 Rfn. Joseph E. Evans	18/ 6/44	Italy.
3530450 Rfn. Thomas Evans	31/ 3/43	S. Tunisia.
6915793 Rfn. Walter T. Evans	14/ 4/43	N. Africa.
6145835 Rfn. Basil W. Evenett	25/10/42	Egypt.
6970147 Rfn. William J. Everett	29/ 7/44	Italy.
6912321 Cpl. Albert E. Fairman	6/ 4/45	N.W. Europe.
14233223 Rfn. William Familton	21/ 7/44	N.W. Europe.
6923052 Rfn. Alfred J. W. Fardon	11/ 1/43	N. Africa.
2056479 Rfn. Albert Faulks	21/ 6/44	Italy.
765452 Rfn. Frederick J. Fawcett	28/ 5/40	Calais.
6969530 Rfn. Herbert A. Featherstone	13/ 6/42	Egypt.
6920293 Rfn. Geoffrey W. Fenn	20/11/41	Egypt.

APPENDICES

Name.		Date and Place.	
6920294	Rfn. David R. Ferrier	19/ 1/42	At sea.
6912742	Cpl. Sidney Ferris..	22/12/43	N. Africa.
6916895	Rfn. Charles Finch	27/10/42	Egypt.
14494526	Rfn. Lionel F. Finch	20/ 4/45	N.W. Europe.
6845056	Sgt. Robert Finch..	20/ 1/45	N.W. Europe.
6913376	Cpl. Reginald F. Findlater	24/10/42	Egypt.
6921301	Rfn. Alfred H. D. Fisher..	1/ 4/45	N.W. Europe.
6087275	Rfn. Frederick M. Fisher..	13/ 6/42	Egypt.
6920671	Cpl. Gerrard Fitzgerald, M.M. ..	3/ 8/44	N.W. Europe.
6918148	Rfn. Desmond F. Fitzpatrick	18/12/42	Italy.
14582925	Rfn. Cyril W. Flint	8/12/44	Italy.
6914217	Rfn. Edgar J. Flint	27/10/42	Egypt.
6915470	Rfn. John Fogarty	9/ 5/42	Egypt.
5338931	Rfn. Russell Fokes	29/ 7/44	N.W. Europe.
6967972	Rfn. John B. Foley	25/ 5/40	Calais.
6913039	L./Cpl. Herbert C. Ford ..	15/ 9/40	Egypt.
6915075	Rfn. Raymond E. Forster	31/ 1/40	U.K.
5945849	L./Cpl. Sidney P. Foster ..	19/ 9/44	N.W. Europe.
6921478	Rfn. Victor W. Foster	12/ 4/42	U.K.
6919613	Rfn. Henry J. Fowler	25/ 6/42	Egypt.
5386586	Rfn. Joseph W. Fowler	27/ 4/45	Italy.
6914626	Rfn. Reginald F. Fowler ..	21/ 6/42	Egypt.
6920213	Rfn. William C. Fox	23/ 2/44	U.K.
6913368	Cpl. Joseph Franklin	27/ 2/45	Germany.
6911189	Cpl. David Frazer	22/ 5/40	Calais.
6915305	L./Cpl. Alfred Fredericks	26/ 1/42	Egypt.
6969195	Rfn. Harry Freshwater	30/12/42	N. Africa.
5391946	Rfn. Kenneth F. Frost	14/12/44	Italy.
6917038	Rfn. Gordon R. Fry	18/ 7/44	Italy.
6924520	Rfn. Godwin E. Fryer	10/ 8/44	Italy.
6913575	Rfn. Hubert Gaffey	23/ 5/40	Calais.
6920305	Rfn. George A. Gale	1/ 9/42	Egypt.
6916462	Rfn. Trevor Gallozzie	26/ 4/43	S. Tunisia.
6913006	Cpl. Arthur H. Galt	22/11/41	Egypt.
6918151	Rfn. Sidney A. Gamble ..	12/ 6/42	Egypt.
7017788	Rfn. Edward J. Gardiner..	21/ 6/44	Italy.
14229515	Rfn. Frank Gardner	26/ 8/44	N.W. Europe.
6921313	Rfn. Norman F. Gardner	30/ 7/44	Italy.
6923285	Rfn. Percy Gash ..	13/ 6/44	N.W. Europe.
5675735	Rfn. Ronald G. Gathercole	7/ 7/44	Italy.
6916957	Cpl. George J. W. Gay ..	22/ 4/45	Italy.
6969260	Cpl. Sidney T. George	5/ 5/43	S. Tunisia.
6968588	Rfn. Clement K. Gibbs	11/ 1/45	Italy.
6919623	Rfn. Charles H. Gibson ..	16/ 6/42	Egypt.
6915306	Rfn. Alfred G. Gidley	19/10/40	U.K.
6969759	Cpl. Charles E. Gilbey	1/ 8/44	Italy.
14490175	Rfn. Derek T. Gilburt	8/ 2/45	U.K.
6914164	Rfn. Sidney R. Giles	3/12/41	Egypt.
6970562	Sgt. Duncan Gillibrand ..	29/ 4/43	S. Tunisia.
6912379	Rfn. Malcolm W. Gillies..	11/ 5/43	N. Africa.
6924097	L./Sgt. Arthur Gillings, M.M. ..	19/ 8/44	N.W. Europe.
6915083	Rfn. Leslie L. Gipps	19/ 1/42	At sea.
7018018	Cpl. Alfred T. Godley	13/12/44	Italy.
6921322	L./Cpl. Cecil Golby	1/ 9/44	Italy.

2F

Name.		Date and Place.	
14514284	Rfn. Maurice Goldstein	3/ 9/44	N.W. Europe.
6915727	Rfn. Herbert Goodman	1/ 2/44	Italy.
6921327	Rfn. Walter L. Goodwin	1/ 9/44	N.W. Europe.
6921925	Rfn. William C. Gossington	16/ 5/44	Italy.
3536352	Rfn. Robert D. Goulden	11/ 6/44	Italy.
6921926	Rfn. John F. Govey	7/ 7/44	Italy.
6924531	Rfn. Arthur Gowers	3/10/44	Italy.
6967463	Rfn. James R. Grant	2/ 8/44	N.W. Europe.
6970392	Cpl. Dennis V. Gray	25/10/42	Egypt.
6922215	Rfn. George W. Grayson	19/ 7/44	N.W. Europe.
6914640	L./Sgt. George Green	11/ 5/43	Tunisia.
14655557	Rfn. George E. C. Green	25/ 8/44	Italy.
6920320	Rfn. John G. Green	27/10/42	Egypt.
6914851	Rfn. Maurice Greenberg	17/ 6/42	Egypt.
6968139	Cpl. Ronald Greenfield	6/ 4/41	Egypt.
6968357	Sgt. Maurice K. Greenwood	12/12/44	Italy.
6912806	L./Cpl. Richard W. Greenwood	12/ 8/44	Italy.
6911656	Rfn. Frederick Gregory	28/ 1/43	U.K.
6923293	Rfn. David J. A. Griffin	25/10/42	Egypt.
4863223	Rfn. Harry Griffiths	31/ 3/43	S. Tunisia.
3527702	Rfn. John F. Griffiths	27/ 6/40	Egypt.
6923091	Rfn. William O. Griffiths	10/ 3/43	N. Africa.
6924212	Cpl. John W. Grimes	25/ 4/43	N. Africa.
6923093	Rfn. Jack Grossman	31/ 7/44	N.W. Europe.
7018279	Rfn. Albert E. Groves	8/ 7/44	Italy.
4858000	Rfn. Ernest Gulliver	20/ 6/44	Italy.
6898375	Sgt. Harold E. Gutteridge	20/ 4/45	N.W. Europe.
6921339	Rfn. Arthur S. Guyton	31/ 3/43	S. Tunisia.
6913828	Rfn. Samuel Guzzan	26/10/42	Egypt.
6916470	Rfn. Felix B. Habets	29/ 4/43	S. Tunisia.
6214746	Rfn. Arthur D. Hall	20/ 8/44	N.W. Europe.
6924936	Rfn. Charles A. Hall	7/11/44	N.W. Europe.
5255769	Rfn. Dennis Hall	18/ 9/40	U.K.
6970077	Rfn. George W. Hall	11/ 9/42	U.K.
2082909	Rfn. Jack Hallas	3/10/44	Italy.
6917059	Rfn. Thomas G. Halverson	17/ 8/42	Italy.
6912019	Rfn. Joseph Hamblin	23/ 5/40	Calais.
14440952	Rfn. Neville E. R. Hammond	21/ 8/44	N.W. Europe.
6918731	Cpl. Arthur Hamnett	21/ 1/43	N. Africa.
6969820	Sgt. Frank E. Hancock	6/ 4/45	N.W. Europe.
6970078	Rfn. Donald R. Handley	29/ 5/44	Italy.
6921344	Rfn. Stanley Hann	24/ 3/43	S. Tunisia.
6917837	Sgt. Peter F. Hansen	4/10/43	Italy.
14497417	Rfn. George Harbott	23/ 6/45	N.W. Europe.
6970219	Rfn. Alfred C. Harding	20/ 3/41	U.K.
6970159	Rfn. Arthur Harding	14/ 6/44	N.W. Europe.
6918734	Rfn. Percy H. J. Hardwick	7/12/44	Italy.
6916173	Cpl. Frederick B. Hardy	6/11/44	Italy.
6915947	Rfn. Robert Harford	31/ 7/44	N.W. Europe.
6914339	Sgt. Leonard Harle	4/11/42	Egypt.
6969306	Clr.-Sgt. Frederick E. Harlock	17/ 9/44	Italy.
6914860	Cpl. David J. Harris	25/10/42	Egypt.
14236628	Rfn. Frederick Harris	11/12/44	Italy.
6918168	Rfn. Leslie Harris	9/ 1/43	N. Africa.

APPENDICES

Name.		Date and Place.	
6915725 Rfn. Pinkus Harris	.. ..	26/10/44	Italy.
6921349 Rfn. Thomas G. Harris	.. ..	25/10/42	Egypt.
6912628 Rfn. George A. Hart	.. ..	16/ 9/40	Egypt.
6911762 Rfn. John Hart	.. ..	7/ 3/40	U.K.
14415491 Rfn. Ernest V. Harvey	.. ..	6/ 9/44	Italy.
6910223 C.S.M. Jesse H. Harvey	.. ..	12/ 9/42	At sea.
6921945 Rfn. Reginald V. Harvey	.. ..	12/ 1/43	N. Africa.
14423075 Rfn. Cyril Harwood	.. ..	26/ 7/44	N.W. Europe.
6920232 Cpl. John J. Harwood	.. ..	13/ 6/42	Egypt.
6923309 Rfn. John A. Hassell	.. ..	22/ 2/45	Italy.
6912050 Rfn. Hubert S. Hawdon	.. ..	7/ 2/41	Libya.
6925232 Rfn. William Hawkins	.. ..	2/12/44	N.W. Europe.
6915869 Rfn. William F. Hawkins	.. ..	28/ 5/44	Italy.
6145867 Rfn. John Hayes	.. ..	8/ 5/43	Egypt.
6921950 Rfn. Ronald L. Haynes	.. ..	25/ 7/44	N.W. Europe.
6924113 Rfn. Frederick G. Haynes	.. ..	29/ 5/44	Italy.
14432662 Rfn. James N. Hayward	.. ..	10/ 6/44	N.W. Europe.
6921952 Rfn. Jack Heald	.. ..	3/11/42	Egypt.
5388247 Rfn. William Hedges	.. ..	10/ 6/44	Italy.
6971212 L./Cpl. William C. Heiden	.. ..	3/ 8/44	N.W. Europe.
6917182 Rfn. Frederick C. Hellems	.. ..	10/ 5/41	U.K.
7018285 Rfn. Henry P. Hemmings	.. ..	23/ 8/44	Italy.
6921955 Cpl. Edward M. Henegan	.. ..	31/ 7/44	N.W. Europe.
6918174 Rfn. John H. Hennah	.. ..	31/ 5/42	Egypt.
6967192 Rfn. John S. Hersey	.. ..	7/ 4/41	Egypt.
6969711 Rfn. Geoffrey W. Heslington	.. ..	23/ 7/44	N.W. Europe.
6896364 Rfn. Sidney Hewitt	.. ..	20/ 7/44	N.W. Europe.
6915775 Rfn. Albert T. Hierons	.. ..	10/ 9/44	Italy.
6967088 Rfn. Edwin G. Higgins	.. ..	7/ 8/44	N.W. Europe.
6924223 Rfn. John W. Higgs	.. ..	9/ 5/43	N. Africa.
6923117 Rfn. Benjamin Highbloom	.. ..	18/ 1/43	N. Africa.
6215149 Rfn. Leonard C. Hill	.. ..	22/12/43	N. Africa.
6923315 Cpl. George W. Hillman	.. ..	9/ 8/44	N.W. Europe.
6968360 Rfn. William P. Hills	.. ..	29/ 8/44	Italy.
6917185 Rfn. Albert W. Hine	.. ..	20/ 5/45	U.K.
6967145 Sgt. George J. Hines, M.M.	.. ..	10/ 6/44	N.W. Europe.
7017798 Rfn. Edwin A. H. Hitt	.. ..	20/ 6/44	Italy.
6913215 Rfn. Edgar J. Hobson	.. ..	6/ 2/41	Libya.
6914457 Rfn. Edward B. Hockley	.. ..	28/ 5/40	Calais.
6919648 Rfn. Frederick Hodges	.. ..	27/ 3/43	S. Tunisia.
6921969 Rfn. Harry Hodson	.. ..	10/ 4/43	N. Africa.
14419119 Rfn. Raymond K. Hoer	.. ..	14/ 6/44	N.W. Europe.
14355001 Cpl. Leonard M. Hogger	.. ..	4/ 1/45	N.W. Europe.
6915806 L./Cpl. Victor A. Holland	.. ..	7/ 4/45	N.W. Europe.
6917854 Rfn. Thomas M. Holliday	.. ..	29/ 4/44	Egypt.
6969878 Rfn. Cecil R. Holmes	.. ..	15/ 4/45	N.W. Europe.
6850838 Rfn. Richard H. Holmes	.. ..	30/ 7/44	Italy.
6852387 Rfn. Francis G. J. Holt	.. ..	18/12/45	N.W. Europe.
6920123 Rfn. Thomas H. Homer	.. ..	28/ 5/42	Egypt.
5543241 Cpl. Alexander G. Hone	.. ..	24/ 9/44	N.W. Europe.
6921981 Rfn. Peter B. Hono	.. ..	20/ 2/43	N. Africa.
607215 Rfn. Alexander G. Hooper	.. ..	28/ 1/44	Italy.
6919656 Rfn. Frederick W. Hooper	.. ..	13/ 9/44	U.K.
6919655 Rfn. Harry Hooper	.. ..	25/11/42	N. Africa.

Name.		Date and Place.	
6857482	Rfn. Herbert W. Hopper	17/10/44	N.W. Europe.
6924122	Rfn. Thomas Hopson	18/ 7/44	N.W. Europe.
6924950	Rfn. Edward R. Horne	20/ 6/44	Italy.
6920330	Rfn. Sidney R. Hornett	23/11/41	Egypt.
7018031	L./Cpl. Frederick W. Hornsby	2/ 5/45	Germany.
6918183	Rfn. Leslie G. T. Hornsey	3/11/44	N.W. Europe.
4132586	Rfn. Horace Hough	3/11/42	Egypt.
6920331	Cpl. Thomas R. Hough	13/12/44	Italy.
6921981	Rfn. Peter B. How	20/ 2/43	N. Africa.
6917191	Rfn. Alfred E. Howard	1/12/42	N. Africa.
14426310	Rfn. Alexander P. W. Howard	11/ 6/44	N.W. Europe.
6857485	Rfn. Thomas H. Howard	3/ 8/44	N.W. Europe.
6915102	Rfn. George W. Howell	3/ 6/42	Egypt.
6923320	Rfn. John T. Huckle	17/10/44	N.W. Europe.
6918186	Rfn. Edward W. Huggett	8/ 9/42	Egypt.
6913741	L./Cpl. Gordon G. Huggett	22/11/41	Egypt.
6145875	Sgt. Sidney C. Huggett	20/ 6/44	Italy.
6967593	Rfn. Edward G. Hulme-Jones	2/11/42	Egypt.
6922248	L./Sgt. Bernard H. Hume	19/11/43	Italy.
6916723	Rfn. William J. Hunt	29/ 6/44	N.W. Europe.
6912851	Sgt. William J. Hunt	12/ 9/42	At sea.
6968214	L./Cpl. John E. Hunter	13/ 9/43	Italy.
6916486	Rfn. Charles Hurd	20/ 6/44	Italy.
6915781	Rfn. Reginald S. Hurle	24/10/42	Egypt.
6969585	L./Cpl. Arthur S. Hutcherson	28/ 6/44	N.W. Europe.
3600526	Sgt. Arthur Hutchinson	29/11/42	Egypt.
6208463	Rfn. Henry W. Hutton	3/11/42	Egypt.
6846626	Rfn. Henry H. Hyde	10/ 9/44	N.W. Europe.
6915964	Rfn. Douglas Ingram	27/ 7/42	Egypt.
6921377	Rfn. Robert W. Innell	18/ 6/44	Italy.
6970396	Cpl. Hubert E. Isard	19/ 7/44	N.W. Europe.
6969880	Rfn. Noel Isham	30/ 8/44	N.W. Europe.
6967477	Sgt. James P. Jack	3/11/42	Egypt.
6968128	Rfn. Cyril C. Jackson	28/ 3/45	N.W. Europe.
6844807	L./Sgt. Leslie Jackson	22/11/41	Egypt.
6211077	Rfn. Albert E. James	20/ 2/43	N. Africa.
5572258	Rfn. John W. James	6/ 4/45	N.W. Europe.
6913409	Rfn. Reginald F. James	21/ 9/40	Egypt.
14241997	Rfn. Robert J. James	20/ 6/44	Italy.
6967956	Rfn. William James	1/ 4/41	Cyrenaica.
11405486	Rfn. Harold L. Jarratt	3/10/44	Italy.
6911857	Rfn. George T. Jarrett	14/ 6/42	Egypt.
14236646	Rfn. Samuel E. Jayes	27/ 7/44	Italy.
6914206	Rfn. Leslie Jebb	25/ 5/40	Calais.
6915324	C.S.M. Charles J. Jefford	14/ 6/44	N.W. Europe.
6970221	Sgt. Cecil J. Jeffries	25/ 4/43	N. Africa.
6912477	Rfn. Stanley Jennings	9/ 3/45	Germany.
6924565	Rfn. Christopher Jermy	26/ 8/44	N.W. Europe.
6923153	Rfn. Arthur Jerome	14/ 8/44	N.W. Europe.
6969262	Sgt. Frank H. Jiggins	3/10/43	Italy.
6915106	Sgt. William Jobling	13/ 6/44	Italy.
6911951	Rfn. Frank Johnson	25/ 5/40	Calais.
6916737	Rfn. William C. H. Johnson	13/12/44	Italy.
6792048	P.S.M. Richard A. V. Johnston	25/ 5/40	Calais.

APPENDICES

Name.	Date and Place.	
6913246 Rfn. Stanley C. Johnston..	25/ 5/40	Calais.
6912926 Rfn. Francis M. Jolliffe ..	25/ 5/40	Calais.
14220580 Rfn. Albert E. Jolly	22/ 7/44	Italy.
6915967 Rfn. Charles R. Jones	22/ 7/42	Egypt.
6915690 Rfn. Douglas J. Jones	4/ 5/43	N. Africa.
4122591 Rfn. Herbert G. Jones	28/11/42	Egypt.
6912340 Rfn. Owen G. Jones	23/ 5/40	Calais.
6917208 Rfn. Robert J. Jones	11/ 4/43	N. Africa.
6913383 Rfn. James Jordan	10/ 7/40	Egypt.
6915111 Rfn. John Juch	11/ 4/45	Germany.
6920346 Rfn. Eric Keats	1/ 9/42	Egypt.
6918189 Rfn. Charles Keefe	9/10/43	Italy.
7017168 Rfn. John S. W. Keen	12/ 7/44	Italy.
5382950 Rfn. Reginald C. Keen	28/ 7/44	Italy.
6913961 L./Cpl. John D. Kelly	26/ 5/40	Calais.
6918191 Cpl. Victor C. Kemp	31/ 1/42	At sea.
6914882 Rfn. Sydney A. Kennedy..	6/ 1/42	Egypt.
6924578 Rfn. Roy Kesby	29/ 3/45	N.W. Europe.
6970165 Cpl. John R. Killick	25/ 5/44	Italy.
6968443 Rfn. Alfred P. Killon	12/ 6/42	Egypt.
6925250 Rfn. Albert F. King	31/ 1/45	N.W. Europe.
6915972 Rfn. Arthur R. King	25/10/42	Egypt.
6916751 Rfn. Edward J. King	3/11/42	Egypt.
6968759 Sgt. Eric D. King ..	8/ 1/45	Italy.
6915973 Rfn. Michael G. King	3/11/42	Egypt.
7018305 Sgt. Frederick R. Kingaby	25/ 9/44	Italy.
977147 Rfn. John M. Kirk	26/10/44	Italy.
6846951 Sgt. Charles E. Kitson	18/ 8/44	N.W. Europe.
6916498 Rfn. Kenneth W. G. Knight	6/ 9/44	Italy.
6911122 Sgt. Leslie J. Knight	16/ 5/41	U.K.
6914989 Rfn. George E. Knott	23/ 3/41	Egypt.
6914083 Rfn. Alfred S. Knowles ..	27/12/42	Germany.
6918193 Rfn. Leslie J. R. Kodacz ..	24/10/42	Egypt.
6915117 Rfn. Barnett Kravatsky ..	13/12/44	Italy.
6968795 Cpl. John P. Lacey	31/ 3/43	S. Tunisia.
14434188 Rfn. Edward D. Lagdon ..	29/ 8/44	N.W. Europe.
6202081 Rfn. Albert E. Land	28/12/41	Egypt.
6917369 Sgt. Leonard G. V. Langenschied, M.M.	8/ 4/45	N.W. Europe.
6913358 Rfn. Edward F. Large	24/11/42	Egypt.
6918196 Sgt. Thomas H. M. Lawrence ..	19/ 8/44	N.W. Europe.
6922509 Rfn. Stanley E. Layton	9/ 4/43	N. Africa.
6915975 Rfn. Eric R. Ledford	26/ 4/43	S. Tunisia.
6923340 L./Cpl. Albert E. Lee	31/ 7/44	N.W. Europe.
6912218 Sgt. William W. Lee	30/10/44	N.W. Europe.
5258818 Rfn. Victor Leigh..	28/ 6/45	N.W. Europe.
6914890 Rfn. Ronald J. A. Leon	7/ 6/44	Italy.
6911735 Rfn. John W. Leopard	19/ 1/42	At sea.
6913670 Cpl. Bertram A. J. Leslie..	27/ 3/43	S. Tunisia.
6923345 Rfn. Stanley M. Levine	14/ 6/44	N.W. Europe.
6924983 Cpl. Alfred H. Lewis	13/ 4/45	U.K.
6919837 Rfn. John F. Lewis	12/ 6/42	Egypt.
6912039 Rfn. William E. Lewis	26/ 5/40	Calais.
6912055 Bugler John Lincoln	25/ 5/40	Calais.

Name.		Date and Place.	
14441356	Rfn. Patrick J. Line	11/10/44	N.W. Europe.
14411451	Rfn. Cyril W. F. H. Linsey	23/ 3/44	Burma.
6348456	L./Cpl. Thomas A. Lintott	26/ 4/43	S. Tunisia.
6917384	L./Cpl. Seward J. Lippiatt	2/10/43	Italy.
6912100	Cpl. Stanley R. Littlechild	25/ 5/40	Calais.
6969663	Rfn. George Littlepage	3/ 8/44	N.W. Europe.
14323835	Rfn. John S. Lobar	21/ 6/44	Italy.
6912172	Rfn. Thomas A. Lock	12/ 4/45	N.W. Europe.
6916776	Rfn. William J. Lock	31/ 8/42	Egypt.
6918201	Rfn. Richard W. Long	30/10/41	U.K.
6915980	Rfn. Stanley Long	8/ 7/44	Italy.
6854724	Rfn. Stanley D. Love	15/12/44	Italy.
7017812	L./Cpl. Henry J. Lovell	8/ 7/44	Italy.
6968852	Cpl. Thomas Lovell	13/ 6/44	N.W. Europe.
6922310	Rfn. Thomas G. Lowe	12/ 4/43	N. Africa.
6916780	L./Sgt. Albert E. Lowings	7/ 3/43	N. Africa.
6914227	L./Sgt. James R. G. Lucas	16/ 5/44	Italy.
14233760	Rfn. Albert A. Luchford	18/ 8/44	N.W. Europe.
6911832	L./Sgt. Stanley H. Luchford	26/ 5/40	Calais.
6916783	Rfn. Albert E. Lukey	21/ 1/42	At sea.
6920756	Cpl. Albert W. Lumley	20/ 7/44	N.W. Europe.
6857515	L./Cpl. Francis G. Lynch	18/ 8/44	N.W. Europe.
5255823	Sgt. James Macauley	3/ 9/44	N.W. Europe.
6913776	Rfn. Alfred A. Mackay	4/ 6/44	Italy.
6914237	Rfn. James MacL. Mackay	1/ 4/41	Libya.
6916208	Rfn. James Maddams	13/ 8/40	U.K.
4127604	Rfn. Albert Maddock	13/12/44	Italy.
6923365	L./Cpl. Walter C. Madley	21/ 7/44	N.W. Europe.
6914460	Rfn. John Mahoney	12/ 6/42	Egypt.
6922009	Rfn. Maurice Mahoney	24/ 4/43	N. Africa.
6919677	Rfn. Leopold D. G. Maloney	14/11/42	Egypt.
6916789	Cpl. Ronald J. Manby	1/ 4/45	N.W. Europe.
6912825	Cpl. William J. Manley	20/11/41	Egypt.
6924607	Cpl. Charles G. E. Manners	17/ 7/44	Italy.
6911995	Cpl. Harold W. Marchant	12/ 3/43	N. Africa.
6969335	Rfn. Gordon H. Markham	16/ 4/45	N.W. Europe.
6916513	Rfn. Henry R. Marlow	18/ 2/43	Egypt.
7017820	Rfn. William Marr	2/12/44	Italy.
6923374	Rfn. Albert J. Marsh	30/ 7/44	Italy.
6923376	L./Cpl. Henry T. Marshall	28/ 6/44	N.W. Europe.
1539584	Rfn. Eric P. Marston	30/ 7/44	Italy.
6971151	Rfn. Albert W. Martin	31/ 3/43	S. Tunisia.
6919679	Rfn. Edward E. Martin	12/ 6/42	Egypt.
6970096	Rfn. Frederick Martin	31/ 7/40	U.K.
6916514	Rfn. George Martin	20/ 6/44	Italy.
6916795	Cpl. John R. Martin	21/ 7/44	N.W. Europe.
6970358	Cpl. John P. Maskens	26/ 7/44	N.W. Europe.
6206395	Rfn. George B. Mason	10/ 9/44	N.W. Europe.
14216073	Rfn. Allan W. Masters	14/ 4/43	U.K.
6917410	Rfn. John T. Matthew	31/ 3/43	S. Tunisia.
6968129	Cpl. Gordon H. Matthews	3/11/42	Egypt.
6916596	Rfn. Albert W. May	11/ 8/44	Italy.
6923381	Rfn. Frederick F. May	2/11/42	Egypt.
6923755	L./Cpl. Philip H. May	31/ 7/44	N.W. Europe.

APPENDICES

Name.		Date and Place.
6924614 Rfn. Robert T. May		16/ 5/44 Italy.
6919841 Cpl. Royston McBane		8/12/44 N.W. Europe.
6920904 Rfn. Francis McElroy		11/ 6/44 U.K.
6917400 Rfn. Francis F. McEwan		21/ 9/44 N.W. Europe.
6923361 Rfn. Thomas H. McEwan		9/ 9/44 N.W. Europe.
6967816 Rfn. Frank W. McGuinness		1/10/40 U.K.
4132317 Rfn. William J. McGuinness		24/10/40 Egypt.
6916510 Cpl. Austin J. McHale		25/10/42 Egypt.
6914437 Rfn. William McLauchlan		15/ 2/42 Egypt.
6921437 Rfn. Patrick MacMahon		11/ 1/43 N. Africa.
6920351 Rfn. Henry J. McNee		20/11/41 Egypt.
6970173 Rfn. William McNeil		12/10/42 U.K.
6912665 Cpl. George H. Mead		12/12/40 Egypt.
6967996 Rfn. Sidney V. Mead		8/ 7/44 Italy.
6920373 Rfn. Joseph S. Meadows		18/ 7/44 N.W. Europe.
14408753 Rfn. Ronald A. Mealand		28/ 6/44 N.W. Europe.
6915853 Cpl. Douglas T. Mearns		5/ 8/44 N.W. Europe.
6912041 Rfn. Frederick N. Medhurst		26/ 5/40 Calais.
6845787 Sgt. Joseph J. R. Meilleur, M.M.		19/10/44 N.W. Europe.
4130510 Rfn. Reginald J. Meredith		31/ 5/45 Italy.
6915694 Rfn. John H. Merritt		10/ 3/43 N. Africa.
6917416 Sgt. Kenneth C. Meyer		6/10/44 N.W. Europe.
6920789 Rfn. Charles G. Miles		9/ 6/43 U.K.
6968860 Rfn. Andrew T. Millar		28/12/44 Italy.
6915520 Rfn. Albert G. Miller		20/11/41 Egypt.
6913892 Rfn. Charles D. Miller		26/ 5/40 Calais.
6910535 Rfn. Charles H. Miller		17/ 3/45 Germany.
6969038 Cpl. Colin Miller		6/ 4/45 N.W. Europe.
6924999 Rfn. Denis W. Miller		6/ 7/44 Italy.
6917913 Rfn. John G. Miller		12/ 6/42 Egypt.
6920376 Cpl. Richard W. Miller		10/ 6/44 N.W. Europe.
6925268 Rfn. Ronald S. W. Miller		3/ 8/44 N.W. Europe.
6916220 L./Cpl. Sidney T. Miller		11/ 6/44 N.W. Europe.
6914441 Rfn. William D. Milligan		5/ 6/44 Italy.
6403921 Rfn. George K. Mills		11/12/43 Italy.
6913196 Rfn. Joseph F. Minta		15/11/42 Egypt.
6916221 Cpl. Leslie S. H. Mister		25/11/42 N. Africa.
6923395 Rfn. Frederick C. Mitchell		29/ 6/44 N.W. Europe.
6211382 Rfn. Albert Mitson		31/10/42 Middle East.
14242023 Rfn. Christopher Moakes		31/ 7/44 N.W. Europe.
6915997 Rfn. Edmund A. Moakes		25/ 5/44 Italy.
6898088 Sgt. Charles E. Molloy		3/ 5/45 N.W. Europe.
6913656 Rfn. Herbert H. S. Moody		15/ 8/40 Egypt.
6911900 Rfn. John Moon		5/ 1/45 Italy.
6915354 Cpl. Frederick W. Moore		5/ 5/42 U.K.
6917432 L./Cpl. William P. Moore		21/ 7/44 N.W. Europe.
7017189 Rfn. Albert T. Mordey		16/10/44 Italy.
14265923 Rfn. Robert Moreton		13/12/44 Italy.
3535374 Rfn. Arthur Morgan		3/ 6/44 Italy.
6917921 Rfn. Colin F. Morgan		23/11/41 Egypt.
6919848 Rfn. Thomas T. Morley		15/ 7/43 U.K.
6920149 Rfn. Ivor A. Morris		13/ 6/42 Egypt.
6917436 Rfn. Robert W. Morris		25/10/42 Egypt.
6916004 Rfn. Donald Morrison		30/ 3/43 S. Tunisia.

The Rifle Brigade

Name.		Date and Place.	
6214232	Rfn. Henry J. Moss	25/10/42	Egypt.
6913159	Sgt. John W. Moss	25/ 5/40	Calais.
6922583	Rfn. Felix A. W. Moutell..	2/ 2/43	Libya.
6914269	Rfn. Leslie A. Mower	11/10/45	Germany.
6917709	Sgt. Henry C. Mulford, M.M.	24/10/42	Egypt.
6969102	Rfn. James J. Mulholland	7/ 4/41	Middle East.
7018326	Sgt. John Mulpeter	22/ 4/45	Italy.
6968476	Sgt. Kenneth L. Munday ..	26/10/42	Egypt.
6919852	Rfn. Arthur M. Murphy ..	9/ 4/45	N.W. Europe.
14422557	Rfn. Kenneth T. Musgrave	20/ 7/44	N.W. Europe.
6910513	Rfn. Sydney T. Nally	23/ 5/40	Calais.
6913691	Rfn. Stanley A. Nash	20/ 6/42	Libya.
6924623	Rfn. Lawrence Nedas	21/ 6/44	Italy.
6915359	Rfn. John Nelson ..	9/12/43	Italy.
6914908	Rfn. Leslie W. Nethercott	7/ 6/42	Egypt.
6917446	Rfn. Victor L. Newell	10/ 4/41	Cyrenaica.
6925012	Rfn. Stanley A. Newman..	18/ 7/44	Italy.
6923769	Rfn. Sidney J. Newman ..	22/ 7/44	Italy.
6969427	Rfn. Victor J. Newman	26/11/41	Egypt.
6855002	Rfn. Freddie Newsome	27/ 4/43	S. Tunisia.
6917450	Rfn. Alexander V. Nicholas	29/ 7/44	Italy.
14258618	Rfn. Emrys Nicholas	17/10/44	N.W. Europe.
3450794	Rfn. Albert Nicholson	13/12/44	Italy.
4446029	Rfn. Harold Nicholson	26/ 5/40	Calais.
6914194	Rfn. Henry Nicholson	26/ 5/40	Calais.
6912920	Rfn. William S. Nisbet	23/ 9/40	Germany.
6917927	Rfn. George R. Nobbs	31/ 1/42	At sea.
6912137	C.S.M. Leonard S. Noble	24/10/42	Egypt.
6915601	Cpl. Herbert F. Norris	19/10/44	N.W. Europe.
6923417	Rfn. Richard C. North	2/ 8/44	N.W. Europe.
14441881	Rfn. Ronald A. North	31/ 1/45	N.W. Europe.
6969338	Rfn. Douglas S. Norton ..	21/ 7/42	Egypt.
6916527	Rfn. George A. Noyes	25/10/42	Egypt.
6919897	Rfn. Thomas J. Nutman ..	23/ 9/44	N.W. Europe.
6919899	Rfn. Bernard O'Brien	21/ 7/44	N.W. Europe.
6915010	Sgt. James O'Brien, M.M.	21/ 8/44	N.W. Europe.
6916226	Sgt. Bernard J. O'Connor..	13/ 6/44	N.W. Europe.
6923421	Rfn. Dennis J. O'Connor..	26/ 8/44	Italy.
6968994	Sgt. Patrick O'Halloran ..	13/12/44	Italy.
6923423	L./Cpl. Martin O'Hara	29/ 4/44	Middle East.
6916983	Rfn. John W. Oldfield	3/ 7/42	Egypt.
6918807	L./Cpl. Charles F. Oliver	25/11/42	N. Africa.
6920539	Rfn. Geoffrey F. Oliver ..	21/11/41	Egypt.
6923424	Rfn. Harry Oliver..	26/ 6/44	N.W. Europe.
6918227	Sgt. George W. Ollington..	8/ 4/45	N.W. Europe.
6923425	Rfn. Bernard W. O'Neill ..	8/ 5/45	N.W. Europe.
6922606	Rfn. Edward Orchard	22/ 4/45	Italy.
6917930	Cpl. Charles R. Osborne ..	20/ 9/44	N.W. Europe.
6914914	Rfn. Charles E. Oxley	9/12/43	Italy.
6912094	Rfn. Thomas H. Pace	25/ 5/40	Calais.
6969230	Rfn. Frederick J. Padwick	21/ 4/42	U.K.
6919907	Rfn. Stanley H. Page	9/ 5/43	N. Africa.
6923435	Rfn. Jack Painter ..	9/ 1/43	Middle East.
6851366	Rfn. Frederick W. Palmer	27/10/42	Egypt.

APPENDICES 437

Name.		Date and Place.
6914486 Rfn. Victor H. Palmer	.. ..	25/ 5/40 Calais.
6914181 Rfn. Walter A. Palmer	.. ..	22/ 5/40 Calais.
6916677 Rfn. Albert W. Parker	.. ..	6/ 2/41 Libya.
2617138 Cadet George H. Parker	..	13/ 8/40 U.K.
6916229 Rfn. Henry D. L. Parker	..	29/ 4/43 S. Tunisia.
1138390 Rfn. Ivor J. Parker	.. ..	8/10/44 Italy.
6916674 Sgt. Lionel G. Parker	.. ..	3/10/43 Italy.
6971166 Sgt. William Parker	.. ..	8/ 7/44 Italy.
6923439 Rfn. William J. Parker	.. ..	23/ 1/45 N.W. Europe.
6923781 Rfn. Stanley G. Parkins	.. ..	3/ 8/44 N.W. Europe.
6920159 Rfn. William A. Parnell	.. ..	20/ 6/44 N.W. Europe.
6918230 Cpl. Henry A. Parry	.. ..	28/ 9/44 N.W. Europe.
6968103 Rfn. Stanley Parton	.. ..	27/ 4/43 S. Tunisia.
6920381 Rfn. Alfred C. G. Passmore	..	25/10/42 Egypt.
14666730 Rfn. James Paton	.. ..	14/ 8/44 N.W. Europe.
2066419 L./Sgt. Stanley C. Pattenden	..	25/10/42 Egypt.
6916012 L./Cpl. William H. Payne	..	16/ 5/44 Italy.
6924643 Rfn. Leslie H. Pearce	.. ..	18/ 2/43 N. Africa.
14408122 Rfn. Raymond J. Pearse	..	8/10/44 Italy.
5255843 Rfn. Vincent Pearson	.. ..	31/ 3/43 S. Tunisia.
6844865 Cpl. Charles E. Peck	.. ..	20/ 4/45 N.W. Europe.
6910790 Rfn. Frederick Pedleham	..	29/ 5/40 At sea.
2048192 Rfn. Denis W. Pegg	.. ..	6/ 7/42 Egypt.
6913369 Cpl. Frederick L. Pepper	..	29/10/44 N.W. Europe.
5949563 Rfn. Leslie W. Pepper	.. ..	26/10/42 Egypt.
6925028 Rfn. Richard C. Percival	..	2/10/43 Italy.
6967941 Sgt. Cedric H. Perring	.. ..	3/ 5/43 S. Tunisia.
6923454 Rfn. Edward C. Perry	.. ..	12/ 3/43 N. Africa.
14413130 Rfn. Harry W. Perry	.. ..	21/ 7/44 N.W. Europe.
6848621 L./Sgt. Herbert J. Perry	.. ..	25/ 9/44 Italy.
14556573 Rfn. Herbert H. Pettet	.. ..	23/ 6/44 Italy.
2935573 Rfn. Robert Pettie	.. ..	12/ 6/42 Egypt.
6153422 Rfn. Douglas R. Phelps	.. ..	26/ 7/44 Italy.
6917943 Rfn. Benjamin J. Phillips	..	19/ 1/42 At sea.
6913861 L./Cpl. Ernest Phillips	.. ..	26/ 5/40 Calais.
6916531 Rfn. Frank W. I. Philpott	..	6/11/42 Egypt.
6215191 Rfn. Eric D. Pickett	.. ..	3/11/42 Egypt.
6916014 Rfn. Archibald Pickin	.. ..	21/ 6/44 Italy.
6925280 Rfn. Stanley J. Piddington	..	28/ 6/44 N.W. Europe.
6913721 Rfn. John R. Piggott	.. ..	16/ 4/45 N.W. Europe.
6912315 Rfn. Henry E. Plummer	..	19/ 6/42 Middle East.
5575529 Rfn. Edward B. Pocock	..	9/ 4/42 Egypt.
6917946 Rfn. Percy J. Pogson	.. ..	25/ 3/43 S. Tunisia.
14258636 Rfn. Alan E. Pollard	.. ..	5/ 4/45 N.W. Europe.
6923917 Rfn. Richard Pollard	.. ..	26/ 4/42 U.K.
6917248 Rfn. Douglas E. Poole	.. ..	10/11/43 N. Africa.
14410259 Rfn. Eric E. Popham	.. ..	26/10/45 N.W. Europe.
6919919 Rfn. Reggie J. Porter	.. ..	16/ 6/42 Egypt.
873730 Rfn. Ronald V. Portway	..	29/ 3/45 Germany.
6913746 Rfn. Albert W. Powell	.. ..	15/ 9/40 Middle East.
6917486 Rfn. Arthur C. Powell	.. ..	14/ 8/44 Italy.
6969553 Rfn. Stanley A. Powis	.. ..	22/ 7/42 Egypt.
6913739 L./Cpl. Thomas W. Preston	..	11/ 5/45 N.W. Europe.
6920399 Sgt. William A. Price	.. ..	25/10/42 Egypt.

Name.	Date and Place.	
6917490 L./Cpl. Frank J. Prickler..	16/ 9/42	Egypt.
5344051 Rfn. Alfred Priest..	8/ 7/44	Italy.
6911920 Rfn. Thomas R. Prior	16/ 5/44	Germany.
6915542 Rfn. Henry T. Pritchard ..	15/ 2/44	Italy.
6911069 Rfn. Sidney Proud	29/ 5/40	At sea.
14298264 Rfn. William Proud	6/ 4/45	N.W. Europe.
14499555 Rfn. Ronald W. Prudence	10/ 9/44	N.W. Europe.
6912351 Sgt. William A. Prutton ..	31/ 3/43	S. Tunisia.
6969983 Rfn. James Pullinger	13/12/44	Italy.
6916715 L./Cpl. Thomas K. Purkiss	13/ 6/42	Middle East.
2935722 Rfn. John R. Purvis	2/ 8/44	N.W. Europe.
6917952 Rfn. Gerald A. Pye	31/ 3/43	S. Tunisia.
6925288 Cpl. Joe Quantick..	8/ 4/45	N.W. Europe.
6922653 Rfn. Robert G. Rabey	28/ 3/45	N.W. Europe.
13016231 Rfn. Cyril W. Radford	13/ 6/42	Egypt.
834251 Sgt. Donald A. Radwell ..	26/ 5/40	Calais.
6922656 Rfn. Maurice Rampley	21/ 6/44	Italy.
11269099 Rfn. Albert J. Randall	3/10/44	Italy.
6919929 Rfn. Hillary C. D. Randall	21/ 7/44	Italy.
6914104 Rfn. Horace H. Randall ..	4/ 9/40	Germany.
6917496 Rfn. Harry Read ..	14/ 8/44	N.W. Europe.
6969045 Cpl. Henry T. Read	18/ 7/44	N.W. Europe.
6849464 Rfn. Sidney A. Read, M.M.	20/ 6/44	Italy.
6916245 Sgt. Sidney G. Read	10/ 9/44	N.W. Europe.
6914268 L./Cpl. Patrick J. Reade ..	4/ 7/44	N.W. Europe.
6968518 Rfn. Herbert S. Reading ..	20/ 1/43	Egypt.
6969343 L./Sgt. Norman A. Reed..	28/ 6/44	N.W. Europe.
6913267 Rfn. Colin B. Rees	29/ 1/45	N.W. Europe.
6969344 Rfn. John A. Rees	7/ 4/42	Egypt.
6916543 Rfn. William L. Rees	10/ 6/44	Italy.
6913714 Rfn. Edward M. Rhodes ..	20/11/41	Egypt.
6922667 Rfn. Frederick Richards ..	3/11/42	Egypt.
4121928 Rfn. George Richards	27/ 3/43	S. Tunisia.
6968449 Rfn. Peter A. Richards ..	13/11/42	Egypt.
4264909 Rfn. David Richardson ..	23/ 5/40	Calais.
6911379 C.S.M. George Y. Ridley..	24/ 2/43	S. Tunisia.
5678123 Rfn. Robert J. Ring	13/ 6/44	N.W. Europe.
6917963 Rfn. Terence B. Rink	21/ 1/42	At sea.
6146022 Cpl. Joseph F. Rippin ..	11/ 1/45	Italy.
6023768 Cpl. Alexander R. Ritchie	21/ 6/44	Italy.
6969676 L./Sgt. Jack C. Rivers ..	20/ 2/43	N. Africa.
6398541 Rfn. John W. H. Rixon ..	2/ 9/42	Egypt.
6920171 Rfn. Edward R. Robins ..	5/ 6/43	Italy.
5255854 Rfn. Samuel E. Robins ..	31/ 3/43	S. Tunisia.
6917506 Rfn. Brinley Roberts	25/10/42	Egypt.
6923807 Rfn. Eric F. G. Roberts ..	18/ 7/44	N.W. Europe.
6920914 Rfn. Kenneth R. Roberts..	18/ 7/44	Italy.
6851507 Rfn. William C. Roberts ..	8/ 9/44	N.W. Europe.
6201628 L./Cpl. Albert C. J. Robertson ..	4/11/39	Palestine.
6923499 Rfn. Albert D. W. Robinson ..	7/ 3/43	N. Africa.
6849480 Rfn. Charles W. Robinson	31/ 3/43	S. Tunisia.
14233799 Rfn. Daniel Robinson	10/ 6/44	Italy.
6916548 L./Cpl. George J. Robinson ..	3/11/42	Egypt.
6919946 Rfn. Leslie G. Robinson ..	31/10/42	Egypt.

APPENDICES

Name.	Date and Place.	
6914214 Rfn. Thomas S. N. Robinson	9/ 4/43	N. Africa.
6913884 L./Cpl. Eric Robson	21/11/41	Egypt.
6968281 Rfn. Edward Rochford	5/ 4/41	Cyrenaica.
6923501 Rfn. Thomas A. Rodber	18/ 7/44	N.W. Europe.
6917264 Rfn. Solomon Rodkoff	28/ 6/44	N.W. Europe.
14338639 Rfn. Jack M. Roffey	18/ 8/44	N.W. Europe.
6916569 Rfn. Frank W. Rogers	11/ 5/45	Germany.
6925041 Rfn. Joseph H. Rooke	29/ 6/44	N.W. Europe.
6911515 C.S.M. John H. P. Rooney	24/ 1/42	At sea.
7018349 Sgt. Sidney H. Roots	1/ 9/44	Italy.
6208086 L./Cpl. Alan J. Ross	27/ 6/44	N.W. Europe.
3186147 Rfn. Alexander Ross	26/ 4/42	Egypt.
6912914 Cpl. Cecil Rowling	25/ 5/40	Calais.
6917269 L./Sgt. Lawrence G. Royffe	29/ 6/42	Egypt.
6140865 Rfn. Arthur J. W. Rudkins	8/ 4/45	N.W. Europe.
6917073 Sgt. John A. Russell	3/11/42	Egypt.
7016934 Rfn. George A. Rust	31/ 8/44	U.K.
4273420 Sgt. James R. Rutherford	16/ 5/44	Italy.
4396680 Rfn. George Rutter	25/ 8/44	U.K.
3535771 Rfn. Alfred Rylance	14/11/42	At sea.
6969781 Cpl. Albert Samain	24/ 4/43	N. Africa.
6915826 Rfn. Ernest Sammet	27/ 6/44	N.W. Europe.
6906112 Rfn. James Sands	16/12/45	U.K.
6969497 Rfn. Herbert Sapsford	1/12/42	N. Africa.
14242060 Rfn. Ronald C. Satchell	7/ 7/44	Italy.
6916252 Sgt. James E. A. Saunders	27/10/42	Egypt.
6913452 Sgt. Bertram Savage	27/10/42	Egypt.
6088154 Rfn. Charles C. Savage	9/ 5/41	Egypt.
6912775 Cpl. George F. Savory	22/ 7/44	Italy.
5383328 Rfn. Henry J. Sawyer	11/ 6/44	Italy.
6968957 Rfn. William G. Sawyer	9/ 4/43	N. Africa.
6914714 Rfn. Cecil L. Saxey	18/ 6/44	Italy.
D/40283 Rfn. Albert Say	28/ 4/44	U.K.
6912896 Rfn. Frank L. Sayers	17/ 7/42	Middle East.
6918248 Cpl. Leonard L. Sayers	31/ 5/42	Middle East.
6970113 Rfn. Walter Scotchmer	26/ 7/44	Italy.
6915386 Rfn. Albert E. Scott	20/ 2/42	Middle East.
6915557 Rfn. Kenneth R. Scott	4/ 6/44	Italy.
6913142 Rfn. Raymond Senton	23/11/41	Egypt.
6920490 L./Cpl. William E. Severn	21/ 6/44	Italy.
6918836 Cpl. Albert E. Seymour	26/ 6/44	N.W. Europe.
6917140 Cpl. Charles F. Sharman	19/ 1/42	At sea.
6923820 Rfn. Ernest G. Sharp	3/ 4/43	U.K.
6923822 L./Cpl. Richard Shaw	1/ 8/44	N.W. Europe.
6918251 Rfn. Harry S. Shawyer	5/11/42	Egypt.
6920493 Rfn. William Sheppard	29/ 6/42	Egypt.
6913652 Rfn. Ernest Shipley	15/ 9/40	Egypt.
14558215 Rfn. Stanley Shoesmith	30/ 7/44	Italy.
6854568 Rfn. William C. E. Shoring	17/10/44	N.W. Europe.
6917541 Rfn. George H. Shortland	27/10/42	Egypt.
6923825 Cpl. Harold J. Shutz, M.M.	18/ 9/44	N.W. Europe.
6917136 Rfn. Walter G. Sibley	28/ 1/45	Italy.
6912258 C.S.M. Alfred S. G. Silver	7/ 4/41	Egypt.
6915013 Rfn. Samuel Simmonds	27/10/42	Egypt.

Name.		Date and Place.	
6968115	L./Cpl. Stewart C. Simpson	5/ 4/43	S. Tunisia.
6909290	Sgt. Sidney J. Sims	25/ 5/40	Calais.
6967908	Sgt. William P. Singleton	21/ 6/40	U.K.
6917284	Rfn. Albert E. Sipthorp	4/ 4/44	Germany.
6917988	Cpl. John R. Skelsey	22/ 7/42	Egypt.
6969388	Rfn. John W. Skinner	1/ 4/41	Cyrenaica.
6909327	Cpl. Frederick G. Slater	29/10/39	Palestine.
14621699	Rfn. Leslie Slater	10/ 9/44	N.W. Europe.
6913679	Rfn. Alfred G. Smith	3/12/40	Egypt.
14242075	Rfn. Charles Smith	8/ 8/44	Italy.
6920185	Cpl. Frederick J. Smith	4/ 7/42	Middle East.
7018366	Rfn. George Smith	13/12/44	Italy.
5674709	Rfn. George Harold Smith	27/ 9/44	Italy.
6915744	L./Cpl. George Henry Smith	27/10/42	Egypt.
7018104	Cpl. Goodyear C. F. Smith	20/ 6/44	Italy.
6969389	Rfn. John W. Smith	16/ 6/42	Egypt.
6915791	Rfn. Leonard F. Smith	11/ 4/43	N. Africa.
6854582	Rfn. Norman J. Smith	7/ 7/44	Italy.
6923832	Rfn. Reginald Smith	18/ 8/44	N.W. Europe.
6913803	L./Cpl. Richard K. Smith	27/10/42	Egypt.
6898423	Rfn. Ronald W. Smith	18/ 8/44	N.W. Europe.
6916256	L./Cpl. Victor C. Smith	11/ 1/42	Egypt.
6916935	L./Cpl. William Smith	26/ 7/44	Italy.
4445140	Rfn. William A. Smith	2/12/44	Germany.
7019853	Rfn. William H. Smith	31/ 7/44	Italy.
6916081	C.S.M. William S. Smith	13/12/44	Italy.
6922435	Rfn. James Snaith	3/ 7/44	N.W. Europe.
2124999	Rfn. Roland Snape	3/11/42	Egypt.
6924683	Rfn. Morris G. Snell	31/ 7/44	N.W. Europe.
6924328	Rfn. Norman E. Snuggs	19/ 4/43	N. Africa.
6923835	Rfn. Stanley Southgate	22/12/43	N. Africa.
6913175	Sgt. Robert Spark	22/11/41	Egypt.
6912795	L./Sgt. Edwin A. Speed	27/ 4/40	U.K.
1800195	Rfn. George A. Spencer	21/ 2/45	Italy.
6913080	Rfn. George H. Spencer	1/ 4/42	Germany.
6923930	Rfn. Richard Spencer	18/ 1/43	N. Africa.
6918002	Rfn. William R. Spencer	23/10/42	Egypt.
6913782	Rfn. Frederick A. Spreadbury	23/ 3/42	Egypt.
1570980	Rfn. Oliver Spurr	23/ 6/44	Italy.
6970241	Rfn. Alfred H. Squibb	18/ 4/44	N. Africa.
6912683	Rfn. William J. Squibb	26/ 5/40	Calais.
6919987	Rfn. George W. Squires	29/10/42	Egypt.
11422412	Rfn. Harold Staires	5/ 7/44	Italy.
1823271	Rfn. Harry J. Stamp	28/ 2/45	Italy.
6917559	Rfn. William Stanley	3/11/42	Egypt.
6919990	Cpl. William N. Stares	26/ 7/44	Italy.
1830241	Rfn. James F. Stark	1/ 3/46	Greece.
6923560	Rfn. William A. Steddy	28/ 6/44	N.W. Europe.
14425324	Rfn. James G. W. Stevens	20/ 7/44	N.W. Europe.
6915669	Rfn. Leslie M. Stevenson	9/ 6/42	Egypt.
6921171	Rfn. Robert V. Stewart	2/ 4/45	N.W. Europe.
14411910	Rfn. William Stockbridge	13/ 9/43	U.K.
6920433	Rfn. George H. Stocker	26/10/42	Egypt.
6852085	Rfn. Alex J. Stoneman	9/11/44	U.K.

APPENDICES

Name.	Date and Place.	
6910908 Rfn. Harold W. Stonhill	3/ 2/40	U.K.
6922728 Rfn. Edward A. Stow	11/ 1/43	N. Africa.
1838924 Rfn. Charles W. Street	27/10/44	Italy.
6914729 Rfn. Charles Stringer	22/ 2/43	N. Africa.
6145975 Rfn. James A. Stripp	4/ 7/44	N.W. Europe.
6916376 L./Sgt. Joseph C. P. Strobl	16/ 6/42	Egypt.
6913986 Rfn. Cyril K. H. Strowger	10/ 5/42	Middle East.
6857305 Rfn. Leonard C. Strudwick	10/ 9/44	N.W. Europe.
5253872 Rfn. Arthur W. Stubbs	22/10/40	U.K.
3851871 Rfn. Cecil Styling	25/ 7/44	Italy.
6916562 Rfn. John M. Sullivan	4/ 6/44	Italy.
2817791 Sgt. Ernest A. Surey	3/10/43	Italy.
6145978 Cpl. Haig D. Sutton	27/ 9/44	Italy.
6923850 Rfn. Ernest E. S. Sweetman	29/ 6/44	N.W. Europe.
6920505 L./Cpl. Robert P. Sydes	30/10/42	Egypt.
6917573 Rfn. John H. Tafe	14/ 7/44	Italy.
6923851 Rfn. Robert W. Talbot	21/ 7/44	N.W. Europe.
6925069 Rfn. William J. Talbot	18/ 8/44	N.W. Europe.
6913824 Rfn. George R. K. Tampin	1/ 7/41	Egypt.
6920850 Rfn. John Tandy	23/11/44	Italy.
6921429 Rfn. William J. Tarrant	18/ 9/43	Italy.
6348495 Rfn. George W. Tatman	27/ 6/44	N.W. Europe.
6920001 Rfn. Albert Taylor	9/12/41	At sea.
6969359 Sgt. Arthur W. Taylor	29/ 6/44	N.W. Europe.
6911980 Rfn. Henry S. J. Taylor	28/ 6/40	Germany.
6918533 Rfn. William J. G. Taylor	11/12/44	Italy.
6913104 Rfn. Samuel J. Terry	14/ 6/42	Egypt.
6914093 Rfn. Patrick Thaxter	30/ 1/42	At sea.
4122834 Rfn. John Thelwell	25/ 6/44	N.W. Europe.
6911010 Rfn. Charles C. Thompson	25/ 5/40	Calais.
3970821 L./Cpl. Robert C. Thorne	21/ 1/45	N.W. Europe.
6967924 Rfn. Sidney Thorne	8/ 6/44	Italy.
4206389 Rfn. Alfred H. Tiley	8/ 7/45	Austria.
6919791 L./Cpl. John W. Tillott	3/ 6/42	Egypt.
6924812 Cadet Mark Tindall	27/ 8/42	U.K.
6916568 Rfn. Jack Tinworth	30/ 3/43	S. Tunisia.
6913918 Rfn. William R. Todd	7/ 5/42	Egypt.
6914990 Rfn. William A. Tofield	26/ 9/44	N.W. Europe.
6920863 Rfn. Henry Tomlinson	11/ 6/44	N.W. Europe.
6969606 Rfn. Norman H. Town	4/ 8/44	N.W. Europe.
6913111 C.S.M. James J. Townshend	26/10/42	Egypt.
6923861 Rfn. John C. Townsend	10/ 6/44	Italy.
6916573 Rfn. Frederick C. Trotman	2/11/42	Egypt.
6919766 Rfn. Albert F. Truman	18/10/42	U.K.
6969000 Rfn. Bernard F. Turner	28/ 6/44	N.W. Europe.
5731365 Cpl. Ernest M. Turner	15/12/44	Italy.
3972021 Cadet Harold A. R. Turner	27/12/40	U.K.
6913855 Rfn. James H. Turner	27/10/42	Egypt.
6912681 Rfn. Alfred T. Turpin	14/10/39	Palestine.
6970245 Cpl. Edwin A. Tyler	2/ 5/45	Italy.
6912341 Rfn. Arthur Underwood	23/ 5/40	Calais.
6918872 Rfn. Frederick T. Urry	6/12/42	Italy.
6915706 Cpl. Albert E. Vanner	8/ 2/45	Italy.
6971138 Rfn. Israel Vendor	31/ 3/43	S. Tunisia.

Name.		Date and Place.	
5255892	Rfn. William T. Vickers	31/ 7/44	N.W..Europe.
14402943	Rfn. Richard Vidler	14/12/44	Italy.
14499946	Rfn. Robert B. Vinall	22/ 7/44	N.W. Europe.
6912496	Rfn. Edward W. Vine	25/ 5/40	Calais.
6913527	L./Cpl. Charles A. Viney	28/ 4/43	S. Tunisia.
6916938	Rfn. Edward M. Vintinner	31/ 8/40	U.K.
6969151	Rfn. John Vodden	3/ 2/44	Italy.
14412716	Rfn. Kenneth V. Vodden	25/ 7/44	Italy.
6561642	C.S.M. Harry O. S. Voss	27/ 6/44	N.W. Europe.
6970124	Cpl. Edward J. Vowell	12/ 4/43	N. Africa.
6913590	L./Cpl. Frank C. Wade	22/11/41	Egypt.
6914103	Rfn. Thomas W. Wade	2/11/42	Egypt.
6916053	Cpl. Charles A. Waghorne	29/ 6/44	Italy.
4132984	Sgt. George E. Walley	14/ 6/44	N.W. Europe.
6969559	Rfn. Robert W. Wallis	29/ 7/44	Italy.
6970011	Rfn. Frederick Ward	31/10/42	Egypt.
6912600	Rfn. Albert F. Warner	25/ 5/40	Calais.
6967595	Sgt. Cyril G. Warner	2/11/42	Egypt.
6920438	Rfn. Frank Warner	12/12/41	Egypt.
6917613	Rfn. James R. Warner	3/11/42	Egypt.
6855785	Rfn. Linford Warner	7/ 4/45	N.W. Europe.
6918034	L./Cpl. Ernest H. Warren	20/ 1/42	Egypt.
6919785	Rfn. John C. Warren	15/ 2/42	At sea.
6349149	Rfn. Spencer J. N. Warren	16/ 9/44	Italy.
6918035	Rfn. Alfred Warrener	12/ 6/42	Egypt.
6912293	L./Cpl. Benjamin W. Warwick	25/ 5/40	Calais.
6913401	Rfn. William A. Waslin	29/ 3/45	N.W. Europe.
6919787	Rfn. Charles H. Waters	2/10/43	Italy.
14664888	Rfn. Donald Watkin	23/ 8/44	N.W. Europe.
1116055	Rfn. Alexander W. Watson	8/ 7/44	Italy.
6923947	Rfn. Donald J. Watson	19/ 7/44	N.W. Europe.
6923948	Rfn. Ian Watson	26/ 6/44	N.W. Europe.
6914747	Rfn. John Watson..	27/10/44	Italy.
14309461	Rfn. Thomas Waughman	8/ 7/44	Italy.
5255897	Cpl. Arthur A. Webb, M.M.	30/ 7/44	Italy.
6918284	Rfn. Albert E. Webb	14/ 6/44	N.W. Europe.
14251249	Rfn. Bernard S. Webb	2/ 8/44	N.W. Europe.
3535565	Rfn. Edward Webber	27/ 4/43	S. Tunisia.
6923949	Rfn. Eric Webster..	2/ 8/44	N.W. Europe.
6916276	Rfn. George A. Webster	22/11/41	Egypt.
14235100	Rfn. William J. Weetch	11/ 6/44	Italy.
14439350	Rfn. Walter T. Weight	24/ 7/44	U.K.
6918037	Rfn. Vitalis Weinreich	20/ 7/44	N.W. Europe.
6916277	Cpl. George W. Wells	21/ 6/44	Italy.
6920035	Sgt. Ronald Wells..	5/ 1/45	N.W. Europe.
6913394	Cpl. Richard J. Wenman	27/10/42	Egypt.
6968395	Cpl. James W. West	24/ 7/42	Egypt.
6923707	Rfn. Charles M. Westbrook	20/ 3/43	U.K.
6913281	Cpl. Ronald W. Whatson..	9/ 8/42	Middle East.
6923624	Rfn. Joseph G. H. Wheatley	19/ 7/44	N.W. Europe.
6562247	Rfn. Vincent H. Wheeler..	22/12/42	Italy.
6852346	Rfn. Alfred White	20/ 1/45	N.W. Europe.
6924734	Rfn. Charles E. White	29/ 5/44	Italy.
6918985	Rfn. Dennis H. White	30/11/42	Egypt.

Appendices

Name.		Date and Place.	
6969001 Rfn. Frank C. White	.. ..	31/ 7/42	U.K.
6925093 Cpl. George W. White	.. ..	18/ 1/45	N.W. Europe.
6207341 Cadet Horace H. White	..	30/ 1/43	U.K.
6146011 Sgt. Stephen Whiteley	.. ..	2/ 8/44	Italy.
6897570 L./Cpl. Cyril D. Whitelock	..	13/12/44	Italy.
6970330 Rfn. Jeffrey J. Whitney	.. ..	11/ 9/40	U.K.
14215561 Rfn. William Wickers	.. ..	18/ 7/44	Italy.
6855800 Rfn. Claude H. Wickham	..	8/ 7/44	Italy.
6852348 L./Sgt. Victor L. Wickham	..	6/ 4/45	N.W. Europe.
6847947 Cpl. Ernest Wicks.. ..	..	26/ 7/44	N.W. Europe.
6923632 Rfn. Frederick G. Wicks..	..	26/ 6/44	N.W. Europe.
6913204 Sgt. George C. Wightman, D.C.M.		20/11/41	Egypt.
6916059 Rfn. Frank Wild	..	5/11/42	Egypt.
6913091 Rfn. Frank J. Wilkinson ..	..	28/ 5/40	U.K.
6911902 Rfn. George Wilkinson	.. ..	24/ 5/45	U.K.
6923636 Rfn. Cecil V. Williams	.. ..	14/ 8/44	N.W. Europe.
6912675 Rfn. Harry J. Williams	.. ..	10/ 4/45	N.W. Europe.
6908671 P.S.M. Ivan Williams	.. ..	26/ 5/40	Calais.
6916583 Rfn. Walter L. H. Williams	..	6/ 5/44	Italy.
6911779 Rfn. Herbert G. Williamson	..	25/ 5/40	Calais.
6912010 Rfn. Thomas G. Williamson	..	7/ 5/40	U.K.
7014270 Rfn. William T. Williamson	..	20/ 6/42	Egypt.
6910979 R.S.M. Albert T. Willis ..	..	3/ 7/42	Egypt.
6916580 Rfn. Edwin H. Willis	.. ..	29/ 4/45	N.W. Europe.
14665396 Rfn. Edwin F. Willson ..	..	21/ 8/44	Italy.
6968400 Rfn. Basil G. Wills-Sinclair	..	27/ 4/43	S. Tunisia.
7010006 L./Sgt. Ernest J. Wilson ..	..	11/ 6/40	U.K.
6968074 Sgt. Daniel Wilson, D.C.M.	..	26/ 4/43	S. Tunisia.
5441627 Rfn. Robert Wilson	.. ..	2/11/42	Egypt.
6911893 Sgt. Robert B. Wilson	.. ..	23/ 7/42	W. Africa.
6914755 Rfn. Stanley H. Wilson	.. ..	26/ 3/43	Italy.
6915414 Rfn. William V. Wilson	.. ..	10/ 6/40	U.K.
6923881 Rfn. Frederick Wiltshire ..	..	27/ 6/44	N.W. Europe.
6913474 L./Cpl. Francis H. Winkworth	..	7/12/41	Egypt.
6916065 Rfn. Alfred R. Winser	.. ..	5/ 4/43	S. Tunisia.
6912467 Rfn. Alfred J. Wirtz	.. ..	19/ 2/45	Germany.
14443227 Rfn. Kenneth E. W. Wolton	..	10/ 4/45	N.W. Europe.
6915416 Rfn. Ansell L. Wood	.. ..	25/10/42	Egypt.
6968431 L./Sgt. Charles W. C. Wood	..	25/10/42	Egypt.
6348512 Rfn. George H. C. Wood..	..	14/ 6/45	N.W. Europe.
6968075 L./Sgt. George W. Wood..	..	3/11/42	Egypt.
6923644 Rfn. Harry A. Wood	.. ..	21/ 7/44	N.W. Europe.
6910017 Cpl. William H. Wood	.. ..	8/ 2/45	Germany.
6968529 Rfn. Edward Woodham	.. ..	26/10/45	U.K.
6912405 Rfn. Jack Woolfenden	.. ..	26/ 5/40	Calais.
6925124 Rfn. Percy J. Woollacott ..	..	2/ 1/43	U.K.
6916606 Rfn. John Worley.. ..	..	21/ 6/44	Italy.
5255912 Rfn. Christopher J. Wragg	..	4/ 2/43	Middle East.

Name.		Date and Place.	
6970552 Sgt. Cecil S. Wray..	..	3/11/42	Egypt.
14220742 Rfn. William J. C. Wright	..	19/ 6/44	Italy.
6921554 Rfn. Henry P. Wyatt	..	17/ 3/42	U.K.
6917134 Cpl. Horace C. Yates	..	8/ 4/41	U.K.
6970376 Rfn. Bernard G. Yeomans	..	8/ 5/43	S. Tunisia.
6915587 Rfn. Arthur Young	..	22/11/41	Egypt.
6922817 Rfn. Leonard C. Young ..	..	1/ 1/45	Italy.

60TH RIFLES

The list of officers and riflemen of the 60th Rifles who were killed while serving in the 8th Battalion The Rifle Brigade in North-West Europe includes the following:

Capt. H. Stringer.
Lieut. M. Becke.
Lieut. R. J. Ellis.
Sergt. J. Meilleur, M.M.
Cpl. W. Clark.
Rfn. E. S. Bloomfield.

Rfn. W. Collier.
Rfn. M. Goldstein.
Rfn. H. Hopper.
Rfn. A. Luckford.
Rfn. L. J. Slater.

APPENDICES

APPENDIX "G"

HONOURS AND AWARDS, AND MENTIONS IN DESPATCHES

No guarantee can be given of the completeness or accuracy of this list, but every effort has been made to check it at the War Office. Ranks shown are the substantive, local, temporary or acting ranks held at the time of award, and the dates shown are those of its publication and not of the actual event. For foreign decorations the dates shown are often those on which the insignia have been presented to the recipient or his next-of-kin.

Acton, Capt. T. H.	Mention.	Special Operations.	29/ 8/46
Adams, Capt. C. F.	Mention.	Italy.	29/11/45
Adams, Major R. B.	Mention.	Italy.	29/11/45
Adams, Lieut. R. B. M.	Croix de Guerre. (French.)		3/ 4/45
	Mention.	North-West Europe.	10/ 5/45
Allan, Major A. W.	D.S.O.	Calais.	20/ 9/45
Allberry, Sgt. R. F.	Mention.	Middle East.	6/ 4/44
Alldridge, Rfn. S. E.	M.M.	Italy.	24/ 5/45
Allen, Sgt. R. V.	M.M.	Middle East.	14/ 1/43
Ambler, Major I. A. S.	Mention.	North-West Europe.	8/11/45
Andrews, Major A. J.	Mention.	Middle East.	30/ 6/42
Andrews, Rfn. A. M.	M.M.	Special Operations.	11/ 4/46
Andrews, Clr.-Sgt. H.	Mention.	Middle East.	8/ 7/41
Angel, A./Cpl. G. A.	Mention.	Middle East.	6/ 4/44
Angel, Capt. (Qrmr.) M. M.	M.B.E.	Middle East.	1/ 6/42
Ansell, Major G. E.	Mention.	North-West Europe.	8/11/45
Antoine, Clr.-Sgt. R. C.	Mention.	Middle East.	15/12/42
	Mention.	Middle East.	24/ 6/43
Apsey, Lieut. P. C.	M.C.	North-West Europe.	12/ 4/45
Apsey, Major W. J.	M.C.	Italy.	27/ 1/44
Ashworth, Clr.-Sgt. B.	Mention.	Italy.	23/ 5/46
Atkin-Berry, Lieut. M. I.	M.C.	Italy.	7/12/44
	Mention.	Italy.	11/12/44
Atkins, A./Cpl. D.	Mention.	Middle East.	15/12/42
Ayris, Sgt. H. C.	Mention.	Middle East.	13/ 1/44
Bailey, Sgt. L. W.	M.M.	Italy.	7/12/44
Bailey, Capt. P.	Mention.	Burma.	19/ 7/45
Baines, Major J. N.	M.B.E.	Middle East.	25/11/43
Lt.-Col.	Mention.	North-West Europe.	8/11/45
Baker, Lieut. J. R.	M.C.	North-West Europe.	1/ 3/45
Baldock, L./Sgt. A.	M.M.	North Africa.	15/ 6/43
Baldwin, Sgt. G. W.	M.M.	North-West Europe.	2/ 8/45
Bann, Rfn. W. S.	Mention.	Italy.	29/11/45
Baring, Capt. H. C.	M.C.	Middle East.	13/ 8/42
Major	M.B.E.	Italy.	13/12/45
Barker, Capt. H. A.	O.B.E.	Middle East.	30/12/41
	Mention.	Middle East.	15/12/42
Barnett, Cpl. J. W. C.	M.M.	Middle East.	28/ 1/43
Barret, Rfn. F.	Bronze Cross. (Dutch.)		18/ 7/47
Barrett, Rfn. J. E.	Mention.	Calais.	20/ 9/45
Barrett, Sgt. R. W.	M.M.	Italy.	27/ 1/44
	Bar to M.M.	North-West Europe.	31/ 8/44
Barrett, Sgt. T. J.	M.M.	Middle East.	22/ 7/43

2G

Barrow, Capt. J. L.	Mention.	Middle East.	13/ 1/44
Barry, Major F. P.	Mention.	Italy.	23/ 5/46
	M.B.E.	Italy.	24/ 8/44
	O.B.E.	Italy.	13/12/45
Bartlett, Rfn. R. F.	Mention.	Middle East.	1/ 4/41
Barton, Rfn. C. W.	Mention.	Special Operations.	21/ 2/46
Barton, Cpl. J.	M.M.	North-West Europe.	12/ 7/45
Bass, Lieut. C. C.	M.C.	Middle East.	13/ 9/45
Basset, Lieut. D. W.	Mention.	Middle East.	8/ 7/41
Capt.	M.C.	Middle East.	14/ 1/43
Basset, Major R. T.	M.C.	Middle East.	1/ 4/41
	Bar to M.C.	Middle East.	12/ 2/42
Bastin, C.S.M. W. D.	Mention.	Italy.	29/11/45
Bates, A./Cpl. A. G.	Mention.	Italy.	19/ 7/45
Bates, Lieut. J. D.	M.C.	Middle East.	22/ 7/43
Batt, Sgt. G.	Mention.	North-West Europe.	9/ 8/45
	Mention.	North-West Europe.	4/ 4/46
Baylay, Major B. C.	Mention.	Middle East.	15/12/42
Bell, Major G. N.	M.C.	North-West Europe.	1/ 3/45
Benn, L./Sgt. W. E. C.	Mention.	North-West Europe.	8/11/45
Bennett, Rfn. F.	M.M.	North-West Europe.	1/ 3/45
Bennett, Lt.-Col. F. O. A. G.	Mention.	North-West Europe.	2/ 8/45
	Bronze Star. (American.)		14/11/47
Berry, Cpl. A. J.	M.M.	Middle East.	18/ 2/43
Biddell, Lieut. P. B.	M.C.	Middle East.	5/11/42
	Bar to M.C.	Italy.	27/ 1/44
Billyard-Leake, Capt. C. R., M.C.	Mention.	Middle East.	30/12/41
Bird, Lieut. E. A.	Mention.	Calais.	20/ 9/45
Bird, Lieut. T. A.	M.C.	Middle East.	9/ 5/41
	Bar to M.C.	Middle East.	24/ 9/42
Major	D.S.O.	Middle East.	14/ 1/43
Bishop, A./Cpl. E. W.	M.M.	Middle East.	9/ 9/41
Bishop, C.S.M. K.	Mention.	Italy.	29/11/45
Blackman, L./Sgt. J. W.	M.M.	Calais.	20/ 9/45
Blockley, Lt.-Col. N. R.	Mention.	Persia and Iraq.	5/ 8/43
	O.B.E.	Italy.	24/ 8/44
Blunden, Cpl. C. H.	M.M.	Special Operations.	2/10/42
Boden, Major P. A. D.	M.C.	Middle East.	9/ 9/42
	Bronze Cross. (Dutch.)	North-West Europe.	18/ 7/47
Bodley, Lieut. J. E. C.	M.C.	Italy.	26/10/44
Bolt, Rfn. R. W.	Mention.	Middle East.	13/ 1/44
Bonner, Sgt. W. G.	Mention.	North-West Europe.	4/ 4/46
Bonney, C.S.M. S.	Mention.	Italy.	29/11/45
Booth, Major A. J. G.	M.B.E.	Italy.	19/ 7/45
Borthwick, Major J. T.	Mention.	North-West Europe.	29/ 3/45
	Mention.	North-West Europe.	4/ 4/46
Bosley, Sgt. R. W.	Mention.	Special Operations.	28/ 2/45
Bosvile, Lt.-Col. T. J. B.	D.S.O.	Middle East.	13/ 8/42
	Bar to D.S.O.	Middle East.	28/ 1/43
Brig.	C.B.E.	North-West Europe.	21/ 6/45
	Legion of Honour. (French.)		2/ 8/45
	Legion of Merit. (American.)		8/11/45
	Croix de Guerre. (French.)		1/ 3/49

APPENDICES

Name			Award	Theatre	Date
Bowring, Lieut. P.	..	..	Mention.	Italy.	23/ 5/46
Bradbury, Sgt. G. C.	..	..	M.M.	Middle East.	5/11/42
Bradshaw, Cpl. P. H.	..	..	M.M.	Norway.	27/ 9/40
Brain, Lieut. C. E.	..	..	M.C.	Burma.	27/ 7/44
Bray, Sgt. T. H.	..	..	Mention.	North-West Europe.	22/ 3/45
Brayshaw, Rfn. H.	..	..	G.M.	Home Forces.	16/12/41
Breed, Rfn. J.	..	..	M.M.	Escaped p.o.w.	29/ 9/45
Brett, Sgt. R. A.	..	..	M.M.	Middle East.	14/10/43
Brewster, Sgt. P. N. W.	..		Mention.	Italy.	19/ 7/45
Bridgeman, Lt.-Col. The Viscount, M.C.		..	D.S.O.	B.E.F.	11/ 7/40
			Mention.	B.E.F.	26/ 7/40
			Bar to D.S.O.	B.E.F.	22/10/40
Major-General		..	C.B.	Home Forces.	1/ 1/44
Bridger, Rfn. R.	..	..	M.M.	Middle East.	9/ 9/42
Brightman, Rfn. D. F.	..		Mention.	Italy.	19/ 7/45
Britton, Clr.-Sgt. A. E.	..		Mention.	Italy.	29/11/45
Bromley, Rfn. B. K.	..		Mention.	Middle East.	25/ 1/45
Brooke, Sgt. M. C.	..		Mention.	Middle East.	8/ 4/44
Brown, A./Cpl. G. H.	..		D.C.M.	Middle East.	25/ 4/41
Browne, Capt. Hon. H. G. A.	..		Mention.	Middle East.	26/ 7/40
Brownlow, Major W. S.		..	Mention.	Italy.	29/11/45
Brush, Major E. J. A. H.		..	D.S.O.	Calais.	20/ 9/45
Lt.-Col.	..	..	O.B.E.	Escaped p.o.w.	18/ 4/46
Buckley, Lt.-Col. E. G.	..	..	Gold Cross, George I. (Greek.)		16/ 2/48
Budibent, Sgt. G. A.	..	..	Mention.	Middle East.	8/ 4/43
			M.M.	Middle East.	15/10/44
Burder, Lt. G. C.	..	..	M.C.	North-West Europe.	1/ 3/45
Burford, Lt.-Col. P. G., T.D.	..		Mention.	North-West Europe.	2/ 8/45
			Bronze Star. (American.)		8/12/47
Burgess, Major G. M.	..	..	M.B.E.	North-West Europe.	24/ 1/46
Burling, Capt. H. G.	..	..	Order of King George I. (Greek.)		19/11/48
Burman, Lt. F. W.	..	..	Mention.	Middle East.	8/ 4/43
P.S.M.	..	..	Mention.	Calais.	20/ 9/45
Burnhope, Rfn. S. H.	..		M.M.	Middle East.	14/ 1/43
			Bronze Star. (American.)		23/ 7/48
Butcher, C.S.M. G.	..		M.M.	Italy.	19/ 4/45
Butterfield, Clr.-Sgt. J.	..		Mention.	Italy.	23/ 5/46
Byrne, Rfn. W. P.	..		Mention.	Calais.	20/ 9/45
Cable, A./Cpl. H. G.	..		M.M.	North-West Europe.	12/ 4/45
Cable, Clr.-Sgt. P.	..		Mention.	Italy.	23/ 5/46
Cahill, A./Cpl. T.	..		Mention.	Middle East.	8/ 7/41
Calistan, L./Sgt. C. V.	..		M.M.	Middle East.	13/ 8/42
Sgt.	..	..	D.C.M.	Middle East.	14/ 1/43
Callard, Major W.		..	Mention.	Italy.	23/ 5/46
Cann, A./Cpl. H. E. J.	..		M.M.	Middle East.	14/10/43
Carlton, Cpl. D.	..		M.M.	Italy.	7/12/44
Carter, L./Sgt. M. W.	..		Mention.	Italy.	28/ 6/45
			M.M.	Italy.	28/ 6/45
			Mention.	Italy.	19/ 7/45
Cave, Lt.-Col. F. O.	..	..	Mention.	Middle East.	1/ 4/41
			O.B.E.	Middle East.	16/ 4/42
			Mention.	Middle East.	13/ 1/45
			Mention.	Burma.	26/ 4/45
Cavey, Rfn. G. R.	..	..	M.M.	Middle East.	22/ 7/43

Name	Award	Theatre	Date
Channon, R.Q.M.S. L.	Mention.	Calais.	20/ 9/45
Chapman-Walker, Major W. M.	M.B.E.	Middle East.	6/ 1/44
Chard, Rfn. D. A.	D.C.M.	Middle East.	14/ 1/43
Chichester-Constable, Major P. T.	M.B.E.	Mediterranean.	21/ 6/45
Chichester-Constable, Brig. R. C. J., D.S.O.	Bar to D.S.O.	B.E.F.	22/10/40
	Mention.	Mediterranean.	22/ 2/45
Clark, Cpl. S. C.	M.M.	Middle East.	9/ 5/41
Clark, Rfn. H. J.	Mention.	North Africa.	23/ 9/43
Clarke, Major E. N.	O.B.E.	B.E.F.	11/ 7/40
Brig.	C.B.E.	Home Forces.	23/ 5/46
	Bronze Star. (American.)		18/ 7/47
Clarke, A./Cpl. R. E.	M.M.	Middle East.	1/ 6/43
Clay, Cpl. A. D.	M.M.	Italy.	23/ 8/45
Clay, Lieut. C. J.	Mention.	Calais.	29/ 9/45
Clay, Capt. J. L.	Mention.	Middle East.	13/ 1/44
Coad, S./Sgt. A. V.	D.C.M.	North Africa.	22/ 7/43
Coates, Rfn. R.	M.M.	Italy.	7/12/44
Coates, Rfn. W. G.	Mention.	Middle East.	13/ 1/43
Cobbet, Rfn. W. D.	Mention.	Escaped p.o.w.	2/ 3/44
Cobley, Rfn. R. G. J.	Mention.	Calais.	20/ 9/45
Cockburn, Rfn. E.	M.M.	Middle East.	1/ 6/43
Cohen, Capt. G. S. B.	Mention.	North-West Europe.	4/ 4/46
Cole, Sgt. H. L.	Mention.	Italy.	23/ 5/46
Compton, Cpl. K. E.	Mention.	Italy.	23/ 5/46
Conlon, A./Cpl. M.	M.M.	Middle East.	25/11/43
Conlon, Cpl. P. J.	D.C.M.	Middle East.	9/ 5/41
Connor, A./Cpl. R. A.	Mention.	North Africa.	23/ 9/43
Cooper, Sgt. J.	M.M.	North-West Europe.	29/ 3/45
Cooper, Rfn. R. A. E.	Mention.	Middle East.	13/ 1/42
Cooper, Cpl. R. A.	M.M.	Italy.	19/ 4/46
Cope, L./Sgt. E. W.	M.M.	Middle East.	14/ 1/43
Cope, Lt. J. F.	M.C.	Middle East.	9/ 9/41
Coppin, Sgt. D.	Bronze Cross. (Dutch.)		18/ 7/47
Coryton, Lt. J.	M.C.	North-West Europe.	1/ 3/45
Cosby, Major I. R. S.	Mention.	Italy.	29/11/45
Coulson, Sgt. A. M.	Mention.	Middle East.	13/ 1/44
Coward, Cpl. F. O. C.	M.M.	North-West Europe.	12/ 7/45
Cowan, Lt. J. A. C.	Mention.	Italy.	29/11/45
Cowhey, Sgt. T. V. A.	D.C.M.	Middle East.	12/ 2/42
Cox, Lt.-Col. G.	O.B.E.	Italy.	13/12/45
Cozens, Capt. G. A.	M.B.E.	Greece.	13/12/45
Cripps, Col. R. R., T.D.	Mention.	Italy.	29/11/45
Crocker, R.S.M. T.	M.B.E.	Italy.	28/ 6/45
Cunliffe, Capt. D. F.	M.C.	North-West Europe.	19/10/44
Cunningham, Sgt. E.	M.M.	Middle East.	23/ 4/42
Cunningham, Cpl. R.	M.M.	Middle East.	22/ 7/43
Curtis, C.S.M. E. W.	Mention.	Calais.	20/ 9/45
Curtis, Lt.-Col. W. P. S.	O.B.E.	North-West Europe.	11/10/45
Daly, Major D. W.	Mention.	Burma.	9/ 5/46
Darling, Major D. L.	M.C.	Middle East.	8/ 7/41
	Bar to M.C.	Middle East.	13/ 8/42
	D.S.O.	Middle East.	19/ 8/43
Lt.-Col.	Bar to D.S.O.	Italy.	23/ 8/45
	Mention.	Italy.	19/ 7/45
Davey, Cpl. H.	M.M.	Italy.	7/12/44
Davies, Lieut. D. A. O.	Mention.	North-West Europe.	4/ 4/46
Davies, Major J. E.	M.B.E.	Italy.	28/ 8/44

APPENDICES 449

Daw, Capt. J. G. H. S. W.	Mention.	Middle East.	13/ 1/44
Dawson, A./Cpl. S. G.	Mention.	Italy.	29/11/45
Day, R.Q.M.S. F.	Mention.	Middle East.	13/ 1/44
Day, Capt. M. E.	Mention.	Italy.	29/11/45
De Bell, A./Cpl.	M.M.	Escaped p.o.w.	27/ 4/44
Dent, A./Cpl. S.	Mention.	Escaped p.o.w.	29/ 6/44
Des Graz, Lt.-Col. E. P. A.	Mention.	Middle East.	15/ 3/45
Dewhurst, Major T. L.	M.C.	Italy.	23/ 8/45
Diamond, Rfn. A.	Mention.	Special Operations.	1/11/45
Doe, Sgt. A. F.	Mention.	Middle East.	13/ 1/44
Doherty, Rfn. W. H.	M.M.	Italy.	12/ 4/45
Douglas, Brig. A. S. G., O.B.E.	Mention.	Persia and Iraq.	5/ 8/43
	C.B.E.	Persia and Iraq.	23/12/43
	Order of Alexander Kutuzov, 2nd Class. (Russian.)		21/ 7/44
Douglas, Cpl. M.	Mention.	Escaped p.o.w.	27/ 4/44
Dowsett, Sgt. J.	Mention.	Italy.	29/11/45
Drummond, Sgt. T. J.	M.M.	Middle East.	13/ 8/42
Duck, Rfn. J. M.	Mention.	Calais.	20/ 9/45
Duckworth, Major A. J. S.	Mention.	Italy.	11/ 1/45
Dudgeon, Capt. J. A.	M.C.	Middle East.	28/ 1/43
	Bar to M.C.	Middle East.	1/ 6/43
Dudman, Lieut. (Qrmr.) E. C.	M.B.E.	Middle East.	14/10/43
Duggan, Clr.-Sgt. S.	Mention.	Italy.	29/11/45
Duncanson, Lieut. J. P.	Mention.	Calais.	29/ 9/45
Durey, C.S.M. E. J.	Mention.	North-West Europe.	4/ 4/46
Dyer, Cpl. F.	D.C.M.	Italy.	25/ 5/45
Eagle, Rfn. S. G.	M.M.	Calais.	20/ 9/45
Eakins, Lieut. E. G.	M.C.	Italy.	28/ 6/45
Earley, Lieut. R. W.	Mention.	Italy.	23/ 5/46
Easen, P.S.M. J.	M.M.	Calais.	20/ 9/45
Eastwood, Lieut. H.	Mention.	Italy.	29/11/45
Eastwood, Lt.-Gen. Sir T. R., D.S.O., M.C.	Mention.	B.E.F.	20/12/40
	C.B.	Home Forces.	1/ 1/41
	K.C.B.	Home Forces.	1/ 1/43
	Order of Merit. (Luxembourg.)		26/ 7/44
Edwardes, A./Cpl. E. S.	Mention.	Middle East.	6/ 4/44
Edwardes, Major Hon. M. G.	M.B.E.	Middle East.	14/10/43
Eeles, Major J. E.	Mention.	Italy.	24/ 8/44
	Mention.	Italy.	29/11/45
Eldon, Cpl. E. C.	Mention.	Italy.	24/ 8/44
Elkington, Major J. D. R.	M.B.E.	North Africa.	23/ 9/43
Lt.-Col.	Mention.	Italy.	29/11/45
	O.B.E.	Italy.	13/12/45
Elmes, Rfn. R. E.	Mention.	North-West Europe.	4/ 4/46
Elsmere, Cpl. E. V.	M.M.	Italy.	7/12/44
Emerson-Baker, Lt. J. R.	M.C.	Middle East.	5/11/42
Endean, C.S.M. A.	M.M.	Middle East.	1/ 4/41
	Bar to M.M.	Middle East.	9/ 5/41
Evans, Rfn. J. J.	Mention.	Middle East.	15/12/42
Evans, P.S.M. R. R.	Mention.	Middle East.	8/ 7/41
Fairholm, Capt. P. H. St. J.	Mention.	Italy.	19/ 7/45
Fairweather, Major A. I.	Mention.	Italy.	23/ 5/46
Fairweather, Lieut. R. F.	M.C.	North Africa.	23/ 9/45
Farmer, Sgt. R. J.	Mention.	North-West Europe.	22/ 3/45

Farrer, Cpl. J.	Mention.	North-West Europe.	9/ 8/45
	M.M.	North-West Europe.	9/ 8/45
Faulconbridge, Lieut. A. R.	M.C.	North-West Europe.	23/ 8/45
Faviell-Barrs, Major A. M.	Mention.	North-West Europe.	23/ 8/45
Fearon, Sgt. T.	Mention.	Italy.	23/ 5/46
Fell, Sgt. J. W.	M.M.	Italy.	13/12/45
Fellowes, Lieut. Hon. J. D. C.	Mention.	Calais.	20/ 9/45
Ferguson, Sgt. J. R.	Mention.	North-West Europe.	4/ 4/46
	M.B.E.	North-West Europe.	13/ 6/46
Festing, Brig. F. W.	D.S.O.	Madagascar.	16/ 6/42
Major-Gen.	Mention.	Burma.	5/ 4/45
	C.B.E.	Burma.	5/ 7/45
	Mention.	Burma.	6/ 6/46
	C.B.	Burma.	6/ 6/46
	Legion of Merit. (American.)		6/ 6/46
Field, Cpl. F. C.	D.C.M.	Middle East.	25/ 4/41
Fienburgh, Major W.	M.B.E.	North-West Europe.	24/ 1/46
Fiennes, Capt. Hon. N. T. A.	Mention.	North-West Europe.	22/ 3/45
Fish, Lieut. K. J.	M.C.	Middle East.	17/ 6/43
Fitzgerald, Cpl. G.	M.M.	North-West Europe.	19/10/44
Flower, Major P. T.	M.B.E.	Italy.	28/ 6/45
	Mention.	Italy.	19/ 7/45
Flower, Capt. R. A.	Mention.	Italy.	17/ 6/43
	M.C.	Italy.	24/ 6/43
Foley, Capt. H. T. H.	M.B.E.	Home Forces.	1/ 9/44
Ford, Sgt. F.	Mention.	Middle East.	6/ 4/44
Forshall, Major S.	M.B.E.	North-West Europe.	30/ 9/45
Foster, Capt. O. H. J.	Mention.	Middle East.	30/ 6/42
Fowler, Clr.-Sgt. F.	Mention.	Italy.	23/ 5/46
Francis, L./Sgt. A.	M.M.	Middle East.	14/ 1/43
Francis, Major J.	Order of Leopold. (Belgian.) Croix de Guerre. (Belgian.)		
Francis, Major J. M.	Mention.	Middle East.	24/ 6/43
Francis, Cpl. W. P.	M.M.	Italy.	28/ 6/45
Francks, Major Q. R.	Officer of Leopold. (Belgian.) Croix de Guerre. (Belgian.)		
Franklyn, Capt. R. A. A.	Mention.	Middle East.	8/ 7/41
Freeman, Major J.	M.B.E.	Middle East.	25/11/43
	Croix de Guerre. (French.)		3/ 4/45
Frost, Sgt. T. A. H.	Mention.	Middle East.	2/ 3/44
Fulford, Major F. E. A.	Mention.	Middle East.	30/12/41
Fulton, Cpl. H.	D.C.M.	North-West Europe.	9/ 8/45
Fulton, Cpl. S. W.	M.M.	Middle East.	14/ 1/43
Furey, Major C.	Mention.	Middle East.	30/ 6/42
	M.B.E.	Middle East.	9/ 9/42
Furse, Major P. J. D.	Mention.	North-West Europe.	9/ 8/45
Fyffe, Major L. R. K.	M.C.	Middle East.	1/ 6/43
	Bar to M.C.	Italy.	7/12/44

APPENDICES 451

Fyffe, Major R. A.	M.C.	North Africa.	8/ 4/43
Lt.-Col.	D.S.O.	Italy.	23/ 8/45
Galloway, Rfn. R.	M.M.	Middle East.	9/ 9/42
Garmoyle, Major The Viscount	D.S.O.	Middle East.	20/ 1/42
	Mention.	Middle East.	20/ 1/42
	Bar to D.S.O.	Middle East.	13/ 8/42
Garnett, Lt.-Col. J. C.	Haakon VII Liberty Medal. (Norwegian.)		19/ 3/48
Garnier, Major E. H. C.	M.C.	Middle East.	25/11/43
Gauntlett, Rfn. A. B.	Mention.	Middle East.	13/ 1/44
Gibson, Major B. H.	Mention.	North-West Europe.	4/ 4/46
Gilbert, Capt. B. G.	M.B.E.	Italy.	21/12/44
Giles, Major E.	M.B.E.	Home Forces.	1/ 1/45
Gillan, Rfn. R. C.	D.C.M.	Middle East.	9/ 5/41
Gillings, L./Sgt. A.	M.M.	North-West Europe.	31/ 8/44
Glasgow, R.Q.M.S. R. W.	M.B.E.	North-West Europe.	11/10/45
Glenney, Capt. D. C.	Mention.	North-West Europe.	8/11/45
Godfrey-Faussett, Lt.-Col. P.	Mention.	North-West Europe.	9/ 8/45
	O.B.E.	North-West Europe.	24/ 1/46
Godwin, L./Cpl. J. E.	Mention.	Special Operations.	28/ 2/46
Goodey, R.S.M. E. C.	D.C.M.	Calais.	20/ 9/45
Goodwin, Rfn. J.	Mention.	Escaped p.o.w.	1/ 3/45
Gordon, C.Q.M.S. J. L.	Mention.	Middle East.	13/ 1/44
Gordon-Duff, Major J. B.	M.B.E.	Malta.	6/ 1/44
	Mention.	Malta.	6/ 4/44
Gordon-Duff, Capt. T. R.	M.C.	Calais.	20/ 9/45
Gore, Lt.-Col. A. C.	D.S.O.	North Africa.	23/ 9/43
Brig.	Bar to D.S.O.	Italy.	23/ 8/45
Goschen, Major Sir E. C., Bt.	D.S.O.	Italy.	7/12/44
	Mention.	Italy.	23/ 5/46
Gough, Capt. C. F. H.	Mention.	B.E.F.	20/12/40
Goy, C.S.M. G. A.	Mention.	Italy.	29/11/45
Green-Wilkinson, Lieut. J. C. C.	M.C.	Middle East.	18/ 3/43
Griffiths, L./Sgt. N. B.	D.C.M.	Middle East.	3/11/42
Groom, Sgt. T. W.	Mention.	Italy.	19/ 7/45
Groom, Rfn. W. C. R.	Mention.	Italy.	19/ 7/45
Groves, L./Cpl. W. A.	M.M.	North-West Europe.	12/ 7/45
Guise, Cpl. A. G.	D.C.M.	Middle East.	13/ 8/42
Gurr, Rfn. F.	M.M.	Calais.	20/ 9/45
Hall, Lieut. F. C.	Mention.	North Africa.	24/ 2/44
Hamilton, C.S.M. F. M.	Mention.	Italy.	29/11/45
Major	Bronze Star. (American.)		28/ 1/49
Hamilton-Russell, Major A. G. L.	Mention.	Calais.	20/ 9/45
Hamlyn, Capt. G.	Mention.	North-West Europe.	10/ 5/45
Hancock, Capt. K. S.	Mention.	Middle East.	6/ 4/44
Handibode, Sgt. M.	Mention.	Italy.	29/11/45
Harington, Major J. T.	M.B.E.	Greece.	4/ 1/45
	D.S.O.	Greece.	4/ 1/45
Harris, Clr.-Sgt. J. G.	Mention.	Italy.	29/11/45
Harris, Sgt. R.	Mention.	Italy.	19/ 7/45
Hart, Lt.-Col. L. E. O. T., M.B.E.	Legion of Honour. (French.)		18/ 7/47
	Croix de Guerre. (Belgian.)		16/ 1/47

Hart, Lt.-Col. L. E. O. T., M.B.E.	Haakon VII Liberty Medal. (Norwegian.)		19/ 3/48
	Croix Militaire. (Belgian.)		14/ 5/48
Haslam, Major J	Mention.	North-West Europe.	9/ 8/45
	M.B.E.	North-West Europe.	24/ 1/46
Hastings, Capt. R. H. W. S.	Mention.	Middle East.	2/ 7/41
	Mention.	Middle East.	15/12/42
	M.C.	Middle East.	25/ 2/43
Lt.-Col.	D.S.O.	North-West Europe.	31/ 8/44
	Bar to D.S.O.	North-West Europe.	21/ 6/45
	O.B.E.	North-West Europe.	24/ 1/46
Hawdon, Rfn. H. S.	Mention.	Middle East.	8/ 7/41
Hawkes, Lieut. J. M.	Mention.	Middle East.	24/ 6/43
Capt.	Mention.	Middle East.	13/ 1/44
Hawkins, C.Q.M.S. A. J. F.	Mention.	Middle East.	13/ 1/44
Hayden, Sgt. J. J.	M.M.	North-West Europe.	29/ 3/45
Hayes, Cpl. S.	Mention.	Italy.	23/ 5/46
Hayman, Major P. T.	M.B.E.	Mediterranean.	21/ 6/45
Head, Lieut. D. E.	Mention.	Italy.	29/11/45
Hedley, Sgt. G. E.	Mention.	Calais.	20/ 9/45
Hegarty, Cpl. D. J.	M.M.	Italy.	23/ 8/45
Hems, P.S.M. F. G.	Mention.	Middle East.	8/ 7/41
Henley, Capt. R. A.	M.B.E.	Italy.	13/12/45
Hennell, Cpl. L. H.	M.M.	Italy.	26/10/44
Henniker-Major, Major J. P. C.	M.C.	Mediterranean.	22/ 2/45
Henwood, Rfn. G. W.	M.M.	Italy.	13/12/45
Heries, P.S.M. H. G.	Mention.	Middle East.	8/ 7/41
Hewstone, C.S.M. H. J.	Mention.	North-West Europe.	4/ 4/46
Hicks, Lt.-Col. K. B.	Mention.	Italy.	24/ 8/44
	O.B.E.	Mediterranean.	21/ 6/45
Hill, Rfn. C. W.	M.M.	Middle East.	1/ 6/48
	Mention.	Italy.	23/ 5/46
Hine, Sgt. J. A.	M.M.	Middle East.	5/11/42
	Bar to M.M.	Middle East.	14/ 1/43
Hines, Sgt. G. J.	M.M.	Middle East.	15/10/42
Hodge, Lieut. P. S.	Mention.	North-West Europe.	4/ 4/46
Hollands, Sgt. W. A.	M.M.	North-West Europe.	19/10/42
Hollis, Major R. D.	Bronze Star. (American.)		11/ 7/45
	Croix de Guerre. (French.)		2/ 8/45
	Mention.	North-West Europe.	2/ 8/45
Holt-Wilson, Lieut. A. B.	M.C.	Middle East.	20/ 1/42
Hopkins, Rfn. E. A.	Mention.	North-West Europe.	22/ 3/45
Hopkinson, Lt.-Col. H. S. P.	Mention.	Middle East.	1/ 4/41
	Mention.	Middle East.	30/12/41
	O.B.E.	Burma.	28/ 6/45
Hopper, Major J. O.	Mention.	Italy.	22/ 3/45
Hore-Ruthven, Capt. Hon. A. P. H.	Mention.	Middle East.	1/ 4/41
Horton, Cpl. J. A.	M.M.	Italy.	20/ 9/45
Hosier, Rfn. H. H.	Mention.	Middle East.	8/ 7/41
Hoskier, Capt. F. R. B.	Haakon VII Liberty Medal. (Norwegian.)		19/ 3/48

APPENDICES 453

Name	Award	Theatre	Date
Hoskyns, Lt.-Col. C. B. A.	Mention.	Calais.	20/ 9/45
Houdret, Capt. P. C. G. B.	M.B.E.	Italy.	20/ 9/45
Hough, Lieut. A. D. V.	Mention.	Escaped p.o.w.	15/ 6/44
Howorth, Lieut. D.	M.C.	North-West Europe.	21/12/45
Hughes, Sgt. W. J.	Mention.	Escaped p.o.w.	15/ 6/44
Humly, Rfn. S.	M.M.	Calais.	20/ 9/45
Hunt, Major G. H.	O.B.E.	B.E.F.	11/ 7/40
Colonel	C.B.E.	Italy.	20/ 9/45
Hunter, Lt.-Col. J. A., M.C., M.B.E.	D.S.O.	North-West Europe.	1/ 3/45
Hunter, Lieut. J. M.	M.C.	Middle East.	25/11/43
Huntsman, Lieut. J. H.	Mention.	Italy.	29/11/45
	Silver Star. (American.)		23/ 5/47
Hurley, Capt. R. C.	M.C.	Italy.	20/ 7/44
Husselby, C.S.M. J. E.	Mention.	Italy.	23/ 5/46
Hussey, Sgt. W.	M.M.	Middle East.	9/ 9/42
Innes, Lieut. P. C.	M.C.	Middle East.	13/ 8/42
	Mention.	Middle East.	15/12/42
Irvine, Rfn. T.	M.M.	Middle East.	22/ 7/43
Irvine, C.S.M. W. J.	Mention.	Italy.	19/ 7/45
Irwin, Lieut. J. B. D.	M.C.	Middle East.	14/ 1/43
Jacobs, Rfn. H. G.	Mention.	Middle East.	13/ 1/44
James, L./Sgt. A.	Mention.	North-West Europe.	22/ 3/45
James, Lieut. C. P.	M.C.	North-West Europe.	2/ 8/45
Jarvis, P.S.M. E. H.	D.C.M.	Middle East.	9/ 5/41
Jepson-Turner, Lieut. B. W.	M.C.	Middle East.	26/11/42
Major	Croix de Guerre. (French.)		23/ 4/45
Jepson-Turner, Lieut. R. L.	D.S.O.	Middle East.	13/ 8/42
Johnson, Lt.-Col. R. E. W., T.D.	O.B.E.	Italy.	13/12/45
Johnson, A./Cpl. T.	Mention.	Calais.	20/ 9/45
Johnston, Capt. C. G.	Mention.	Escaped p.o.w.	15/ 6/44
Johnston, Lieut. M. E.	Mention.	North-West Europe.	8/11/45
Johnston, P.S.M. R. A. V.	Mention.	Calais.	20/ 9/45
Jones, C.S.M. B. W.	Croix de Guerre. (French.)		5/ 1/43
Jones, Capt. E. A.	Mention.	Italy.	29/11/45
Jones, Rfn. K. F.	Mention.	Middle East.	15/12/42
Jones, C.S.M. R. M.	M.M.	Middle East.	14/ 1/43
Jordan, Rfn. F. G.	M.M.	North-West Europe.	1/ 3/45
Kane, Lieut. G. J.	Mention.	Calais.	20/ 9/45
Keighley, Major F. H. V.	Mention.	North-West Europe.	10/ 5/45
	O.B.E.	North-West Europe.	24/ 1/46
Kelly, Capt. J. T.	Mention.	Burma.	9/ 5/46
Kelly, Rfn. P.	Mention.	Middle East.	6/ 4/44
Kelsey, C.S.M. E.	Mention.	Italy.	29/11/45
Kennedy, Sgt. P. A.	Mention.	Special Operations.	28/ 2/46
Kerr, Major M. G.	Mention.	Special Operations.	27/ 5/41
King, Sgt. A. L.	Mention.	Italy.	23/ 5/46
King, Rfn. T. D.	Mention.	Italy.	11/ 1/45
King-Salter, Major E. J. C.	D.S.O.	Norway.	22/ 4/43
	O.B.E.	Home Forces.	1/ 1/46
Kingsmill, Cpl. G. H. W.	M.M.	North-West Europe.	1/ 3/45
Kinnaird, Capt. Hon. K. G.	Mention.	North-West Europe.	4/ 4/46
Kirk, Clr.-Sgt. A. J.	M.M.	Italy.	7/12/44
Kittoe, Lt.-Col. R. M. C.	O.B.E.	Italy.	13/12/45
Klanke, Cpl. E. G.	M.M.	Italy.	7/12/45
Ladmore, Rfn. L. R.	M.M.	North-West Europe.	2/ 8/45

Name	Award	Theatre	Date
Lane, C.Q.M.S. G.	Mention.	Italy.	29/11/45
Lane, Lt.-Col. G. E. W.	O.B.E.	Home Guard.	15/12/44
Lane, Cpl. G. J.	M.M.	Calais.	20/ 9/45
Langenscheid, Sgt. L. G. V.	M.M.	North-West Europe.	1/ 3/45
	Mention.	North-West Europe.	22/ 3/45
Langrish, Sgt. H. R.	Mention.	North-West Europe.	8/11/45
Lawson, C.S.M. W. J.	M.M.	Italy.	13/12/45
	Mention.	Italy.	23/ 5/46
Ledley, P.S.M. A.	M.M.	Calais.	20/ 9/45
Lee, Rfn. J.	Mention.	Middle East.	13/ 1/44
Lee, Sgt. W. W.	M.M.	North-West Europe.	21/12/44
Lemar, Sgt. A.	Mention.	Italy.	19/ 7/45
Lentaigne, Lieut. J. W. O'N.	M.C.	Middle East.	13/ 8/42
Leyland, Lieut. J. C. M.	M.C.	Middle East.	19/ 8/43
Liddell, Lieut. C. A.	M.C.	Middle East.	25/ 4/41
Lincoln, Rfn. A. C.	Mention.	North-West Europe.	22/ 3/45
Ling, Lieut. A. J.	M.C.	Middle East.	20/ 1/42
Lipman, Cpl. C.	Mention.	Italy.	11/ 1/45
Lloyd, Lieut. W. R. B.	M.C.	North-West Europe.	1/ 3/45
Longrigg, Lieut. J. S.	Mention.	Italy.	29/11/45
Longstaff, Sgt. G. E. M.	Bronze Star. (American.)		14/ 5/48
Longstaff, Rfn. R.	Mention.	Italy.	29/11/45
Lonsdale, Major J. F.	D.S.O.	Italy.	19/ 4/45
Love, Cpl. E. G.	Mention.	Italy.	23/ 4/46
Lowe, Sgt. J. E.	Mention.	North-West Europe.	22/ 3/45
Luke, Major P. A. C.	M.C.	North-West Europe.	12/ 4/45
Lyden, Sgt. J.	Mention.	Middle East.	6/ 4/44
Lytton-Milbanke, Lt.-Col. Hon. N. A. S.	O.B.E.	Italy.	13/12/45
MacAlpine, Lieut. J. W.	M.C.	Italy.	23/ 8/45
Macauley, A./Sgt. J.	Mention.	North-West Europe.	22/ 3/45
MacPherson, Sgt. A. H.	Mention.	Middle East.	8/ 7/41
Mahoney, Sgt. K.	Mention.	Calais.	20/ 9/45
Maidlow, Capt. J. H. T.	Mention.	North-West Europe.	9/ 8/45
Main, Sgt. D. A.	D.C.M.	Middle East.	1/ 6/43
2/Lieut.	M.C.	Italy.	7/12/44
Malkin, Cpl. J. A.	B.E.M.	Italy.	19/ 4/45
Manning, Sgt. A. H.	M.M.	Middle East.	25/11/43
Mansel, Sgt. A. F.	M.M.	Middle East.	18/12/43
Marchant, Rfn. A. G.	Mention.	Italy.	23/ 5/46
Marten, Major F. W.	M.C.	Middle East.	14/10/43
Mason, Major J. L.	Mention.	Italy.	29/11/45
Massy-Beresford, Brig. T. H., M.C.	D.S.O.	Far East.	13/12/45
Matthews, Sgt. H. J.	M.M.	Calais.	20/ 9/45
May, Capt. E. P.	M.C.	North-West Europe.	1/ 3/45
May, Lieut. G. T.	M.C.	Middle East.	22/ 9/43
McBrien, Capt. W. R.	Mention.	Middle East.	13/ 1/44
McColl, 2/Lieut. R. S.	M.C.	Middle East.	15/10/42
McGrigor, Capt. C. E.	Mention.	Italy.	23/ 5/46
Mee, S./Sgt. C. E. C.	Mention.	Escaped p.o.w.	15/ 6/41
Meldrum, Major H. T.	D.S.O.	Middle East.	18/12/43
Mellor, Lieut. A. H. S.	Mention.	Middle East.	8/ 7/41
Merrick, Capt. G. E.	M.C.	Italy.	23/ 8/45
Mersh, Cpl. A.	Mention.	Italy.	19/ 7/45
Metcalfe, Sgt. L. A.	Mention.	Italy.	19/ 7/45
Meyer, A./Sgt. K. C.	M.M.	North-West Europe.	21/12/44
Micaleff, Rfn. J.	M.M.	Mediterranean.	15/ 3/45
Mieville, Lieut. C. H.	M.C.	Italy.	24/ 8/44
Miles, A./Sgt. H. H.	M.M.	Middle East.	14/ 1/43

APPENDICES

Name	Award	Theatre	Date
Millar, Lieut. G. R.	M.C.	Escaped p.o.w.	27/ 4/44
Capt.	D.S.O.	Special Operations.	22/ 3/45
	Legion of Honour. (French.)		5/11/45
Millar, Lieut. R. J.	Mention.	North-West Europe.	8/11/45
	M.C.	North-West Europe.	24/ 1/46
Miller, Sgt. C. F.	Mention.	Middle East.	6/ 4/44
Miller, Cpl. R. W.	M.M.	Italy.	27/ 1/44
Millwood, Sgt. D. N.	Mention.	North-West Europe.	10/ 5/45
Milner, Major C. F.	M.C.	North-West Europe.	12/ 7/45
Milton, Rfn. S. J.	Mention.	Escaped p.o.w.	26/ 7/45
Minkoff, Sgt. A. R.	M.M.	Italy.	20/ 9/45
Mitchell, Lieut. J. I.	M.C.	Italy.	23/ 8/45
	Mention.	Italy.	29/11/45
Mitchell, Capt. J. R. S.	Mention.	Italy.	11/ 1/45
Mitchell, Lieut. P. A. N.	M.C.	North-West Europe.	12/ 7/45
Mole, Lieut. H. A.	Mention.	Burma.	19/ 9/46
Montford, Lt.-Col. I. C., D.S.O.	O.B.E.	Italy.	21/12/44
	Mention.	Italy.	25/ 5/46
Moore, Sgt. W. F.	Mention.	Italy.	23/ 5/46
Morgan, Rfn. G.	M.M.	Middle East.	5/11/42
Morgan, Major P. R. C.	Mention.	Italy.	24/ 8/44
Morgan-Grenville, Lt.-Col. Hon. T. G. B., D.S.O., M.C.	Mention.	North-West Europe.	22/ 3/45
	O.B.E.	North-West Europe.	24/ 1/46
Morhaim, Rfn. R.	Mention.	Italy.	19/ 7/45
Morley, Major G. W. R.	Mention.	Middle East.	24/ 6/43
Lt.-Col.	O.B.E.	Italy.	21/12/44
	Bronze Star. (American.)		20/ 3/47
Morpeth, Lieut. Viscount	M.C.	Italy.	28/ 6/45
Morris-Keating, Capt. P. S.	Mention.	Middle East.	24/ 6/43
Mosley, 2/Lieut. M. H.	M.C.	Middle East.	9/ 5/41
Mosley, Lieut. N.	M.C.	Italy.	12/ 4/45
Moss, Rfn. M. A.	Mention.	Special Operations.	6/ 6/46
Mulford, Sgt. H. C.	M.M.	Middle East.	15/10/42
Munday, R.S.M. L. E. B.	Mention.	Special Operations.	21/ 2/46
Murphy, L./Cpl. M. J.	Mention.	Calais.	20/ 9/45
Murray, Sgt. H. R.	M.M.	North-West Europe.	12/ 4/45
Naper, Lieut. N. W. I.	M.C.	Special Operations.	28/ 2/46
Nauman, Major J. E. B.	Mention.	Middle East.	13/ 1/44
Newman, A./Sgt. D.	M.M.	Middle East.	14/ 1/43
Nichol, Lt.-Col. H. R.	Mention.	Mediterranean.	22/ 2/45
Niven, Lt.-Col. J. D.	Legion of Merit. (American.)		8/11/45
Noonan, L./Cpl. J. P.	M.M.	North-West Europe.	2/ 8/45
Norman, Major G. E. M.	Mention.	Italy.	11/ 1/45
Northover, Rfn. J. F.	Mention.	Italy.	29/11/45
O'Brien, Rfn. J.	M.M.	Middle East.	9/ 5/41
O'Brien, Capt. Hon. P. L. A.	Mention.	India.	8/ 7/43
O'Grady, Sgt. H. J.	Mention.	Italy.	29/11/45
O'Hara, Sgt. W.	Mention.	Italy.	23/ 5/45
Oliver, Cpl. J.	Mention.	Italy.	19/ 7/45
Osborne, Cpl. E.	M.M.	North-West Europe.	1/ 3/45
Page, R.S.M. W. G.	Mention.	North-West Europe.	4/ 4/46
Pain, L./Sgt. H. E.	M.M.	Italy.	7/12/44
Paley, Major A. G. V.	O.B.E.	Middle East.	1/ 4/41
Lt.-Col.	D.S.O.	North-West Europe.	29/ 3/45
Palmer, Major A. G. D.	M.C.	Middle East.	1/ 4/41

Pammington, L./Sgt. F. S.	Mention.	Italy.	29/11/45
Parker, Major F. A.	Mention.	North Africa.	16/ 9/43
Lt.-Col.	O.B.E.	Italy.	28/ 6/45
Parker, Capt. R. J.	Mention.	Italy.	23/ 5/46
Pawson, Lieut. H. A.	Mention.	North Africa.	23/ 9/43
Payne, Rfn. G. R.	M.M.	Middle East.	5/11/42
Pearce, C.S.M. A. E.	Croix de Guerre. (French.)		3/ 4/45
Pearson, L./Sgt. S. G.	Mention.	Italy.	23/ 5/46
Pearson, Capt. T. C. H.	D.S.O.	Middle East.	9/ 5/41
Lt.-Col.	Bar to D.S.O.	Middle East.	19/ 8/43
Peel, Capt. P.	M.C.	Calais.	20/ 9/45
Perry, Rfn. A. J.	M.M.	Middle East.	1/ 4/41
Petley, Major H. H.	Mention.	Italy.	19/ 7/45
Pettit, Cpl. R. L.	M.M.	Middle East.	22/ 7/43
Pevalin, Cpl. S. W.	D.C.M.	Middle East.	13/ 8/42
Phillips, Sgt. D. M.	Mention.	Special Operations.	21/ 2/45
	Mention.	Calais.	20/ 9/45
Piggott, L./Cpl. L. E.	M.M.	North-West Europe.	24/ 1/46
Pinnock, R.S.M. E. T.	Mention.	Middle East.	8/ 7/41
	M.M.	Middle East.	10/ 2/43
Pittman, Sgt. A.	Mention.	Italy.	29/11/45
Plummer, Sgt. C. W.	Mention.	Italy.	29/11/45
Pocock, Rfn. F. A.	Mention.	North-West Europe.	9/ 8/45
Pontifex, Capt. D. M.	Mention.	Italy.	23/ 5/46
Pool, Sgt. E.	Mention.	Italy.	29/11/45
Poole, Major R. D. D.	Mention.	Middle East.	30/12/41
Pratt, L./Sgt. G.	D.C.M.	North-West Europe.	4/ 4/46
Prickett, A./Sgt. R. J.	Mention.	Italy.	23/ 5/46
Prior, Major H. H. V.	Mention.	Burma.	9/ 5/46
Prior, A./Cpl. W. C.	Mention.	North-West Europe.	4/ 4/46
Pritchard, Cpl. R. G. A.	M.M.	Italy.	28/ 6/45
Prittie, Lieut. Hon. T. C. F.	Mention.	Calais.	20/ 9/45
	M.B.E.	Special Operations.	5/12/46
Puddifoot, L./Cpl. E. G.	Mention.	Middle East.	24/ 6/43
Purdon, Col. D. J.	Mention.	Middle East.	15/12/42
	Mention.	Middle East.	6/ 4/44
	Legion of Merit. (American.)		17/10/46
Purvis, Capt. I. B.	Mention.	North-West Europe.	4/ 4/46
Puxley, Sgt. T. A.	M.M.	North-West Europe.	21/ 6/45
Rathbone, Lt.-Col. L. M. B.	O.B.E.	Home Forces.	1/ 1/45
Rawlings, C.S.M. W. A. C.	Mention.	Italy.	29/11/45
Ray, A./Sgt. J. F.	Mention.	Middle East.	13/ 1/44
Raynor, Lieut. W. B. G.	Mention.	Italy.	19/ 7/45
	M.C.	Italy.	13/12/45
Read, Rfn. S. A.	M.M.	Middle East.	1/ 6/43
Redfern, Lieut. T. E.	M.C.	Middle East.	13/ 8/42
Reeve, Major-Gen. J. T. W., D.S.O.	C.B.E.	China.	1/ 7/41
	C.B.	Home Forces.	1/ 7/46
	Order of Phœnix. (Greek.)		19/11/48
Renton, Lt.-Col. J. M. L., O.B.E.	Mention.	Middle East.	1/ 4/41
	D.S.O.	Middle East.	9/ 5/41
Brig.	Bar to D.S.O.	Middle East.	13/ 8/42
Restorick, Clr.-Sgt. F. W.	Mention.	Italy.	29/11/45
Richardson, Lieut. (Qrmr.) A. W.	Mention.	Middle East.	13/ 1/44
	M.B.E.	Italy.	28/ 6/45

APPENDICES 457

Name	Award	Theatre	Date
Richens, Sgt. F. J.	Mention.	North-West Europe.	4/ 4/46
Riddell, Major J. C.	Silver Star. (American.)		25/ 3/49
Rigglesworth, Major A. W.	Mention.	Italy.	19/ 7/45
Riley, C.S.M. J. A.	Mention.	Special Operations.	24/ 1/46
Roberts, C.S.M. F. H.	Mention.	Italy.	29/11/45
Roberts, C.S.M. R. G.	Mention.	Italy.	23/ 5/46
Roberts, C.S.M. W. H.	Mention.	B.E.F.	10/ 3/40
Robinson, Major J. C.	Bronze Star. (American.)		17/10/46
Rodwell, Sgt. P. L.	Mention.	North-West Europe.	8/11/45
Rogers, Capt. K. A.	M.B.E.	Italy.	28/ 6/45
Rolt, Lieut. A. P. R.	M.C.	Calais.	20/ 9/45
	Bar to M.C.	Escaped p.o.w.	1/11/45
Roots, Sgt. W. F. J.	M.M.	Italy.	8/ 2/45
Rose, Major C. M.	Mention.	North-West Europe.	9/ 8/45
Rowan, Major A. P.	Mention.	North-West Europe.	8/11/45
Rowett, Rfn. W.	M.M.	Middle East.	13/ 8/42
Russel, Major P. C. E.	Mention.	North-West Europe.	4/ 4/46
Russell, Capt. S. H.	O.B.E.	Home Forces.	22/ 1/41
Russell, Major W. R. V.	M.C.	Burma.	28/10/42
Rutley, Rfn. D. H. S.	Mention.	Middle East.	15/12/42
Sandell, R.Q.M.S. C.	Mention.	Middle East.	26/ 7/40
Sargeant, Major E. H.	Mention.	North-West Europe.	10/ 5/45
Saunderson, Lieut. A.	Mention.	Calais.	20/ 9/45
Sawyer, Rfn. V. O.	Mention.	Italy.	19/ 7/45
Scanes, Rfn. W. J.	Mention.	Middle East.	6/ 4/44
Seabrook, Rfn. V. J.	Mention.	Calais.	20/ 9/45
Sedgwick, Lieut. J. P.	M.C.	North-West Europe.	19/10/44
Selway, Major N. C.	Mention.	Italy.	19/ 7/45
Severn, Capt. C. D. G.	Mention.	Italy.	19/ 7/45
Shepherd, Major H. B.	Mention.	North-West Europe.	4/ 4/46
Shepherd-Cross, Major P. C.	M.C.	Italy.	7/12/44
Shilcock, Rfn. A. C.	M.M.	Middle East.	9/ 5/41
Shuckard, Rfn. H. D.	Mention.	Middle East.	6/ 4/44
Shutz, A./Cpl. H. J. M.	M.M.	North-West Europe.	1/ 3/45
Simmonds, C.S.M. S. J.	Mention.	Middle East.	13/ 1/44
Simond, Capt. C. K.	M.B.E.	North Africa.	16/ 9/43
	Mention.	North-West Europe.	8/11/45
	Mention.	North-West Europe.	4/ 4/46
Simpson, Rfn. T. C.	M.M.	Middle East.	13/ 8/42
Sinclair, Capt. T. C.	Mention.	Middle East.	1/ 4/41
	M.C.	Middle East.	8/ 7/41
	Bar to M.C.	Middle East.	12/ 2/42
Lt.-Col.	Mention.	Middle East.	6/ 4/44
	Mention.	Italy.	19/ 7/45
Skingle, Rfn. R. D.	Mention.	Italy.	19/ 7/45
Skipper, Sgt. J. A.	M.M.	North-West Europe.	12/ 4/45
Sladen, Lieut. D. R.	Mention.	Calais.	20/ 9/45
Small, Rfn. A.	Mention.	North Africa.	23/ 9/43
Smith, Sgt. N. W.	Mention.	Italy.	23/ 5/46
Smith, Sgt. T. F.	Mention.	Escaped p.o.w.	15/ 6/44
Smith, Lieut. (Qrmr.) W.	M.B.E.	Italy.	20/ 9/45
Soboleff, 2/Lieut. I. S. K.	M.C.	Middle East.	13/ 8/42
Major	Mention.	North-West Europe.	9/ 8/45
	Mention.	North-West Europe.	4/ 4/46
Soffe, Rfn. R. G.	Mention.	North-West Europe.	9/ 8/45
Southby, Lt.-Col. A. R. C.	O.B.E.	Italy.	13/12/45
	Medal of Freedom. (American.)		14/ 5/48

Name	Award	Theatre	Date
Sowter, Rfn. R.	Mention.	Italy.	23/ 5/46
Sparrow, Lieut. G. E.	M.C.	Italy.	8/ 2/45
Steels, L./Cpl. W.	Mention.	Calais.	20/ 9/45
Steer, Lieut. B.	Croix de Guerre. (French.)		4/ 2/46
Steggles, Cpl. V. E.	M.M.	North Africa.	8/ 7/45
Stephens, Lt.-Col. F.	D.S.O.	Middle East.	31/12/42
Stevens, P.S.M. H. L.	D.C.M.	Calais.	20/ 9/45
Stewart-Wilson, Lieut. R. S.	Mention.	Italy.	11/12/44
	M.C.	Italy.	7/12/46
Stileman, Lieut. D. M.	Cross of Merit. (Polish.)		4/12/44
Stockdale, T.S.M. W. R.	D.C.M.	Special Operations.	2/10/42
Stokes, Major D. R.	M.B.E.	Italy.	21/ 8/44
Stonell, L./Sgt. H.	M.M.	North-West Europe.	12/ 7/45
Stopford, Brig. M. G. N., M.C.	D.S.O.	B.E.F.	11/ 7/40
	Mention.	B.E.F.	26/ 7/40
	C.B.	Home Forces.	1/ 6/43
Lt.-Gen.	K.B.E.	Burma.	28/ 9/44
	G.C.B.	Burma.	1/ 1/47
General	Legion of Merit. (American.)		19/11/48
Straight, Capt. (Qrmr.) W.	Mention.	Calais.	20/ 9/45
Straker, Capt. J. J.	M.C.	North-West Europe.	1/ 3/45
Strange, Rfn. J.	Mention.	Escaped p.o.w.	1/ 3/45
Street, Major W. V., M.C.	O.B.E.	Middle East.	30/12/41
Lt.-Col.	D.S.O.	Mediterranean.	31/ 8/44
Sugg, L./Cpl. C. D.	Mention.	Italy.	19/ 7/45
Surtees, Lieut. J. F. H.	M.C.	Calais.	20/ 9/45
Suter, Major W. E.	Mention.	Middle East.	24/ 6/43
Sutton - Nelthorpe, Col. O., D.S.O., M.C.	C.B.E.	Home Forces.	11/ 6/42
Swann, Clr.-Sgt. J. E.	D.C.M.	Middle East.	14/ 1/43
Tapping, Sgt. W. H.	Mention.	Italy.	23/ 5/46
Taylor, Major J. A., M.C.	Mention.	Calais.	20/ 9/45
Taylor, Sgt. W.	Mention.	Italy.	29/11/45
Taylor, Sgt. W. J.	Mention.	Calais.	20/ 9/45
Taylor, Lt.-Col. W. J. K.	O.B.E.	North-West Europe.	13/ 6/46
Temperley, Col. C. E., O.B.E., M.C.	Mention.	Italy.	19/ 7/45
	Bronze Star. (American.)		18/ 7/47
Tendler, Cpl. A.	Mention.	North Africa.	23/ 9/43
Thompson, Sgt. A.	M.M.	Italy.	23/ 8/45
Thomson, Major J. H.	Mention.	North-West Europe.	22/ 3/45
	M.B.E.	North-West Europe.	24/ 1/46
Thornborough, Sgt. C. H.	Mention.	Italy.	29/11/45
	Mention.	Italy.	17/ 1/46
Thrift, Lieut. A. H.	M.C.	Italy.	19/ 4/45
Tibbet, Major G. R.	Mention.	North-West Europe.	4/ 4/46
Toms, 2/Lieut. J. E. B.	M.C.	Middle East.	13/ 8/42
	Bar to M.C.	Middle East.	14/ 1/43
Townshend, Capt. H. R.	M.B.E.	North-West Europe.	24/ 1/46
Trappes-Lomax, Major S. R.	M.C.	Middle East.	28/ 1/43
Traylor, Clr.-Sgt. F. H.	Mention.	Mediterranean.	22/ 2/45
Trevelyan, Lieut. W. R.	Mention.	Italy.	19/ 7/45
Triggs, Sgt. S. J.	M.M.	North-West Europe.	19/10/45
Trinder, Rfn. D. J.	M.M.	Middle East.	19/ 8/43

APPENDICES 459

Name	Award	Location	Date
Tritton, Major Sir G. E., Bt.	Bronze Star. (American.)		18/12/45
Tully, Sgt. G. A.	Mention.	Escaped p.o.w.	16/ 6/44
Turner, Lt.-Col. V. B.	V.C.	Middle East.	19/11/42
Van der Weyer, Lieut. A. J. B.	Mention.	Calais.	20/ 9/45
Vatcher, Lieut. H. F. W. L.	Mention.	Italy.	23/ 5/46
Verney, Lt.-Col. U. O. V.	O.B.E.	Italy.	30/ 6/46
Walker, Rfn. F. A.	Mention.	Middle East.	24/ 6/43
	M.M.	Middle East.	14/10/43
	Mention.	North-West Europe.	30/ 8/45
Waller, Capt. J. de W.	M.C.	Special Operations.	7/11/46
Walters, Lt.-Col. C. E.	Mention.	Italy.	23/ 5/46
Warner, Cpl. V. W.	M.M.	Middle East.	20/ 1/42
Warren, Major C. P., M.C.	M.B.E.	Middle East.	11/ 7/40
	Order of the Nile. (Egyptian.)		31/ 4/41
	Legion of Merit. (American.)		15/ 8/46
Webb, Rfn. A. A.	M.M.	Middle East.	22/ 7/43
Webster, Sgt. J. J.	M.M.	Middle East.	13/ 8/42
Weeks, Lt.-Gen. Sir R. M., C.B.E., D.S.O., M.C., T.D.	K.C.B.	War Office.	2/ 6/43
	Legion of Merit. (American.)		17/11/47
Welch, Sgt. J. L. D.	Mention.	Calais.	20/ 9/45
Weld-Forester, Lieut. C. R. C.	Mention.	Calais.	20/ 9/45
	Mention.	Escaped p.o.w.	1/11/45
Wells, Rfn. L. F.	Mention.	Escaped p.o.w.	1/ 3/45
Wells, A./Cpl. M. W.	Mention.	Special Operations.	28/ 2/46
Welsh, Sgt. D. W.	Mention.	B.E.F.	3/ 2/44
Weyman, Rfn. H. A. G.	Mention.	Escaped p.o.w.	15/ 6/44
Wheeler, Capt. H. C.	Mention.	Escaped p.o.w.	9/11/44
Wheeler, L./Sgt. J.	Mention.	Italy.	23/ 5/46
Whigham, Capt. I. H. D.	Mention.	Middle East.	15/12/42
Major	Mention.	Italy.	24/ 8/44
	M.B.E.	Italy.	19/ 4/45
Whitaker, Lieut. T. A. A.	M.C.	North-West Europe.	1/ 3/45
Whitchelo, Cpl. H. R.	Mention.	Italy.	23/ 5/46
White, L./Sgt. A.	M.M.	North-West Europe.	5/ 4/45
White, C.S.M. G. F.	M.B.E.	Middle East.	30/12/41
Wightman, Sgt. G. C.	D.C.M.	Middle East.	19/ 8/41
Wigley, Cpl. N. D.	Mention.	Italy.	19/ 7/45
Wilkie, C.S.M. A. A.	Mention.	Burma.	19/ 9/46
Williams, Brig. E. S. B.	C.B.E.	Home Forces.	1/ 6/43
Williams, P.S.M. I.	Mention.	Calais.	20/ 9/45
Williams, Major I. E.	Mention.	Italy.	29/11/46
Willis, C.S.M. A. T.	Mention.	Middle East.	8/ 7/41
Wilsmer, A./Cpl. R.	Mention.	Special Operations.	9/11/44
Wilson, Major A. J.	M.C.	Italy.	23/ 8/45
	Mention.	Italy.	29/11/45
Wilson, Sgt. D.	D.C.M.	Middle East.	1/ 6/43
Wilson, Major D. O.	Mention.	Middle East.	15/12/42
Wilson, Major H.	Mention.	Italy.	19/ 7/45
Wilson, Lt.-Gen. Sir H. M., D.S.O.	K.C.B.	Middle East.	11/ 7/40
	G.B.E.	Middle East.	4/ 3/41
	Mention.	Middle East.	1/ 4/41

460 THE RIFLE BRIGADE

Wilson, Lt.-Gen. Sir H. M., D.S.O.	Military Cross. (Greek.)		10/ 4/42
General	Mention.	Middle East.	24/ 6/43
	G.C.B.	Italy.	8/ 6/44
	Virtuti Militari. (Polish.)		4/12/44
Field-Marshal	Bronze Star. (American.)		8/12/45
	D.S.M.		24/ 1/46
	Legion of Merit. (American.)		4/ 4/46
Wilson, Major P. M.	Mention.	Persia and Iraq.	5/ 8/43
Wilton, Sgt. G.	Mention.	Special Operations.	6/ 6/42
Witt, Major J. C.	Mention.	North-West Europe.	4/ 4/46
Wohlegemuth, Rfn. J. W. ..	Mention.	Middle East.	6/ 4/44
Wood, Lieut. J. K.	M.C.	Italy.	19/ 4/45
Worboys, C.S.M. G. A.	Mention.	Middle East.	13/ 1/44
R.S.M.	Bronze Star. (American.)		16/ 1/47
Worsley, Major R. E.	Mention.	Italy.	23/ 5/46
Wright, Lt.-Col. E. F. L. ..	O.B.E.	North-West Europe.	13/ 6/46
Wright, Sgt. P.	Mention.	Italy.	23/11/45
Wright, Sgt. S.	Mention.	Italy.	23/11/45
Wrixon-Becher, Capt. Sir W. F., Bt.	M.C.	Middle East.	1/ 6/43
Wyeth, Rfn. W. J.	M.M.	Middle East.	24/ 9/42
Yetman, Lieut. E. R. C. ..	M.C.	North-West Europe.	26/12/44

60TH RIFLES

At various times and in all theatres officers and riflemen of the 60th Rifles served with the Regiment. Those who were awarded decorations while serving with the 8th Battalion in North-West Europe include the following:

Lieut.-Colonel J. A. Hunter, M.B.E., M.C.	D.S.O. Mention in Despatches.
Major P. J. Bradford..	D.S.O. M.C.
Lieut. M. M. J. Raymond	M.C.
Sergt. J. Barton	M.M.
Sergt. H. Stonell	M.M.

INDEX

INDEX

Acroma, 53, 113, 119, 122, 131
Acton, Maj. T. H., 16-19, 22
Adams, Lt. R. B. M., 370
Adige River, 338, 340, 342
Afragola, 245
Afrika Korps: arrive in M.E., 61; 64, 71, 103, 104, 111, 133, 136, 142, 146, 161, 184-5, 220; end of, 236, 237
Agedabia, 63, 65, 98, 103, 107, 187-8, 194
Agheila, 60, 62, 64; second advance to, 94; 99, 134-6, 187-8, 194, 213, 233, 376
Ahaus, 402
Akarit, Wadi, 195, 202, 204, 220, 231, 236
Alam Halfa, 110, 144-6, 393
Alamein, 4, 5, 34, 42, 64, 77, 110, 120, 130, 181, 183, 185, 192, 224, 230, 233, 239, 250, 324, 329, 376, 404
Alamein Line, 131, 133
Alatri, 263, 264
Albert Canal, 386
Aldridge, Rfn., 307
Alexander, F.-M. Lord, 261, 339
Algiers, 213
Allan, Maj. A. W., 9, 20-3
Allen, Sgt., 156
Aller River, 403
Allford, Lt. C. A. W., killed, 296
Amecourt, 372
Americans: land in Africa, 161; 191, 204, 213, 217, 218, 220, 225, 262, 290, 303, 367-8, 372, 384, 386, 391, 393
American Fifth Army, 242, 243
Amiens, 373, 374, 407, 414
Amoroso, Col., 178
Anderson, Lt. M. C., 371; killed, 374
Andrews, Maj. A. J., 63
Anneullin, 374
Anson, Maj. H. E., 102
Antelat, 65, 102, 186, 187
Antoine, Clr.-Sgt., 76
"Antonio," Rfn., 46
Antwerp, 375, 379, 383, 405, 414
Anzio, 254, 260, 262, 414
Apennines: winter in, 299-312, 251, 254, 262
Apsey, Lt. P. C., killed, 402
Apsey, Maj. W. J., 118, 121, 232, 245, 247, 348, 364
Aqena Nuova Canal, 248, 249

Arce, 257, 260
Archangel, s.s., 8
Ardennes, 389-91, 393, 396
Arezzo, 263, 283, 286
Argenta Gap, 332
Argentan, 361
Argoub el Hanech, 216
Argoub el Megas, 227-9
Armies—
 First Army: 161, 187; train in England, 207; Africa, 218, 206, 229-30; impression of Eighth Army on, 223, 229, 230, 235, 414
 Second Army: 373
 Fifth Army: 252, 261, 263, 254, 268, 290, 312, 332, 333
 Eighth Army: 119; in retreat, 122; 123-7, 133, 134-6, 141-3, 148, 157, 161, 164, 184, 191, 193, 195, 199, 201, 202, 204, 206, 214, 220, 223-4, 231, 234, 235, 242, 243, 252, 254-5, 261, 263, 268, 287, 294, 303, 312-3, 331, 333, 340
Arnhem, 382, 384
Arno Valley, 253, 282
Arras, 374
Arromanches, 347, 355
Atkin, Clr.-Sgt., 76
Aunay, 375
Australian Forces, 63, 70, 224, 156
Aversa, 246, 249
Avranches, 350
Ayres, Sgt.: at Snipe, 172, 175

Badinsky, Gen. K., 371
Baldwin, Sgt., 392
Bampfield, Lt. A. G. H., 15
Barclay, Capt. C. F. M., 53
Bardia, 42, 53, 61, 72, 182-3, 185-6
Baring, Maj. H. C., 122; joins 61st Inf. Bde., 260
Baron, 357
Barrett, Sgt., 228, 353
Barrow, Maj. H., R.A., 77
Barum, 409
Bas Perier, 369-70, 385
Bass, Capt. C. C., 65
Basset, Maj. D. W., 162, 267
Basset, Maj. R. T., 33 (footnote), 70-1, 73, 77, 82-7
Bassum, 403
Bates, Maj. J. D., 399

463

Battalions—
1st Battalion: Calais, 7-30; 81, 101; re-formed, 102; arrives at Suez 102; 103, 107, 109; visit of H.M. King of Hellenes, 109; 117-20, 122, 129, 131, 135, 142; Col. F. Stephens commands, 143; 144, 146; "Desert Rats," 147; 148-50, 153, 154, 181, 182, 193, 196, 197, 205, 206, 213, 217, 227, 229, 230, 232, 233, 235, 236; Italy, 238; inspected by H.M., 239; Col. Stephens leaves, 242; Col. V. Paley commands, 242; 247; leaves Italy, 250; 253, 267, 268, 337; Norfolk, 344; embarks, 346; arrives France, 347; 349, 352-4, 360, 362, 364-66, 375, 382, 386, 395, 397; visit of Sir J. Burnett-Stuart, 400; Germany, 402; Col. V. Paley leaves, 403; Col. Boden commands, 413

2nd Battalion: 31-82; hands over to 1st Bn., 101; Col. Renton in command, 111; 113, 116, 119-20, 122-3, 125; Maj. Hon. M. G. Edwardes to command, 128; 135, 144-9, 153-5, 157-9; Snipe, 162; 164; D. Order Snipe, 165; 166, 182, 191, 193; visit of Lord Wilson, 194; 195, 199, 200, 201, 202; move to First Army, 206; 221, 223, 226-7, 229-31, 232, 235, 236; Italy, 238; inspected by H.M., 239; visit of Lord Wilson, 239; 252; Taranto, 259; joins 61st Inf. Bde., 259; 260, 266-7, 270-1, 273-4, 276-8, 281, 284-6, 288, 290-1, 294, 296, 299, 303, 306, 308; Tossignano, 311-3; 316, 320; re-formed, 324; appreciation of service, 324; 328, 333, 335, 338-40; first British troops to enter Austria, 342; 345, 413, 414

7th Battalion: 135, 136, 141-5, 147-8, 153-5, 157-8, 160, 163-4, 181-2, 193, 195, 196, 198-200, 201-5; to First Army, 206; 213, 221, 223, 227, 229-30, 234-6; Nile Delta, 238; inspection by H.M., 239; Eden visits, 240; Gen. Lord Wilson visits, 240; Taranto and joins 61st Inf Bde., 259; 260, 263-6, 269-70; enters Todi, 271; 274, 281, 284-5, 287-9, 292, 294-5, 297, 300, 307, 309, 317-9, 328, 331, 332; under command of 26th Armd. Bde., 332; crosses Po, 340; 413

8th Battalion: 207, 220, 267-8, 337; history, 344; 346, 349-55; arrives France, 355; Hill 112, its first experience, 356; 358-60, 362; good record, 363; withdrawn to refit, 364; 366; draft from 8th/60th, 367; 370, 382, 383, 388, 390; Brussels, 391; under 6th Airborne, 393; 405, 413

9th Battalion: Tower Hamlets Rifles, 413; 9, 60; Port Said, 61; 62, 66, 78, 81, 94, 99, 100, 103, 105, 107, 109, 111, 113, 120, 129-30, 131, 135; disbanded, 138; appreciation, 140; 146, 236-7

10th Battalion: 161, 206-9, 212, 214, 219-20, 222; pig taken by Eighth Army, 225; 226-7, 229, 232-4, 238; inspected by H.M. and P.M., 239; Liri Valley, 240; 251, 252, 254-5, 258, 262, 267-8, 272-4, 280, 283, 285, 287-9, 291, 295, 297, 301, 304-5, 319, 321-2, end of Bn., 328; 329, 345, 375

Battipaglia, 243, 303
Baylay, Maj. B. C., 100
Becher, Sir W. B. W.-, Bt., 203, 227
Beckwith, Capt. H. A. H., killed, 229
Beda Fomm, 141
Beelev, Rfn., V.C. (60th Rifles), 84
Beirut 239, 241
Beja, 211
Belefaa Ridge, 121
Bell, Maj. G. N., 360, 371, 391
Belli Circus, 410
Belsen, 409
Benghazi, 55, 62, 97, 100, 108, 126, 147, 186-7, 190, 193, 337
Bergen-op-Zoom, 394
Bergonzoli, Gen., 58, 59
Béthune, 377
Bickersteth, Capt. P. M. G., 398
Biddell, Lt. P. B., M.C., 108, 121, 145, 246; wounded, 247
Binks, Sgt. R.A., 170, 172, 174
Bir Aslag, 118, 121
Bir el Gubi, 82, 83, 88, 95, 116, 117, 131
Bir el Tmer, 122
Bir Hacheim, 13, 105, 112-3, 116-20, 122-6, 128, 130, 141, 188
Bir Suweiyat, 74
Bir Taieb el Essem, 92
Bir Temrad, 107
Bir Thalata, 128
Birch, Lt. R. M., killed, 365
Birch, Maj. Whirley, R.A., 77, 115
Bird, Maj. T. A., 42, 54, 55, 77, 87, 112, 124, 138, 172, 174, 176, 177
Bird, Capt. M. G., 159

INDEX

Bird, 2/Lt. E. A., 12, 20, 21
Bizerta, 211, 239, 241
"Blackcock," Operation, 397, 399
Blacker, Capt. I. F. E., 278; killed, 279; 281
Blackman, Cpl., 18, 19
"Bladeforce," 209-11, 214, 222, 232
Boars, wild, 393
Bocconi, 292, 294
Boden, Maj. P. A. D., 78, 100, 130, 131, 223 (footnote), 395; commanding 1st Bn., 398; commanding 1st Bn., 403
Bodley, Lt. J. E. C., 234, 256
Boisselles, 393
Bologna, 290, 294, 303
Bomford, Lt. R. L., killed, 258
Bond, Lt. H. M. G., 248
Bone, 213, 254
Booth, Maj. A. J. G., 279, 329
Borgo, 319, 325; Gap, 314-16; 318, 303
Born, 397
Bosvile, Brig. T. J. B., 102, 119; commanding 7th Motor Bde., 143; 176, 202, 237
Bou Arada, 213-6, 221; Vale, 223; 226-7, 229
Bou Ficha, 239
Bouthardi, 205
Bowden, Sgt., 357
Bradbury, Sgt., 136
Bradford, Maj. P. J., 370, 407
Bras, 361-3, 366
Brausch, Gen. von: surrenders, 235; 236
Bray, Sgt., 351
Bree, 394
Brett, Sgt.: Snipe, 172; 175
Bretteville L'Orgueilleuse, 356
Breuil, 376
Brigades—
  2nd Armd.: 77, 105-7, 117-8, 120, 166, 174-5, 203
  2nd Para.: 254
  3rd Indian Motor: 119
  4th Armd.: 55, 58, 71-2, 83, 89, 95, 99, 146, 227, 233, 356
  4th Light Armd.: 189
  7th Armd.: 71, 72, 77, 82, 84, 89, 111, 112, 116, 123, 124, 127, 189, 206, 249
  7th Motor: 77, 72, 79, 82-4, 89, 111-2, 116, 123-4, 127, 143, 144, 146, 148, 153-4, 157-8, 165, 171, 175-6, 182, 195-6, 198, 201-2, 205, 225, 235, 260
  8th Armd.: 189
  9th Armd.: 259
  21st Indian: 318
  22nd Armd.: 80-3, 88, 99, 121, 142, 143-6, 150, 182, 184, 189, 192, 193, 196, 205, 220, 232, 244, 364, 365, 375, 395, 396, 397
  24th Armd.: 170-2
  26th Armd.: 227, 233, 255, 267-8, 270, 284, 286-7, 294, 297, 331-2
  29th Armd.: 301, 345, 361
  28th (Irish) Inf.: 297, 313
  61st Inf.: 259-62, 267-9, 271-2, 282, 284, 289, 293, 299; Christmas card from Germans, 326; 329, 330, 332, 339, 375
  131st Inf.: 151, 386, 397, 398
  150th Inf.: 120
  159th Inf.: 372
"Brockforce," 394
Brockhuizenvorst, 390
Brooke, Maj. J. A. R., 275
Brown, Maj. J. F., 318, 320-1, 323
Brown, Sgt.: Snipe, 171; 172
Brown, Sgt.: Snipe, 174
Brown, Cpl., 45
Browne, Maj. Hon. H. G. A.: killed, 146
Brownlow, Maj. W. S., 159
Brush, Lt.-Col. E. J. A. H., 17, 18, 21, 26
Brussels, 390, 391
Bug Bug, 41, 46, 66, 68, 69, 70, 107, 112, 123
Bunsoh, 404
Burder, Lt. G. C., 387; killed, 404
Bure, 393
Burg el Arab, 142
Burgsteinfurt, 405
Burnett-Stuart, Gen. Sir J., 400
Burma, 414
Burton, Maj., R.A., 59
Butler, Lt. R. M., 349
Buxtehude, 404
Byass, Col. F., 85

Cable, Cpl., 399
Caen, 346, 350, 353-7, 359-62, 365-6, 376
Caesar, Lt. J. V., killed, 354
Cairo, threat to removed, 146
Calais, 25, 27, 29, 39, 250, 311, 344, 347, 404; messages, 414
Calistan, Lt. C. V., 72, 172-3, 178; killed, 287
Cameron, Capt., R.A.M.C., Calais, 24
Campbell, Brig. J. C., 4; character, 38; 39, 44, 55, 66, 69, 71, 74-5, 77, 80, 89, 92, 94, 98, 128; killed, 138; 237, 349, 350, 389
Camurcino, 286
Canadians, 256-7, 313, 364-6, 376
Cancello, 247
Cantalupo, 270
Cap Bon Peninsula, 64, 230-3, 235
Capua, 247, 253

Capuzzo, 39, 40, 69, 72
Cardito, 245, 249, 403
Carpiquet, 356, 357
Carter, Capt. G. J., 97
Casa Collina, 306
Casa Colombaia, 303
Casa Frascoleto, 303, 316-7, 319
Casa Mescola, 319
Casola Valsenio, 304, 323
Cassino, 254-6, 259, 272, 314
Castagneto, 291
Castel del Rio, 297
Castelvieto, 278
Castiglion-Florentino, 284
Cattolica, 330, 342
Cauldron, The, 120, 123-4
Caunchy, 377
Caunter, Brig. J. A. L., 55
Cavalry—
  K.D.G.: 55, 77, 98, 112, 280
  Bays: 77, 102, 118, 121
  5th D.G.: 375, 386-8
  Royals: 76, 97
  Greys: 77, 146, 150
  3rd Hussars: 69, 77
  7th Hussars: 53, 77, 85, 338
  8th Hussars: 77, 349, 398, 404
  9th Lancers: 77, 102, 118
  10th Hussars: 77, 102, 118, 235, 345
  11th Hussars: 39, 41, 55-6, 68, 76, 81-3, 106, 185-6, 232, 248-9, 387, 403
  12th Lancers: 77, 112
  16th/5th Lancers: 217, 220-1, 266-7, 276, 283, 286-7, 288
  17th/21st Lancers: 209, 211, 215, 218, 220, 266, 269, 276-87, 288, 294-7, 331-2, 334-5
  23rd Hussars: 4, 356-7, 382-4, 368-70, 372, 405, 410
  27th Lancers: 339-40
Cavanazza, 338
Cave del Predil, 340
Cemetery Hill, 64
Cerqueto, 271
Chabot, Capt. K. N. O., 372
Chapel Hill, 393
Chard, Rfn.: Snipe, 172
Charleroi, 391
Charruba, 104
Chenedolle, 369
Chetniks, 341, 342
Cheux, 356-9
Chiana Valley, 283
Chichester, Maj. O. R. H., 39, 74, 88
Chouigi Pass, 211
Christian, Capt. C. E., 248
Christopher, Lt.-Col. J. R. C., R.A., 71
Churchill, Rt. Hon. W.: 109; visit, 143; visit, 191; 240, 241

Clark, Lt. E. G.: killed, 284
Clarke, Lt. A.: killed, 376
Clarke, Cpl.: killed, 395
Clayton, Maj. M. G., 100
Cleret, G., 379
Clifton, C./Sjt., 21
Cogalina, 327
Coghill, Maj. H., 15
Cohen, Lt. L. H. L., 192; wounded, 199
Colt-Williams, Lt. R., 73
Combe, Maj.-Gen. J. F., 55, 60
Connaught, H.R.H. The Duke of, 32, 59
Connelly, Sgt., 406; killed, 409
Consett, Lt.-Col. C. d'A. P., 71, 77
Cope, Lt. J. F., 62
Cope, Cpl.: Snipe, 175
Copeland, Maj. J. R., 84; killed, 240
Corbett-Winder, Lt.-Col. J. L., 150
Corciano, 278-80
Cormons, 341-2
Corps—
  21st Army Group: 288, 346, 392
  V: 332
  VIII: 355, 356, 358, 403
  IX: 228
  X: 147, 148, 161, 193, 242, 244, 280, 290
  XII: 397
  XIII: 83, 96, 104, 106, 148, 255, 260, 290, 312
  XXX: 80, 117, 119, 188, 224, 346, 373
Cortona, 284
Coryton, Capt. J., 385
Coryton, Lt. W. P.: killed, 143
Cowan, Admiral Sir W., 116
Coward, Cpl., 402
Craye-sur-Mer, 355
Crete: German reinforcements to M.E. from, 144
Crevecoeur-le-Grand, 373
Criss, P.S.M., 16, 17
Croara, 302, 312
Crocker, Gen. Sir J.: wounded by Piat, 228
Crocker, R.S.M., 255, 339
Croissy-sur-Selle, 373
Cross, Cpl., 12
Crowder, Lt. M. K., 90; Snipe, 177
Cubitt, Capt. M. F. V., 46, 58
Cubitt, Sgt., 249
Cullen, Sgt., 172; Snipe, 174
Culme-Seymour, Lt. (later Maj.), 121
Culnane, Cpl.: killed, 408
Cunliffe, Maj. D. F., 356
Currie, Lt.-Col. J. C., 96-8
Cyrene, 62
Cyrenaica, 193

INDEX

Dabaa, 132
Darlan, Admiral, 210
Darling, Lt.-Col. D. L., 33 (footnote), 57, 68, 228, 260, 271, 274; wounded, 276; 335, 340, 342
Davies-Scourfield, Maj. J., 90, 112
De Heidenbloom, 387
De Rips, 385, 388
Deir el Ragil, 135, 137, 144
Derna, 53, 65, 68, 190, 194, 404
Des Graz, Lt.-Col. P. A.: killed, 120
Desert, description of, 34
"Desert Rats," 223, 225
Deurne, 385, 388
Dewhurst, Maj. T. L., 289, 335
Dido, H.M.S., 213
Digby, Rev. Wingfield, 24
Dinant, 391-2, 414
Dinther, 386
Divisions—
   1st Armd.: 77, 80, 102, 104, 108, 112, 146-7, 153, 166, 198, 200-2, 204, 223, 225, 229, 230, 235, 344
   2nd Armd.: 60-2, 99
   4th British: 230, 233
   4th Indian: 46, 72, 80, 97, 99, 183, 198, 199, 204, 230-1
   5th Indian: 135
   6th Armd.: 207, 209, 214, 220, 225-6, 230-34, 254, 255, 258, 259, 263, 272, 331, 332, 333, 340
   6th Airborne: 393
   7th Armd.: 68-71, 80-1, 88, 94, 101, 102; reorganized, 111; 119; Renton commanding, 128; 147, 229, 230-1, 241-2, 247, 249, 272, 346, 354, 360, 364, 365, 367, 375, 376, 382, 386, 388, 395, 397, 400, 402, 405
   8th Indian: 254, 256, 270, 288, 302, 319
   8th Armd.: 142
   10th Armd.: 239
   10th Indian: 258, 281, 290
   11th Armd.: 345, 356, 360, 364-7, 375, 382-5, 394, 400, 402, 405
   15th Scottish: 356, 367, 370, 386, 410
   43rd: 372.
   44th: 150, 266
   46th: 243, 248
   49th: 394
   50th: 107, 120, 122, 147, 197, 198, 346
   51st: 147, 156, 163, 166, 190, 204, 205, 388
   56th: 243, 247-8
   78th: 230, 257, 264, 332
Dixon, Lt. A. T., 383

Djebel Akdar, 62, 342
Djebel Beida, 203
Djebel Hadoudi, 203
Djebel Saikhra, 198, 245
Djedida, 212
Dodgy Column, 129
Doherty, Rfn., 307
Dolling, Sgt.: Snipe, 171; 172
Dorrien-Smith, Maj. F. A., 121, 232; killed, 354
Dortmund, 402, 406
Douglas, Brig. A. S. G., 85, 95, 97
Downing, Lt. S. J. F., 265
Dudgeon, Maj. J. A., 142, 182
Dumy, Y., 378
Dunphie, Maj.-Gen. C. A. L.: leaves Bde., 219
Duncanson, Lt. J. P., 13, 19, 22, 28

Eagle, Rfn., 22
Eakins, Lt. E. G., 308
Easen, P.S.M., 16, 26
Ebn Ksour, 219
Echt, 397
Eden, Rt. Hon. A., 240
Edwardes, Maj. Hon. M. G., 103; commanding 2nd Bn., 128
Edwards, Lt. B. W. M.: killed, 198
Egleston, Capt. M. K. M. F., 228
El Adem, 126
El Aggareb, 205
El Agheila, 100, 197
El Ala, 217
El Alamein: myth of El Alamein Line, 134; 145-5, 142, 144, 146; Battle of, 148; 149, 151, 162-3
El Arrousa, 212
Elbe, 147, 404-5, 409, 410
El Duda, 84
El Hamma, 5; the Gap, 196; 200, 201-2, 204
Elkington, Maj. J. D. R., 209
Elkington, Lt. R. F. R.: killed, 216
Elkington, Sgt., 394
Ellon, 359, 375
El Ruweisat, 143
Elvet el Tamar, 131
Emerson-Baker, Capt. J. R., 145, 266
Ems, 402, 406
Enfidaville Line, 206, 231, 235
"Epsom," Exercise, 356
Eritrea, 71
Erskine, Maj.-Gen. G. W. E. J., 356, 375
Erskine, Brig. I., 68
Escaut Canal, 386
Esquay, 357
Etrepagny, 372
Evelegh, Maj.-Gen. V., 266, 288

Faella, 287
Fairweather, Maj. R. F., 218, 322
Falaise, 356, 358, 360, 365, 371, 376
Fallingbostel, 404
Fano, 329
Farfa, 269
Fellowes, Hon. J. D. C., 17, 19, 26
Ferrara, 253, 332, 337
Ferrieres, 368
Fervaques, 376
Field, A./Cpl., 45
Fiuggi, 266
Flers, 371
Fletcher, Lt. F. T. F. C. G., 15
Fletcher, Capt. G. E., 104, 198; killed, 199
Florence, 253, 289, 304, 326
Flower, Maj. R. A., 77, 163, 165-6, 174, 266
Flower, Maj. P. T., 39, 89
Flower, Lt. P. E.: killed, 156
Folgore, Italian Div., 150
Fondouk, 221-2
Fontana Liri, 258
Fontanelice, 302, 304, 313, 319, 339
Foreign Formations and Units—
  Adolf Hitler Panz. Div., 352, 362
  Ariete Div., 129, 234
  Hermann Goering Div., 114, 229, 235, 262
  Regiment Hardegg, 389
  Young Fascists, 238
  1st German Para. Corps, 333
  1st German Para. Div., 255, 287, 333
  1st S.S. Panz. Div., 262, 263
  4th Alpine Bn., 265
  4th German Para. Div., 333
  Seventh German Army, 373
  Tenth German Army, 294
  10th Panz. Div., 220-1, 235
  12th S.S. Regt., 409
  15th Panz. Div., 75, 89, 114, 146, 183, 238, 255, 276-7
  21st Panz. Div., 75, 85, 88, 107, 114; Snipe, 174; 183, 201, 238, 376
  26th Panz. Div., 255
  33rd Recce Regt., 75
  44th Austrian Div., 266
  65th German Div., 339
  90th German Light Div., 114, 146, 185, 234, 236-8, 255
  90th Panz. Div., 255
  97th German Corps, 340
  133rd (12th Bn.) Regt. of Littorio Div.: Snipe, 178
  194th German Arty. Regt., 285
  271st German Div.: H.Q. staff captured, 371
  275th German Div., 333
  305th German Div., 277, 292
  334th German Fusilier Regt., 313
  715th German Fusilier Bn., 289, 290, 292, 339
  735th German (2nd Bn.) Regt., 306, 313
  755th German Regt., 306, 313, 321
  1028th German Regt., 290
Foreshew, Lt. T. J., 245, 353
Forest of Olives, 204-5
Forêt d'Eveque, 368
Forêt de Montfort, 377
Forli, 393
Fort Maddalena, 39
Fossa Cembalina, 334
Foster, Maj. O. H. J., 316, 321
Foy Notre Dame, 392, 393
Francis, Maj. J. M., 143
Francis, Cpl.: Snipe, 172
Franklyn, Capt. A. A., 43, 82; killed, 97
Francolise, 247, 248
Free French, 107, 112, 122, 124-5, 130
French Volunteers: for Regt., 377
Frewen, Lt. E. P. V.: killed, 234
Freyberg, Gen. Sir B. C., Bt., 234, 239
Fruin, Sgt., 374-5
Fulford, Lt.-Col. F. E. A., 33 (footnote)
Fulignano, 259
Fulton, Cpl., 367
Fyffe, Lt. D. O.: killed, 409
Fyffe, Maj. L. R. K., 275-6
Fyffe, Lt.-Col. R. A., 241; to command R.W.K., 254; commanding 2nd Bn., 276; commanding 10th Bn., 288; goes blindfolded to arrange surrender of Germans, 339

Gabes, 201, 202
Gafsa, 204
Gambut, 123
Garigliano, River, 244, 248-50
Garmoyle, Brig. Viscount, 4, 74, 33 (footnote), 54, 68, 77, 82-3, 85, 90, 94, 97, 101, 112, 116, 119, 124; to command 7th Motor Bde., 128; killed, 138; 143, 237
Garnier, Maj. E. H. C., 121, 135, 186, 245
Gartside, Lt., R.A.M.C.: Calais, 24
Gazala, 102, 104, 107-8, 111-2, 115, 130-1, 233, 404
Gebel Saikhra, 404
Geffen, 387, 404
Geldrop, 384
German propaganda, Italy, 325
Gerwen, 384

Gibbons, Capt. E. W. L., 78; killed, 202
Glasgow: 1st Bn. arrive at, 344
Gloucester, H.R.H. Gen. Duke of: visit to 9th Bn., 109
Goodey, R.S.M., 25
"Goodwood," Operation, 360
Gordon-Duff, Capt. T. R., 12, 14, 16
Gore, Brig. A. C., 207; to Kasserine, 217; 241; Forms 61st Inf. Bde., 259-60; wounded, 286; 414
Gort, Gen. Viscount, 29
Goschen, Sir Edward G., Bt., 209, 256, 274, 279
Goschen, Maj. G. W., R.A., 59, 69, 77
Gothic Line, 5, 280-3, 290, 311, 342
Gott, Lt.-Gen. W. H. E., 32; character, 38; 54, 68, 70, 74, 81, 93-4, 114; killed, 138; 144-5, 237
Goubellat, 216, 235, 225, 227
Gough, Rev. H., 227
Graham, Lt. N., R.E., 165
Grand Brogel, 384
Grassina, 304
Gray, Lt. D. J., 289
Greek mutiny, 240
Green, Lt.-Col. R., R.A., 289
Greenfield, Maj. P., R.A., 77
Grentheville, 361-2
Griffiths, Lt. N. B., 145
Grubbenvorst, 389
Guards Formations—
  Guards: 269, 270, 274, 278
  Guards Brigade: 70-2, 78, 94, 99, 101, 103, 140, 195, 234, 269-70, 271, 274, 278
  Guards Armd. Div.: 360, 382-4, 375
  1st Guards Bde.: 258, 271, 280, 286, 289-90, 293, 301-2, 318-9, 331
  5th Guards Armd. Bde.: 395
  24th Guards Bde.: 219
  201st Guards Bde.: 95
  Grenadier Guards: 270, 290, 291
  Coldstream Guards: 41-3, 68, 70, 219, 265, 269, 303
  Scots Guards: 68, 122
  Irish Guards: 230
  Welsh Guards: 270
Gunn, Lt. Ward, V.C., 82, 85, 86-7
Gurkhas, 204, 231
Gurr, Rfn., 26
Gwynn, Capt., R.A.M.C., 322

Habata, Bir, 74
Halfaya, 43, 50-1, 53, 69-70, 72, 101, 185
Hamburg, 404
Hamilton-Russell, Maj. A. G. L., 11, 14, 16-7, 21-2, 26

Hammam Lif, 72, 233, 239
Hancock, Sgt., 108; killed, 408
Hannay, Lt. P. V. C., 258
Hanover, 406
Harding, Gen. Sir J., 181, 183, 184
Harding, Lt.-Col. R. P., 357, 368
Harington, Maj. J. T., 57
Hart, Sgt., 6, 7, 398
Harvey, Brig. C. B., 345, 406
Hasseiat, 100, 107
Hastings, Maj. R. H. W. S., 77, 112
Hatert, 389
Hawkins, Rfn., 407
Haywood-Farmer, Lt. E. C.: drowned, 248
Heard, Rev., 24
Hedges, Lt. N. L., 226
Heesch, 387
Heeze, 384
Helchteren, 383-4
Hellenes, H.M. The King of the: visits 1st Bn., 109
Henley, Maj. R. A., 215
Henniker-Major, Maj. J. P. E. C., 127
Hicks, Lt.-Col. K. B., 141, 158, 194
Hill, 112, 356-8, 366, 372
Hillyer, Sgt., 172, 174
Himeimat, 134-5, 137, 145, 146, 148, 150, 152-3, 192, 226
Hinde, Brig. W. R. N., 375
Hine, Sgt., 172, 175
Hines, Sgt., 349
Hitler Line, 256, 257
H.M. The King: inspects Bns., 239; effects of his visit, 253; 280
Hobart, Lt.-Col. P. C., 388
Hobbs brothers, R.A., 77
Hogg, Capt. Hon. Q. McG., 68, 70
Holland, Col., 19, 24
Holtum, 397
Holt-Wilson, Lt. A. B., 157, 172, 175, 177
Homs, 188-9, 197, 239, 241, 403
Hone, Cpl., 357; killed, 385
Hooper, Rfn., 211
Hope, Lt.-Col. J. C., 329, 330; killed, 337
Horrocks, Lt.-Gen. Sir Brian, 241, 373
Hoskyns, Lt.-Col. C. B. A., 11, 14, 18, 21, 23; died of wounds, 24
Hubert Folie, 366
Hughes-Onslow, Lt. T. N., 410
Hull, Maj.-Gen. R. A., 210
Hunt, Lt.-Col. G. H., 156, 194
Hunter, Lt.-Col. J. A., 359, 362, 364, 368, 371, 393; fishing success, 410
Huntsman, Lt. J. H., 320
Hutchinson, Sgt., 398
Huth, Maj. P. H., 398

Infantry—
  Queen's: 186, 193, 399
  Buffs: 191
  R. Northumberland Fusiliers: 63, 64
  R. Warwickshire Regt.: 369
  Devonshire Regt.: 398
  R. Leicestershire Regt.: 218
  Lancashire Fusiliers: 212
  R. Hampshire Regt.: 248
  Welch Regt.: 14, 21, 338
  Black Watch: 165
  Northamptonshire Regt.: 211
  K.S.L.I.: 363
  D.L.I.: 70, 399
  Cameron Highlanders: 45
  R. Ulster Rifles: 295
  Argyll and Sutherland Hrs.: 286
Innes, Lt. P. C., 77, 126-7, 163
Isard, Cpl., 363
Isenbruch, 395

Jarvis, P.S.M., 58
Jebltrozza, 220
Jefford, C.S.M., 352
Jepson-Turner, Lt. R. L., 122, 135
Jepson-Turner, Maj. B. W., 348
Jillings, Sgt., 246
Johnstone, P.S.M., 21
Jones, Capt. E. A. T., 99
Jordan, Rfn., 387
June battle, 70, 71, 74

Kairouan, 206
Kane, 2/Lt. G. J., 22
Kasserine, 217, 219
Keightley, Gen. Sir C., 234
Keith, Capt. J. A. S., 338, 341
Kelly, Maj. N. L., 186, 198, 199; killed, 205
Keren, 231
Kerr, Lt.-Col. M. G., 103
Kesselring, Gen., 299
Kidney Ridge, 166
Kiel Canal, 404
Killick, Sgt., 385
King, Lt. D. M., 386
Kingsley, Lt. A. G.: killed, 291
Kingsmill, Cpl., 372
King's Royal Rifle Corps: 84, 88, 90, 130, 150, 220, 413
  1st Battalion: 32, 38, 53, 68, 76, 131, 220, 229, 259, 286, 329, 332, 337
  2nd Battalion: 111-2, 143, 158; Snipe, 166
  8th Battalion: 345, 354; company to 8th R.B., 370
  9th Battalion: 111, 115-6; to be disbanded, 138
Kisby, Sgt., 371
Kitson, Sgt., 371

Klagenfurt, 342, 413
Knightsbridge, 118, 120-2, 131, 135
Knollys, Maj. V. C., 15, 19, 22
Kournine, 226, 227, 229, 230

L'Aigle, 371
La Bassée, 377
La Fauconnerie, 205
Laguna, 314
Lake Comacchio, 294
La Masure, 350
Lane, Cpl., 21
Langenscheid, Sgt., 387
Lanone River, 312
Lascelles, Lt. Hon. G. D., 398
La Verdure, 208
Le Beny Bocage, 368, 370
Le Duc Canal, 384
Lee, Sgt., 376
Leese, 408
Leicester Ridge, 219
Leine River, 409
Le Kef, 210, 219, 223; arrival of 7th Motor Bde., 225
Lens, 377
Lentaigne, 2/Lt. J. W. O., 118, 121; killed, 136
Le Pont Mulot, 353
Leptis Magna, 241
Leslie-Melville, Lt. Hon. G. D. E., 407
Leunen, 389
Leyland, Lt. J. C. M., 227
Liddell, Maj. C. H., 45, 66, 78, 99, 100, 163
Lightly, Lt. J. M. F., 174
Lignano, 385, 386
Lille St. Hubert, 384
Ling, Lt. A. J., 88
Liri Valley, 255, 258, 260, 262, 272, 342, 414
Lisieux, 377
Livarot, 376
Livingstone-Learmouth, Lt.-Col. L., 77
Livry, 349
Lockwood-Wingate, Lt. P., 156
L'Olmo, 275
Lomas, Maj. J., R.A., 77
Longstop Hill, 230
Lonsdale, Maj. J. F., 256, 333
Loom, 390
Louvain, 394, 405
Lowrison, Lt. F. J.: killed, 264
L.R.D.G., 196
Lübeck, 411, 414
Lukas, Col. K.: runs opera, 247
Luke, Maj. P. A. C., 397-9
Lumsden, Lt.-Gen. H., 4, 11, 121, 135, 137
Lüneburg, 403
Lyne, Maj.-Gen. L. O., 395

Index

Maabus el Rigel, 121
Maas, 388-9, 391, 394, 399, 400
Maastricht, 388, 395
Maaten Bagush, 183
Macaulay, Sgt., 374
McColl, Capt. R. S., 129
McCrea, Maj. M., 356, 357, 372
McGaw, Lt.-Col. A. J. T., 61
McGrigor, Capt. J. N.: killed, 90
Mackenzie, Maj. K. O., 356, 358
McNaughton, Maj.-Gen., 12
Macnaughton, Lt. A. D. H., 254
McSwiney, Lt. P., R.A., 86
Maeseyck, 400
Maggio, 284-5
Maktar, 220
Maktila, 45
Maletti, Gen., 46
Mansel, Maj. J. C., 329
Maraua, 65
Mareth, 181-2, 191-3; battle, 194; 194-6, 198, 201, 202, 204, 220
Marines, Royal: at Calais, 15; 26
Marradi, 292
Marriott, Maj.-Gen. J. C. O.: on 9th Bn., 140
Marseilles-en-Beauvais, 373
Marten, Maj. F. W.: his account, 70; 72-4, 176, 338, 340
Martin, Sgt., 305
Mason, Lt. F. C. W., 394; killed, 406
Massy-Beresford, Brig. T. H., 102
Mateur, 211, 212
Mather, Lt. A. N., 364; killed, 376
Matildas break through, 72
Matmata Hills, 191, 195, 199
Matruh, Mersa, 131
Matthews, Lt. D. H., 353
May, 2/Lt. G. T., 190, 352
May, Capt. E. P., 407
Mazingarbe, 377
Mechili, 54, 104, 106-7
Medawwar Fort, 54
Medenine, 191-2, 194-5, 197, 199, 200, 220
Medjerda River, 231, 233
Medjez el Bab, 212, 219, 229, 235
Meijel, 385-6
Meldrum, Maj. H. T., 136; assumes command, 276
Melet, 391
Mena House Guard, 240
Mena Road, 33, 67, 112, 340
Mentana, 268
Merrick, Capt. G. E., 341
Mersa Aula, 107
Mersa Brega, 60, 62, 101, 103, 187
Mersa Matruh, 33, 37-9, 41, 44, 46, 77, 81, 94, 102, 128, 135, 182
Mescola, 302-3
Metcalfe, Sgt., 221
Meuse, 384, 391, 397

Meyer, Sgt., 377
Miles, Sgt.: Snipe, 172; 175
Millar, Capt. G. R., 103
Miller, Lt.-Col. (now Maj.-Gen.) E. A. B., 23
Miller, Lt. R. C. S., 26
Milner, Maj. C. F., 352, 397, 402
Mister, Cpl., 211
Misurata, 189
Mitchell, Lt. J. I., 334, 338
Mitchell, Lt. P. A. N., 398, 402; killed, 403
Mittel Brett, 339
Moll, 306
Mondragone, 248
Monselice, 339
Montagu-Douglas-Scott, 2/Lt. M., 46, 69
Monte Acqua Salata, 302
Monte Battaglia, 301
Monte Camurcino, 284
Monte Capello, 301
Monte Castiglion, 284
Monte Dela Serra, 296
Monte Erbolini, 291
Monte Freddo, 295
Monte Giovi, 288
Monte Lacugnano, 273-6
Monteloro, 304-6
Monte Malbe, 275-6, 279, 281
Monte Morrone, 267
Monte Penzola, 302, 312, 318
Monte Peschiena, 290
Monte Rentella, 278-80, 282
Monte Roncosole, 302
Monte Rotondo, 268-9
Monte San Croce, 281
Monte Taverna, 302, 308-9, 313
Montfort, 397, 399
Montgomery, F.-M. Lord, 5, 144, 151, 154, 180, 188-90; visits 2nd and 7th Bns., 195; 198, 254, 309, 345, 391
Morgnania, 234
Morpeth, Viscount, 284, 305, 319
Morton, Cpl., 25
Mosley, Capt. M. H., 34, 57, 77; killed, 160; 162-3
Mott-Radclyffe, Maj. C. E., M.P., 265, 270, 275
Mount Pincon, 349
Mrassas, 233
Msus, 65; Stakes, 102; 104, 106-7, 186, 188
Mteiffel, 124
Munday, R.S.M., 104
Muraglione Pass, 291
Murphy, Rfn., 26
Murray, Maj.-Gen. H.: report of Tossignano, 323; 342
Murray, Sgt., 399
Musaid, 72

Naples, 244, 252
Narni, 270
Naumann, Lt. A., 211
Naumann, Maj. J. E. B.: Snipe, 177; 318
Neeroeteren, 395
Newman, Sgt., 172; Snipe, 174
Newton, Capt. O., K.R.R.C., 77
New Zealanders, 80, 96, 135-7, 142, 146, 157, 189, 196-8, 200, 201, 205, 224, 286, 335, 338-40, 341
Nibeiwa, 44, 46, 71
Nicholson, Brig. C., 8, 10, 13, 15, 18, 20
Nicolas, 379
Nienburg, 403
Nieustadt, 395-7
Nijmegen, 395
Nile Delta, 238, 239, 340
Ninove, 374
Nobel, C.S.M., 163
Nordrebber, 409
Norrie, Lt.-Gen. Sir Willoughby, Bt., 80
Norway, 8
Noyes, Cpl.: Snipe, 169

O'Brien, Rfn., 58
O'Brien, Sgt., 213
O'Connor, Gen. Sir R. N., 41
O'Connor, Sgt., 350
Ochtrupp, 402-3
Octaviano, 244
Odgers, Maj. C. N. F., 275, 281
Odon, 354, 356-8
Ophasselt, 374
Orlando, 296
Orne, 5, 354, 356, 360, 364, 371
Orsara, 308
Overische, 391

Radua, 253, 339
Paley, Brig. A. G. V.: takes command of 1st Bn., 242; 245, 247, 249; to the staff, 403; 404
Palmanova, 399
Palmer, Maj. A. G. D., 43, 46, 57, 71, 74, 82, 92, 97, 124, 152; wounded, 153; 190, 337
Panaro River, 332, 335
Paniez, N., 378
Parker, Capt. A. M., 378
Parker, Lt. R. J., 258, 333, 340
Parker, Sgt., 246
Pawson, Lt. H. A., 216-7
Pearson, Lt.-Col. T. C. H., 56-7, 59; commanding 2nd Bn., 157; 159-60, 166, 171, 182, 236, 239
Pearson, Sgt.: Snipe, 169; 173
Peel, Maj. P., 11, 15, 18, 21, 26

Perrin, Sgt.: killed, 229
Persse, Maj. J. A.: killed, 100
Persse, Lt. J. H.: killed, 201
Perugia, 5, 253, 270-80, 414
Pevalin, Sgt., 127
Pfeiffer, Capt., 314
Phillips, Sgt., 25
Picton, Maj. A. D., 78, 194
Pigeons, issue of, 392
Piglio, 266
Pila, 274-5
Pinney, Maj. B., R.A., 87
Pinnock, Capt. E. T., 237, 329
Pistoia Div., Italian Army, 199
Plezzo, 339
Po, 256, 312, 332, 335-8, 340-2
Poggio Renatico, 335
Po Morto di Primaro, 333
Pontassieve, 283, 287
Pontifex, Capt. D. M., 340
Poole, Lt.-Col. R. D., 55, 102
Poole, Lt. J. J., 387
Poperinghe, 390
Pratt, Cpl., 383
Pratt, Sgt., 408
Presles, 369-70
Price, Lt. M. H., 17, 26
Prittie, Maj. Hon. H. D. G., 112, 244; opera, 297
Prittie, Hon. T. C. F., 22
Pritty, Capt. G. S., 352
Purdon, Lt.-Col. D. J., 33 (footnote), 78, 106, 140, 141
Putanges, 371

Qattara Depression, 134, 137, 148

Ramsden, Lt. J. R., 371
Ramsdoncksveer, 388
Ramsdorf, 402
Rapido, 255, 267
Ravenna, 293
Raymond, Lt. M. M. J., 408
Read, Sgt., 383
Reader-Harris, Maj. J. W., 266, 286, 318, 320-2
Redfern, Lt. T., 121
Reed, Lt. F., 14
Reeswijz, 386
Reeve, Maj.-Gen. J. T. W., 2
Reeve, 2/Lt. J. M. W.: killed, 127
Regimental Dinner at Tunis, 237
Remnant, Lt. B. J. F., 399
Renaix, 374
Renacci, 287
Reno, 335
Renton, Maj.-Gen. J. M. L., 5, 32, 41, 54-5, 68, 111, 116; commanding 7th Armd. Div., 128; 237
Rethem, 403

INDEX

Retma, 116, 119, 160
Rhine, 402
Ridley, C.S.M.: killed, 192
Rieti, 269
Rimini, 294
Rio Sgarba, 315
Roberts, Maj.-Gen. G. P. B.: commanding 22nd Armd. Bde., 143; 184, 220, 345
Robinson, Lt. M. H. W.: killed, 402
Roer River, 397, 400
Roermond, 395
Rogers, Maj. Coxwell, 26
Rogers, Capt. K. A., 229
Rolt, Maj. A. P. R., 11, 16, 17, 19, 21-2, 26
Rome, 247; condition of country, 253; 254, 255, 258, 260; advance on, 262; 263; falls, 267; 268, 269, 272, 280, 375
Rommel, Gen., 72, 93-6, 114, 135, 145, 148, 158, 181-2, 185
Rosendaal, 394
Ross, Lt. T. R. C., 145
Rotterdam, 383
Rowan, Maj. A. P., 356
Rowett, Rfn., 127
Royal Air Force: good support, 130; 146, 151, 155, 160, 196, 201, 205, 231, 242-3, 353, 360-1, 393, 405, 408
Rundstedt, Gen. von, 299, 390
Russell, Lt. G. A.: killed, 158
Ruweisat Ridge, 134-5, 137, 144-5
Ryan, Lt. G. V.: killed, 388

St. Cyprien, 231
St. Honorine de Ducy, 359
St. Joost, 398-400, 403
St. Lo, 366
St. Martin de Besaces, 367
St. Odilienberg, 397-8
St. Oudenrode, 386
St. Vito, 341
Sahms, 410
Salerno, 239, 242-3
Salt, Lt. J. N., 156
Sampher, Sgt., 171
San Agostino, 335
San Angelo, 254
San Benedetto, 292, 297, 300
San Giuseppe Vesuviano, 244
San Margherita, 305, 308
San Nicolo, 333
San Nicoso Ferrarese, 333
Sanderson, Lt. A., 25
Santerno River, 301-3
Saunnu, 101, 105, 107
Savill, Cpl.: Snipe, 172
Savone River, 248

Sbikha, 225
Schei, 389
Scheldt, 375
Schilbracht, 395
Schilberg, 397
Schleswig-Holstein, 404
Second Front: commences, 268; 344
Sedgwick, Lt. J. P.: killed, 394
Segnali, 115
Segni, 334
Seine, 367, 370-2, 377
Selway, Maj. N. C., 220-1, 287-8
Senio Line, 301-2; Valley, 332.
Sept Vents, 367
Sergeant, Maj. E. H., 399
Sfax, 204-5, 211
Sharpe, Capt. J., R.A., 77
Shepherd-Cross, Maj. P. C., 157, 171, 264, 270, 334
s'Hertogenbosch, 387
Shipton, Lt.-Col. E. A., 61
Shutz, Cpl., 374
Sicily, 239
Sidi Ayed, 214
Sidi Aziz, 69, 70
Sidi Barrani, 39, 43, 46, 68, 231
Sidi Omar, 69, 72, 73, 74
Sidi Omar Nuovo, 72
Sidi Rahman, 159, 181
Sidi Rezegh, 4, 5, 39, 64; battle of, 80; 83, 96, 110, 119, 125, 131, 132, 158, 182, 186, 236, 240, 414
Sidi Saleh, 4, 5; action of, 56; 81, 97, 160, 191, 200, 230, 237, 324
Silvertop, Lt.-Col. D., 360
Simeon, Lt. J. E., 118
Simond, Capt. C. K., 156
Sinclair, Maj. T. C., 57, 69, 71, 90, 96; 2nd Bn., 239; 276, 281, 296, 317
Sittard, 397.
Skipper, Sgt., 399
Sladen, 2/Lt. D. R., 12, 14, 20
Sloughia, 211
Smail, Lt.-Col. A. T., 76
Smiley, Maj. C. M., 22
Snipe, 5, 42, 93, 141, 154, 157, 160; action of, 162; conference, 176; 230, 238, 287
Soboleff, Maj. I. S. K., 118, 122
Sofafi, 74
Sollum, 33, 37, 39-41, 43, 50-1, 71, 128, 135, 182, 185
Somma Vesuviano, 244
Somme, 373-4, 377
Sorinne, 393
Souk el Arba, 210
Sousse, 202, 204, 211
South Africans, 85, 92, 101, 107, 112, 117, 120, 122, 125, 131, 135, 269

South African Armd. Car Regt., 4th, 76, 77, 116
Southby, Lt.-Col. A. R. C., 254, 274, 288
Sparanise, 247
Sponek, Gen. Graf von: surrender of, 234
Stacey, R.S.M., 404
Steer, Lt. C., 378
Steimbke, 409
Stephens, Lt.-Col. F., 143, 152, 186-8, 197, 205; in Tunis, 232; leaves Bn., 242; 403
Stevens, P.S.M., 12, 20
Stevens, Lt. G. L., 289
Stewart-Wilson, Lt. R. S., 257, 336-8
Stileman, Capt. D. M., 367
Stolzenau, 406
Stone, Cpl., 408
Straight, Capt. W., 13
Straker, Capt. J. J., 367, 388
Street, Maj. V. W., 327
Sturgess, Lt. R. W., 214
Sudlow, Ltd. D. L., 357, 373, 393
Suez Canal, 144
Surtees, Maj. J. F. A., 12, 22, 26
Susteren, 397
Suter, Maj. C. W., 397
Suter, Capt. W. E., 142-3
Swann, Sgt.: Snipe, 175; 177
Swanwick, Lt. T. K., 408
Syke, 403

Tagliamento, 340, 341
Takruna, 206
Talbot, Capt. G. S. W., 109; killed, 354
Taranto, 259
Tarvisio Pass, 342
Taylor, Maj. J. A., 9, 18, 20, 21; wounded, 23; 24
Taylor, Rev. J., 369, 385
Tebourba, 212
Tecklenburg, 406
Teege, Col. (German Army): account, 178
Tel el Aqqaqir, 158, 160
Terni, 269
Territorial Army, Infantry—
   Queen Victoria's Rifles: 7, 10, 12, 14, 16-8, 20, 22, 24
   Monmouthshire Regt.: 362-3
   Herefordshire Regt.: 384
Testour, 210, 214
Teutoburger Wald, 402, 406
Thala, 217-8, 222, 393
Thomas, Lt. G. A., 20
Thompson, Sgt., 338
Thrift, Lt. A. H., 264, 275
Tiber Valley, 268-9, 270
Tiel, 394

Tilburg, 387
Tilly-sur-Seulles, 348
Tito, Marshal, 341-2
Tmimi, 213
Tobruk, 33, 53, 68, 69, 71, 72, 73, 80-4, 92-3, 95-7, 102, 107, 112, 115-6, 119, 122-3; fall of, 125; 126, 131, 135, 141, 185-7, 213, 376
Todi, 271
Toms, Lt. H. J. L.: killed, 221
Toms, Maj. J. E. B., 127, 172-4
Tossignano, 252, 299, 303-4, 306; attack, 310; 311-2, 315, 317, 318
Tournai, 374
Townsend, Capt. H. R., 394
Trappes-Lomax, Maj. S. R., 143, 159
Trasimene Lake, 253, 272, 275-6, 280-2
Travemunde, 411
Treneer-Michell, Lt.-Col. E. D., 345, 358-9
Trevisio, 339, 340
Trida, 305
Trieste, 341
Triggs, Sgt., 369, 373-4, 384, 406
Trigh Capuzzo, 83, 96
Tripoli, 55, 60, 147, 181, 189, 190, 191, 193-5, 196, 197, 233, 236, 239-41, 414
Trivigliano, 265, 266
Trondheim, 8
Tryon, Capt. R. G. L., 13
Tucker, Clr.-Sgt., 76
Tummar Camp, 44, 71
Tunis, 5, 147, 187, 190, 192, 204, 206, 209-13, 220, 222; fall of, 223; 225, 230-1, 233; dinner, 237; 238; Victory March, 239; 267, 324, 342, 375, 414
Tunis, Gulf of, 233
Tunisia, 194-6, 204, 208, 220, 230, 234, 252, 245
Turner, Col. V. B., V.C., 72, 104, 118; commanding 2nd Bn., 137; 157; Snipe, 164; 172; 173; wounded, 176; 177, 178; V.C., 180
Two Tree Hill, 215-6, 222

Udenhout, 387
Udine, 340-2

Vanoystaeyen, D., 378
Various Units—
   Rhodesian A./Tk. Bty.: 115, 116
   R.A.S.C.: at Calais, 15; 77
   15th Light Fd. Amb.: 77
Vassy, 371
Vena del Gesso, 302, 303, 314, 315, 318

INDEX

Venice, 253
Venlo, 391
Venray, 388
Verner, Lt. J. W.: killed, 227
Vernon, 371
Vickers M.G.: reintroduced, 110
Villa Capponi, 327
Villa Mengoni, 307
Villa Perazzi, 289
Villers Bocage, 311, 346, 349-52, 354; battle of, 355; 357, 362, 366
Vimont, 362
Vlierden, 385
Vloed Beek, 395-8
Volturno River, 244, 246, 247
Voules, Lt. E. M., 327

Waal, 394
Wadi Akarit, 202, 204
Wadi Faregh, 101
Wadi Halazin, 38
Wadi Soffegin, 189
Wadi Zem Zem, 191
Wadi Zigzaou, 196, 197
Waind, Lt., R. N., 24
Walsrode, 404
Warner, Cpl., 86
Wavell, F.-M. Lord, 71, 73, 97; campaign, 414
Webb, Rfn., 228
Weld-Forester, Lt. C. R. C., 11, 26
Welman, Capt. E. M. P., 215
Welsh, Sgt., 25, 26
Wesel, 405
Weser, 5, 403, 406, 409
Weser River, 242; crossing, 407; 414
West, Lt. J. W. D., 156
Westnedge, Lt. B. J.: killed, 256
Weyer, 2/Lt. A. J. B. Van Der, 20
Whatson, Cpl., 138
White House Feature, 228
Whigham, Lt.-Col. I. H. D., 39, 78, 89, 92
White, Lt. F. L., 159
Whitaker, Maj. L. I. T., 121
Wickham, Sgt., 408
Wilcox, Capt. M., R.A.M.C., 369
Wilding, Lt. P. J.: killed, 279
Willems, 374
Williams, Brig. E. S. B., 5, 32
Williams, Maj. G. C.: killed, 397

Williams, P.S.M., 20
Willis, R.S.M., 136
Wilson, Maj. D. O., 78
Wilson, F.-M. The Lord, 32, 37, 55, 59; visits 2nd Bn., 194; 239, 259
Wilson, Maj. A. J., 211, 291, 322, 336
Wingate, Chindits, 74
Wingate, Gen., 389
Wingfield, Brig. A. D. R., 395
Wintour, Lt. H. J. F., 170
Withers, Maj. H., R.A., 71, 77, 112
Witt, Maj. J. C., 348, 397
Wolfhound, H.M.S., 16
Wood, Lt. K., R.A., 73
Wood, Lt. J. K., 318
Woodcock Position (Snipe), 166, 169, 174
Woods, Sgt. R. A.: Snipe, 172; 174
Worboys, R.S.M.: wounded, 204
Wightman, Sgt., 69
Wright, Maj. J. P., 349, 352
Wrigglesworth, Maj. A. W., 96, 296
Wurm, River, 397
Wyldbore-Smith, Maj. F. B., 245

Yeomanry—
  Derbyshire: 210, 211, 215, 255, 268-9
  Essex: 63, 66
  Fife and Forfar: 263, 356, 363, 372-3
  R. Gloucestershire Hussars: 77, 100
  London, County of: 3rd, 400; 4th, 100, 153, 189, 198, 205, 245-6, 248-52, 254, 375
  Lothians and Border Horse: 234, 258, 265, 268, 270, 273, 276-7, 286, 331, 333-6
  Norfolk: 352, 397
  Northamptonshire: 361-3
  Northumberland Hussars: 105
  R. Wiltshire: 264
Yetman, Lt. E. R. C.: 367, 393; killed, 409

Zehmoula, 192
Zliten, 189
Zomeren, 384, 400

www.ingramcontent.com/pod-product-compliance
Lightning Source LLC
Chambersburg PA
CBHW071353300426
44114CB00016B/2044